THE CAMBRIDGE COMPANION TO
PIAGET

Jean Piaget (1896–1980) was listed among the 100 ı..ჟ̣ı important persons in the 20th century by *Time* magazine, and his work – with its distinctive account of human development – has had a tremendous influence on a range of disciplines from philosophy to education, and notably in developmental psychology. *The Cambridge Companion to Piaget* provides a comprehensive introduction to different aspects of Piaget's work in a manner that does not eschew engagement with the complexities of subjects or debates yet is accessible to upper-level undergraduate students. Each chapter is a specially commissioned essay written by an expert on the subject matter. Thus, the book will also be of interest to academic psychologists, educational psychologists, and philosophers.

Ulrich Müller is associate professor of developmental psychology at the University of Victoria. His research focuses on the development of problem solving and social understanding in infants and preschoolers. He currently serves on the board of directors of the Jean Piaget Society and is an associate editor of *New Ideas in Psychology*. He is the editor of *Developmental Perspectives on Embodiment and Consciousness* (with Willis Overton and Judith Newman) and *Social Life and Social Knowledge: Toward a Process Account of Development* (with Jeremy I. M. Carpendale, Nancy Budwig, and Bryan Sokol). He received the Early Scientific Achievement Award from the Society of Research in Child Development in 2005.

Jeremy I. M. Carpendale is professor of developmental psychology at Simon Fraser University. He has published in the areas of cognitive, social cognitive, and moral development. His work focuses on the nature and development of thinking about social and moral matters and the role of language and social interaction in such development. He is an associate editor of *New Ideas in Psychology* and author of *How Children Develop Social Understanding* (with Charlie Lewis). He is an editor of several books, including *Social Life and Social Knowledge: Toward a Process Account of Development* (with Ulrich Müller, Nancy Budwig, and Bryan Sokol).

Leslie Smith is a freelance researcher based in the Lake District in northwest England and professor emeritus at Lancaster University. He is currently an associate editor of *New Ideas in Psychology*. His main interests are in Piaget's theory, children's mathematics learning, and the normativity of human development. His published work includes a dozen books, most recently *Norms in Human Development* (as editor, with Jacques Vonèche). His monograph *Piaget's Developmental Epistemology* is in preparation for publication by Cambridge University Press.

The Cambridge Companion to
PIAGET

Edited by

Ulrich Müller
University of Victoria

Jeremy I. M. Carpendale
Simon Fraser University

Leslie Smith
Freelance Researcher, Lake District, UK

CAMBRIDGE
UNIVERSITY PRESS

CAMBRIDGE UNIVERSITY PRESS
Cambridge, New York, Melbourne, Madrid, Cape Town, Singapore,
São Paulo, Delhi, Dubai, Tokyo

Cambridge University Press
32 Avenue of the Americas, New York, NY 10013-2473, USA

www.cambridge.org
Information on this title: www.cambridge.org/9780521727198

© Cambridge University Press 2009

First published 2009

Printed in the United States of America

A catalog record for this publication is available from the British Library.

Library of Congress Cataloging in Publication data

The Cambridge companion to Piaget / editors, Ulrich Müller, Jeremy I. M.
Carpendale, Leslie Smith.
   p. cm. – (Cambridge companions to philosophy)
Includes bibliographical references and index.
ISBN 978-0-521-89858-4 (hardback) – ISBN 978-0-521-72719-8 (pbk.)
1. Piaget, Jean, 1896–1980. 2. Cognition in children. 3. Child psychology.
I. Müller, Ulrich, 1964– II. Carpendale, Jeremy I. M., 1957– III. Smith,
Leslie, 1943–
BF723.C5C35 2009
154.4′13092–dc22   2009010977

ISBN   978-0-521-89858-4 Hardback
ISBN   978-0-521-72719-8 Paperback

CONTENTS

CONTRIBUTORS

Marylène Bennour
Archives Jean Piaget
Genève, Switzerland

Maximilian B. Bibok
Department of Psychology
Simon Fraser University
Canada

Trevor Bond
Faculty of Education Studies & Graduate Programmes Office
Hong Kong Institute of Education
China

Jan Boom
Department of Developmental Psychology
Universiteit Utrecht
The Netherlands

Robert L. Campbell
Department of Psychology
Clemson University
United States

Jeremy I. M. Carpendale
Department of Psychology
Simon Fraser University
Canada

Michel Ferrari
Ontario Institute for Studies in Education
University of Toronto
Canada

Kurt W. Fischer
Graduate School of Education
Harvard University
United States

Stuart I. Hammond
Department of Psychology
Simon Fraser University
Canada

Yeh Hsueh
College of Education
The University of Memphis
United States

Thomas Kesselring
Institut für Philosophie
Universität Bern
Switzerland

Richard F. Kitchener
Department of Philosophy
Colorado State University
United States

John G. Messerly
Department of Philosophy
Austin Community College
United States

David Moshman
Educational Psychology
University of Nebraska
United States

Ulrich Müller
Department of Psychology
University of Victoria
Canada

L. Todd Rose
Center for Applied Special Technology (CAST)
Wakefield, MA
United States

Leslie Smith
Professor Emeritus, Lancaster University, and freelance researcher
Lake District
United Kingdom

Bryan W. Sokol
Department of Psychology
St. Louis University
United States

Anastasia Tryphon
Faculty of Psychology and Educational Sciences
Université de Genève
Switzerland

Jacques Vonèche
Faculty of Psychology and Educational Sciences
Université de Genève
Switzerland

ULRICH MÜLLER, JEREMY I. M. CARPENDALE, AND
LESLIE SMITH

1 Introduction

Overview

This introduction is in three parts. In the first part, we comment on the relevance of epistemology for psychology and vice versa. In this context, we briefly elaborate on Piaget's epistemological framework, address some common misconceptions that arise from an overly psychological interpretation of his theory, and introduce the different chapters of this volume. In the second part, Leslie Smith provides a short biography of Piaget. The third part, also by Leslie Smith, points out a number of problems that readers of the English translations of Piaget's work will encounter.

INTRODUCTION I. THE CONTEXT OF PIAGET'S THEORY

Ulrich Müller, Jeremy I. M. Carpendale, and Leslie Smith

The reception of Piaget's work and Piaget's reaction toward this recognition present an interesting puzzle. On the one hand, Piaget is widely recognized for his work on child psychology. For example, in an article on Piaget appearing in a series of papers summarizing the work of eminent developmental psychologists, Harry Beilin (1992, p. 191) wrote the following: "No one affected developmental psychology more than Jean Piaget (1896–1980). From his earliest publications in the 1920s to the time of his death, the influence he exercised was extraordinary. His theory...has no rival in developmental psychology in scope and depth.... The number of experiments conducted by Piaget and his colleagues has never been tabulated, but it is unrivaled in the history of developmental psychology." On the other hand, Piaget expressed mixed feelings about the reception of his work. For example, toward the end of his career, Piaget (Bringuier, 1977/1980, p. 54) made this comment on the recognition of his work: "I am pleased by it, of course. But it is pretty catastrophic when I see how I'm understood."

We submit that one of the reasons Piaget did not feel well understood is that psychologists as well as philosophers generally failed to grasp that at the heart of Piaget's research program lies a unique way of integrating empirical research and epistemology. Psychologists have generally ignored the epistemology, that is, theoretical framework, that drives Piaget's work. Philosophers, on the other hand, have dismissed the relevance of Piaget's empirical work for epistemological questions because "philosophical and psychological questions... are different from each other, and... there are no grounds for the belief that philosophical questions can be answered by appeal to empirical evidence or vice versa" (Hamlyn, 1971, p. 19).

Epistemology and Psychology

In his Foreword to a major commentary on his work, Piaget (1963, p. viii) remarked that his interpreters tended to focus on the empirical side of his work and did not pay enough attention to the epistemological foundation of his approach. One reason for the one-sided reception of Piaget's work by psychologists may be a failure to see the relevance of, or need for, examining the assumptions on which theories are based. However, as noted by Piaget (1970/1983, p. 105), it is not possible to study the psychology of human development without making epistemological assumptions that have to be addressed in the study itself, for example, assumptions about the relations between mind and world, and biological and psychological functioning.

One outcome of this lack of appreciation of the relevance of epistemology for the study of psychology and psychological development is that epistemological assumptions often remain tacit. Practically, this amounts to many psychologists basing their theories on assumptions that originate in the empiricist tradition (Piaget, 1970/1972a, p. 10). According to Piaget, the central idea of empiricism is that "the function of cognitive mechanisms is to submit to reality, copying its features as closely as possible, so that they may produce a reproduction which differs as little as possible from external reality" (Piaget & Inhelder, 1969/1976, p. 24). Essentially, empiricism explains our knowledge of the world in terms of sensory experience and the causal play of associations (Piaget, 1965/1972, pp. 53–56). In contemporary psychology, the functionalist framework carries on the legacy of the empiricist tradition. The central idea of functionalism is that mental states (e.g., beliefs, desires) are determined by their causal relations to other mental states, sensory inputs, and behavioral outputs. According to the functionalist framework, mental states function as mediators between input and output.

Piaget argued that these empiricist assumptions are conceptually flawed and are not consistent with empirical findings (Piaget & Inhelder, 1969/1976). The idea that knowledge consists of a copy of reality is, according to Piaget, flawed because there would be no way to evaluate the accuracy of such copies which cannot be directly compared to reality itself: "[I]n order to make a copy we have to know the model that we are copying, but according to this theory of knowledge the only way to know the model is by copying it, until we are caught in a circle, unable ever to know whether our copy of the model is like the model or not. To my way of thinking, knowing an object does not mean copying it – it means acting upon it" (Piaget, 1970, p. 15; cf. Piaget & Inhelder, 1966/1971, pp. 385–386). Notice that this objection applies with equal force to any theory of mind based wholly on representation – a commitment ubiquitous in modern psychology – in that the knower can only ascertain the degree of fit between a representation and reality by recourse to another representation, never to reality (see Bickhard, 1993, 1999, 2009).

As an alternative view to this passive interpretation of knowledge, Piaget (1970/1983, p. 104) proposed that "in order to know objects, the subject must act upon them, and therefore transform them." Piaget's constructivist view implies that knowledge does not pre-exist in the world to be imposed on the children, nor is it already innately pre-prepared in children. In consequence, this version of constructivism is incompatible with nativism, normally regarded as the standard alternative to empiricism. In this context, Piaget's distinction between particular properties of an organism and general properties of organization is relevant. Particular properties of an organism (e.g., eye color) are due to hereditary transmission. General properties of organization (e.g., classification abilities) are due to something else: "Amoeba, sponges, fish, and mammals transmit all their characteristics [and this is] a truly hereditary transmission; but they also transmit quite equally the most general properties of life in virtue of organization, and that is not transmission in the same sense. [This is because] at every step of hereditary transmission, a *living* organization is present as the necessary condition of particular transmissions because it determines the *activities* arising in that transmission" (Piaget, 1967/1971, p. 323; our emended translation).

Piaget's third way (i.e., alternative to empiricism and nativism) is that knowledge develops through the child's actions on the world. In addition, knowledge is always tied to a particular framework (see Chapter 3, this volume), a paradigm case of which are the structures that emerge as any knowing subject interacts with the world. More specifically, the relation between subject and world is characterized by the functional processes of assimilation and accommodation. At the psychological level, assimilation captures the intrinsic directedness of consciousness and refers to the incorporation of new elements into already existing schemes – and schemes are organized wholes composed of affect, sensation, motor movement, perception – thereby giving meaning to those elements (Piaget, 1975/1985, p. 16); for example, in grasping a new toy, this toy is assimilated to the grasping scheme, the toy attains the functional meaning of being "graspable." Accommodation refers to the modification of existing schemes to take account of particular features of the new object or situation (e.g., in the very same assimilatory act, the pre-existing grasping scheme needs to be modified to take hold of the new toy). In the context of the functions of assimilation and accommodation, structures take a dynamic function in a double sense. First, structures do not exist independently of structuring activity: "Assimilation is hence the very functioning of the system of which organization is the structural aspect" (Piaget, 1936/1953, p. 410). Second, structures change as a result of the subject's interaction with the world: Every genesis originates from one structure and results in another structure, and, conversely, every structure has a genesis (Piaget, 1964/1967).

Two questions follow: First, which structures are in fact constructed by the mind? Second, what is the process enabling this to happen?

As to the first question, influenced by the Bourbaki group of mathematicians (see Aczel, 2007), between 1940 and 1965 Piaget (1970, p. 23) identified three cognitive structures that characterize children's thinking at different points in development. His evidence during this period was gained with a view to finding out whether these structures are in fact constructed. Piaget interpreted his evidence as confirmation that this is the case. But there are important qualifications usually disregarded in commentary. (a) It is an empirical question for investigators to check out the evidential basis of these three structures. "The average subject knows his own intelligence only in its performances, for the operative structures elude him, as moreover nearly all mechanisms affecting his behaviour and, even more, his organism. That structures exist is, therefore, something for the observer to ascertain and analyse them" (Piaget, 1973, p. 46; our emended translation). Thus, the key question is whether these three structures can be identified at points in development, not whether each and every aspect of a child's mental life can be described in these terms. (b) To the question "Are there any general stages?" Piaget gave the clear and specific answer "No." If a general stage is such that it includes "at the same time, for a given level, the totality of the organic, mental and social aspects of development... [then] there are no general stages. [Rather] in the various neurological, mental and social fields, we see an intermingling of processes of development which are evidently interrelated, but to different extents or according to multiple temporal rhythms, there being no reason why these processes should constitute a unique structural whole at each level" (Piaget, 1960, pp. 14–15). For Piaget, at any developmental level there is no singleton structure for all action and thought, emotion, will and all the rest of the human psyche. Rather, there are various functional instances of these formal structures that characterize thinking throughout human development. (c) Piaget provided formal descriptions of the cognitive structures he identified, but at different points in his career he employed alternative formal models (see Chapter 10, this volume; see also Piaget & Garcia, 1987/1991), and it has been argued that his greater contribution was his insight regarding the role of operations (i.e., the active processes of coordinating actions and thoughts) rather than the particular logical models he employed (Apostel, 1982).

As to the second question, throughout, and especially during 1965–1980, this was the central issue in Piaget's work. Note that it is largely bypassed *in toto* in most Anglo–Saxon work in psychology. Piaget's research on this dynamic process was also overlooked. A key claim of his constructivism is that cognitive structures always have a process that enabled their construction. It is therefore a fundamental error to detach a structure from its formative process, as in some critical commentary on Piaget's position. Several chapters in this book (Chapters 3, 4, 5, 6, 9, 14, 17) focus on the process of construction.

One primary reason for common misinterpretations of Piaget's theory and for overlooking the epistemological core of Piaget's theory appears to be that the epistemological framework guiding contemporary research is fundamentally different from Piaget's epistemological framework. For Piaget, a structure is not some internal mediating device triggered by incoming information; rather, a structure is the activity of form-giving that is always intentionally directed toward the world. The operations Piaget describes are coordinated internalized actions with implicatory and meaningful relations, that is, "implication between the meanings of actions" (Piaget, 2004/2006, p. 5). Actually, his position is long-standing and evident in his first book on infancy: "Every act of intelligence presupposes a system of mutual implications and interconnected meanings" (Piaget, 1936/1953, p. 7; cf. Mays, 1987, p. 235).

Working within an empiricist framework, however, contemporary developmental psychologists have misconstrued Piaget's concept of structure as a functional device, that is, as "a hypothetical construct that is related to an observable performance as an antecedent to consequent" (Chapman, 1987, p. 289). This leads to a common interpretation of Piaget's notions of stage and structure. According to this common, or "received view" of Piaget's theory, stages are thought to be global structures that define a child's thinking. Once a child has developed the structure of concrete operational reasoning, he or she should be able to use it to solve all tasks in that domain (for sources of this interpretation, see Chapman, 1988; Lourenço & Machado, 1996). Therefore, once a child has entered a stage, such as the concrete operational stage as defined by passing concrete operational reasoning tasks, that child would be expected to pass all such tasks because they all require the "same" structure of reasoning. A prediction of homogeneity and synchrony in development follows from this interpretation. However, the abundant evidence of horizontal décalage, or inconsistency in reasoning, clearly does not fit this prediction. A classic example of asynchrony in development is that children develop conservation first for quantity then weight and then volume (Piaget & Inhelder, 1941/1974). From this interpretation of Piaget's theory, horizontal décalage has been viewed as a significant empirical difficulty for Piaget's theory, even thought to cast into doubt the structuralist framework of his theory (Siegel & Brainerd, 1978).

However, Piaget actually never claimed that stages are characterized by homogeneity or developmental synchrony, and, in fact, in many places Piaget made the opposite point that variability should be expected (Piaget, 1960; see Chapman, 1988). Furthermore, the idea of horizontal décalage is entirely consistent with, and should be expected on the basis of, Piaget's grounding assumption that thought originates in action, from which it follows that forms of thinking should, at first, be context- and content-specific. That is, the form of thought cannot be separated from its content, and although structures involving different content, such as length and weight, may be of the same logical form, they develop independently in a functional sense through the child's activity with these different areas of content. Using the analogy between developmental levels and contour lines depicting height on a map (Smith, 2002a), Reinhold Messner has climbed all 14 mountains more than 8,000 m high. But he does not live at the 8,000 m contour. Contours are levels of physical heights of things such as mountains on Earth; they are not levels of earthlings. Developmental levels are levels of intellectual construction; they are not levels of knowers. Thus, "although issues of homogeneity–heterogeneity and synchrony–asynchrony are important in their own right, they are irrelevant for testing the empirical implications of Piaget's theory because the theory itself allowed for developmental asynchrony" (Lourenço & Machado, 1996, p. 152).

Piaget used structure to characterize "the morphological properties of a certain type of thinking or reasoning" (Chapman, 1987, p. 289). The different interpretations of the concept of structure have important theoretical and methodological ramifications: "Functionalists are likely to seek the causal or functional antecedents of particular cognitive performances, but formalists are more likely to be interested in the formal properties" (p. 289). The formal properties Piaget wanted to describe were forms of thinking, that is, different ways in which children approach the same kind of problem. In other words, this is what is common to all children at a specific level of thinking – what Piaget referred to as "the epistemic subject." His tasks were "meant to study the epistemic development of certain concepts in the child, not to determine the cognitive level of any particular child or group of children" (Sinclair, 1982, p. 180).

This misunderstanding of Piaget's notions of stage and structure is related to another misinterpretation of Piaget's theory of cognitive development, which is that the particular ages at which children acquire concepts are criterial for a particular level of thinking (e.g., Gelman & Baillargeon, 1983; Halford, 1989). According to Piaget (1956, p. 34), however, "stages can be characterized in a given population chronologically, but that chronology is extremely variable." That is why in Piaget's account "age is an indicator, but not a criterion of developmental level" (Smith, 1991, p. 77). The criterion is defined in terms of the coordinated operations or structure required by the task that is used to assess a particular level of thinking. Thus, "if a child solves a task earlier than reported by the protocol [i.e., Piagetian research], no serious conceptual damage is inflicted on the theory" (Lourenço & Machado, 1996, p. 147). Furthermore, central to Piaget position was the sequence in which different forms of thinking emerge and the mechanisms involved in level transitions, and not the age at which they emerge.

Psychologists do not see the need to work through Piaget's complex ideas about equilibration and allied processes unless they first recognize the flaws, or at least undefended assumptions, in the view of knowledge they take for granted. Because psychologists generally take knowledge as unproblematic, the complexity of Piagetian theory seems simply superfluous. Theories of cognitive development, however, are necessarily based on assumptions about the nature of knowledge. How else can true knowledge be demarcated from true belief, and both from their usurpers, such as misconception, "false memory," pseudo-reasoning, and misunderstanding? This question is fundamental and notably complex for adult minds – witness the perennial problems of relativism and skepticism. As well, an adequate account of cognitive development has to address this question from the perspective of the developing child from infancy to adulthood. It is exactly such an account that Piaget set out to present.

Genetic Epistemology

Piaget called his answer genetic epistemology, the aim behind which is "to explain knowledge, and in particular scientific knowledge, on the basis of its history, its sociogenesis, and especially the psychological origins of the notions and operations upon which it is based" (Piaget, 1970, p. 1). Traditionally, epistemology has been a branch of philosophy, concerned with the nature, scope, and validity of knowledge. For Piaget, epistemology is no longer the sole preserve of philosophy; instead he advocated the use and relevance of empirical methods in approaching epistemological questions.

One reason for a developmental approach to knowledge is that knowing itself is not static but rather is a process. At issue for Piaget was ascertaining what in fact this process is, and for that, evidence was required as well as epistemological theory. In this context, Piaget (1970/1972a, p. 2) approvingly quotes the neo-Kantian philosopher Natorp (1910, pp. 14–15):

> Like Kant, we start with the actual existence of knowledge and seek the basis from there. But what is this existence since, as we know, knowledge is constantly evolving? Progression, method is everything... in consequence, the existence of knowledge cannot be comprehended except as a *fieri* [i.e., to be made, to become; our note]. This *fieri* alone is the fact. Any entity (or object) which knowledge attempts to crystallize must dissolve again in the current of development. It is in the last phase of this development, and in this alone, that we have the right to say: "this is (a fact)." What we can and must seek, then, is the law underlying this process.

But if constant evolution is constitutive of scientific knowledge, as witnessed in the natural and human sciences, and even in logic and mathematics (Piaget, 1950, 1965/1972, 1970/1972a, 1970/1972), then the study of the conditions of the possibility of knowledge must include the development of knowledge. The study of the development of knowledge, in turn, falls under the purview of the empirical sciences.

The epistemological analysis of the development of knowledge can proceed along two pathways: the historico–critical and the psychogenetic
pathway:

> Clearly, then, epistemological analysis must sooner or later achieve a
> historical or historico–critical dimension; the history of science being
> an indispensable tool for a philosophical understanding of science. The
> question is whether history involves a pre-history. But there is a complete
> absence of documentation on the formation of concepts in the case of pre-
> historic man, for although we have knowledge of his techniques we lack
> sufficient complementary information on his cognitive functions. The
> only course open to us, therefore, is to follow the example of biologists
> who supplement their scanty stock of phylogenetic knowledge by tur-
> ning to embryogenesis: in the case of psychology this means studying the
> mental ontogenesis of the child at every age. (Piaget, 1970/1972b, p. 11)

Furthermore, empirical methods are relevant for another reason: All
epistemologies make statements or contain assumptions about the process of knowledge acquisition. For example, whereas classical empiricism emphasized the importance of sense data and association, rationalism highlights the activity of the intellect. Thus, "all epistemologies
raise questions of fact and thus implicitly adopt psychological positions" (Piaget, 1970/1972a, pp. 4–5), but they lack effective methods
to answer these questions (Piaget, 1970, p. 7). To answer these factual
questions, "psychological findings become relevant and should be taken
into account" (Piaget, 1970, p. 8).

Genetic epistemology fundamentally is an interdisciplinary enterprise. It draws on expert knowledge from the individual sciences and
the help of logicians, mathematicians, and cyberneticists in modeling and formalizing levels of knowing and growth processes (Piaget,
1970/1972a, p. 6). Piaget's emphasis on interdisciplinary collaboration
reflects his belief in the interdependence of the different sciences – an
interdependence that Piaget conceived of not as a linear order but as a
cyclical system (see Brown, 2003):

> Thus man cannot understand the universe except through logic and
> mathematics, the product of his own mind; but he can only understand
> how he has constructed mathematics and logic by studying himself psy-
> chologically and biologically, or in other words, as a function of the
> whole universe. This is the true meaning of the circle of sciences: it
> leads eventually to the conception of unity through interdependence
> between the various sciences, such that disciplines on opposite sides
> of this cyclic order maintain reciprocal relationships with each other.
> (Piaget, 1970/1972a, p. 83)

Because the different sciences constitute a cyclical system and not a linear order, concepts from a higher level (e.g., the biological concept of life) cannot be reduced to those of a lower level (e.g., physicochemical processes). According to Piaget, the coordination of two different levels leads to an enrichment and transformation of the lower level (Piaget, 1970/1972b, pp. 92–93).

This summary has highlighted only the key features of Piaget's genetic epistemology. A more systematic treatment of several aspects of this topic can be found throughout this volume. At any event, our introduction should suffice to bring home the point that Piaget's genetic epistemology has an interdependent focus on epistemological principles and psychological evidence in one and the same account, thereby ensuring its distinctiveness in being reducible to neither epistemology nor psychology, neither severally nor jointly.

Organization of the Volume

The goal of this volume is to provide a comprehensive introduction to key aspects of Piaget's work that is accessible to advanced undergraduate students. Given that Piaget was a prolific writer whose publication period spans more than 60 years (with posthumous volumes and articles still being published), the coverage of aspects of Piaget's work had to be selective. For further reading there are several excellent monographs on Piaget available in English that focus more on either his theoretical work (e.g., Kitchener, 1986; Smith, 1993, 2002b), his empirical work (Ginsburg & Opper, 1988), or both (Chapman, 1988; Vuyk, 1981).

This volume highlights the theoretical or epistemological aspects of Piaget's work and elaborates the relations between empirical research and epistemological issues. Piaget's genetic epistemology is comprehensive and ambitious in that it addresses the relations between, on the one hand, psychology and biology, and, on the other hand, psychology and sociology; Piaget's "biology" and "sociology" are discussed in separate chapters. A number of chapters highlight Piaget's work on developmental processes, a topic particularly salient in his later (i.e., 1970s) writings. Particularly relevant for current discussions in cognitive and affective neuroscience is Piaget's conceptualization of affectivity, consciousness, and morality. As the authors of these chapters point out, the current debates in these areas would benefit from the assimilation of Piaget's writings on these topics. Finally, this volume includes two chapters that present reformulations of Piaget's theory that preserve its strengths while suggesting modifications that address its weaknesses.

Our volume starts in Chapter 2 with a review of several currents of European philosophy, psychology, and biology that might be largely unknown today but that influenced Piaget's thinking. Undoubtedly, the sociocultural context or zeitgeist and the historical events left their mark on Piaget's work. Marylène Bennour and Jacques Vonèche provide several examples of how the sociocultural and intellectual context influenced the formation of Piaget's ideas. They trace these influences at each of four different stations of Piaget's life: Neuchâtel, where Piaget was born and spent his adolescence; Zurich, where Piaget studied, with Bleuler, among others, and attended lectures by Jung; Paris, where Piaget worked as a research assistant of Simon and became acquainted with Janet (and through Janet, with Baldwin's writings); and finally, Geneva, where he worked for most of his life, primarily at the university, later creating the International Center for Genetic Epistemology. The chapter shows how the myriad of influences are taken up in Piaget's own work, and that, when confronted with conflicting ideas, Piaget's originality consisted in finding a third way (or *tertium quid*) that reconciled these conflicting views in a new and ingenious way.

Chapter 3 deals with Piaget's genetic epistemology. In this context, the term "genetic" does not refer to genes, and to bring out the difference, Leslie Smith characterizes Piaget's work as developmental epistemology dealing with two features of human development that run in apparently contrary directions. One is biological origins, that is, empirical genesis. The other is valid constitution, that is, normative legitimation whereby sound knowledge is demarcated from pseudo-counterparts. Fundamentally at issue is the intellectual instrument that in fact makes this possible from the knower's perspective. Epistemology as a branch of philosophy deals with the validity of our knowledge, and psychology as an empirical science deals with the empirical origins of our knowledge. According to Piaget, neither is sufficient to address appropriately the fundamental issue. A key principle is that norms are empirically investigable as normative facts at every level from the cradle to the grave. Initially, norms are implicit in an agent's actions, becoming explicit as reasons for actions in their conscious realization as norms-in-use. This analysis includes distinctive implications for a number of challenges to it.

John Messerly in Chapter 4 summarizes Piaget's writings on biology and his theory of evolution as a self-organizing and constructive process. For Piaget (1967/1971, p. 354), cognitive processes are the outcome of a continuous evolution, and cognitive self-regulation uses the general systems of organic autoregulation that can be found on all morphogenetic, physiological, and nervous/neural levels. Furthermore, Piaget (e.g., 1970/1972b, pp. 52–58) claimed that the relation between biological organism and environment raises the same kind of problems and has found the same kind of answers as the relation between mind and world. That is why his epistemology needs to address the relation between the organism and the environment at different levels. Piaget's early biological research led him to develop a distinctive theory of biological evolution, which he extended from the organic world to the psychological world, allowing him to link biological and intellectual adaptation. This theory – which is neither Lamarckian nor Darwinian – is based on the idea of a "phenocopy," and it led Piaget increasingly to emphasize the role of behavior as instrumental in moving both biological and psychological evolution. Piaget was aware that his theory of evolution was unorthodox, and he even called it a "hazardous hypothesis." The chapter takes up a number of criticisms of Piaget's theory of evolution and concludes that Piaget viewed evolution as a self-organizing and constructive process.

In Chapter 5, Richard Kitchener presents and evaluates Piaget's sociological theory. Generally, Piaget is believed to have given only scant attention to the social dimension of development. In fact, many psychologists have considered Piaget's theory to be the prototypical individualist theory. Kitchener counters this claim by demonstrating that sociology or social psychology played an important part in Piaget's larger research program. In fact, as the chapter elaborates, Piaget advanced, at somewhat different points in his career, three different theories of the nature of the social influence on cognitive development and its influence on cognitive development. However, Piaget never fully integrated these different accounts, leaving his sociological theory incomplete at best. The chapter concludes by sketching a possible synthesis of these different accounts of the social.

In Chapter 6, Jan Boom analyzes Piaget's central construct, equilibration, which Piaget regarded as the fundamental aspect of all cognitive development. For Piaget, equilibration is a process that improves existing structures in the constant construction of novel knowledge. Three of its features are: (a) the tendency of living systems to change in maintaining themselves, (b) learning processes constrained by obstacles and lacunae to be overcome by serially better levels of equilibrium, and (c) knowledge improvement due to processes of abstraction and reflection on the part of the epistemic subject. Whatever views are taken about Piaget's interpretations, alternative positions are apparently in worse states, including models in dynamic systems theory, connectionism, and developmental neuroscience. At present, a convincing alternative to Piaget's account awaits formulation.

According to Piaget, knowledge consists neither of preformed, innate structures nor of structures passively absorbed from the environment. Rather, knowledge needs to be constructed. Construction processes were a concern to Piaget throughout his entire career, becoming the prime focus of his thinking during the late period (1965–1980). Robert Campbell in Chapter 7 elaborates on three important processes of construction that received considerable attention in Piaget's later work: reflecting abstraction, generalization, and dialectics. This chapter explicates the role of each of these processes in the construction of new knowledge and ponders their interrelations. Piaget did not accomplish the task of synthesizing these different constructive processes into an overarching system. Piaget's late work has received little attention, undeservedly because it is full of distinctively fascinating ideas and empirical results.

In Chapter 8, Trevor Bond and Anastasia Tryphon review the method that Piaget used in his psychological work. Piaget used the terms "clinical" (1926/1960) and "critical" (1924/1947) to refer to his method. The critical method consists essentially of a combination of observation, experimentation, and verbal exchange, and throughout the investigation the researcher continuously adapts his or her questions to the answers of the participant with a view to ascertaining the nature and degree of their validity from the knower's perspective. Bond and Tryphon trace the beginnings of Piaget's method to his adaptation of Burt's reasoning test in Paris and document how Piaget's collaborators, notably Bärbel Inhelder, contributed to the refinement of the method. A detailed comparison between an unpublished research protocol produced by a research assistant and a published protocol reveals several features of the critical method not well captured in the published version. The central conclusion in this chapter is that Piaget's method is grounded in his epistemology and is designed to lay bare the validity of the operational mechanisms of thought. Furthermore, the data generated by the critical method have been subjected to rigorous quantitative analyses, and modern psychometric methods have lent strong support to Piaget's developmental theory.

In Chapter 9 Ulrich Müller examines Piaget's work on infant cognitive development – what Piaget termed sensorimotor intelligence. Sensorimotor intelligence is a practical intelligence that involves perception–action cycles on the basis of which infants interact with the world. For Piaget, sensorimotor intelligence provides a bridge between biological functioning – which it extends – and rational thought – into which it develops. After discussing the place of sensorimotor functioning within the context of Piaget's epistemological framework, the chapter summarizes the substages of sensorimotor intelligence, illustrates how these substages manifest themselves in infants' practical knowledge of the physical world, and reviews why sensorimotor development prepares and lays the groundwork for the emergence of symbolic thought. The final section of this chapter evaluates a number of criticisms that have been leveled at Piaget's theory of sensorimotor intelligence.

An overview of Piaget's empirical work on children's cognitive development is continued in Chapter 10 by Maximilian Bibok, Ulrich Müller, and Jeremy Carpendale. Their chapter reviews Piaget's work extending from the emergence of symbolic thought to the end of the concrete–operational period in late childhood. In the 1960s, Piaget (Piaget, Grize, Szeminska, & Vinh Bang, 1968/1977; Piaget, Henriques, & Ascher, 1990/ 1992) adopted the mathematical concept of morphisms to characterize the formal properties of children's cognitive organization. The chapter shows that morphisms provide an elegant way to describe the different forms of thought in childhood and the transitions between them. The different levels of thinking are illustrated in the areas of conservation, transitive reasoning, classification, and number. Under this interpretation, Piaget's theory of cognitive development stands up rather well against frequently raised criticisms. At the same time, it is acknowledged that Piaget's several accounts provided different conceptualizations of cognitive development in childhood that he never fully integrated.

In Chapter 11, David Moshman focuses on Piaget's account of formal operations, the type of reasoning that emerges in adolescence. Moshman begins with Piaget's original account of formal reasoning as presented in the 1920s (Piaget, 1924/1928). The next sections review the research reported in *The Growth of Logical Thinking from Childhood to Adolescence* (Inhelder & Piaget, 1955/1958). The chapter summarizes the main features of formal operational thinking as well as the implications that the emergence of formal operations has for adolescent personality. The final section of this chapter is a critical evaluation of Piaget's account of formal operations with specific reference to ways in which it should be expanded.

Piaget's theory of moral development is the topic of Chapter 12 by Jeremy Carpendale. Consistent with his larger epistemological framework, Piaget criticized individualistic approaches as well as collectivist approaches to morality. Instead, Piaget offered a third way of thinking about morality and its development: Morality arises within the relations between people. This directs attention to the nature of social relations. Piaget outlined two general types of relationships, based on constraint or cooperation, although any actual relationship consists of some mixture of the two. Relationships of constraint, as exemplified by authoritarian parent–child relationships, are based on unilateral respect and authority. Such relationships give rise to a morality of constraint – the view of morality focused on by socialization approaches. But from Piaget's perspective this type of morality is incomplete because it amounts to conformity without understanding. In contrast, cooperative relationships among equals, as exemplified by peer relationships, are based on mutual respect and involve an obligation to explain one's position as well as listen to others. Relationships of this type are best suited for reaching mutual understanding and the development of knowledge in general and moral and social understanding in particular. Carpendale concludes that Piaget's approach to moral development is essential for ongoing discussion because his central problem of how children come to construct and respect moral norms is missing in current debates.

Piaget's views about the development of consciousness and related epistemological problems are explicated in Chapter 13 by Michel Ferrari. Ferrari examines Piaget's views about two fundamental epistemological problems central to any theory of consciousness: (1) the general problem of the subject–object relationship in any type of knowing, and (2) the specific problem of the physical–mental relationship within the knowing subject. Piaget adopts a unique form of internal interactionism that develops over the course of the lifespan to address the first issue, and a sophisticated form of parallelism that draws on cybernetics and structuralism to address the second. Overall, Piaget aimed for an eventual integrative monism that coordinates information from neuroscience and cognitive science while providing compelling reasons why such a monism may always exist in name only. Although Piaget's approach to these problems did not solve them, his examination of the problems – and his proposed coordination of philosophy, psychology, cybernetics, and neuroscience – proposes a cross-fertilizing cooperation between these disciplines that is certainly one of the most promising directions for the scientific study and understanding of consciousness.

Chapter 14 by Bryan Sokol and Stuart Hammond deals with Piaget's theory of affectivity. Piaget's theory did not, as is sometimes claimed, ignore the affective dimension of psychological life. However, the chapter argues that Piaget held a somewhat ambivalent position toward affectivity and that, by and large, Piaget's theory of affectivity remained underdeveloped. The authors describe the stages of affective development that Piaget proposed in a series of lectures (1953–1954) at the Sorbonne, now published as *Intelligence and Affectivity* (1981). Piaget held that the stages of affective development parallel his well-known stages of cognitive growth, but he cautioned that "the comparison between affective states and acts of intelligence cannot be pushed too far" (1954/1981, p. 15). The chapter concludes with the suggestion that the theoretical framework of action theory is well suited for the further elaboration of Piaget's insights into affective development.

Piaget's educational model including his pedagogy, that is, theory of teaching, is presented in Chapter 15 by Leslie Smith. Although in the 1960s the name of Piaget became coupled with the notion of ages and stages and, worse, deferring teaching until children were "ready," this chapter sets out to show how and why this model included the central principle that teaching should be directed on learning beyond children's current abilities. In addition, Piaget believed that children should be offered the opportunity, freed from authoritarian coercion, to construct anew for themselves – and possibly in new ways – the knowledge and values of their culture. On this interpretation, Piaget's view necessitates that teachers realize that social interaction between children plays an essential role in the development of individual autonomy. This role of individual autonomy is shown in the context of young children's work in mathematics. In addition, this chapter argues that Inhelder and Piaget's work on children and adolescents has implications for classroom-based learning. Intervention work in the context of science and mathematics in both secondary and primary schooling is presented as replicable empirical evidence of these implications.

Yeh Hsueh, in Chapter 16, examines the reception that Piaget's work received in the United States between 1925 and 1971. He divides his historical review into three periods: the early 1920s to 1939, 1940 to 1955, and 1956 to 1971. The first period is characterized by several reviews of early Piaget's work that also inspired empirical research. During this period, Harvard University awarded Piaget his first honorary doctoral degree; interestingly, the degree was not in psychology but in recognition of his contributions to promoting the understanding of social learning in a changing society. In the second period, interest in Piaget's work waned, partly due to the behaviorist climate in North America. Several factors, not the least of which was the cognitive revolution, led to a rediscovery of Piaget in the late 1950s, and Piaget's work reached its peak recognition in the 1970s. Throughout, the chapter shows how the social, political, and economic climate in the United States influenced the reception of Piaget's work.

In Chapter 17 Thomas Kesselring shows the closeness of Piaget's epistemology to the philosophy of Hegel and Kant. Similar to Hegel,

Piaget raised the question about regularities in cognitive development; similar to Kant, Piaget was concerned with the genesis of necessary knowledge. In this context, Kesselring offers a reconstruction of Piaget's stage theory. For Piaget, "stages are an *indispensable instrument for the analysis of formative processes*" (1977, p. 817, italics in original). Piaget's stage theory, however, has been the object of numerous criticisms. In this chapter, these objections are summarized and evaluated. To address these criticisms, the author suggests a reinterpretation of Piaget's stage theory. According to this proposal, development is characterized by the construction of increasingly more complex blueprints, which, in turn, generate patterns of action and thought specific to particular levels of development. This reinterpretation leads to a reconstruction of Piaget's stage theory and the developmental processes involved in the transition from one to another stage, also providing answers to the Hegelian and Kantian questions.

Finally, in Chapter 18 Todd Rose and Kurt Fischer outline neo-Piagetian theories. These theories emerged as responses to an interpretation of Piaget's account of stages as being static in nature. From the perspective of this interpretation, variability in forms of reasoning used by the same child is a significant problem for Piaget's position. It is this variability in reasoning that is central to the Rose and Fischer discussion. In doing so they emphasize psychological structure as dynamic organization and discuss factors associated with variability in reasoning. Neo-Piagetian theory can be evaluated in its own right in terms of its contribution to understanding cognitive development.

The chapters in this volume are written in a critical rather than an apologetic spirit. Each chapter evaluates and discusses problems of Piaget's theory. At the same time, the contributors to this volume share the contention that Piaget's theory provides the starting point and foundation for deep reformulations of his theory, reformulations that might lead to better solutions to the problems with which Piaget struggled. In this sense, we hope to keep Piaget's ideas alive instead of turning them into "dead relics" (Chandler, 1999, p. x), and to promote a search for a *tertium quid* that synthesizes Piaget's theory and opposing theories:

> It is my conviction, illusory or otherwise – and the future alone will show which part is truth and which simple conceited obstinacy – that I have drawn a quite clear general skeleton, but one still full of gaps of such a kind that, in filling them, one will be led to differentiate its connections, in various ways, without at the same time altering the main lines of the system. The history of the experimental sciences abounds in examples that are instructive in this regard. When one theory succeeds another, the initial impression is that the new one contradicts the old

and eliminates it, whereas subsequent research leads to retaining more of it than was foreseen. My secret ambition is that the hypotheses one could oppose to my own will finally be seen not to contradict them but to result from a normal process of differentiation. (Piaget in Bringuier, 1977/1980, p. 144)

INTRODUCTION II. JEAN PIAGET: FROM BOY TO MAN

Leslie Smith

Jean Piaget was born on August 9, 1896, in Neuchâtel, and he died on September 16, 1980, in Geneva. His work commands international acclaim with a world ranking of 4th as a Psychologist, and 77th as a Scientist. The historical context of Piaget's achievements is surveyed in Chapter 2 and a review of his reception, notably in the United States, in Chapter 16 (this volume). What follows here is a short overview of his early formation as a boy in Neuchâtel leading to his work as a young man in Geneva.

Neuchâtel, "an orderly little town" (Vidal, 1994), is in a francophone canton of Switzerland near the Jura mountains, but also a milieu where "cultural and religious values were often in conflict" (Barrelet & Perret-Clermont, 2008, p. xii). Jean's younger sisters were Madeleine and Marthe. Their father, Arthur Piaget, was a history professor at the local university, known for his commitment to systematic study and critical independence (de Tribolet, 2008, p. 27; Vidal, 1994, p. 13). "He taught me," Piaget (1952, p. 237) tells us, "the value of systematic work, even in small matters," but ruefully added that, as a young boy, his work was abundantly manifest in notebooks such as "Our Birds" that attracted his father's comment that it amounted to a shopping list. His mother, Rebecca Jackson, was the first woman elected to Neuchâtel's school commission (Vidal, 1994, p. 15). Well known for her socialist and pacifist views, her influence on her son led eventually to Piaget's (1915) commitment to universal suffrage for women.[1] Piaget (1952, p. 238) tells us that his mother was an intelligent and fundamentally good woman but that her neurotic temperament made family life difficult, a view later confirmed by Marthe (Vidal, 1994, p. 14). It had a direct impact in that "I started to forego playing for serious work very early." His work soon paid off, and Piaget (1952, p. 238) was "launched," as he put it:

- his first journal publication by the age of 10 years (Piaget, 1907), followed by some 30 more before he made a "psychological turn" (Archives Piaget, 1989);
- appointment as "famulus" to Paul Godet, the director of the local Natural History Museum (Piaget, 1952, p. 238);

- membership in 1910 of the local club, Friends of Nature, where he was even then regarded as "professor of conchology." His first address was on Godet's evidence about mollusks unique to Lake Neuchâtel (Vidal, 1994, pp. 24, 44);
- secretary in 1911 of the Toad Committee, whose work was invariably acknowledged as "perfect" in content, style, and length (p. 45);
- correspondence with the director of the Natural History Museum in Geneva where he was invited to become a curator, aged 16 years. Though by now internationally regarded as "a mature professional in malocological taxonomy," Piaget turned the job down (p. 36);
- avid contributions to the club's sessions combining seriousness and mockery; notice his tongue-in-cheek nickname, Tardieu, derived from Tardy the Snail (Vidal, 1994, pp. 44–46).

Notice two things here. One is the personal origin of Piaget's interest in biology manifest in these early achievements. The other is a club minute in 1915: the Friends' aim was *not* "to philosophize...but to observe" (Vidal, 1994, p. 46). This was not lost on the adult Piaget (1965/1972, p. 76), whose work amounted to a "scientific philosophy."

In his formal education, "Jean Piaget was an outstanding pupil, particularly gifted in intellectual work" (Schaller-Jeanneret, 2008, p. 37). His primary schooling started in 1904 without preparatory kindergarten education and continued with secondary education at the Collège Latin in 1907 concurrently with his own extra-mural work and achievements. In 1912, at age 17, he transferred to the gymnasium, where he followed an academic pathway as a preparation for university. This pathway included philosophy that Piaget studied as follows (Schaller-Jeanneret, 2008, p. 43):

> 1913–1914 Psychology, facts of consciousness. Psychological analysis of judgment. The emotions. The will. Reflections.
> 1914–1915 Descartes: *Discourse on Method*. Aristotle's logic (terms, propositions, syllogisms); elements of modern logic; principles and methods of science.

As such, it is interesting on three counts. First, Piaget's philosophy teacher at school was Arnold Reymond (1908), whose doctoral thesis on logic and mathematics included coverage of the work of Gottlob Frege, the founder of modern logic at the end of the 19th century. It is likely that Piaget was introduced to the "new logic" while still at school (Smith, 1999a, 1999b). Second, Reymond became a philosophy professor at Neuchâtel University where Piaget studied during 1915–1918. Evidently Piaget was not known as a participative student during his early semesters (Schaer, 2008, p. 51). No doubt this is because his interests were more extensive than his registered science subjects that included zoology, embryology, geology, physical chemistry, and mathematics, notably group theory (Piaget, 1952, p. 242). Crucially, Piaget combined his science training with regular involvement in philosophy classes (Bessire & Béguelin, 2008, p. 65), including Reymond's. Indeed, one of his papers had attracted Reymond's prescient comment "what you (Piaget) call the passage from nominalism to realism is the most original in your paper" (Vidal, 1994, p. 86). This comment about two standard answers in philosophy to the problem of universals was astute in view of its elaboration in Piaget's (1918) first book in favor of constructivism, incompatible with both (Smith, 2009). In 1918, Piaget gained his *licence* – that is, undergraduate degree – in natural sciences. His work was rated "outstanding," with maximum marks in both oral and written examinations in botany, paleontology, and zoology, and with near maximum in the oral examination in human anatomy and physiology (Schaer, 2008, p. 52). This was followed in the same year by his doctor of science degree – that is, PhD – on Valaisian mollusks (Piaget, 1921a; Schaer, 2008, p. 52). Third, in 1925 and in succession to Reymond, Piaget was appointed professor of philosophy of science and psychology at Neuchâtel University, thereby maintaining in academia his joint interests in philosophy and science (Piaget, 1925). And in these joint interests lay what Piaget (1952, p. 239) called "a series of crises," personal and intellectual problems of great magnitude.

In 1912, Piaget was completing a course in religious instruction, fully recognizing that the commitments of his mother and father were polar opposites – his mother had a devout commitment to the Protestant faith; his father was committed to honest criticism without regard for religion. Personally, Piaget felt the painful pull of both. Although not unique, it was significant. Piaget's own theological beliefs led to his membership in the Swiss Christian Students Association with two outcomes. One was its joint meetings with the Swiss Philosophical Society, whose members included Pierre Bovet and Arnold Reymond – both influential in changing the course of Piaget's career during 1912–1918. The other outcome was later, a text on the psychology and epistemology of development (Piaget, 1923). But the personal problem was compounded by an intellectual problem that went to the foundations, later expressed as "the reconciliation of science and faith" (Piaget, 1918, p. 21). Where does truth lie when two disciplines collide? For a devout Protestant, the answer had to include religious truth; for his father, truth depended on the use of systematic and public methods. Piaget was not unique in facing the general problem of the relations between science and religion, and it remains unresolved today (Plantinga, 2007).[2] Piaget (1952, p. 240) tells us that the conflict came to a head during a holiday with his god-father at Lake Annecy. He was shown a copy of Bergson's (1911) famous book that led him to remark: "it was the first time that I heard philosophy discussed by anyone not a theologian; the shock was terrific, I must admit." Piaget had made a stunning realization. On the one hand, biological ideas required a good rationale whose tenability inevitably led to philosophy. On the other, Piaget (1952, p. 239) realized that he required some "protection against the demon of philosophy" (1952, p. 239) – the ideas central to an empirical science required good evidence, and philosophy was not in the business of providing evidence at all.

Piaget was beginning to understand that this duality appeared elsewhere. If biology required a tenable rationale as an empirical science dealing with the origin of living things, then what about the problem of knowledge in epistemology? Origins are all very well, but Kant (1787/1933, B368) had long ago pointed out that pseudo-concepts, such as the concept of fate, have an origin without being rationally legitimate. The many kinds of human knowledge are a fact of life too, so do they have only an origin in the human mind or a proper constitution too? For the young Piaget, there was an impasse. On the one hand, Bergsonian biology was theoretically rich but empirically bankrupt. On the other, religion had its basis in dogma rather than reason but, even so, its central concern was fundamentally right in dealing with the nature of life itself with special attention to values and norms.

This dual conflict came to a head. Suffering a personal breakdown, he went to Leysin in the Vaud Alps for a convalescence amounting to "uncommon voyages of self-discovery and self-renewal" (Vidal, 1994, p. 164). His first book, *Recherche*, was written during this convalescence, that is, "September 1916 to January 1917" (Piaget, 1918, p. 7).[3] Its main proposal was about how to reconcile "two cults that snuff each other out" (Piaget, 1918, p. 41). The advance for Piaget (1952, p. 240) was to combine biology and theory of knowledge through an intermediary whose identification dawned only slowly. The intermediary was psychology subject to two constraints, that is, "[two ideas] which are still dear to me, and which have never ceased to guide me" (Piaget, 1952, p. 241). One: "logic has its origin in a sort of spontaneous organisation of acts" (Piaget, 1952, p. 241). Two: "at all levels – living cell, organism, species, concepts, logical principles, etc. – the same problem about the relationships between parts and wholes is found" (Piaget, 1952, p. 242). Taken together, they implied a third: "the state of equilibrium between

the whole and the parts... corresponded to states of conscious legitimation [*conscience*] of a normative character: logical necessity or moral
obligation, as opposed to lower forms of equilibrium that characterize
non-normative states of consciousness [*conscience*] such as perception
etc., or organismic events" (p. 242).[4]

Prima facie, neither of Piaget's "dear ideas" seems particularly convincing. Piaget tells us that he interpreted his first idea as a version of
pragmatism (p. 241); yet even during the relevant period, 1914–1918,
pragmatism was open to multiple interpretations in the hands of Marx,
James, and Peirce. Which version was Piaget's? And his second idea,
despite Reymond's remark about originality, can be easily read as vacuous in view of the fundamental heterogeneity that distinguishes the
biological action of cells and the actions of human agents guided by
logical principles. But that is to miss their novelty in Piaget's hands
and their serial elaboration throughout the rest of his work. Piaget had
realized that action is amenable to empirical investigation, even though
biological action in the cell and psychological acts of an agent are not
the same thing. So this unit of analysis makes possible scientific investigation based on an empirical methodology. Further, Piaget had also
realized that although biology required an empirical methodology, evidence alone was not enough. What is required as well is an inventory of
problems along with a suitable unit of analysis. His proposal about part–
whole relationships had two specific strengths. One was its interdisci-
plinarity with the potential to span problems in a range of sciences with
special attention to whether these were the same problem in relevant
respects. The other was that knowledge entails a knower in that knowing is an ipsative process that includes itself. Effectively, these ideas
became central to Piaget's (1918, p. 118) scientific research-program.[5]
The central aim was "to explain knowledge, and in particular scientific
knowledge, on the basis of its history, its sociogenesis, and especially
the psychological origins of the notions and operations upon which it is
based" (Piaget, 1970, p. 1). In *Recherche*, the central argument was about
the contribution of states of equilibrium to the formation of knowledge,
and summarized as such by Piaget (1952, pp. 242–243). But that argument was incomplete, notably as to the process in which different states
are linked.[6]

The argument was also incomplete in another respect. Piaget (1952,
p. 243) tells us that in formulating his equilibrium theory, his understanding of how to test it empirically was non-existent. That is why
in 1918 he decided to extend his training by making a "psychological turn." A rationale for the inclusion of psychology is explicit in
Recherche in that psychology occupies a place in Piaget's (1918, p. 99)

"circle of science." Thereby its contribution is essential, even though he made it clear that existing approaches were regarded as inadequate. "The use of questionnaire methods by the Americans has been marked by hypertrophy whose outcome has been delightful puerilities, all the more so due to an army of scientists who translate their findings in mathematical terms allowing them to demonstrate the simplest and most natural results (and only those, mind you) by a complicated apparatus of curves and calculations" (Piaget, 1918, p. 63). What was required instead was a better conception of psychology, a conception that would do justice to "living organization [and thereby] permitting psychology to be at the same time both experimental and yet explanatory of the manifestations of the mind whose value is attested in metaphysical psychology" (1918, p. 160). Note well: "a better conception" – Piaget did not believe that he already had this at his disposal.[7]

This "psychological turn" was in three moves. One was an application in 1918 to the Faculty of Arts at Neuchâtel to study for a doctorate in philosophy with a psychological component. His project had a title that was accepted but without the work being formally completed.[8] Instead, Piaget gained his science doctorate. A second was his move to Zurich with a view to training in psycho-analytic approaches to the mind. This led to his exposure to Bleuler, Jung, Lipps, and Pfister (Vidal, 1994, p. 225). The third was a move to Paris. Piaget had been recommended to Théodore Simon – Alfred Binet's collaborator – who was planning a French standardization of Cyril Burt's IQ tests. Simon required a research assistant, and he invited Piaget to take this on. As well, Simon took a relaxed stance in directing his project that was devolved to Piaget who was given considerable freedom. Hard-working since his childhood with a lively inquiring mind, Piaget was at long last in a position to gain his own evidence about children's minds and their development. He set to work "without much enthusiasm" (Piaget, 1952, p. 244) – recall his comment on psychometrics in *Recherche*. But taken together, they provided the springboard that enabled Piaget to gain the psychological evidence required by his research-program. Piaget would interpret his evidence by going beyond both biology and sociology. His interpretation was based on an Hegelian argument, a *tertium quid* or third alternative that broke new ground over an existing duality.

Firstly, sociology. Piaget's (1920) first psychology paper was "Psycho-analysis as to Its Relations with Child Psychology." Its main thesis was about a fundamental phenomenon in the human mind, manifest as "the conscious and unconscious [that] are everywhere inter-linked, often in an inextricable manner. [And so] the special mechanisms that psycho-analysis has discovered in the study of feelings have effectively their importance too in the development of reason" (p. 19). Under this thesis, affectivity and intelligence are inter-linked through common mechanisms that merit special attention in child psychology (pp. 56–58). The implication is that sociology as the science of interpersonal relations could not supplant psychology as the science of intrapersonal relations due to this fundamental duality intrinsic to the human mind.

Secondly, biology. Burt's (1919) evidence was based on psychometric tests with graded questions such as item 12 for 8-year-olds in England:

> Edith is fairer than Olive, but she is darker than Lily.
>
> Who is darker – Olive or Lily?

His evidence was in terms of their age of success (see Table 1.1.):

TABLE 1.1. *Performance on Burt's Psychometric Test by Age and Gender*

Test Item	Testing Age	Average Age		Standard Deviation	
		Boys	Girls	Boys	Girls
12	8	11.8	10.1	6.0	5.5

Burt's interpretation of this evidence was that

> all the elementary mental mechanisms essential to formal reasoning are present before the child leaves the infants' department, i.e., by the mental age of seven, if not somewhat before. Development consists primarily in an increase in the extent and variety of the subject-matter to which these mechanisms can be applied, and in an increase in the precision and elaboration with which these mechanisms can operate. (1919, p. 127)

Evidence such as this fueled Burt's (1955) well-known view that the mechanism of human intelligence is innate. Yet Piaget was struck by the fact that children could not successfully answer questions based on logic. This surprising fact cried out for explanation.[9] The conclusion drawn by Piaget was that nativism is inadequate and should be replaced with a better alternative.

Piaget was grappling with a problem that would be central to his work for the rest of his life about the hypothesis explanatory of mental construction. He made his own monumental first step, adapting item 12 thus (Piaget, 1921b):

> Edith is fairer than Susan. Edith is darker than Lily.
>
> Who is the darkest, Edith, Susan, or Lily?

His evidence was based on French children ($n = 37$), and it revealed that 35 did not give the correct answer after one reading, 22 failed to do so at all, and 15 gave the correct answer after multiple readings. A check was made on Gw, aged 13 years, who helped his father by selling newspapers. His protocol ran thus. Note that he spontaneously used the premises in his own explanations (see Table 1.2).

TABLE 1.2. *Protocol of Gw*

Trial	Response Fairer < Darker	Reasons
1	Lil < Edi < Suz	[Gw correctly recalls the premises] *Edi is fairer than Suz and darker than Lil*
2	Suz < Edi < Lil	*Last time, I realized that "Edi is fairer than Suz" meant she was fairer than Suz, but because of "darker than Lil" she was the darkest of the three.* [In the grip of this contradiction] *Edi is average, Suz is fair but a bit less than Edi, Lil is dark but less than Edi* [therefore] *Lil is the darkest and Suz the fairest*
3	?	[Still under the grip of contradiction] *Edi will really be the darkest of the three, since she is darker than Lil, but on the other hand she is fairer*
4	?	[Doubt about Suz, since she is less fair than Edi]
5a	Lil < Edi = Suz	*Sometimes Suz is the darkest, sometimes it's Edi,* [so] *Suz is the same as Edi, and Lil is fairer*
5b	Lil < Edi < Suz	(Asked to identify the color of the girls' hair, his reason contradicted his response) *Edi is brown, Lil is dark, Suz is light dark that is almost black*

Source: Piaget, 1921b, p. 146.

Piaget's interpretation of this evidence was in terms of his *tertium quid*. Even in adolescence, youngsters give contrary answers to the same question – trials 2 and 5 – and also give reasons that are incompatible with their own responses – trials 2 and 5 – apparently without being aware of this. For Piaget (1921b, p. 172), "a long evolution is necessary separating what is implicit from what is explicit." That is, mental evolution is a fact of life, and so the open question concerns the laws of mental construction. In 1923, Piaget formulated a key distinction about three ways to study logical reasoning. Logic as the formal science of truth provides one way, that is, the normative study of truth-preserving deduction. Developmental psychology (*psychologie génétique*) as an empirical science provides a second way, that is, the factual study of the origins of the mechanisms used by children in their mastery of deduction. But Piaget saw a third way – his *tertium quid* – distinct and yet linked to both. "It can be asked not only how children eventually succeed [*arrive*] at deduction, but how they control the truth of their deductions, how the idea of truth presents itself to children at all. Is that a matter of logic or psychology?" (Piaget, 1923, p. 57). Crucially, this third way would focus on "developmental logic" (*logique génétique*) (p. 57) with a view to establishing the "developmental laws of thought" (*lois génétiques de la pensée*) (p. 64) (see Chapter 3, this volume).

In 1921 Piaget was offered a research post in Geneva. Except for the interval 1925–1929 in Neuchâtel where he gained his first chair, Piaget lived and worked in Geneva for the rest of his life. In 1923, he married a member of the research team – Valentine Châtenay, "my wife and loyal collaborator" (Piaget, 1952, p. 246) – who contributed to his second book (Piaget, 1923/1959). Their three children – Jacqueline, born in 1925, Lucienne in 1927, and Laurent in 1931 – made a famous contribution to Piaget's three infancy books (see Chapter 9, this volume).[10] In 1929, Piaget was appointed to a chair at the University of Geneva, where he remained for the rest of his richly varied and successful career, whose main features are briefly listed in Table 1.3 (cf. Smith, 1997, 2001).

Publications

Piaget wrote some 100 books and 600 published papers (Archives Piaget, 1989). Posthumous publications continue to appear. Piaget (1970/1983) was at pains to remind that his work was unfinished business in that he was the "chief revisionist" of his program. Indeed, in his autobiography Piaget (1952, p. 247) pointed out two defects in his early work in psychology. One: its unit of analysis was dependent on language, yet logic has its formation in action in advance of language. Two: there was no account of any "framework" such as a cognitive structure or network of norms. Further, Piaget invoked different models for the interpretation of his work, thereby demonstrating that his research-program was productive (Lakatos, 1974; see Chapter 11, this volume). In general, Piaget remarked that he saw the future of psychology "with optimism. We see new problems everyday" (quoted in Smith, 1993, 2006). Indeed, his work displays a remarkable capacity for development.

Jean Piaget died on September 16, 1980, in Geneva, Switzerland. He displayed an exceptional interdisciplinary expertise in the elaboration of a research program that is already a major contribution to human knowledge.

TABLE 1.3. *Jean Piaget 1921–1980: Principal Appointments and Prizes*

Jean Piaget 1921–1980*

Principal Appointments

1921–1925	Research Director, Institut Jean-Jacques Rousseau, Geneva
1925–1929	Professor of Psychology, Sociology and the Philosophy of Science, University of Neuchâtel
1929–1939	Professor of the History of Scientific Thought, University of Geneva
1929–1967	Director, International Bureau of Education, Geneva
1932–1971	Director, Institute of Educational Sciences, University of Geneva
1938–1951	Professor of Experimental Psychology and Sociology, University of Lausanne
1939–1952	Professor of Sociology, University of Geneva
1940–1971	Professor of Experimental Psychology, University of Geneva
1952–1963	Professor of Genetic Psychology, Sorbonne, Paris
1955–1980	Director, International Centre for Genetic Epistemology, Geneva
1971–80	Emeritus Professor, University of Geneva
1974–	Jean Piaget Archives Foundation, Geneva
1976	80th Birthday: Piaget defended his 1975 book on *Equilibration* in front of an "international and interdisciplinary" jury

Other Appointments

President	Swiss Commission UNESCO
	Swiss Society of Psychology
	French Language Association of Scientific Psychology
	International Union of Scientific Psychology
Co-Director	Department of Education, UNESCO
Member	UNESCO and 20 Academic Societies
Editor	*Archives de Psychologie* and 7 other journals

Honorary Doctorates

1936	Harvard, USA
1946	Sorbonne, France
1951	Rio de Janeiro, Brazil
1953–1975	28 other Universities

Prizes

1963	City of Geneva Prize
1967	Award for Distinguished Scientific Contribution, American Psychological Association
1970	Fonème Prize
1972	Erasmus Prize
1972	Stanley Hall Medal
1980	Balzan Prize
1966–1975	5 other Prizes

* *Source:* A Jean Piaget en l'honneur de son 80ème anniversaire, Centre de Télévision, Genève, 1976.

INTRODUCTION III. READING PIAGET IN ENGLISH

Leslie Smith

There are several reasons why reading Piaget is both an enlightening and challenging experience: (a) he was a prolific author, publishing some 100 books and 600 papers (Archives Piaget, 1989);[11] (b) he wrote primarily for himself as Piaget's (1970/1983) self-styled "chief revisionist," rather than for others with varying levels of access to and views of his *oeuvre*; (c) he was a polymath with books on biology, epistemology, logic, psychology, and sociology, all requiring interdisciplinary interpretation – more on this in the next section; (d) he was a seminal thinker from his first book *Recherche* (1918) setting out his "research-program" to his final papers *Reason* (2004/2006) with his "guiding hypothesis."

As well, English readers face two problems in that English translations may have unwelcome features in being selective or problematic. Let's take each in turn with regard to Piaget's books. But please note that the examples given are merely examples – an analysis that is systematic within any book is beyond the scope of this note. What follows is in three parts: (1) selective English translation, (2) problematic English translation, and (3) reading Piaget in English.

Selective English Translation

Although he published a small number of books in English (1953, 1968, 1970), Piaget invariably published in French, not, of course, "in Swiss" (cf. the remarks made by students at the Sorbonne in 1965/1972, p. 24). And then the problems begin:

- The time-lag between the date of French/English publications is variable, ranging from simultaneous (1932/1932) to 33 years (Piaget & Inhelder, 1941/1974).
- A translation is often re-issued with a later date of English publication; however, this usually amounts to re-cycling the original translation, not to a new translation (1947/1950 and 1947/2001).
- Only one book has been re-translated (1975/1985), its first translation (1975/1978) being seriously defective.
- The pagination of British and U.S. publications can differ (1932/1932; 1932/1965), as too the dates of U.S. and British editions (1936/1952 and 1936/1953).
- Text added to later French editions is sometimes not included in the earlier English translation; for example, a rationale of Piaget's

"critical method" in the Preface (Piaget, 1947; cf. Smith, 1993, §11) of an augmented edition of an earlier book (1924/1928). Although that is understandable, other cases are not; for example, an analysis of research on conservation in a Preface (Piaget & Inhelder, 1961) included in the second edition of an earlier French book whose English translation appeared in 1974, that is, a decade later (1941/1974; cf. Smith, 2002b, ch. 5).

- In 1955, Piaget founded his International Center for Genetic Epistemology (Centre International de l'Épistémologie Génétique – CIEG). Its publications formed a series called Studies in Genetic Epistemology (Études d'Épistémologie Génétiques – EEG) and included some 40 coauthored volumes. Most of the volumes published during 1957–1967 have not been translated – a catastrophic omission in view of the critical attention that Piaget's work was accorded during this period. Check for yourself the list of authors and titles in the bibliographies in Endnote 11. Alternatively, try to find any empirical study in the 1960s of children's development of reasoning by mathematical induction, an important and essential form of reasoning. In fact, there are no empirical studies other than in EEG 17 (Inhelder & Piaget, 1963. For a review and confirming replication, see Smith, 2002b with commentary in Rips, Bloomfield, & Asmuth, 2008). The volumes published from 1968 onward – see Piaget (2004/2006, p. 2) – have fared better, but three currently remain untranslated (two of these are reviewed in Chapter 7, this volume).
- Overall, Piaget published 88 authored or edited books in French; yet 38 (43%) are still unavailable in English; see Table 1.4. The pattern is the same or worse for Piaget's papers.

Problematic English Translation

Again, there are several manifestations, including: pseudo-translation, incomplete translation, inconsistent translation within the same book, inconsistent translation between different books, mistranslation, and typographical error.

PSEUDO-TRANSLATION. Here are three examples.

La Formation du Symbole. The main argument of Piaget's third book on infancy concerns the development of the symbolic function, that is, *Symbol Formation* (1945/1962). Its English translation as *Play, Dreams and Imitation in Childhood* severs Piaget's link with Peircean semiotics (Peirce, 1910; cf. Chapter 3, this volume).

TABLE 1.4. *Books in French Unavailable in English*

Date	Books in French Editions Unavailable in English	Pages
1918	*Recherche* The research program that dominated the rest of Piaget's life	210
1942	*Classes, relations, nombres* The logical model essential to the empirical study of number development (1941/1952)	323
1949	*Traité de logique* The generalized logical model covering development from childhood to adolescence, thereby essential to Piagetian texts during 1940–1970	423
1950	*Introduction à l'épistémologie génétique,* 3 Vols. The *chef d'oeuvre* that elaborates Piaget's genetic epistemology, i.e., developmental epistemology. It should be read in conjunction with his 1967 book	1060
1967	*Logique et connaissance scientifique* The interdisciplinary encyclopedia of developmental epistemology written by Piaget – whose contribution was one third – and peers with its rationale for his dialectical constructivism	1345
1957–1973	Etudes d'Epistémologie Génétique (EEG): This series led to annual volumes edited by Piaget. Although eight have been translated into English – the most recent is Piaget (1977/2001) – most (29) have not	circa 4000
1978	*Recherches sur la généralisation* This book on generalization was explicitly linked to its predecessor on abstraction (Piaget, 1977/2001)	262
1980	*Les formes élémentaires de la dialectique* Effectively, Piaget's final book on dialectic	249

Orage. This French word is "storm" in English. Piaget asked a good question about children's identity criteria in the demarcation of one storm from others in the same series of storms. In a translation (1975/1978) that should not be used, this question was converted into a ridiculous question about how young children distinguish oranges over an interval of time (cf. Smith, 1993, p. xiv). The correct translation *storm* is in Piaget (1975/1985, p. 123).

Pensée de l'enfant; chez tout adulte. In Piaget's (1971/1974, p. 34) account, infant intelligence is non-representational; further, some types of reasoning can be found throughout human development. The following translation does scant justice to this: *"What I maintain then is by no means particular to infant thought; it is found again not only in every adult thought but also in the development of scientific thought."* Yet in his French text, Piaget is drawing a child/adult, not an infant/adult, contrast; further, this is generalized to people, not to thoughts. Thus his claim should read: *"What I maintain is in no way confined to children's thought; it is re-found not only in every adult but even in the development of scientific thought."*

INCOMPLETE TRANSLATION. A paradigm case is the *Child's Conception of Number* (Piaget, 1941/1952), whose omissions are several and major.

First, its French title is *La Genèse du Nombre chez l'Enfant*. Thus, its literal English translation is *The Genesis of Number in the Child*, or alternatively *The Origin of Number in the Child*. It was co-authored with Alina Szeminska. Naturally enough, her name is explicit in the French text, yet her name is omitted from its English counterpart. This monstrous omission is indefensible both in itself and in view of her on-going work with Piaget (for example, Piaget, 1977/2001, ch. 1).

Second, about 15–20% of the French text has been omitted (French = 317 pages; English = 243 pages, see Chapman, 1988, p. 152). The translators alert their readers to the fact that their translation is incomplete but mischievously add "when no essential idea was involved." This is blatantly false. Furthermore, they add that their translation is stated to be with "the author's [sic] permission" (Piaget, 1941/1952, p. ix). Note this singularity; yet the French text was co-authored. Actually, Piaget (1963/1967, p. 83) gave this account of what happened: "The mathematician who did the English translation of my book, *The Child's Conception of Number* (1952) asked me to delete from the English edition the formulas I had given at the end of the French edition because they seemed shocking to him and to English logicians." Piaget then added that his formal model was independently formalized (Grize, 1967; cf. Piaget 1961/1966, pp. 172–174) and that logicians such as Quine had particizpated in CIEG programs during its presentation without identifying major objections; indeed, it was given specific support (Papert, 1963).

Third, prime examples of omission are the use of its logical model – *passim*; Piaget's "at the end" really means "at the later parts of most chapters"; omission through interpretation – instead of six logical formulae whose clarity is evident whatever position is taken about their validity, non-formal counterparts with questionable clarity and even accuracy are presented (Piaget, 1941/1952, p. 91); omission of Piaget's distinction between intensive–extensive–metric quantification (reviewed in Smith, 1993, p. 166).

Fourth, this book is an empirical study strictly dependent on its logical model (Piaget, 1942; reviewed in Chapman, 1988, and in Smith, 2002b). This model was serially and explicitly put to use in the interpretation of the evidence. By deleting "the formulas," the translators set up an empirical target in quasi-detachment from its underlying model. In the sequel, psychologists completed the detachment, submitting the evidence to alternative scrutiny without regard for its Genevan model (e.g., Bruner, Olver, & Greenfield, 1966); this was not lost in Piaget's (1968, p. 31) acid remark that "there are certain elementary distinctions which he [Bruner] does not make."

Fifth, two other defects in this translation are worth noticing. One: in view of the first word in the French title *genèse*, the English title could read *Origins of Number in the Child*. Two: the opening words on the first page of chapter 1 are *Toute connaissance* and should read: *All knowledge* – more on *connaissance* later. However and taken together, two fundamental features of Piaget's work have been severed in this English translation, namely that it is an epistemology dealing with both the origin of knowledge and, by implication, its constitution (see Chapter 3, this volume).

INCONSISTENT TRANSLATION WITHIN THE SAME BOOK. The same French word is sometimes translated in different ways within the same book. Two of Piaget's infancy texts are marked in this respect.

The Construction of Reality in the Child. In this translation (Piaget, 1937/1954), the English word *image* has become ambiguous in three ways in the first ten pages.

Représentation. The translation uses two different English words (*interpretation, image*) in place of the same French word: "*[An infant's] own interpretation of things. . . . the child's image of the world*" (p. xii). Because Piaget's account of infancy is action-based, not representation-based, English *interpretation* makes good sense; *image* does not.

Image. The French *image* is correctly translated by its English equivalent: The associationist theory of vision invoked in this context requires there to be a *mental image* (Piaget, 1937/1954, pp. 5–6).

Tableau/Tableaux. In Piaget's account of infancy, the question is raised about intelligent mastery of the actual world. Piaget's action-based proposal was as follows. First, what the young infant looks at is not thereby the same as what that infant grasps or tastes or listens to. That is, during early infancy, identity-criteria are not mastered merely in exposure to that object – the object looked at is not thereby the object grasped. Second, the actions of young infants are directed on something other than an independently existing object. Third, this is a *tableau* (plural *tableaux*). This French term is translated by two different English words – *pictures* and *images* – even on the same page (Piaget, 1937/1954, p. 8). The use of *images* is positively misleading in view of its two companion uses previously noted. Further, it leads to misconception under an empiricist interpretation in view of the incompatibility of empiricism and constructivism (Piaget, 1969; cf. Smith, 1987, 1998). Piaget's (1936/1952, p. 37) action-based account of intelligence is explicitly demarcated from a representational theory of mind (Bickhard, 2009; Müller, Sokol, & Overton, 1998).

In short, within ten pages, one English word is used for three French words. Further, two French words are non-uniformly translated. Crucially, Piaget's constructivist account of infant intelligence is rendered problematic by its conflation with rival empiricist accounts that Piaget was at pains to reject.

THE ORIGINS OF INTELLIGENCE IN THE CHILD. The French title is *La Naissance de l'Intelligence chez l'Enfant* and so literally reads *The Birth of Intelligence in the Child* (1936/1952). The same translator invariably translated *tableaux* as *images* (p. 64). For the reasons just given, this is misleading and incorrect. Further examples of inconsistency occur in both directions.

Expérience. This word has two English counterparts in *experiment* and *experience.* An experiment requires a human action directed on changing the course of nature and as such is not part of the physical order (von Wright, 1971). In Piaget's account, infants' development includes the capacity *to experiment in order to see* (Piaget, 1936/1952, p. 266). The English text later converts this to *experience* (p. 348) in a context where Piaget was at pains to distance his account from empiricist interpretations in which experience is central. Thus, the same French term is differently translated in English, and the change is substantive.

Intentionnalité, Intention. An action can be intentional in the absence of a prior, conscious intention (Anscombe, 1963). This difference is invoked in Piaget's account of the intentionality of action that precedes the formation of spontaneous intention (Piaget, 1936/1952, p. 147 and p. 321, respectively). The use of the same English word *intention* in place of these two French words merges a fundamental distinction that is invoked in the French text. Once again, this difference is substantive.

INCONSISTENT TRANSLATION BETWEEN DIFFERENT BOOKS. Examples include the following.

Schème, Schéma. This example is at the heart of Piaget's account, and it is ubiquitous. No doubt its basis is due to a Kantian influence on Piaget. Yet in general, Piaget's *modus operandi* was to adapt the principles that he would put to novel use, as too in this particular case.

The German term *Schema* – English translation: *schema* (plural: *schemata or schemas*) – was used by Kant (1787/1933, B180) to refer to the intermediary between sensory inputs (that are nonconceptual) and conceptual categories (that are non-sensory). Kant specifically denied that this could be accomplished by what he termed an *image* (see Smith, 1998). Rather, a schema was introduced as an intellectual instrument whose function was their interlinkage. Such is Kant's (1787/1933, B180) "schematism of understanding," though he candidly confessed that how this occurred was a mystery "in the depths of the human soul." Kant's basic argument ran like this. Properly constituted norms are required for knowledge true of reality; whatever sensory inputs are, they are not normative; but *a priori* categories are properly constituted as normative principles – for example: The category of causality is the principle that every event has, and has to have, a cause. Thus, for Kant, the schematism of the understanding was a necessary intermediary linking the sensory origin of knowledge with its normative constitution. Note that Kant's categories were *a priori*; but they were neither innate nor learned (see Chapter 3, this volume).

Kant's argument influenced Piaget, but notice three things. One: the German *Schema* is standardly translated in French as *schème* (Kant, 1787/1971, p. 151) – recall that in English its standard translation is *schema* (Caygill, 1995). Two: the French *schéma* has a common sense usage such as the English *outline, diagrammatic representation* – Piaget used the French *schéma* in this way, for example, *schema of organization* (Piaget, 1936/1953, p. 5), *subtle schema* (Inhelder & Piaget, 1955/1958, p. 27). Three: Piaget parted company from Kant, notably in his use of the French *schème* (English: *scheme*). Piaget (1961/1966, pp. 152–153) made the same commitments as Kant: Normative properties are required for knowing reality, and so, following Kant, such properties are not learned (Piaget, 1964, p. 176) nor are they innate (Piaget, 1936/1953, pp. 1–2). But Piaget adapted Kant's commitment to apriority: For Piaget, there are no *a priori* categories available for use at the outset of development. Instead, any human action is regulated by a framework (1936/1953, p. 6; French: *cadre*. Commentary on this notion is in Chapter 3, this volume), where a framework is a "system of mutual implications and interconnected meanings" (p. 7). Crucially, any framework is constituted by its normative properties. Unlike Kant, for whom normative categories are *a priori* and fully formed in their use, for Piaget any framework has a formation in time through its serial use; that is, human development is the successive replacement of frameworks, from simple to complex (Smith, 2006, 2009).

In short, a Piagetian scheme is a normative framework. A scheme used during infancy, such as an action scheme, is a simple framework; a scheme used in adolescence, such as an operational scheme, is complex. English readers face problems with both.

Schèmes: Actions. The translation in the infancy texts uses *schemata* (Piaget, 1936/1953, p. 6), and a few lines later, in Piaget's explicit adaptation of Kant, the *schemata of motor behavior.* This is confusing and should read *schemes* and *schematism of behavior*, the former to mark Piaget's technical term in line with his constructivism, the latter to secure its Kantian basis, "a sort of functional *a priori* of reason" (Piaget, 1936/1953, p. 9). In line with Piaget's constructivism, *scheme* is explicit in several translations (Piaget, 1961/1966, p. 170; 1966/1971, p. 37; 1977/2001, p. 30), though not in all because *schema* is confusingly still given for the French *schème* (Piaget, 1967/1971, p. 6; 1974/1980, p. 20).

Operational schemes. Adolescent thought is also regulated by *schèmes opératoires;* in the standard translation, this becomes *operational schemata* (Inhelder & Piaget, 1955/1958, p. 307), thereby removing Piaget's link between frameworks in infancy and adolescence. It should read *operational schemes* – compare Piaget's explicit definitions using *schèmes*, inclusive of actions and operations (Piaget, 1961/1966, pp. 235, 246).

MISTRANSLATION. Cases of mistranslation include the following, no doubt not a complete list.

Compréhension. This word has two meanings. One is epistemological and the English word is the same – *comprehension*: see Piaget's (1974/1978) book title. The other is logical, and the English word is *intension* in that any concept has a sense or meaning (intension), whether or not there are any cases falling under it (extension) – for example, a unicorn is not a mermaid (their intensions are different), even though there are none (their extensions are empty). In some translations, *comprehension* is given when *intension* is required (Piaget, 1941/1952, p. 161; 1974/1980, p. 19).

Connaissance. The English term is *knowledge* – it is unsurprisingly and explicitly so used in Piaget's (1967/1971) book title. It is surprising that *notion* is used in the opening lines of a famous book: *Every notion, whether it be scientific or merely a matter of common sense, presupposes a set of principles of conservation, either explicit or implicit* (Piaget, 1941/1952, p. 3); this was noted previously and should read: *All knowledge, whether scientific or merely a matter of common sense, presupposes a set of conservation principles, that are either explicit or implicit.* Because a notion is not the same as knowledge – concepts are used in false guesses – the difference is fundamental. Further commentary follows shortly (see *prise de connaissance*).

Conscience. This French term – as too the old English word *conscience* (Ferrari, Pinard, & Runions, 2001; see also Chapter 13, this volume) – has two meanings corresponding to the English words *consciousness* and *conscience*. Usually, the appropriate meaning is identified contextually, that is, cognitive and moral contexts, respectively. However, note three things. One: In Piaget's book on moral judgment, the French term *conscience* is correctly translated by English *conscience* and *consciousness* (Piaget, 1932/1932, pp. 2, 3, respectively); elsewhere in this book, alternatives for the English *conscience* include *bona fide* (p. vii) and *sense* (p. 105). Two: There is a commonality between logical and moral rules that was specifically noted by Piaget (1932/1932, p. 343); the commonality lies behind his remark that "logic is the morality of thought just as morality is the logic of action" (Piaget, 1932/1932, p. 404; cf. "logic as comparable to ethics" in Carl, 1994, p. 13). This commonality is invoked in English expressions such as *I hear what you say but in all conscience I disagree*; that is, this is something I have to do. The French *conscience* captures this, and in other contexts the same translator uses *mind*, for example, *how the mind comes to respect these rules* (Piaget, 1932/1932, p. 1; cf. pp. 1, 146, 195). There is good intent behind this use of *mind*; all the same, the link with *conscience* is lost. An alternative might be *consciousness of legitimacy* (in Brouwer, 1912/1983, p. 79; see also Chapter 3, this volume), that is, *conscious legitimation*. Three: The same translator in reference to the lag between action and thought makes intelligent use of *conscious realization* for *prise de conscience* (Piaget, 1932/1932, p. 56). More on this later (see *prise de conscience*).

Ensemble des Parties. This logical notion refers to a set S with subsets, such that the power set of S is the set of S's subsets. Thus, its English translation is *power set* (see Campbell in Piaget, 1977/2001, p. 122). By contrast, the English translation *structured whole* is vague and confusing (Inhelder & Piaget, 1955/1958, 16; *pace*, p. xix).

Prise de Connaissance, Prise de Conscience. An early translation of *prise de conscience* was *conscious realization* (Piaget, 1932/1932, p. 56) to denote the knower's dawning consciousness of something, that is, becoming aware of it. As the title of one of Piaget's books, it has been translated as *The Grasp of Consciousness* (1974/1976). But this is ambiguous because it could imply that consciousness has a capacity size, measurable by what is comprehended in it, whereas Piaget's focus is on the process of becoming conscious. Two consequential translation errors are evident. One is its predominant but not invariable translation by English *cognizance*. This severs Piaget's link between *being conscious* (p. 332, lines 1–2) and *cognizance* (p. 333, line 3). Also severed are links to Piaget's account of consciousness elsewhere (e.g., in infancy, see Piaget, 1936/1953, p. 37). Two: Worse still, *awareness* is also used for *connaissance* – for example: *awareness of what is happening outside the subject*

(Piaget, 1974/1976, p. 342). This latter should, of course, read *knowledge*. And to cap it all, *cognizance* is used for *connaissance* too: *cognizance of its results, either success or failure* (p. 334) – this too should read *knowledge*. Piaget's (1974/1978) companion text is also marked by comparable errors.

Piaget's basic point is this. All human actions are intentional such that an agent has some awareness or consciousness of an action through its goal (Piaget, 1960/1974, p. 63). For Piaget, this is interpreted as a process of becoming consciously aware of something (*prise de conscience*). As well, an agent has some knowledge of the outcome of an action. For Piaget, this is interpreted as a process of gaining knowledge of something (*prise de connaissance*). For example (Piaget, 1974/1976, ch. 2), children were asked to use a sling to hit a target – the children have an awareness of the action–goal and also knowledge as to whether the target is hit or not. Thus, there are two intellectual processes with different objects because an action–goal is not an action–outcome. The open question is how children's intelligent grasp of the similarities and differences between action–goals and action–outcomes develops, that is, the formation of the identity-criteria of these analytically distinct "objects." The ambiguous and shifting use of *cognizance* masks an epistemological distinction that is important in its own right. As well, the distinction is central to Piaget's model of equilibration (1974/1976, p. 335; 1975/1985, p. 45), and so to his periphery–center model (1974/1976, p. 335).

In my view, these translations (Piaget, 1974/1976; 1974/1978) are unreliable. The twin errors are serious, and taken together Piaget's account is unintelligible in these English texts that are thereby unreliable with regard to their central constructs.

TYPOGRAPHICAL ERROR

$$N(N-1) - (N-1)$$

The English translation of this formula from the French text is correct (1977/1995, p. 176). However, footnote 33 was added, alerting readers to an error: when $N = 100$, the number of relationships is 9801, and not 4851 as stated in the French text (p. 196). Evidently, the French text contained a typographical error, and should read:

$$\frac{N(N-1)}{2} - (N-1)$$

Reading Piaget in English

What follows are some suggestions about how to read Piaget's texts in English translation.

[i]   In any English text, identify the word(s) used to refer to a key construct and then search for its other uses in the same text.

[ii]   In the same text, identify and search for companion constructs in the same family.

[iii] Repeat [i] and [ii] using other Piagetian texts.

[iv]   Check Piaget's French texts – search for the French counterparts to the English terms. It is possible to do this without actually translating the French by analogy with FIND in word-processing.

[v]   Consult bilingual colleagues, linguists, or researchers to gain a second opinion.

In general, two things are required on the part of international publishers. In French, make available a standard edition of Piaget's books, both in hard copy and electronic formats. In English re-translate Piaget's books with a view to a standard edition inclusive of page references to its French counterpart.

NOTES

1.   Universal suffrage for women at the federal level in Switzerland was not achieved until 1971.

2.   Disputes between biologists about the standing of religion and biology are ongoing, Gould (2001) arguing for their compatibility, Dawkins (2006) their incompatibility.

3.   *Search* – Piaget's (1918) book has a précis in Gruber & Vonèche (1995). If Piaget (cf. 1952, p. 243) ignored *Recherche*, it was in 1918 through lack of psychological evidence for the philosophy required by its main argument.

4.   *Conscience* – see Chapter 3, note 15.

5.   A research-program comprises an ontology about which problems are at issue and a methodology about appropriate methods to be used in their investigation. The program is not to be confused with any specific theory or model falling under it (Lakatos, 1974).

6.   The process was later named equilibration: "thus development is in a sense a progressive equilibration, an unending change from a lesser state of equilibrium to a more advanced state" (Piaget, 1943, p. 123; cf. 1975/1985).

7.   Piaget is here referring to his own empirical work in biology in the decade 1910–1920. His stance was generalized to cover his work over the next 60 years.

8.   The title of Piaget's project was "An essay on value judgments and biological methods in the sciences of the mind" (Bessire & Béguelin, 2008, p. 66).

9.   Abduction is a logical inference starting from a "surprising fact C" to its explanation under the hypothesis "if A were true, C would be a matter of course" (Peirce, 1910/1955, p. 151).

10. Not, of course, to any of the others – see Chapter 9, this volume.
11. Two useful Web sites are:
   http://ael.archivespiaget.ch
   http://www.fondationjeanpiaget.ch/fjp/site/bibliographie/index_livres_
   alpha.php.

REFERENCES

Aczel, A. (2007). *The artist and the mathematician: The story of Nicolas Bourbaki, the genius who never existed.* London: High Stakes Publishing.

Anscombe, G. E. M. (1963). *Intention* (2nd ed.). Oxford: Blackwell.

Apostel, L. (1982). The future of Piagetian logic. *Revue Internationale de Philosophie, 36,* 567–611.

Archives Piaget. (1989). *Bibliographie Jean Piaget.* Geneva: Foundation Archives Jean Piaget.

Barrelet, J.-M., & Perret-Clermont, A.-N. (2008). Preface. In A.-N. Perret-Clermont & J.-M. Barrelet (Eds.), *Jean Piaget and Neuchâtel: The learner and the scholar* (pp. v–xv). Hove, UK: Psychology Press.

Beilin, H. (1992). Piaget's enduring contribution to developmental psychology. *Developmental Psychology, 28,* 191–204.

Bergson, H. (1911). *Creative evolution.* London: Macmillan.

Bessire, M.-J. L., & Béguelin, S. (2008). Did Jean Piaget's 'conversion' from malacology to psychology happen in the Faculty of Arts? In A.-N. Perret-Clermont & J.-M. Barrelet (Eds.), *Jean Piaget and Neuchâtel: The learner and the scholar* (pp. 62–74). Hove, UK: Psychology Press.

Bickhard, M. H. (1993). Representational content in humans and machines. *Journal of Experimental and Theoretical Artificial Intelligence, 5,* 285–333.

Bickhard, M. H. (1999). Interaction and representation. *Theory & Psychology, 9,* 435–458.

Bickhard, M. (2009). Interactivism. In J. Symons & P. Calvo (Eds.), *The Routledge companion to the philosophy of psychology* (pp. 346–359). London: Routledge.

Bringuier, J.-C. (1980). *Conversations with Jean Piaget.* Chicago: University of Chicago Press. (Original work published in 1977)

Brouwer, L. E. J. (1983). Intuitionism and formalism. In P. Benacarraf & H. Putnam (Eds.), *Philosophy of mathematics: Selected readings* (2nd ed., pp. 77–89). Cambridge: Cambridge University Press. (Original work published in 1912)

Brown, T. (2003). Reductionism and the circle of the sciences. In T. Brown & L. Smith (Eds.), *Reductionism and the development of knowledge* (pp. 3–26). Mahwah, NJ: Erlbaum.

Bruner, J., Olver, R., & Greenfield, P. (1966). *Studies in cognitive growth.* New York: Wiley.

Burt, C. (1919). The development of reasoning in school children. *Journal of Experimental Pedagogy, 5,* 68–77, 121–127.

Burt, C. (1955). Evidence for the concept of intelligence. *British Journal of Educational Psychology, 25,* 158–177.

Carl, W. (1994). *Frege's theory of sense and reference.* Cambridge: Cambridge University Press.

Caygill, H. (1995). *A Kant dictionary*. Oxford: Blackwell.

Chandler, M. (1999). Foreword. In E. L. Scholnick, K. Nelson, S. A. Gelman, & P. H. Miller (Eds.), *Conceptual development: Piaget's legacy* (pp. ix–xi). Mahwah, NJ: Erlbaum.

Chapman, M. (1987). Piaget, attentional capacity, and the functional implications of formal structure. In H. W. Reese (Ed.), *Advances in child development and behavior* (Vol. 20, pp. 229–334). Orlando, FL: Academic Press.

Chapman, M. (1988). *Constructive evolution*. Cambridge: Cambridge University Press.

de Tribolet, M. (2008). Arthur Piaget (1865–1952): Background of Jean Piaget's father. In A.-N. Perret-Clermont & J.-M. Barrelet (Eds.), *Jean Piaget and Neuchâtel: The learner and the scholar* (pp. 25–35). Hove, UK: Psychology Press.

Ferrari, M., Pinard, A., & Runions, K. (2001). Piaget's framework for a scientific study of consciousness. *Human Development, 44*, 195–213.

Gelman, R., & Baillargeon, R. (1983). A review of some Piagetian concepts. In P. H. Mussen (Series Ed.) and J. H. Flavell & E. M. Markham (Vol. Eds.), *Handbook of child psychology* (Vol. 3, pp. 167–230). New York: Wiley.

Ginsburg, H., & Opper, S. (1988). *Piaget's theory of intellectual development*. Englewood Cliffs, NJ: Prentice-Hall.

Grize, J.-B. (1967). Remarques sur l'épistémologie mathématique des nombres naturels. In J. Piaget (Ed.), *Logique et connaissance scientifique* (pp. 512–525). Paris: Gallimard.

Gruber, H., & Vonèche, J. (Eds.). (1995). *The essential Piaget*. Northvale, NJ: Jason Aronson Inc.

Halford, G. S. (1989). Reflections on 25 years of Piagetian cognitive development psychology, 1963–1988. *Human Development, 32*, 325–337.

Hamlyn, W. (1971). Epistemology and conceptual development. In T. Mischel (Ed.), *Cognitive development and epistemology* (pp. 3–24). New York: Academic Press.

Inhelder, B., & Piaget, J. (1958). *The growth of logical thinking*. London: Routledge & Kegan Paul. (Original work published in 1955)

Inhelder, B., & Piaget, J. (1963). Itération et récurrence. In P. Gréco, B. Inhelder, B. Matalon, & J. Piaget (Eds.), *La formation des raisonnements récurrentiels* (pp. 47–120). Paris: Presses Universitaires de France.

Kant, I. (1933). *Critique of pure reason* (2nd ed.). London: Macmillan. (Original work published in 1787)

Kant, I. (1971). *Critique de la raison pure*. Paris: Presses Universitaires de France. (Original work published in 1787)

Kitchener, R. F. (1986). *Piaget's theory of knowledge*. New Haven, CT: Yale University Press.

Lakatos, I. (1974). Falsification and the logic of scientific research programmes. In I. Lakatos & A. Musgrave (Eds.), *Criticism and the growth of knowledge* (pp. 91–196). Cambridge: Cambridge University Press.

Lourenço, O., & Machado, A. (1996). In defense of Piaget's theory: A reply to 10 common criticisms. *Psychological Review, 103*, 143–164.

Mays, W. (1987). Piaget on logic and number. In J. Russell (Ed.), *Philosophical perspectives on developmental psychology* (pp. 220–239). Oxford: Basil Blackwell.

Müller, U., Sokol, B., & Overton, W. (1998). Reframing a constructivist model of the development of mental representation: The role of higher-order operations. *Developmental Review, 18*, 155–201.

Natorp, P. (1910). *Die logischen Grundlagen der exakten Wissenschaften* [The logical foundation of the exact sciences]. Leipzig and Berlin: B. G. Teubner.

Papert, S. (1963). Sur la logique Piagétienne. In L. Apostel, J-B. Grize, S. Papert, & J. Piaget (Eds.), *La filiation des structures* (pp. 107–130). Paris: Presses Universitaires de France.

Peirce, C. S. (1955). Logic as semiotic: The theory of signs. In J. Buchler (Ed.), *Philosophical writings of Peirce* (pp. 98–119). New York: Dover Publications. (Original work written 1910)

Piaget, J. (1907). Un moineau albinos. *La rameau de sapin: Organe du Club jurassien, 41*, 36.

Piaget, J. (1918). *Recherche*. Lausanne: La Concorde.

Piaget, J. (1920). La psycho-analyse dans ses rapports avec la psychologie de l'enfant. *Bulletin Mensuel Sociéte Alfred Binet, 20*, 18–58.

Piaget, J. (1921a). *Introduction à la malacologie Valaisanne*. Thèse doctorale, Université de Neuchâtel. Sion: Imprimerie F. Aymon.

Piaget, J. (1921b). Une forme verbale de la comparaison chez l'enfant. *Archives de Psychologie, 18*, 141–172.

Piaget, J. (1923). La psychologie des valeurs religieuses. *Sainte-Croix 1922* (pp. 38–82). In Association Chrétienne d'Etudiants de la Suisse Romande, Lausanne: La Concorde.

Piaget, J. (1925). Psychologie et critique la connaissance. *Archives de psychologie, 19*, 193–210.

Piaget, J. (1928). *Judgment and reasoning in the child*. London: Routledge & Kegan Paul. (Original work published in 1924)

Piaget, J. (1932). *The moral judgment of the child*. London: Routledge & Kegan Paul. (Original work published in 1932)

Piaget, J. (1942). *Classes, relations, nombres: essai sur les groupement de la logistique et sur la réversibilité de la pensée*. Paris: Vrin.

Piaget, J. (1943). Le développement mental de l'enfant. *Juventus Helvetica: Notre Jeune Génération, 2*, 123–140.

Piaget, J. (1947). Avant-propos de la Troisième Edition. In J. Piaget, *Le Jugement et le raisonnement chez l'enfant* (pp. 9–10) (3rd ed.). Neuchâtel: Delachaux et Niestlé.

Piaget, J. (1949). *Traité de logique*. Paris: Colin.

Piaget, J. (1950). *Introduction à l'épistémologie génétique*. 3 Vols. Paris: Presses Universitaires de France.

Piaget, J. (1950). *The psychology of intelligence*. London: Routledge & Kegan Paul. (Original work published in 1947)

Piaget, J. (1952). *The child's conception of number*. London: Routledge & Kegan Paul. (Original work published with A. Szeminska in 1941)

Piaget, J. (1952). *Autobiography*. In C. Murchison (Ed.), *History of psychology in autobiography*, Vol. 4 (pp. 237–256). New York: Russell & Russell.

Piaget, J. (1952). *The origins of intelligence in the child*. New York: International Universities Press. (Original work published in 1936)

Piaget, J. (1953). *The origins of intelligence in the child*. London: Routledge & Kegan Paul. (Original work published in 1936)

Piaget, J. (1953). *Logic and psychology*. Manchester: Manchester University Press.

Piaget, J. (1954). *The construction of reality in the child*. London: Routledge & Kegan Paul. (Original work published in 1937)

Piaget, J. (1956). Les stades du développement intellectuel de l'enfant et de l'adolescent. In P. Osterrieth, J. Piaget, R. de Saussure, J. Tanner, H. Wallon, & R. Zazzo (Eds.), *Le problème des stades en psychologie de l'enfant* (pp. 33–42). Paris: Presses Universitaires de France.

Piaget, J. (1959). *Language and thought of the child* (3rd ed.). London: Routledge & Kegan Paul. (Original work published in 1923)

Piaget, J. (1960). *The child's conception of the world*. Totowa, NJ: Rowman & Allanheld. (Original work published in 1926)

Piaget, J. (1960). The general problems of the psychobiological development of the child. In J. M. Tanner & B. Inhelder (Eds.), *Discussions on child development*, Vol. 4 (pp. 3–27). London: Tavistock Publications.

Piaget, J. (1962). *Play, dreams, and imitation in childhood*. London: Routledge & Kegan Paul. (Original work published in 1945)

Piaget, J. (1963). Foreword. In J. Flavell, *The developmental psychology of Jean Piaget* (pp. vii–ix). New York: Van Nostrand.

Piaget, J. (1964). Development and learning. *Journal of Research on Science Teaching, 2*, 176–186.

Piaget, J. (1965). *The moral judgment of the child*. New York: The Free Press. (Original work published in 1932)

Piaget, J. (1966). Part II. In E. Beth & J. Piaget (Eds.), *Mathematical epistemology and psychology* (pp. 131–304). Dordrecht: Reidel. (Original work published in 1961)

Piaget, J. (1967). The thought of the young child. In J. Piaget, *Six psychological studies* (pp. 77–87). London: University of London Press. (Original work published in 1963)

Piaget, J. (1967). Genesis and structure in the psychology of intelligence. In J. Piaget, *Six psychological studies* (pp. 143–158). New York: Random House. (Original work published in 1964)

Piaget, J. (1967). *Logique et connaissance scientifique*. Paris: Gallimard.

Piaget, J. (1968). *On the development of memory and identity*. Barre, MA: Clark University Press.

Piaget, J. (1969). Quelques remarques sur les insuffisances de l'empirisme. *Studies Philosophica, 28*, 119–127.

Piaget, J. (1970). *Genetic epistemology*. New York: Columbia University Press

Piaget, J. (1971). *Biology and knowledge*. Edinburgh: Edinburgh University Press. (Original work published in 1967)

Piaget, J. (1972a). *Psychology and epistemology: Towards a theory of knowledge*. Harmondsworth, UK: Penguin Press. (Original work published in 1970)

Piaget, J. (1972b). *The principles of genetic epistemology*. New York: Basic Books. (Original work published in 1970)

Piaget, J. (1972). *Insights and illusions in philosophy*. London: Routledge & Kegan Paul. (Original work published in 1965)

Piaget, J. (1973). *Main trends in psychology*. London: George Allen & Unwin. (Original work published in 1970).

Piaget, J. (1974). Child praxis. In J. Piaget, *The child and reality* (pp. 63–92). London: Frederick Muller Ltd. (Original work published in 1960)

Piaget, J. (1974). Affective unconscious and cognitive unconscious. In J. Piaget, *The child and reality* (pp. 31–48). London: Frederick Muller Ltd. (Original work published in 1971)

Piaget, J. (1976). *The grasp of consciousness*. Cambridge, MA: Harvard University Press. (Original work published in 1974)

Piaget, J. (1978). *Success and understanding*. London: Routledge & Kegan Paul. (Original work published in 1974)

Piaget, J. (1978). *The development of thought*. Oxford: Blackwell. (Original work published in 1975)

Piaget, J. (1980). *Experiments in contradiction*. Chicago: University of Chicago Press. (Original work published in 1974)

Piaget, J. (1983). Piaget's theory. In P. Mussen (Ed.), *Handbook of child psychology* (4th ed., pp. 103–128). New York: Wiley. (Original work published in 1970)

Piaget, J. (1985). *Equilibration of cognitive structures*. Chicago: University of Chicago Press. (Original work published in 1975)

Piaget, J. (1995). *Sociological studies*. London: Routledge. (Original work published in 1977)

Piaget, J. (2001). *The psychology of intelligence*. London: Routledge. (Original work published in 1947)

Piaget, J. (2001). *Studies in reflecting abstraction*. Hove: Psychology Press. (Original work published in 1977)

Piaget, J. (2006). Reason. *New Ideas in Psychology, 24*, 1–29. (Original work published in 2004)

Piaget, J., & Garcia, J. (1991). *Toward a logic of meaning*. Hillsdale, NJ: Erlbaum. (Original work published in 1987)

Piaget, J., Grize, J.-B., Szeminska, A., & Vinh Bang (1977). *Epistemology and psychology of functions*. Dordrecht-Holland: D. Reidel. (Original work published in 1968)

Piaget, J., Henriques, G., & Ascher, E. (1992). *Morphisms and categories: P Comparing and transforming*. Hillsdale, NJ: Erlbaum. (Original work published in 1990)

Piaget, J., & Inhelder, B. (1961). Introduction à la seconde édition. *Le développement des quantités physiques chez l'enfant*. Neuchâtel: Delachaux et Niestlé.

Piaget, J., & Inhelder, B. (1971). *Mental imagery in the child*. London: Routledge & Kegan Paul. (Original work published in 1966)

Piaget, J., & Inhelder, B. (1974). *The child's construction of quantities*. London: Routledge & Kegan Paul. (Original work published in 1941)

Piaget, J., & Inhelder, B. (1976). The gaps in empiricism. In B. Inhelder & H. Chipman (Eds.), *Piaget and his school* (pp. 24–35). New York: Springer. (Original work published in 1969).

Plantinga, A. (2007). *Religion and science.* Retrieved March 22, 2009, from http://plato.stanford.edu/entries/religion-science/.

Reymond, A. (1908). *Logique et mathématiques: Essai historique et critique sur le nombre infini.* Doctoral thesis, University of Geneva.

Rips, L., Bloomfield, A., & Asmuth, J. (2008). From numerical concepts to concepts of number. *Behavioral and Brain Sciences, 31,* 623–642.

Schaer, J.-P. (2008). Studies at the University of Neuchâtel. In A.-N. Perret-Clermont & J.-M. Barrelet (Eds.), *Jean Piaget and Neuchâtel: The learner and the scholar* (pp. 51–61). Hove, UK: Psychology Press.

Schaller-Jeanneret, A.-F. (2008). Early schooling. In A.-N. Perret-Clermont & J.-M. Barrelet (Eds.), *Jean Piaget and Neuchâtel: The learner and the scholar* (pp. 36–50). Hove, UK: Psychology Press.

Siegel, L., & Brainerd, C. (1978). Preface. In L. Siegel & C. Brainerd (Eds.), *Alternatives to Piaget* (pp. xi–xiv). New York: Academic Press.

Sinclair, H. (1982). *Piaget on language: A perspective.* In S. Modgil & C. Modgil (Eds.), *Jean Piaget: Consensus and controversy* (pp. 167–177). New York: Praeger.

Smith, L. (1987). The infant's Copernican revolution. *Human Development, 30,* 210–224.

Smith, L. (1991). Age, ability and intellectual development in Piagetian theory. In M. Chandler & M. Chapman (Eds.), *Criteria for competence* (pp. 69–91). Hillsdale, NJ: Erlbaum.

Smith, L. (1993). *Necessary knowledge.* Hove, UK: Erlbaumm Associates Ltd.

Smith, L. (1997). *Jean Piaget.* In N. Sheehy, A. Chapman, & W. Conroy (Eds.), *Biographical dictionary of psychology* (pp. 447–452). London: Routledge.

Smith, L. (1998). On the development of mental representation. *Developmental Review, 18,* 202–227.

Smith, L. (1999a). What Piaget learned from Frege. *Developmental Review, 19,* 133–153.

Smith, L. (1999b). Epistemological principles for developmental psychology in Frege and Piaget. *New Ideas in Psychology, 17,* 83–147.

Smith, L. (2001). *Jean Piaget.* In J. A. Palmer (Ed.), *50 modern thinkers on education: From Piaget to the present* (pp. 37–44). London: Routledge.

Smith, L. (2002a). Piaget's model. In U. Goswami (Ed.), *Blackwell handbook of childhood cognitive development* (pp. 515–537). Oxford: Blackwell.

Smith, L. (2002b). *Reasoning by mathematical induction in children's arithmetic.* Oxford: Elsevier Pergamon Press.

Smith, L. (2006). Norms and normative facts in human development. In L. Smith & J. Vonèche (Eds.), *Norms in human development* (pp. 103–137). Cambridge: Cambridge University Press.

Smith, L. (2009). Wittgenstein's rule-following paradox: How to resolve it with lesson for psychology. *New Ideas in Psychology, 27,* 228–242.

Vidal, F. (1994). *Piaget before Piaget.* Cambridge, MA: Harvard University Press.

von Wright, G. H. (1971). *Explanation and understanding.* London: Routledge & Kegan Paul.

Vuyk, R. (1981). *Overview and critique of Piaget's genetic epistemology.* London: Academic Press.

2 The Historical Context of Piaget's Ideas

INTRODUCTION

The aim of this chapter is neither to trace an intellectual genealogy of Piaget nor to sketch the zeitgeist of his times, because such approaches represent a conception of biography and the history of ideas that is not ours for many reasons: verification is difficult, the reconstruction of facts is problematic, and the image of the genesis of ideas is mechanical.

So we are going to limit ourselves here to some selected examples of clear and documented influences upon Piaget during the course of his life in different locations memorable for his growth: Neuchâtel, Zurich, Paris, and Geneva.

NEUCHÂTEL (1896–1919)

Piaget's scientific and philosophical socialization, in childhood and adolescence, took place within two different groups: The Friends of Nature (Les Amis de la Nature), a society of young men interested in natural history, and the YMCA of Switzerland. The Friends of Nature was a movement started by Pierre Bovet (the future director of the J.J. Rousseau Institute). Bovet's idea was to keep the minds of young adolescents busy with scientific preoccupations rather than to let them indulge in drinking binges and sword contests in the tradition of German universities. Bovet was supported in his efforts by Samuel Cornut, Piaget's godfather and a gentleman of letters who, during a trip to Lake Annecy in Savoy, offered Bergson's (1907/1911) *Creative Evolution* to the young Piaget.

The book was a revelation for Piaget, who, so far, had been more involved in his study of mollusks than in philosophy. After observing an albino sparrow in his hometown at the age of 11, Piaget decided to publish his observation in a local journal for amateur naturalists, and with this paper (few lines long) in hand, the boy decided to offer his services to

Paul Godet, the director of the natural history museum in Neuchâtel. The director was a friend of Piaget's father and consequently agreed to employ the boy in the classification of mollusks during his time out of school. Godet, already retired, continued to head the museum. Godet was totally unaware in those years (1913–1915) of the scope of the Darwinian revolution or of the rediscovery of Mendelian heredity because he had been trained in natural history in the Lamarckian tradition. Being a Lamarckian meant believing in a transcendental order (i.e., a hierarchy that cannot be changed) of species and in circumstantial transformations under the influence of the milieu provoking an adaptive response that becomes inherited by repetition and learning. Thus, Paul Godet wanted to reach the ideal transcendental order of species through perfect classifications. His method was based on visual features such as shape, color, (thickness), size, and so on, which were used as determinants to establish a species. With Darwin and Mendel, the determinant of a species is essentially sexual reproduction.

The question of whether cross-reproduction was possible and the issue of genetic distribution were either unknown to Godet or frowned upon. Naturally, a member of the Friends of Nature like Piaget, raised as he was to look at birds, flies, flowers, and mollusks to avoid sex, drinking, and sabre fighting, could not possibly be interested in the sort of pansexualism spread by the Darwin family.

Piaget's only contact with Darwin came through the reading of Bergson's (1907/1911) *Creative Evolution*, which (unlike the two Darwinian factors of random variation and consecutive selection, which are directionless) is meaningful and purposefully directed toward the metaphysical goal of "Life in abundance." For Bergson as well as for Lamarck there is a sense to evolution, a hierarchy of beings from the inferior to the superior culminating in spiritual life. This allows for a reconciliation of science and faith with the superiority of metaphysics over physics because all scientific nomenclatures are nominalistic, that is, ideal lines of demarcation "like meridians for the geographer" (Piaget, 1912/1984, p. 106). They are useful but not truthful.

The discovery of Bergson by Piaget coincided with his undergoing a religious education to prepare for his confirmation in the Protestant Church, during which he read a Protestant theologian, Auguste Sabatier, whose ideas about religion were close to those of Bergson. So close indeed that Piaget wrote a paper about the two. What Piaget found common to the two authors was the opposition between a religious belief anchored in authority (church, Bible, or dogma) and one based upon spiritual freedom of interpretation and, thus, inner revelation of a God felt as immanent to man and universe. The parallel between Bergson and

Sabatier is that God can be identified with life and life is abundance, as in Bergson's "élan vital" (vital impulse). The same push is at work in the two cases. Therefore, Piaget could describe his encounter with *Creative Evolution* as a pure revelation because he was putting together science and faith, life and God, evangelism (authority) and liberalism within Protestantism, Darwinism and Lamarckism in biology, pragmatism, conventionalism, and nominalism on one philosophical side, and realism, Kantianism, mechanism, and vitalism on the other.

As his teacher in philosophy, Arnold Reymond, put it, Piaget was then under the illusion that he had achieved a complete system of the world. This is especially evident in the novel *Recherche* (Piaget, 1918). The book is a sort of Bildungsroman whose hero Sébastien, a young man in an identity crisis typical of adolescence, discovers his own revelation about science and religion and ridicules all the thinkers who came before him. "Apparently the author has read everyone and everything in the scientific, philosophical and theological domains. Lists of authors follow lists of authors. Bergson did not understand Bergson! Boutroux did not get the gist of Boutroux and so on" (A. Reymond, personal archives). Most of these authors are forgotten nowadays. So it is rather pointless to insist on this part of this book. Instead, it is necessary to mention that *Recherche* contains Piaget's first theory of equilibration (Vonèche, 1993), mentions the central role of action, and indicates a proximity to Gestalt theory (but places a greater importance on the activity of the subject than does Gestalt theory).

In a chapter about the influences upon Piaget, it seems beside the point to insist upon the originality of his own ideas and the quality of his insights, especially because they have been splendidly summarized by the master himself in his various autobiographies. Rather it is important to report Reymond's critical remarks, even if one does not necessarily share them, because a man that Piaget saw almost daily had obviously a strong influence on the young Piaget and on the fact that *Recherche* became a book carefully hidden by Piaget and omitted in his bibliography for 50 years. In his autobiography published in 1952, Piaget alludes to this in his typical oblique way: "My strategy proved correct: No one spoke of it [*Recherche*] except one or two indignant philosophers" (Piaget, 1952a, p. 243).

It represents also a local illustration of a broader conflict in evolutionary theory and among evolutionists between gradualists who were convinced of the old saying *Natura non facit saltus* (Nature does not make jumps) and who gathered around Pearson and Wheldon and their journal, *Questions of the Day and the Fray*, discussing small variations of species that were statistically significant and Mendelians who believed in genes and were gathered around W. Bateson and his journal *Reports of the Royal Society's Committee on Evolution*. The mere mention of this journal suffices to indicate where the power to convince stood in the fray of that day. In that day, young Piaget was fighting against a Polish research fellow working in Lausanne, W. Roszkowski, a devoted Mendelian.

For Piaget, there was no difference between *germen* and *soma* in an individual. In addition, his epistemology was, like that of most naturalists, one of the gaze (une épistémologie du regard, in M. Foucault's apt phrase). This means that at the time, Piaget refused to accept levels of reality beyond the visible ones. Thus, for him, a variation is a variation, period, regardless of any form of qualification such as hereditary or individual (fluctuating). For his opponent hereditary variations only can be considered as species; fluctuating ones cannot.

Piaget's answer to Roszkowski's argument proceeds by a form of *reductio ad absurdum*. He accepts, at first, the distinction between hereditary and fluctuating variations. Then he marshals evidence showing that some species that apparently are hereditary can be considered fluctuating. This leads to the absurd conclusion that, in the end, all species can be considered as fluctuating, which, in turn, proves his point: Well-defined and stable species arise gradually, and the same processes of adaptation that first produce fluctuating (reversible) variations, if continued, produce hereditary species. It is interesting that Piaget, although Lamarckian, does not consider the alternative conclusion that the concept of species is indeed entirely artificial, an idea advanced by Lamarck himself. This controversy put an end to Piaget's career as a naturalist.

ZURICH

When Piaget left for Zurich, he knew precious little about psychology in general and experimental psychology in particular. But, in his autobiography (Piaget, 1952a, p. 243) he claimed having gone to Zurich with the intention "of working in a psychological laboratory." This sounds rather bizarre because Geneva had an excellent laboratory created and directed by Théodore Flournoy, and France, Germany, and Great Britain had several psychological laboratories. So the choice of Zurich seems rather peculiar. As a matter of fact, during the semester he spent in Zurich from October 1918 to March 1919, he spent most of his time doing psychiatry under the direction of Eugen Bleuler and attended lectures by C. G. Jung and O. Pfister. Pfister and Piaget shared a common interest in the relation between science (especially psychoanalysis in this case) and religion (Pfister was a Protestant minister by training).

As a matter of fact, Pfister attended Piaget's three lectures on psycho-analysis in Paris (partially translated in Piaget, 1977) and wrote a report about them in *Imago* (1920). These lectures dealt with Freud, Adler, and the Zurich school of psychoanalysis, respectively. They demonstrated a good knowledge of these three directions in psychoanalysis, which Piaget presents as a system of dialectics between Freudian pansexual-ism and Adlerian achievement need, resulting in the Zurich school that "reconcile[s] these two equally interesting tendencies in psychoanalytic theory" (Piaget, 1920/1977, p. 59). Whereas Freud was focusing on the past and Adler on the present, Jung would reconcile past and present. But Piaget went beyond that and formulated, for the first time, his theory of development according to which growing up mentally means moving out of autism and into socialized reason. Thus, from 1920 on, mental development is the growth of rationality for Piaget.

PARIS

Piaget went to Paris upon P. Bovet's warm recommendation to stan-dardize in French Cyril Burt's test of intelligence for Dr. T. Simon of the famous Binet–Simon scale of intelligence in children. The young Piaget was given afternoons to test the children. This way of interviewing chil-dren during afternoons lasted for the rest of Piaget's life: Mornings were reserved to the study of logic, epistemology, and history of science. Later hours were used for psychological experimentations.

The most direct and personal influence on Piaget in Paris was cer-tainly Pierre Janet. Janet was one of the stars of French psychology, which is hard to believe now that he is either unknown or forgotten. A physician by training as well as a philosopher, Janet spent his life study-ing psychiatric patients so carefully that he invited some of them to reside in his house. He had an extended circle of friends and colleagues that included James Mark Baldwin, who had been forced to resign from Johns Hopkins University in Baltimore and was living in exile in France at the time. Although Piaget never met Baldwin (Piaget, 1982), appar-ently he became deeply interested in his work through Janet's influ-ence. Piaget imported in his theory some of Baldwin's concepts such as adualism, circular reactions in psychology, phenocopy in biology and, most importantly, several ideas into his very little known social psy-chology and sociology. Piaget was also influenced by Janet's ideas that psychology is the science of action, that representation in the child consists of the reversal from external to internal, that thinking is inter-nal discussion, and that affectivity is the motor of action and thought. Moreover, the idea that action is rooted in the sensorimotor system is also something that Piaget owes to Janet. Of course, this last point connects with Piaget's debt to Henri Poincaré, the famous mathematician and physicist. Poincaré's geometry is based on the idea of movements divided into placements and displacements coordinated by the relations between visual and proprioceptive sensations into a mathematical group. Piaget (1937/1954) used Poincaré's notion of group of displacement to describe the development of object permanence and the practical concept of space that, at the age of 2, results in the construction of a group of spatial displacements.

The genesis of the group of displacement in Piaget's mind deserves to be narrated because it illustrates the way in which Piaget worked. In his mother's family home in Paris, he once observed one of his young cousins playing with a ball. At one point, the ball rolled under the sofa. The child stopped running after the ball as soon as it was out of sight. The young Piaget was puzzled. So he fetched the ball from under the sofa and threw it to the child. After a short while, the ball rolled again under the sofa and, once again, the child did not look for it and immediately changed focus, to Piaget's bemusement. Here comes the heart of Piaget's creativity: He connected this observation with Poincaré's geometry. Piaget was reading at the time the two most famous books of Poincaré, *La Science et l'Hypothèse* (1909) and *La Valeur de la Science* (1912). This group of displacement was to be revisited in the studies by Piaget and his wife Valentine on their own three children in the mid-1920s and early 1930s. One must add that a Piagetian group of displacements is quite different from Poincaré's formulation. It has, for instance, no real mathematical quality.

Paris was also the period during which Piaget read widely about logic and especially mathematical logic. He had already been introduced to logic as a discipline somewhat distinct from philosophy by Arnold Reymond. In Paris, Piaget read the then-famous French logician Goblot (1918) and Whitehead and Russell's (1910) *Principia Mathematica* (he had already read Russell's [1903] *The Principles of Mathematics* in Neuchâtel) as well as Couturat's (1896) logical investigations. It is not clear what Piaget understood of all this. What most probably struck Piaget in Goblot's writings was the rapprochement between psychology and logic as well as the consideration of epistemology as a positive science. From Couturat (1896), Piaget probably retained the opposite point of view that "the real science of intelligence is not psychology but metaphysics" (p. 580), and that epistemology is a critique of reason and its progresses. Once again, we find here the general strategy used by Piaget throughout his life: the search for a *tertium quid* between two opposing points of view. A third way between Lamarckism and Darwinism was found in the notion of phenocopy, which is equivalent to Baldwin's notion of organic selection. In a similar way, Piaget reconciled the views of Durkheim and Tarde in sociology (i.e., the opposition between society and individuals as the final explanation of sociological processes). The same holds for mathematics and the opposition between Russell's Platonism (eternal ideas) and Poincaré's conventionalism. And so on.

Such a general strategy of discovery and explanation by the opposition of two camps allows Piaget to redefine the entire paradigm of explanation as well as the research program. Piaget also used this strategy in opposing Bergson to Brunschvicg. For Piaget, Bergson was on the side of antirationalism and Brunschvicg on that of critical rationalism. Opposing the two perspectives allowed Piaget to elaborate the first outline of his future epistemology reconciling life and reason in a third position superseding the original opposition.

Piaget retained Brunschvicg's rejection of positivism and empiricism in general. Piaget recognized the lawmaking role of human reason but without Kant's *a priori* conditions because he already held a view that was more relativistic than Brunschvicg. This raises the question of the role of Kantianism in Piaget's thinking. In the many discussions about this problem with one of us, Piaget denied any influence "except, maybe, a very indirect one . . . something like what Boring would have called the *Zeitgeist* and we all know that the *Zeitgeist* is everywhere, that is nowhere" (personal communication). We know of another example, however, where Piaget tends to cover his tracks carefully (see Piaget, 1982). With this in mind, it is difficult to inquire seriously on the topic, even though the notion of scheme so central to Piaget's system clearly comes from Leibniz via Kant, as well as a few others presumably. But discussing them in the present state of affairs would mean not abiding to our initial precautionary rule.

Brunschvicg (1912) exerted a methodological influence upon Piaget in the sense that Brunschvicg considered that a relativistic and interactionist epistemology relies on two different and complementary methods: history and psychology. To Brunschvicg, history of science is the laboratory of the epistemologist and psychological investigations of the genesis of ideas its complement at the synchronic level. This dual nature of any epistemological theory becomes one of the tenets of genetic epistemology from this moment on, although Piaget did not share Brunschvicg's idealism because he rooted his own epistemological theory in biology and the theory of evolution as he understood it, that is, as a productive *tertium* between Darwinism and Lamarckism. In this sense, Piaget's epistemology is closer to Baldwin's although it remains more restricted in its scope: Piaget's incursion in the realm of morality is limited to moral reasoning and to the demonstration that "morality is the logic of action as well as logic is the morality of thinking" (1932/1968, p. 13).

Binet influenced Piaget in many ways. For instance, in his study of perceptual mechanisms (1961/1969), Piaget is the first one to reuse Binet's distinction between what Piaget calls primary and secondary optico-geometric illusions. The former ones are called primary by Piaget (innate for Binet) because they decrease in intensity with development. The latter increase in function of development (acquired for Binet). One of us has shown that the passage from primary to secondary illusions is linked to the integration of time (Vonèche, 1970), which is typical of cognitive development going from the timeless here-and-now to ever more complex spaces and times.

Another more profound aspect of Binet's influence on Piaget is the conception of intelligence and cognition as organs (Binet & Simon, 1909). There are, at least, two ways in which Binet's conception influenced Piaget: one is by rooting the study of cognitive development in biology; the other is by considering that the basis of behavior rests upon the body's exchanges with the environment, which means that cognitive autoregulations are an integral part of all the genetic, morphogenetic, physiological, and neuronal regulations of the body. Moreover, they seem to draw from the other organic systems of the body to reorganize them in a new set of functional relations that are more complete, stable, and flexible than those of each individual organ (see Piaget, 1967/1971). As far as rooting cognition in biology, Piaget's claim is equivalent to that of Binet. Both consider that cognitive processes are adaptive (like any other organic adaptation) by assimilation and accommodation (the two opposite poles of adaptive behavior). The parallel between Piaget's and Binet's ideas is exceptional: The comparison of intelligence to an organ whose components (memory, attention, judgment, etc.) correspond to the organic cells runs deeper since Binet and Simon (1909) wrote that "the principle of adaptation is not contained in any one of the intellectual faculties [that was the way the components of intelligence were called in the psychology of the time, M. B. & J. V.] there is an idea that goes beyond the components... There is a functional dimension that forces one to consider thought as action." This programmatic statement by Binet, made only 2 years before his untimely death, was indeed implemented by Piaget.

Binet's influence is also methodological. When one thinks of it, Piaget stripped down the test method thanks to the help of the psychoanalytic method. Binet's method consists of standardized questions. Freud's approach is free associations. Piaget once again composes the two things into a *tertium*. He has in mind a certain aim: testing the mental capacities of the growing mind (its competencies in today's parlance), but this is not done rigidly by standardized questions; it follows the meanders of the child's flow of thoughts. It is exactly what Binet wanted when he wrote "what we want to read is not what the individual thinks but what she does, thus her power and not her consciousness" (Binet & Simon, 1909, p. 107). In addition, in Binet's approach tests are a hodge-podge of questions; in Piaget's approach, they are organized according to a number of logical operations. What Piaget did was to put Binet back on his feet, to use Marx's famous sentence about Hegel.

COMING TO GENEVA

The *Maison des Petits* was an institution created by Bovet and Claparède within the Rousseau Institute for the education of young children with the idea that one does not teach anything to children because they discover the world for themselves. In any case, the only task of education consists in giving opportunities to children, encouraging independent critical thinking by establishing a sort of Socratic dialogue between the child and the adult. Such an attitude fitted with Piaget's own.

In addition, Piaget found there a wealth of information about children and learning devices of all sorts. Piaget owes a lot to the pedagogy of *centres d'intérêt* (interest centers) introduced by Decroly and Claparède in Belgium and Switzerland at the moment when Dewey introduced it in the United States. This threesome was opposed to the orthopaedic approach to education recommended by Binet because their pedagogy was functional and experimental. This generated a new conflict in Piaget. Should he follow Binet and direct his research in the domain of remedial psychology for which tests of intelligence were invented, or should he join the functionalists?

Piaget's choice was rapidly made on epistemological grounds. Differential and remedial psychology as practiced by Binet and Simon meant an interest in the particular that could have seduced the gradualist in Piaget. But the true epistemologist is fascinated only by the universal and abstract. Thus Piaget sided with Claparède. In addition, there was a nice passage for the crossing-over: biology and the rooting of intelligence (cognition) in biology. This was a point of agreement between Binet and Claparède. Thus, Piaget could move from Binet's orthopaedic educational psychology to Claparède's functional psychology thanks to the orthogenetic notion of interest, which is biological in nature according to Claparède. Interest is, in Claparède's vocabulary, the psychological equivalent of biological need. The question then arises: Can we assimilate the need for food to the need to understand, and explanation to the

need for truth? For Claparède such an assimilation is perfectly legitimate: The need for food and the need for intelligence are two different
forms of vital adaptation. If this is so, how should the difference between
the need for food (which remains the same throughout life) and the need
for intelligence (which varies with age in children) be recognized and
accounted for? Because Claparède was a pragmatist (in the philosophical sense) and a functionalist (in the medical and psychological sense),
things were fairly simple: "A tadpole is not yet a frog, but it is not
imperfect, functionally speaking. Indeed, when compared to an adult
frog, it misses a lot of things (structurally): legs and lungs for instance.
But it fits perfectly its present condition which is to live in fresh water.
If it had legs, it would walk on earth and do without lungs" (Claparède,
1946, p. 22). The old Panglossian ring of *the best of all worlds* so typical
of pragmatism is so clear in this passage that the reader does not need
the transfer to child development made by Claparède (1946, p. 22): "If
the young child is not reasonable, it is simply that there no need for
reason in its present condition."

Since *Recherche*, Piaget was aware of the shortcomings of pragmatism, "a philosophy for cuckolds" (personal communication). Nevertheless, he adopted this functional dimension in his own system because
there is one formidable advantage to it. If we consider cognitive development as organized change, we need an invariant against which to
measure change, otherwise it would never be noticed. Function plays
this role perfectly well because it is immutable, though ever-changing
structures can be pegged against it!

Piaget was aware that this change in perspective requires one further
step to account for the specificity of intelligence: Function and structure have to be logical as well as biological. Thus, logic is biology by
other means. The continuity between Binet's and Claparède's teachings
is not only preserved, it is reorganized into a system of transformations
amenable to an analysis and evaluation in terms of a hierarchy of logical structures that follow each other during mental development in a
sequence ordered by the relative power of every successive new logical
structure. By so doing, Piaget maintains the invariance of the functions
of biologic as well as the transformations of the structures of the growing mind. Thus, Piaget's early pledge to "devote my life to the biological
explanation of knowledge" (personal communication) is accomplished.

However, implementation of this project took some time for two
reasons: The first of which is the fact that this project is identified ex
post facto in Piaget's (1952a) autobiography. The second one stems from
the first: Not having identified clearly his research program, he groped
at the beginning and looked for another pathway to the explanation of

knowledge. At first, in a very classical way, he dealt with language as a way of understanding logic and the growth of intelligence. One has to remember here the weight of the verbal factor in the scales of intelligence at the time (early 1920s) as well as the fact that many important figures, both in philosophy and psychology at the time, somehow fused language and thought.

It was indeed Piaget's important contribution to the question to disentangle the two. He approached the growth of language in terms that differed radically from the mainstream of the time. Most developmental psychologists considered then that the right way to understand the mastery of language by young children was simply to count the number of words used at a given age, then plotting the curve over time, and there it was.

Piaget, under the influence of J. M. Baldwin and Janet, thought that language was essentially a means of communication among fellow creatures. So he watched children interacting with each other and discovered that up to the age of about 7 they practiced what he called *collective monologue* (children talk *at* each other and not *to* each other), whose function is to accompany actions and not to substitute them. Their language is thus egocentric in nature and not really social. This led Piaget to consider that development consists of a movement from the solipsism of the baby to the egocentrism of the child to end up with the decentration of the adult. Such was the logic of the growth of knowledge – essentially a process of socialization – and Piaget decided to study his own first baby (Jacqueline, born in 1925) with this idea in mind.

His research (1932/1968) on moral judgment was going in the same direction, influenced by Bovet's conception of obedience as prompted by a sentiment of admiration for authority figures and a desire to emulate them by imitation and internalization. Piaget drew from this his two forms of morality: heteronomy and autonomy, heteronomy corresponding to Bovet's descriptions and autonomy to a new level of operational thinking corresponding to full socialization.

At this point in his thinking, Piaget was deeply and lastingly influenced by the discussion of one of his papers at the annual conference of the French Philosophical Society (1928) by the famous French developmental psychologist and psychiatrist Henri Wallon.

In his discussion of Piaget's paper, Wallon (1928, pp. 133–134) proposed the following: "Instead of making of socialization the agent, the factor of relative thinking, I would reverse the terms and I would say that when, due to its cognitive and organic development, the child becomes capable to hold simultaneously in mind two different points of view... then its sociability will be translated into terms of relative thinking."

This was acceptable to Piaget because it skipped over the sempiternal discussion about nature and nurture by focusing on a *tertium*, mental structures.

The most important influence on Piaget's theory of intelligence comes from Claparède's study of *The Genesis of Hypothesis* (1933). In 1917, Claparède developed a theory of intelligence in a paper called *La psychologie de l'intelligence*, based on a reappraisal of Thorndike's theory of trial and error (groping). Claparède distinguished two forms of groping: nonsystematic groping and systematic groping. Nonsystematic groping characterizes empirical intelligence. It happens haphazardly, without any direction, and it is selected afterward pretty much in the way natural selection works in Darwin's theory of evolution. Systematic groping, on the contrary, is systematic, oriented, under the control of thought, especially in the form of a certain awareness of relationships among objects and with the subject. Thus, the general reaction of a human being in front of novelty is neither instinctive (in the sense of a built-in system of response prior to any contact with the environment) nor acquired (in the sense of conditioning or learning) but groping. This act of groping in general, systematic or not, is, for Claparède, the sign of intelligent behavior.

Between 1917 and 1933, Claparède refined his theory. Like Binet, he considers intelligence as the form, *par excellence*, of adaptation to new situations by opposition to instinct or habit. Like Binet, Claparède distinguishes three moments in this process of adaptation: (1) questioning, (2) hypothesizing, and (3) control. Questioning means giving a direction to the search of adaptation. Hypothesis consists of either actual trials and errors or mental groping. Control is either the actual confrontation with the facts (empirical intelligence) or the use of representational relations previously established to verify the hypothesis (systematic intelligence). In this view, the two types of groping are no longer considered entirely different but as the two opposite ends of a chain of intelligent behavior. This reformulation allows Claparède to consider that the basic mechanism of intelligence is the grasp of an implication (in the logical sense) between actions and goals or, in other words, the grasp of a relation of necessity between act and aim, as in the means–ends relations. Therefore, rather than considering learning and intelligence as a long chain of stimulus–response reactions, Claparède (1933) considers the organism "as a machine for implication" (p. 106), and he explains conditioning in terms of implication: "The [Pavlovian] dog reacts to A [conditioned reflex] as if B [unconditioned reflex] were contained in, involved by A" (p. 106). Claparède (1933) even goes further:

"One could say that living involves implication" (p. 107). But the question remains: How is it possible for the dog to take the bell for the meal or, in Claparède's functionalist terminology, why does the bell function as the meal? For Claparède, this is a necessary relationship from trial one. Unfortunately, Claparède does not explain this necessity. Piaget's solution to this difficulty is fairly simple: the postulation of organized totalities composed by internal elements (*schèmes*) that are mutually implicative and by an operation (that he calls *assimilation*) inherent to the *schèmes* as well as to their mutual implication. Hence, *schèmes* assimilate each other constantly, which is why the bell can be taken for the meal as long as the meal is sometimes served when the bell is rung. If the bell is presented without the meal a sufficient number of times, it is no longer assimilated to the meal.

The notion of grasp of consciousness was also adapted by Piaget from Claparède. Claparède's concept of grasp of consciousness is expressed in a sort of law according to which the degree of awareness of an action is inversely proportional to its habitualness. Claparède rediscovered here the ancient Aristotelian law that what is last in the analysis is first in genesis.

Piaget (1928, p. 106) retains mainly the epistemological dimension of this law: Reason attempts to master experience by grasping objects before grasping the way they were constructed. Thus, reason proceeds from the most external features of experience toward the origins of the intellectual labor necessary to construct experiences under the pressure of contradictions raised by such a primitive realistic view of the state of affairs. In 1974, Piaget (1974/1976) re-elaborated his notion of grasp of consciousness. He spoke then of a process going from (successful) action to understanding (Piaget, 1974/1978). He conceived of understanding as resulting from a double process of internalization and externalization of actions. Internalization culminates in logico-mathematical structures and externalization in causality (i.e., the attribution of mental, logical, and mathematical structures to reality).

SETTLING IN GENEVA

Between 1933 and the end of World War II, Piaget transformed the Institute. So far the curriculum had been rather loose, with students coming for various periods of time from a few weeks to several years, obtaining various diplomas whose academic status was sometimes unclear. In addition, the atmosphere was very democratic, warm, and informal. Personal and academic aspects of life at the Institute were not separated. The reputation of the Institute in the city of Geneva was very bad.

"They" were very progressive politically; homoerotic relations were supposed to be openly practiced; "they" were nudists and in favor of free love; "their" children were scandalously undisciplined.

All this changed with Piaget's takeover. From semester one until the end of the course of study, students were associated with research, first by taking protocols of children's interviews, then as experimenters. This regimen had a double effect: The students had to be interested in what Piaget did (which was a difficult constraint for many), but in counterpart they could influence Piaget's thinking and the direction of research in ways most of them did not perceive clearly. Of course, this form of influence cannot be formalized, not even traced properly, because it all took place in the evanescence of free and passionate discussions.

There was a small group of people to whom Piaget read daily what he had written and from whom he requested opinions, criticisms, and discussion thereof. Some of these influences are recognized in Piaget's various autobiographies (see Vonèche, 2001), but the most important ones are indeed assimilated by Piaget so thoroughly that he sincerely thought their ideas were his.

During World War II, Piaget lived in isolated Switzerland and his contacts with foreign colleagues were limited. But in the 1950s, this desolate landscape changed drastically. American research renewed its connection with Geneva, and the American government invited Piaget to lecture in American universities, because the American government was impressed by the quality of European research in human development compared to that of the United States. Piaget declined the invitation and sent Bärbel Inhelder instead. She found the work of a trio of young Americans at Harvard, Jerome Bruner, Roger Brown, and George Miller, interesting. Their cognitive orientation due to the seminal work of H. E. Gruber seemed to fit the Genevan brand of psychology "in the arid behaviouristic landscape of America then" (Bärbel Inhelder, personal communication, 1983). After discussing with Bruner, Piaget noticed major differences in their views and was offended by Bruner's attacks on the Genevan method, considered sloppy, and on the very concept of conservation. So he fought back with a ferocious review (Piaget & McNeill, 1967) of Bruner's (Bruner, Oliver, & Greenfield, 1966) book *Studies of Cognitive Growth* as well as with a research program he launched on perception, mental imagery memory, and language. This was to counteract the division of cognitive processes into enactive, iconic, and symbolic made by Bruner. Similarly, Miller's book with Pribram and Galanter on *Plans and Structures* (1960) was considered by Piaget as closer to what he was doing than anything else in the United States. Information theory and stochastic models of learning, as well as the use of Markov chains, influenced Piaget's formulation of his theory of equilibration of the 1950s (which was abandoned rather quickly) as well as his modeling of conservation of physical quantities.

Analytical philosophy in the Anglo–Saxon world prompted a series of papers by Piaget against empiricism, logical or not. Phenomenology in Continental Europe had little further influence on Piaget because he was already closer in many ways to German thinking than to other trends in philosophy. He was indeed influenced by Brentano's notion of intension (tension toward rather than intention) that shows through his own and Claparède's notions of implication, assimilation, and *schèmes*. Piaget went so far as to consider himself (and rightly so) a subjective Gestaltist as well as a subjective behaviorist, (*l'équilibration toujours!*).

The creation, in 1955, thanks to the Rockefeller Foundation, of the International Center for Genetic Epistemology, transformed the ways and means of Piaget's research. Because the Rockefeller and Ford Foundation had already financed Claparède and Piaget before the war, it was perfectly normal for them to come back with their own backing to support Piaget's research. He could hire a large number of assistants and invite for periods ranging from a few days to a full year a series of eminent international scholars in the fields of mathematics, physics, logic, history of science, biology, and psychology. All these people were influential on Piaget, because with such a group Piaget had the opportunity to discuss extensively all his ideas and theirs. But this influence is not easily noticeable. Bärbel Inhelder's role is primordial but never apparent because, after tremendous discussions (that one of us had the opportunity to observe over a long period) on a specific research topic or on general ideas, Inhelder and Piaget ended up agreeing on a common position that they both defended with the same arguments and constancy – a perfect *entente cordiale*.

The experiments that led to the book on *The Growth of Logical Thinking from Childhood to Adolescence* (Inhelder & Piaget, 1955/1958) provide a good example of how a team of researchers changed Piaget's position. Initially, these experiments were intended as a study of induction in children. Soon, the team of experimenters discovered that most children up to 12 or 13 were incapable of formulating a coherent principle or law organizing the elements presented in the experiments. In addition, successful subjects reached the correct solution not by way of empirical induction, as expected, but by hypothetico-deductive reasoning, the use of combinatorial systems (more or less complex), and the consideration of reality as one special case among all possible cases.

This state of affairs disturbed everyone. Heated discussions followed for 1 year until Piaget reached the conclusion that the results could fit one of his earlier essays on logic (on which he had worked to make his transatlantic voyage to Brazil more pleasant!): *Essai sur les transformations des operations logiques* (1952b). The conjunction of experimental results with logic led to the stage of formal operations as the final stage of mental development, and the induction volume remained a draft.

Piaget's research on formal operations has been often criticized, especially by logical positivists who believe in falsification. Falsification is not something acceptable to Piaget, because, in spite of claims to the opposite, it relies heavily on empirical verification (note this last word, by the way), because one single instance of a black swan falsifies the statement that all swans are white.

The only relevant aspect of falsification to an antipositivist like Piaget is its meaning, that is to say the inferences made possible by the very *act* of falsifying as well as the deductive anticipations permitted by the action of looking for counterexamples or, more accurately, for one counterexample. Notice the crucial change of vocabulary: counterexamples exist only within a system of schemes coordinated among themselves within the whole of the system and with the whole itself. Thus, falsification is no longer an object (a black swan, for instance, or even an act such as finding a black swan) but the meaning hidden behind and, at the same time, revealed by the act or the object (i.e., What does looking for a black swan mean to someone stating that all swans are white?).

This is possible only within a system of coordinated implications in which truth value varies according to the scope of the implicatory system. What Piaget attempted to do all his life was develop an embryology of truth values in the growing mind and in the history of science. This is possible only through an increasing coordination of actions and operations in the individual and society. This also means that the locus of mind is no longer the brain, as vile materialists attempt to make us believe, but humankind in general through ever-increasing cooperation, as we illustrate in the next example.

Piaget's work on causality is another example of how a team of researchers influenced Piaget's thinking. Piaget had worked on physical causality as a young man (1926/1972, 1927/1972), but he later was utterly dissatisfied with his work, which he considered too naïve. So with the help of all the researchers of the Centre for Genetic Epistemology, he studied the question in 1966. For 3 long years, he was not pleased with the solutions the group was imagining until, one day, one of the children was presented with a classical physical apparatus called *Newton's balls* that consists of a series of five or six balls, each suspended to an independent string. Contrary to naïve expectations, when an impulse is given to the first one, the last one alone in the row moves.

Upon observing the last one move, this child told the experimenter: "I am the one to give the movement and it runs unseen through the balls, because it has to." This answer pleased Piaget because it illustrated, according to him, Maine de Biran's theory of causality, which views causality as an extension to the objects of human power. Young psychologists in the group who had been trained in general psychology told him about attribution theory. Logicians mentioned possible similarities between transmission of movement and transitivity. Piaget got started, and after long discussions he came up with his theory of causality as the attribution to objects of some of the operations of the subject (Piaget, 1971/1974). As these examples illustrate, one should think of the Genevan School as an artists' colony, a medieval or Renaissance workshop, rather than Aristotle's group with one and only one mastermind.

CONCLUSION

This chapter represents an attempt to demonstrate that Piaget's creativity relies upon a dialectical process of opposition between two camps, considered thesis and antithesis, resolved in a new synthesis redefining the entire field. A number of examples of this research strategy were provided such as the opposition between Darwin and Lamarck, Bateson and Pearson, or Binet and Claparède. Others could have been elaborated such as opposition between Durkheim and Tarde in sociology or between Russell against Poincaré in mathematics, which shows that this strategy was widely used by Piaget.

Opinions may diverge about the pertinence and effectiveness of attempting to solve epistemologically important scientific problems in this way. Nevertheless, the fact remains that Einstein, when told by Piaget in Princeton about the famous experiments on the conservation of physical quantities, exclaimed: "Genial, so eine einfache Idee!" (Wonderful, such a simple idea!).

REFERENCES

Bergson, H. (1911). *Creative evolution*. New York: Henri Holt. (Original work published in 1907)

Binet, A., & Simon, T. (1909). L'intelligence des imbéciles. *Année Psychologique, 15*, 1–147.

Bruner, J., Oliver, R. O., & Greenfield, P. M. (1966). *Studies in cognitive growth*. New York: Wiley.

Brunschvicg, L. (1912). *Les étapes de la philosophie mathématique*. Paris: Alcan.

Claparède, E. (1917). La psychologie de l'intelligence. *Scientia, 11*, 353–368.

Claparède, E. (1933). La genèse de l'hypothèse. *Archives de Psychologie, 24*, 1–155.

Claparède, E. (1946). *L'éducation fonctionnelle ou psychologie de l'enfant et pédagogie expérimentale.* Neuchâtel: Delachaux & Niestlé.

Couturat, E. (1896). *L'infini mathématique.* Paris: Alcan.

Goblot, E. (1918). *Traité de logique.* Paris: Alcan.

Inhelder, B., & Piaget, J. (1958). *The growth of logical thinking from childhood to adolescence.* New York: Basic Books. (Original work published in 1955)

Miller, G. A., Galanter, E., & Pribram, K. H. (1960). *Plans and the structure of behaviour.* New York: Holt.

Pfister, O. (1920). Jean Piaget, la psychoanalyse et la pèdadogie. *Imago, 6*, 294–295.

Piaget, J. (1918). *Recherche.* Lausanne: La Concorde.

Piaget, J. (1928). Les trios systèmes de la pensée de l'enfant: Etude sur les rapports de la pensée rationnelle et de l'intelligence motrice. *Bulletin de la Societé Française de Philosophie, 28*, 97–141.

Piaget, J. (1952a). Autobiography. In E. G. Boring, H. S. Langfeld, H. Werner, & R. M. Yerkes (Eds.), *A history of psychology in autobiography* (Vol. 4, pp. 237–256). New York: Russell & Russell.

Piaget, J. (1952b). *Essai sur les transformations des operations logiques.* Paris: Presses Universitaires de France.

Piaget, J. (1954). *The construction of reality in the child.* New York: Basic Books. (Original work published in 1937)

Piaget, J. (1968). *The moral judgement of the child.* London: Routledge & Kegan Paul. (Original work published in 1932)

Piaget, J. (1969). *The mechanisms of perception.* London: Routledge & Kegan Paul. (Original work published in 1961)

Piaget, J. (1971). *Biology and knowledge.* Chicago: University of Chicago Press. (Original work published in 1967)

Piaget, J. (1972). *The child's conception of the world.* Totowa, NJ: Littlefield Adams. (Original work published in 1926)

Piaget, J. (1972). *The child's conception of physical causality.* Totowa, NJ: Littlefield Adams. (Original work published in 1927)

Piaget, J. (1974). *Understanding causality.* New York: Norton. (Original work published in 1971)

Piaget, J. (1976). *The grasp of consciousness.* Cambridge, MA: Harvard University Press. (Original work published in 1974)

Piaget, J. (1977). Psychoanalysis in its relations with child psychology. In H. E. Gruber & J. J. Voneche (Eds.), *The essential Piaget* (pp. 55–59). New York: Basic Books. (Original work published in 1920)

Piaget, J. (1978). *Success and understanding.* London: Routledge & Kegan Paul. (Original work published in 1974)

Piaget, J. (1982). Reflections on Baldwin, an interview conducted and presented by J. Jacques Vonèche. In J. M. Broughton & D. J. Freeman-Moir (Eds.), *The cognitive-developmental psychology of James Mark Baldwin: Current theory and research in genetic epistemology* (pp. 80–86). Englewood Cliffs, NJ: Ablex.

Piaget, J. (1984). La vanité de la nomenclature (edited by F. Vidal). *History and Philosophy of the Life Sciences, 6*, 75–106. (Unpublished lecture, held 1912)

Piaget, J., & McNeill, D. (1967). Cognitions and conservations: Two views. *Contemporary Psychology, 13*, 530–533.

Poincaré, H. (1909). *La science et l'hypothèse*. Paris: Flammarion.

Poincaré, H. (1912). *La Valeur de la Science*. Paris: Flammarion.

Russell, B. (1903). *The principles of mathematics*. London: Allen & Unwin.

Vonèche, J. (1970). *Les effets consécutifs figuraux*. Bruxelles-Louvain: Vander.

Vonèche, J. (1993). Piaget's first theory of equilibration (1918). In D. Maurice & J. Montangero (Eds.), *Equilibrium and equilibration* (pp. 3–15). Geneva: Fondation Archives Jean Piaget.

Vonèche, J. (2001). Identity and narrative in Piaget's autobiographies. In J. Brockmeier (Ed.), *Narrative and identity* (pp. 219–246). Amsterdam, Philadelphia: John Benjamins.

Wallon, H. (1928). L'autisme du malade et l'égocentrisme enfantin: Intervention aux discussions de la these de Piaget. *Bulletin de la Societe Française de Philosophie, 28*, 131–136.

Whitehead, A. N., & Russell, B. (1910). *Principia mathematica*. Cambridge, UK: Cambridge University Press.

3   Piaget's Developmental Epistemology

Developmental epistemology is not to be confused with developmental psychology and the latter is not identical with child psychology. (Instead) it bridges the gap between developmental psychology and epistemology in general, which it helps to enrich. . . . Developmental epistemology is thus by nature an interdisciplinary research, where developmental psychology plays a necessary but not sufficient role.

Adapted from Jean Piaget (1966/1973)[1]

I INTRODUCTION

Knowledge leads to problems that emerge within and between disciplines. Where does truth lie when different disciplines such as science and religion clash as "two cults that snuff each other out" (Piaget, 1918, p. 41)? What Piaget wanted to know was the nature of the intellectual instrument – the *ipse intellectus* (Piaget, 2004/2006, note 30) – operative in human knowing and responsible for rational (dis)agreement. If there is no such instrument, rational exchange is impossible; that is, there is no such thing as knowledge true of reality at all nor even misconception. Piaget's (1918, p. 152) proposal was that scientific laws (*lois*) are understood through different kinds (*genres*) of knowing.

Effectively, this was his "research-program" (p. 118) whose resolution was to dominate the rest of his life. It charted a novel course between science and philosophy in being inter-dependent with both (1925, p. 131). Piaget (1950, p. 13) later called his proposal genetic epistemology, or the study of the "mechanisms in the growth of the different kinds of knowledge" (1957, p. 14). This subtle definition is elaborated in section 4, but two things can be noticed right now. First, the study deals with changes in human development in terms of sequences and mechanisms. Second, the study deals with these changes as facts and norms. The study is factual in being empirical and so based on evidence. The study is also normative in two inter-dependent respects. Firstly, its focus is on how the knower distinguishes what is right from what is wrong – not merely in morality but also in mathematics, indeed in human experience generally. Secondly, its focus is also on the formation of such knowledge through lesser and better states, with special attention to how this is understood from the knower's perspective. I (Smith, 2006b, p. 115) call Piaget's proposal developmental epistemology (DE).[2]

One conclusion is already evident. Piaget repeatedly re-stated DE as a commitment to a "circle" (1918) or "spiral" (1950) or "family" (1979) of sciences. This means that DE is "necessarily interdisciplinary" (1965/1972, p. 29) – interdisciplinary in combining normative epistemology and empirical psychology, necessarily so in view of its joint focus on both in the same account without collapsing the distinction between facts and norms.

My chapter is in four parts. The first two parts are critiques of psychology and epistemology. My argument will be that though both are essential to DE, each has deficiences that require remediation. Specificially, DE's psychology will be a psychology of normative facts, and its epistemology will be a dialectical constructivism. The third part is an analysis of DE's principles. Their central function is a resolution of Piaget's dominating problem, which is to show how human knowledge has both an empirical origin and a normatively tenable constitution. Its central notions are action and their frameworks comprising networks of norms. Reasons for actions secure a bridge-head from the implicit use to their conscious realization. Human knowledge with its origin in action has a proper constitution in virtue of its degree of fit with scientific frameworks in human history. Although the fit is typically unrecognized by the knower, demonstrations of the knower's expertise provide intersubjective grounds of knowledge true of reality. The final part sets out a summary and main implications of this argument as well as challenges to it.

2 PSYCHOLOGY

The focus in this section is how and why psychology makes a necessary, but not a sufficient, contribution to DE. Its contribution is necessary because evidence is required about the availability of the intellectual instrument used in knowing the world, but not sufficient because psychology, as a causal science, has principled limits that preclude its adequate explication of key notions of human knowledge, notably its constitution, truth, and necessity.

Evidence

DE's "first principle [is] to take psychology seriously" (Piaget, 1970, p. 9). This principle seems clear-cut as a commitment to the psychology of human development. No doubt this is one reason why Piaget's work has been influential in psychology. However, this principle also has substantial qualifications.

An account of human knowing requires a psychology of the knower because there is no knowledge without a knowing subject, and this is so in both psychogenesis and sociogenesis (Piaget, 1967a, p. 38; 1967c, p. 395). But the psychology invoked in philosophy is typically "armchair" psychology, dependent on reflection devoid of evidence. Reflection, whether banal or insightful, could not amount to law without the proper controls required for empirical testing. As an empirical science, psychology aims to ensure such controls are undertaken (Piaget, 1963/1968, pp. 153–156). That is why DE requires a psychology.

The qualification concerns what sort of psychology this would be. Piaget's argument referred to experimental evidence, yet Piaget explicitly declined to take any interest in the experimental investigation of causal variables (see Piaget, 1941/1952, p. 149). In DE, causal variables are not in the frame of reference because mental functioning operates through implication, not causation – through norms, not causes. It was long ago noticed that Piaget's work amounts to the "psychology of normative facts" (Isaacs, 1951). "The truth of $2 + 2 = 4$ is not the 'cause' of the truth $4 - 2 = 2$ in the same way that a cannon causes the movement of two billiard balls. [The truth] of $2 + 2 = 4$ 'implies' that of $4 - 2 = 2$ which is quite a different matter" (Piaget, 1963/1968, p. 187). In DE, the distinction between causality and normativity is fundamental to the type of psychology at issue.

Origins and Constitution

As an empirical science, psychology can describe any display of the human mind at work. Developmental psychology has a particular contribution to make in charting *origins*, for example, number development in childhood (Carey, 2008; Sophian, 2007). But a second step is also required: The mind's work is not always good work. Kant (1787/1933, B368) argued that pseudo-rational concepts have an origin without being properly constituted – his example was the concept of fate. Such concepts have an empirical origin, even though they are illegitimate in being either vacuous or antinomic. For example, the Queen offered to hire Alice on the understanding that "there is jam every other day, but never jam today" (Carroll, 1871) – is this serious, or is it a joke? Cantor's set theory led both to transcendental numbers and to Russell's (1919) paradox – to intellectual triumph and to disaster. Charting the origins of human knowledge is all very well, but establishing its constitution is an essential requirement too. Cultures are littered with such concepts from astrology through phlogiston to zoism. That is why an account of human knowing should also deal with the *constitution* of knowledge, that is, its proper legitimation (Kant, 1787/1933, B116-116). How is valid knowledge distinguished from invalid counterfeits? Why are its operative principles legitimate and not disreputable? Is its functioning rational or capricious?

Kant argued that he had identified a set of *a priori* categories valid for all human knowledge.[3] For Kant (1787/1933, B1), these categories had a debut in – not a derivation from – experience. In DE, the formation of human knowledge comprises both factual origins and normative constitution (Piaget, 1970/1972, p. 92). Following Kant, Piaget argued that psychology deals with questions about origins but not about constitution, because "psychology knows nothing of the distinction between fact and norm" (Piaget, 1925, p. 197). That is why psychology is not enough, why it has to be combined with a normative theory. In DE, constitution is factual and normative, occurring as a temporal process of "continuous construction" throughout human development (Piaget, 1970, p. 77).[4]

Truth

Human knowledge is objective in that knowledge entails the truth of what is known, a principle attested over two millennia (Moser, 1995). In DE, infant activity is confined to "success or practical adaptation, whereas the function of verbal or conceptual thought is to know and state truths" (Piaget, 1937/1954, p. 360). Thus, the notion of truth is formed *after* infancy, where its origin is open to psychological investigation (Piaget, 1928/1995, p. 184). Less clear is how causal psychology can explain its constitution (Piaget, 1923, p. 57).

The formation of the notion of truth is not merely a causal matter. Weather-cocks blow in the wind without knowing which way the wind is blowing – no weather-cock understands the meaning of its own causality (Peirce, 1910/1955). Parrots reliably use language without knowing its significance – they say "this is red" without realizing that "this is colored" (Brandom, 2000). Human thinking can be causally manipulated – a veritable *Truman Show* – leaving anyone in a mental state well short of knowledge; that is, beliefs can be false under causal conditions reliably productive of them while masquerading for knowledge by their owner's lights (Plato, 1935). Indeed, the thinking of any person can be true without any realization that it is so, still less why it is so. Surely knowledge is more than that (Gettier, 1963).

The key distinction can be brought out as follows (Frege, 1977, p. 7):

(a)   thinking, i.e. grasping a thought;
(b)   making a judgment, i.e. recognizing or acknowledging its truth;
(c)   expressing a judgment.

Frege's argument was that (a) my thinking about the Pythagorean theorem, for example, is different from (b) my recognizing the truth of the Pythagorean theorem, that is, judging it to be true. What I think may be true, or false, or even have no truth-value at all in being manifest as wishful thinking, suppositions, questions, or imperatives. But even if a thought has a truth-value, this is not something I have to understand for me to think it. To make a judgment is to recognize a thought to be true, that is, recognize the thought as true. Thus, if I make a judgment, I have to acknowledge in some way my thought to be true or false, that is, I have to make a controlled use of the notion of truth. Both (a) and (b) are different from (c), my stating that the Pythagorean theorem is true, in that I can think or make a judgment without expressing this. For Frege (1979, pp. 2–4), causal psychology deals with the origin of thoughts under (a) but has no business with the logic central to judgments under (b). This is because human error has a causal aetiology, and yet the notion of truth is a logical – not a psychological – notion. The capability for judgment-making operates through the logic of reasons, not the psychology of causes, and to suppose otherwise would result in a "hitherto unknown type of madness" (Frege quoted in Smith, 2006b, p. 106).[5]

Piaget did not accept this omnibus rejection of psychology due to his interdisciplinary commitment (see previous section). Psychology can investigate the thinking of children or adults cross-culturally, whether their thinking is true or false. But he did accept that causal psychology is insufficient, and that is why Isaacs' remark (quoted in section 1) is astute. What DE requires is specific evidence about how the notion of truth has a formation during childhood, that is, how the norms of truth are used correctly.

Necessity

Whatever is true is true, but not all truths are necessary truths. It is true that adding two pebbles to two pebbles makes four pebbles; but adding two drops of water to two drops can make one pool (Piaget, 1967d, p. 582). What this means is that the action of adding actual objects together can have alternative outcomes; the sum of adding two and two can be other than four – that is a real possibility, and no contradiction arises from this. Yet the mathematical addition $2 + 2 = 4$ has an invariant outcome that could not be otherwise. Social contexts provide ubiquitous cases of the same point: If one bottle of beer costs £1, six individual bottles may cost £6, whereas a six-pack costs £5. Even so, $6 \times 1 = 6$ is not only true but necessarily true. For Aristotle, necessity is anything that could not be otherwise; for Leibniz, a necessity is anything whose negation implies a contradiction (Piaget, 1977/1986). Paradigm examples of necessities are mathematical truths, such as $2 + 2 = 4$, and logical inferences, such as

> The wine is Sauvignon, red or white
> It is not red Cabernet Sauvignon
> therefore
> It is white Sauvignon Blanc

Given these premises, this conclusion is a necessity – its negation is impossible in entailing contradictions. Of course, the premises could be false – the wine might be rosé; or the conclusion could be a preference – trout is on the menu; it could even be a causal regularity – in Marlborough, we always have white wine, though we do have red wine available. Maybe, but that is all irrelevant as to the relation linking these premises/conclusion, namely the necessitating relation of entailment. And the point is that human knowledge includes necessary knowledge.

Piaget regarded the formation of necessary knowledge as DE's central problem:

> the distinction between what is *necessary* and what is *simply given*, or between what is necessary and what is conventional, is infinitely more difficult to establish than Kant supposed (Piaget, 1925, p. 195);

> the main problem of any epistemology is in fact to understand how the mind succeeds in *constructing necessary relationships*, which appear to be independent of time, if the instruments of thought are merely psychological operations that are subject to evolution and are constituted in time (Piaget, 1950, p. 23);

> the emergence of *logical necessity* constitutes the central problem in the psychogenesis of logical structures (Piaget, 1967c, p. 391);

> *necessity is not an observable*, based on a reading from objects.... From this arises our interest in the study of *its formation during psychogenesis*. (Piaget, 1977/1986, p. 302);

> at issue is how to explain) the advance from a temporal construction to an atemporal necessity (Piaget & Garcia, 1983/1989, p. 15).

The reason why the formation of necessity is a problem in DE is that human knowledge has its origin in the actual world, that is, the world in which everything is the case (Wittgenstein, 1972). Anything that is the case is thereby true. But a modal fallacy is committed in inferring a necessity from a truth. It is true that the Earth has one moon – but not a necessity because the facts could have been otherwise. Indeed, that is why empirical investigations are required to check the facts. Although necessary truths have an origin in experience, their derivation has to lie elsewhere, as Kant (1787/1933, B1) convincingly argued against Humean empiricism. Piaget sided with Kant against Hume but then went on to add two complications serving to augment the psychogenetic problem. One is the early development of pseudo-necessities. The other is the difference between verifying and demonstrating necessities (Piaget, 2004/2006, notes 12, 25). Both are taken up in the next section.

3 EPISTEMOLOGY

The focus in this section is on why and how epistemology makes a necessary, but not sufficient, contribution to DE. Its contribution is necessary for the analysis of the intellectual instrument used in knowing the world, but not sufficient primarily because it has traditionally been unable to resolve questions about the actual availability of this instrument for all knowers, including children. DE is an epistemology with a particular commitment to dialectical constructivism.

Theory of Knowledge

As a branch of philosophy, epistemology is theory of knowledge and standardly regarded as a normative discipline dealing with problems about knowledge and reality (Piaget, 1961/1966, p. 149). These problems require "norms, for if we try to deal with problems of principles and foundations, we have to discuss norms" (Piaget, 1965/1972, p. 165*). Knowledge has normative properties that require an organization with a proper legitimation – that is why causal psychology is not enough. Thus, an analysis of knowledge has to show how these normative requirements are met. Epistemology makes a necessary contribution as a principal resource from which all Piaget's problems were recast in his research-program (Piaget, 1918, p. 118; 1952, p. 240). But normative epistemology is not sufficient for DE on several counts.

In DE, all epistemologies are classified through two principles: Human knowledge implies a knowing subject and known object, and human knowledge has a structure and genesis. Each principle leads to a triad, making a ninefold taxonomy (Piaget, 1967e, p. 1240; see Table 3.1).[6] Two main objections are marshaled against the first two columns, leading to DE's preferred categorization as dialectical constructivism.

TABLE 3.1. *Piaget's Taxonomy of Epistemologies*

	Structure	**Genesis**	**Constructivism**
O Object	realism Plato	empiricism Locke	dialectic of nature Marx
S Subject	apriorism Kant	conventionalism Poincaré	historical relativism Brunschvicg
S-O interaction	phenomenology Husserl	identification Leibniz	dialectic Piaget

Briefly, DE's argument against epistemologies in the first column is its complete rejection of the preformation of any structure of knowledge independently of a knowing subject. The truths arising from such a structure would be independent, whereas in DE "any truth [is] relative to a determinate level of thought under development, including fundamental logical truths" (Piaget, 1950, p. 46). DE's argument against epistemologies in the second column is its rejection of the formation of knowledge without any organization. In DE, the same fact, for example, an apple falling to the ground, is a "fact" only through its variable interpretation due to the right questions being asked – for Newton, this was one thing, for Adam/Eve something else (Piaget, 1965/1972, p. 126). In general, what appeared true or necessary at one point in history – such as Aristotle's logic or Euclidean geometry – does not always appear so in the sequel (Piaget, 1925, p. 196; 1962/2000, p. 243; 1967e, p. 1267). DE's overriding commitment is to an epistemology providing an overall coordination of both principles in the same account. This is because the formation of all knowledge depends on its normative constitution and its empirical origin. Further, DE is dialectical in view of the coordination between known object and knowing subject, where this includes an individual evolution (psychogenesis) and a social history (sociogenesis).

Availability

In DE, non-empirical epistemologies are argued to be incapable of addressing the factual implications of their own analyses, even denying the relevance of empirical evidence at all (Piaget, 1965/1972, pp. 11–19). "Platonic, rationalist or apriorist epistemologies suppose themselves to have found some fundamental instrument of knowledge that is, extraneous, superior or prior to experience. [But such doctrines] have omitted to verify that it was actually at the subject's disposal. Here whether we like it or not is a question of fact" (Piaget, 1952/1977, p. 5*).[7] An epistemology provides an analysis of an intellectual instrument by whose use knowledge can be gained. An essential question to ask is whether this instrument is in fact available to all knowing subjects. There can be no answer to this question in normative – non-empirical – epistemologies, neither severally nor jointly. Yet an answer is required for an adequate resolution of the issue central to DE, namely how in fact the different kinds of knowledge grow.

4 DEVELOPMENTAL EPISTEMOLOGY

This section is an analysis of DE's main principles for the study of the formation of knowledge, including its origins and constitution through its development. A sociogenetic framework can serve as a template against which a psychogenetic framework is compared, although the latter can contribute in the sequel to the formation of new sociogenetic frameworks. This strategy is in line with the "spiral of sciences" intrinsic to DE (see section 1). An important implication is that necessitating reasons can be investigated as normative facts in the interpretation of equilibration as a developmental mechanism, a notoriously problematic construct.

Definition

DE is a scientific epistemology dealing with the formation of knowledge.[8] Its formation includes two processes. One is sociogenesis dealing with the different kinds of knowledge relative to their historical development within societies and their cultural transmission through generations (Piaget, 1967c, p. 397). The other is psychogenesis dealing with elementary notions emergent during the development of individuals (Piaget, 1967b, p. 65). The unit of analysis in both is a framework (*cadre*). In sociogenesis (Piaget & Garcia, 1983/1989, p. 248), frameworks include formal structures and knowledge systems. In psychogenesis (Piaget, 1936/1953, p. 6; 1977/2001, p. 320), frameworks include action-schemes and cognitive structures. Complementary to its definition in section 1, DE's aim is

> to grasp knowledge in its growth (for this formation is itself a mechanism of growth, without an absolute beginning) and assuming that such growth always simultaneously gives rise to questions of facts and of norms, it tries to combine the only adequate methods for deciding such questions. (Piaget, 1965/1972, p. 76*; see also 1950, p. 13; 1970, p. 1; 1970/1972, p. 15)

This definition is complex, so here is my analysis of its main features.

Sequences

In DE, all knowledge has its formation in sequences of construction and re-construction. Constructions occur as advances from one level (*niveau*) to the next in an invariant order. However, variability in knowing within any level is *not* excluded; that is, there are multiple developmental routes at any level en route to the next. By analogy with contour lines on a map with as many contours as the scale and map size require, contours/levels do not determine routes (Smith, 2002b). Constructions are without end; that is, there is neither a first nor last level (1977/1986, p. 302).[9] Crucially, constructions are indefinitely successive, occurring as a series of steps (*étapes*) of variable size, none of which is complete. Paradigm cases include children's reasoning restricted to "contiguous" steps in analogical reasoning without generalization (Piaget, 1977/2001, pp. 147–148) and/or modal reasoning about "limited co-necessities" (Piaget, 1977/1986, p. 302) (see examples of Ad Hoc Necessity and Pseudo-necessity in Appendix 1).

A stage (*stade*) is a particular level, defined through three criteria – the level is prepared by the previous level and integrated in its successor level; the triple occur in an invariant order independent of age; all actions at that level have the same organization (Piaget, 1967/1971, p. 17). The third criterion does not state that all of an agent's actions are at that level, merely that if they are, their organization is the same. As well, the framework corresponding to a stage in an individual's development has the same organization as that of a public framework in the history of science. A stage is comparable to a 250 m contour shown in bold on a map, that is, emboldened on pragmatic grounds in that no contour/level in itself differs from any other. Indeed in DE, achievement occurs at a variable speeds dependent, *inter alia*, on pedagogy (see Chapter 15, this volume).[10]

So interpreted, construction is compatible with human creativity in the construction of novel knowledge, that is, "new relationships and new instruments of thought" (Piaget, 1975/1985, p. 67). In DE, novelty amounts to a new step not already contained in its predecessors. This is an important consequence in that DE's central aim is to make explicit the steps and levels between children's and scientific knowledge (Piaget, 1967a, p. 15).

Mechanisms

DE's central assumption is that "common mechanisms" are operative in the formation of all knowledge (Piaget & Garcia, 1983/1989, pp. 26–28).[11]

These mechanisms are operative in the actions of knowing subjects – no knowing subject, no knowledge. Thereby is the origin of all knowledge secured in actions. The mechanisms in the constitution of knowledge include reasons for action. Action is discussed right now; reasons as well as their common link through norms are discussed in the next section.

Actions are intentional, meaningful, and normative, and they secure the origin of knowledge as a capability amounting to what an agent knows how to do.

First, intentionality. In DE, "an action is not some sort of movement but rather a system of movements coordinated in virtue of a result or an intention" (Piaget, 1960/1974, p. 63*). A category mistake is made in conflating the intentionality of action and the causality of bodily movement.[12] Thus, Lucienne's reflex movement in grasping her mother's finger (Piaget, 1936/1953, p. 89) is not an action, whereas her retrieval of a watch hidden under a box is (Piaget, 1936/1953, p. 287). An action is goal-directed in that its agent is aware of the goal "in the action" without requiring prior, conscious intention.[13]

Second, meaning. "An assimilatory scheme [i.e., primitive framework] confers meaning on the objects that it assimilates and assigns goals to the action it organizes" (Piaget, 1975/1985, p. 16; cf. 1977/1986, p. 305). When Lucienne "grasps her coverlet in her right hand" (Piaget, 1936/1953, p. 99), this action has meaning – for Lucienne there and then. In DE, infants' actions have meanings as a consequence of Peircean semiotics. Piaget (1936/1953, p. 191*) adopted Peirce's (1910/1955, p. 102) three types of signifiers – index (indice), symbol, sign. Thus, Lucienne's action can have indexical meaning. But Piaget also adapted Peirce's account. For Peirce (1910/1955, pp. 99–100), meaning is always triadic and based on two relations, one between a signifier S and its object O, another between that same object O and an interpretant, I, usually a person.[14] In DE, a framework is an interpretant, and human development consists in the change in frameworks over time, covering indexical, symbolic, and sign-based signification. In consequence, action as knowing how to do something is a predecessor of understanding as knowing what something is (Piaget, 2004/2006, note 3).

Third, norms. A scheme is a primitive framework for determining what is to be done, or otherwise not done; for example, Lucienne initially did not suck her fingers, although later her fingers found her mouth (Piaget, 1936/1953, p. 54). Piaget's comment was that her fingers went in the "right" (bonne) direction – for Lucienne, this action-scheme was determinative of what she was doing. The control is normative in that human intelligence is a control system "consisting in the sum-total of rules of control which intelligence makes use of for its own direction" (Piaget, 1932/1932, p. 405).

The control is not a causal control in bio-psychology but rather normative regulation in intelligent action. Human intelligence amounts to activities and acts in a system; that is, the system is a framework with an organization consisting in norms. The organization has a normative characterization in terms of meaningful implications (square, therefore rectangular) and obligations (red traffic light, so have to stop). This is so for all intentional activities. "Every act of intelligence presupposes a system of mutual implications and interconnected meanings" (Piaget, 1936/1953, p. 7).

In general, "the evolution of norms therefore raises a problem whose roots extend right down to the sources of action and primitive relations between conscious legitimation [*conscience*] and organism" (Piaget, 1950, p. 30).[15] All actions are norm-laden; that is, a human agent is "always 'norm-laden' [*toujours normé*]" (Piaget, 1965, p. 159). This is true from birth onward: "From the beginning and even among our youngest subjects, a physical fact is recorded only within a logico-mathematical framework, however elementary it may be" (Piaget, 1977/2001, p. 320). The norms initially operative in infancy are about successful adaptation (Piaget, 1936/1953, p. 240) and only subsequently about "norms of coherence and the unity of logical thought" (p. 11). Human agency does not exclude the independent operation of psycho-biological causation nor is it reducible to it. The meaning of an action is not the causality of bodily movements, nor is an action's meaning captured by studying the causal processes – for example, in neuroscience – underlying bodily movements because these have no meaning in themselves. Nor are norms reducible to causes. Crucially, an action is self-initiated by its agent, who has the capability to re-act, that is, repeat the action or change it. In DE, the serial exercise of this capability is regulation, that is, reinforcement or correction (Piaget, 1975/1985, p. 16). What are reinforced or corrected are the norms in the framework as an initially unwitting accompaniment of the agent's intentionality and meaning.

Norms and Normative Facts

In 20th-century psychology, three positions about norms were evident as (Smith, 2006a, pp. 9–15):

(a)   norm-denial – norms are like phlogiston, non-existent;
(b)   norm-reduction to causality – norms are psychometric averages or social regularities;
(c)   norms as norm-laden in a distinctive sense.

DE is incompatible with (a) and (b) due to its commitment to (c); so what sense is this? DE's stance is elegantly summarized in the difference between the causality of number-making and the normativity of number-implication: "2 does not 'make' 4, its meaning 'implies' that 2 + 2 = 4 (Piaget, 1967/1971, p. 49). In general, normative capabilities are not the same as causal capacities in three respects. One is norm-recognition: A norm is presupposed in the recognition of a norm – a signpost lacks an interpretant and so does not recognize the direction it signifies (Brandom, 2000). Another is norm-commitment: A norm already accepted causally by "normative pressure" can be later confirmed or rejected in an agent's autonomous commitment (von Wright, 1983). A third is norm-creation: Whatever the causal facts may be, any norm can be created, and then revised, rejected, or replaced by another norm (Piaget, 1975/1985).

My analysis of (c) depends on two conditions about a norm's double accessibility, namely that a norm is manifest in a pattern of action or understanding in virtue of its binding force on the norm-user (Smith, 2006b, p. 116). The pattern is publicly available in norm-use and so open to third-person investigation. The binding-force amounts to "has to" whereby the pattern is obligated or necessitated for the norm-user as a first-person committal. In learning the rules of a game, "it remains to be understood why a player applies the rules thus learnt, and accepts them as valid: by pure convention, [or] as an obligation" (Piaget, 1961/1966, p. 143*). Norms are often socially transmitted and training can be perfectly successful. Even so, compliance with a norm and autonomous commitment to a norm as a norm are not the same thing.

Norms comprise multiple varieties (for examples in children's mathematics, see Appendix 1; further examples in game-playing are in Smith, 2006a). Firstly, norms are not confined to morality; mathematical norms are valid norms, as indeed are the principles in any aspect of experience. Secondly, there are many inventories of norms (Brandom, 2000); a sextet due to von Wright (1963) includes rules, commands, directives, customs, moral principles, and ideals. Thirdly, norms have a history, even a future. New norms can come into existence – veritable acts of creation – and old norms can be annulled (von Wright, 1983). Fourthly, human development includes the formation of pseudo-norms and "false absolutes" (Piaget, 1962/2000, 2004/2006). In short, any norm-user is both a creative agent and a committed patient in a normative maze. Moral dilemmas are a reminder that no norm is a singleton, and this generalizes to all varieties of norm – for example, in arithmetic, the addition rule is one norm with implications for other norms such as subtraction, multiplication, and division.

In Piaget's account, an operation is a norm-use such that "an operation is never isolated. It is always linked to other operations, and, as a result it is always part of a total structure" (Piaget, 1964, p. 177).

Norms cannot annul causes, but they can lead to actions that reinforce or correct causes. And norms function in distinctive ways (Smith, 2006a):

- determination in laying down what something is; e.g., handling a ball in soccer is a foul, whereas in rugby it is an intrinsic part of the game;
- legitimation in judging what is right or wrong, e.g., the entailments from addition to multiplication in $(3 + 4) = 7 \Rightarrow (3 \times 4) = 12$;
- necessitation or "has to be" as obligation in action, e.g., Luther's "I cannot do otherwise," or necessitation in understanding, e.g., Spinoza's "1, 2, 3, so the next number in the same proportion has to be 6."

Norms are not derivable from facts, otherwise psychologism arises (see section 5). But the use of a norm is a normative fact in which a norm is invoked unwittingly or wittingly by the user. In turn, a normative fact is not a causal fact, otherwise the norm-causes distinction collapses. Rather, normative facts are "facts in experience permitting the observation that a particular agent considers him- or herself to be obligated by a norm, irrespective of its validity from the observer's point of view" (Piaget, 1950/1995, p. 30). Examples of normative facts are in Appendix 2.

From a third-person perspective, the normative facts of other agents are available for public investigation. But there are two constraints. One is that even though normative facts are open to third-person observation, the corresponding norm is not. The other is that normative facts are facts dependent on interpretation through a normative theory available in sociogenesis.

Origins and Constitution Re-Visited

What is now required is an account of two bridges, one for the individual's advance from success to understanding, the other for the fit between individual and public frameworks.

Psychogenetic bridge. This bridge runs from action to understanding. Actions as such do not have a truth-value, whereas understanding based on knowledge is true of reality. Consequently, this bridge is required in advances from action to thought.

Schematically, the transition is manifest as vertical *décalage* or the temporal lag from *pratique* to *conscience*, that is, from the use of a norm to its conscious legitimation.[16] A norm can be used without recognition of

- its presence in regulating an action;
- its implications in the context of other norms in the framework;
- its obligations for action;
- its necessitations for understanding.

"The subject never achieves clear knowledge of his own actions except by way of their results on objects [and] succeeds in understanding objects only by means of inferences linked to coordinations of the same actions" (Piaget, 1975/1985, p. 45). Such is the cognitive unconscious in that norms can be used without their conscious realization that is initially non-existent, then lacunary and distorting, and always incomplete (Piaget, 1971/1974, p. 35). That is why multiple mechanisms – this plural was noted and in section 1 – are invoked in DE, including equilibration, egocentrism, abstraction.

In DE, there are no norms as ideal objects, no "answer book" available in advance for any individual to consult. "[There are no] ideal kinds of objects, given once and for all from within or without us: they no longer have ontological meaning" (Piaget, 1970/1972, p. 70). Nor is there a short-cut through consciousness because the emergence of norms is a slow process. Instead, DE's commitment is to knowing as the "search for truth" (Piaget, 1965/1972, p. 21) in that the knower sets out "to attain truth" (Piaget, 1967/1971, p. 361*). This commitment leaves open whether the search is successful (Piaget, 1975/1985, p. 6), but it strictly requires the search to be made by the knower – otherwise that individual would be wholly reliant on extrinsic authority. However, there is no teleology of final causes – no search for truth as truth known in advance to the knower (Piaget, 1965/1972, p. 42; 1975/1985, p. 139).

Norms are operative from early infancy, but that leaves open which norms these are and how they are used. For example (Piaget, 1932/1932; cf. Smith, 2006b):

- Toddlers play with marbles without any regard for the rules of the game (p. 25).
- Children begin to learn to play marbles by the rules (pp. 28–30).
- Youngsters play marbles successfully by the rules (pp. 35–40).

Thus, norm-use is mastered partially and sequentially. In general, a knower should have an epistemic expertise sufficient to resolve the fatal ambiguity between "I think I know X" and "I know X," that is, Frege's distinction between (a) thinking and (b) judging (see section 2).[17] In DE, any knowing subject has dual aspects (Piaget, 1961/1966, p. 238). One is the psychological subject distinguished by the individual differences between one subject and any other (Piaget, 1965/1972, pp. 48–49). The other is the epistemological subject distinguished by intersubjective identities, that is, the self-same principles that are common ground between different subjects. That is why in DE, public methods, such as experimentation and formal proof (1963/1968), are intersubjective in being "valid for all" (Piaget, 1924/1928, p. 24).[18] The distinction between these dual aspects is crucial. One leads to a psychology of causal facts about individual differences under variable contingencies, contexts, and cultures. The other leads to a psychology of normative facts about how the same norms are constructed, permitting rational agreement or rational disagreement.

Norms are elaborated through reason-giving in terms of implications and obligations in the agent's action framework (Piaget, 2004/2006, note 3). Initially, reasons remain implicit. But following Baldwin, DE amounts to no "sophism of the implicit" (Piaget, 1928/1995, p. 189) in view of its strict requirement for norms to be operative in actual reasoning. Norms implicit in the agent's framework become explicit as implications or obligations in the agent's reasons. What is required is some acknowledgment of "what has to be, what couldn't be otherwise," at least under that framework. That is why DE's main problem is the formation of necessary knowledge (see section 2). Without norms, knowledge is impossible; without necessities and obligations, norms are impossible.

There are many varieties of reason (see Appendix 1). Their diversity reinforces the case for DE as a science, and the detection of an agent's normatively charged reasons reinforces the case for DE as an epistemology. The language of modal logic – *must, can't, have to, necessary* – is often on display in children's expressions of their reasons. Even so, this is not sufficient – reasons expressed in modal language can be unsound. Nor is it necessary – reasons can be sound without being expressed in modal language. Sound reasons are necessitating, including reasons as preconditions, consequences, and linkages (see Appendix 3).

Reasons are constituting on three counts. Firstly, reasons are the criteria as to how knowledge is constituted by the knower. Without reasons, nobody is in a position to know whether a response is true or false and is thereby precluded from resolving the fatal ambiguity in (a) and (b). That is why in DE "the key question for analysis is the examination of what subjects regard as proof or 'reason' for what they regard as a truth" (Piaget, 2004/2006, p. 7). Secondly, a reason used as verification is not the same as a reason used in demonstration (Piaget, 2004/2006, p. 7; see Appendix 3). Reasons can be learned, amounting to "inert knowledge" (Whitehead, 1932); they can also be productive, generating novel knowledge. Thirdly, reasons can be necessitating in action or understanding, serving three functions. One is to make explicit what was implicit in the norms in the framework. "The role of reason is thus to introduce new necessities into systems where they were merely implicit or remained unacknowledged" (Piaget, 2004/2006, p. 8). A second is to integrate any norm with others in the framework, that is, the "normative character of necessary integrations" (1977/1986, p. 313) – see the previous section on sequences. A third is to demonstrate, and set out the rationale why, something is the case or even has to be.

An important implication of this argument is that if reasons are normative facts, they are empirically investigable. And if reasons are mechanisms, they contribute to – and are even part of – its central construct, equilibration (Piaget, 1975/1985, p. 3). This means that DE's central construct is both intelligible (Smith, 2002b) and testable (Smith, 2006b).

Sociogenetic bridge. This bridge runs from an individual to a public framework. Truth is important because scientific laws are laws true of reality. And DE's aim is to explain how knowledge of these laws is developed. But truth cannot be a wholly individual matter. If I can develop true knowledge, and you can too, what happens if we disagree? A framework valid only for any single individual runs into the problem of having to reconcile contradictions within and between frameworks. How, then, does DE avoid anarchy where "anything goes"?

Behind this question is Piaget's (1936/1953, p. 8) accord problem.[19] The problem has two parts, the "accord of thought with itself," that is, coherence (Piaget, 1975/1985, p. 13), and the "accord of thought with things," that is, objectivity (cf. Piaget, 1967/1971, p. 65).

DE's proposal is to focus on the interplay between psychogenetic and sociogenetic frameworks and to do so in terms of dialectical constructivism. The proposal does not amount to their mere addition, because "society no more knows how to create reason than does the individual" (Piaget, 1933/1995, p. 227). Instead, the proposal is for an investigator's focus on the relations between frameworks directed on establishing convergences and divergences between norms and normative facts. For example, children's number reasoning can be checked against mathematical frameworks such as category theory (see Chapter 10, this volume); the converse check should also be made from psychogenetic evidence to sociogenetic norms (see Piaget & Garcia, 1983/1989).

DE provides no overarching solution to the accord problem, valid once and for all and for all knowledge. Although some philosophers – notably Kant – claimed to have provided such a rationale in terms of *a priori* categories, no such stance could be tenable in DE with its express commitment to constructions "without end." That is why DE contains no *a priori a quo* (*from which*): Norms are not preformed and ready for use at the outset of life; instead, there are principles *a priori ad quem* (*to which*): Norms in sociogenesis serve as a limit for psychogenetic sequences (Piaget, 1961/1966, p. 282; 1965/1972, p. 57). The interplay between frameworks in psychogenesis and in sociogenesis is a dialectic on several counts. The interplay is not a causal correlation but a rational coordination of normative facts and norms. New normative frameworks can lead to the detection of new normative facts. New normative facts can contribute to the formation of new frameworks of norms. This sequence of turn-takings can continue indefinitely, even when frameworks judged to be consistent and complete are recast in the sequel – for example, the logic of Aristotle, the geometry of Euclid, the physics of Newton.[20]

What DE provides is a defeasible solution, that is, a solution valid unless revised, rejected, or recast in the sequel on jointly factual and normative grounds. This solution is methodological in being a recursive analysis of the reciprocal relations between facts and norms, cases and principles. As a control over adequacy, three conditions should be met (Piaget, 1963/1968, pp. 159–161):

- Normative facts are lawful.
- A law is deducible within a normative system.
- The system has an actual instantiation.

These conditions entail the interplay of empirical verification (normative facts) and demonstration (normative theories) in the same explanation. Notice, though, that DE does not entail that all norm-use is "optimizing" (Piaget, 1975/1985, pp. 3–6). A use satisfying these conditions could amount to regression, or steady-state, or progression.

5 IMPLICATIONS AND CHALLENGES

I have argued that Piaget's DE is a necessarily interdisciplinary study of the formation of knowledge, that is, the actual origins and constitution of the different kinds of knowledge. The study of origins requires evidence from an empirical psychology; the study of constitution requires norms in a normative epistemology. DE maintains a joint focus on the relations between these disciplines with special reference to the coordination of normative facts and norms in the same account. Complementary to this joint focus is the reciprocal interplay between the knowing frameworks whose formation occurs in individuals and the knowledge systems whose formation is in the history of science. In DE, there is no over-arching rationale as the grounds of the objectivity and coherence of human knowledge. Instead, the accord between norms and normative facts – principles and cases – is an endless series of mutual adjustments co-extensive with human life.

IMPLICATIONS

My Argument has Four Main Conclusions.

1. DE is necessarily interdisciplinary. Critical commentary on DE is vulnerable to premature closure without adequate regard for the integrity of the interdisciplinary whole. One manifestation is to detach a disciplinary part for individual scrutiny. Another is to survey the whole "from without." In Piaget's (1963) view, both are endemic, a trend that has continued with rare exceptions.

2. In DE, the normative problem "How is knowledge possible?" is converted into an empirical counterpart "How does knowledge develop?" for study in a psychology of normative facts about how in fact knowledge is organized through its development. Because norms are not reducible to causes, that is why a psychology exclusively directed on causal facts would be seriously incomplete. Currently this is most psychology.

3. DE is a dialectical constructivism directed on the relations between normative facts and norms, where these relations include reference to both the origin and constitution of knowing as coordination – not merely correlation – due to knowing subjects and known objects.

4. In DE, the formation of knowledge is sequential through indefinitely many levels of construction whose mechanisms of advance are actions and reasons, both in psychogensis and sociogenesis. Actions are organized through normative frameworks, that is, obligations and implications that are operative but implicit in action frameworks and becoming explicit in the agent's reasons. So interpreted, equilibration becomes a testable process about the formation of necessitating reasons. There is no over-arching rationale that guarantees the objectivity of knowledge; there is a methodology by whose use progress can be made toward rational (dis)agreement.

Challenges

Because of space limitations, my argument has been limited in two respects. One is its focus on psychogenesis to the virtual exclusion of sociogenesis. The other is its focus on DE's exegesis without due regard for its evaluation. However, some key challenges can be identified:

Does DE imply psychologism and so is inherently flawed? No (see section 4). Psychologism is the exclusively factual justification of normative laws, and psychologism is a fallacy (Kusch, 2007). DE does not commit this fallacy (Smith, 2006b). Instead, it leads to the open question of how to explain the formation of mature norms from primitive norms (cf. Bickhard, 2009; Brandom, 2000).

Piagetian stage theory – hasn't this been scientifically discredited? No (see Chapters 1 and 15, this volume). DE implies developmental levels, not stages. Almost all the research (Case, 1992) on Piagetian stages confounds chronological age, a pseudo-criterion, and DE's official criteria summarized in section 4. Claims such as "There are four Piagetian stages emergent at ages. . . . " or "Children can conserve at four years" are incorrect or incomplete, and usually both.

Is not causal psychology sufficient – witness its success in Theory of Mind (TOM) research on false belief? No. A central conclusion in TOM research is children's understanding of false belief (Wellman, 2002). Yet this conclusion is indeterminate in view of its conflation of Frege's distinction between thinking and judging (see section 2). That distinction requires the *children's* understanding of the normativity of belief. But normativity is not causality, and so is non-interpretable in causal models currently used in TOM research.

Is not a psychology of the origins of knowledge without its constitution sufficient? No. It is not sufficient for psychologists to attribute "their" knowledge to children in experimental conditions. If adult psychologists have a constituting expertise, how did they gain it? Nobody wholly reliant on the causal laws of psychology would be able to demarcate truth from falsity at all.

Reasons are important in their way but surely not essential? No. Necessitating reasons are criteria whose use amounts to the actual mechanisms that revise and recast the norms operative in action frameworks. Statistical analyses of response frequencies in human development (Lewis, 2005; Siegler, 2007) are supplementary indicators of reason-giving acts in knowledge constitution.

Conclusion

Piaget's DE is a novel research-program for a scientific epistemology. As such, it should be evaluated by the extent to which its problem-shift is degenerative or progressive (Lakatos, 1974). I want to end with Piaget's verdict on this: "The most criticized author in the history of psychology [and] I came through alive" (in Smith, 2002b, p. 515).[21]

APPENDIX I VARIETIES OF REASONS

Non-Necessity – Contradiction

Seven disks A–G were presented in pairs, visually identical but each subliminally smaller in size than its successor. Disks were presented pairwise such that the size difference was detected only in the final A–G comparison. ALA did not respect the transitivity of relations when asked about their relative size (Piaget, 1974/1980, p. 7).

JP   So what about them all together?
ALA   A, B, C, D, E, F are the same, G is bigger, and G is the same as F

Pseudo-Necessity

A three-dimensional, box-shaped figure whose five visible sides are white was presented. PHI was asked the color of the invisible, rear side. A fallacy is committed in merging a necessity with a contingency (Piaget, 1981/1987, p. 31).

PHI   White
JP   Could there be any other color?
PHI   No
JP   Why?
PHI   The box is all white and so the back can't be another color

Ad Hoc Necessity

This type of necessity is constrained by prevailing contingencies, contexts, or cultures.

In an analogy task, drawings were presented in a jumbled order. The children's contribution was in two parts, first to place the drawings in pairs that go well together, and second to bring together two pairs that go well together (Piaget, 1977/2001, p. 142).

CAN   (Builds his pairs in a regular fashion: vacuum cleaner
      socket) otherwise you can't vacuum; (bird feather) other-
      wise it can't fly; (and dog fur) otherwise he'll be cold. (Nev-
      ertheless, CAN did not succeed on any problem requiring
      relations among relations.)

Limited Necessity

Multiplication is logically equivalent to repeated addition. Children
with the ability to add were presented two collections of chips, A and
B. The task was to take chips two at a time from A and three at a time
from B so as to make equal piles (Piaget, 1977/2001, p. 61).

MIL   (Tries two times 2 As and one times 3 Bs, then realizes)
      No, it isn't right. You'll still have to put another 3 Bs and
      another 2 As. That way both will have 6

Unlimited Necessity

The task dealt with the systematic classification through a power set.
The children were shown objects for grouping in three ways: squares–
circles, big–small, red–green. They were then asked to select objects
through specified combinations of properties (Piaget, 1978, p. 24).

JP   Can you show me everything other than the big, green
      square?
BLA   (Correct enumeration)
JP   And the contrary of that?
BLA   (He indicates the small, red square). Ah, no – the right
      answer is small, red circle. (Asked to explain what a con-
      trary is.) You have to do it in the right way: red – not the
      color, small – not the size, round – not the shape.

APPENDIX 2 NORMS AND NORMATIVE FACTS

In a conservation task, children aged 5–7 years were shown two lines of
blue or white buttons under the usual two conditions, initial one–one
spatial correspondence (Figure 3.1a) followed by the lengthening of the
white line (Figure 3.1b).

The children were asked whether there was the same in each line
or more in one than the other. They were also asked to explain their
answer.

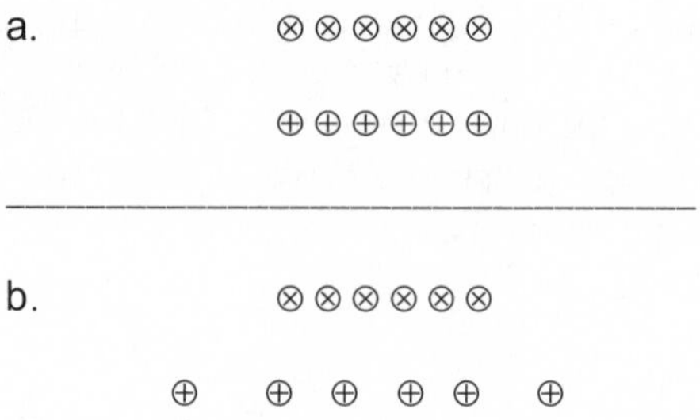

a.   ⊗ ⊗ ⊗ ⊗ ⊗ ⊗

               ⊕ ⊕ ⊕ ⊕ ⊕ ⊕

---

b.   ⊗ ⊗ ⊗ ⊗ ⊗

      ⊕   ⊕   ⊕   ⊕   ⊕   ⊕

Figure 3.1. Conservation of number. Alignment of buttons before (a) and after (b) transformation. ⊗ = blue; ⊕ = white.

Norms in Non-Conservation

Some children (10%) answered that there were "More Blues."

- More blues because you've taken two away.
- Fewer whites because these two aren't there.

These reasons are revealing – the two end white buttons were still there, they could be clearly seen in being moved 1 cm along the table. These children believed that these two buttons were no longer part of the Blue line and, in consequence, there were only four blue buttons left in the line. "6 Blues, 4 Whites, therefore more Blues." This amounts to a case of normative misconception, not to miscounting: moving a button 1 cm meant its disqualification from line membership. A norm about the spatial coincidence of endpoints was invoked to determine which buttons were still in the line and which were not. An analogy (not used by the children) is that a soccer player can stand on the touch line after being sent off by the referee – there on the touch-line but not there on the pitch.

Norms in Conservation

Three quarters of the children answered correctly "the same in each." More interesting were their reasons in two respects.

(a) Some children specifically argued: (*the same*) "*because them ones are not out;*" that is, spatial variation does not alter the equality.
(b) Some children invoked norms of necessity because "it's always got to be the same, because it's just stretched out so it's a longer length, and it will still be the same if you stretched out the blue ones as well."

These amount to the explicit use of modal notions in a sound justification about why spatial change has no bearing on equality of quantity. The key point is that reasons reveal which norms are in fact operative in mental functioning, and so their detection requires their characterization as normative facts.

Source: Smith, 2002a, pp. 67–78.

APPENDIX 3 NECESSITATING REASONS

Pseudo-Reasons, Verifications, Demonstrations

The children were asked to build three pillars A, B, C out of equal-sized blocks such that a wooden rail would run from A to B and another from B to C in a single slope – for example, three towers made from 3, 2, 1 blocks respectively. A marble was then placed at the top, without a push, for its descent. At issue were variable conditions under which the children should ensure a decreasing order of height in the pillars. Three things to notice are initial displays of unsound pseudo-reasons, later displays of procedural conditions sufficient for success; eventual displays of necessitations relative to the intension (meaning) of the reasons for this success (1983/1987, pp. 37, 42*, 45).

PSEUDO-REASONS

San   (3,2,1. What if I add 1A, 1B, 1C, i.e. 4,3,2.) That wouldn't work, it would be too high. (And from 3,2,1: what if I take away 1A, 1B, 1C?) That wouldn't go: there wouldn't be any downhill

VERIFICATION

Dom   (For 3,2,2 begins by adding one block to A and notes that with 4,2,2) it doesn't roll like a marble. . . . (He concludes immediately.) It takes another one on A and [hesitating] one here (on B, confidently. Why?) Because with four A, three B, and two C, I'll always have a drop.

DEMONSTRATION

Lau   (With 2,2,1, removes 1B then 1C, thus 2,1,0. Is it the same speed as 3,2,1, presented earlier?) That amounts to the same, because there was only one less to take away. (For 3,3,1) We have to either add one there (A) or take one off (B). (For 4,3,3). We have to add one there (A) and one there (on the second, i.e., B. And what if you want to make only on change?) Take off there (B: 3)

NOTES

1. References to Piaget's work include dual dates to French and English publications respectively; pagination is to the latter and * indicates my emended translation. Translations from work unavailable in English are mine.
2. *Genetic* can be misleading – Piaget's focus would be not on DNA, but on genesis, i.e., origin. Psychogenesis and sociogenesis deal with individual and public origins. This focus took Piaget well beyond child psychology (Kitchener, 1986, p. 1; cf. Piaget, 2004/2006, p. 10).
3. *A priori* in being independent of experience but not in being innate (Kitcher, 1990, pp. 15–16). Compare Kant (1770, 2–395): "the categories of understanding do not function as innate concepts."
4. Piaget also parted company from Kant – see section 4.
5. On Frege and Piaget, see Smith (1999a, 1999b, 2006b).
6. This taxonomy is an advance over earlier accounts of its rows (Piaget, 1947/1950) and columns (Piaget, 1964/1968).
7. Evidence-free accounts still abound (Dummett, 1981, p. 678; Husserl, 1965, p. 101/111; Wittgenstein, 1972, 4.1121).
8. "Alternative characterizations are "biological epistemology" (1967/ 1971, p. 64), "constructivist epistemology" (1981/1987, p. 3).
9. "*Construction sans fin... régression sans fin*" (1967d, p. 577/587).
10. See Chapman (1988, pp. 340–368).
11. These mechanisms bear neither on the content of concepts nor its representational machinery nor independent variables for experimental manipulation *pace* (Carey, 1987; Case, 1992; Fodor, 1975; Siegler, 2007).
12. A bodily movement (arm rising) and an action (raising my arm) are not the same thing (Wittgenstein, 1958: §621).
13. The "horizon of intentionality" is variable (von Wright, 1983).
14. An interpretant is a system capable of standing both for the original object and for other objects, thus augmenting signifying scope in generating new meanings (cf. Atkin, 2006). See also the critique of representation in Bickhard (2009).
15. On this translation, see Brouwer (1912, p. 79). The dual meanings of French *conscience* are English *consciousness* and *conscience*.
16. *Practique*, usually translated as *practice* (1932/1932, p. 19), is translated as *use* to secure a link with Wittgenstein on rule-following (Smith, 2009). *Conscience* – see note 15.
17. Conflating (a) and (b) is failing to detect a "fatal ambiguity" (Frege in Smith, 2006, pp. 3, 106).
18. See Frege (in Smith, 1999b, p. 96) "capable of being the common property of several thinkers."
19. French *accord*; also translated as *harmony* (Piaget, 1967/1971, p. 344), *correspondence/agreement* (1975/1985, p. 19). See also Piaget

(2004/2006, p. 16) on *adéquation as adequacy;* "knowing reality means constructing systems of transformations that correspond, more or less adequately, to reality" (1970, p. 15; cf. Chapman, 1988).

20.   For a comparable position, see Goodman (1979; cf. Smith, 2008).

21.   Alive? Alive and well, surely (Smith, in preparation).

REFERENCES

Atkin, A. (2006). *Peirce's theory of signs.* Retrieved March 23, 2009, from http://plato.stanford.edu/entries/peirce-semiotics/.

Bickhard, M. (2009). Interactivism. In J. Symons & P. Calvo (Eds.), *The Routledge companion to philosophy of psychology* (pp. 346–359). London: Routledge.

Brandom, R. (2000). *Articulating reasons: An introduction to inferentialism.* Cambridge, MA: Harvard University Press.

Brouwer, L. E. J. (1983). Intuitionism and formalism. In P. Benacarraf & H. Putnam (Eds.), *Philosophy of mathematics: Selected readings* (2nd ed., pp. 77–89). Cambridge: Cambridge University Press. (Original work published in 1912)

Carey, S. (1987). Theory changes in childhood. In B. Inhelder, D. Caprona, & A. Cornu-Wells (Eds.), *Piaget today* (pp. 141–163). Hillsdale, NJ: Erlbaum.

Carey, S. (2008). *The origin of concepts.* New York: Oxford University Press.

Carroll, L. (1871). *Through the looking-glass and what Alice found there.* London: Macmillan.

Case, R. (1992). *The mind's staircase.* Hillsdale, NJ: Erlbaum.

Chapman, M. (1988). *Constructive evolution.* Cambridge: Cambridge University Press.

Dummett, M. (1981). *Frege: Philosophy of language* (2nd ed.). London: Duckworth.

Fodor, J. (1975). *The language of thought.* Cambridge, MA: Harvard University Press.

Frege, G. (1977). *Logical investigations.* Oxford: Blackwell.

Frege, G. (1979). *Posthumous papers.* Oxford: Blackwell.

Gettier, E. P. (1963). Is justified true belief knowledge? *Analysis, 23,* 121–123.

Goodman, N. (1979). *Fact, fiction, and forecast* (3rd ed.). Hassocks, UK: Harvester Press.

Husserl, E. (1965). Philosophy as rigorous science. In E. Husserl, *Phenomenology and the crisis of philosophy* (pp. 71–148). New York: Harper & Row. (Original work published in 1910)

Isaacs, N. (1951). Critical notice: Jean Piaget, *Traité de logique. British Journal of Psychology, 42,* 185–188.

Kant, I. (1933). *Critique of pure reason* (2nd ed.). London: Macmillan. (Original work published in 1787)

Kitchener, R. F. (1986). *Piaget's theory of knowledge: Genetic epistemology and scientific reason.* New Haven, CT: Yale University Press.

Kitcher, P. (1990). *Kant's transcendental psychology.* New York: Oxford University Press.

Kusch, M. (2007). *Psychologism.* Retrieved March 23, 2009, from http://plato.stanford.edu/entries/psychologism/.

Lakatos, I. (1974). Falsification and the logic of scientific research programmes. In I. Lakatos & A. Musgrave (Eds.), *Criticism and the growth of knowledge* (pp. 91–196). Cambridge: Cambridge University Press.

Lewis, C. (2005). Cross-sectional and longitudinal designs. In B. Hopkins (Ed.), *The Cambridge encyclopedia of child development* (pp. 129–132). Cambridge: Cambridge University Press.

Moser, P. (1995). *Epistemology*. In R. Audi (Ed.), *The Cambridge dictionary of philosophy* (pp. 233–238). Cambridge: Cambridge University Press.

Peirce, C. S. (1955). Logic as semiotic: The theory of signs. In J. Buchler (Ed.), *Philosophical writings of Peirce* (pp. 98–119). New York: Dover Publications. (Original work published in 1910)

Piaget, J. (1918). *Recherche*. Lausanne: La Concorde.

Piaget, J. (1923). La psychologie des valeurs religieuses. *Sainte-Croix 1922* (pp. 38–82). In Association Chrétienne d'Etudiants de la Suisse Romande, Lausanne: La Concorde.

Piaget, J. (1925). Psychologie et critique de la connaissance. *Archives de Psychologie, 19,* 193–210.

Piaget, J. (1928). *Judgment and reasoning in the child*. London: Routledge & Kegan Paul. (Original work published in 1924)

Piaget, J. (1931). Le développement intellectuel chez les jeunes enfants. *Mind, 40,* 137–160.

Piaget, J. (1932). *The moral judgment of the child*. London: Routledge & Kegan Paul. (Original work published in 1932)

Piaget, J. (1941). Le mécanisme du développement mental et les lois du groupement des opérations. *Archives de Psychologie, 28,* 215–285.

Piaget, J. (1950). *Introduction à l'épistémologie génétique*. Vol. 1. *La pensée mathématique*. Paris: Presses Universitaires de France.

Piaget, J. (1952). *The child's conception of number*. London: Routledge & Kegan Paul. (Original work published in 1941)

Piaget, J. (1952). Autobiography. In C. Murchison (Ed.), *History of psychology in autobiography*, Vol. 4 (pp. 237–256). New York: Russell & Russell.

Piaget, J. (1953). *The origins of intelligence in the child*. London: Routledge & Kegan Paul. (Original work published in 1936)

Piaget, J. (1954). *The construction of reality in the child*. London: Routledge & Kegan Paul. (Original work published in 1937)

Piaget, J. (1957). Epistémologie génétique, programme et méthodes. In W. Beth, W. Mays, & J. Piaget (Eds.), *Epistémologie génétique et recherche psychologique* (pp. 13–84). Paris: Presses Universitaires de France.

Piaget, J. (1963). Foreword. In J. Flavell, *The developmental psychology of Jean Piaget* (pp. vii–ix). New York: Van Nostrand.

Piaget, J. (1964). Development and learning. *Journal of Research in Science Teaching, 2,* 176–186.

Piaget, J. (1965). Discussion: Genèse et structure en psychologie. In M. de Gandillac & L. Goldman (Eds.), *Entretiens sur les notions de genèse et de structure* (pp. 156–159). Paris: Mouton & Co.

Piaget, J. (1966). Part II. In E. Beth & J. Piaget, *Mathematical epistemology and psychology* (pp. 131–304). Dordrecht: Reidel. (Original work published in 1961)

Piaget, J. (1967a). Introduction et variétés de l'épistémologie. In J. Piaget (Ed.), *Logique et connaissance scientifique* (pp. 3–61). Paris: Gallimard.

Piaget, J. (1967b). Les méthodes de l'épistémologie. In J. Piaget (Ed.), *Logique et connaissance scientifique* (pp. 62–134). Paris: Gallimard.

Piaget, J. (1967c). Epistémologie de la logique. In J. Piaget (Ed.), *Logique et connaissance scientifique* (pp. 375–402). Paris: Gallimard.

Piaget, J. (1967d). Les problèmes principaux de l'épistémologie des mathématiques. In J. Piaget (Ed.), *Logique et connaissance scientifique* (pp. 554–598). Paris: Gallimard.

Piaget, J. (1967e). Les courants de l'épistémologie scientifique contemporaine. In J. Piaget (Ed.), *Logique et connaissance scientifique* (pp. 1225–1274). Paris: Gallimard.

Piaget, J. (1968). Explanation in psychology and psycho-physiological parallelism. In J. Piaget & P. Fraisse (Eds.), *Experimental psychology: Its scope and method*. Vol. 1: *History and method* (pp. 153–192). London: Routledge & Kegan Paul. (Original work published in 1963)

Piaget, J. (1968). Genesis and structure in the psychology of intelligence. In J. Piaget, *Six psychological studies* (pp. 143–159). London: University of London Press. (Original work published in 1964)

Piaget, J. (1970). *Genetic epistemology*. New York: Columbia University Press.

Piaget, J. (1971). *Biology and knowledge*. Edinburgh: Edinburgh University Press. (Original work published in 1967)

Piaget, J. (1971). *Structuralism*. London: Routledge & Kegan Paul. (Original work published in 1968)

Piaget, J. (1972). *Insights and illusions in philosophy*. London: Routledge & Kegan Paul. (Original work published in 1965)

Piaget, J. (1972). *Principles of genetic epistemology*. London: Routledge & Kegan Paul. (Original work published in 1970)

Piaget, J. (1973). Preface. In A. Battro (Ed.), *Piaget: Dictionary of terms* (p. 2). New York: Pergamon Press. (Original work published in 1966)

Piaget, J. (1973). *Main trends in psychology*. London: George Allen & Unwin. (Original work published in 1970)

Piaget, J. (1974). Child praxis. In J. Piaget, *The child and reality* (pp. 63–92). London: Frederick Muller Ltd. (Original work published in 1960)

Piaget, J. (1974). Affective unconscious and cognitive unconscious. In J. Piaget, *The child and reality* (pp. 31–48). London: Frederick Muller Ltd. (Original work published in 1971)

Piaget, J. (1977). Genetic epistemology. In J. Piaget, *Psychology and epistemology* (pp. 1–22). London: Penguin. (Original work published in 1952)

Piaget, J. (1977). *Epistemology and psychology of functions*. Dordrecht: Reidel. (Original work published in 1968)

Piaget, J. (1978). *Success and understanding*. London: Routledge & Kegan Paul. (Original work published in 1974)

Piaget, J. (1979). Relations between psychology and other sciences. *Annual Review of Psychology, 30*, 1–8.

Piaget, J. (1980). *Experiments in contradiction*. Chicago: University of Chicago Press. (Original work published in 1974)

Piaget, J. (1983). Piaget's theory. In P. Mussen (Ed.), *Handbook of child psychology* (4th ed., pp. 103–128). New York: Wiley. (Original work published in 1970)

Piaget, J. (1985). *Equilibration of cognitive structures*. Chicago: University of Chicago Press. (Original work published in 1975)

Piaget, J. (1986). Essay on necessity. *Human Development, 29,* 301–314. (Original work published in 1977)

Piaget, J. (1987). *Possibility and necessity: The role of possibility in cognitive development* (Vol. 1). Minneapolis: University of Minnesota Press. (Original work published in 1981)

Piaget, J. (1987). *Possibility and necessity: The role of necessity in cognitive development* (Vol. 2). Minneapolis: University of Minnesota Press. (Original work published in 1983)

Piaget, J. (1992). *Morphisms and categories*. Hillsdale, NJ: Erlbaum. (Original work published in 1990)

Piaget, J. (1995). Genetic logic and sociology. In J. Piaget, *Sociological studies* (pp. 184–214). London: Routledge. (Original work published in 1928)

Piaget, J. (1995). Individuality in history. In J. Piaget, *Sociological studies* (pp. 215–247). London: Routledge. (Original work published in 1933)

Piaget, J. (1995). Explanation in sociology. In J. Piaget, *Sociological studies* (pp. 30–96). London: Routledge. (Original work published in 1950)

Piaget, J. (2000). Commentary on Vygotsky's criticisms. *New Ideas in Psychology, 18,* 241–259. (Original work published in 1962)

Piaget, J. (2001). *Studies in reflective abstraction*. Hove: Psychology Press. (Original work published in 1977)

Piaget, J. (2006). Reason. *New Ideas in Psychology, 24,* 1–29. (Original work published in 2004)

Piaget, J., & Garcia, R. (1989). *Psychogenesis and the history of science*. New York: Columbia University Press. (Original work published in 1983)

Piaget, J., & Garcia, R. (1991). *Toward a logic of meanings*. Hillsdale, NJ: Erlbaum. (Original work published in 1987)

Plato (1935 367 BCE). *Theaetetus*. In F. M. Cornford (Ed.), *Plato's theory of knowledge* (pp. 15–164). London: Routledge & Kegan Paul. (Original work published 367 BCE)

Russell, B. (1919). *Introduction to mathematical philosophy*. London: George Allen & Unwin Ltd.

Siegler, R. S. (2007). Cognitive variability. *Developmental Science, 10,* 104–109.

Smith, L. (1999a). What Piaget learned from Frege. *Developmental Review, 19,* 133–153.

Smith, L. (1999b). Epistemological principles for developmental psychology in Frege and Piaget. *New Ideas in Psychology, 17,* 83–117, 137–147.

Smith, L. (2002a). *Reasoning by mathematical induction in children's arithmetic*. Oxford: Elsevier Pergamon Press.

Smith, L. (2002b). Piaget's model. In U. Goswami (Ed.), *Blackwell handbook of childhood cognitive development* (pp. 515–537). Oxford: Blackwell.

Smith, L. (2006a). Norms in human development: Introduction. In L. Smith & J. Vonèche (Eds.), *Norms in human development* (pp. 1–31). Cambridge: Cambridge University Press.

Smith, L. (2006b). Norms and normative facts in human development. In L. Smith & J. Vonèche (Eds.), *Norms in human development* (pp. 103–137). Cambridge: Cambridge University Press.

Smith, L. (2009). Wittgenstein's rule-following paradox: How to resolve it with lessons for psychology. *New Ideas in Psychology, 27,* 228–242.

Smith, L. (in preparation). *Piaget's developmental epistemology.* Cambridge: Cambridge University Press.

Sophian, C. (2007). *The origins of mathematical knowledge in childhood.* New York: Erlbaum.

Spinoza, B. (1994). *Treatise on the emendation of the intellect.* In B. Spinoza (Ed.), *A Spinoza reader* (pp. 48–55). Princeton, NJ: Princeton University Press. (Original work published in 1662)

von Wright, G. H. (1963). *Norm and action.* London: Routledge & Kegan Paul.

von Wright, G. H. (1983). *Practical reason.* Oxford: Blackwell.

Wellman, H. M. (2002). Understanding the psychological world: Developing a theory of mind. In U. Goswami (Ed.), *Blackwell handbook of childhood cognitive development* (pp. 167–187). Oxford: Blackwell.

Whitehead, A. N. (1932). *The aims of education.* London: Williams & Norgate Ltd.

Wittgenstein, L. (1958). *Philosophical investigations* (2nd ed.). Oxford: Blackwell.

Wittgenstein, L. (1972). *Tractatus logico-philosophicus* (2nd ed.). London: Routledge & Kegan Paul.

4   Piaget's Biology

PIAGET AS BIOLOGIST AND PHILOSOPHER

Jean Piaget, who spent more than 50 years investigating how children learn and develop, is universally recognized as one of the world's great child psychologists. But for Piaget these studies were merely the means he used to understand the philosophical question that motivated him: *What was the relationship between biology and knowledge*? Or, to put it more fully, is there any connection between the relationship of biological organisms and their physical environment that parallels the relationship between human minds and their epistemological environment? The search for the connection between biology and knowledge motivated Piaget's work, and his years of careful study of children provided the material from which he could, hopefully, answer his question. In other words, the study of children was undertaken specifically to bridge the gap between biology and knowledge. What Piaget uncovered after years of arduous toil was that the parallels between biological organisms in physical environments and human minds in epistemological environments were striking. Eventually his theory and the evidence led him to propose that there are functional invariants – organization, adaptation, assimilation, accommodation, and equilibration – that exist in both realms.

Moreover, because *evolution* is basic to both biology and epistemology, he realized that if a particular version of evolution applied to both domains, he would bridge the gap between them. But is there one conception of evolution that explains the existence of both biological organisms and human thought, particularly scientific thinking? Piaget thought there was, and thus his *conception of evolution* is central to all his theorizing. In this chapter I will explain Piaget's biological theorizing, assess the theory, and reflect on the broader implications of his conception of evolution.

94

THE EARLY BIOLOGICAL RESEARCH

In the 1920s, Piaget conducted biological research on mollusks, the subject of his doctoral dissertation (Piaget, 1921). This research pertained to the influence of heredity and environment on morphogenesis (Piaget, 1929a, 1929b). (The problem exists not only in biology but in learning theory and epistemology.) Piaget was aware of a snail, *Limnaea stagnalis*, that had an elongated shell in tranquil waters. In the great lakes of Switzerland where the waters are turbulent, the snail has a globular shape that can be explained as a phenotypic adaptation to the action of the waves, which force the snails to clamp themselves to the shore. By observing 80,000 individuals, Piaget found that the snail's globular shape became hereditarily fixed. Not only did they not revert to the elongated shape when bred in still waters, but a pure species could be bred according to the Mendelian laws of crossbreeding. It seemed these findings were not easily explained by Darwinian principles of random mutation and natural selection because the mutations were not random and the environment did not select against the acquired trait. So how might one explain the behavior of this aquatic mollusk, the *Limnaea stagnalis*? We could suppose that the mollusks' shortened and globular shape is a phenotypic adaptation to the turbulent waters. However, because this shape becomes hereditarily fixed – not reverting to the elongated shape when bred in still waters – it is not merely an adaptation of the phenotype. Might, then, Lamarckism provide the solution to the problem?

The mollusks' acquired hereditary traits, which were stimulated by environmental action, and the phenotypic adaptation, a shortened and globular shape, became a part of the genotype when this trait was hereditarily transmitted. If this took place, *Limnaea stagnalis* would provide an example of Lamarck's inheritance of acquired characteristics. However, Piaget found this solution untenable. When bred under experimental conditions, contractions of the shape occurred, but they were not transmitted to the genotype. The influence of environmental factors upon heredity depends, he thought, on the intensity and duration of the environmental stimuli, correlative with an activity of the organism in response to the environmental stress.

Perhaps then mutationism, the Darwinian solution, does resolve the problem after all; that is, genotypic changes bring about phenotypic ones. Random changes in the genotype produce some individuals with traits – in this case, globular shapes – that increase their chances for survival in turbulent waters. These chance mutations occur independently of the environment, and so there is no environmental action on genotypes. But significant problems present themselves for this solution. First, mollusks with globular shapes can exist in various lacustrine environments, but in fact they exist only where they are best adapted. If chance mutations explain adaptation then the globular variety should be randomly distributed. The fact that they exist only where environmental conditions are favorable suggests the organism's active response to the environment. And second, the environment does not select against the acquired trait because the globular shape does not disappear when the mollusks are reintroduced into still waters, even when observed over long periods of time.[1]

Piaget concluded that neither the Lamarckian nor the Darwinian solution could explain these biological facts. Evolution does not result solely from either the exogenous or the endogenous activity of the organism. Moreover, this conclusion coincided with the one he was drawing at about the same time based on his studies of children's learning. He was beginning to believe that evolution, both biological and cognitive, results from a continual and dynamic interaction between organism and environment.

THE THEORY OF THE PHENOCOPY

Piaget later came to believe that his early conception of evolution as organism/environment interactionism applied to the history and epistemology of the sciences as well as to the development of cognitive structures in children. By the time he wrote *Biology and Knowledge* (1967/1971), he had firmly placed knowledge within an evolutionary perspective that is neither neo-Lamarckian nor neo-Darwinian, reasserting his view that knowledge results from an interaction of the organism and environment.

In addition, he continued to argue that phenotypic adaptation could bring genotypic restructuring. In his research on *Limnaea stagnalis*, he had encountered similar results with the plant genus *Sedum*. A particular variety, *Sedum parvulum*, exhibited distinctive features as a response to harsh environmental conditions. In some species of *Sedum* these features exist as nonhereditary adaptations, because the plants revert to their usual form when transplanted to normal environments. In the Sedum *parvulum* these features were hereditarily fixed, because their distinctive features remain when transplanted to different environments. In the case of hereditary fixations, new genotypes replaced phenotypic adaptations. This was true in the *parvulum*, just as it had been in the *Limnaea stagnalis* (see Piaget, 1974/1980, pp. 17–45).

To explain how phenotypic adaptation leads to genotypic restructuring, Piaget redefined the notion of *phenocopy* to refer to a genotype that copies a phenotype.[2] He was careful to distinguish his interpretation of phenocopy from Lamarckism. As opposed to Lamarck, Piaget recognized that acquired characteristics are not always inherited and that the organism is not passive with respect to the environment.

Essentially, Piaget's model of phenocopy may be summarized as follows. First, the organism responds to a change in the external environment with a somatic modification. If this modification does not cause disequilibrium, the phenotypic adaptation does not become hereditarily fixed. Second, if there is a disequilibrium between the exogenous modification and the endogenous hereditary program, then disequilibrium is transmitted to the internal environment. Third, if epigenetic development cannot re-establish equilibrium, the disequilibrium may descend all the way to the genome. Fourth, at the level of the genome, mutations respond to disequilibrium. The response of the genome is random in the sense that mutations do not necessarily restore equilibrium, but they are directed toward restoring the equilibrium of the organism. Fifth, the endogenous variations are then selected by both the internal and external environments until stability is restored. And finally, these variations result in endogenous reconstruction; that is, they become hereditarily fixed. One may note a significant similarity between genomic and cognitive variations; both are directed toward responding to the needs of the organism.

The model is distinct because of its focus on how the phenotype and genotype interact. Not only do changes in DNA, cells, and tissue ultimately affect the organism's body and behavior, but the reverse is also true. Piaget defended this view – that nonspecific messages are sent back to the genome – with evidence from molecular genetics that suggests that information can move from RNA back to DNA. The model also explained why the genotype does not always copy the phenotype. It copies a phenotype only if the disturbance at the phenotypic level is sufficient to cause disequilibrium at the level of the genome. Because evolution results from this *interaction* of organism and environment, both the organism's passive reception of the environment and random genetic mutations are rejected as the sole causal agents of evolution. In this sense, biological (and cognitive) evolution is a constructive process involving directedness due to the demand of the system to maximize equilibrium – the tendency of the organism "not simply to return to the former state, but to go beyond it in the direction of the best possible equilibrium compatible with the situation" (Piaget, 1974/1980, p. 111). He also compared his equilibration theory with contemporary theories of self-organizing systems (Piaget, 1975/1985). Equilibration is the process by which living systems become increasingly organized; living systems are self-organizing systems.[3]

Thus, Piaget's evolutionary biology disputed neo-Darwinism. He compared the neo-Darwinian view that chance mutations cause evolutionary change to supposing that "the apple which chanced to fall beside Newton was the source of the great man's theories of gravitation" (Piaget, 1974/1980, p. 119). Instead, he argued that Newton's genius resulted from a constructive process of hereditary and environmental interaction, and a long history of reflecting abstractions.[4] His earlier studies had led him to believe that the evolution of knowledge resulted from the subject's internalization and reconstruction of the objects of knowledge. Analogously, he believed that his biological experimentation demonstrated that morphogenesis resulted from phenocopy, the internalization of aspects of the environment. Between construction of biological form and construction of human knowledge lie an intermediate realm – *behavior*. It is to this subject that I now turn.

A Phenocopy of Behavior

Piaget's evolutionary biology placed great importance on the organism's behavior, which he defined as "action directed by organisms toward the outside world in order to change conditions therein or to change their own situation in relation to these surroundings" (Piaget, 1976/1978, p. ix). Behavior includes sensorimotor activity, animal and plant reflexes, and acts of human intelligence. However, it excludes internal activity like muscle contraction, blood circulation, and respiration. Behavior is distinguished from the latter activities because it aims at transforming or utilizing the external environment.

In *Behavior and Evolution* (1976), he hypothesized that behavior is the most significant determinant of evolution. He believed that this was not a radical hypothesis and that modern ethology supported it. But how does one conceptualize the relationship between behavior and evolution? Lamarck assumed that behavior is the source of evolutionary variations, because acquired characteristics are inherited. Darwin assumed that behavior played no significant role in evolution because internal changes are the source of evolutionary variations. According to the neo-Darwinians, behavior is not the cause of evolution; it is the effect.[5] But if genetic variations are isolated from behavior, how does one explain the organism's adaptation to the world? Piaget found the neo-Darwinian answer – that adaptation results from a long process of fortuitous mutations – unacceptable.

His theory of the phenocopy was one way to account for the role of behavior in evolution. He compared his theory with those of the psychologist J. M. Baldwin, the biologist C. H. Waddington, and the neurobiologist Paul Weiss. All argued that the organism's activity – construed variously as reacting to, accommodating to, or choosing the environment – influences evolution. The goal of *Behavior and Evolution* was to examine the possible role behavior played in evolution. Whether one construed behavior as the product of genetic variation or as the producer of evolutionary change, there can be no doubt that behavior and evolution are inextricably linked, inasmuch as biology is concerned with the relationship between endogenous change and exogenous activity. But because, according to Piaget, some endogenous variations must respond to the organism's need to expand and restructure its environment, chance is an unlikely source of variation. In this context, the relationship between endogenous variations and exogenous activity is the central issue to be resolved.

This led Piaget to advance his own theory of behavior's role in evolution. According to his theory, the phenocopy mediates between adaptive behavior and the genotype in evolutionary transformations. I have already discussed the role phenocopy plays in the hereditary fixation of morphological traits, but Piaget also examined the theory in the context of behavior in order to show how phenotypical behaviors can become hereditarily fixed. Whether one speaks of phenocopy regarding morphological or behavioral traits, the process is one whereby the organism's activity modifies the genome. Still, Piaget noted that not all behavior results in genotypic alteration – for example, human language is not inherited. This led him to believe that between noninherited and inherited behavior exist many intermediate categories.

Additionally, Piaget proposed the following account of the interaction between the organism's behavior and the genome. The process begins when the organism responds to a prolonged change in the environment with a new or modified behavior. If the new behavior results in internal disequilibrium, the disequilibrium is communicated to the genome.[6] Piaget made it clear that the message is nonspecific – something is not functioning normally – and he appealed to Weiss's observation that genes are not isolated but interact with higher levels of organized systems to support his claim. The genome responds to disequilibrium by "trying out" new variations. This process is not random, because the variations respond to the organism's needs, but it is not preprogrammed either, inasmuch as it may take many variations for the genome to respond properly. These variations are then selected by the internal environment in order to restore equilibrium between the genome and the internal environment. Because the internal environment has been modified by new behaviors that embody the external environment, there is a convergence between the new genotype and the phenotypical behavior.

Notice that the new phenotype does not become fixated in the genome, as the Lamarckians claimed, but that endogenous construction brings about equilibrium between endogenous and exogenous forces. Whereas the neo-Darwinians claimed this construction is random, Piaget claimed it is partially directed. The phenocopy supplies the internal environment with information about the external environment and accounts of behavioral or morphological adaptation.

BEHAVIOR: THE MOTOR OF EVOLUTION

Piaget had long argued that the behavior of an organism accommodates to, acts upon, interacts with, and restructures its environment. This realization led Piaget (1976/1978, p. 139) to affirm the major thesis of *Behavior and Evolution*: "It is of the essence of behavior that it is forever attempting to transcend itself and that it thus supplies evolution with its principal motor."

He had offered this thesis as a contrast to neo-Darwinism, arguing vehemently that physicochemical transformations do not cause the extraordinary increase in complexity that characterizes higher organisms. The reason is that, physiologically, the organism's basic characteristic is conservation rather than change and mutation, and well-adapted organisms have no reason to change.[7] It thus appears that evolutionary causation is found in the relationship between the organism's openness to the environment and its organizational propensities. Behavior innovatively responds to environmental obstacles by organizing and adapting to them, and it strives to improve itself, extend itself, and increase control over the environment.

By describing the process whereby behavior responds innovatively to environmental stimulus, Piaget returned to the notions of assimilation and accommodation.[8] He made an important distinction between physiological assimilation, which repeatedly incorporates substances or energies into the organism, and behavioral assimilation, which extends itself by the organization of past actions. Thus, the former is characterized by repetition; the latter by extension or transcendence. Physiological and behavioral accommodations are also distinguished in that the former are merely passive replacements that abolish pre-existing structures, whereas the latter actively refine and integrate previous behavioral schemes. These distinctions reveal that behavior has a capacity for change that physiology lacks.

Physiologically, primitive organisms are as well adapted as higher ones, but behaviorally, there is a great disparity between lower and higher organisms. Behavior in vertebrates, most notably their insatiable curiosity, opposes the conservative proclivities of physiology. It continually seeks to transcend itself and favors the construction of new behavioral schemes. Still, this provides no assurance that behavior is the motor of evolution, for behavior may be dependent on the nervous system. In response to this objection, Piaget cited evidence that behavior plays a role in the formation of the nervous system as much as the reverse.

Such considerations allowed him to reaffirm his thesis that great evolutionary transformations cannot be explained solely by chance mutations. To see why, consider the two alternatives. Either the organism's structure and behavior evolve independently, both resulting from chance occurrences that are later selected by the environment, or morphology and behavior are coordinated in the evolutionary process. If the latter is the case, then behavior is the motor of evolution because it mediates between the organism and environment and tends to supersede itself. As Piaget said, the choice between the two conceptual models is striking: "Either chance and selection can explain everything or else behavior is the motor of evolution" (Piaget, 1976/1978, p. 147). Clearly he did not think that chance and selection were sufficient.

Note the obvious contrast between rational and random evolution. Whereas Piaget's affirmation of a logical and law-governed process is problematic, the neo-Darwinians must account for the biological and cognitive functioning of higher vertebrates by a process that is fundamentally irrational. Given the alternative, Piaget's solution is appealing. One should note that he did not deny that some evolutionary variations, particularly morphological ones, are the outcome of chance. But he argued that behavior, say nest-building in birds, could not be explained this way. Can one suppose that inept birds built frail, conspicuous nests until mutations produced more skillful nest-builders? Piaget thought the position that evolution results exclusively from chance to be absurd, and he supported this contention by pointing to particular differences between behavioral and mutational adaptation.

The main difference is that behavior is teleonomic.[9] Whereas mutations are random and generated independent of the environment, behavior is goal-oriented and aims at reshaping the environment. Mutations promote survival, sturdiness, and reproductive capacity, whereas behavioral adaptations are judged according to their success in attaining a goal. The distinction between behavioral and ordinary variations shows why behavior is the most significant factor in the evolutionary process.

> To the extent that evolutionary "progress" depends at once on the growth of the power of organisms over their environment and on the relative

independence they acquire as a result of their actions . . . behavior must be considered the motor of all these transformations. And no matter how neurological, physiological, or even biochemical the preconditions may be, the fact remains that behavior itself creates those higher unitary activities without which macro-evolution would be incomprehensible. (Piaget, 1976/1978, p. 151)

Piaget concluded *Behavior and Evolution* by recognizing important distinctions between variational and organizing evolution. Variational evolution is random, takes place primarily at the genetic level, and is subject to a posteriori selection. In contrast, organizing evolution is teleonomic – it affects the entire organism and strives to establish a rapport or equilibrium between the organism and the environment. Organizing evolution brings about new behavioral forms and the organs that serve them as behavioral instruments. Selection results from an equilibrium achieved between the internal and epigenetic environments and phenotypic traits. Piaget claimed that genetic reconstruction of learned behavior in no way implied a return to Lamarckism, inasmuch as the internal environment selects the hereditary variations that respond to the organism's needs. In other words, it is not the action of the environment but action by the organism on the environment that stimulates the internal change to which variations respond. Future advances in genetics may result from reconciling the two types of evolution, necessitating a reconciliation of the discrete units that are subject to variational evolution and the overall dynamic organization characteristic of all living things. *Behavior and Evolution* reached two admittedly speculative conclusions. "The first that there is an organizing evolution as well as a variational one; and the second is that behavior is its motor" (Piaget, 1976/1978, p. 159).

A Summary of Piaget's Conception of Evolution

Piaget's biological theorizing brings his thought full circle. He could now see the essential connections between biology and knowledge and the role that a conception of evolution played in both. Essentially, both organic and cognitive evolution are characterized by self-regulation or equilibration, the universal characteristic of all life that drives evolution from the simplest organic forms to the most complex forms of scientific and mathematical thought. Cognitive evolution is the adaptation of the subject's intellectual structures to reality, whereas biological evolution is the adaptation of the organism's biological structure to the environment. In the cognitive case, adaptation consists in the assimilation of new perceptions, ideas, and events into existing schemes and the subsequent accommodation of those schemes to the materials assimilated. The process aims at achieving cognitive equilibrium.[10] Analogously, biological adaptation consists in the assimilation of elements of the environment and the subsequent accommodation of the organism in terms of the phenocopy.

Thus, the connection between the biological and the cognitive is in terms of the adaptational or organizational principles that apply at all levels of biological functioning. These principles apply to cognitive functioning as well, because cognition extends biological functioning. In other words, because thought is an activity of the organism, it must be governed by the same laws of organization as the organism itself. Thus, both biological and cognitive structures result from the organism's basic functioning, which is itself a continual process of organization and adaptation moving toward more equilibrated states. This is the essence of Piaget's conception of evolution.[11]

CRITICISMS OF PIAGET'S BIOLOGICAL THEORIES

Unfortunately, Piaget's biological theory has not been generally well received. The eminent neurobiologist Jean-Pierre Changeux (1980, p. 196), for example, argued that the concept of phenocopy "corresponds to a decrease in the genetic potentialities of the organism." In discussing Piaget's biological observations, Changeux claimed that *Limnaea*, which adapt to different environments, exhibit multiple phenotypes, whereas the so-called phenocopy displays only one. According to Changeux (1980, p. 196), "the phenocopy would not correspond to the acquisition of a new competence, but to a loss of genetic potentialities." In other words, *Limnaea* in whom the phenotypic adaptations become hereditarily fixed have in fact lost the genes that determine other phenotypes. Changeux, like virtually all contemporary biologists, categorically rejected Piaget's biological theory: "Modern theories of evolution are based on the spontaneous and random mutations of the DNA molecule and on the recombination of its segments; ... and it seems difficult to imagine, at present, a molecular mechanism for Piaget's mutations ... " (Changeux, 1980, p. 195).

Or consider the noted molecular biologist Antoine Danchin, who criticized Piaget's biological theory as hopelessly out of date: "Although it may have been possible, before the existence of molecular biology, to believe in an 'instructive' or 'creative' principle that would explain the determination of traits in a living organism, producing an adaptive phenocopy ... this point is today merely an episode in the history of ideas" (Danchin, 1980, p. 357). Danchin's explanation of phenocopy echoed Changeux's. Phenotypic adaptations occur, and in some cases become invariant, when organisms confront specialized environmental conditions. In these cases, the organism loses "the regulatory aptitudes that allowed it to change its phenotype according to the environment" (Danchin, 1980, p. 359). This loss of phenotypic variability is not detrimental in such cases because the specialized environment remains constant. Other organisms retain phenotypic variability, which they exhibit when transferred back to their original environment. According to Danchin (1980, p. 359), individual phenotypes can be understood "without allowing the intervention of even the least instructive notion on the part of the environment." Phenocopy does not indicate a constructive evolutionary process, "but simply a particular realization of a given program according to a strict determinism" (Danchin, 1980, p. 360). He argued that all of the available evidence contradicts Piaget's views.

MORE RECENT DEVELOPMENTS

Yet some recent developments seem to lend support for Piaget's biological views. For example, the zoologist and National Academy of Sciences member Mary Jane West-Eberhard (2003, pp. 3–4) states:

> One of the oldest controversies in evolutionary biology . . . concerns the relations between nature and nurture in the evolution of adaptive design. In modern evolutionary biology there is still a gap between the conclusions of a genetic theory for the origin and spread of new traits, and the observed nature of the traits being explained, the manifest phenotype, always products of genes and environment . . . The gap is especially clear in discussions of adaptively flexible morphology and behavior. How are complex adaptively flexible traits constructed during evolution? . . . It is not surprising that students of human behavior have been among the first to complain about the failure of evolutionary biology to deal effectively with complex adaptive plasticity. Anthropologists, for example, have good reasons to question the explanations of a strongly gene-centered sociobiology. Human behavior is *essentially* circumstantial. We know intuitively that our phenotypes are molded by our environments – by mothers, fathers, schoolteachers, economics, and accidents of history. But in this respect human nature is like every other phenotype of every other animal or plant. If this is true, then how can students of social evolution so often predict cultural patterns and insect behavior from models based on genes alone? A phenotype is the product of both genotype and environment. To state the problem in more general terms: if recurrent phenotypes are as much a product of recurrent circumstances as they are of replicated genes, how can I accept a theory of organic evolution that deals primarily with genes? How does the systematic incorporation of environmental influence evolve?

And she concludes that development is the key or "missing link be-tween genotype and phenotype, a place too often occupied by metaphors in the past" (West-Eberhard, 2003, p. 19). In short, although recent evolutionary biology has focused mostly on how genes and traits are propagated or lost, it says little about how new traits originate. West-Eberhard provides a detailed account of how evolutionary novelty can be explained by recent research from development, physiology, and be-havior. Thus, like Piaget, she denies that evolutionary novelty can be explained by mutations alone.

Others, like the anthropologists Sue Taylor Parker and Terrence W. Deacon, concur. Parker (2004) argues that new phenotypic models pro-vide insight into the role of behavior and development in evolution. Although some details of Piaget's model are problematic, she still claims that there is evidence that environmentally induced epigenetic changes can modify genetic expression and thus may be inherited. In addition:

> . . . two larger themes in Piaget's biology books are partially vindicated by a recent new synthesis of development and evolution. The first theme is Piaget's dissatisfaction with the exclusive role of mutation in the classic neo-Darwinian account of the origins of adaptive variation, which par-tially parallels West-Eberhard's critique. The second theme which finds support is his emphasis on the role of development, especially behavioral adaptation, in the origins of adaptations. This theme finds parallels in West-Eberhard's phenotype-centered model of the origins of novel traits (Parker, 2004, p. 81). And Deacon (2004, pp. 116–117) agrees that con-temporary research is confirming some of Piaget's insights:

> Piaget's appeal to both Baldwin and Waddington can now be seen to be insightful anticipations of a necessary complexification of evolution-ary theory, though neither a repudiation of Darwinian mechanism nor a return to Lamarckian paradigms. To explain the apparent auto-regulatory power of biological evolution does, as he suspected, require incorporating the role of epigenetic processes as mediators between genotype and phe-notype selection . . . Dissatisfied with both Darwinian and Lamarckian logic and reaching for a constructivist intermediate, Piaget anticipated the contemporary convergence of developmental psychology and evolu-tionary biology. Even today this synthesis is only just beginning to bear fruit . . . .

CONCLUSION: VARIATIONAL AND CONSTRUCTIVE EVOLUTION

Piaget maintained that the order or structure of the milieu pierces the so-called genetic envelope. And it is this exchange that results in constructive evolution. In contrast, contemporary geneticists typically insist that the genetic envelope cannot be penetrated and that it alone determines the range of regulations and behaviors available to the organism. So molecular biology is reductionistic; the microscopic determines, and is unaffected by, the macroscopic. In other words, there exists an asymmetry of determinism between the two worlds – the causality and explanation is unidirectional. This can be seen in the claim of molecular biologists that randomness and chance cause evolution. The illustrious molecular biologist Jacques Monod (1971, pp. 112–113) provided the classic statement:

> Pure chance, absolutely free but blind at the very root of the stupendous edifice of evolution: this central concept of modern biology is no longer one among others possible or even conceivable hypotheses: it is the sole conceivable hypothesis, the only one that squares with observed and tested fact.

Moreover, Monod (1971, pp. 113–115) claimed that the indeterminacy or uncertainty operative in genetic mutations is "essential" as opposed to "operational." This uncertainty does not result from our inability to determine the causes of mutations – operational uncertainty – but from purely accidental coincidences – essential uncertainty. The ultimate source of essential uncertainty is the same as for quantum events. The only alternative to accepting essential uncertainty, according to Monod, is to adopt fatalism.

Monod's description of evolution is paradigmatic of the received view in contemporary biology. I characterize the theses of this position to be (a) evolution proceeds because of chance, (b) evolution is essentially variational and irrational, (c) there is no teleology to evolution, and (d) evolution implies complete freedom, because no laws govern its process. The first thesis is definitional and follows from the overwhelming evidence of molecular biology. The second and third follow from the first, and the fourth follows from the claim that evolutionary change is "essentially" uncertain. I call this evolution *variational*.

Piaget's constructive evolution provides a vivid contrast. He did not deny, for example, that chance could plausibly explain the color of the butterfly; but he did not believe it could sufficiently explain more complex human behaviors. Can one really suppose that the extraordinary correspondence of mathematics to reality arose by chance? Does chance explain the development of science or the increase in genes from bacteria to higher animals? Piaget did not think so. Although recognizing the contributions of the microscopic and the effects of programming and environmental influence, he denounced one-way causality and the omission of the process of equilibration/self-regulation in evolutionary transformations. It is by organizational and adaptive behaviors that the organism exploits the interaction of the microscopic and macroscopic forces.

I thus take the essential theses of constructivist evolution to be (a) evolution proceeds by organization, (b) evolution is primarily rational, (c) there is a teleonomic direction to evolution, and (d) there is limited freedom in evolution because laws govern and constrain the process. The first point is definitional, the second and third follow from the first, and the fourth is a consequence of the functional invariants. I call such evolution *constructive*.

So is this constructive evolution primarily variational or organizational? Although the complexity of the relationship between the organism's internal and external environment in driving evolution is a matter of dispute, I argue that one should allow scientific research to continue to unravel this complicated relationship. How the issue will be finally resolved is a matter of dispute. Still, I suspect that future research will eventually confirm Piaget's major insight – evolution is, in large part, a self-organizing and constructive process.[12]

GLOSSARY OF TERMS

phenotypic	the observable properties of an organism that are produced by the interaction of the genotype and the environment.
adaptation	the development of physical and behavioral characteristics that allow organisms to survive and reproduce in their habitats.
genotypic	all or part of the genetic constitution of an individual or group.
phenocopy	(for Piaget) a genotype that copies a phenotype.
somatic	relating to the body, especially as distinct from the mind.
endogenous	originating within an organism or tissue.
exogenous	originating outside an organism or system.
genome	the complete set of genetic material of a human, animal, plant or other living thing.

NOTES

1. I note at the outset that Piaget will reject the so-called Weismann barrier. Weismann advocated the germ plasma theory, according to which (in a multicellular organism) inheritance only takes place by means of the germ cells – the gametes such as egg cells and sperm cells. Other cells of the body – somatic cells – do not function as agents of heredity. The

effect is one way: Germ cells produce somatic cells and more germ cells, but *the germ cells are not affected by anything the somatic cells learn or any ability the body acquires during its life.* Genetic information cannot pass from soma to germ plasm and on to the next generation. This unidirectional process is referred to as the Weismann barrier.

2. Piaget (1974/1980, p. 8) defines phenocopy as "a product of convergence between a phenotypic variation and a genotypic mutation which comes to take its place."

3. Note that Piaget used the notion of equilibrium to refer to the state of an organism. From the 1940s onward, he used the notion of equilibration to refer to the process whose particular phases were states of equilibrium.

4. Reflective abstraction is a concept introduced by Piaget to describe the construction of logico-mathematical structures by an individual during the course of cognitive development (see Piaget, 2001).

5. A classic statement of this view may be found in Jacques Monod (1971).

6. Piaget does not make it clear how this communication with the genome takes place. The idea is that external changes in the environment exert a nonspecific influence on the genotype moving it to act creatively to adapt to this new environment. Exactly how this takes place biologically is unclear, and Piaget no doubt was hoping that further biological research might illuminate the specifics and thereby resolve the issue.

7. Note that conservation here is used in the biological sense – genes generally do a good job of copying themselves – not in the cognitive sense of, say, the conservation of number during childhood.

8. These notions play an important role in his early studies of children, particularly in *The Origins of Intelligence in Children* (Piaget, 1936/1953, see Chapter 9, this volume).

9. My use of the word "teleonomic" follows the usage of C. H. Waddington and Ernest Mayr. According to Waddington, it does not denote that the end state is external to the process and steers evolution; it is a "quasi-finalistic" term implying only that the process is goal-oriented (see Waddington, 1975, p. 223). Mayr (1988, p. 45) defines teleonomic similarly: "A teleonomic process or behavior is one which owes its goal-directedness to the operations of a program." Teleonomy is to be contrasted with, and so distinct from, the stronger term "teleology." In the case of teleology, the final causes *completely determine* processes and events.

10. In *Biology and Knowledge* and elsewhere, Piaget (1967/1971) stated his view that a living process is open in that any level of cognitive equilibrium can be recast in the sequel.

11. A more detailed presentation can be found in Messerly (1996).

12. I would like to express my deep gratitude to Ulrich Müller and Les Smith for their efforts in improving this essay.

REFERENCES

Changeux, J.-P. (1980). Genetic determinism and epigenesis of the neuronal network: Is there a biological compromise between Chomsky and Piaget?

In M. Piattelli-Palmarini (Ed.), *Language and learning: The debate between Jean Piaget and Noam Chomsky* (pp. 185–197). Cambridge, MA: Harvard University Press.

Danchin, A. (1980). A critical note on the use of the term 'phenocopy.' In M. Piattelli-Palmarini (Ed.), *Language and learning: The debate between Jean Piaget and Noam Chomsky* (pp. 356–360). Cambridge, MA: Harvard University Press.

Deacon, T. W. (2004). Beyond Piaget's phenocopy: The baby in the Lamarckian bath. In S. T. Parker, J. Langer, & C. Milbrath (Eds.), *Biology and knowledge revisited: From neurogenesis to psychogenesis* (pp. 87–122). Mahwah, NJ: Erlbaum.

Mayr, E. (1988). *Toward a new philosophy of biology.* Cambridge, MA: Harvard University Press.

Messerly, J. (1996). *Piaget's conception of evolution: Beyond Darwin and Lamarck.* Lanham, MD: Rowman & Littlefield.

Monod, J. (1971). *Chance and necessity: An essay on the natural philosophy of modern biology.* New York: Knopf.

Parker, S. T. (2004). Piaget's phenocopy model revisited: A brief history of ideas about the origins of adaptive genetic variations. In S. T. Parker, J. Langer, & C. Milbrath (Eds.), *Biology and knowledge revisited: From neurogenesis to psychogenesis* (pp. 33–86). Mahwah, NJ: Erlbaum.

Piaget, J. (1921). *Introduction à la Malacologie Valaisanne.* Thèse pour l'obtention du grade de Docteur ès Science, Université de Neuchâtel, 1918. Sion: F. Aymon.

Piaget, J. (1929a). Les races lacustres de la 'Limnaea stagnalis' L. Recherches sur les rapports de l'adaptation hereditaires avec le milieu. *Bulletin Biologique de la France et la Belgique, 63,* 424–455.

Piaget, J. (1929b). L'adaptation de la limnaea stagnalis aux milieux lacustres de la Suisee Romande. *Revue Suisse de Zoologie, 36,* 263–531.

Piaget, J. (1953). *The origins of intelligence in children.* London: Routledge and Kegan Paul. (Original work published in 1936)

Piaget, J. (1971). *Biology and knowledge.* Chicago: University of Chicago Press. (Original work published in 1967)

Piaget, J. (1978). *Behavior and evolution.* New York: Random House. (Original work published in 1976)

Piaget, J. (1980). *Adaptation and intelligence.* Chicago: University of Chicago Press. (Original work published in 1974)

Piaget, J. (1985). *The equilibration of cognitive structures: The central problem of intellectual development.* Chicago: University of Chicago Press. (Original work published in 1975)

Piaget, J. (2001). *Studies in reflecting abstraction.* Hove: Psychology Press. (Original work published in 1977)

Waddington, C. H. (1975). *The evolution of an evolutionist.* Ithaca: Cornell University Press.

West-Eberhard, M. J. (2003). *Developmental plasticity and evolution.* Oxford: Oxford University Press.

5 On the Concept(s) of the Social in Piaget

THE PROBLEM

The problem I want to raise in this chapter is the following: Does Piaget's theory of cognitive development include a theory of the social? If so, is the theory coherent and/or adequate?

There exists a common set of criticisms of Piaget's theory of cognitive development (Boden, 1980; Hamlyn, 1971, 1978; Meacham & Riegel, 1978; Rotman, 1977; Russell, 1979; Tripp, 1978; Vygotsky, 1934/1986; Wallon, 1928, 1942, 1951; Wilden, 1977): (1) Piaget has no theory of the social contribution to cognitive development; (2) he has such a theory, but it is inadequate because his theory is impoverished and inadequately stresses the social; (3) he may have had a sufficiently complex theory of the social, but it is a false or mistaken one. The question I want to pursue is: Are these criticisms justified?

A common reply to his set of criticisms made by Piagetian scholars (Apostel, 1986; Chapman, 1986; Kitchener, 1981, 1991; Mays, 1982; Smith, 1982, 1995) is that the critics simply have not read Piaget, in particular, his recently translated *Sociological Studies* (Piaget, 1977/1995). For contained therein is such a social theory. Hence, the critics are wrong about (1). These scholars are less sanguine about question (2), although some argue that the theory is a plausible one (although perhaps needing a few tweaks here and there). It is, however, difficult to find many that argue that (3) itself is false and that Piaget has a perfectly fine account in no need of revision. So, the real question concerns the very existence or degree of adequacy of any such alleged sociological account in Piaget's works.

What were the critics responding to in Piaget's work? Did they just not read him? This, of course, is true of many of his critics, but not all. Did they read him but perhaps gave an incorrect or inadequate interpretation? If so, why?

THE SOLUTION

In this chapter I will argue that both the critics and the defenders of Piaget are (partially) correct. Piaget does have a theory of the sociological dimension of cognitive development. In fact, he has several – at least three: (a) an early social epistemology, in which the social played a crucial epistemic role; (b) a Spinozist (or logicist) double aspect view, in which there is a single underlying state of equilibrium manifested in several different areas; and (c) an internalist rationalist account, in which any external influence, social or otherwise, is dependent upon and derivative from purely individualist cognitive mechanisms. I will argue that Piaget himself was unclear about these three accounts, which he often seemed to hold simultaneously. The most adequate account is the early one; the second one should be rejected or substantially revised; the third version might be defensible (if substantially revised). Such a revised version might be combined with the first and perhaps the second, but such a combination awaits future completion. I sketch a possible line of development.

THE EPISTEMOLOGICAL THEORY

Piaget's earliest research centered on what he called "Studies in Childhood Logic." After completing his doctorate, Piaget went to Zurich to study psychoanalysis (see Ducret, 1984; Vidal, 1986), where he became acquainted with the ideas of Jung, Pfister, Bleuler, Freud, Adler, and Silberer. Eugen Bleuler's concept of autistic thinking was a signature theme in Piaget's social epistemology.[1]

BLEULER AND EGOCENTRIC THOUGHT

Bleuler gave several closely related definitions of autism, but the core idea was that it was *a detachment from reality associated with a rich fantasy life*:

> One of the most important symptoms of schizophrenia is the preponderance of inner life with an active turning away from the external world. The most severe cases withdraw completely and live in a dream world; the milder cases withdraw to a lesser degree. I call this symptom *autism*. (1912/1951, p. 399)

Bleuler stressed there were two types of thinking: *autistic thinking* and *logical or realistic thinking*. Autism was not to be identified with autistic thinking, however, which could be quite normal (as in the case of play or dreams) (Bleuler, 1911/1950, p. 374).

The idea of autistic thinking was seized upon by Piaget early in his thinking (Piaget, 1920, 1923a). For just as Bleuler suggested, childhood thinking could be seen as having features of autistic thinking as opposed to the rational thinking present in ordinary adult life. Piaget's major hypothesis was that there was another way of thinking, *egocentric thinking*, in between autistic thinking and logical thought.

Freudian *symbolic thought* is characterized as an absence of logical consequence, a predominance of the image over the concept, and a lack of awareness of the connections relating the successive images to themselves (Piaget, 1923a, p. 275). It is almost always autistic in nature – individualistic, incommunicable, and independent of social life. "The thought of the child," Piaget suggested, "is intermediate between symbolic thought and logical thought" (Piaget, 1923a, p. 284). Here there is an absence of the need for discussion, of logical deduction and verification, with a predominance of syncretistic or visual schemes over logical analysis (p. 285). In symbolic thought and autistic thought, there is no awareness of self because there is no awareness of others.

The child's thought is fundamentally egocentric, Piaget says. Although the child attempts to adapt to reality, his thought is largely autistic because it is not logical, rational, or objective without an attempt (or ability) to justify his statements or beliefs. The child is simply not communicating with another child or adult.

Adapted information is an exchange of thought with others, an attempt to convey a belief to another. Adapted information can give rise to dialogue, where two individuals are talking about the same state of affairs but disagree over it. Such cases are rare in childhood because what one finds there (primarily) is *primitive argument*, a clash of affirmations without an attempt at logical justification; instead there is simply a conjunction of statements.

At this stage the child is not yet aware of other persons and their points of view, nor is the child aware of her own point of view. In short, egocentrism is "the inability to differentiate between one's own point of view and other people's" (Piaget, 1924/1928, p. 272). By not knowing his own perspective, the child consistently confuses what is just his point of view for all points of view. This is a kind of unconscious solipsism. All of this begins to change when other individuals come to disagree with him.

> Only by means of friction against other minds, by means of exchange and opposition does thought come to be conscious of its own aims and tendencies and only in this way is it obliged to relate what could till then remain juxtaposed. (Piaget, 1924/1928, p. 11)

> Anyone who thinks for himself exclusively and is consequently in a
> perpetual state of belief, *i.e.* of confidence in his own ideas will naturally
> not trouble himself about the reasons and motives which have guided his
> reasoning process. Only under the pressure of argument and opposition
> will he seek to justify himself in the eyes of others, and thus acquire the
> habit of watching himself think, *i.e.* of constantly detecting the motives
> which are guiding him in the direction he is pursuing. (Piaget, 1924/1928,
> p. 137)

Encountering this shock, which is an obstacle or barrier (Claparède's
Law), the child is forced to attempt to provide a justification to another
person. This justification must be in the form of a reason for the belief. If
the child is to convince others, he must provide a reason the other person
would accept. But to do this, the child must understand the difference
between her point of view and that of others, hence becoming aware of
a diversity of different epistemic points of view.

Several epistemological distinctions are important here. First, there
are several kinds of knowledge: knowledge-that (propositional knowledge), knowledge-how, direct acquaintance, etc. Piaget's primary concern
is with knowledge-that or *understanding*; this kind of knowledge he also
calls logical, conceptual, or cognitive as distinct from knowledge-how
(*success*) (Piaget, 1974/1978). It eventuates in propositional knowledge with the aid of certain kinds of conceptual abilities and formal–
operational structures. This was the focus of his early theory of egocentrism and is the centerpiece of his genetic epistemology.

Social interaction is essential for cognitive knowledge (knowledge-
that) because, absent social interaction, the epistemic subject would
not see a need for justification. Hence, justifications are always justifications given to others, a social concept belonging to a group of other
social concepts: responsibility, excuses, blame, etc. Reasons are given
with an eye to convincing the other person, who is demanding a justification. The stages of egocentrism, socialization, and objectivity "are
determined by ages which happen to correspond to the ages of important changes in the child's social life, viz. 7–8 . . . and 11–12" (Piaget,
1924/1928, pp. 112–113).

Later, Piaget came to suggest that autistic thinking was an early
stage of childhood (the first 2 years of life) prior to egocentrism, which
in turn was a precursor to conceptual–logical thought. He came to see
this first stage differently as a consequence of his observations of his
own children, coming eventually to label it *motor intelligence* (sensorimotor intelligence) and attributing to it a certain kind of low-level
rationality – a logic of action (Piaget, 1928b). Children of 0 to 2 years of
age are not completely autistic: Although they may be autistic at the
reflective, conceptual level, they manifest a certain kind of rationality

in their actions. Now, it was egocentrism, the stage between motor intelligence and cognitive intelligence, that was seen as a stage of irrational thought, with motor intelligence having a practical rationality and cognitive intelligence having a theoretical rationality.

If this earlier (motor) stage of intelligence and knowledge was rational, although in a different sense from later cognitive rationality, it cried out for an account of what made it rational; this the social dimension could not do because it was absent during this period. Hence, another account of rationality was needed.

STUDIES IN CHILDHOOD RATIONALITY

Early in his career (1921), Piaget planned a series of books to be entitled *Studies on Childhood Logic*, which consisted of two works on childhood reasoning (Piaget, 1923/1926, 1924/1928) and a proposed third volume on *New Research on the Logic of the Child*, which never appeared. But why did the third volume never appear? What had happened to change Piaget's earlier theory of social egocentrism?

Several things can be briefly mentioned: First, his research on his young children (0–2 years) resulted in his new theory of motor intelligence. Second, there was a set of criticisms raised against his theory (Isaacs, 1930; Wallon, 1928, 1942, and others) at a famous 1928 conference (Piaget, 1928b). These partially motivated Piaget to turn to the development of his theory of groupings, which provided, he believed, an answer to his critics and a more comprehensive theory of rationality.

Piaget's research on his own children started in 1925, resulting in several monumental works (1936/1952; 1937/1954), which moved him in the direction of *sensorimotor intelligence* (or *motor intelligence*) and changed his views about social epistemology.

Intelligence, Piaget says, is the faculty in individuals that is concerned with adapting to the world and forming an adequate representation of things (1923a, p. 276). Now if there is something called motor intelligence, it is concerned with adapting to the world and forming adequate representations of it. Hence, it is concerned with *knowing* the world. But it seems to be a different kind of knowledge. If so, how does it relate to his earlier social epistemology?

Piaget may be correct that the social is necessary for conceptual knowledge (theoretical rationality), but the social does not seem to be necessary for motor knowledge (practical rationality). The organism must adapt to its environment, but this means adapt to physical objects, which provide *resistance* to the knower. Ordinary physical objects provide resistance to one's action, and this constitutes a mechanism for verifying motor intelligence. Indeed, Köhler's (1917/1925) apes can engage in a certain kind of rational behavior, and even rats can engage in what Tolman called "vicarious trial and error" – thinking about which path to follow in a maze. Now, all of this is consistent with the view that the social is necessary to move from the lower level to the next higher level. What, then, has become of Piaget's claim that the social is explanatorily essential to rationality? At most, it is true of cognitive rationality, but cognitive rationality has something in common with practical rationality. This commonality is what Piaget's theory of groupings is designed to address, namely, an account of the rationality present in both.

THE SPINOZIST, DOUBLE-ASPECT ACCOUNT

During this early period, Piaget began moving to a different conception of the nature of the social in the development of knowledge – this was his *theory of social and logical parallelism (isomorphism)* or what I'll call a double-aspect view. According to this view, it is no longer correct to assert that the social is necessary, essential, or a presupposition of the growth of knowledge in the way he had earlier thought. Now, we are told that the social and the logical (or individual) are two sides of the same coin: There is a correlation, parallelism, or identity between the social and the individual (Piaget, 1977/1995, pp. 82, 84, 87–88, 89, 94, 145–146, 148, 244, 278, 280, 307, 310): They are two aspects of one underlying reality or process (Piaget, 1977/1995, pp. 145, 294, 309); there is one reality viewed from two different standpoints (Piaget, 1977/1995, p. 89); there is a correlation or parallelism between the two (Piaget, 1977/1995, p. 244); the two aspects are interdependent (Piaget, 1945/1951, p. 239); they are isomorphic to each other (Piaget, 1954/1981, p. 9), and so forth. The social is inseparable from the individual, we are told, and hence because of this parallelism, it is fruitless to ask which came first or which causes the other. This is reminiscent of the metaphysics of the 17th-century philosopher Baruch Spinoza, who maintained (1677/2000) that reality (God) consisted of nature, which is all that there is (pantheism), but that there are two aspects in which nature is manifested: a physical aspect and a mental aspect. These aspects are in a kind of perfect parallelism or correspondence with each other so that Descartes mind–body dualism and interactionism is sidestepped. I believe this label, with modification, might be a suitable term for Piaget's second theory of the social.

The stimulus for this development, at least partially, was Piaget's work on the child's conception of space and geometry, which led him to Poincaré (1905/1958) and the latter's *group of displacements*. This explicitly led to Piaget's account of the child's construction of space and geometry, but it also led to his more general theory of groupings. In effect, therefore, his early social epistemology directly led him to his theory of groupings. For example, Piaget asks the question of whether the nonrelational character of childish ideas about right–left, brothers–sisters, etc., can be traced back to egocentrism and answers yes:

> There are three very definite stages in this evolution of right and left. During the first the child places himself at his own point of view, during the second at the point of view of others, and during the third at a completely relational point of view in which account is taken of objects in themselves. The process is therefore precisely that of the gradual socialization of thought – ego-centrism, socialization, and finally complete objectivity. The curious thing is that the three stages are determined by ages which happen to correspond to the ages of important changes in the child's social life, viz. 7–8, diminution of ego-centrism, and 11–12, the stage of rules and of thought which has become sufficiently formal to reason from all given points of view. (Piaget, 1924/1928, pp. 112–113)

Clearly the theory of groups and groupings was historically tied up with the relation between one's own perspective and the perspective of others and their operational transformations.[2] But more than this, such a theory would also be able to explicate the kind of rationality present in sensorimotor intelligence and in the highest form of conceptual rationality. Hence, Piaget's early theorizing directly led to his theory of groupings.

Piaget's earliest publications on theory of groups and groupings appeared in two brief articles in 1937 (Piaget, 1937) and 1938 (Piaget, 1938)[3] and then in book form (Piaget, 1942). From the beginning (i.e., 1937) his thinking about groups was tied up with an algebra of logic (Piaget, 1953) as an offshoot of Poincaré's group of displacements. Such an approach was based upon the 19th century logic of Boole; in the 20th century the dominant logic was symbolic logic or logistics, associated with Frege, Whitehead, and Russell.

Piaget's first major work on groupings (1942), *Classes, Relations and Numbers*, has as a subtitle *An Essay on the Groupings of Logistics and the Reversibility of Thought*. Early on in that work, Piaget says, "In effect, we are working on a treatise on logistics" (1942, p. 1). "The aim of the present work," Piaget goes on to say, "is to construct an operatory logistics of classes, relations, and numbers, that is to say, a logistics whose structure would be parallel to and not heterogeneous to mental structures" (Piaget, 1942a, p. 2). The key theoretical notion here was groupings, based on the model of mathematical groups. Groups and groupings are formalistic notions, as is logistics, and constitute a model of closely related notions: a state of equilibrium and the underlying structure of such a state. Although there is some controversy here, I believe the concept of groupings must be interpreted in a formalistic way. Such an approach gives us one clear sense of what a structure is and constitutes one interpretation of Piaget's dual-aspect model.

STRUCTURAL ISOMORPHISM

Piaget's (e.g., 1942) early interest in structure and the theory of relations was furthered by his early reading of Russell (1919) and Carnap (1929). Suppose we have two systems or subject matters, each of which is concerned with a relation or set of relations, for example, the two relations of "husband of" (H) and "wife of" (W) (exclude recent redefinitions of "marriage"). Suppose there is a set of elements (people) {E} in H and ■ {E'} in W such that some elements of {E} have the relation of H (e.g., Bill and Hillary) and some do not; and some elements of {E'} have the relation of W (e.g., Hillary and Bill) and some do not. Suppose we have a mapping (one–one) of elements of {E} onto elements of {E'} such that whenever two terms of {E} have H, their correlates have W (and vice versa). The set of all elements that has H is the structure of H and the set of all elements that has W is the structure of W. Here, the two structures are the same: They are isomorphic to each other. When two relations have the same structure, all their logical properties are identical.

Now suppose there are two systems, for example, individual cognition and social interaction, in which they are in respective states of equilibrium E_1 and E_2. E_1 has an underlying structure and so does E_2. Suppose this structure consists of a particular kind of *grouping structure* G, which consists of a set of relations {R = R_1, R_2, ... Rn}. If G is present in both, they have the same structure and can be said to be isomorphic to each other.

Throughout Piaget's writings, one finds a common theme often stated. Individual interaction in an environment can be characterized as reaching a certain state of equilibrium E_1, and individual interaction with others can also be characterized as reaching a certain state of equilibrium E_2. Both states of equilibria, E_1 and E_2, can vary in degree, which matches the corresponding stage of development. Each state of equilibrium E_1 has an underling structure to it, which can be formally modeled by a grouping structure (i.e., group, grouping, lattice), each of which consists of a set of relations (e.g., operations). The state of individual equilibrium can be equivalent to the state of social equilibrium in which case the structure of the one is isomorphic to that of other because

G is the same in both. When this happens, one can say that there is a structure common to both systems. If so, one cannot ask which is more important or has temporal or causal priority because they are isomorphic to each other; one cannot ask which system causes the other any more than one can ask which relation, husband or wife, is the first or which one caused the other. Hence, the individual aspect of the person and the social aspect of the person are two inseparable aspects of one underlying process in the sense that they have the same underlying formal structure and are isomorphic to each other (Piaget, 1977/1995, pp. 35, 43, 87–89, 94, 145–146). "In sum, the social relationships equilibrated into cooperation constitute *groupements* of operations exactly like the logical actions exercised on the external world by the individual, and the laws of *groupements* define the form of ideal equilibrium common to both social and individual actions" (Piaget, 1977/1995, p. 146).

CRITICISMS OF LOGICIST FORMALISM

Although this language bespeaks (perhaps) of a kind of Spinozist dual-aspect view, interpreted in purely formal terms (something Spinoza did not claim), Piaget's theory of grouping structure has a difficult time incorporating the material aspect of this view, for a grouping structure is a purely formal notion. Piaget is clear about this: His theory of grouping is a logistics approach in which one constructs a formal model of equilibrium (Piaget, 1949/1966, pp. 3, 271).

Equilibrium, no doubt, is taken by Piaget to have *both* a formal and a material (content) aspect. Formal structures qua formal have no causal powers. It can, therefore, make little sense to say "that the logical groupings constitute not only the effect but the very cause of the formation of operations" (Piaget, 1941, p. 217). This is because groupings, qua formal structures, have no causal powers, although groupings qua material structures do. But then we need an explication of what the latter notion is. The important question left unanswered is: What is the cause of the equilibrated system? How does one explain the construction of this system? Here it is not the concept of a state of equilibrium but the process of equilibration that is crucial.

In an interesting article, Döbert (2004) has argued that, contrary to the previous line of thought (in which it is claimed that Piaget's moving from his first theory of the social to his second theory was a mistake), this move was progressive from a structuralist perspective. Such a perspective led Piaget to his theory of groupings, in which the sociological component was de-emphasized and this was an advance. This is because rationality requires order and coordination, and this requires something like a grouping structure.

I have argued against such a notion. True, logical structure is necessary for rationality, but it is not sufficient. This is (again) because rationality and epistemology – Piaget's concern – is broader than a formal–syntactical model. Of course, one wants an adequate formal model of rationality and intelligence, and grouping structures might be such a model. But to argue that this is all you need is inadequate.

A CAUSAL INTERPRETATION

Now, Piaget may not intend this "dual-aspect" view to be interpreted in such a purely formal manner. Perhaps he means to say (Piaget, 1977/1995, pp. 88, 145, 641) that it is the case that there is an actual real process in which there is simultaneously operating both individual causal mechanisms and social causal mechanisms (as well as biological causal ones). Perhaps his claim is that there is, as a matter of fact, no social interaction that is not, at the same time, individual psychological intelligence, and (conversely) every case of intraindividual intelligence is also a case of some kind of social interaction (Piaget, 1977/1995, p. 33). Even if there is a dual aspect of content, we still need to know what causes each of these (Piaget, 1977/1995, pp. 143, 215).

Such a view would be more in keeping with the Spinozist model, because Spinoza was not claiming that, in his dual-aspect view, there was merely an underlying formal mechanism instantiated in two different domains. Spinoza claimed a perfect correspondence or parallelism between the mental and the physical, including (of course) all of the causal properties of both, which were identical in some sense. They are two sides of a coin.

Such a claim is sometimes made by Piaget:

> ... there are not three human natures, the physical person, the mental person, and the social person, superimposed or succeeding one another ... but there is on the one hand the organism, determined by hereditary characteristics as well as by ontogenetic mechanisms, and on the other hand the set of human behaviors, each of which has, from birth and in differing degrees, a mental aspect and a social aspect. (Piaget, 1977/1995, p. 33)

I do not believe such a view can be defended, however. For first, this is incompatible with his early social epistemology, in which he claimed that one could untangle the social and the individual aspects of intelligence because the first stage of individual development was that of autism/egocentrism (modeled after psychoanalysis), in which the social was absent; it appeared only later at 7–8 (Piaget, 1924/1928,

p. 209)!⁴ This was one of the major bones of contention between Piaget and Wallon, who insisted the child is social from birth.

Second, even if it were true that, as a matter of fact, humans are always social, this would be a contingent claim. The question would be not what happens to be true of virtually all humans, but whether the social is absolutely essential to cognitive development. This is the point of thought experiments such as Robinson Crusoe: If an individual could survive in the absence of all social contacts, how far could he develop intellectually?⁵ Can we factor out the respective contributions of the individual and the social? Yes, Piaget says (1977/1995, p. 194) if we want to know when the social becomes influential. As Piaget seems to think (1977/1995, p. 94), such a Robinson simply could not advance much beyond sensorimotor intelligence (1977/1995, pp. 38, 94, 135, 154, 195, 221, 278; 1949/1966, p. 158).

According to Piaget the normative principle of optimizing equilibration is a principle operating from birth to adulthood. Although he sometimes is unclear about this, we can propose that it is constant in its functioning across the developmental trajectory, resulting in different structures over time.

Alongside of this, there is the influence of the social on cognitive development. Here, the operation of a social principle is not constant. In the first stage, there is no significant epistemic input from the social. This progressively changes in the next and succeeding stages, because there is a geometric increase in the influence of the social. Hence, the more advanced the development, the greater the influence of the social (Piaget, 1977/1995, p. 38). In the second and third stages, it is the shock of social discussion, whereas subsequently it is the influence of language, and so forth. What these precise social influences are is something to be worked out – something Piaget never did. But it is clear that some social influences are epistemically positive (e.g., discussion) and others are epistemically negative (e.g., ideology).

COGNITIVE INTERNALISM

Finally, I want to mention a third account of the social that can be found in Piaget, one in which *the social is dependent on the psychological*. Starting out from a Durkheimian perspective, in which (perhaps mistakenly) one imagines it is social pressure that determines epistemic structures and logical reasoning, one can ask the question: How does this happen? How does social pressure and social conformity work? Piaget's view is that the social does not and cannot act directly on behavior or on a passive mind. Instead, any social influence will be mediated by a psychological process or mechanism that interprets the external social influence (Piaget, 1977/1995, pp. 33, 37, 295).

As a cognitivist, Piaget believes that every environmental influence must be mediated by an internal cognitive process of interpretation, selection, judgment, etc.; this is the thrust of the centrality of assimilation.[6] But if that is the case, then it is easy to be led to the view that it is the individual, the autonomous individual, who is in control of development and who is in charge of letting in and interpreting social influences (Piaget, 1977/1995, p. 36).

If this is so, then it is the psychological realm that is primary and the social will be secondary. On this view, what is driving development will be individual, psychological processes, not social ones. This seems to be the basis for the claim (e.g., by Wallon) that Piaget is really a Rousseauian.

In his later works (Inhelder & Piaget, 1955/1958, pp. 243–244; 1959/1969) the primacy and autonomy of equilibrium is explicitly set forth.

> ... the development of operational behaviour is an autonomous process rather than a secondary consequence, depending on the development of perception or of language.... When we speak of the autonomy of this development, we wish to be understood in the very precise sense that the development can be explained without necessary reference to various factors which undoubtedly do play a part in its concrete realization, e.g., maturation, learning and social education, including language. For the key to its explanation lies in the concept of equilibration, which is a wider notion than any of these and comprehends them all. (Inhelder & Piaget, 1959/1969, p. 292)

THE PRINCIPLE OF ASYMMETRY

According to an influential view (Laudan, 1977), there is a *principle of asymmetry* operating in the case of cognitive change: When the cognitive change is a rational one, the fact that it is rational is a sufficient explanation of the change, and nothing extrarational is possible or needed. But when the cognitive change is an irrational one, this requires a special, nonrational explanation, for example, one involving external sociological factors such as class interest or funding priorities. Sociology, therefore, can explain why an irrational change occurred, but it cannot explain why it was rational. That falls to logic.

In the case of Piaget, a similar principle of asymmetry sometimes seems to be operating. When there is cognitive change toward optimizing equilibration – *équilibration majorante* – (Piaget, 1975/1985, p. 3), the reason for this is simply that it is rational to do so: It is more equilibrated. But what about cognitive change that is irrational? Here, sociological factors (e.g., ideology) seem to be relevant. On this account, therefore, the social explains deviations from *équilibration majo-rante*. Although affectivity "is constantly at work in the function-ing of thought," Piaget says, "it does not create laws of equilibrium" (1954/1981, p. 7). Indeed, "in our opinion, affectivity only makes ratio-nal thought deviate into all sorts of paralogisms; it does not form coherent systems as is the case with reason" (p. 60). Similar things could be said for other social factors, for example, in traditional class-room instruction, spontaneous (natural) concepts, and in theories not allowed to develop naturally; instead "correct" adult concepts and the-ories are simply impressed on the child's mind (Piaget, 1977/1995, p. 203).[7]

On this purely cognitivist account, epistemic change involves *internalist* explanations, whereas invocations of social and economic factors are *externalist explanations*. In the history of science, these two terms have been employed to characterize two ways of explaining his-torical change: Internalist factors are logical in nature, appealing to mat-ters of evidence, confirmation, and reason, whereas external factors are basically irrational ones, invoking extrarational factors such as class interest, economic motivations, and psychological factors such as the motivation to win the Nobel Prize. Something like this can be found in Piaget.

COGNITIVE IMMANENCE

In Piaget's earliest writings, he expressed a kind of awe for Henri Berg-son's (1907/1911) *élan vital*. In place of it, however, he substituted the law of equilibrium (equilibration): Over the course of intellectual devel-opment there is a push, press, or tendency toward an ever-increasing degree of equilibrium – a vection as it were. This is a kind of law of rational change, a principle governing how reason operates over time.

This law of equilibrium, Piaget repeats, is not something external, imposed upon intellectual change from without; it is not a transcendent, Platonic principle. On the contrary, much like Kant's notion of the moral law, which is not internal to the individual, the law of equilibration is an immanent principle in experience (Piaget, 1977/1995, pp. 94, 154, 190, 216, 227, 243). Such a concept of the immanent versus the transcendent goes back to Piaget's earliest years and his youthful speculations about theology.[8]

There is an immanent principle of normativity to be found within certain experiences – what he calls *logical experience* (Piaget, 1923b;

1977/1995, p. 185). It has a "givenness," which presents itself to the individual (Piaget, 1977/1995, pp. 170–171, 185), resulting in *normative feelings* – feelings of necessity. But as such, it is distinct from ordinary psychological processes and experiences. In a certain sense, therefore, psychological processes are "external" to this normativity. Hence, norms are not prescriptions external to the individual. They are themselves present within these special logical experiences. This is the source of the principle of equilibration and reversibility – a normative principle immanently present in some of our experiences. In this sense, logic does not prescribe norms from an external point of view (Piaget, 1977/1995, p. 94). Laws of logic are constructed by the individual on the basis of experience. What, then, is the role of external factors? Can they, nevertheless, be necessary for epistemic development?[9]

Appropriating a philosophical school of the 17th century, we could say that environmental factors, such as intersubjective discussion, are not causes of rationality and rational change; instead they are the *occasion* for such change. The underlying causal factor, for example, the felt disequilibrium, is an internal factor present in the individual. Individual thought, Piaget says,

> is a system that aims towards equilibrium (...) but never attains it (...). So the problem, then, is not to know what creative causality will make reason penetrate the individual from the outside, but simply what circumstances will permit the rational equilibrium immanent in the individual to further realize itself. (1977/1995, p. 227; see also Piaget, 1977/1995, pp. 227, 289)

The cause of rational change, if we are to use that term, is thus not external at all but internal.

This account seems to be a kind of Rousseauian account, where the individual left to himself proceeds naturally and rationally toward epistemic improvement. This is the individualism that Wallon ascribes to Piaget. Piaget, of course, denies it, but I think there is reason to believe that such an account, as I have explicated, can be found running throughout Piaget's works.

Conclusion

I have suggested that Piaget has at least three different accounts of the nature of the social and its role in the cognitive development of the individual. Piaget's account of social epistemology was clearly set forth in his early works and can also be found in subsequent works. He never really abandoned it, but it became somewhat subdued (later). This is the most famous of his theories of the social; it is the one that Piagetian scholars cite in defending Piaget against his critics.

Piaget began on a somewhat different course around 1928. Although he did not abandon his early theory, it was overlaid with another theory of the social, his Spinozist theory. His first view was modified as a result of his research on the child's first 2 years of life, giving rise to his theory of motor intelligence, and as a result of various criticisms. This led (initially) to a two-level theory of cognition: sensorimotor knowledge and cognitive knowledge. To explain the continuity in development from the sensorimotor level to the conceptual level, Piaget had recourse to his major theoretical construct – his theory of equilibration. This was accompanied by his growing interest in the *structure* of equilibration – his theory of grouping. This theory was the basis for his claim that individual rationality and social interaction are two aspects of a single process. Given the predominance of Piaget's theory of groupings, this account was given the lion's share of attention in his later works.

Piaget's third theory has been present in Piaget's writings from the very beginning (1918, 1923b, 1928a). It has been a motif present throughout his entire career, but present alongside his other accounts. This account is an individualistic one based on a kind of rationalist (internalist) model.

Because these three models were never successfully integrated into one overall account, both the critics of Piaget and his defenders have textual evidence for their claims. In a sense, therefore, both camps are correct but only partially so, for they are ignoring other passages in Piaget in which he proposes alternative views. The source of their dispute, I think, is that they were focusing on different passages in Piaget.

In closing, what can be said about the relations between these three models? Can they be integrated into one overall account? If so, what aspects must be eliminated? What additions must be made? I can provide only the sketchiest account of one possible synthesis.

I have argued that Model I is absolutely essential and must be retained (Kitchener, 2004). But what about the others? The dual-aspect theory can be interpreted in at least two different ways. As a strictly formalistic, logicist theory it is inadequate. There is, of course, nothing wrong with a purely formal (syntactical) account of logic and reasoning. But if logic and reasoning are thought to be reducible to logistics, this account is inadequate. Simply put, reasoning is not the same as formal logic, and Piaget was interested in reasoning. It is tempting to equate reasoning with logic and to interpret logic in a purely formal way. But this picture is inadequate and overlooks the point many have made that a theory of logic cannot be narrowly syntactical; instead it must include semantics and pragmatics. I do not think Piaget would deny this, but he often writes in a misleading way about the theory of logic.

If the formalist interpretation of the second model won't work, what about its causal interpretation? Here, things are much better because this approach would stress the importance of *equilibration* – the underlying process of attaining and revising particular states of equilibrium (formally modeled).

But what is an adequate account of equilibration? How does it explain the transition from one state to the next? Piaget's book on equilibration (1975/1985) does not help much. For the important issue here concerns real causal processes (versus normative principles of implication) and their relationship (Mischel, 1971; Smith, 1993, 2006). This takes us to the third theory.

According to this theory, the notion of equilibration is that of an internal, endogenous, normative principle or law of evolution immanent in experience. This normative principle is thus "in" the experience of the individual, not transcendent of it, and like Kant's moral law "constrains without determining." How adequate is such a view? This raises the crucial issue of "causes versus reasons," the fact–norm distinction.

The principle of asymmetry claims there is a fundamental explanatory difference between rationality and irrationality. The explanation of rationality requires principles different from those explaining irrationality. Almost invariably, the explanatory principles underlying rationality are autonomous principles of normative rationality belonging to rationality theory. These are almost without exception noncausal principles. Explanatory principles of irrationality fall into a different category: Here one wants to explain why individuals formed an irrational belief. These are external factors – factors external to the autonomous rational mind – factors that took the mind "off course," resulting in a deviation from rationality. Reasons are, therefore, in a category different from causes.

This view has been challenged by social scientists, psychologists, and philosophers on several grounds, which I cannot set forth here (Kitchener, forthcoming). The short of it is the following: Such a dualism is antithetical to a naturalistic view of the world. Causes are clearly part of the natural world, operating in space–time. But rational, normative principles seem transcendent of the natural world, entities in a Platonic supernatural realm. If we have learned anything from the history of science, it is to reject such spooky entities for reasons I won't go into here. The problem is to construct a theory of norms and reasons consistent with a scientific naturalism. Such an account, I suggest, would be a causal account.

Suppose it is rational to prefer theory T_2 to T_1 on the grounds of greater simplicity. It may be rational to believe this, but in order to explain an individual's actual belief (rather than, say, his possible belief), it would seem to be necessary to bring in the subject's cognitive awareness or higher-order belief about the rationality of such a change. Arguably, this seems to be sufficient to explain belief change, in fact, sufficient to explain all belief change rational or irrational. If so, then a theory of psychological belief does the explanatory work here, not normative principles.

Furthermore (and this is much more debatable) cognitive change is a causal process, for example, my belief that it was Monday caused me to get up and prepare a class lecture. If this is the case, then *mental causes explain everything* – this is the thesis of *the omnipotence of mental causation*. Does it matter whether the cause was rational or not? Not for the purposes of explanation!

What about the equilibration model? On the previous account, it is not disequilibrium itself (i.e., a disequilibrated state of cognitive elements) that does the motivating. It is the need, feeling, or dislike of disequilibrium that is the driving force. It does not matter whether it is real disequilibrium or just felt disequilibrium. If someone does not care about contradicting himself, he will not be motivated to change (Piaget, 1954/1981, pp. 3, 5, 18; 1975/1985, pp, 3, 10–11, 68, 129). What matters is the internal psychological state that motivates.[10] Likewise with equilibrium: If an individual feels that a set of cognitive operations is equilibrated, wouldn't that be sufficient for him to cease his construction of formal operatory structures?[11]

If so, then the third model of the social seems to be inadequate because it assumes something like the principle of asymmetry. To improve upon that model, one would need *a principle of symmetry* where both rational and irrational beliefs and belief change are to be explained by the same set of underlying causal principles. Such an account would also allow us to incorporate the first model. For on that model, the social has a crucial part to play in epistemic development because (in brief) other individuals challenge the cogency of your beliefs by questioning your supporting reasons.

Here, one can say that this shock or disagreement is motivational, driving you to modify the reasons for your belief only if you believe you ought to give the other person good and convincing reasons and you have a desire to do so. Here, social influences operate through the internal cognitive state of belief + desire. Model III and Model I are thus (arguably) compatible.

What about Model II – the dual-aspect model? First, interpreted purely formally via grouping theory, one's belief set may have the structure of a grouping, and one may even believe it has such a structure. Hence, it is formally logical. Likewise with a set of interpersonal relations found, say, in exchange theory. Both sets are equilibrated. But again why did one come to construct a formal grouping? How does one explain this? The law of equilibration claims that one will do so as the ideal outcome of certain kinds of experiences. But again one must be motivated to do so, and it seems that this motivation is the real explanation of the process (together with beliefs about what an ideal equilibrium would be).

Piaget's project was to show how norms (can) develop from causal facts (Smith, 2006). But this seems to underwrite a kind of dualism of the natural versus the normative, and Piaget himself (sometimes) expressed doubts about this way of putting it, sometimes (at least) favoring a causal account of the process (Piaget, 1954/1981, 1975/1985). Rather, the task would better be expressed as showing how norms are possible in such a naturalistic perspective, how it is possible for norms to emerge from empirical facts (Kitchener, 2006).

Bloor (1974) argues that every explanatory principle must be causal and adds that the normative (rationality, truth) must be entirely eschewed. But one does not have to take such an extreme course. One could deny a dualism of reasons and causes and argue that both are natural. One could do this either by being a nonreductionist (as Dewey was) or by being a reductionist and arguing that norms are just complex kinds of causal relations (Kitchener, forthcoming). That latter is the more daunting task, but it is one worth contemplating.

NOTES

1. Bleuler (1911/1950) contains a brief discussion of autism, elaborated in his important but rarely read monograph on autism (1912/1951), which is the work importantly discussed by Vygotsky (1934/1986). Bleuler (1919/1970) is not about clinical autism at all but about inadequate medical diagnosis.

2. Cf. also his remarks: " ... the purely perceptual point of view is always completely egocentric. This means that it is both unaware of itself and incomplete, distorting reality to the extent that it remains so. As against this, to discover one's own viewpoint is to relate it to other viewpoints, to distinguish it from and co-ordinate it with them. Now perception is quite unsuited to this task, for to become conscious of one's own viewpoint is really to liberate oneself from it. To do this requires a system of true mental operations, that is, operations which are reversible and capable of being linked together" (Piaget & Inhelder, 1948/1967, p. 193). Clearly this necessitates, Piaget thinks, something like his theory of groupings.

3. Which one was first is debatable.

4. Piaget claims both that there is no social influence in the earliest stage (e.g., 1977/1995, pp. 84, 221, 290), and that there are such social

influences from birth (e.g., 1977/1995, pp. 216–217, 278). The latter concession involved a shift in the meaning of "social" for Piaget.

5. Are there actual cases of a completely asocial individual? Stories about wolf-children naturally come to mind (see, e.g., Yousef, 2001). I know of no one who has given a thorough survey of this issue. However, the evidence certainly indicates significant impairment in cognitive development.

6. Of course, there is also the need to accommodate oneself to the social environment.

7. On this account, however, the social does have a minor role. (1) External social factors can explain the precise instantiations of this increase in equilibrium and the precise manifestations it takes, for these particularities do involve environmental factors. (2) External social factors might be invoked to explain temporal factors, why, for example, it was so slow in happening and how it might accelerate the process (Piaget, 1977/1995, p. 37).

8. In an early article on the two types of religious attitudes – immanence and transcendence – Piaget said: "There exists outside of subjective consciousness, outside of this subjectivity, something greater than just obedience to collective representations – a normative and rational reality, hence an autonomous indication of rationality" (1928a, p. 15).

9. This raises the question of whether norms are autonomous or explainable psychologically (see Piaget, 1923, 1977/1995, p. 170). I think Piaget vacillates on this question.

10. In moral theory, this is the issue of motivational internalism versus externalism. Does a rational belief about a moral norm inherently motivate an individual to behave in a certain way (internalism), or does motivation require, in addition, desire, feeling, or sentiment (externalism)? Internalism usually goes with rationalism (e.g., Kant), whereas externalism goes with empiricism (Hume) and/or functionalism (Dewey, James, Claparéde). Although this is controversial, I believe Piaget is an externalist. If so, then it is misleading to view his moral theory as an example of rationalism.

11. Now, for pragmatists and functionalists there is an objective measure of what a problem is: It is an (external) obstacle that prevents one from reaching a goal: for a child or an animal imagined water will not slake one's thirst. But this line of thought will not be applicable to higher-order purely cognitive needs.

REFERENCES

Apostel, L. (1986). The unknown Piaget: From the theory of exchange and cooperation toward the theory of knowledge. *New Ideas in Psychology, 4,* 3–22.

Bergson, H. (1911). *Creative evolution.* New York: Henry Holt. (Original work published 1907)

Bleuler, E. (1950). *Dementia Praecox or the group of schizophrenias.* New York: International Universities Press. (Original work published 1911)

Bleuler, E. (1951). Autistic thinking. In D. Rapaport (Ed.), *Organization and pathology of thought* (pp. 399–437). New York: Columbia University Press. (Original work published 1912)

Bleuler, E. (1970). *Autistic undisciplined thinking in medicine and how to overcome it.* Darien, CT: Hafner. (Original work published 1919)

Bloor, D. (1974). *Knowledge and social imagery.* London: Routledge.

Boden, M. (1980). *Jean Piaget.* New York: Viking.

Carnap, R. (1929). *Abriss der Logistik.* Vienna: Julius Springer.

Chapman, M. (1986). The structure of exchange: Piaget's sociological theory. *Human Development, 29*, 181–194.

Döbert, R. (2004). The development and overcoming of universal pragmatics in Piaget's thinking. In J. Carpendale & U. Müller (Eds.), *Social interaction and the development of knowledge* (pp. 133–154). Mahwah, NJ: Erlbaum.

Ducret, J.-J. (1984). *Jean Piaget: savant et philosophe* (Vol. 2, pp. 495–507). Geneva: Droz.

Hamlyn, D. (1971). Epistemology and conceptual development. In T. Mischel (Ed.), *Cognitive development and epistemology* (pp. 3–24). New York: Academic.

Hamlyn, D. (1978). *Experience and the growth of understanding.* London: Routledge & Kegan Paul.

Inhelder, B., & Piaget, J. (1958). *The growth of logical thinking from childhood to adolescence: An essay on the construction of formal operational structures.* London: Routledge & Kegan. (Original work published 1955)

Inhelder, B., & Piaget, J. (1969). *The early growth of logic in the child.* New York: Norton. (Original work published 1959)

Isaacs, S. (1930). *The intellectual growth of young children.* New York: Harcourt Brace.

Kitchener, R. F. (1981). Piaget's social psychology. *Journal for the Theory of Social Behavior, 11*, 253–277.

Kitchener, R. F. (1991). Jean Piaget: The unknown sociologist. *British Journal of Sociology, 42*, 421–442.

Kitchener, R. F. (2004). Piaget's social epistemology. In J. Carpenter & U. Müller (Eds.), *Piaget's sociological studies* (pp. 45–66). Mahwah, NJ: Erlbaum.

Kitchener, R. F. (2006). Genetic epistemology: Naturalistic epistemology vs. normative epistemology In L. Smith & J. Vonéche (Eds.), *Norms in human development* (pp. 77–102). Cambridge: Cambridge University Press.

Kitchener, R. F. (forthcoming). *Developmental epistemology: Cognitive development and naturalistic epistemology.* Book manuscript.

Köhler, W. (1925). *The mentality of apes.* London: Routledge & Kegan Paul. (Original work published 1917)

Laudan, L. (1977). *Progress and its problems.* Berkeley: University of California Press.

Mays, W. (1982). Piaget's sociological theory. In S. Modgil & C. Modgil (Eds.), *Jean Piaget: Consensus and controversy* (pp. 31–50). New York: Praeger.

Meacham, J. A., & Riegel, K. F. (1978). Dialektische Perspektiven in Piagets Theorie. In G. Steiner (Ed.), *Die Psychologie des 20. Jahrhunderts, Vol. 8: Piaget und die Folgen* (pp. 172–183). Zurich: Kindler.

Mischel, T. (1971). Cognitive conflict and the motivation of thought. In T. Mischel (Ed.), *Cognitive development and epistemology* (pp. 311–356). New York: Academic Press.

Piaget, J. (1918). *Recherche*. Lausanne: La Concorde.

Piaget, J. (1920). La psychanalyse dans ses rapports avec la psychologie de l'enfant. *Bulletin mensuel: Sociètè Alfred Binet, 20*, 18–34, 41–58.

Piaget, J. (1923a). La pensée symbolique et la pensée de l'enfant. *Archives de Psychologie, 18*, 275–304.

Piaget, J. (1923b). La psychologie et les valeurs religieuses. In Association chrétienne d'étudiants de la Suiss romande (Eds.), *Sainte-Croix 1922* (pp. 38–82). Lausanne: La Concorde.

Piaget, J. (1926). *Language and thought of the child*. London: K. Paul, Trench, Trubner. (Original work published 1923)

Piaget, J. (1928a). *Deux types d'atitudes religieuses: Immanence et transcendance*. Geneva: Association chrétienne d'etudiants de Suisse romande.

Piaget, J. (1928b). Les trios systèmes de la pensée de l'enfant: Etude sur les rapports de la pensée rationnelle et de l'intelligence motrice. *Bulletin de la Société Française de Philosophie, 28*, 97–141.

Piaget, J. (1928). *Judgment and reasoning in the child*. London: K. Paul, Trench, Trubner. (Original work published 1924)

Piaget, J. (1937). Les relations d'égalité résultant de l'addition et de l soustraction logiques constituent-elles un groupe? *L'Enseignement Mathématique, 36*, 99–108.

Piaget, J. (1938). Les groupes de la logistique et la réversibilité de la pensée. *Revue de Théologique et de Philosophie, 27*, 291–292.

Piaget, J. (1941). Le méchanisme du développement mental et les lois du groupements des opérations. *Archives de Psychologie, 28*, 215–285.

Piaget, J. (1942). *Classes, relations et nombres: Essai sur les groupements de la logistique et sur la réversibilité de la pensée*. Paris: J. Vrin.

Piaget, J. (1951). *Plays, dreams, and imitation in childhood*. London: W. Heinemann. (Original work published 1945)

Piaget, J. (1952). *The origins of intelligence in children*. New York: W. W. Norton. (Original work published 1936)

Piaget, J. (1953). *Logic and psychology*. Manchester: Manchester University Press.

Piaget, J. (1954). *The construction of reality in the child*. New York: Basic Books. (Original work published 1937)

Piaget, J. (1966). *The psychology of intelligence* (2nd ed.). Totowa, NJ: Littlefield & Adams. (Original work published 1949)

Piaget, J. (1978). *Success and understanding*. London: Routledge & Kegan Paul. (Original work published 1974)

Piaget, J. (1981). *Intelligence and affectivity: Their relationships during child developmemt*. Palo Alto, CA: Annual Reviews. (Original work published 1954)

Piaget, J. (1985). *The equilibration of cognitive structures: The central problem of intellectual development*. Chicago: University of Chicago Press. (Original work published 1975)

Piaget, J. (1995). *Sociological studies*. New York/London: Routledge. (Original work published 1977)

Piaget, J., & Inhelder, B. (1967). *The child's conception of space*. New York: Norton. (Original work published 1948)

Poincaré, H. (1958). *The value of science*. New York: Dover (Original work published 1905)

Rotman, B. (1977). *Jean Piaget: Psychologist of the real*. Ithaca, NY: Cornell University Press.

Russell, B. (1919). *Introduction to mathematical philosophy*. London: George Allen & Unwin.

Russell, J. (1979). *The development of knowledge*. New York: St. Martin's.

Smith, L. (1982). Piaget and the solitary knower. *Philosophy of the Social Sciences, 12*, 173–182.

Smith, L. (1993). *Necessary knowledge: Piagetian perspectives on constructivism*. Hillsdale, NJ: Erlbaum.

Smith, L. (1995). Introduction to Piaget's *Sociological studies*. In J. Piaget, *Sociological studies* (pp. 1–22). London: Routledge.

Smith, L. (2006). Norms and normative facts in human development. In L. Smith & J. Vonèche (Eds.), *Norms in human development* (pp. 103–137). Cambridge: Cambridge University Press.

Spinoza, B. (2000). *Ethics*. New York: Oxford University Press. (Original work published 1677)

Tripp, G. M. (1978). *Betr. Piaget. Philosophie oder psychologie?* Köln: Paul-Rugenstein.

Vidal, F. (1986). Jean Piaget et la psychanalyse: Premières rencontres. *Le Bloc-Notes de la Psychoanalyse, 6*, 171–189.

Vygotsky, L. (1986). *Thought and language*. Cambridge, MA: MIT Press. (Original work published 1934)

Wallon, H. (1928). L'autisme du malade et l'égocentrisme enfantin: Intervention aux discussions de la these de Piaget. *Bulletin de la Societe Française de Philosophie, 28*, 131–136.

Wallon, H. (1942). *De l'acte à la pensée*. Paris: Flammarion.

Wallon, H. (1951). Post scriptum en réponse à M. Piaget. *Cahiers Internationaux de Sociologie, 10*, 175–177.

Wilden, A. (1977). *System and structure: Essays in communication and exchange*. London : Tavistock.

Yousef, N. (2001). Savage or solitary? The wild child and Rousseau's Man of Nature. *Journal of the History of Ideas, 62*, 245–263.

6   Piaget on Equilibration

EQUILIBRATION AS A CENTRAL CONCEPT IN PIAGET'S THEORY

According to Piaget, models of equilibration are involved in all questions about cognitive development. Cognitive development, for him, is a succession of constructions with constant elaborations of novel structures. Moreover, for Piaget, this implies a process that improves existing structures and replaces temporally achieved equilibria through re-equilibrations. This process is designated by Piaget as equilibration, and coming to grips with it is the central issue for many of his works.

Piaget's account of equilibration is not only crucial for understanding his approach, it also sets his theory apart from most other theories concerning cognitive development. Moreover, Piaget, in his long career, has developed his own terminology that suits his own intentions better, but this terminology makes the challenge for new uninitiated readers even more daunting. It might be in order, therefore, to characterize the equilibration idea avoiding Piagetian jargon. So, I will first give a brief expository definition and elaborate upon it by expanding on all terms used in – and left out of – this brief definition.

Subsequently, I will go deeper into matters now based on Piaget's own formulations and review some of the central issues and perspectives involved. This review is roughly structured along these perspectives with a focus, first, on biological systems, next on the psychological subject, and third on the epistemological subject. Finally, conclusions and evaluation will follow.

A Tentative Definition of Equilibration

As a preliminary definition (avoiding Piaget jargon) I propose: "Equilibration is the tendency of the subject to develop increasing control over experience." In expanding (see the following) the terms used in this preliminary definition, my aim is merely expository.

The term "subject" might already presuppose more than is required. The notion of equilibration is applied by Piaget from very broad to very specific, for example, to inorganic evolution, to organisms and physiological mechanisms, to nonhuman functioning, to schemes, to sensorimotor regulations, or to thinking. The definition given previously is limited to the level of human cognition proper (roughly the last three in this list). What would be minimally presupposed for equilibration to be possible, though, is a complex system that is in a permanent exchange with its environment. That system has to have an identity, or a center, or a unity in some sense. Such a system is trying to maintain itself and expand its field of control. Such a center – in the preliminary definition shown previously – could be located in the nervous system, although Piaget himself is careful not to locate this process. Anyway, in the normal case, we can say the subject, or the knower, has one brain, one history, and memory.

Experience involves all exchanges with the environment outside the body. I am reluctant, however, to frame experience in terms of information, because that almost immediately leads away from what Piaget had in mind. It would be no problem to think of experience as induced by the environment through sensory organs, but it can also be self-generated with outputs to the motor systems such that both are intertwined.

Development is understood here in the sense (of Piaget and others) of a general, systematic, highly idealized, constructive process that can be reconstructed (afterward) as directed and progressive. I emphasize that development so understood is an interpretation of developmentalists to conceptualize common features of individual human change. Development is currently often understood in developmental psychology in a much looser sense: Almost any systematic change over time during childhood will do. However, my definition of development states that, in as far as directed and progressive changes in thinking do occur over time in individuals, we may denote them as development (but some other conditions have to be fulfilled also).

Tendency is used because Piaget proposed that the development of cognitive functioning is inherent in living things, occurring without any requirement for external rewards. Increasing control is understood here as that which needs to be explained in this chapter, and in particular the development of it concerns us. Control can vary enormously – from almost none to a high degree of it. Control is an individual matter given the one subject or single center referred to previously. Control points to directed activity. The increasing part of control is the hardest to conceptualize. Equilibration is a process that is supposed to lead to increasingly better equilibrium.

Improvement and direction, however, were modernist ideas that were heavily contested in the last decades of the previous century. Postmodernism has discredited the whole notion of progress and instead favored (cultural) relativism. Nativism, especially in the variety of Fodor and Chomsky, gave a severe blow to the credibility of Piagetian theory in the 1980s. Evolutionary theories are less clear about progress than they often suggest, but certainly neo-Darwinists are univocal that improvement can never be the result of directed change. We will see what Piaget's account of equilibration has to offer despite these attacks on what for Piaget was an important aspect of development.

In the brief definition mentioned previously several terms or issues were deliberately not included; it is worthwhile to notice what is missing from it.

The definition does not say control over the environment. It might be tempting, but it is certainly too simple to say that with growing equilibration we come closer to understanding the objectively given external world. In fact, no fixed endpoint for cognitive development is implied in Piaget's account of equilibration. To the contrary, every new level once attained opens up new possibilities (Piaget, 1975/1985, p. 150; 1981/1987, p. 4). Nevertheless, Piaget has been ambiguous on this point and often suggested that he has increasing control over the environment in mind. But note that, even if we were to know, to understand, or to be able to explain, what this kind of control is, we still could not predict a subject's behavior. Piaget was well aware of the fact that he did not offer a standard causal explanation of behavior.

Stages are not mentioned in the working definition previously. They are apparently hardly mentioned by Piaget himself in his last writings on equilibration. However, stage theory is fully compatible with his equilibration account and, as theoretical constructions, stages still play an important role, as we will see in the following. Stages in such a sense, it can be argued, need not be discarded despite the critical debate over empirical corollaries of Piaget's general stage theory (Lourenço & Machado, 1996). Relevant for now is that Piaget never implied development to consist in a sequence with a fixed endpoint, and he spoke of provisional stages in that respect (Piaget, 1975/1985, p. 139).

Knowledge is not mentioned in my definition. Although equilibration certainly is at the core of Piaget's theory of knowledge development (genetic epistemology just means that), the term "knowledge" might bring with it – for the present-day social science student – inappropriate connotations of passive static information that resides in memory and has to be processed and manipulated by a central processor. In contrast, for Piaget the organism is in constant interaction with its environment and the subject is also constantly exercising its schemes, as in having them interacting with each other. This implies the functioning of knowledge and memory but in a manner unlike their implementation in a computer. Some more advanced varieties of neural networks might come closer to what Piaget had in mind (see Boom, 2004; Mareschal et al., 2007).

What I hope to achieve in this chapter is more clarity over what cognitive equilibration is. We need to raise the level of abstraction to arrive at a concise description or explanation of equilibration, which is insightful, while at the same time not lose contact with the concrete lowest level. The danger of free speculation, idealistic in its negative meaning, was clearly felt by Piaget. This illustrates precisely what equilibration is all about: the delicate balance between increasing abstraction and generalization on the one hand and honoring the ties to reality on the other hand. Development is not just one aspect of this balance but at the very heart of it.

Piaget's Formulations

Piaget's main work on equilibration is his *L'équilibration des Structures Cognitive* originally published in 1975 in French. This book is one of the rare books that has been translated into English twice: The first translation (cf. Piaget, 2004/2006, table 1) is not to be recommended due to many grave errors and a general lack of understanding of Piaget's ideas. Fortunately, the second, 1985 translation by Brown and Thampy, *The Equilibration of Cognitive Structures*, is good. Nevertheless, the theme of equilibration can be found throughout Piaget's work from his early publication *Recherche* (1918; see Vonèche, 1993) to one of the last (Piaget & Garcia, 1983/1989). The final version of his equilibration account is developed in his last works: some 15 books, not all translated (see Piaget, 2004/2006). An excellent overview of the development of Piaget's theory is provided by Chapman (1988) and more specifically about equilibration in a paper from 1992 (Chapman, 1992). Nevertheless, the most elaborate theoretical statements can be found in the book on equilibration and in his book on abstraction (1977/2001; see Chapter 7, this volume).

Piaget provides rather divergent descriptions of equilibration in his 1975/1985 book. This points to the fact that the equilibration concept is difficult to grasp because it concerns a wide range of phenomena, from very simple and concrete (e.g., sensorimotor schemes) to extremely complex (e.g., advanced mathematics and logic) and, to make things even more complex, the level of analysis of these phenomena itself also varies enormously. The level of analysis varies in terms of abstraction, in terms of aims (description, explanation, or understanding), and in terms of scientific perspective (roughly: biological, psychological, or epistemological). I will use these three perspectives to structure my following overview.

DYNAMIC SYSTEMS: OR SEEN FROM THE VIEWPOINT OF A BIOLOGICAL SYSTEM

As a biologist, Piaget considered cognitive development to be part of a much more general tendency of living systems to grow, change, improve and maintain themselves. He sought to characterize the most general properties of such systems with a view to their general applicability, especially to cognitive development, the history of science, and biology. For Piaget, developmental changes are organized, for example, as action schemes in infancy or as operational schemes in adolescence. He postulated that every scheme tends to incorporate external elements compatible with it (Piaget, 1975/1985, p. 6).

In the opening chapter Piaget describes equilibrium as "...a process leading from certain states of near equilibrium to others, qualitatively different, through multiple disequilibria and reequilibrations" (Piaget, 1975/1985, p. 3). Equilibrium must be taken as a dynamic equilibrium: as a property of a process that is constantly changing as far as its elements are concerned but that has found a stable form. This stability is also described elsewhere in the book as closure of the structure. The systems are "...open in the sense that they involve exchanges with the environment and closed in the sense that they constitute cycles" (Piaget, 1975/1985, p. 4).

These quotes make clear that equilibration can be characterized as self-organization. According to Piaget's equilibration account, the system must maintain its identity and stability while at the same time modifying itself and enlarging itself, and this is precisely the sort of thing self-organization is conceived to be in nonlinear dynamic systems theory. Although nonlinear dynamic systems theory has become popular slightly too late for Piaget, there is a remarkable affinity between Piagetian ideas and nonlinear dynamic systems theory.

For example, Piaget was familiar with and fond of Prigogine's work. Prigogine was an early pioneer in chaos theory, which is a branch of dynamic systems theory (Glansdorff & Prigogine, 1971). Piaget recognized the importance of dynamic systems:

"It is important to recall at the outset that by a cognitive equilibrium (which is analogous to the stability of a living organism) we mean something quite different from mechanical equilibrium (a state of rest resulting from a balance between antagonistic forces) or thermodynamic equilibrium (rest with destruction of structures). Cognitive equilibrium is more like what Glansdorff and Prigogine call 'dynamic states'; these are stationary but are involved in exchanges that tend to 'build and maintain functional and structural order in open systems' far from the zone of thermodynamic equilibrium" (Piaget, 1977/2001, pp. 312–313).

Several other places can be found where Piaget suggests the importance of dynamic system theories: "If we could have rewritten today the pages which follow, we would have placed much more emphasis on the self-regulating processes of equilibration" (Piaget, 1977/1995, p. 26). On the final page of one of his last books Piaget reiterates the analogies between Prigogine's work on dissipative structures and equilibration (Piaget & Garcia, 1983/1989). They state that interchanges with the outside stabilize the structures through regulations, stability is a function of complexity, and the stable states can only be understood in terms of their history as they have gone through a series of (un)stable predecessors. For more hints on why Piaget's theory is an incipient "systems theory," see Chapman (1992).

However, self-organization as spontaneous organization toward a higher level of order is still an elusive concept. Piaget apparently did not have the opportunity to elaborate more on self-organization himself. Unfortunately, his clear endorsement of notions from dynamic systems theory remain somewhat isolated from his descriptions based on his own empirical research, to which we will turn now.

LEARNING PROCESS: OR SEEN FROM THE VIEWPOINT OF THE INDIVIDUAL

In the concluding chapter Piaget admits that the basic idea was banal: "However diverse the goals pursued by action or thought..., the subject seeks to avoid incoherence and for that reasons always tends toward certain forms of equilibrium, but without ever achieving them, except in terms of provisional stages,... " (Piaget, 1975/1985, p. 139). Related to what a knowledge structure (which is the entity that is in equilibrium) does, closure refers to the situation in which all kinds of input are anticipated or can be dealt with: All conceivable obstacles and lacunae are no longer really disturbing because their possibility is already integrated into the structure. So, this is a desirable end state but difficult to attain, requiring a lot of hard construction work (in the cognitive sense) and even worse: When it seems to be attained, it invariably turns out that the new structure has opened up new possibilities that eventually will lead to new disequilibrations. These new possibilities and new problems may take a long time before being discovered, if ever, but the seed is sown.

The workings of equilibration in concrete tasks are analyzed by Piaget in great detail. I will first review the distinctions Piaget makes among three different forms of equilibrium. Next, the basic notions involved in functional analysis of simple equilibration (regulations, schemes, structures, and compensations) will be addressed. Finally, I briefly address the main points of Piaget's analysis of concrete interactions between subject and object.

Three Different Forms of Equilibration

Before delving deeper into the way the subjects can develop, it is important to acknowledge that Piaget distinguished three forms of interaction corresponding to three forms of equilibration. Interactions between subject and object come down to interactions between schemes and external objects and these need to be regulated. The first form of equilibration is operative in their regulation. Such subsystems, which may be independent initially, are not automatically aligned, for example, because they are constructed at different speeds, or because it takes time and effort to incorporate all suitable elements into them. This may cause disequilibria engendering the need for reciprocal assimilation between these subsystems, which is the second sort of equilibrium, pertaining to interactions between substructures. Accommodations may lead to a differentiation of a scheme (or structure or system) into subsystems. These subsystems can cause multiple disequilibria and therefore need to be assimilated, into a new total system, which involves a kind of integration, leading to a qualitative new level. Therefore, Piaget sometimes refers to this form of equilibration as equilibration between differentiation and integration. This third sort of equilibration adds a hierarchical dimension to the simple horizontal relations involved in the second form of equilibration between subsystems of equal rank because it concerns interactions between a total system and subsystems (Piaget, 1975/1985, p. 7).

The largest part of the equilibration book is devoted to structural and functional analysis of the first form of equilibrium. The only serious elaboration offered by Piaget regarding the last two forms of equilibrium is that in all three forms of equilibration, a balancing of affirmations and negations is needed. Affirmations refer to attributing positive characteristics (a) to something, and they must be contrasted with negations, which refer to attributing negative characteristics (non-a) to something. A negation is not just the absence of a characteristic but a specific attribution of this absence.

A nice example from *Experiments in Contradiction* concerns capital letters seen in a mirror (Piaget, 1974/1980). When shown a capital letter like K in a mirror, young children readily notice it is "the wrong way around" and can predict what happens to other letters; however, when shown a symmetrical letter like M they are surprised because it does not turn. Some children even maintain that this cannot be a real letter from the alphabet! According to Piaget the problem for these children is that they have not constructed the class of reversed letters in a one-to-one correspondence to the nonreversed letters. Somehow for them the class of reversed letters contains fewer letters than the class of normal letters.

As an example of the other forms of equilibration, think of coordinating two subsystems S_1 and S_2. Their coordination requires the discovery of what part they have in common $S_1 . S_2$ and also what is not in common: that is, the opposition between $S_1 .$ not-S_2 and $S_2 .$ not-S_1. Integration of a subsystem into a total system not only requires that positive properties are positively identified but also that the properties they lack in common be distinguished in the negative sense.

Interactions Between Subject and Object

Development starts with interaction between subject and object, although the subject is initially not aware of the terms of this interaction, neither of himself nor of objects. So let's rephrase: An organism acts upon its environment and in doing so may encounter resistance. The reaction to this resistance can be what Piaget calls a regulation. A regulation is defined as an elementary part of the activity repertoire of the organism, which occurs when the repetition of an action is modified by its own result (Piaget, 1975/1985, p. 16). A regulation can manifest itself as negative or positive feedback; for example, resistance becomes experienced as an obstacle or as a lacuna (the feeling that something is missing). Regulations play a role at all developmental levels; however, not all reactions are regulations and not all succeed in (partly) dealing with the resistance. The more general characteristics of an activity repertoire are what we should think of when Piaget talks about schemes. Schemes make it possible to repeat an action in virtue of feedback provided by previous executions of similar actions.

When the subject encounters resistance this can, from the point of view of the cognitive structure involved, be described as a perturbation or disturbance of that structure. Structures are dynamic cognitive structures for Piaget; that is, they indicate the more permanent features of a system that consists of a never-ending, cyclic series of changes or exchanges with the environment. As seen previously, such a system is both open due to input from the environment (exchanges) and closed because it maintains some identity throughout these changes. However, a perturbation implies that the system cannot act like this any longer. For example, when to accommodate new input requires a major change in the structure, such that the identity of it cannot be upheld without modification. Thus, the system can change and is capable of transforming itself. Note that the terms "scheme," "structure," and "system" are often used interchangeably, although there are slight differences in connotation, as just indicated.

Successful regulations are denoted as compensations by Piaget (1975/1985, p. 24). Therefore, compensations of resistance in the empirical domain require some form of contact between subject and object. Compensations are fundamental for Piaget (Vuyk, 1981, p. 154). Compensatory regulation is the very mechanism of optimizing equilibration (Chapman, 1988, p. 293). Compensations can be defined as actions opposed to and tending to cancel or neutralize some effect either by canceling or undoing it (inversion) or by neutralizing it (reciprocity). However, when the compensations are not complete but only partial, contradictions will arise (as in the example with capital letters in a mirror discussed previously). In the famous conservation of liquid task, one reaction is compensation by complete negation when the child argues that you can pour the water back in the original container, but another reaction can be compensation by reciprocity or pointing to the fact that increase in height is neutralized by decrease in width. The increase is not undone but effectively neutralized in this last case by an internal modification. Also, the original scheme is still functioning after such a differentiation. However, it will not do to return to a previous equilibrium because of the very contradictions that resulted in disequilibrium in the first place. Compensations, if realized, lead to a new and somehow better equilibrium precisely because it surpasses the contradictions that could not be reconciled previously. It is this that Piaget claims to be the case in development and what he has to explain or make plausible. Piaget argues that compensations in their richly varying forms and levels lead to reversibility and always involve constructions (see the following).

Application to Interactions: Observables and Coordinations

Piaget introduced the distinction between observables and coordinations in his account (Piaget, 1975/1985, chapter 2). The notion of observables pertains to what for a given subject are the perceptual facts. The notion of coordination, in contrast, stands for inferences that go beyond the readily perceptible. For example, two events can be observed, and those two observables might be coordinated by thinking of a causal connection between them. The causal connection is not something that can be seen; it is inferred. Exactly what is perceptible and what needs to be inferred, however, depends on the development of the subject. What is difficult for a 4-year-old to construct might be so evident to a 10-year-old that for this older child it is in effect an observable fact. In addition, it should be noted, Piaget warns us, that coordinations may be implicit and perceptions may be illusory.

The point is that what is to count as observable is not absolutely given; it is based on previous constructions (stage dependent). Nevertheless, for the person concerned, or seen from the perspective of a certain stage, it is a given. And more important, it functions as a given in the sense that it can be at variance with accompanying coordinations. Disturbances do not result from discrepancy with some absolutely given external reality but derive from discrepancy between what is observable (e.g., as indicated by changes to the object) on the one hand (based on previous constructions) and knowledge and expectations derived from the actions of the subject on the other hand. Restoring the balance (e.g., between expectations and observables) may require differentiation of the schemes employed. Action scheme x can be used in situation y but not in situation z, but action scheme x' (x slightly modified) might be adequate for z. According to Piaget, each compensation of a disturbance is always also a construction because a successful reaction to a disturbance is always a differentiation of a scheme. Previous scheme x is not in itself wrong and need not be discarded; on the contrary, the disturbance is precisely due to the fact that the scheme x is employed in a situation where it is not entirely adequate. A more adequate reaction might therefore be a differentiation between schemes x and x', a precondition being that the difference between what is needed and what is available is not too great.

Not just any perturbation leads to a compensation. Piaget distinguishes three sorts of reactions to perturbations characterized by increasing degrees of compensations. Alpha reactions are characterized by the absence of any attempt to integrate the perturbations into the system in question. Minor perturbations do not move the system far from equilibrium, and a simple modification may be sufficient to achieve re-equilibrations. By contrast, when the perturbation is stronger, the subject may ignore or even actively ignore the perturbation. Alpha reactions involve a centration on the affirmations and a total neglect of negations. Beta reactions integrate the perturbing element that has sprung up into the system. What was a perturbation for the system becomes a variation within a reorganized structure. New relationships are established that connect the elements incorporated with those already existing. It involves partial compensations, superior to alpha reactions, through the reworking of the conceptualizations involved. The aim is not to cancel the change introduced by the perturbing object but to integrate it with a minimization of costs. Gamma reactions consist in anticipation of variations that otherwise could become perturbations. If every possible transformation is fully compensated by an inverse or converse transformation, and every possible affirmation by a corresponding negation, then variations are no longer perturbations. The closure of the structure eliminates all contradictions from the outside and from within. But it is not a simple resultant of opposing factors because it has an intrinsic necessity.

In sum, compensations cannot be understood in terms of an adaptation to a fixed, subject-independent reality. Even if Piaget would admit that there is a subject-independent reality at the ontological level, and although he assumes that the overall stage pattern is such that objectivity is approached as a limit, this limit plays no role in his account of the construction of knowledge. At the epistemological level he remains a constructivist. Compensations are instrumental for the adaptation to a subject-dependent reality.

Piaget's equilibration account contains many more subtle distinctions; for example, we should distinguish between subject-related and object-related observables and coordinations. Observable features of our own actions and of objects are the first to be equilibrated. Second to be equilibrated are inferential coordinations drawn from the subject's own actions or from relationships attributed to objects in attempts to explain them causally. The latter are, at first, not available to consciousness. For Piaget, becoming conscious is a result of reconstructions involving inferential coordinations.

In his latter books he returned to these topics (see Piaget, 2004/2006, table 1; Piaget & Garcia, 1983/1989; cf. Vuyk, 1981). In particular his theory of reflecting abstractions is relevant in clarifying these important forms of equilibrations.

EPISTEMOLOGICAL: OR SEEN FROM THE VIEWPOINT OF KNOWLEDGE IMPROVEMENT

In the preface of *The Equilibration of Cognitive Structures* Piaget furnishes the context for his equilibration account: "Knowledge does not proceed either from experience with objects alone or from an innate program preformed in the subject but results instead, from a succession of constructions producing new structures" (Piaget, 1975/1985, p. xvii). He constructed a rather complex model of development based on the joint emergence of adaptive improvement and constructive novelty in which he sought to avoid the problems of both empiricism and rationalism (see Boom, 1997). From this perspective, it is not the psychological subject but the epistemic subject (the subject as knower) that is central.

The first process (adaptive improvement) involves the compensation of perturbations coming directly or indirectly from outside the subject, although it does not go as far as classical empiricism by treating the subject as a *tabula rasa*. It results, according to Piaget, in increasing coherence or equilibrium in relation to the world external to the subject. This process of adaptation through interaction is addressed in the part of his theory concerned with achieving equilibrium. The account of achieving equilibrium by itself is confined to improvement in the sense of adaptation as far as within-stage change is concerned. It is suitable to explain changes such as this in as far as it provides, as we have seen previously, a very detailed description of how, by regulations (e.g., feedback and feedforward loops), cognitive structures become more adapted. However, adaptation in the case of going to the next stage cannot be explained in this way, and therefore claims about novelty are, in this respect, difficult to uphold. The second process (constructive novelty) is addressed in Piaget's theory of reflecting abstractions (Piaget, 1975/1985, 1977/2001).

In order to understand what reflecting abstraction is, let us consider the following first: If we reflect on something, we take something we did or something we observed in a prereflexive manner out of its normal context by thinking about it. Usually this implies that we become conscious of what is involved in what we at first took for granted. By thinking about it, we may see new connections and new distinctions. These same elements can be found in Piaget's definition of reflecting abstraction. But whereas reflection typically pertains to adult thinking and is used in the context of becoming conscious of something, Piaget tried to define a more general mechanism that preserves the idea of restructuring previous cognitive structuring.

The general definition given by Piaget reads: "Reflecting abstraction proceeds from the actions or operations of a subject and transfers to a higher plane what is taken from a lower level of activity. Because of this transfer, the differentiations necessarily bring about novel generalizing compositions at the new level" (Piaget, 1977/2001, p. 29; my amended translation). Reflecting abstraction involves two steps: first, projecting (or bringing, or reflecting or transposing) the structure implied in the coordination to the next higher level where the coordination ceases to be a coordination and becomes an action-observable; second, reorganizing this structure, which meanwhile has become a substructure. Piaget gives a detailed description of the different forms this process can have and distinguishes it from empirical abstraction, which is the name for a process by which material properties of an object or action are abstracted. Empirical abstraction (concerning, e.g., weight, color, movement, and force) does not go beyond the observable features, is not by itself creative, and is always dependent on earlier reflecting abstractions.

The first step consists in bringing structures of the lower level to the next level, thereby constituting this higher level (Piaget, 1977/2001, p. 303ff). In the more technical description, this is the process by which a coordination pertaining to actions of a subject at level x becomes an action-observable for level x + 1. In this way a new level is linked to the foregoing level. The step is constructive because a new level of abstraction is constituted. To give an example of an elementary form of this kind of projection, consider the case when a concept is formed. "Concept" is here taken in the elementary and restricted sense of a class. Take, for example, the concept *toy*, defined as every small thing one can play with. The sensorimotor equivalent for this concept is the collection of objects that can be assimilated to the action scheme of playing. In this first step, projection, the observable properties of these actions are interiorized and a reunion of these objects in a whole is possible based on their common qualities. The projection in this example thus comes down to the formation of a concept.

The second step, called by Piaget reflection [French *réflexion*] or reorganization, is needed because the transposition of the structures of the lower level to the next higher level introduces multiple new disequilibria (p. 314). These disequilibria are the result of all the kinds of new relations that must be accounted for due to the first step. This second step is constructive in a double sense, according to Piaget. In the first place, with the projection, generalization over several instances has become possible. "Even if the coordination that projection thereby transfers from the plane of action to the conceptual plane remains the same, this very projection creates a new morphism or correspondence between the coordination on the conceptual plane and the practical situations in which the coordinated action is repeatedly carried out" (Piaget, 1977/2001, p. 308). In the second place, these first organizations also lead to the discovery of related content, which was not assimilable into the earlier structure but which has now become assimilable by further slight transformation of the structure and so becomes integrated within a larger and therefore partly novel structure (Piaget & Garcia, 1983/1989, p. 2). In other words, this step consists in interactions in the form of reciprocal assimilations and accommodations between sub-structures. (For further details and nuances, see Chapter 7, this volume.)

Reflecting abstraction can perhaps be interpreted also as looking for the (implicit) reasons for success of actions from the previous stage (Piaget, 1974/1978, 2004/2006). This interpretation is consistent with Piaget's suggestion that finding reasons means fitting the facts into a structural framework where necessary relations are (or could be) distinguished from actual and possible relations, which in turn implies a balance between the affirmations and negations involved. In trying to find the reasons behind success, there is a refocusing on the activity itself (or the relevant operations, etc.).

Both processes, that of purely endogenous constructions made by the epistemic subject and that of compensation for disturbances from outside, are integrated by Piaget into his equilibration account. According to this theory, novelty and improvement are joint characteristics of development, neither of which is sufficient by itself to explain change; that is, the two processes when taken in isolation are not sufficient.

The theory of reflecting abstractions, in which the endogenous constructions of the (epistemic) subject are strongly emphasized, seems suitable to explain novelty in development, but regarding improvement in development, the role played by this mechanism is less clear. How can the constructions inherent in reflecting abstractions compensate for disturbances from outside, especially for the empirical domain? Remember that progress in stage development, implying that the next stage is in some respects better, is related to the claim that the central deficits of the previous stage are resolved in the subsequent one. The new stage is supposed to fill lacunae and compensates for obstacles (contradictions and disturbances), even for potential problems.

Piaget's solution seems to be that the accommodation of cognitive structures to content leads to refinement and elaboration of those structures. This is a constructive process in itself, although limited in scope because the stage boundaries cannot be transcended this way. However, this elaboration of structures ensures the essential contact with the "environment," and this contact, in the long run, accounts for the fact that constructions due to reflecting abstractions converge with increasing adaptation.

EVALUATION

The account of equilibration in the broad sense involves multiple levels of analysis (biological, psychological, epistemological). One could argue that Piaget has not been able to fully integrate these levels and that his account is unfinished (at best). However, regarding fundamental questions concerning the normative aspects of development such as the construction of necessary knowledge (Smith, 1993; see Chapter 3, this volume), alternatives to Piaget's account fare no better, and Piaget's account is far from obsolete.

No doubt living organisms are dynamic systems on the edge of stability. Piaget's vision that the development of knowledge concerns a special variety of such dynamic systems is a useful heuristic for further exploration. More recent progress in dynamic systems theory could perhaps supplement Piagetian theory. The foundations were laid in Prigogine's nonequilibrium thermodynamics (Nicolis & Prigogine, 1977), Thom's (1975) catastrophe theory, and Haken's (1983) (theory of) synergism. The application of dynamic systems and self-organization perspectives to development were pioneered by van der Maas and Molenaar (1992), van Geert (1994), and Thelen and Smith (1994), but promises have not been substantiated so far, perhaps because the field had difficulty accommodating the complex modeling involved or because the levels of abstraction were too far apart. In as far as modeling was focused on temporal unfolding of growth in a few simple interconnected variables, this constitutes a basic but highly abstract level of analysis. Elsewhere, I spell out the connection between Piaget's interactionism and these extremely general dynamic properties (Boom, 2004). However, connecting such an abstract level of analysis to the more concrete level of analysis of development in actual empirical task behavior has turned out to be difficult and has so far not led to the breakthroughs hoped for (but see Shultz, 2003, Chapter 5).

Connectionist models of development (which can be seen as varieties of dynamic systems models, although they have their own tradition and history) are still actively pursued with their focus on task behavior. Some of these models (albeit a minority) are inspired by, or consistent with, important elements of Piaget's theory (Elman et al., 1996; Sirois & Shultz, 2003).

The recently emergent field of developmental neuroscience is successful, promising, and popular. An explicit connection to Piagetian theory is acknowledged by those who combine developmental neuroscience with constructivist ideas and connectionist modeling just mentioned (Johnson, 1997; Mareschal et al., 2007). Unfortunately, a more precise rendering of the fit between these ideas and equilibration in Piagetian theory is presently lacking.

There were hopes that a combination of dynamic systems theory, constructivist connectionism, and developmental neuroscience would be instrumental in further developing an account of equilibration or

perhaps even replacing it, but promising contributions notwithstanding (e.g., Molenaar & Raijmakers, 2000), no convincing alternative to
Piaget's account has been formulated.

From a Piagetian perspective with its focus on the subject, equilibration is a long sequential process involving a tendency to overcome disturbances and lacunae in cognitive functioning. It was not possible to do
justice to the numerous experiments and books in which these aspects
of equilibration are well documented and carefully analyzed. We could
benefit from paying more attention to these studies, although it is clear
that Piaget's choice of topics was inclined by relevance to his overall
theory. Curiously, most criticism of Piaget's equilibration account has
remained only global, for example, arguing that it is not testable because
it is not precise enough (Klahr, 1999). In fact, the notion of equilibration
has been neglected in developmental psychology, at least in comparison
to the critical attention given to Piaget's stage theory. Most handbooks
pay little attention to this notion, and if they do they conclude it is too
vague to be of practical use. Informed criticism by Chapman (1992) concludes that Piaget has neglected intersubjective interaction, but even so,
Piaget's theory, and in particular his questions and general intuitions,
remain relevant for contemporary psychology.

From the perspective of (genetic) epistemology, Piaget has postulated
a tendency toward progressively better equilibrium that involves the
joint working of reflecting abstractions and compensations by regulations. This is perhaps the overall main theme in his equilibration theory.
Although novelty and improvement are logically independent concepts
in that a novel stage is not necessarily a better one and a better stage
is not necessarily qualitatively and structurally new (though it must be
different in some respect), Piaget insisted on their intrinsic relatedness.
Whether this aspect of his account is convincing depends on the question of whether the integration pursued by Piaget is deemed possible.
One may doubt this, but so far no alternative theory has even come
close in breadth and scope (but see Becker, 2008). Reflecting abstraction is important (but not sufficient) for understanding improvement
in a formal, rationalistic sense, but this progress is restricted in meaning. The claim defended by Piaget only pertains to underlying cognitive
competencies. The cognitive structures of the higher stage contain the
structures of the previous stage as substructures in a reorganized and
better organized form, but reflecting abstraction in isolation can say
nothing about adaptation (within-stage or over several stages). This is
why, in the end, for Piaget, the relation between the stages is defined in
reference to the process or mechanism (though not in any mechanistic
sense) of optimizing equilibration: A next stage can only be novel and

better in virtue of the general properties of the developmental process (Boom, 1991, 2004).

REFERENCES

Becker, J. (2008). Conceptualizing mind and consciousness. *Human Development, 51*, 165–189.

Boom, J. (1991). Collective development and the learning paradox. *Human Development, 34*, 273–287.

Boom, J. (1997). Cognitive development. In W. Van Haaften, M. Korthals, & T. Wren (Eds.), *Philosophy of development: Reconstructing the foundations of human development and education* (pp. 101–118). Dordrecht: Kluwer.

Boom, J. (2004). Individualism and collectivism: A dynamic systems interpretation of Piaget's interactionism. In J. I. Carpendale & U. Müller (Eds.), *Social interaction and the development of knowledge: Critical evaluation of Piaget's contribution* (pp. 67–85). Mahwah, NJ: Erlbaum.

Chapman, M. (1988). *Constructive evolution: Origins and development of Piaget's thought.* Cambridge: Cambridge University Press.

Chapman, M. (1992). Equilibration and the dialectics of organization. In H. Beilin & P. B. Pufall (Eds.), *Piaget's theory: Prospects and possibilities* (pp. 39–59). Hillsdale, NJ: Erlbaum.

Elman, J. L., Bates, E. A., Johnson, M. H., Karmiloff-Smith, A., Parisi, D., & Plunkett, K. (1996). *Rethinking innateness: A connectionist perspective on development.* Cambridge, MA: MIT Press.

Glansdorff, P., & Prigogine, I. (1971). *Thermodynamic theory of structure, stability and fluctuations.* London: Wiley.

Haken, H. (1983). *Advanced synergetics.* Berlin: Springer.

Johnson, M. H. (1997). *Developmental cognitive neuroscience.* Oxford: Blackwell.

Klahr, D. (1999). The conceptual habitat: In what kind of system can concepts develop. In E. K. Scholnick, K. Nelson, S. A. Gelman, & P. H. Miller (Eds.), *Conceptual development: Piaget's legacy* (pp. 131–161). Mahwah, NJ: Erlbaum.

Lourenço, O., & Machado, A. (1996). In defense of Piaget's theory: A reply to 10 common criticisms. *Psychological Review, 103*, 143–164.

Mareschal, D., Johnson, M. H., Sirois, S., Spratling, M. W., Thomas, M. S., & Westerman, G. (2007). *Neuroconstructivism: How the brain constructs cognition.* Oxford: Oxford University Press.

Molenaar, P. C. M., & Raijmakers, M. E. J. (2000). A causal interpretation of Piaget's theory of cognitive development: Reflections on the relationship between epigenesis and nonlinear dynamics. *New Ideas in Psychology, 18*, 41.

Nicolis, G., & Prigogine, I. (1977). Self-organization in non-equilibrium systems: From dissipative structures to order through fluctuations. New York: Wiley.

Piaget, J. (1918). *Recherche.* Lausanne: La Concorde.

Piaget, J. (1978). *Success and understanding.* Cambridge, MA: Harvard University Press. (Original work published in 1974)

Piaget, J. (1980). *Experiments in contradiction.* Chicago: University of Chicago Press. (Original work published in 1974)

Piaget, J. (1985). *The equilibration of cognitive structures: The central problem of intellectual development*. Chicago: University of Chicago Press. (Original work published in 1975)

Piaget, J. (1987). *Possibility and necessity, Vol. 1: The role of possibility in cognitive development*. Minneapolis: University of Minnesota Press. (Original work published in 1981)

Piaget, J. (1995). *Sociological studies*. London: Routledge. (Original work published in 1977)

Piaget, J. (2001). *Studies in reflecting abstraction*. Hove: Psychology Press. (Original work published in 1977)

Piaget, J. (2006). Reason. *New Ideas in Psychology, 24*, 1–29. (Original work published in 2004)

Piaget, J., & Garcia, R. (1989). *Psychogenesis and the history of science*. New York: Columbia University Press. (Original work published in 1983)

Shultz, T. R. (2003). *Computational developmental psychology*. Cambridge, MA: MIT Press.

Sirois, S., & Shultz, T. R. (2003). A connectionist perspective on Piagetian development. In P. T. Quinlan (Ed.), *Connectionist models of development* (pp. 13–42). Hove: Psychology Press.

Smith, L. (1993). *Necessary knowledge*. Hove: Erlbaum.

Thelen, E., & Smith, L. B. (1994). *A dynamic systems approach to the development of cognition and action*. Cambridge, MA: MIT Press.

Thom, R. (1975). *Structural stability and morphogenesis*. Reading, MA: Benjamin.

van der Maas, H. L. J., & Molenaar, P. C. M. (1992). Stagewise cognitive development: An application of catastrophe theory. *Psychological Review, 8*, 395–417.

van Geert, P. (1994). *Dynamic systems development: Change between complexity and chaos*. Hempstead: Harvester Wheatsheaf.

Vonèche, J. (1993). Piaget's first theory of equilibration (1918). In D. Maurice & J. Montangero (Eds.), *Equilibrium and equilibration* (pp. 3–15). Geneva: Fondation Archives Jean Piaget.

Vuyk, R. (1981). *Overview and critique of Piaget's genetic epistemology*. London: Academic Press.

7 Constructive Processes

Abstraction, Generalization, and Dialectics

GENETIC EPISTEMOLOGY AND CONSTRUCTIVISM

The key principle of Jean Piaget's genetic epistemology is *constructivism*. Constructivism rejects old-fashioned rationalism: Knowledge is not made out of special knowledge-parts preformed in each individual knower at birth. It also rejects empiricism: Knowledge does not consist of epistemic pieces impressed on the knower by the environment, whether physical or social. Instead, the knower has to *construct* knowledge.

Genetic epistemology is a developmental theory of knowledge. It is about what knowledge consists of and how knowledge develops.

Knowledge

What knowledge consists of is not the unique preoccupation of this chapter. However, there is no harm in re-emphasizing certain points, because Piaget's conception is so far removed from those that prevail in contemporary cognitive psychology, artificial intelligence, or philosophy of mind. One can make a reasonable decision (as Boom has, in Chapter 6 of this volume) to characterize his developmental theory in terms of control over experience, where experience is understood in terms, not of information, but of exchanges with an external environment.

But Piaget wanted to keep hold of knowledge rather than yield it to those whose conceptions he thought were inadequate, and we will continue in that vein. In genetic epistemology, knowledge is not a matter of images. It does not take the form of propositions. It does not consist of symbolic data structures in the mind that correspond to structures in the world.

Rather, knowledge is pragmatic, or action-oriented. In Piaget-language, knowledge is fundamentally *operative*; basically, the knowing subject knows what to do with something under certain conditions or what that thing will do under different conditions.

Operative knowledge consists, in turn, of *cognitive structures*. The most basic type of structure, already available to infants, is the sensorimotor action scheme. A typical early scheme (Piaget, 1936/1952) is the one that specifies how to get the mobile that hangs over the baby's crib to move (for instance, by kicking it). Over the course of development, more powerful and sophisticated kinds of structures get constructed, such as the groupings of concrete operations that, during middle childhood, enable children to perform elementary reasoning about classification, number, and putting things in order.

Development

In rejecting old-fashioned empiricism, Piaget (1970) maintained that knowledge cannot, in general, be a copy of what we know. We would have to know the object of our knowledge in advance of copying it; otherwise, we would be in no position to judge whether our copy was accurate.

Rather, development[1] is what structures do. Without any external prompting, operative structures demand to be applied. When the knowing subject applies a structure to the environment, or *assimilates* the environment to it, the structure may work: It may fulfill the knower's goals as expected. But in some cases assimilation will be unsuccessful: Applying the scheme will not lead to attaining the goal as expected. For instance, if a young child has acquired a fly-swatting scheme, applying it to another housefly is routine assimilation, and normally the goal will be reached: The worst that usually happens is missing the fly and needing to try again. But if the child attempts to apply it to a different kind of flying insect, say a hornet, the result will probably be unsuccessful assimilation: Swatting a hornet results in getting stung.

When assimilation has not been met with success, the child needs to modify the scheme in order to *accommodate* it to the environment. For instance, the child may inhibit swatting until she has checked whether the insect looks like a fly (in which case swatting is truly indicated) or like a hornet (in which case moving away quietly may be indicated instead). Accommodating the scheme to the environment may mean putting restrictions on it (e.g., use this fly-swatting scheme only with nonstinging insects) or differentiating it into one or more subschemes. Sometimes entirely new schemes will need to be constructed for successful accommodation to take place.

Piaget thought that development tends toward a balance, or equilibrium, between assimilation and accommodation. Hence, his most general treatment of developmental construction was a theory of *equilibration* (Piaget, 1975/1985). Equilibration may take more complicated forms depending on the type of structure. It will also vary depending on whether structures are assimilating and accommodating the physical environment or other structures within the knowing subject (for details, see Chapter 6 in this volume).

Beyond Equilibration

Although he put other projects on hold so he could complete a book-length treatise on the subject, Piaget (1975/1985) realized that equilibration was not the whole story. From 1968 through 1979, he directed research on many different constructive processes: consciousness; affirmations, negations, and contradictions; abstraction; generalization; opening onto new possibilities and closing off necessities; dialectics; and the search for reasons (for overviews, see Vuyk, 1981, and Ducret, 2000).

Each of these constructive processes is internally related[2] to each of the others. The interdependencies among them are far too numerous and varied to fit into a single chapter. Here, I have chosen three on which to concentrate: abstraction, generalization, and dialectics. Abstraction enjoyed a special place in Piaget's thinking, yet it has not gotten enough recognition; generalization is tightly bound to abstraction; and the dialectical spirit pervaded all of Piaget's later work. What is more, the work on generalization and dialectics remains unavailable in English, despite its important role in the overall theory.

Each of these processes requires a basic distinction for its formulation: empirical versus reflecting abstraction; inductive versus constructive generalization; discursive reasoning versus dialecticalizing. Abstraction and generalization also come in higher-order variants, such as reflected abstraction or synthesizing generalization. Abstracting and generalizing are tightly internally related in Piaget's theory, though disparities in the number of higher-order variants, and in the error-proneness of those variants, prevent them from merging. All three processes are internally related to equilibration and under some interpretations could collapse into it, but each has properties that block such a collapse – which is just as well, for Piaget seems to have intended that each constructive process retain its own identity. Finally, Piaget's ideas about all three processes afford many further opportunities for developmental research. But only abstraction has received some attention from other researchers, and much more needs to be done.

ABSTRACTION

Basic equilibration pertains to interactions with the physical environment; the more refined forms pertain to mutual adjustments and integrations within the knowing subject. But none of them directly explains how we come to know our own processes of knowing or the coordinations of our own actions. How, for instance, do we become able to give a correct description of how we navigate through a wire maze? This is a task that we master at a practical level long before we can correctly describe how we do it (Piaget, 1977/2001, chapter 11). How do we become able to recognize the number of times that we added some number of objects (Piaget, 1977/2001, chapter 2)? How do we build new cognitive structures that are actually *about* old structures? For instance, Piaget believed that when we construct formal operations, these are actually operations to the second power or operations *on* concrete operations.

Empirical abstraction, which covers properties of objects in the environment, is plainly inadequate here. It will enable us to recognize what all white objects have in common, or what all squirrels have in common, or even what all mammals have in common, but it will not tell us anything about the way we get through a wire maze. To answer such questions Piaget introduced *abstraction réfléchissante*, or reflecting abstraction; it abstracts properties of our processes of knowing, or of the inner coordinations among our actions. There are two phases to it. Projection (*réfléchissement*) takes a structure at a lower developmental level (such as the action coordination of interest) and projects it onto a higher level (where the coordination may now be understood consciously and explicitly). Reflection (*réflexion*) reorganizes the structure at the higher level; our explicit understanding of something about our actions is not a mere copy of our previous cognitive structure, and to function properly it needs to be integrated with other new structures at the higher level.

A prime example comes from the development of multiplication. Multiplication looks like repeated addition – yet children find it much harder than addition. According to Piaget's analysis, children have to be able to recognize how much they are adding each time. This is *empirical abstraction*; even the youngest children in the multiplication study (Piaget, 1977/2001, chapter 2) easily recognized the number of poker chips that they were adding to the row each time. To multiply successfully, however, Piaget maintains that children must also attend to the number of *times* that they add that amount. Only through *reflecting abstraction* can children understand how many times they added poker chips to one row or how many times the experimenter added chips to the other. The same goes for realizing that adding two and doing that three times has produced the same number as adding three and doing that twice.

Reflected and beyond. Even when they recognized that $2 \times 3 = 3 \times 2 = 6$, Piaget found that children still had difficulty predicting what would happen when, say, another 2×3 and another 3×2 are added. To predict those results correctly, children need to construct the multiplicative operation n times x, where each x is an additive operation rather than just a number of poker chips added. This step calls for *reflected abstraction (abstraction réfléchie)*; it is reflecting abstraction to the second power or reflecting abstraction applied to the products of reflecting abstraction.

There can be reflecting abstraction of a third order, the kind that reflects on reflected abstraction (examples are given in Piaget 1977/2001, chapter 5). Piaget called this third-order process *metareflection (métaréflexion)* or *reflective thinking (pensée réflexive)*. He speculated about even higher orders of reflecting abstraction.

Stages. Equilibration, in Piaget's final thoughts about the subject, had grown virtually independent of stages of cognitive development (see Chapter 6 in this volume). Reflecting abstraction cannot be pried free so easily: It presupposes *some* sequence of developmental levels. Projection is what brings a cognitive structure up from level N-1 to level N; reflection does the reorganizing at level N.

Piaget did come to accept that reflecting abstraction, reflected abstraction, and metareflection might not align with the sequence of major stages or periods. In the mathematically oriented chapters of *Studies in Reflecting Abstraction*, reflecting abstraction showed up at Stage IB (the second half of preoperations), reflected abstraction could be seen at Stage IIB (the latter part of concrete operations), and metareflection had to wait until Stage III (formal operations). But in the chapters on serial order, Piaget sometimes put reflecting abstraction at Stage IA and reflected at Stage IIA. In chapter 18 of the same book, he somewhat notoriously claimed that reflecting abstraction is going on in toddlerhood, during the upper sensorimotor substages.

Consciousness

Our references to knowledge of the inner coordinations of one's actions emphatically suggest a connection between reflecting abstraction and *la prise de conscience* (becoming conscious or cognizant). Noticing what squirrels have in common – shape, size, manner of running, eating habits, dentition – does not require us to become conscious of something about our actions that we were not conscious of before; noticing that we had to make a backward movement to get all the way through the wire maze does.

If the prototypical results of reflecting abstraction are becoming consciously aware of that backward movement (Piaget, 1977/2001, chapter 11) or of where you had to stand so that you could hit the bowling pin when you released a ball hanging from a string attached to a hook on the ceiling (chapter 13), the answer is obviously yes.

However, when Piaget (1950/1973) first brought up reflecting abstraction, he maintained that becoming conscious always involves reflecting – but not the other way around. In *The Grasp of Consciousness* and *Success and Understanding* (1974/1976, 1974/1978) he distinguished between reflecting abstraction, which need not involve consciousness, and reflected abstraction, which does. And in chapter 18 of his *Reflecting Abstraction* volume, Piaget described reflecting abstraction being used by 1- and 2-year-olds, when they learn to push a rotating bar away from them in the "wrong" direction in order to bring a desired object toward them. He was definitely not attributing conscious knowledge to these toddlers.

Perception

We have seen how abstraction was meant to be internally related to several other constructive processes that Piaget was simultaneously struggling to characterize during his final decade (for further details, see Campbell, 2001). Yet it was also meant to be "backward compatible" (Campbell, 2001) with older parts of his theories.

Most obstinate among these was his account of perception, a vestige of old-fashioned empiricism. Piaget (1961/1969) thought that perception yields a series of centrations, or snapshots; although it plays a key role in our operative schemes, the knowledge that we can get from perception alone is not really operative, and it cannot be the source of any genuinely new constructions.

Piaget has been criticized for walling perceiving off from interacting with the world, thus excluding it from the realm of operative knowledge (e.g., Bickhard & Richie, 1983; O'Regan & Noë, 2001). Our worry is narrower here. Suppose that the properties of objects (or, on occasion, of the consequences of our actions) that we come to know through empirical abstraction are properties that we can perceive. Piaget could still have theorized that abstracting the whiteness of white objects, or the length of physical objects in general, already involves schemes and assimilation to schemes. Had he done so, he would have been able to tie empirical abstraction to operative knowledge. Instead, he viewed empirical abstraction as never going beyond perception, leaving him with questions about the kind of process that abstraction is.

Is Abstraction Always the Same Kind of Process? Is reflecting abstraction qualitatively the same as empirical abstraction, except for the properties being abstracted? Or is it a different kind of process, with distinct dynamics? If empirical abstraction is just abstraction applied to objects and their perceivable properties, and reflecting abstraction is just abstraction applied to actions, then Piaget's occasional insistence on reflecting abstraction early in development is richly warranted because reflecting abstraction should be at work as early in our development as empirical abstraction is. There would also be no reason to expect reflecting abstraction to involve consciousness.

Contradicting this, however, is Piaget's division of reflecting abstraction into projective and reflective phases, which have no analogue in empirical abstraction. Further militating against sameness of process is Piaget's hierarchy of reflecting abstraction, reflecting on the products of reflecting abstraction (reflected abstraction), reflecting on the products of reflected abstraction (metareflection), and so on; no such hierarchy is generated by empirically abstracting from the results of previous empirical abstraction.

Does Abstraction Collapse into Equilibration? One of the difficulties for a model like Piaget's, in which every process is internally related to every other, is preventing each process from being *totally* internally related to at least one other process. For if the identity of Process A is constituted by *all* of its relations to Process B, then there is no way to prevent A from losing that separate identity and collapsing into B. If Processes A and B are of lesser importance in Piaget's theory, the collapse of A into B may merely signal a need to consolidate them. The problem becomes much more pressing when B is equilibration – a fundamental process, if not the fundamental process.

So just how tightly is abstraction related to equilibration? Does reflecting abstraction correspond to assimilation, whereas empirical abstraction corresponds to accommodation? At times, Piaget (e.g., 1977/2001, pp. 293, 297) maintained that there is reflecting abstraction whenever there is an assimilating framework. But genetic epistemology is quite firm on the subject: As soon as babies are learning anything at all, they have schemes and are assimilating contents to them. Therefore, if having an assimilating framework already means doing reflecting abstraction, abstraction will collapse into equilibration, of which reflecting abstraction will merely be the assimilating aspect, whereas empirical abstraction will become the accommodating aspect.

The Problem of Error

It's odd to have to ask how a constructivist conception of knowledge can account for error (in Chapter 6 of this volume, Boom wonders whether higher forms of equilibration necessarily make the knower better adapted). Reflecting abstraction leads to structures at the next higher level, but errors are possible at any developmental level, and there is no reason to suppose that every new cognitive structure will be true or successful. Reflected abstraction, at least, is linked to consciousness, and we are capable of consciously misconceiving something about our actions and their coordinations. More broadly, abstraction is almost indissolubly linked to generalization (see the following). Generalizations can go wrong in several ways: They can be too broad or too narrow, they can confound different dimensions, they can fasten on a dimension that turns out to be irrelevant, and so on.

Indeed, Piaget occasionally identified errors that he believed were produced by reflecting abstraction. Some other developmentalists call them "growth errors": wrong answers that stem from more advanced or sophisticated thinking (e.g., 1977/2001, pp. 48–49, 212, 228). But Piaget also claimed at times that the reflective phase of reflecting abstraction is error-proof (pp. 321–322). To make his claim plausible, Piaget had to deny (e.g., pp. 239–240) that an overly broad or overly narrow generalization that ultimately gets corrected was ever really an error; he tried to argue, roughly, that in such cases the structure was correct, but its application was mistaken. Tellingly, Piaget would not repeat this argument in his *Studies in Generalization*.

GENERALIZATION

Failure to pick the argument up again is significant because of the extensive internal relations between abstraction and generalization. So much so that Piaget and his team carried out their research programs on these topics in successive years (1971 and 1972, though the books were not published until 1977 and 1978).[3]

This should not be surprising, as every act of abstracting establishes classes of greater or lesser generality, and every act of generalizing presupposes an abstraction.

Inductive Generalization. If I conclude that all white surfaces reflect the entire spectrum of visible light, I am generalizing over white objects.

But classifying white objects together presupposes my abstraction of whiteness as a dimension. The generalization about white objects is what Piaget calls *inductive*;[4] it has an obvious reciprocal dependency on *empirical* abstraction.

Constructive Generalization. Suppose, however, that I am generalizing, not about properties of objects out in the environment but about properties of the inner coordinations among my actions. Suppose that I recognize that whenever I add three poker chips at a time and do this action two times, the result will be the same one that I get when I add two poker chips at a time and do that action three times. Moreover, if I repeat 3 × 2 and 2 × 3 a second time, I will once again get equal numbers of poker chips. The abstraction that I have performed here is not empirical, but *reflecting* (or reflected, when I correctly predict what will happen with two repetitions). The generalizations that I make are correspondingly *constructive*.

Piaget calls the relevant type of generalization "constructive" for two reasons: It involves building reorganized cognitive structures at a higher developmental level, and these have genuinely novel properties. Because new structural forms are involved, as well as new contents to which those forms may apply, Piaget and Henriques credit constructive generalization with "double constructive power" (1978, p. 221).

Integrations and Differentiations. In Piaget's (1975/1985) theory of equilibration, the third and highest form involves the differentiation of systems into subsystems and the integration of subsystems into new overarching systems (see Chapter 6 in this volume). Generalization is tied right into this interplay of integrations and differentiations: "In constructing the new on the basis of the known (instead of just finding the known in new objects, as it did back in its inductive beginnings), constructive generalization naturally proceeds by differentiating and integrating; for novelties are not just piled on top of what preceded them – they are in part derived from it" (Piaget & Henriques, 1978, p. 227). Further details of differentiating and integrating will come into focus in the following.

Is There a Hierarchy for Generalization?

A source of awkwardness for Piaget is that generalization lacks an obvious principle of hierarchy. Abstraction moves up a ladder from empirical, to reflecting, to reflected, to metareflective and beyond. Once constructive generalization has been differentiated from inductive, however, it is not clear how there might be further steps. Many of the chapters in the *Generalization* book just treat constructiveness as a matter of degree.

In a secondary elaboration, however, Piaget moves generalizing into a closer alignment with abstracting. Piaget and Henriques (1978) classify types of generalization according to the integrations that they produce.

Coordinating Integrations. Inductive generalization produces coordinative integrations (*intégrations coordinatrices*), which bring subsystems together into a larger system that has no new properties of its own. The subsystems are actually richer in distinctive characteristics, though the total system will naturally have more subdivisions than any of them do. For instance, subclassifying domestic dogs into collies and poodles and *bichons frisés* is a matter of inductive generalization, which from Piaget's standpoint is short on constructive power.

Totalizing Integrations. Constructive generalization produces totalizing integrations (*intégrations totalisantes*). These yield a total system whose properties are qualitatively different from those of any of its subsystems. The new system properties enrich the cognitive structures that were there before the total system emerged and enhance their power.

But an alignment with abstraction calls for a finer breakdown than this.

Completive Integrations. So Piaget proposes that basic constructive generalizing produces completive integrations (*intégrations complétives*). These "integrate a poorer structure into a richer one, which comes down to adding new operations" (Piaget & Henriques, 1978, p. 232). An example is the development of power set structures with clearly defined unions and intersections out of disjoint classifications (chapter 1 in the *Generalization* volume).

Synthesizing Integrations. More advanced constructive generalizing produces synthesizing integrations (*intégrations synthétisantes*). These involve "extracting a common structure or concept out of several structures or notions that were previously conceived as heterogeneous" (p. 232). Generalizations (in chapter 12) that bring together linear and angular speed into a single common concept are a prime example.

Extrinsic and Intrinsic Variations

Each type of integration, in its turn, has a counterpart form of abstraction. But Piaget does not travel a direct route from one to the other; he winds through a new set of claims about extrinsic and intrinsic differentiations.

> While constructive generalizations bring with them continual differentiations [. . .] these also exist within inductive generalizations. Except in

that case the differentiations are imposed by external objects, instead of being endogenous. Here, then, is a new fundamental opposition between the two forms of generalization: it depends on whether the differentiations are exogenous, and due to new, unpredicted observables, or, on the contrary, the differentiations are linked to transformations internal to the system. (Piaget & Henriques, 1978, pp. 227–228)

Piaget prefers to contrast extrinsic with intrinsic *variations*:[5,6]

> *Intrinsic* differentiations or variations can be determined through necessary deductions from the meaning of [a] property. *Extrinsic* differentiations or variations are entrained from the outside through considerations of fact (observations and empirical abstractions). Variations in the length of the sides of a Euclidean triangle, and the equality or inequality of these sides, are therefore intrinsic: a side with no length is a contradictory notion, and two lengths must either be equal or unequal. By contrast, whether mountains are 1,000 or 2,000 or 3,000 meters high is a matter of extrinsic variation: even if we enumerate all of the possible causes of erosion, we have nothing to go on but observations and denotations. The same goes for the possibility of a vertebrate having or not having mammary glands in addition to having a spinal column. This differentiation remains extrinsic insofar as the biochemical reasons are not known that would allow a deductive connection bringing these two characters together. (pp. 228–229)

In chapter 7 of the *Generalization* book, children are asked to find the shortest path that a snail could take from the top of a wall to a lettuce plant in the middle of a garden. The youngest children try different paths and notice which one is shortest only after the fact (if they do at all). At the highest level, children realize that the shortest path is the sum of two line segments – and that one of these segments must still be the same length when the wall is pushed over sideways, so the snail ends up crossing it horizontally instead of vertically. Variations in path length begin as extrinsic phenomena and end up intrinsic.

Lining Up the Ladders

"There is no point," Piaget says, "in drawing further attention to the kinship between intrinsic variations and reflecting abstraction, or between extrinsic variations and empirical abstraction" (Piaget & Henriques, 1978, p. 230).

Coordinative integration, then, produces no novelty; it depends on extrinsic variations and goes with empirical abstraction.

Completive integration produces limited novelty on the basis of intrinsic variations and need not involve consciousness; it goes with reflecting abstraction.

Synthesizing integration produces strongly structured outcomes on the basis of intrinsic variations and does involve consciousness; it goes with reflected abstraction.

As Piaget puts it, "completive integrations, which are obviously the core of constructive generalization, are the prerequisite for synthesizing integrations, because the structures to be compared and synthesized first had to be constructed. What's more, becoming conscious or thematizing requires a reconstruction on the reflective plane of what was functioning on the instrumental plane without being explicitly represented" (p. 234). His preferred procedure for testing for reflected abstraction (Piaget, 1977/2001) was asking children to compare related tasks that they had already mastered and to state how they are similar or different.

Unfortunately, the ladder for types of integration is missing a rung. There is no analog to metareflection; reverting for a moment to the way he thought before completing *Studies in Reflecting Abstraction*, he makes a quick reference to "reflecting abstraction ... and its final stage, reflected abstraction" (Piaget & Henriques, 1978, p. 235). But he also claims that "the higher forms of synthesizing integration" function on the "plane of reflective thematizing" (p. 235) – a typical way of referring to metareflection. Here is a clear source of difficulty.

Error Again

Another disparity between abstraction and generalization is that Piaget felt no compulsion to make constructive generalization error-free. The *Generalization* volume reports several examples of growth errors. For instance, in lining up cardboard rectangles of various lengths and widths to meet a total length target (chapter 3), participants at Level IIB (late concrete operations) make more mistakes than their counterparts who are still functioning at Level IIA. "On the one hand, these subjects make more deductions than those in IIA and often perform calculations before noting results. [...] On the other, precisely because they aim to reason before acting, they run an increased risk of error and grope for solutions more often" (p. 41).

So constructive generalization can lead to new kinds of errors – even, for a time, to an increase in errors overall. Piaget did not carry over to constructive generalization his occasional assertions that the reflective phase of reflecting abstraction is error-proof.

Same Process, Different Contents?

Over the boundaries between inductive and constructive generalization, and between empirical and reflecting abstraction, there are comparable tensions. Just as he sometimes extended reflecting abstraction to any case where there was an assimilating framework, Piaget was sometimes willing to stretch constructive generalization. At one point, he asserted that not just completive but synthesizing generalization is already at work during the early concrete operational period because "the construction of the first natural numbers is accomplished by synthesizing inclusions of classes... and relations of order... and there we have an example of synthesizing integration whose mechanism remains unconscious" (Piaget & Henriques, 1978, p. 235).

The question about one process or two is less crisply posed for generalization. Reflecting abstraction (Piaget, 1950/1973, 1974/1976, 1977/2001) works in two phases: projection and reorganizing reflection. Constructive generalization seems to have just the reorganizing phase. It is because reflecting abstraction has two phases, and because empirical abstraction uses neither of them, that the suggestion lacks plausibility that abstraction could be a single process that happens to apply to different contents. It is easier to make out inductive and constructive generalization (Piaget & Henriques, 1978) as the same process applied to different contents – at the cost of putting their internal relations with empirical and reflecting abstraction under strain.

Differentiation and Integration. Much clearer, in Piaget's presentation, is the way generalizing relates to both differentiating and integrating:

> Generalizing is partly involved in every differentiation, insofar as variations are being compared, not just the final states to which they lead. Generalizing is just as implicated in every integration. [...] For instance, as far back as the sensorimotor level, when two schemes such as grasping and vision are integrated through reciprocal assimilation, objects that are both visible and graspable are consequently contrasted with those that can be seen but not grasped (e.g., the moon) and those that can be grasped but not seen (e.g., objects behind a manipulable screen). But the special case in which both positive qualities are brought together is now tightly linked to generalizations about distances, occlusions, displacements, and so on. The same goes at every level for integration into overarching systems; it always involves generalizing, whether it is constructive or even inductive. (Piaget & Henriques, 1978, p. 230)

Does Generalizing Collapse into Equilibrating? There are enough disparities between abstracting and generalizing, as Piaget understood them, to prevent their reciprocal internal relations from melding them together into a single scale of processes. But it would be no great disaster for Piagetian theory were they to merge; they were meant, at the very least, to be closely coupled.

A more serious worry is that generalizing might collapse back into equilibrating. If reflecting abstraction requires nothing more than an assimilating framework, abstracting collapses into equilibrating. If constructive generalization is already happening as soon as there are schemes to which content can be assimilated, generalizing will share that fate. However, Piaget usually identified constructive generalization with the third and most advanced kind of equilibration (see also Chapter 6 in this volume):

> [...] the continual reequilibrations that constructive generalization must reach are of a particular type. Among the forms of equilibrium for cognitive functions that we have identified elsewhere, it is the third that predominates. [...] [This] is of a different nature, pertaining to the totalizing or synthesizing character of generalization when it integrates. We will call it equilibrium between differentiations and integrations. Once subsystems are constructed by differentiation, it remains for integration to bring about the formation of total structures that incorporate them, adding laws of composition specific to these totalities as such and transcending the particular properties of the subsystems. (p. 242)

DIALECTICS

The final process that we will consider, a good deal more briefly than the first two, is dialecticalizing. For Piaget, dialectics provided not just a type of developmental process but also a metaperspective on his entire enterprise.

The Dialectical Metaperspective

First, the metaperspective. Although he rejected the "dialectical logic" of Hegel or Marx, Piaget (1972/1973, 1980) took it for granted that genetic epistemology is dialectical:

> The sort of situation in which the subject of some mode of knowing is modified by the object that he is studying, while modifying it in return, is the very prototype of a dialectical interaction. There are two principal methods for approaching such interactions; we are also accustomed to call these two sorts of methods dialectical. On the one hand, we seek to clarify these interactions via their development, in other words to place them within a historical or genetic perspective. On the other, we seek to analyze them in terms of disequilibria and reequilibration – we could also say, in terms of autoregulations and cycles of causal interactions. (1972, pp. 59–60)

In a broad sense, dialectical thinking (e.g., Sciabarra, 2000) is a type of systems thinking that views components of the system as significantly internally related to one another – in other words, the nature of one process is partly a matter of how it relates to other processes. From Piaget's standpoint, it is hard to say anything meaningful about either historical change or individual development without being dialectical in this broad sense:[7]

> When dialectics makes evident the specific nature of historical developments with their continual conflict, opposition, and transcendence (*dépassement*), it often confines itself to teasing out the mechanisms that everyone can acknowledge. The dialectical spirit is undoubtedly more widespread than membership in one or another school of thought. (1972, p. 85)

We have already seen how important internal relations are to Piaget's theories about constructive processes.

Dialecticalizing

Piaget undertook his only empirical program of research on the dialectical aspects of development in 1977, eventually readying for publication a slender volume on *Elementary Forms of Dialectic*. A worry at the forefront of his thinking was that dialecticalizing (*dialecticisation*) could collapse into equilibration, turning all aspects of development (rather trivially) dialectical. It became crucial how

> [...] to distinguish between the construction of cognitive structures, which alone is dialectical, from what can be drawn out of them once they are constructed, using nothing beyond simple deductions – using a purely discursive method, as we will follow Kant in calling it.
>
> Throughout cognitive development, dialectical phases alternate with discursive phases that are not reducible to dialectics. The discursive phases may lead at times to contradictions, but these come about because of insufficient analysis; no dialectic is needed to overcome such contradictions when better definitions or better inferences will allow the matter to be seen more clearly. (Piaget, 1980, p. 213)

Discursive Activity. Discursive activity, then, merely draws consequences deductively from cognitive structures already constructed. One may dispute the conclusion that it has no constructive power at all, but one can also see why Piaget did not credit discursive reasoning as highly productive of new knowledge. Still, discursive reasoning is very different from empirical observations or extrinsic variations, which Piaget also found lacking in constructive power. What prevents abstraction and generalization from collapsing back into equilibration is the fact that reflecting abstraction or constructive generalization involve qualitatively different processes from empirical abstraction or inductive generalization. What prevents dialecticalizing from collapsing into equilibration is the possibility of pure deductive activity – a traditional preoccupation of philosophical rationalism rather than empiricism.

Causal and Inferential. Another difference is that equilibration has a causal aspect to it, whereas Piaget envisions dialectics as strictly inferential. In the former, Piaget wants to include both our practice of attributing causality to external objects and our execution of mental operations through physical actions on the world. Of the latter, Piaget says, "the [meaning] implications of which this consists are inseparable from the causal aspect but range over the meanings of these operations taken up (*assumées*) [by the knowing subject], not over the way they are effected materially" (1980, p. 227).

Interdependencies. Although all three forms of equilibration are supposed to be dialectical, dialecticalizing specifically involves the construction of interdependencies – and these, in turn, are characteristic of the subsystem-to-system form. Among the common properties of dialectical processes

> most general [...] is the construction of interdependent relationships, not previously established, between two systems *A* and *B*. *A* and *B* are initially conceived either as opposed to each other or simply as foreign to each other. When unified, *A* and *B* end up being considered subsystems of a new totality *T*, whose overarching characteristics belonged neither to *A* nor to *B* before they were unified. For instance, in the equalization tasks of Chapter 2 the younger subjects do not see right away that adding elements to one of the collections implies subtracting them from another, when only coordinating these two operations will guarantee that the total system is noncontradictory. (Piaget, 1980, pp. 214–215)

Piaget rejects the Hegelian triad of thesis – antithesis – synthesis and does not require that actual contradictions arise while dialecticalizing. Still, it should not come as a surprise that Piagetian dialectics has a special affinity with balancing affirmations and negations (Piaget, 1974/1980, 1975/1985) nor that interdependencies transcend the structures that preceded them:

> [...] Each new interdependency generates new kinds of transcendence, when, added to those that preceded it, it leads to a new totality *T2* whose predecessor *T1* now becomes a subsystem.

For instance, in the case of spatial perspectives (Chapter 10) the child discovers the inverse relations before-behind when the observer makes a 180° excursion around the house; for the child this new interdependency leads to totality T_1, which already transcends the static totality T_0 (without modifying the projective relations). But there is nothing more to that transcendence than the new interdependency.

By contrast, when the child goes beyond this to grasp that left-right relations can also be inverted, hence that a new totality T_2 incorporates T_1 as a subsystem, the concept of transcendence takes on a new meaning. This is so in particular when, as may be the case here, there is what must be called a transcendence of the very instruments of transcendence (which is a form of constructive generalization). (pp. 215–216)

Although Piaget saw the dialectics project through to completion, his theoretical treatment is sketchier than those he provided for abstraction or generalization. Still, *Elementary Forms* allows us to connect a few more dots.

Error and the Ladder. There is no indication that Piaget considered dialectical processes to be incapable of leading to error. That particular temptation does not seem to have reached beyond his *Reflecting Abstraction* book. And dialecticalizing may progress, but it has no defined set of levels. The closest Piaget came to positing any higher-order dialectics is the passage quoted immediately preceding, where he refers to "transcendence of the very instruments of transcendence."

NEW POSSIBILITIES

To use Piaget's own manner of speaking, we may observe that his thinking about constructive processes was still undergoing re-equilibration. He had not sorted out all of the pseudodependencies from the genuine interdependencies; had not yet thematized and put on the reflective plane a lot of what it was doing with reasonable success on the instrumental plane; had not fully synthesized all of its subsystems into an overarching system; and had not epistemically converted some extrinsic variations into intrinsic variations by providing reasons for them.

The completion of anything resembling Piaget's late theory of developmental processes would require much effort by others.[8] But even those with no special commitment to that theoretical edifice will find many directions worth exploring empirically.

Further Research on Abstraction

Piaget's ideas on the three processes of interest have been put to use only sparsely. In empirical research, the focus has been entirely on reflecting abstraction. In addition to a few studies directly modeled after his (e.g., Piché & Laurendeau-Bendavid, 1982), a German research team collected an extremely rich set of longitudinal data on young children's progress at one set of geometric tasks (Schmid-Schönbein, 1985). Adult problem-solving research has occasionally drawn on the abstraction theory (e.g., Moses, 1994), sometimes incorporating interactivist and Vygotskian theory alongside Piaget's (e.g., Granott, forthcoming). There has even been a retrofit to Kohlbergian moral stages, which were not conceived with reflecting abstraction in mind (Boom, Brugman, & van der Heijden, 2001).

Meanwhile, reflecting abstraction has been a topic of continuing interest among mathematics educators and mathematical learning researchers (e.g., Simon & Tzur, 2004).

The modest spread of the abstraction theory seems to be a consequence of two factors. First, abstraction got a 20-year head start over the other two ideas, having been initially proposed in 1950 and discussed in some works that were translated into English during Piaget's lifetime (for a capsule history, see Campbell, 2001). Second, it emerged within Piaget's mathematical epistemology, and he always seemed most comfortable with the notion in mathematical domains. It is hard to improve on his formulation that "[reflecting] abstraction is the general constructive process of mathematics: it has served, for example, to evolve algebra out of arithmetic, as a set of operations on operations" (Piaget, 1970/1983, p. 125; the translators called it "reflective" abstraction).

Possibilities That Remain Open

Hardly any subsequent empirical research seems to have been influenced by Piaget's generalization theory or by his account of developmental dialectics. Piaget did not take generalization on systematically until he published his book on the subject, and his important comments on dialectics all come from his final decade. Neither *Studies in Generalization* nor *Elementary Forms of Dialectic* has been translated, restricting the non-Francophone contingent to summaries in comprehensive treatises by Vuyk (1981) and Chapman (1988). Meanwhile, to many in the Francophone world, Piaget is a figure looming up out of the past: Houdé (2007), a leading developmental psychologist in France, gives reflecting abstraction all of one footnote in his recent roundup of developmental psychology.[9]

The late works on which this chapter has concentrated are nonetheless full of fascinating ideas and empirical results just waiting for investigators to take them up. How, for example, could any serious student of human knowledge and its development not be intrigued by chapter 1 of *Elementary Forms?* Using nothing fancier than a game of 20 questions, Piaget and his collaborators examine a proactive dialectical spiral of predicates, concepts, judgments, and inferences, along with its retroactive twin, which runs from inferences to judgments to concepts all the way back to predicates. A great many possibilities remain to be generated by Jean Piaget's theories of abstraction, generalization, and dialectics.

NOTES

1. For present purposes, I am assuming that development is progressive change over time, always involving some advance or improvement. The possibility of regressive change is addressed by Leslie Smith (see Chapter 3, this volume).

2. If Process A is internally related in some way to Process B, the relation with B is essential to A; A would not be the same process otherwise. If Process A is externally related to Process B, on the other hand, the relation could be taken away or altered and A would still be the same process.

3. An extremely detailed summary of Piaget's research on processes is available in French from Ducret (2000); see also the chronological table of research programs and books in Piaget (2006).

4. Piaget and Henriques (1978) used the word "inductive" in a descriptive fashion, purposely avoiding such questions as whether science uses induction or some kind of inductive argument is logically valid.

5. The notion of meaning (*signification*) in Piaget's late works is affected by revisions that he was making to his logic. A *meaning implication* (*implication signifiante*) is roughly an "if-then" statement in which the meaning of the consequent is contained within the meaning of the antecedent (Piaget, 1977/1986); in a more precise treatment, "$p \to q$ if one meaning m of q is embedded in the meaning of p and if this meaning is transitive" (Piaget & Garcia, 1987/1991, p. 3, Davidson and Easley translation). Piaget sometimes employed a type of "relevance logic" for meaning implication, but his allusions do not always imply a commitment to this particular formalism.

6. The provision of reasons for them is what turns extrinsic variations intrinsic. This does not mean that the altitudes of mountains would change if reasons were provided for them; it does mean that a previously unrecognized relation between variations in altitude and other known properties of the environment (such as processes of erosion) becomes known, and the other known properties explain the differences in altitude. A study of reasons was Piaget's very last research project (Henriques, Dionnet, & Ducret, 2004; Piaget, 2006).

7. One could be pardoned for translating *dépassement* as "*Aufhebung*," or "sublation" – both technical terms for what the Hegelian synthesis does. The synthesis incorporates the thesis and the antithesis, including their

contradictions, subsuming them and surpassing them; when everything is done, the thesis and the antithesis no longer exist separately (Sciabarra, 2000).

8. For instance, although there is more to it, and it was not arrived at in this way historically, the interactivist theory of knowing levels (Campbell & Bickhard, 1986) can be understood as an account of reflecting abstraction and constructive generalization that locks both of them tightly to *la prise de conscience*.

9. Houdé's book, which appeared in a series of concise overviews aimed at the general public, is intended to replace Piaget and Inhelder's (1966/1969) work of the same title.

REFERENCES

Bickhard, M. H., & Richie, D. M. (1983). *On the nature of representation: A case study of James J. Gibson's theory of perception.* New York: Praeger.

Boom, J., Brugman, D., & van der Heijden, P. G. M. (2001). Hierarchical structure of moral stages assessed by a sorting task. *Child Development, 72,* 535–548.

Campbell, R. L. (2001). Reflecting abstraction in context. In J. Piaget, *Studies in reflecting abstraction* (pp. 1–27). Hove: Psychology Press.

Campbell, R. L., & Bickhard, M. H. (1986). *Knowing levels and developmental stages.* Basel: Karger.

Chapman, M. (1988). *Constructive evolution: Origins and development of Piaget's thought.* Cambridge: Cambridge University Press.

Ducret, J.-J. (2000). *Jean Piaget 1968–1979: Une décennie de recherches sur les mécanismes de construction cognitive.* Genève: Service de la Recherche en Éducation.

Granott, N. (forthcoming). Emergent representation out of actions in social systems: Discovery in collaborative problem solving. *New Ideas in Psychology.*

Henriques, G., Dionnet, S., & Ducret, J.-J. (2004). *La formation des raisons: Étude sur l'épistémogenèse.* Sprimont, Belgium: Mardaga.

Houdé, O. (2007). *La psychologie de l'enfant* (2nd ed.). Paris: Presses Universitaires de France.

Moses, N. (1994). The development of procedural knowledge in adults engaged in a "tractor-trailer" task. *Cognitive Development, 9,* 103–130.

O'Regan, J. K., & Noë, A. (2001). A sensorimotor account of vision and visual consciousness. *The Behavioral and Brain Sciences, 24,* 939–973.

Piaget, J. (1952). *The origins of intelligence in children.* New York: International Universities Press. (Original work published in 1936)

Piaget, J. (1969). *The mechanisms of perception.* London: Routledge & Kegan Paul. (Original work published in 1961)

Piaget, J. (1970). *Genetic epistemology.* New York: Columbia University Press.

Piaget, J. (1973). *Introduction à l'épistémologie génétique, Vol 1: La pensée mathématique* (2nd ed.). Paris: Presses Universitaires de France. (Original work published in 1950)

Piaget, J. (1973). *Main trends in psychology.* London: Allen & Unwin. (Original work published in 1972)

Piaget, J. (1976). *The grasp of consciousness*. Cambridge, MA: Harvard University Press. (Original work published in 1974).

Piaget, J. (1978). *Success and understanding*. Cambridge, MA: Harvard University Press. (Original work published in 1974)

Piaget, J. (1980). *Experiments in contradiction*. Chicago: University of Chicago Press. (Original work published in 1974)

Piaget, J. (1980). *Les formes élémentaires de la dialectique*. Paris: Gallimard.

Piaget, J. (1983). Piaget's theory. In W. Kessen (Ed.), *Handbook of child psychology* (4th ed., Vol. 1: *History, theory, and methods*, pp. 103–128). New York: Wiley. (Original work published in 1970)

Piaget, J. (1985). *The equilibration of cognitive structures: The central problem of intellectual development*. Chicago: University of Chicago Press. (Original work published in 1975)

Piaget, J. (1986). Essay on necessity. *Human Development, 29*, 301–314. (Original work published in 1977)

Piaget, J. (2001). *Studies in reflecting abstraction*. Hove: Psychology Press. (Original work published in 1977)

Piaget, J. (2006). Reason. *New Ideas in Psychology, 24*, 1–29.

Piaget, J., & Garcia, R. (1991). *Toward a logic of meanings*. Hillsdale, NJ: Erlbaum. (Original work published in 1987)

Piaget, J., & Henriques, G. (1978). *Recherches sur la généralisation*. Paris: Presses Universitaires de France.

Piaget, J., & Inhelder, B. (1969). *The psychology of the child*. New York: Basic Books. (Original work published in 1966)

Piché, Y., & Laurendeau-Bendavid, M. (1982). La prise de conscience de la négation dans la genèse de la réversibilité. *Revue canadienne des sciences du comportement, 14*, 35–49.

Schmid-Schönbein, C. (1985). "He, sind ja beide gleich groß!" Eine prozeßanalytische Rekonstruktion des Verständnisses von "gleich sein." In T. B. Seiler & W. Wannenmacher (Eds.), *Begriffs- und Wortbedeutungsentwicklung* (pp. 167–189). Berlin: Springer.

Sciabarra, C. M. (2000). *Total freedom: Toward a dialectical libertarianism*. University Park: Pennsylvania State University Press.

Simon, M. A., & Tzur, R. (2004). Explicating the role of mathematical tasks in conceptual learning: An elaboration of the Hypothetical Learning Trajectory. *Mathematical Thinking and Learning, 6*, 91–104.

Vuyk, R. (1981). *Overview and critique of Piaget's genetic epistemology, 1965–1980* (2 vols.). London: Academic Press.

8   Piaget and Method

Piaget's method of data collection has always appeared quite unorthodox to psychologists raised on the Anglophone diet of standardized, objective, and experimental scientific method where results were routinely presented following some sort of routine statistical analyses. Piaget's books revealed him as merely chatting to few children – mainly his own and apparently, just a few others – about the moon, about their drawings of bicycles, and most famously, how skinny glasses held more juice than fat ones did. Interesting for sure – but hardly replicable, scientific psychological experiments: The questions changed, the procedures changed, and none of the results showed means and standard deviations. Considering the number of published papers and books, we remain surprised by the small space Piaget gave to explaining his method. Although the hundreds of protocol extracts, meant to illustrate his theory, correspond to almost half of the pages of each published volume, the mention of any detailed data collection, setting, or precise method eventually used in the reported investigations is rare and generally very vague: "You place in front of the child a *certain number of flowers . . .* "; " *. . . it is useful . . .* to have the child draw a picture . . . " (see Tryphon, 2004). This lack of clarity has given rise to many criticisms of Genevan researchers' "bad habits," such as nonrigorous experimental conditions, small, nonrepresentative samples, and lack of quantitative analyses (Flavell, 1963).

It would be easy to blame readers for their lack of understanding of Piaget's method, but a number of features of the Genevan research program conspire against all but the most ardent researchers in coming to grips with what is often loosely called the clinical interview method. First, Piaget was primarily an *epistemologist* who adopted a Kantian/structuralist philosophical stance rarely acknowledged by the *psychologists* who formed the preponderance of his audience. Second, his own written work reveals very little of his method – even to the avid reader. Almost in passing, Piaget provided some description in just a few places (e.g., Piaget, 1926/1929 and 1947; Piaget & Rosello, 1922), and Inhelder reflected on her role in developing the research techniques in her autobiography (Inhelder, 1989). So, this chapter will show that, with the benefit of hindsight, we can have a better understanding of Piagetian method now than we *could* have had at the time we first encountered it.

In trying to describe and explain the Genevan *méthode*, our procedure will be to provide an historically informed reconstruction of the method(s) developed by the Genevan school. We will rely on published (but often little-cited) accounts as well as documents that we have uncovered during our research at the Archives Jean Piaget. We aim to reveal that the tip of the Piagetian iceberg of research known to many – the quotes from interviews with children that adorn his empirical publications – was supported by a much larger, usually concealed, philosophically driven research program – known only to those who had direct personal involvement in it. So Piaget's method does exist, or rather, just like Piaget's theory or like knowledge itself, a Genevan method developed over time.

Attempting to make a link between Piagetian research and Piagetian method is a hazardous and difficult enterprise. Even more so, as one can find a large number of adjectives accompanying the term method throughout Piaget's writings. From the "historic–critical" (Piaget, 1925a) to simply "critical" method (Piaget, 1947), from "genetic" (Piaget, 1925a) to "clinical" method (Piaget, 1925b; Piaget & Rosello, 1922); all these descriptors appear, quite often in inconsistent ways, in various writings, and at different dates in Piaget's *oeuvre*. At each point, those titles might have different meanings. It seems necessary to distinguish two different levels at which Piaget's method can be discussed. They reflect two different aspects of Piagetian research: one at the epistemological level and the other at the psychological level. The terms "historic–critical" and "genetic" (i.e., developmental) refer to how psychology, considered a science, can provide answers to a general epistemological question concerning the construction of knowledge. On the other hand, the clinical (or critical) method is restricted to the means by which empirical data are collected, as opposed to other methods used by psychologists, such as observation, testing, etc. So, this chapter focuses on the psychological dimension of Piaget's theory and, more specifically, on his clinical (or critical) interview method. This chapter shows Piaget's interview technique to be philosophically well grounded, aimed, over a lifetime of research, at developing a new theory of the development of rational thought. It spite of the paucity of description in his own work and the barrage of complaints from critics, Piaget's method is justifiable in its own right. It remains a powerful tool for psychologists and educators, provides the foundations for large-scale investigations of Piaget's claims, and satisfies the most stringent psychometric analysis.

THE GENEVAN *MÉTHODE*

> What's in a name? That which we call a rose
> By any other name would smell as sweet.
> Romeo and Juliet (II, ii, 1–2)

The specific objective for which Piaget and his colleagues aimed in their investigations was arranging each empirical study "to lay bare the operational mechanisms of thought" (Inhelder, 1962, p. 19), whereas the general purpose of the entire research program was to study the formation of necessary concepts and intellectual operations. It was not, as commonly believed, to investigate the cognitive development of any particular sample of subjects (Bond & Jackson, 1991, p. 33; Smith, 1993). Herein lies the reason underlying the insistence of some Piagetian scholars (e.g., Smith, 1993) on the use of the term *method of critical exploration* to emphasize the epistemological purposes of the Genevan research. The substantive difference between *critical* and *clinical* is that a *clinical* method is content with ascertaining whether any response/reason is actually that of the person being interviewed (as in psychoanalysis), whereas a *critical* method focuses on the nature of the respondent's belief: how the response is justified in terms of the evidence and possible competing explanations (i.e., Piaget's much-maligned use of countersuggestions). Empiricists seem horrified that the interviewer's challenge might influence the powerless child to change his mind. But that is the essence of the Piagetian *oeuvre*: not *what* the child knows, but *how* the child knows it; not the child's *judgment*, but the *justification* of that response (cf. Brainerd, 1973; Smith, 1992).

> In short, the aim is to monitor aspects of their modal understanding with respect to a coherent, and so durable, set of beliefs which can remain self-identical through challenges and transformations . . . The key question is not whether consistency is present, but whether it can be maintained through irrelevant transformation. In this way conservation is a constitutive feature of rational thought . . . (Smith, 1992, p. 57)

The term "critical" was substituted for "clinical" by Piaget in his foreword to the third edition of *Judgment and Reasoning in the Child*, written in 1947:

> Thus we have totally renounced the method of pure and simple conversation, after our research on the first two years of development, and have adopted a mixed method, whose superior fecundity has been proved

since. This 'critical method' (if it is allowed to baptize this way the outcomes of procedures that we had originally borrowed from the psychiatrists' 'clinical method') consists.... (Piaget, 1947, p. 7, our translation)

By this terminological change, Piaget aimed to avoid the criticisms
of his early publications concerning the pathological aspect of the term
"clinical" (Baumgarten, 1927) or the suggestive aspect of the investigator's questions (Isaacs, 1930; see Piaget's reply to Isaacs's criticism in
Piaget, 1931). Nevertheless, the term "clinical" continued to be used
in the subsequent work of the Genevan school when discussing the
interview method (Bang, 1966; Droz, Berthoud, Calpini, Dällenbach, &
Michiels, 1976).

Piaget himself located the origin of his method during the 2 years
he spent in Paris between 1919 and 1921 (Piaget, 1952). Indeed, after
a semester in Zurich, where he attended two psychology laboratories
and became acquainted with psychological methods and psychoanalysis (Ducret, 1990), Piaget left Switzerland to pursue his studies at the
Sorbonne. At the same time he was appointed at the Binet-Simon laboratory to standardize Burt's (1883–1971) reasoning tests to identify children with special educational needs – as well as gifted children. The
tests' scoring indicated the child's mental age; the test items, which
involved copying figures, answering logical questions, interpreting pictures, and so on, were intended to evaluate the child's performance
across various domains of intelligence.

While working on these tests, Piaget realized that the errors committed by the children were more informative about their intellectual
level than were the correct answers. The problem with a standardized
test is that the child's answer can be categorized only as "right" or
"wrong." However, in talking more extensively with the children about
the problems, Piaget realized that, whether any given answer was right
or wrong, the more important question was to discover why a particular
child gave a particular answer, especially when a presumably "wrong"
answer given by a child could be found consistently in the responses
of other children. He was seeking to reveal the child's understanding of
the question – rather than merely to count the "rights" and "wrongs."
Thus he started to interview children and began to develop his own data
collection method: "Thus, I engaged my subjects in conversations pat-
terned after psychiatric questioning, with the aim of discovering something about the reasoning process underlying their right, but especially
their wrong answers" (Piaget, 1952, p. 244).

The first explicit reference to the term "clinical method" appeared
in a 1922 article by Piaget and Rosello. Piaget had accepted the post

of "chef de travaux" offered by Claparède at the Institut Jean-Jacques
Rousseau in Geneva and continued his own research. Referring to the
two methods generally used in child psychology at that time, that is,
the method of individual monograph[1] and the testing method, both of
which the authors judged as inadequate, they proposed a third inspired
by pathology: the clinical method. However, the method was not clearly
explained in the 1922 paper (where children were asked to describe the
eidetic images they formed – following Jaensch's and Binet's procedures).
It was mentioned rather vaguely and used in presenting the results – and
to question the validity of the types of image descriptions studied and
proposed by Binet.

> "Clinical investigation is under-valued in contemporary child psychol-
> ogy. Whatever the claims for their superiority, both book-length indi-
> vidual case studies and testing methods present some problems, which
> consist either in leading to purely qualitative results, or, on the other
> hand, providing a snap-shot of results that are too far removed from daily
> life. A third method should then be recommended, which would lead
> to a typology of children, in the way the clinical method in pathology
> led to a classification of syndromes. This clinical method would present
> the same dangers for child psychology as for pathology, and the classifi-
> cations might be regarded as inadequate in either case, but the benefits
> would be the same: science needs schemes which unify observations
> and provide landmarks, even if these landmarks are mobile" (Piaget &
> Rosello, 1922, p. 208, our translation).

Piaget revealed a little more about his method in "La Représentation
du monde chez l'enfant" (The child's representation of the world), a
short article published in 1925 (i.e., a short paper with the same title as
the 1926 book!):

> In a few words, the method to follow in the study of children's represen-
> tation of the world is this: observe the child naturally, note the child's
> utterances and questions, and then, inspired by these questions inter-
> view other children directly; finally, return to pure observation in order
> to verify the results of the previous interviewing. The method is thus a
> sort of shuttle between pure observation and interviewing, interviewing
> intended to increase the volume of data and direct observation intended
> to situate them in their spontaneous mental context. Thus, we avoid
> two problems: The results of observation only are too poor to allow
> an advanced analysis. The results of interviewing only are too much
> influenced by the questions and unintentional suggestions, to allow an
> interpretation safe from any objection. On the other hand, the two meth-
> ods combined will result in something solid, comparable to the clinical
> method in psychiatry. (Piaget, 1925b, p. 192, our translation)

The core of Piaget's method becomes clear in this citation: a combination of observation and experimentation, that is, a continuous adaptation of the investigator's questions to the subject's answers and the reformulation of new questions. This description became more developed in Piaget's introduction to *The Child's Representation of the World* (1926), his only book referring extensively to the clinical method, where he clearly states that the investigator needs to be guided by the answering subject.

Until the mid-1930s the method remained restricted to a verbal exchange between the two protagonists of the investigation, as witnessed in all the protocols of the first six monographs published by Piaget (1923/1926, 1924/1928, 1926/1929, 1927/1930, 1932/1932, 1936/1952). Piaget himself later acknowledged the limits of this verbal method. "It was only later, by studying the patterns of intelligent behavior of the first two years, that I learned that for a complete understanding of the genesis of intellectual operations, manipulation of, and experiences with objects had first to be considered" (Piaget, 1952, p. 247). This statement might be seen as a convenient reconstruction of the past; his autobiography being written in 1952, long after the publication of the great amount of his empirical work published in English.

It is clear that the observations Piaget made of his own children had some influence on this part of his working method, because verbal interaction was quite restricted with his infant children. But this is not the only explanation. In addition to the change in his interests mentioned previously, two other factors can help account for this change. First, after returning to Geneva in 1929, he became codirector of the Institute, and this status gave him better opportunity to conduct his research, which at that time, in addition to sensorimotor development, was already concerned with the study of operations underlying the child's construction of knowledge. Second, Piaget began to work with Alina Szeminska, Edith Meyer, and Bärbel Inhelder, three students, and later collaborators: All three participated actively in the elaboration and progressive modification of the Genevan research. Given that we lack the space in this chapter to discuss the ways in which each of them participated in developing the method, we will focus only on the role of Bärbel Inhelder, who later became Piaget's key colleague.

Although Bärbel Inhelder (1913–1997) was the youngest of the three previously mentioned collaborators, she was the one who played the most important role, not only in the 1930s, when objects were first introduced in Piaget's investigations, but even more so later, in the 1950s, when she undertook her work on the inductive method of adolescents. According to her autobiography, Inhelder commenced her collaboration with Piaget in summer 1933, that is, her first study year, with the dissolving sugar task, published in the journal of the Jean-Jacques Rousseau Institute (Inhelder, 1936). The documents available at the Archives Jean Piaget in Geneva suggest that Inhelder's claim should not be read too literally. It appears rather more plausible that Inhelder was guided by Szeminska and under the latter's influence developed her interview skills.

At this point, it should be noted that although at different times Piaget stated that his method had changed, no dramatic changes can be noticed in the publications mentioned previously. It is true that the method ceased to be exclusively verbal and that the investigative settings were devised to include more objects. However, these were more often manipulated by the investigator than by the child, whose role consisted of observing the changes introduced in the tasks and commenting on them. It is only with Inhelder's return to Geneva in 1943 that a significant change in method took place. Inhelder took charge of all the empirical research left unfinished when her colleagues left Geneva at the start of the war. Not only did she contribute directly to the publication of the books on physical quantities, geometry, and space, but she also started her own research program into adolescents' methods of experimentation (see Bond, 2001; Inhelder, 1954/2001). It is also important to note that with Inhelder's presence in the Institute in the 1940s, Piaget actually stopped interviewing children himself, except on the rare occasions during his classes when he needed to do so to illustrate his theory. In this case he would "order" one or two schoolchildren from a local teacher and ask the child(ren) questions in the presence of his students or, instead, have a student ask the questions (Tryphon, 2004).

THE GENEVAN *MÉTHODE* RECONSTRUCTED

Thus, Inhelder's first endeavor was to collect and complete the data that would be assembled, edited, theorized, and presented later by Piaget in those various publications where each published protocol is only a part of a much longer interview transcript (*procès-verbal*).[2] The published books include data from only a small number of the subjects actually studied for each task. For some tasks, this amounted to several dozens of subjects, and, certainly, Piaget's published accounts do not provide the necessary information for informed replications. Our suggestion is that it is only by reading many of these original *procès-verbal* that one can reconstruct the methodological parts of the research processes that resulted in the edited protocols which were actually published.

To do this we will take as our exhibit A the book published in 1958 as *The Growth of Logical Thinking from Childhood to Adolescence* (*GLT*), originally *De la Logique de L'enfant à la Logique de L'adolescent* (*LELA*-1955), and the research program that yielded that publication (see Chapter 11, this volume; Bond, 2001). Our choice has both theoretical and pragmatic reasons that will gradually unfold in the chapter. The Genevans' chosen technique for the investigation of the development from concrete to formal thinking was Inhelder's modification of Piaget's interview style:

> "In order to grasp the constructive mechanisms of reasoning, I developed and practiced what had been called the clinical, and since, the critical exploratory method. This method favoured an exchange of views based on the manipulation of real objects, in contrast with the mostly verbal method of Piaget's earlier research" (Inhelder, 1989, p. 215, commenting on the period 1932–1938).

We can safely presume that the published *GLT* reports consisted of stylized and edited summaries of the pertinent aspects of each investigation, but how did the record of an interview session *procès-verbal* become a published protocol in that book? For example, the 15 lines of Ker (10;0; *GLT*, p. 97) come from four-and-a-half typed A4 pages in its original form, but the celebrated but lengthier Gou protocol (33 lines in *GLT*, p. 102; see Figure 8.1) is condensed from just a two-and-a-half page *procès-verbal* report.

The interviews by this time followed a relatively standard format: Pairs of investigators conducted each interview, one actively participating in the investigation (*interrogatrice*) while the second (*secrétaire*) took the copious notes that were later typed up in triplicate as *procès-verbal* transcripts. Many of the protocols now filed in the Archives Jean Piaget in Geneva list Inhelder and the appropriate *assistant*[3] as the pair of investigators (sometimes Inhelder did the recording); others record *assistants* and students sharing these roles, with the occasional (recorded) interruption of Mlle Inhelder, who apparently was not too far away. (None of the remaining thousand or so of these *GLT* protocols refer to "*le patron* Piaget" at all, further corroborating Inhelder's claim to personal responsibility for the direction of the adolescence research and the claim [*GLT*, p. *xxiii*] for their independence at this stage of the research. Piaget's work on the logical analysis was conducted later than and separately from Inhelder's own research into children's experimental procedures [Inhelder; Noelting, personal communication]). Each of the

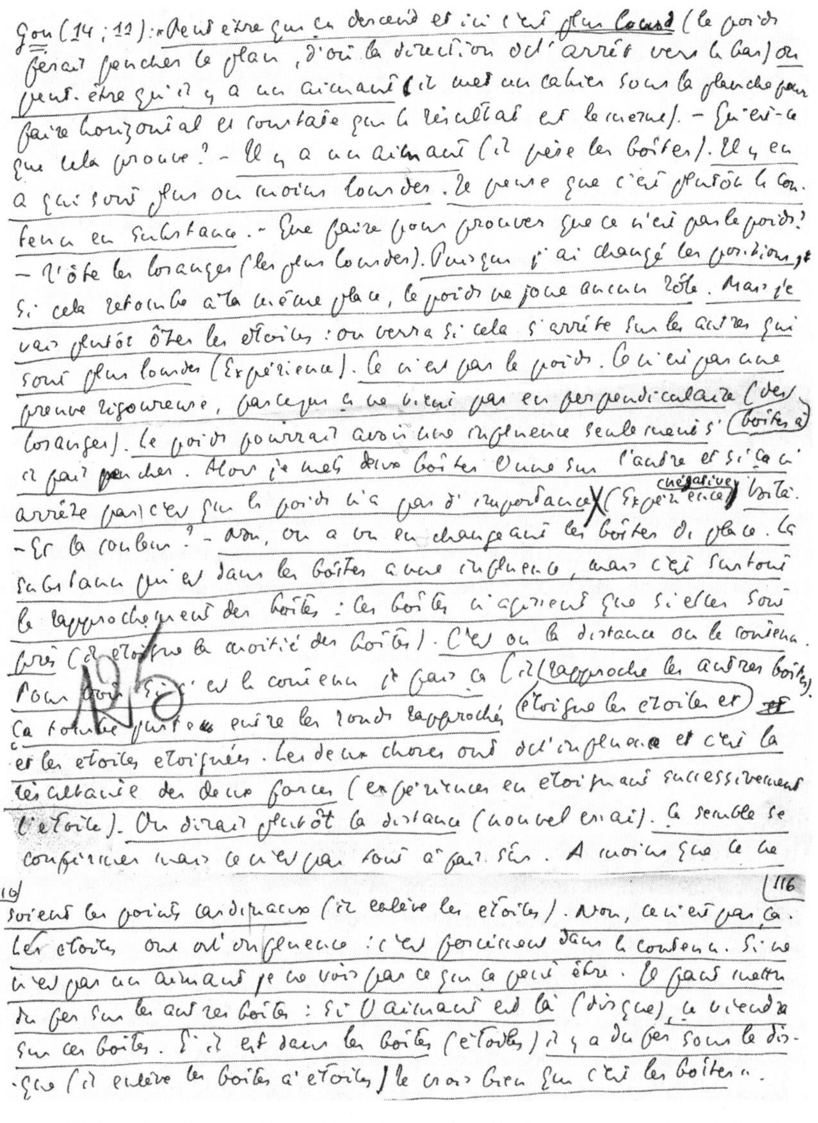
Gou (14;11): «Peut-être que ça descend et ici c'est plus lourd (le poids
ferait pencher le plan, d'où la direction de l'arrêt vers le bas) ou
peut-être qu'il y a un aimant (il met un cahier sous la planche pour
faire horizontal et constate que le résultat est le même). – Qu'est-ce
que cela prouve? – Il y a un aimant (il pèse les boîtes). Il y en
a qui sont plus ou moins lourdes. Je pense que c'est plutôt le contenu en substance. – Que faire pour prouver que ce n'est pas le poids?
– J'ôte les losanges (les plus lourdes). Puisque j'ai changé les positions et
si cela retombe à la même place, le poids ne joue aucun rôle. Mais je
vais plutôt ôter les étoiles: on verra si cela s'arrête sur les autres qui
sont plus lourdes (Expérience). Ce n'est pas le poids. Ce n'est pas une
preuve rigoureuse, parce que ça ne tient pas en perpendiculaire (des
losanges). Le poids pourrait avoir une influence seulement s'il (boîtes à)
il fait pencher. Alors je mets deux boîtes l'une sur l'autre et si ça s'
arrête parce que le poids n'a pas d'importance (Expérience négative) boîte.
– Et la couleur? – Non, on a vu en changeant les boîtes de place. La
substance qui est dans les boîtes a une influence, mais c'est surtout
le rapprochement des boîtes: les boîtes n'agissent que si elles sont
près (il éloigne la moitié des boîtes). C'est ou la distance ou le contenu.
Pour voir si c'est le contenu il faut ça (il rapproche les autres boîtes).
La tombe juste entre les ronds rapprochés (éloigne les étoiles et)
et les étoiles éloignées. Les deux choses ont de l'influence et c'est la
résultante des deux forces (expériences en éloignant successivement
l'étoile). On dirait plutôt la distance (nouvel essai). Ça semble se
confirmer mais ce n'est pas tout à fait sûr. A moins que ce ne
110 116
soient les points cardinaux (il enlève les étoiles). Non, ce n'est pas ça.
Les étoiles ont de l'influence: c'est forcément dans le contenu. Si ce
n'est pas un aimant je ne vois pas ce que ça peut être. Il faut mettre
du fer sur les autres boîtes: si un aimant est là (disque), il viendra
sur ces boîtes. S'il est dans les boîtes (étoiles) il y a du fer sous le disque (il enlève les boîtes à étoiles) je crois bien que c'est les boîtes».

Figure 8.1. Extract from Piaget's own handwritten manuscript of the Gou protocol as it would appear in *LELA* (pp. 109 and 110 of the manuscript).

psychology students then submitted an assessable report that addressed the ten or so cases personally conducted while each of Inhelder's *assistants* produced annual reports that summarized and analyzed all of that year's investigations on each problem.

Interestingly, the extracts from the Gou and the Ker protocols appeared both in *GLT* and in the drafts of the book Inhelder was writing: "In addition, the specific problems of experimental induction analyzed from a functional standpoint (as distinguished from the present structural analysis) will be the subject of a special work by the first author" (*GLT*, p. *xxiv*). The edited summaries of the protocols for Inhelder's planned book are often quite different from those published in *GLT*. The various edited summaries appear to be directed to different ends: Those in *GLT* reflected Piaget's focus on the skills characteristic of his developing epistemic subject, which were amenable to his logical analysis; Inhelder's drafts focused on the experimental strategies that teachers anywhere might recognize as used by children in secondary school science laboratories (see Inhelder, 1954/2001). The *GLT* versions (Piaget's handwritten draft of this text – see Figure 8.1 – is one of but a minority that are known to be in existence) are obviously taken directly from the original typed *procès-verbal*; they could not have been prepared from Inhelder's already existing summaries. A comparison with the original transcripts will show that the published protocols do scant justice to the breadth and depth of the abilities demonstrated by the subjects; remember, Piaget was focused on a few core intellectual competencies of these children. Worse than that, they do serious injustices to the Genevan *méthode* for those of us trying to understand it directly from the evidence provided: There is no adequate record of the investigative procedures or a detailed description of the interviewers' questions and directions sufficient for the reader to grasp the quintessentially interactive nature of the procedure (see Bond, 1994).

There is little doubt that the published protocols are faithful *summaries* of the original typewritten records; all of what appears in print is to be found in the originals. But, what is missing – the aspects related to procedures; more accurate use of ellipses (for example) in the published accounts – would have been more faithful to original investigations. More importantly, the ellipses would have alerted the reader that some other (undisclosed) events had taken place. The following character-by-character comparisons of the published Gou "invisible magnetism"[4] protocol with the original typewritten version and Piaget's own (handwritten) manuscript for the book will reveal what is *omitted* in the published records; that is more instructive to our appreciation of the Genevan *méthode*. What is *common* to all accounts need delay us no further; in spite of implied criticism to the contrary, the correspondences reflect painstaking care in the preparation of the published summaries.

In summary, the *procès-verbal de l'expérience des aimants* for the subject known as Gou recorded some 19 systematic experimental variations and the stopping point for each of those trials. About two thirds of the original spoken record can be attributed to Gou, whereas one third of the conversation recorded the questions and comments of the "interrogatrice," Mlle. Claude Penard (see Figure 8.2). The edited summary of the interview (*GLT*, p. 102) (mis)represented the balance of the dialogue as follows: Gou's actions and dialogue have been edited to about half their original length, whereas Penard's questioning was reduced to just over 10% of her contribution (see especially Figure 8.3 for our English translation, where the underlined sections are those that actually appear in *GLT*). The published protocol then revealed her contribution as about one-and-a-half lines of the 33-line published transcript. The original interviewer–subject interaction proportion of 1:2 is distorted to 1:20 in print. How could the reader have inferred what was going on?

One might presume that the excised portions of the protocol consisted of the usual, "Why?" "You're sure?" "What do you think?" and "Why did you do that?" so common in even the most rudimentary replications. Certainly, questions of exactly those types fell to Piaget's editorial hand, but other crucially informative questions suffered the same fate. Clearly, Penard's questions directed Gou to consider the roles of hypotheses and proof in his experimentation: Questions such as, "What does that prove?" "What do you think of your hypothesis about magnets?" "You have proof?" are less easily presumed from the published records. More importantly, the complete absence of the introductory (nine) questions and answers allows the reader to substitute any imagined (less satisfactory or less demanding) strategy for the one actually implemented by Penard. In response to the inquiry as to the possibility of predicting stoppage on the blue zones, Gou posited, "It depends if I pull more or less strongly." Two trials (each resulting in "blue") resulted in the suggestion of the factor of "tilting" by Gou; only after the third successive "blue" result does the first line of the *GLT* account record the hypotheses concerning weight/tilting or the presence of a magnet. What the Genevans' published accounts of the "invisible magnetism" investigation do not make clear is the role that the investigator plays in ensuring that the individual has every opportunity to display the abilities under investigation. In the original Gou *procès-verbal*, Penard's dialogue makes this role very explicit: "You can do what you like with the boxes to verify this hypothesis," "Could you have other evidence?" "Is that sufficient proof like that?" indicate the insistence of Penard that Gou satisfy himself of the *necessity* of his experimental variations and the *sufficiency* of the evidence he adduced to support or reject his conjectures.

<u>Procès-verbal de l'expérience des aimants</u>   +

<u>Xavier GOUACHE 14 ans, 11 mois</u>   Interrogatrice: Mlle Penard
                                        Secrétaire: Mlle Bourquin.

<u>(aimants sur bleu)</u>

I) Est-ce que l'on peut prévoir l'ar-   Ca dépend si je tire plus ou moins fort.
rêt des ailes bleues ?
                    <u>(bleu)</u>
II) Et si l'on recommence, est-ce   Je pense que ça va toujours du même
que vous pouvez prévoir quelque chose   ? côté;
Pourquoi ?   Je ne sais pas, elles étaient déjà là
                                         quand je suis arrivé, peut-être que cela
                                         descend.

                <u>(bleu)</u>
III)   – C'est exactement la même place.
Si on fait une troisième fois ?   Cela retombera à la même place.
Pourquoi ?   Peut-être que cela descend et ici c'est
                                         plus lourd (roulettes) ou peut-être, il
                                         y a un aimant.
Que pourriez-vous faire si c'est   Mettre quelque chose sous la planche
bien penché ?   (il met un cahier sous la planche
                <u>(bleu)</u>   – Ca revient la même chose
IV) Qu'est-ce que cela prouve ?   Il y a un aimant.
Vous pouvez tout faire avec les   Il y a de la cire là (étoiles). Je pense
boîtes pour vérifier cette hypothè-   que c'est selon la quantité ou la diffé-
se.   rence des metaux dans les boîtes (l'en-
                                         fant soupèse les boîtes).
Que constatez vous ?   Il y en a qui sont plus ou mois lourdes.
Vous pensez que le poids a une influ-   Je pense plutôt que c'est le contenu
ence ?   en substance.
Que pourriez-vous faire pour prouver   J'ôte les losanges.
que ça n'est pas le poids ?
Pourquoi ?   Puisque j'ai changé de positions les boî-
                                         tes, si cela retombe à la même place, le
                                         poids ne joue aucun rôle. Mais je vais
                                         plutôt ôter les étoiles.
Pourquoi ?   On verra si cela s'arrête sur les autres
                                         boîtes qui sont plus lourdes

                <u>(arrêt sur ronds)</u>   – Ca n'est pas le poids.
Vous êtes sûr ? Auriez vous une   Ca n'est pas une preuve rigoureuse parce
autre preuve ?   que cela ne vient pas en perpendiculaire.
                                         Le poids pourrait avoir de l'influence
                                         seulement sil fait pencher.
Au moyen des boîtes, auriez vous   Je mets deux boîtes l'une sur l'autre et
une autre preuve ?   si cela ne s'arrête pas là c'est que le
                                         poids n'a pas d'importance.
Et la couleur à une importance ?   Non, on a vu en changeant les boîtes de
                                         place.
Que pensez-vous de votre hypothèse   Je ne croit pas que ça soit ça.
des aimants ?
Et qu'est-ce que cela pourrait être ?   La position sous l'aiguille. Non, cela
                                         n'est pas ça, il faudrait aussi que le
                                         terrain descende (l'enfant met les aimants
                                         sur vert)
Pourquoi faites-vous cela ?   Pour voir les relations des boîtes entre
                                         elles. On verra si c'est l'aiguille.
                <u>(vert)</u>   – Alors c'est la boîte.
Qu'est-ce que cela prouve relative-   Si c'était l'aiguille, cela serait reve-
ment à l'aiguille ?   nu sur bleu.

Figure 8.2. Extract from the original record of interview (*procès-verbal*) of the
Gou protocol held in the AJP, Geneva.

Xavier GOUACHE 14 years, 11 months

Investigator: Miss Penard
Recorder: Miss Bourquin

(magnets on blue)

I) Can you predict its stopping on the blue sector?

That depends on whether I push more or less strongly.

(blue)

II) And if we were to recommence, can you predict anything?
Why?

I think that it always goes to the same place;

I don't know, they were already here when I arrived, perhaps that slopes.

(blue)

III)
If you try a third time?
Why?

What will you be able to do if it's really tilted?
(blue)

- It's exactly the same place.
It will come back to the same place.
Perhaps that slopes and here it's heavier (. .) or perhaps, there is a magnet.
Put something under the board (he puts a note-pad under the board)
- It returned to the same place.

IV) What does that prove?
You can do anything you like with the boxes to verify that hypothesis.

There's a magnet.
There's some wax in there (stars). I think that it's according to the amount or the differences in the metals in the boxes (the child feels the weight of the boxes).

What do you notice?
You think that weight has an influence?

There are those which are heavier or lighter.
I rather think that it's the nature of the contents.

What can you do to prove that it isn't weight?

I remove the diamonds.

Why?

If it comes back to the same place now that I have changed the positions of the boxes, weight plays no part. But instead, I am going to remove the stars.

Why?
(stops on the circles)

We'll see if it stops on the other boxes which are heavier.

You're sure? Is there another proof?

- It's not weight.
It's not a rigorous proof because it doesn't come to the perpendicular.
Weight could have an effect only if it causes tilting.

Do you have any other evidence, just using the boxes?

I put two boxes, one on top of the other, and if it doesn't stop there, then weight is not important.

And colour is important?

No, you can see that by changing the place of the boxes.

What do you think about your magnet hypothesis?
And what could it be?

I don't believe that that's it.

The position under the pointer. No, it's not that, it would be necessary also that the base slops (the child put the magnets on green).

Why do you do that?

In order to see the relationships between the boxes themselves
We'll see if it is the pointer.

(green)
What does that proves it with regard to the pointer?

- Then it's the box.
If it was the pointer, it would have come back to the blue.

Figure 8.3. Page of our English translation of the French *procès-verbal* for Gou. Underlined text indicates the parts included in *GLT*.

Given the absence of a comprehensive treatise on the Genevan method and the editing out of large portions of the crucial interactions, it is easy to see how the investigatory strategies adopted by researchers contributing to the secondary Piagetian literature were limited by a *reactive* principle in contrast with the *proactive* and highly collaborative investigative procedures of the Genevan *méthode* especially as evidenced in these examples of complete transcripts. Elsewhere, children were obliged to respond to the problems posed by the investigator, whereas the original investigations involved both child and investigator working together, planning ahead so that no opportunity for original discovery by either was overlooked. Although some might claim to have been able to interpolate these features into the published Genevan research accounts, the detail and style of the material omitted from those accounts has come as a surprise to a number of well-informed Piagetians.

The point at issue here is not whether the published Gou protocol is adequate to illustrate aspects of Piaget's theory or whether the evidence it contained is sufficient for Piaget's claims on it (see Bond & Jackson, 1991, for a defense of Piaget's use of the Gou protocol). What is essential to this chapter on Piaget's method is that this analysis of the Gou protocol provides substance to our claim that in the absence of specific Genevan training in the procedure, the published accounts of the implementation of the Piagetian data collection technique do not provide adequate insight into the Genevan *méthode*. Is it merely that the interactive, proactive nature of the method is not sufficiently emphasized, leading to general misunderstanding? Indeed, it would be difficult to deny the claim that the published accounts are routinely misleading. Certainly, there are not sufficient details of procedures or questions to allow for the successful replication of the tasks typical of the Piagetian *oeuvre* by the vast groups of developmental psychologists who were genuinely interested in Piaget's work. Although Anglophones might be justly criticized for not having understood Piaget's data collection method, the cryptic investigatory accounts in the Genevan literature have contributed very little to an enlightened understanding of the Piagetian method of data collection.

Although Piaget is routinely regarded by students and their professors around the world as a child psychologist, it is now clear to us that he sought to answer long-standing epistemological questions (Smith, 1993), which he addressed by collecting psychological evidence. Vonèche and Vidal (1985) brought the impact Piaget actually had (as a child psychologist) into sharp contrast against the impact he always wanted to have (as philosopher/epistemologist). Following this distinctly psychological approach, our access to the original reports of the original *GLT*

TABLE 8.1. *Genevan Subjects by Age and Stage*

Age	Report of Claude Penard					LELA/GLT Chapter 6					LELA/GLT			
	I	IIA	IIB	IIIA/B	N	I	IIA	IIB	IIIA/B	N	<III	IIIA	IIIB	N
<6,0	1				1									
6,0	2				2	1				1				
6,6		1			1	1				1				
7,0	4				4	1				1	8			8
7,6	1				1						17			17
8,0		2			2	2				2	13			13
8,6		1			1						6			6
9,0		1	1		2	1				1	11			11
9,6		4	2		6	2				2	12			12
10,0		1	3		4	1				1	13			13
10,6			4		4		2			2	11	2		13
11,0		1	4		5						4	3		7
11,6		1	2	1	4			1		1	5	6		11
12,0											1	7		8
12,6			1		1						1	16	1	18
13,0			1	2	3							8	3	11
13,6				3	3							4	3	7
14,0												5	9	14
14,6								1		1		3	8	11
15,0													7	7
15,6													5	5
N	8	12	18	6	44	2	7	3	1	13	102	54	36	192

IIA/B: Early/mature concrete operations; IIIA/B: Early/mature formal operations.

investigations yielded the data we used to construct tables of the incidence of the various types of thinking among the samples of Genevan schoolchildren. If it took two-and-a-half pages of interview to produce a half-page published Gou protocol, what data were used for the whole chapter? We used the annual report by Mlle. Claude Penard (n.d.) of the sample (*n* = 45) of children aged from 5;8 to 13;11 years who attempted to solve the "invisible magnetism" problem in 1948. We will attempt to elucidate the links between Piaget's epistemological analyses and the psychological research of Inhelder and her team, which provided the data.

Table 8.1 is constructed to show the extent of the original adolescence research and the potential representativeness of the cases eventually published in *GLT*. The set on the right of the table (adapted from Reuchlin, 1964) shows the ages and stage allocations of all cases (*N* = 192) actually reported in *GLT*. The left-hand set classifies the Penard magnetism sample (*N* = 44) according to age and stage. The center set provides details for those exemplar cases (*N* = 13) drawn from

Penard's sample that provide the data for Piaget's analysis in chapter 6 of *GLT*. Penard's sample (age 6 years to 13 years, 6 months) shows that the Genevans were monitoring the *transition* between the less complete forms of childhood problem solving to the more complete forms of thought available to the adolescent – not just adolescent thinking per se.

Piaget's groundbreaking research was, in its essence, pure discovery: "But our problem was quite different: it was concerned, by contrast, with seeking to find the secrets of thinking which we did not know in advance" (Piaget & Inhelder, 1961, p. xii, our translation). The Genevan *méthode* played a crucial role in this discovery process. However, the replications of these investigations – especially outside the European setting – were conceptualized as a form of testing Piaget's ideas: Did they apply to other children? In other places? When investigated by other researchers? And, of course, the most trivial of tests: Did the ages for the stages match across investigations? Of course, such attempts at reproducibility are at the heart of Western scientific method where the crucial element is the ability of any investigation to produce commensurate results when replicated by another investigator working independently. It is then reasonable to expect that the published results of the Genevan researchers would be evaluated by others by reproducing the original investigations. Here lie the twin problems for secondary Piagetian research. First, the original investigative descriptions focus on the child's intellectual competence – not on the procedures required to uncover them. Second, for researchers of Piaget's ideas in the Anglo-American research tradition, a key part of data collection and analysis procedures was the application of quantitative analytical procedures to what Piaget had insisted was best discovered and described qualitatively.

PIAGET MEETS PSYCHOMETRICS

Piaget is routinely regarded as having very little knowledge of, and even less interest in, psychometrics. Many suggest that Piaget regarded the role of quantifying cognitive development as another "American question." In an interesting review of the book *Measurement and Piaget* (Green, Ford, & Flamer, 1971) devoted to the proceedings of a conference in 1969, Wohlwill summarized rather succinctly the lack of interest by Piagetians in nomothetic aspects of cognitive development in his title "And Never the Twain Did Meet." He then painted a picture of the archetypal Piaget "deliberately relegating the problems of 'psychometricizing' Piagetian tasks and data to a province beyond his concern, on the grounds that he has 'no interest whatever in the individual,'" and described other developmentalists as "quite ready to let the topic

TABLE 8.2. *Percentage of Subjects Solving (with Proof) the Combination of Liquids Task (Number of Subjects Are Given in Parentheses)*

Ages	12	13	14	15	16
Elementary school	7.1 (42)	8.2 (49)	11.6 (43)	50 (12)	
Secondary school	10 (10)	12.5 (8)	18.8 (16)	42.1 (19)	66.6 (19)

of measurement lie in the limbo to which Le Patron had relegated it" (Wohlwill, 1972, pp. 334–335). This has long been the received view of Piaget's attitude to psychometrics and can be readily supported by references to Piaget's own words on the matter (after Bond, 1995a, 1995b). Indeed, the use of quantitative techniques in the Genevan research was very limited, almost naïve: A small number of his texts from the middle period (1940–1960s) contain quantitative indices such as very basic summary tables with percentages (see Table 8.2) and rarely more. However, these inclusions and his assertions about variations in research agendas in Geneva suggest that Piaget wavered a little on the need to respond to issues raised by his critics about the role of quantification. He described (e.g., 1962) a new role for "all sorts of controls, both statistical and non-verbal," claimed "Dr B. Inhelder has made use of the longitudinal method," and refers to Laurendeau and Pinard (1962; see also Laurendeau & Pinard, 1968, 1970), which "both supports the generality of my early results and makes a trenchant methodological criticism of my early critics." In other places, he specifically eschewed the use of quantitative methods. The infamous quote from the number book summarizes his views nicely: "Statistical precision could no doubt easily be obtained, but at the cost of no longer knowing exactly what was being measured" (Piaget & Szeminska, 1941/1952, p. 193). This confirms Piaget's preoccupation with epistemological rather than psychometric issues.

However, wider reading of the research conducted under Genevan auspices provides a far more detailed and interesting account. It reveals that although psychologists elsewhere were addressing the problems inherent in applying quantitative principles to the investigation of Piagetian theory, considerable progress was already being made in Geneva by Nassefat (1963), Uzan (1978), and in France by Longeot (1967, 1978). Edelstein and Schroeder (2000, p. 840) later reflected, "These analyses (i.e., of individual differences in Francophone post-Piagetian research) are viewed as preoccupied by the 'American question' of measurement and method, instead of attempting a theoretical account of the issues raised by intraindividual and interindividual variability in development."

REPLICATIONS OF THE GENEVAN MÉTHODE

In the United Kingdom, Lovell (1961; Lovell & Shields, 1967) reported on 200 subjects (8 years to adulthood) tested on a total of ten of the problems described in *GLT*. Replications in Australia (Dale, 1970; chemical combinations task, and Somerville, 1974; pendulum) and in the United States (Lawson, 1979, p. 67; chemicals, rods, and balance tasks) provided psychometric support for the Inhelder and Piaget (1955/1958) accounts for those tasks with any differences concerned mainly with quantitative detail (see also Bond, 1998). These results remain a remarkable testament to the transportability of Genevan epistemology into American, British, and Australian psychological research, using the original tasks analyzed by quantitative rather than qualitative methods. One important conclusion, however, was that the Genevan *méthode* technique of individual interview was too demanding on time, skills, and resources to allow the sort of grand-scale replication studies needed for a close examination of Piaget's claims (e.g., those in *GLT* or in any of his major empirical works). But already we leave ourselves open to the charge that we are counting the wrong thing: Note previously that the *intellectual operation* – not the human child – was Piaget's unit of analysis (see Jackson, 1987). It can then be argued that Piaget and his colleagues, for instance in *GLT*, worked with possibly tens of thousands of those things we should all acknowledge as "data," and the tedious critical objection commonly leveled at the Genevans on account of their "thin" and "inadequate" data could accordingly be dismissed in a couple of sentences.

MOVING TO STANDARDIZATION
AND QUANTITATIVE ANALYSES

Given that large-scale testing is impossible without the development of suitable group-testing instruments that would replicate the original Genevan tasks as faithfully as possible, Shayer and his CSMS (Concepts in Secondary Mathematics and Science project team at Chelsea (now King's) College in the United Kingdom (Shayer, Küchemann, & Wylam, 1976; Shayer & Wharry, 1974; Shayer & Wylam, 1978) set to work on the development of their Piagetian Reasoning Tasks (*PRTs*). Shayer's conclusion was that after a fine-grained statistical analysis of seven Piagetian Reasoning Tasks and a total sample well in excess of 14,000, "Not one of the seven Tasks investigated in detail gives any grounds for questioning the scientific integrity of the work reported by Piaget" (Shayer & Wylam, 1978, p. 3); recall that *GLT* used behavioral descriptions of about 200 subjects from a total sample of 1,500 to provide Piaget's reported sample of behaviors). Gerald Noelting (developer of the chemicals experiment for chapter 4 *GLT*) subsequently developed three more original tasks to reveal the use of formal operational schemata of proportions, combinatorial thinking, and propositional logic. Those results asserted the structural integrity of his tasks and revealed evidence of unequivocal stage-like developmental changes in the data (Noelting, Rousseau, & Coudé, 1996; Noelting, Coude, Rousseau, Bond, & Brunel, 2000). Studies into claims about Piagetian phenomena, including their very existense, have been more – or less – successful in corroborating key aspects of Genevan genetic epistemology, and the two preceding exemplars provide powerful supportive evidence for the generalizability and transfer of key constructs. So, how does a scientific community of scholars resolve the disparity between this evidence and the "death by a thousand cuts" that Piaget's work has suffered at the hands of naysayers? Piaget's *méthode* of discovery is, obviously, not essential for investigating Piagetian theory. Our suggestion is that, in an absence of a broader understanding of Piagetian epistemology, including the *méthode* by which the original data were captured, investigations into Piaget's psychology will remain only more – or less – successful. Of course, Noelting had insider information about how the Genevans conducted their research. And Shayer? Perhaps Shayer saw more than others did as he read *GLT* one page at a time, line by line with Piaget's (1947) *Traité de Logique* on one side and Wittgenstein's *Tractatus* on the other.

The Methodological Tension and Its Modern Resolution

From the orientation of Anglophone critics, the Genevan *méthode* was seen to be open to manipulation of the investigator (thereby lacking both objectivity and replicability) and incapable of providing quantitative data: "results obtained by such a flexible procedure as the *'méthode clinique'* do not lend themselves to statistical treatment" (Wallace, 1965, p. 58). Genevan doctoral candidate Nassefat developed a *"méthode d'interrogatoire standardisé,"* admitting that the Genevan *méthode* technique gave more information than did his standardized method but at the expense of not being able to quantify the ensuing information (Nassefat, 1963, pp. 30–31), echoing Piaget's earlier preference for qualitative understanding of cognitive development rather than statistical summaries of children's task performances.

Two apparently unfinished (unreported) projects were already part of the Genevan scheme of things: The statistical standardization of certain tasks into a developmental scale (Inhelder with Bang) and a longitudinal study of cognitive development (Inhelder with Noelting) are worthy of particular note because of their sheer size and scope. Inhelder (1963) reported, "[t]he need for widely applicable diagnostic instruments and the need to make the instruments available led us to undertake, with Vinh-Bang, the attempt to standardize the interrogation procedures and to evaluate the results by statistical methods capable of constituting a tableau of developmental results which could be related into an operational scale" (p. 314). "The experiments that revealed the most about operativity were then set up as tests, standardized and statistically evaluated by Vinh-Bang" to develop "a diagnostic instrument in the form of a genetic scale . . . on which our colleague Vinh-Bang has been working for about ten years . . . " (p. 308). Preliminary results from these investigations appear in a number of places in the Genevan literature; the analysis revealed in Table 8.2 shows rates for complete success (with proof) – presumably level IIIB (mature formal operations) – for Noelting's chemical combinations problem (Piaget & Inhelder, 1963/1969, p. 155/p. 191).

Inhelder (1963, p. 317) continued,

> "But this framework is not sufficient for diagnostic applications because it is also necessary to take into account all types of nuances which can be brought out only through a rather thorough longitudinal study. In this context let us note research which we have carried out with G. Noelting with groups of children between four and fifteen years of age, following their evolution at regular intervals during a period of five years. These observations permitted us to distinguish a succession of transitory behaviour within each of the behavior classes and to understand the developmental relationships among them . . . ".[5]

Video of selected Noelting interviews are part of a DVD set produced in Geneva (Ducret, Grzeskowiak, & Perruchoud, 1996). Although we have seen – with our own eyes – the data sheets for each of these projects in the hands of the respective principal investigators, to our knowledge no substantial quantitative analyses have actually been undertaken.

MODERN MEASUREMENT THEORY MEETS PIAGET'S METHOD

Although Rasch measurement[6] has been applied to numerous Piagetian-based research projects (e.g., Bond & Fox, 2007; Gray & Fox, 1996, 1997), the focus in this chapter is explicitly on the use of modern measurement principles to data collected using the Genevan *méthode*. Bunting

(Bond & Bunting, 1995; Stafford, 2004) prepared a set of descriptive performance criteria extracted directly from the content of chapter 4 in *GLT* (pp. 67–79). Subsequently, 58 Genevan *méthode* protocols were collected, recording the attempts of a sample of Australian adolescents to solve the pendulum problem from *GLT*, and the highly detailed performance criteria were used to score quantitatively each of the protocols. The results of partial credit analysis, one of the family of Rasch measurement models, provided a fine-grained description of these abilities not previously countenanced under qualitative or quantitative analytical techniques. The results substantiated central constructs of Piagetian theory at the formal operational stage but also indicated where the *GLT* descriptions do not entirely match with the quantitative interpretations. As a result, two modifications were suggested as being worthy of consideration and further investigation: the inclusion of a timing device and the elimination of the impetus variable. Moreover, a second analysis (Stafford, 2004) included in the original research report revealed that the Genevan *méthode* and the *PRTIII* versions of the pendulum problem (the latter taken from Shayer's standardization battery) were measuring the identical underlying trait, although, not surprisingly, the Genevan *méthode* was more sensitive than the *PRTIII* at eliciting displays of formal operational thinking on the pendulum problem.

The results of a number of diverse applications of the Genevan *méthode* of qualitative data collection (e.g., various conservations, Drake, 1998; Bond, 2003; number concepts, Grobecker & Bond, 1999; conservation of area, Bond & Parkinson, 2009; moral judgments, Dawson, 2000; Bond & Fox, 2007) matched with modern psychometric techniques have yielded remarkable corroborations of Piagetian developmental theory.

EVALUATION: SHUTTING THE STABLE DOOR AFTER THE HORSE HAS BOLTED?

The popular history version of Piagetian theory might be caricaturized thus: Piaget's work in Geneva first attracted the attention of influential Americans immediately after the 1939–1945 conflagration in Europe, Africa, and the Pacific – as a possible basis for education that would help prevent the rebirth of some forms of political totalitarianism. But it was during the post-Sputnik era (1957+) that Piaget's ideas became almost unquestionably popular in the United States. The reporting of Piagetian-informed research filled volumes of journals such as *Science Education* and *Journal of Research in Science Teaching* (see Chapter 17 for a more thorough review). Three decades later revealed that the Piagetian zenith was quite past and his theory had fallen from educational fashion as quickly as it had become the center attraction. In particular, although early investigations showed promising results, Piaget's theory, and his investigatory methods, it seemed, did not stand up to the statistical rigor that remains a central tenet of Anglo-American empiricism. One might be given to wonder what Piaget might have said about the quantitative results adduced in this chapter in defense of his key ideas. Although it is quite likely that he could have been interested enough in the metrical/quantitative results, it is more likely that he could regard his *méthode critique* evidence as compelling in its own right and in need of no other justification. Certainly the Genevan *méthode* fell to the wayside, accused of three fatal flaws: invalid in its own right and neither suitable for large-scale administration nor amenable to the style of quantification required in that research environment.

To provide an adequate evaluation of the Genevan *méthode* technique, we can now recognize the methodological framework within which Inhelder and Piaget were operating – a framework best described as rationalist, genetic, and hermeneutic. The rationalist orientation is most clearly illustrated by the privileged role of each child's own explanations of the experiments. Does any other school of psychology represent so much of its evidence so clearly in the actual words of children? The dialectical character of transcript after transcript reflects the interactive, exploratory pattern of dialogue involving a competent and willingly collaborative participant. Piaget's subjects are not *tested* in any sense that an empiricist would recognize: Each subject's individual response sets up the conditions for an integrated sequence of reciprocal exchanges between an active, competent interviewee and a tacitly acknowledged authoritative interviewer. The genetic nature of the Genevan *oeuvre* is revealed in the central role that *transition* from less sophisticated to more sophisticated cognitive states plays in the Piagetian accounts. Its hermeneutic characteristics are reflected in the published accounts of the protocols where the experimental chapters consist of passages of edited empirical transcripts sequenced alternately with passages of interpretive analysis (see Bond & Jackson, 1991).

At last there are a considerable number of Anglophone authors who write authoritatively of Piaget's *oeuvre* from Piaget's own philosophical perspective. It has been easy to blame Piaget's critics for trying to assimilate the Genevan approach to their own methods rather than to accommodate their quotidian approaches to the demands of a more Kantian view of knowledge and method, even if Piaget's philosophy was there to encounter in some form in almost every published text. Although access to the rest of the Genevan research agenda (published mostly in

French) might have left us better informed about philosophy and results, the lesson from this chapter is that there was precious little written in any language about how to implement the Genevan *méthode*.

In Bentzen's (2004) well-adopted text, *Seeing Young Children: A Guide to Observing and Recording Behavior*, Piaget's tasks are used in the manner predicted in the title: for observing children and recording their behavior; nothing of our version of the Genevan *méthode* is found in there. Herbert Ginsburg's *Entering the Child's Mind* (1997) provides the only generally accessible account of the Genevan *méthode* and its application to psychology and education: "Piaget's method was not 'unscientific'; rather, it was based on a distinctive theoretical approach" (Ginsburg, 1997). Perhaps it is because he sees Piaget as a genetic epistemologist, rather than merely a developmental psychologist, that Ginsburg claimed that the "clinical interview" is a lasting contribution to a field still dominated by the use of severely limited standardized tests: "In recent years, as understanding of Piaget's work has deepened, the tide has changed and interview methods of one kind or another are considered respectable methods" (Ginsburg, Klein, & Starkey, 1998, p. 408). Ginsburg raised an interesting issue for researchers, thus: "The paradox then is that to be truly 'open,' the interviewer's mind must be prepared. The open mind cannot be an empty mind." "And, as Piaget put it, novice interviewers often 'are not on the look-out for anything, in which case, to be sure, they will never find anything' (Piaget, 1976a, p. 9)" (Ginsburg, 1997, p. 120).

However sensitive Ginsburg's treatise is to the details of implementing Piaget's method, he does very little to illuminate the philosophical and epistemological considerations that drove the Genevan research agenda. Ginsburg et al. noted elsewhere (p. 460 fn.) that educators in the United States seem to have a distaste for the word "clinical" with its connotation of pathology; so, apparently, they substituted words like "flexible" or "informal." Both Duveen (2000) and Mayer (2005) provided well-grounded accounts of Piagetian research and of the development of the Genevan *méthode*. Smith (1993, 2002) provided the epistemological account that seems to have been excised as irrelevant to Ginsburg's audience; Smith's (2002) chapter on "Methods" is focused on just these issues. Ginsburg tells us what to do; Smith tells us why. In contrast, poorly implemented replications of the Genevan *méthode* (e.g., Bynum, Weitz, & Thomas, 1972; Weitz, 1971; Weitz, Bynum, Thomas, & Steger, 1973) and philosophically naïve criticisms of it (e.g., Siegal, 1991, 1999a, 1999b) seem to have negative impacts far beyond what any informed view might expect (see Bond & Jackson, 1991, on Bynum et al.; see Lourenço & Machado, 1996 and Smith, 1999 on Siegal).

The evidence from this chapter reveals that solidly grounded formal operational investigations using the Genevan *méthode*, extensions of it, standardizations of it, and new tests based on it, show remarkable psychometric properties but do not show up at all in recent, apparently authoritative accounts of Piaget's work (see Bond & Tryphon, 2007). Piaget's *méthode* was unfashionable when his theory was in fashion; now, when investigative methods are far more inclusive, Piaget's ideas are regarded as passé. If the fashion of educational and psychological thought is so fickle, is there ever really a chance that it could adopt, or even consider, the term "critical method" introduced by Piaget in his foreword to the (French) third edition of *Judgment and Reasoning* in 1947 (Smith, 1993, pp. 56–60)? This latter term would acknowledge both the method's philosophical underpinnings and rigor, as well as Inhelder's distinctive contribution to this aspect of the Genevan method.

NOTES

1. This is the term used by Piaget; it refers to the books published at the end of the 19th century where the authors described the development of one single child (e.g., Bühler [1918]; Preyer [1882]; Stern [1914]). See also Baldwin (1894); Wallace, Franklin, & Keegan (1994).

2. *Procès-verbal* (see Figure 8.2) and *protocole* are used to indicate the Genevan interview transcripts. In English the terms protocol or transcript are used. The point here is that the published versions have been edited in ways that conceal the application of the Genevan *méthode* in practice.

3. The French *assistant* carries much more of a collegial connotation than does the English term assistant.

4. In this task, the children are asked to discover the principle underlying the consistent stopping behavior of a metal needle as it is spun on a segmented colored disc. Although the force of the push, tilting of the disc, distance and weight of boxes *etc.* might be considered, concealed magnets in one pair of boxes (but not a magnetized needle) determine the stopping point.

5. When it became time to secure funding for Piaget's International Centre for Genetic Epistemology, Vinh Bang, who worked with Piaget, stayed, whereas Noelting's position disappeared (he worked with Inhelder). Noelting consequently went to Quebec.

6. Rasch measurement is a branch of modern Item Response Theory dedicated to the construction of test scales exhibiting interval-level measurement properties. It is now widely used in educational and psychological testing (see Bond & Fox, 2007, for an introduction) and, for example, underlies the large international comparisons of student achievement conducted by OECD-PISA.

REFERENCES

Baldwin, J. M. (1894). *Mental development in the child and the race*. New York: Macmillan.

Bang, V. (1966). La méthode clinique et la recherche en psychologie de l'enfant. In *Psychologie et épistémologie génétiques* (pp. 67–81). Paris: Dunod.

Baumgarten, F. (1927). Rezension von: Piaget (1924) Le jugement et le raisonnement chez l'enfant. *Zeitschrift für Angewandte Psychologie, 28*, 537–542.

Bentzen, W. R. (2004). *Seeing young children: A guide to observing and recording behavior*. New York: Thompson.

Bond, T. G. (1994). Epistemic subject versus quotidien subject: The adolescent research of Inhelder & Piaget. *Education Section Review* (of the British Psychological Society), *18*, 9–14.

Bond, T. G. (1995a). Piaget and measurement I: The Twain really do meet. *Archives de Psychologie, 63*, 71–87.

Bond, T. G. (1995b). Piaget and measurement II: Empirical validation of the Piagetian model. *Archives de Psychologie, 63*, 155–185.

Bond, T. G. (1998). Fifty years of formal operational research: The empirical evidence. *Archives de Psychologie, 66*, 217–234.

Bond, T. G. (2001). Building a theory of formal operational thinking: Inhelder's psychology meets Piaget's epistemology. In A. Tryphon & J. Vonèche (Eds.), *Working with Piaget: Essays in honour of Bärbel Inhelder* (pp. 65–83). London: Psychology Press.

Bond, T. G. (2003). Relationships between cognitive development and school achievement: A Rasch measurement approach. In R. F. Waugh (Ed.), *On the forefront of educational psychology* (pp. 37–46). New York: Nova Science Publishers.

Bond, T. G., & Bunting, E. (1995). Piaget and measurement III: Reassessing the "méthode clinique." *Archives de Psychologie, 63*, 231–255.

Bond, T. G., & Fox, C. M. (2007). *Applying the Rasch model: Fundamental measurement in the human sciences* (2nd ed.). Mahwah, NJ: Erlbaum.

Bond, T. G., & Jackson, I. A. R. (1991). The Gou protocol revisited: A Piagetian conceptualization of critique. *Archives de Psychologie, 59*, 31–53. (Reprinted in L. Smith [1991], *Piaget: Critical assessments*). London: Routledge & Kegan Paul.

Bond, T. G., & Parkinson, K. (2009). Children's understanding of area concepts: Development, curriculum and educational achievement. To appear in M. Wilson, G. Engelhard, & M. Garner (Eds.), *Advances in Rasch measurement* (Vol. 1). Maple Grove, MN: JAM Press.

Bond, T., & Tryphon, A. (2007). Piaget's legacy as reflected in *The handbook of child psychology* (1998 edition). Published online at http://www.piaget .org/news/docs/Bond-Tryphon-2007.pdf.

Brainerd, C. J. (1973). Judgments and explanations as criteria for the presence of cognitive structures. *Psychological Bulletin, 79*, 172–179.

Bühler, K. (1918). *Die geistige Entwicklung des Kindes* (The mental development of the child). Jena: Gustav Fischer.

Bynum, T. W., Weitz, L. J., & Thomas, J. A. (1972). Truth-functional logic in formal operational thinking: Inhelder and Piaget's evidence. *Developmental Psychology, 7*, 129–132.

Dale, L. G. (1970). The growth of systemic thinking: Replication and analysis of Piaget's first chemical experiment. *Australian Journal of Psychology, 22*, 277–286.

Dawson, T. L. (2000). Moral reasoning and evaluative reasoning about the good life. *Journal of Applied Measurement, 1*, 346–371.

Drake, C. (1998). *Judgments versus justifications in Piagetian research: On empirical contribution to a philosophical argument*. Unpublished honours thesis, James Cook University, Townsville, Queensland, Australia.

Droz, R., Berthoud, S., Calpini, J.-C., Dällenbach, J.-F., & Michiels, M. P. (1976). Méthode expérimentale – méthode clinique. *Revue Européenne des Sciences Sociales, 14*, 305–324.

Ducret, J.-J. (1990). *Jean Piaget*. Neuchâtel: Delachaux et Niestlé.

Ducret, J.-J., Grzeskowiak, M., & Perruchoud, A. (Eds.). (1996). *Jean Piaget. Cheminements dans l'oeuvre scientifique*. Geneva: FPSE & SRED. (Faculty of Psychology and Educational Sciences and Educational Sciences Service.)

Duveen, G. (2000). Piaget ethnographer. *Social Science Information, 39*, 79–97.

Edelstein, W., & Schroeder, E. (2000). Full house or Pandora's box? The treatment of variability in post-Piagetian research. *Child Development, 71*, 840–842.

Flavell, J. (1963). *The developmental psychology of Jean Piaget*. Princeton, NJ: Van Nostrand.

Ginsburg, H. P. (1997). *Entering the child's mind. The clinical interview in psychological research and practice*. Cambridge, MA: Cambridge University Press.

Ginsburg, H. P., Klein, A., & Starkey, P. (1998). The development of children's mathematical reasoning: Connecting research with practice. In W. Damon (Ed.), *Handbook of child psychology, Vol. 4: Child psychology in practice* (5th ed., pp. 401–478). New York: Wiley.

Gray, W., & Fox, C. (1996). *Rasch scaling of a set of Piagetian-based written problems representing different forms of thought and different logical operations*. Paper presented at the 16th Annual Symposium of the Jean Piaget Society, Philadelphia.

Gray, W., & Fox, C. (1997). *Use of Piagetian theory to investigate misfitting persons and misfitting items according to Rasch analysis*. Paper presented at the Annual Meeting of the American Educational Research Association, Chicago.

Green, D. R., Ford, M. P., & Flamer, G. B. (Eds.). (1971). *Measurement and Piaget*. New York: McGraw-Hill.

Grobecker, B., & Bond, T. (1999). Children's construction of addition. *Archives de Psychologie, 67*, 95–122.

Inhelder, B. (1936). Observations sur le principle de conservation dans la physique de l'enfant. *Cahiers de la Pédagogie Expérimentale et de Psychologie de L'enfant, 9*, 1–16.

Inhelder, B. (1962). Some aspects of Piaget's approach to cognition. *Monographs of the Society for Research in Child Development, 27*(2), 19–40.

Inhelder, B. (1963). Afterword. In B. Inhelder (Ed.), *The diagnosis of reasoning in the mentally retarded* (pp. 305–331). New York: John Day Company.

Inhelder, B. (1989). Autobiography. In G. Lindzey (Ed.), *History of psychology in autobiography* (Vol. 8, pp. 208–243). Stanford, CA: Stanford University Press.

Inhelder, B. (2001). The experimental approaches of children and adolescents. In A. Tryphon & J. Vonèche (Eds.), *Working with Piaget: Essays in honour of Bärbel Inhelder* (pp. 193–209). London: Psychology Press. (Original work published in 1954)

Inhelder, B., & Piaget, J. (1958). *The growth of logical thinking from childhood to adolescence*. London: Routledge & Kegan Paul. (Original work published in 1955)

Isaacs, S. (1930). *Intellectual growth in young children*. London: Routledge & Sons.

Jackson, I. (1987). On situating Piaget's subject: A triangulation based on Kant, structuralism, and biology. *Philosophy of the Social Sciences, 17*, 471–486.

Laurendeau, M., & Pinard, A. (1962). *La pensée causale*. Paris: PUF.

Laurendeau, M., & Pinard, A. (1968). *Les premieres notions spatiales de l'enfant: Examen des hypotheses de Jean Piaget*. Paris: Delachaux & Niestle.

Laurendeau, M., & Pinard, A. (1970). *The development of the concept of space in the child*. New York: International Universities Press.

Lawson, A. E. (1979). Relationships among performances on group administrated items on formal reasoning. *Perceptual and Motor Skills, 48*, 71–78.

Longeot, F. (1967). *Psychologie differentielle et theorie opératoire de l'intelligence*. These: Université de Paris.

Longeot, F. (1978). *Les stades opératoires de Piaget et les facteurs de l'intelligence*. Grenoble: PUG.

Lourenço, O., & Machado, A. (1996). In defense of Piaget's theory: A reply to 10 common criticisms. *Psychological Review, 103*, 143–164.

Lovell, K. (1961). A follow-up study of Inhelder and Piaget's *The growth of logical thinking*. *British Journal of Psychology, 52*, 142–153.

Lovell, K., & Shields, J. B. (1967). Some aspects of a study of the gifted child. *British Journal of Educational Psychology, 37*, 201–208.

Mayer, S. J. (2005). The early evolution of Jean Piaget's clinical method. *History of Psychology, 8*, 362–382.

Nassefat, M. (1963). *Etude quantitative sur l'évolution des opérations intellectuelles: le passage des opérations concrètes aux opérations formelles*. Neuchâtel: Delachaux & Niestle.

Noelting, G., Coude, G., Rousseau, J. P., Bond, T., & Brunel, M.-L. (2000). Can qualitative stage characteristics be revealed quantitatively? *Archives de Psychologie, 68*, 259–275.

Noelting, G., Rousseau, J.-P., & Coudé, G. (1996). *Operatory stages as a composition of relations and the onset of formal operations*. Paper presented at the 26th Annual Symposium of the Jean Piaget Society, Philadelphia.

Penard, C. (n.d.). *Rapport – expérience des aimants*. Unpublished report, Archives Jean Piaget.

Piaget, J. (1925a). Psychologie et critique de la connaissance. *Archives de Psychologie, 19*, 193–220.

Piaget, J. (1925b). La représentation du monde chez l'enfant. *Revue Théologique et de Philosophie, 13*, 191–214.

Piaget, J. (1926). *The language and thought of the child.* Neuchâtel; London: Kegan Paul Trench Trubner. (Original work published in 1923)

Piaget, J. (1928). *Judgment and reasoning in the child.* London: Kegan Paul Trench Trubner. (Original work published in 1924)

Piaget, J. (1929). *The child's conception of the world.* London: Kegan Paul Trench Trubner. (Original work published in 1926)

Piaget, J. (1930). *The child's conception of physical causality.* London: Kegan Paul Trench Trubner. (Original work published in 1927)

Piaget, J. (1931). Le développement intellectuel chez les jeunes enfants. *Mind, 40*, 137–160.

Piaget, J. (1932). *The moral judgment of the child.* London: Kegan Paul Trench Trubner. (Original work published in 1932)

Piaget, J. (1947). Avant-propos de la Troisième Edition. In J. Piaget, *Le Jugement et le raisonnement chez l'enfant* (pp. 9–10) (3rd ed.). Neuchâtel: Delachaux et Niestlé.

Piaget, J. (1952). *The origins of intelligence in children.* New York, NY: International Universities Press. (Original work published in 1936)

Piaget, J. (1952). *The child's conception of number.* London: Routledge and Kegan Paul. (Original work published with A. Szeminska, 1941)

Piaget, J. (1952). Autobiography. In E. G. Boring, H. S. Langfeld, H. Werner, & R. M. Yerkes (Eds.), *History of psychology in autobiography* (Vol. 4, pp. 237–256). Worcester, MA: Clark University Press.

Piaget, J. & Inhelder, B. (1961). *Introduction à la séconde édition. Le développement des quantités physiques chez l'enfant* (2nd ed.). Neuchatel: Delachaux et Niestlé.

Piaget, J. & Inhelder, B. (1969). Intellectual operations and their development. In P. Fraisse, & J. Piaget (Eds.), *Experimental psychology: Its scope and method, Vol. VII Intelligence* (pp. 147–203). London: Routledge and Kegan Paul. (Original work published in 1963)

Piaget, J., & Rosello, P. (1922). Notes sur les types de description d'images chez l'enfant. *Archives de Psychologie, 18*, 208–223.

Preyer, W. (1882). *Die seele des kindes* (The mind of the child). Leipzig: Grieben.

Reuchlin, M. (1964). L'intelligence: Conception génétique opératoire et conception factorielle. *Revue Suisse de Psychologie Pure et Appliquée, 23*, 113–134.

Shayer, M., Küchemann, D. E., & Wylam, H. (1976). The distribution of Piagetian stages of thinking in British middle and secondary school children. *British Journal of Educational Psychology, 46*, 164–173.

Shayer, M., & Wharry, D. (1974). Piaget in the classroom Part 1: Testing a whole class at the same time. *School Science Review, 192*, 447–458.

Shayer, M., & Wylam, H. (1978). The distribution of Piagetian stages of thinking in British middle and secondary school children: 11–14/16 year olds and sex differentials. *British Journal of Educational Psychology, 48*, 62–70.

Siegal, M. (1991). *Knowing children: Experiments in conversation and cognition.* Hove: Erlbaum.

Siegal, M. (1999a). Language and thought: The fundamental significance of conversational awareness for cognitive development. *Developmental Science, 2*, 1–14.

Siegal, M. (1999b). Beyond methodology: Frequently asked questions on the significance of conversation for development. *Developmental Science, 2*, 29–34.

Smith, L. (Ed.). (1992). *Jean Piaget: Critical assessments*. London: Routledge.

Smith, L. (1993). *Necessary knowledge. Piagetian perspectives on constructivism*. Hove: Erlbaum.

Smith, L. (1999). Necessary knowledge in number conservation. *Developmental Science, 2*, 23–27.

Smith, L. (2002). *Reasoning by mathematical induction in children's arithmetic*. Oxford: Elsevier Pergamon Press.

Somerville, S. C. (1974). The pendulum problem: Patterns of performance defining developmental stages. *British Journal of Educational Psychology, 44*, 266–281.

Stafford, E. (2004). What the pendulum can tell educators about children's scientific reasoning. *Science & Education, 13*, 757–790.

Stern, W. (1914). *Psychologie der frühen kindheit* (Psychology of early childhood). Leipzig: Quelle & Meyer.

Tryphon, A. (2004). De l'expérience à la publication: Le cas de Jean Piaget. *Bulletin de Psychologie, 57*, 595–610.

Uzan, S. (1978). *Le raissonnement logico-mathematique d'adolescents en situation scolaire et d'apprentis en milieu professionnel*. Thèse: Université de Geneve.

Vonèche, J., & Vidal, F. (1985). Jean Piaget and the child psychologist. *Synthèse, 65*, 121–138.

Wallace, J. G. (1965). *Concept growth and the education of the child*. Slough: National Foundation for Educational Research.

Wallace, D. B., Franklin, M. B., & Keegan, R. T. (1994). The observing eye. A century of baby diaries. *Human Development, 37*, 1–29.

Weitz, L. J. (1971). *A developmental and logical analysis of Piaget's sixteen binary operations*. Ann Arbor, MI: University Microfilms.

Weitz, L. J., Bynum, T. W., Thomas, J. A., & Steger, J. A. (1973). Piaget's system of sixteen binary operations: An empirical investigation. *Journal of Genetic Psychology, 123*, 279–284.

Wohlwill, J. F. (1972). And never the Twain did meet. Review of *Measurement and Piaget. Contemporary Psychology, 17*, 334–335.

9   Infancy

Piaget's work on infancy is based on the diligent observation of and experimentation with his own three children, Lucienne (born 1925), Jacqueline (born 1927), and Laurent (born 1931) and comprises three volumes, *The Origins of Intelligence in Children* (OI; 1936/1952), *The Construction of Reality in the Child* (CR; 1937/1954), and *Play, Dreams and Imitation in Children* (PDI; 1945/1962). These volumes, which have been characterized as "three of the most remarkable and original documents in psychology" (Russell, 1978, p. 92), can justly be said to have revolutionized the way in which developmental psychologists think about and study infants (Vonèche & Vidal, 1985). Even though there was certainly research on and theorizing about infant development before these volumes were published (e.g., Baldwin, 1894/1906; Bühler, 1918; Koffka, 1924; Stern, 1914/1930), Piaget's work on infant development was unparalleled in terms of its originality, scope, and systematicity, and, as I will argue, it still is today.

The work on infancy followed an already impressive line of research that Piaget had conducted on cognitive and moral development in preschool and school-age children (see Chapter 16, this volume). According to Piaget (1952, 1954/1973), his infancy research changed the way he approached development. In his early work, he focused on verbal exchanges in order to understand the logical, rational thought of the child. However, when he later studied the development of intelligence in infants, he realized that to fully understand the origins of the operations of verbal thought one has to first examine the manipulation and experimentation with objects (Piaget, 1952). The study of infant development showed that there is an action logic that is more basic than, and a prerequisite for, verbal rational thought (Piaget, 1954/1973). Piaget termed this action logic *sensorimotor intelligence,* and the three volumes on infancy "form one entity dedicated to the beginnings of intelligence, that is to say, to the various manifestations of sensorimotor intelligence and to the most elementary forms of expression" (OI, p. ix).

For the most part, Piaget's books on infancy cover topics that today are considered to fall into the domain of cognitive development, and this is the heading under which they are covered in developmental psychology textbooks (e.g., Berk, 2007; Cole, Cole, & Lightfoot, 2005). It would, however, be myopic and amount to a serious misunderstanding to believe that Piaget's work on infancy is just about infants' cognitive development. In fact, within Piaget's developmental epistemology, sensorimotor intelligence development takes up a systematic place: It is the centerpiece that bridges biological and psychological development.

In the first section of this chapter, I discuss the role of sensorimotor intelligence within Piaget's theory. This discussion highlights the epistemological framework of sensorimotor intelligence because, as Piaget (1970, p. 705) noted, the study of infant development "raises all the main issues in the theory of knowledge." In the second section, I briefly summarize the major substages of sensorimotor intelligence and show how these substages manifest themselves in infants' practical understanding of the physical world, with a focus on the development of object permanence and spatial cognition. In the third section, I summarize Piaget's account of symbolic representation. Finally, I examine several criticisms that have been raised with respect to Piaget's theory of sensorimotor intelligence.

SENSORIMOTOR INTELLIGENCE: THEORETICAL ISSUES

The way in which Piaget conceptualized sensorimotor intelligence is intricately connected with his thinking about biological functioning and with the central issue his developmental epistemology was aimed at addressing: the emergence of necessary knowledge (e.g., Piaget, 1950a, p. 23; see Chapter 3, this volume). Accordingly, for Piaget sensorimotor intelligence must be conceived of in a way that is consistent with and extends biological functioning and that brings into view the later emergence of necessary knowledge (OI, pp. 412–419).

The issue of the relations between biological factors (i.e., heredity) and cognitive development is addressed at the outset of OI. Piaget acknowledged that "certain hereditary factors condition intellectual development" (OI, p. 1), but he distinguished between two different interpretations of heredity. In the first sense, heredity refers to specific innate structures (e.g., structure of sense organs); in the second sense, it refers to a general way of functioning (or what Piaget called functional invariants). Piaget considered the second, functional sense of heredity

as far more important for cognitive development.[1] This type of heredity refers to the "functional nucleus of intellectual organization which
comes from the biological organization in its most general aspect" (OI,
p. 3). This general way of functioning "will orient the whole of successive structures which the mind will then work out in its contact
with reality" (OI, p. 3). By contrast, though acknowledging the importance of innate structures, Piaget believed that their role consists in
both enabling and placing constraints on the organism's functioning.
Furthermore, innate structures only mark the starting point that will be
transformed and transcended in the course of the interaction between
organism and environment (OI, p. 2).

The same functional invariants – organization, adaptation, assimilation, and accommodation – characterize biological and psychological
functioning (OI, pp. 6–8): Psychological functioning is always organized
and occurs within a framework. At every level, "intellectual functioning involves an element of assimilation, that is of structuring through
incorporation of external reality into forms due to the subject's activity"
(OI, p. 6). At the same time, the incorporation of new elements leads
to a modification of the structure, and thus to accommodation. Finally,
intellectual adaptation consists of "putting an assimilatory mechanism
and a complementary accommodation into progressive equilibrium"
(OI, p. 7).

Psychological functioning is the outcome of and extends biological self-organization because it does not depend on the material incorporation of the elements with which it interacts (Piaget, 1967/1971,
pp. 26–27). As a result, compared to biological functioning, psychological functioning leads to the extension of the environment we can interact with, increasing integration of the past and the dissociation of form
and content (Piaget, 1966/1976, pp. 52–55).

Having clarified the relations between organic and cognitive development, the question then becomes: How is rational thought related to
sensorimotor intelligence (Piaget, OI, p. 411–412)? Sensorimotor action
not only "plunge[s] deep into organic life," it also constitutes an "intermediary zone between the organic self-regulatory mechanisms and the
later logical mathematical operations and their underlying structures"
(Piaget & Inhelder, 1969/1976, p. 35). To be able to derive rational
thought from sensorimotor functioning, the latter must be conceptualized in a way that one can recognize the seeds of what will become
rational thought. I briefly explain the way in which Piaget conceived of
the continuity between sensorimotor intelligence and rational thought
by expanding on the implications that the functional invariants have for
the conceptualization of sensorimotor intelligence.

Sensorimotor intelligence is a practical intelligence on the basis of which infants interact with the world through perception–action cycles. Infants employ action schemes like sucking, pushing, hitting, and grasping to explore and manipulate the world. A scheme is the general structure of an action that consolidates through practice and is applicable to situations that vary as a function of modifications of the environment (Piaget, 1960/1973, p. 66).[2] Schemes are inseparable from and used in assimilation; this is why assimilation is a dynamic, structuring activity: "Assimilation is hence the very functioning of the system of which organization is the structural aspect" (OI, p. 410). The structuring activity of assimilation involves a need and is directed toward specific goals (OI, pp. 44–45). Because schemes are structures with varying degrees of generality, bringing them to bear in particular situations always requires an adjustment or accommodation. Accommodation thus particularizes the general schemes, supplies them with specific content, and modifies them in doing so (OI, p. 416). Furthermore, assimilation always uses the existing structure of the organization; its functioning carries the history of the subject's interaction with the world into each particular act and structures the content supplied by accommodation accordingly. For example, an infant who has differentiated various ways of interacting with a ball will have different action potentialities available compared to an infant who has not.

The structuring activity of assimilation is inherently directed and gives meaning to the things interacted with (Piaget, 1965/1971, pp. 131–132). Meaning is always bound to an organization: "The characteristic feature of meaning is to be relative to other meanings, that is, to involve a *minimum* system or organization" (Piaget, 1965/1971, p. 158, emphasis in original; see also Piaget & Garcia, 1987/1991, p. 4). To characterize the relations between meanings, Piaget used the term *implication in the wide sense*: "Enlarging the meaning of the word 'implication' we therefore find a relation by implication to be the basic relationship between two states of consciousness, whereas physiologic connections are characterized by causal relationships" (Piaget, 1954, p. 143). Implications in the wide sense are basic because they arise from the structuring activity of assimilation, which directs and organizes "external data" and integrates them into a system of schemes (OI, pp. 399–407). Implications in the wide sense are already found at the sensorimotor level. For example, when infants grasp an object to shake it, the sensorimotor scheme of shaking implies the scheme of grasping, and the assimilation of the object to these schemes constitutes an implication (Piaget, 1950b, p. 149; Piaget & Garcia, 1987/1991, p. 5). Therefore, at the sensorimotor level, actions have a meaning for the agent.[3]

Piaget's way of conceptualizing psychological functioning has two important consequences. First, the notion of causality does not apply to states of consciousness, not even at the level of sensorimotor intelligence, because causality is based on an external (independent) relation between cause and effect (von Wright, 1971; see Chapter 13, this volume). Accordingly, neurophysiological approaches to sensorimotor intelligence (Elman et al., 1996; Munakata, McClelland, Johnson, & Siegler, 1997) remain incomplete because they fail to capture the meaning-conferring, implicatory function of the structuring activity of assimilation (Piaget, 1950b, p. 149). Second, it is easier to see how logical necessity can develop out of implications in the wide sense than how it can possibly emerge out of cause–effect (e.g., stimulus–response) relations. In fact, Piaget (1963/1968, p. 188) termed necessary knowledge *implication in the strict sense* (e.g., 2 + 2 implies 4) and considered it a particular instance of implication in the wide sense.

To further stress the functional continuity between sensorimotor intelligence and rational thought, Piaget drew analogies between the former and the latter. Assimilation is compared to judgment:

> A judgment is nothing other, from a functional point of view, which is common to reflective intelligence and sensorimotor intelligence, than the assimilation of a datum to a scheme. . . . Assimilation [is] an act of judgment inasmuch as it unites experimental contents and logical form. (OI, pp. 267, 410)

Moreover, sensorimotor action patterns that subordinate one scheme as means (e.g., pushing away an obstacle) to another scheme (e.g., grasping an object) as end are compared to the subordination of premises to conclusions at the level of verbal intelligence. However, even though sensorimotor intelligence and reflective intelligence share the same functional invariants, they are structurally different. At the sensorimotor level, meaning is originally embedded in and bound up with unreflective activities; objects have a functional, practical meaning; they are things at hand, utensils for practical use or manipulation (Overton, 1994).

> Sensory-motor intelligence aims at success and not at truth; it finds its satisfaction in the achievement of the practical aim pursued, and not in recognition (classification) or explanation. It is an intelligence only lived and not thought. (PDI, p. 238; cf. OI, p. 240)

Piaget's conceptualization of the working of (sensorimotor) intelligence clashes with the way empiricists view intelligence. Piaget himself was ardent in his opposition to empiricism (e.g., Piaget & Inhelder, 1969/1976). Empiricism is not just an empirical method but also a theory of experience. Essentially, it conceives of human beings as passive and sense perception as providing replicas or copies of reality that are based on association. As key proponents of empiricism, Piaget identified Hume, Locke, and behaviorist stimulus-response theories, but he also thought that empiricism is trenchant in psychology (and, one might add, even today, see Müller & Giesbrecht, 2008). According to Piaget, empiricists misconstrue the fundamentally active relation between infant and environment as a passive, causal relation: "Even before language begins, the young infant reacts to objects not by a mechanical set of stimulus-response associations but by an integrative assimilation to schemes of action, which impress a direction on his activities and include the satisfaction of a need or an interest" (Piaget, 1965/1971, p. 131; see also OI, p. 411). Furthermore, Piaget (1970) rejected the idea that knowledge is a copy of reality. Rather, he was influenced by Kant's (1787/1929) idea that objectivity is constituted by the subject (see Chapter 3, this volume). Kant argued that our intuition (i.e., sensibility) and understanding use *a priori* (i.e., independent of all experience) forms and categories, which are the condition of the possibility for experiencing objectivity. Piaget subscribed to the ordering and organizing function of the mind, but he believed that the forms and categories are not *a priori* but undergo development as a result of the subject's interaction with the world (OI, pp. 376–395).

To summarize, sensorimotor functioning is a practical intelligence that links biological functioning and rational thought. It is based on and extends the functional invariants (organization, adaptation, assimilation, and accommodation) characteristic of biological functioning. These invariants are *a priori*, but they generate, through their functioning, structural change. Sensorimotor intelligence is intrinsically directed to, interacts with, and establishes a meaningful relation to, the world. Intelligence exhibited by human beings originates and perpetuates itself "neither with knowledge of the self nor of things as such but with knowledge of their interaction, and it is by orienting itself simultaneously toward the two poles of that interaction that intelligence organizes the world by organizing itself" (CR, pp. 354–355). Sensorimotor intelligence cannot be reduced to causal mechanisms and associations, but it requires an active agent who unites a logical form with a particular content. Sensorimotor intelligence functions in many ways analogous to rational thought. However, the major difference between sensorimotor intelligence and rational thought is that the former aims at success, whereas the latter aims for truth.

PRACTICAL KNOWLEDGE IN INFANCY

The three volumes on infancy focus on different aspects of infants' cognitive development. Whereas OI examines the coordination and differentiation of sensorimotor schemes of practical intelligence, CR studies how practical intelligence constructs the concepts of object, space, causality, and time. PDI, in turn, is mainly devoted to the emergence of symbols in the context of the development of imitation and play.

It is important to keep two key aspects of Piaget's account in mind. First, in Piaget's account, there are no innate modules with adultlike competencies that are suddenly switched on, nor is there any special processing mechanism that, out of the blue, comes online (see OI, p. 100; Piaget, 1967/1971, p. 327, fn.). Rather, structural change is produced in the course of the infant's interactions with the world, and developmental continuity is provided by the functional invariants. Second, self and world cannot be known independently of each other: "[I]t is through progressive construction that the concepts of the physical world and of the internal self will become elaborated as a function of each other, and the processes of assimilation and accommodation are only instruments of this construction without ever representing the actual result of it" (OI, p. 136). Because of the correlative nature of the organization of the subject and the world, it is necessary to "reconstruct the subject's point of view" (CR, p. xii) in order to understand the meaning that infants attribute to objects and events (see also Piaget & Inhelder, 1969/1976, p. 32). The reconstruction of the subject's point of view is guided by the idea that the complexity of actions determines the complexity of meaning, and it is assisted by the method of contextualizing infants' actions within a developmental sequence and interpreting the earlier levels in the light of later levels (CR, p. 221).

Sensorimotor Intelligence

Piaget distinguished six substages in the development of sensorimotor intelligence. Even though he provided age ranges for each substage, age is not the defining feature of each substage (see Smith, 1993, sect. 18). Rather, the substages are defined by the structure of the pattern of activity, and it is this structure that is summarized in the following subsections (for an excellent, more detailed summary, see Chapman, 1988). In addition, the substages should not be taken to be homogenous because at each substage, the infant can display behaviors that belong to previous substages (CR, p. 299).

SUBSTAGE 1: THE USE OF REFLEXES (0–1 MONTH). For Piaget, psychological life begins with the use of hereditary reflexes (OI, pp. 39, 223). Reflexes are general action patterns such as sucking, looking, and touching (Piaget, 1975/1985, p. 69). Each reflex constitutes an "organized totality" (OI, p. 38) that comprises perceptions, coordinated movements, and a need; it is not just a "summation of movements" (OI, p. 38). The reflexes of interest to Piaget are distinguished from simple reflexes (e.g., sneezing reflex) in that they change as a result of experience and thus have a history (OI, p. 40).

At this initial substage, assimilation and accommodation are not differentiated from each other because accommodations have not yet begun to modify the functioning of the assimilatory schemes. The use of the reflexes, however, leads to their gradual accommodation to external reality. For example, sucking is initially elicited whenever infants come into contact with any region of the breast, but crying and the termination of the search for the nipple ensues if the nipple is not immediately found (OI, Obs. 2, 3). However, when, after several days, infants come into contact with regions of the breast adjacent to the nipple, they will search for the nipple until they succeed (OI, Obs. 5).

The exercise of the reflexes already reveals three fundamental functional characteristics of sensorimotor functioning: functional assimilation, generalizing assimilation, and recognitory assimilation. Functional assimilation means that the need for repetition is inherent in the reflex. The repeated exercise of the reflex, in turn, leads to its consolidation and strengthening (OI, p. 32). The concept of functional assimilation implies that need or "the motive power of activity" (OI, p. 44) does not exist external and independently of the global functioning of the organism. Rather, the need is part of the assimilatory scheme and constitutes its subjective aspect (OI, p. 45). Needs themselves are not static but become more complex with the differentiation and integration of sensorimotor schemes (OI, p. 170).

Generalizing assimilation refers to the phenomenon that infants incorporate increasingly varied objects into their schemes (e.g., the sucking scheme is applied to fingers, blankets). Generalizing assimilation follows from the self-organizing and spontaneous nature of functional assimilation: Functional assimilation implies that a scheme "is not limited to functioning under compulsion by a fixed excitant, external or internal, but functions in a way for itself. In other words, the child does not only suck in order to eat but also to elude hunger, to prolong the excitation of the meal, etc., and lastly, he sucks for the sake of sucking" (OI, p. 35).

Recognitory assimilation goes hand in hand with generalizing assimilation because the application of schemes leads to their differentiation and particularization. For example, recognitory assimilation manifests itself in different sucking behaviors that depend on the infant's internal state (i.e., hunger versus satiation, see OI, Obs. 6). Because sucking varies depending on whether the infant is hungry or not, Piaget argued that the sucking actions have a basic meaning for the infant:

> The increasing calm which succeeds a storm of crying and weeping as soon as the child is in position to take nourishment and to seek the nipple is sufficient evidence that, if awareness exists at all, such awareness is from the beginning the awareness of meaning. But one meaning is necessarily relative to other meanings, even on the elementary plane of simple motor recognition. (OI, p. 38)

Still, at this substage, meaning and thus consciousness is closely tied to the infant's activities and consists of an "awareness of attitudes, of emotions, or sensations of hunger and of satisfaction" (OI, p. 37).

SUBSTAGE II: THE FIRST ACQUIRED ADAPTATIONS AND THE PRIMARY CIRCULAR REACTIONS (1–4 MONTHS). As soon as their action schemes incorporate new objects, infants begin to differentiate assimilation and accommodation and move to the second substage of sensorimotor intelligence characterized by acquired adaptations and primary circular reactions. As examples of acquired adaptations, Piaget described systematic thumb sucking and tongue protrusion (OI, Obs. 11–24), looking behaviors (OI, Obs. 28–39), hearing and phonation (OI, Obs. 40–49), and prehension (OI, Obs. 50–93).

Piaget used the term *primary circular reaction* to refer to these behavior patterns. Circular reactions are defined as "functional use leading to the preservation or the rediscovery of a new result" (OI, p. 55). The reactions are primary because they are centered on the infant's body. They are circular because they form cycles of movements that repeat an interesting sensation discovered by chance.

During this substage, infants start to reciprocally assimilate or coordinate two different schemes. For example, infants grasp what they are seeing, and they move in front of their eyes what they are grasping. This coordination leads to the fusion of two different schemes, "a new totality, self-enclosed," and previous needs are reorganized as a function of this new totality (OI, p. 143). Still, the coordination of primary schemes such as looking and hearing is relatively simple in that it applies to one and the same object (OI, pp. 143, 232), and the schemes are not hierarchically coordinated but fused in a new global scheme (OI, p. 231).

Based on the observation that 3- to 4-month-old infants start to open their mouth as soon as they see the bottle or objects that remind them of the meal (OI, Obs. 27), Piaget engaged a detailed discussion of whether acquired adaptations can be explained by empiricist learning principles such as passive associative transfer or classical conditioning. According to Piaget, infants' reactions to the bottle or other stimuli cannot be explained by external stimulus-response relations because the stimuli have a meaning for the infants to begin with; without this meaning, it would not be possible to explain why these stimuli become relevant or how the associations could be confirmed or strengthened (OI, p. 127). Rather, the conditioned reflex is part of an assimilatory scheme; the incorporation of a signal into an assimilatory scheme is confirmed as long as the signal is part of a process fulfilling a need: "It is this active relationship between the subject and the objects that are charged with meanings which creates the association and not the association which creates this relationship" (OI, p. 131).

SUBSTAGE III: SECONDARY CIRCULAR REACTIONS (4–8 MONTHS). In contrast to primary circular reactions, secondary circular reactions are centered on the effect that infants' actions – often by chance – produce in the external world. Essentially, secondary circular reactions aim at reproducing the effect by repeating the action that generated this effect in the first place. For example, Piaget's daughter Lucienne (0;3 [5])[3] moved her legs vigorously, thereby shaking her bassinet. The movement made the dolls swing that were hanging from the hood. Lucienne looked at the dolls, smiled, and repeated the movement (Obs. 94).

Secondary circular reactions differentiate out of primary circular reactions: "Everything thus goes back to movements of legs or feet, arms or hands, and it is these 'circular' movements of prehension which become differentiated in movements directed at pulling, shaking, swinging, displacing, rubbing, etc." (OI, p. 178). It is because infants understand that the unforeseen event is related to their activity that the external event arouses interest and the schemes (e.g., leg movement, sight of interesting event) are reciprocally assimilated, with the result that the action is reproduced (OI, pp. 172, 178).

However, secondary circular reactions do not yet constitute true acts of intelligence (OI, p. 182) because the relations (e.g., shaking to make the bassinet move) were discovered fortuitously by the child and not constructed on purpose: "The need arises from discovery and not the discovery from the need" (OI, p. 182). Furthermore, secondary circular reactions aim at repeating the interesting effect. By contrast, according to Piaget, "in a true act of intelligence, the need which serves as motive power not only consists in repeating, but in adapting, that is to say, in assimilating a new situation to old schemes and in accommodating these schemes to new circumstances" (OI, p. 182).

SUBSTAGE IV: THE COORDINATION OF SECONDARY SCHEMES (8–12 MONTHS). The novelty of substage IV consists in the coordination of two secondary schemes. For example, when Piaget (Obs. 122) presented his son Laurent (0;7 [13]) with a matchbox and obstructed the access to the matchbox by placing his hand in front of it, Laurent started to hit Piaget's hand to lower it and then removed the obstacle. The coordination of secondary schemes differs from the behaviors displayed at the previous substage in two ways (OI, p. 229). First, whereas secondary circular reactions simply tried to reproduce an interesting event, the coordination of secondary circular reactions becomes necessary when infants in pursuit of their goals encounter an obstacle that requires them to accommodate existing schemes to a new situation. Second, whereas secondary circular reactions lead to the differentiation between means and ends only after the fact, means and ends are differentiated in substage IV from the outset. At substage IV, then, children coordinate two independent schemes, the scheme assigning an end to the action (e.g., grasping the matchbox) and the scheme used as a means (e.g., hitting the hand to lower it).

The differentiation between means (or transitional schemes, as Piaget also called them) and ends involves the coordination of two acts of assimilation: the choice and pursuit of goals and the assimilation of the means to the goal (OI, p. 230). The obstacles or intermediate objects are thus reciprocally assimilated to the transitional scheme and the goal scheme. The schemes cease "to work by simple fusion in order to give rise to diversified operations of inclusion or of hierarchical implication, of interference and even of negation" (OI, p. 232). Negation, for example, is involved when infants remove an obstacle to grasp the desired object because the obstacle acquires the meaning "object to be removed" (OI, p. 235). As a result of the reciprocal coordination, the schemes become more mobile and "fit for new coordinations and syntheses" (OI, p. 238).

For Piaget (OI, p. 154), the differentiation of means and end and, thus, the setting of goals in advance are the criteria for ascribing intentionality (see Chapter 1, Part 3, this volume). At the same time, the differentiation between means and ends also leads to the differentiation between value and ideal:

> As soon as there is intention, in effect, there is a goal to reach and means to use, consequently the influence of consciousness of values [the value or the interest of the intermediary acts serving as *means* is subordinated

to that of the goal] and of the ideal [the act to be accomplished is part of an ideal totality or *goal*, in relation to the real totality of the acts already organized]. (OI, p. 149, emphasis in original)

As a result of the differentiation between means and ends, objects do not have only one value any longer (nor are they characterized by the contrast value vs. nonvalue), but they can serve as obstacle, useful means, or end in themselves, and ends, as a consequence of the more complex coordination they require to be attained, become "more remote and so determine more 'ideal' totalities" (OI, p. 244).

SUBSTAGE V: TERTIARY CIRCULAR REACTIONS (12–18 MONTHS). At substage V, infants use what Piaget called tertiary circular reactions to explore novel features of objects for their own sake and form new schemes through active experimentation. The search for novelty is illustrated in an observation of Jacqueline (0;11 [20]), who slid a variety of objects down her coverlet, varying their positions (Obs. 145). Whereas secondary circular reactions vary actions to reproduce a specific event, tertiary circular reactions gradate and vary actions to "ferret out new phenomena" (OI, p. 274). The interest in novelty is due to the increasing number of schemes infants have at their disposal.

An example that illustrates the discovery of new means through active experimentation is infants' discovery that a stick can be used as a tool to draw objects toward themselves (OI, Obs. 157–161). Piaget examined this behavior by presenting his children with a desirable object out of reach and a stick. His children initially tried to grasp the object directly. Later, they intentionally searched for the stick and used the previously acquired striking scheme to hit the object. In the course of many trials, the striking scheme was gradually accommodated to the particulars of the problem situation and Piaget's children successfully retrieved the target object.

A behavior characteristic of tertiary circular reactions and the discovery of new means is groping, "the accommodation of earlier schemes which become differentiated as a function of the present experiment" (OI, p. 289). In the process of discovering new means, groping arises in the context of encountering an obstacle to one's goal. Previously acquired schemes (e.g., striking in the behavior with the stick) are then activated and gradually differentiated until the problem is solved. But groping should not be mistaken for blind trial and error learning because groping is directed by the initial goal and the initial means as well as by schemes activated in the process of groping (Piaget termed the latter *auxiliary schemes*, OI, p. 296). The end scheme provides the goal, which orients the search, coordinates the progress of groping, and provides the background on which the successive attempts are evaluated. The auxiliary schemes, in turn, provide an outline of the solution and assimilate the chance events discovered in the process of groping (e.g., realizing that the object can be displaced when struck, OI, p. 301). Chance thus plays a role in groping, but the effective utilization of chance events depends on the structuring activity of the subject (OI, p. 303).

SUBSTAGE VI: THE INVENTION OF NEW MEANS THROUGH MENTAL COMBINATION (>18 MONTHS). At substage VI, infants become capable of solving new problems, not through an extended process of groping but by the sudden invention of new means. In contrast to tertiary circular reactions, which are controlled "a posteriori by the facts themselves," the sudden invention of new means is "controlled *a priori* by mental combination" (OI, p. 340). Lucienne (1;6 [23]) displayed this sudden invention when she played with her doll carriage for the first time. When she pushed the carriage over the carpet and ran up against a wall, she pulled the carriage, walking backward. However, because this position was not convenient to her, she paused and, without hesitation, walked around to the other side of the carriage to push it (OI, Obs. 181).

The invention of new means relies on the same processes as the groping behaviors characteristic of stage V: When infants, in pursuit of a goal, encounter an obstacle, auxiliary schemes are activated and reciprocally coordinated with the schemes setting out the goal and the initial means. However, instead of accommodating these schemes in a trial and error fashion, these schemes "entering into action remain in a state of latent activity and combine with each other before (and not after) their external and material application" (OI, p. 347). Thus, at stage VI, the coordination of schemes occurs mentally or deductively, and Piaget believed that this contrast "between directed groping and actual *invention* is primarily due to a difference in speed" (OI, p. 341, emphasis in original). In other words, thanks to the increasing mobility, diversification, and consolidation of schemes, the structuring activity of assimilation occurs more rapidly in mental invention than in groping, with the result that "the structuring activity no longer needs to depend on the actual data, [but] can make a complex system of simply evoked schemes converge" (OI, p. 343).

Piaget argued that it would be mistaken to attribute this sudden invention to the simple internalization of experience because, by so doing, one would overlook the internal structuring activity of assimilation – and the structuring activity of assimilation is always internal – which organizes and reorganizes the schemes (OI, p. 348). The sudden invention of new means relies on symbolic representations, specifically mental images, that emerge at substage VI. In fact, invention and symbolic representation are interdependent: "To invent is to combine mental, that is to say, representative, schemes and, in order to become mental, the sensorimotor schemes must be capable of intercombining in every way, that is to say, of being able to give rise to true inventions" (OI, p. 341).

Construction of the World

For Piaget, the differentiation and coordination of sensorimotor schemes leads to the construction of increasingly complex relations between objects in the world (OI, p. 211). Nondifferentiated and isolated action schemes produce meaning that is "absolutely immediate" (CR, p. 7) and remains centered on the subject's body because the body serves as the common and constant reference point of action, even though the infant is not aware of this centration (Piaget, 1970/1972a, p. 21). With the coordination of sensorimotor schemes, meaning becomes increasingly detached from the immediate situation and is less centered on infants' activity (CR, p. xi). The completion of sensorimotor development leads to a Copernican revolution (Piaget, 1970/1972a, p. 21; see Smith, 1987) in the sense that, for the infant, his own action is no longer the whole of reality and instead now becomes "one object among others in a space containing them all; and actions are related together through being coordinated by a subject who begins to be aware of himself as the source of actions" (Piaget, 1970/1972a, pp. 22–23).

Because during sensorimotor substages I and II assimilation and accommodation have barely been differentiated, infants lack a clear differentiation between their actions and the effects of these actions in the world (Piaget, 1975/1985, p. 70). As a consequence, infants experience the world during these substages as "a collection of centers of creation or reproduction in which the child localizes his own impressions of effort and activity, but one cannot say that he conceives of these centers as either external or internal to himself" (CR, p. 228). Furthermore, objects at these substages are experienced as direct extension of the previous action. This is why infants' search for objects only extends the previous action (CR, Obs. 4, 5). Thus, when an object leaves their visual field, infants' behavior (including their eye movements) is characterized by passive expectation and not active search because active search requires the coordination of secondary schemes and the removal of obstacles (CR, pp. 10–11).

With respect to space, the first two substages are characterized by uncoordinated heterogeneous spaces (visual space, auditory space,

buccal space, etc., CR, p. 101). Within these different spaces, however, the infant demonstrates coordinated behavior patterns that an
observer might interpret as constituting groups of displacement. Piaget
adopted the concept of a group from the French mathematician Poincaré
(1905/1958). A group is "constituted by every coordinated totality of displacements capable of returning to the point of departure and such that
the final state does not depend on the route followed" (CR, p. 107; see
Chapman, 1988, p. 108). For example, when Laurent (0;1 [3]) coordinated
hand and mouth movements and rediscovered the correct movements
to place the hand back into the mouth after having lost contact, his
behavior already constituted a practical group (CR, Obs. 67). However,
according to Piaget, there is no evidence that infants are aware of these
groups because, as other observations showed, infants do not yet place
themselves in space and do not yet understand spatial relations between
things (CR, p. 105). Thus, at these substages "action creates space but is
not yet situated in it" (CR, p. 102). Still, the practical groups demonstrate
that the construction of relations between actions is a fundamental feature of intellectual functioning: "The logic of relations is immanent in
all intellectual activity; every perception and every conception are the
making of relationships. If the logic of relations is only tardily reflected
as a normative system, it is virtually preformed in the functioning of
every act of intelligence" (CR, p. 209).

The coordination of vision with prehension and the emergence of secondary circular reactions promote the differentiation between assimilation and accommodation. As a consequence, meaning becomes gradually detached from infants' immediate motor activity and inserted into a
network of relations that grows increasingly independent (i.e., objective)
of the infants' activity (OI, pp. 74–75).

> When an object can be simultaneously grasped and sucked or grasped,
> looked at and sucked, it becomes externalized in relation to the subject
> quite differently than if it could only be grasped. In the latter case it is
> only an aliment for the function itself and the subject only attempts to
> grasp through the need to grasp. As soon as there is coordination, on the
> contrary, the object tends to be assimilated to several schemes simulta-
> neously. It thus acquires an ensemble of meanings and consequently a
> consistency, which endow it with interest. (OI, p. 121)

However, because secondary circular reactions do not yet fully differentiate means from ends, relations between objects are used but not
analyzed, and infants are not able to comprehend more than one object
at a time (OI, p. 232). As a result, object permanence is still tied to the
action in progress, with the difference that, in contrast to the first two

substages, infants now can anticipate objects in new positions (CR, Obs. 6–11).

During the third substage, spatial relations are centered on the infant's actions and constitute what Piaget (CR, p. 114) termed *subjective groups*. Infants can only rediscover their own positions relative to objects and do not yet relate objects to each other or place their own body in a space common with the other objects. Therefore, infants conceive of objects' positions as relative to their actions and not as relative to their actual displacements in a common and objective space (CR, p. 121). For example, Laurent (0;7 [0]) made no attempts to turn his bottle over when it was presented to him upside down with the nipple invisible; he only turned the bottle over when the nipple was partly visible (CR, Obs. 78). Laurent's failure to recognize that his bottle had a reverse side illustrates that spatial relations (in front, behind) are not conceived of as relative to the object but remain dependent on the infant's own perspective (CR, p. 130).

At substage IV, the differentiation between means and ends leads to the construction of relations between two objects simultaneously (OI, p. 233). The ability to construct means–end relations has repercussions for infants' understanding of space. Infants' actions are organized in simple reversible groups such as hiding an object under a screen and retrieving it (CR, Obs. 85). However, the spatial groups at this level remain midway between subjective and objective groups because infants cannot yet understand relations that are completely independent of their actions. The infant "does not yet recognize positions and displacements as being relative to one another, but only as relative to himself" (CR, p. 183). The lack of understanding relations as relative to objects is apparent in the A-not-B error: Infants search for an object at a location where they previously found it and not at the location where they saw the object disappear (CR, Obs. 39–45). "The object screen is therefore not considered by the child as something with which the hidden object is in relationship: the screen is still perceived as relative to the subject and not as relative to the object" (CR, p. 192).

Tertiary circular reactions involve the construction of more complex relations between objects because infants successively coordinate the auxiliary means with the goal and the situation at hand. The means are no longer a simple function of the goal but become increasingly objectified (OI, pp. 277–278). As a result, infants start to discover and use complex interrelations among objects (CR, p. 186). For example, infants start to search for objects placed behind themselves and other people (CR, Obs. 104–105). Infants also start to construct objective groups of spatial displacements that coordinate spatial relations among locations.

For example, infants move from location A to location B, then from location B to location C, and finally from location C back to location A (CR, Obs. 117). However, infants do not yet succeed at tasks requiring the symbolic representation of spatial relations (CR, p. 202). For example, infants do not place their own body in the same space as other objects, as is evident in Jacqueline's (1;6 [15]) attempts to grasp a cloth on which she was standing (OI, Obs. 168; see also CR, Obs. 118, 119, 121, 122). Similarly, even though infants succeed at tasks that involve visible displacements of objects, they still fail at tasks that involve invisible displacements (CR, Obs. 55–57).

Finally, with the emergence of symbolic representation, the spatial groups are not only objective but become also representative (CR, p. 205). Infants can use detours in which part of the detour is not visible. For example, when Jacqueline's (1;6 [8]) ball rolled too far under a bed to be reached from the side at which it disappeared, she walked around the bed and retrieved the ball from the other side of the bed (CR, Obs. 123). Piaget also argued that infants now locate their own body in the same space as other objects (see Moore, Mealiea, Garon, & Povinelli, 2007). Finally, at stage VI infants solve object permanence tasks in which objects are invisibly displaced. For example, when Piaget hid a small pencil in his hand, moved his hand successively to hiding places A, B, C, and left the pencil under C, Jacqueline (1;7 [23]) was able to retrieve the pencil. According to Piaget, the retrieval of invisibly displaced objects presupposes the emergence of symbolic representation (CR, pp. 83–86).

SYMBOLIC REPRESENTATION

A central claim put forward in OI, CR, and PDI is that sensorimotor development culminates in the emergence of symbolic representational thought. For Piaget, symbolic representational thought is a structuring activity that synthesizes concepts or schemes and symbolic representational items (PDI, p. 67). Symbolic representational items consist of signifiers (i.e., items that convey meaning) that are differentiated from their referents, and signifieds (i.e., the meaning carried by the signifier). Piaget termed a system of such signifiers the *semiotic function* (Piaget & Inhelder, 1966/1969, p. 51). The semiotic function subsumes both symbols and signs. Following the tradition of de Saussure (1916/1986, pp. 67–69), Piaget (Piaget & Inhelder, 1966/1969, p. 56) defined symbols such as mental images as motivated signifiers (i.e., they resemble the things signified), and signs, such as words, as arbitrary and conventional signifiers. The semiotic function makes it possible for children to think about absent objects as well as past, future, and even fictitious events.

For Piaget, signifiers and signified are not limited to symbolic representational intelligence but already present at the sensorimotor level because meaning is always constituted by signifiers and signified (OI, pp. 189–190). However, in contrast to the signifiers at the symbolic–representational level, signifiers at the sensorimotor level are not differentiated from what they refer to (OI, pp. 191). Piaget (OI, p. 191) used the generic term *indications* to refer to undifferentiated signifiers. Signifieds at this level are sensorimotor schemes that confer meaning on the elements interacted with (OI, p. 189). An indication is an "objective aspect of external reality" (OI, p. 193), "a perceptible fact which announces the presence of an object or the imminence of an event (the door which opens and announces a person)" (OI, pp. 191–192).

Piaget distinguished between different types of indications that correspond to different substages of sensorimotor development (OI, pp. 189–196, 247–252, 327–328). For example, during substage II, indications result from the coordination of different primary schemes such as sight and hearing, and infants use sound as an indicator for sight; that is, they recognize "that the thing heard is to be looked at" (OI, p. 194). Whereas indications that result from the coordination of primary schemes remain related to infants' own activity, the coordination of secondary schemes promotes the objectification of the signifier and the gradual detachment of meaning from the immediate spatial–temporal field. Thus, infants at substage IV anticipate events that are independent of their own actions. For example, Jacqueline (0;9 [15]) started to cry as soon as she saw the person seated next to her get up and move away a little because she took these behaviors as indications of the imminent departure of this person. For Piaget, to account for these more complex undifferentiated signifiers, we do not need to attribute symbolic representations to the infant; rather, these indications arouse a specific object-related expectation (OI, p. 252).

At sensorimotor stage VI, the first symbolic representations arise in the form of mental images. The transition from motor symbols to mental images is captured in an observation of Piaget's daughter Lucienne (OI, Obs. 180). When confronted with a box the opening of which was too narrow to remove a chain it contained, Lucienne (1;4 [0]) used the opening and closing of her mouth and then widened the opening of the box to pull out the chain. Piaget interpreted the opening and closing of the mouth as a differentiated signifier that signified the motor operations required for the successful solution of the problem. Piaget was adamant that symbolic representations are only "tools of nascent thought" (OI, p. 248) supporting the dynamic process of invention (i.e., the structuring activity of assimilation).

The problem that Piaget tackles in PDI is explaining how children generate detached signifieds and differentiated signifiers. Essentially, he drew on the distinction between the assimilatory and the accommodatory functions and suggested that symbolic representational activity arises from the synthesis of these two complementary functions.

Specifically, concomitant to the differentiation and coordination of schemes, the activities of assimilation and accommodation become further differentiated. During the second year of life, the detachment of actions from immediately given stimuli results in the emergence of pretend play. Pretense, according to Piaget, is best characterized as the primacy of assimilation over accommodation because objects are freely assimilated to infants' needs (PDI, pp. 103, 148–149). The assimilatory function, and specifically pretend play, supplies the detached signifieds for symbolic representational activity (PDI, pp. 3, 104, 276).

At the same time, accommodation becomes more active and directed toward novelty as such, which manifests itself, among others, in the imitation of novel behaviors (PDI, pp. 52–61). Imitation itself is characterized by the primacy of accommodation over assimilation (PDI, pp. 277–282). Differentiated signifiers are supplied by deferred imitation. For example, Piaget's daughter, Jacqueline (1;4 [3]), when placed in her playpen, imitated the temper tantrum she had observed a boy throwing in his playpen on the prior day (PDI, Obs. 52). Through this action, Jacqueline provided herself, though perhaps not consciously (PDI, p. 70), with a signifier (imitative action) that is differentiated from that which it signifies (absent model). Later, with the interiorization (i.e., latent activity of schemes due to increased speed) of such an imitative action, a mental image results, marking the beginning of symbolic representation (Piaget & Inhelder, 1968/1973). Mental images are not just extending sensations, as postulated within the empiricist tradition (and as implied by the notion of internalization), but arise from the interiorization of motor and perceptual activities (PDI, p. 77).

CRITICISM OF PIAGET'S THEORY

Many aspects of Piaget's theory of infant development have been severely criticized. I briefly cover three lines of criticism: (a) Piaget did not properly explain the process of interiorization and the emergence of symbolic representations, (b) Piaget largely ignored the importance of social interaction for the development of knowledge, and (c) Piaget severely underestimated infants' abilities.

First, it has been claimed that Piaget's account is flawed because it does adequately explain the emergence of symbolic representations

(Bickhard & Campbell, 1989; Judge, 1985; Müller, Sokol, & Overton, 1998a, 1998b). However, Piaget's account has been defended against these criticisms (see Morgado, 2002; Smith, 1998). Either way, it is fair to say that Piaget did not explain the process of interiorization in sufficient detail (Vonèche & Vidal, 1985), and this important aspect of Piaget's account (as well as that of others, see Vygotsky, 1978, p. 57) awaits further elaboration.

The second line of criticism is directed to a lack of social factors and the failure to capture major transitions in social development in Piaget's account (Hamlyn, 1978; Rodríguez, 2009; Tomasello, 1996). Social factors are certainly not absent in Piaget's work on infancy. First, the statement that "human intelligence is subject to the action of social life at all levels of development from the first to the last day of life" (Piaget, 1977/1995, p. 278) clearly includes the sensorimotor stage. Second, the social learning processes of imitation (PDI, pp. 8–88), the special role of persons (e.g., OI, pp. 277–278; CR, p. 318), and changes in infants' understanding of the agency of persons (CR, Obs. 137–139, 142, 143, 152, 153) are discussed at some length. Third, Piaget also pointed out the importance of social interaction and communication for the development of symbolic representational thought: "Outside this social relation there is no apparent reason why pure representation should follow action" (CR, p. 367; see Sinclair, 1982). However, the construction of the social world does not receive the same level of attention in Piaget's work on infancy as the construction of the physical world. Piaget also did not provide a detailed analysis of how communicative interaction leads to symbolic representation. Overall, the still open question is whether Piaget's relative lack of attention to social interaction in infancy invalidates his account of infancy or whether his theoretical framework can be revised to capture social development (e.g., Carpendale & Lewis, 2006; Chapman, 1991; Müller & Carpendale, 2000, 2004).

The major thrust of the criticism leveled against Piaget's theory of infant development comes from the neonativist enterprise that argues that core knowledge and the abilities to represent and reason about physical reality (e.g., objects, causality, space) are innate (see Bremner, 2001; Cohen & Cashon, 2006, for reviews). The issue is not whether Piaget's observations and experiments can be replicated; the issue is whether Piaget's method of assessing infant competencies (i.e., his reliance on sensorimotor action such as manual search) systematically underestimated infants' competencies. Neonativists consider looking time to be a more sensitive measure of infants' "true competence." A common method that is used in this line of research is the violation of expectation (VOE) paradigm (see Bremner, 2001). In the VOE paradigm, infants are familiarized with an event sequence (e.g., a screen rotating back and forth through an arc of 180°, see Baillargeon, 1987). Following habituation to this event, infants are presented with test events that either do or do not violate the physical principle under study (e.g., the screen either stops at the box or appears to pass through it). It is assumed that if infants look longer at the impossible than at the possible event, they understand the physical principle under study. Using the VOE paradigm, it has indeed been found that already 3- to 4-month-old infants look longer at "impossible" than at "possible" events (see Baillargeon, 2004a; Bremner, 2001).

Neonativists' rich interpretation of an infant's looking time behavior has not gone unchallenged (e.g., Cohen & Cashon, 2006; Haith & Benson, 1998; Kagan, 2008; Rakison, 2007).[4] It has been argued that possible and impossible events in the VOE paradigm are confounded with other factors, which in turn might explain the looking time differences (e.g., Bogartz, Shinskey, & Speaker, 1997; Cashon & Cohen, 2000; Rivera, Wakeley, & Langer, 1999). Furthermore, it has been argued that because the VOE paradigm only assesses whether infants perceptually discriminate between two different events, it is generally compatible with a perceptual interpretation and does not warrant the ascription of advanced cognitive processes to infants (Cohen & Cashon, 2006; Haith & Benson, 1998; Kagan, 2008; Müller & Overton, 1998a; Rakison, 2007; but see Baillargeon, 2004a, 2004b). A further problem for the rich interpretation of looking time data is that it fails to explain why infants' precocious knowledge is not revealed in their actions (e.g., in the A-not-B task) even several months after they have acquired the necessary motor skills (Bremner, 2001; Müller & Overton, 1998a).

Aside from the controversy over how to interpret looking time data, contemporary neonativism is rooted in an epistemological framework entirely different from Piaget's epistemological framework. More specifically, contemporary neonativism is based on a causal representational or mechanist theory of meaning, which itself is rooted in the empiricist tradition (Goldberg, 1991; McDonough, 1989). According to causal representational theories, meaning and behavior are explained through internal representations that mediate between input and output. These representations are causally produced by input (i.e., perceptual information) and, in turn, effect some output (i.e., bodily movements). For example, in Baillargeon's (2004a, 2004b, 2008) account of physical reasoning, representations of events are triggered by some input and run through some computations performed by the physical reasoning system, which then produces an output (i.e., increased attention to the physically impossible event). Baillargeon (2004b, p. 422) explicitly states that reasoning in her theory is performed by some device: "It seems very unlikely that infants possess explicit beliefs about anything. What they do possess is an abstract computational system, a physical reasoning system that monitors physical events and flags those that do not unfold as expected for further scrutiny." In causal representational theories such as Baillargeon's, representations become entities that take on a life of their own and the "person as agent becomes superfluous" (Judge, 1985, p. 51).

This necessarily cursory discussion indicates the fundamental differences in the way in which contemporary neonativist theories (exemplified by Baillargeon's theory) and Piaget conceptualize the working of the mind (for a more detailed treatment, see Müller & Newman, 2008; Müller & Overton, 1998a, 1998b; Müller et al., 1998a). Basically, in the tradition of empiricist causal representational theories, Baillargeon's theory conceptualizes the mind as passive and relations between infants and the world as external, whereas Piaget's theory conceptualizes the mind as active and the relation between infant and world as internal. It is not surprising that, given these different epistemological frameworks, terms such as *representation* or *reasoning* take on different meanings in Baillargeon's and Piaget's theories (Müller & Giesbrecht, 2008).[5] Unfortunately, Baillargeon (2008) is not aware of the epistemological commitments resulting from her theory. For example, Baillargeon does not address how her theory avoids the symbol-grounding problem (i.e., the problem of explaining how representative items can have meaning) (Bickhard, 1993, 1999; Heil, 1981; Müller & Overton, 1998a; Smythe, 1992). Nor is it clear how the notion of objectivity can have any meaning within a causal representational framework (Straus, 1963). Finally, Baillargeon (2008) contradicts herself by claiming on the one hand that a computational device produces infants' responses in the VOE paradigm and, on the other hand, that infants engage in their attempts at understanding the physical world in an explanation-based learning process. In essence, Baillargeon illegitimately mixes an account that is based on external relations between infant and world with an internal account of this relation (see Hacker, 1991).

CONCLUSION

In Piaget's developmental epistemology, sensorimotor intelligence serves as a bridge between biological functioning and rational thought. On the one hand, the beginning of sensorimotor intelligence, the system of reflexes, is linked to the morphological and anatomical structure of the organism. One the other hand, sensorimotor intelligence already entails a logic of action and meaning implications and thus the seeds of what later will become rational thought and necessary knowledge (OI, p. 418). Furthermore, biological functioning, sensorimotor intelligence, and rational thought are based on the same self-organizing processes (i.e., functional invariants). The functional invariants guarantee the continuity of development while, in constant interaction with the world, constructing increasingly complex forms (i.e., structural change).

Piaget's work on infancy addresses several fundamental epistemological questions such as the relation between structure and function, matter and form, cognition and affect, biology and cognition, and it presents a systematic theory of the process of signification, the structure of consciousness, the role of action and experience in development. The breadth of Piaget's approach to infancy and the depth of dealing with fundamental epistemological questions are still unparalleled. Contemporary causal representational approaches to infant development, such as Baillargeon's, represent, in this respect, a step backward because they ignore epistemological questions and are unaware of their own epistemological commitments. As a result, contemporary approaches are fraught with fundamental conceptual problems (see Müller & Newman, 2008; Müller & Overton, 1998a, 1998b; Müller et al., 1998a).

However, in several aspects Piaget's theory of infancy remains incomplete and in need of elaboration and possibly revision. Findings from contemporary research using looking time measures also create lacunae that must be addressed by Piagetians. This likely will lead to modifications of Piaget's theory. For example, it might be necessary to incorporate into his account some concepts that originate in information-processing theory (such as short-term and working memory, Chapman, 1988). At the same time, the potential of Piaget's theory of sensorimotor intelligence for contributing to recent theoretical developments such as the emphasis on embodied, action-based theories of meaning has still to be realized (Clark, 2006; Gallagher, 2005; Gallese & Lakoff, 2005).

Future research on infancy would certainly benefit from taking more serious and exploring the theoretical and empirical implications two key insights of Piaget's theory of infancy. First, higher mental functions are grounded in and emerge out of a practical, prereflective form of intelligence. Second, there is no structure independent of activity and vice versa: "The essential is, therefore, not the scheme in so far as it is a structure, but the structuring activity which gives rise to the schemes" (OI, p. 350). Piaget's view of infants as active agents that confer increasingly complex meanings on the things interacted with has yet to be fully assimilated in developmental psychology and in philosophy.[6]

NOTES

1. Strictly speaking, the general way of functioning is not hereditary because it is already operative at the level of the genes (Piaget, 1970/1972a, p. 57). Rather, it is a functional *a priori* that reflects the continuity of life.

2. In the following, I use the terms *scheme* and *schemes* (see Chapter 1, Part 3) to refer to the general structure of actions. Quotes from the translations of Piaget's work that use the terms *schema* or *schemata* have been changed accordingly. In Piaget's work, the term *schema* [schéma] refers to individualized images (Piaget & Inhelder, 1966/1971, pp. 366, 382; see Chapter 1, Part 3, this volume). Broadly speaking, schemes are linked to the operative or transformative aspect of intelligence, and schemas are linked to the figurative aspect of intelligence. The figurative aspect of intelligence includes perception, images, and, to some extent, language (Piaget, 1961/1969, p. 283). The operative and figurative aspects of intelligence are interdependent: The operative aspect represents the structuring activity of assimilation, the figurative aspect provides the material for this activity. For example, perception provides an undifferentiated signifier that attains meaning by being assimilated to action schemes (e.g., Piaget, 1970/1972b, pp. 45–62).

3. Children's ages in years, months, and days. Thus, (0;3 [5]) reads: 0 years, 3 months, and 5 days.

4. In her recent work, Baillargeon (2008; Hespos & Baillargeon, 2008) claims that the VOE paradigm and action-based tasks generate converging findings. However, this claim is problematic for the reason that it systematically ignores the different levels of complexity that, in Piaget's theory, underlie manual search behavior and looking behavior. Specifically, following Kant (1787/1929, B 236), Piaget (CR, pp. 322–326) distinguished between a sequence of perception (subjective succession) and the perception of a sequence (objective succession). Arguably, the VOE paradigm engages only the former, less complex sequence of perception, and manual search the more complex perception of a sequence (see Müller & Overton, 1998a). Unfortunately, this important distinction between subjective and objective succession seems to have been lost on contemporary infancy researchers.

5. The term *representation* is not defined in Baillargeon's theory. It is thus unclear whether she might accept that the findings generated with the VOE paradigm can be explained on the basis of undifferentiated signifiers (see Müller & Giesbrecht, 2008).

6. SSHRC of Canada and the Human Early Learning Network supported the preparation of this chapter.

REFERENCES

Baillargeon, R. (1987). Object permanence in $3\frac{1}{2}$- and $4\frac{1}{2}$-month-old infants. *Developmental Psychology, 23*, 655–664.

Baillargeon, R. (2004a). Infants' reasoning about hidden objects: Evidence for event-general and event-specific expectation. *Developmental Science, 7*, 391–414.

Baillargeon, R. (2004b). Can 12 large clowns fit in a Mini Cooper? Or when are beliefs and reasoning explicit and conscious? *Developmental Science, 7*, 422–424.

Baillargeon, R. (2008). Innate ideas revisited: For a principle of persistence in infants' physical reasoning. *Perspectives on Psychological Science, 3*, 2–12.

Baldwin, J. M. (1906). *Mental development in the child and the race: Methods and processes* (3rd revised ed.). New York: Macmillan. (Original work published in 1894)

Berk, L. (2007). *Infants and children: Prenatal through middle childhood* (6th ed.). Boston: Allyn & Bacon.

Bickhard, M. H. (1993). Representational content in humans and machines. *Journal of Experimental and Theoretical Artificial Intelligence, 5*, 285–333.

Bickhard, M. H. (1999). Interaction and representation. *Theory and Psychology, 9*, 435–458.

Bickhard, M. H., & Campbell, R. L. (1989). Interactivism and genetic epistemology. *Archives de Psychologie, 57*, 99–121.

Bogartz, R. S., Shinskey, J. L., & Speaker, C. J. (1997). Interpreting infant looking: The event set x event set design. *Developmental Psychology, 33*, 408–422.

Bremner, G. (2001). Cognitive development: Knowledge of the physical world. In G. Bremner & A. Fogel (Eds.), *Blackwell handbook of infant development* (pp. 98–138). Oxford: Blackwell.

Bühler, K. (1918). *Die geistige Entwicklung des Kindes* (The mental development of the child). Jena, Germany: Fischer.

Carpendale, J. I. M., & Lewis, C. (2006). *How children develop social understanding*. Oxford: Blackwell.

Cashon, C. H., & Cohen, L. B. (2000). Eight-month-old infants' perceptions of possible and impossible events. *Infancy, 1*, 429–446.

Chapman, M. (1988). *Constructive evolution*. Cambridge: Cambridge University Press.

Chapman, M. (1991). The epistemic triangle: Operative and communicative components of cognitive development. In M. Chandler & M. Chapman (Eds.), *Criteria for competence: Controversies in the conceptualization and assessment of children's abilities* (pp. 209–228). Hillsdale, NJ: Erlbaum.

Clark, A. (2006). Cognitive complexity and the sensorimotor frontier. *Aristotelian Society Supplementary Volume, 80*, 43–65.

Cohen, L. B., & Cashon, K. H. (2006). Infant cognition. In W. Damon & R. Lerner (Series Eds.), D. Kuhn & R. Siegler (Vol. Eds.), *Handbook of child psychology, Vol. 2: Cognition, perception, and language* (6th ed., pp. 214–251). New York: Wiley.

Cole, M., Cole, S. R., & Lightfoot, C. (2005). *The development of children* (5th ed.). New York: Worth Publishers.

de Saussure, F. (1986). *Course in general linguistics*. La Salle, IL: Open Court Classics. (Original work published in 1916)

Gallagher, S. (2005). *How the body shapes the mind*. Oxford: Clarendon Press.

Gallese, V., & Lakoff, G. F. (2005). The brain's concepts: The role of the sensory-motor system in conceptual knowledge. *Cognitive Neuropsychology, 22*, 455–479.

Goldberg, B. (1991). Mechanism and meaning. In J. Hyman (Ed.), *Investigating psychology* (pp. 48–66). London: Routledge.

Hacker, P. M. S. (1991). Seeing, representing and describing: An examination of David Marr's computational theory of vision. In J. Hyman (Ed.), *Investigating psychology* (pp. 119–154). London: Routledge.

Haith, M. M., & Benson, J. B. (1998). Infant cognition. In W. Damon (Series Ed.), D. Kuhn & R. Siegler (Vol. Eds.), *Handbook of child psychology, Vol. 2: Cognition, perception, and language* (5th ed., pp. 199–254). New York: Wiley.

Hamlyn, D. W. (1978). *Experience and the growth of understanding*. London: Routledge & Kegan Paul.

Heil, J. (1981). Does cognitive psychology rest on a mistake? *Mind, 90*, 321–342.

Hespos, S. J., & Baillargeon, R. (2008). Young infants' actions reveal their developing knowledge of support variables: Converging evidence for violation-of-expectation findings. *Cognition, 107*, 304–316.

Judge, B. (1985). *Thinking about things: A philosophical study of representation*. Edinburgh: Scottish Academic Press.

Kagan, J. (2008). In defense of qualitative changes in development. *Child Development, 79*, 1606–1624.

Kant, I. (1929). *Critique of pure reason*. London: Macmillan. (Original work published in 1787)

Koffka, K. (1924). *The growth of the mind*. London: Routledge & Kegan Paul.

McDonough, R. (1989). Towards a non-mechanistic theory of meaning. *Mind, 98*, 1–21.

Moore, C., Mealiea, J., Garon, N., & Povinelli, D. J. (2007). The development of body self-awareness. *Infancy, 11*, 157–174.

Morgado, L. (2002). The role of representation in Piagetian theory: Changes over time. In T. Brown & L. Smith (Eds.), *Reductionism and the development of knowledge* (pp. 159–174). Mahwah, NJ: Erlbaum.

Müller, U., & Carpendale, J. I. M. (2000). The role of social interaction in Piaget's theory: Language for social cooperation and social cooperation for language. *New Ideas in Psychology, 18*, 139–156.

Müller, U., & Carpendale, J. I. M. (2004). From joint activity to joint attention: A relational approach to social development in infancy. In J. I. M. Carpendale & U. Müller (Eds.), *Social interaction and the development of knowledge* (pp. 215–238). Mahwah, NJ: Erlbaum.

Müller, U., & Giesbrecht, G. (2008). Methodological and epistemological issues in the interpretation of infant cognitive development. *Child Development, 79*, 1654–1658.

Müller, U., & Newman, J. L. (2008). The body in action: Perspectives on embodiment and consciousness. In W. F. Overton, U. Müller, & J. L. Newman (Eds.), *Developmental perspectives on embodiment and consciousness* (pp. 313–341). New York: Taylor & Francis.

Müller, U., & Overton, W. F. (1998a). How to grow a baby: A re-evaluation of image-schema and Piagetian approaches to representation. *Human Development, 41,* 71–111.

Müller, U., & Overton, W. F. (1998b). Action theory of mind and representational theory of mind: Is dialogue possible? *Human Development, 41,* 127–133.

Müller, U., Sokol, B., & Overton, W. F. (1998a). Reframing a constructivist model of the development of mental representation: The role of higher-order operations. *Developmental Review, 18,* 155–201.

Müller, U., Sokol, B., & Overton, W. F. (1998b). Constructivism and development: Reply to Smith's commentary. *Developmental Review, 18,* 1228–1236.

Munakata, Y., McClelland, J. L., Johnson, M. H., & Siegler, R. S. (1997). Rethinking infant knowledge: Toward an adaptive process account of successes and failures in object permanence tasks. *Psychological Review, 104,* 686–713.

Overton, W. F. (1994). Contexts of meaning: The computational and the embodied mind. In W. F. Overton & D. S. Palermo (Eds.), *The nature and ontogenesis of meaning* (pp. 1–18). Hillsdale, NJ: Erlbaum.

Piaget, J. (1950a). *Introduction à l'épistémologie génétique* (Vol. 1). Paris: Presses Universitaires de France.

Piaget, J. (1950b). *Introduction à l' épistémologie génétique* (Vol. 3). Paris: Press Universitaires de France.

Piaget, J. (1952). *The origins of intelligence in children.* New York: International Universities Press. (Original work published in 1936)

Piaget, J. (1952). Autobiography. In C. Murchison (Ed.), *History of psychology in autobiography* (Vol. 4, pp. 237–256). New York: Russell & Russell.

Piaget, J. (1954). *The construction of reality in the child.* New York: Basic Books. (Original work published in 1937)

Piaget, J. (1954). The problem of consciousness in child psychology: Developmental changes of awareness. In H. A. Abramson (Ed.), *Conference on problems of consciousness* (Vol. 4, pp. 136–177). New York: Josiah Macy Foundation.

Piaget, J. (1962). *Play, dreams and imitation in childhood.* New York: W.W. Norton & Co. (Original work published in 1945)

Piaget, J. (1968). Explanation in psychology and psychophysiological parallelism. In P. Fraisse & J. Piaget (Eds.), *Experimental psychology: Its scope and method* (Vol. 1, pp. 153–191). London: Routledge & Kegan Paul. (Original work published in 1963)

Piaget, J. (1969). *The mechanisms of perception.* New York: Basic Books. (Original work published in 1961)

Piaget, J. (1970). Piaget's theory. In P. H. Mussen (Ed.), *Carmichael's manual of child psychology,* Vol. 1 (3rd ed., pp. 703–730). New York: Wiley.

Piaget, J. (1971). *Insights and illusions of philosophy.* London: Routledge & Kegan Paul. (Original work published in 1965)

Piaget, J. (1971). *Biology and knowledge.* Chicago: University of Chicago Press. (Original work published in 1967)

Piaget, J. (1972a). *The principles of genetic epistemology.* London: Routledge & Kegan Paul. (Original work published in 1970)

Piaget, J. (1972b). *Psychology and epistemology: Towards a theory of knowledge.* Middlesex: Penguin Books. (Original work published in 1970)

Piaget, J. (1973). Language and intellectual operations. In J. Piaget (Ed.), *The child and reality* (pp. 109–124). New York: Viking Press. (Original work published in 1954)

Piaget, J. (1973). Child praxis. In J. Piaget (Ed.), *The child and reality* (pp. 63–91). New York: Viking Press. (Original work published in 1960)

Piaget, J. (1976). Biology and cognition. In B. Inhelder & H. Chipman (Eds.), *Piaget and his school* (pp. 45–62). New York: Springer Verlag. (Original work published in 1966)

Piaget, J. (1985). *The equilibration of cognitive structures.* Chicago: University of Chicago Press. (Original work published in 1975)

Piaget, J. (1995). *Sociological studies.* London: Routledge. (Original work published in 1977)

Piaget, J., & Garcia, R. (1991). *Toward a logic of meanings.* Hillsdale, NJ: Erlbaum. (Original work published in 1987)

Piaget, J., & Inhelder, B. (1969). *The psychology of the child.* New York: Basic Books. (Original work published in 1966)

Piaget, J., & Inhelder, B. (1971). *Mental imagery in the child.* New York: Basic Books. (Original work published in 1966)

Piaget, J., & Inhelder, B. (1973). *Memory and intelligence.* New York: Basic Books. (Original work published in 1968)

Piaget, J., & Inhelder, B. (1976). The gaps in empiricism. In B. Inhelder & H. Chipman (Eds.), *Piaget and his school* (pp. 24–35). New York: Springer Verlag. (Original work published in 1969)

Poincaré, H. (1958). *The value of science.* New York: Dover Publications. (Original work published in 1905)

Rakison, D. H. (2007). Is consciousness in its infancy in infancy? *Journal of Consciousness Studies, 14,* 66–89.

Rivera, S. M., Wakeley, A., & Langer, J. (1999). The drawbridge phenomenon: Representational reasoning or perceptual preference? *Developmental Psychology, 35,* 427–435.

Rodríguez, C. (2009). The 'circumstances' of gestures: Proto-interrogatives and private gestures. *New Ideas in Psychology, 27,* 288–303.

Russell, J. (1978). *The acquisition of knowledge.* London: Macmillan.

Sinclair, H. (1982). Piaget on language: A perspective. In S. Modgil & C. Modgil (Eds.), *Jean Piaget: Consensus and controversy* (pp. 167–177). London: Holt, Rinehart, and Winston.

Smith, L. (1987). The infant's Copernican revolution. *Human Development, 30,* 210–224.

Smith, L. (1993). *Necessary knowledge.* Hove: Erlbaum.

Smith, L. (1998). On the development of mental representation. *Developmental Review, 18,* 202–227.

Smythe, W. E. (1992). Conceptions of interpretation in cognitive theories of representation. *Theory and Psychology, 2,* 339–362.

Stern, W. (1930). *Psychology of early childhood.* New York: Henry Holt and Company. (Original work published in 1914)

Straus, E. W. (1963). *The primary world of senses.* London: Glencoe. (Original work published in 1956)

Tomasello, M. (1996). Piagetian and Vygotskian approaches to language acquisition. *Human Development, 39,* 269–276.

Vonèche, J., & Vidal, F. (1985). Jean Piaget and the child psychologist in Jean Piaget. *Synthese, 65,* 121–138.

von Wright, G. H. (1971). *Explanation and understanding.* Ithaca, NY: Cornell University Press.

Vygotsky, L. S. (1978). *Mind in society: The development of higher psychological processes.* Cambridge, MA: Harvard University Press.

MAXIMILIAN B. BIBOK, ULRICH MÜLLER, AND
JEREMY I. M. CARPENDALE

10 Childhood

This chapter provides an overview of Piaget's work on cognitive development in childhood, extending from the emergence of symbolic thought
at approximately 2 years of age to the emergence of hypothetico-
deductive thought beginning in early adolescence. Piaget's research on
cognitive development spans 6 decades, starting with his early research
on children's understanding of part–whole relations (Piaget, 1921) and
concluding with the posthumously published books on the logic of
meanings (Piaget & Garcia, 1991) and categories and morphisms (Piaget,
Henriques, & Ascher, 1990/1992). What unites this massive research
program is Piaget's view of knowledge as constructed through activity
(see Chapters 1, 7, this volume).

Two matters complicate a summary of Piaget's theory of cognitive
development in childhood. First, Piaget and his collaborators charted
children's development in areas as diverse as classification, ordering (seriation), number, geometry, movement, time, causality, physical quantity, memory, imagery, and physics (conservation). Second, Piaget studied developmental changes in the development of reflective abstraction,
the grasp of consciousness, the role of contradiction, and generation
of possibility and necessity mainly in early and middle childhood (see
Chapters 6, 7, 13, this volume). Thus, it is not possible to cover all the
areas tackled by Piaget, and we limit ourselves to describing his work
on topics that have received considerable attention in the child developmental literature, specifically conservation, seriation, classification,
and number.

Rather than the particular age at which a specific form of thought
emerges in development, Piaget was more interested in the developmental sequences constituted by different forms of thought and the processes
involved in transforming one form of thought into another (Lourenço &
Machado, 1996; Piaget, 1956; Smith, 1991). Piaget used different logical–
mathematical models to precisely describe the logical characteristics of

different forms of thought as they emerge in the course of development. Whereas in his work from the 1930s to 1970s he relied on qualitative algebra and group theory to model different forms of thinking, he later adopted the mathematical concepts of categories and morphisms.

In this chapter we begin with a description of the logical–mathematical models, with a focus on Piaget et al.'s (1990/1992) morphism model.[1] Next we describe two periods of preoperational thought. The first (symbolic and preconceptual thought) is characterized by the emergence of symbols and the second (intramorphic) by unidirectional thought. We then discuss the two-step transition from preoperational to concrete operational thought. First, preoperational (intermorphic) cognitive functions become decontextualized. Second, they become systematically coordinated, resulting in (transmorphic) concrete operations (Piaget, 1970). We then illustrate the developmental advances in the areas of conservation, transitive reasoning, classification, and number. We conclude by discussing criticisms that have been leveled against Piaget's conceptualization of cognitive development during childhood.[2]

OPERATIONS AND MORPHISMS

The central goals of Piaget's theory were to describe and explain the fecundity and rigor of thought (Piaget, 1936/1952, pp. 417–419; see Chapman, 1988, p. 144). Fecundity refers to the continuous construction of novel forms of thought in the course of development. Rigor refers to the reversibility (i.e., systemic coordination) and deductive necessity of thought (see Chapter 3, this volume). A key insight of Piaget's was that the condition that makes possible the fecundity and rigor of thought is the organization of cognitive processes into coordinated systems or structures (Piaget, 1947/1976, 1975/1985). Piaget held that an understanding of deductive necessity emerges in childhood (approximately at the ages 6 to 7) at a level of thought that he termed concrete–operational; that is, it only operates upon concrete materials (i.e., tangible) and thus possesses certain inherent limitations (see Inhelder & Piaget, 1955/1958, pp. 248–251; Piaget, 1947/1976, p. 146).

The importance of operations in Piaget's theory follows from his epistemological framework. In contrast to empiricist theories, in which knowledge is derived from perception, Piaget emphasized the role of action and operations (transformation) in the construction of knowledge. Operations are defined as "interiorized actions (e.g., addition, which can be performed either physically or mentally) that are reversible (addition acquires an inverse in subtraction)" (Piaget, 1970, p. 705). Whereas Piaget had previously focused on the role of transformations in the emergence of concrete operations, in his later work he emphasized the role of comparisons and correspondences. Because Piaget used mathematical models to describe the organization of thought, this change in emphasis is reflected in his use of different mathematical formalizations.[3]

From the 1940s to 1970s, Piaget used algebraic or set theoretical concepts to describe this organization of operations, which he called "groupings" (Piaget, 1942, 1947/1976). Groupings are characterized by five features (Piaget, 1942, 1947/1976, pp. 40–42). First, they constitute closed systems: Any two elements of a grouping can be combined and can produce a new element of the same grouping (e.g., the numerical operation of adding two numbers produces another number). Second, every change is reversible because an inverse operation is defined within the system (e.g., adding can be reversed by subtraction). Third, the same result can be obtained in different ways because the combination of operations is associative (e.g., $[2 + 5] + 4 = 2 + [5 + 4]$). Fourth, when an operation is combined with its inverse, it is annulled (e.g., $+ 2 - 2 = 0$). Fifth, the addition of a class to itself (or to a larger class that includes the first class) leaves the result unchanged. For example, adding the class of flowers to itself yields the class of flowers; adding the class of flowers to the class of plants yields the class of plants. Piaget termed this fifth characteristic tautology $(A + A = A)$ or resorption $(A + B = B)$.

Near the end of his career, Piaget began to use the mathematical concept of morphisms derived from category theory (Eilenberg & MacLane, 1945; MacLane, 1971) to formally conceptualize cognitive development (Piaget & Garcia, 1991; Piaget et al., 1990/1992, p. 132). Morphisms (structural correspondences) are "comparisons [that] consist essentially in discovering common forms between two structures, two objects, two states, or [two] terms [that are] to be compared, whatever their number or their nature" (Piaget, 1979, p. 27). Morphisms are cognitive functions that allow individuals to transfer a form or conceptual mapping to objects. Morphisms, therefore, are cognitive functions that permit individuals to redraw the conceptual mappings they place upon objects to that of other conceptual mappings. Throughout this process, morphisms preserve the *state* of the structural relations among objects, which, in turn, were supplied by the previously utilized morphisms (Piaget, 1977, p. 351). Morphisms, therefore, allow for the comparison of objects by abstracting from them structural relations (Piaget, 1977, p. 351). Morphisms, however, do not transform states but leave them intact (Piaget, 1979, p. 18).

For example, children can conceptually frame two objects, arranged side by side, by imposing an alphabetical conceptual mapping, such as

"A" and "B," upon the objects. This conceptual mapping, in turn, can be translated through a cognitive function into a calendrical conceptual mapping, such as "Monday" and "Tuesday." Despite such translation, the structural relation between the two objects mapped by the morphisms has nonetheless remained the same – "A" comes *before* "B," and "Monday" comes *before* "Tuesday." Morphisms, therefore, permit the evaluation of identity, similarity, and equivalency across objects based upon the correspondences between their structural relations (Piaget & Garcia, 1991, p. 131).

Through the application of morphisms, objects are said to be *enformed*: "the active imposition of a form on an object by the knowing subject. In a derived sense, the same word designates...the fact that some knowledge content is subsumed under a well-defined form" (Piaget et al., 1990/1992, p. 189). The morphisms individuals transfer to objects, therefore, necessarily determine how they will conceptualize those objects. In turn, such conceptualizations will already determine the possible cognitive manipulations that individuals can perform upon those objects. For example, both the Roman and Arabic number systems are conceptual mappings that individuals can apply to objects. However, unlike the Arabic numeral system, the Roman system lacks notation for the value of zero and thus never developed a positional notation (e.g., 20 equals 2 in the 10th position). Consequently, fractional values are essentially impossible under this system, as well as the addition of large sums. Morphisms, therefore, allow for certain cognitive manipulations to take place while at the same time precluding the use of other cogitive manipulations.

In Piaget's morphism model, transformations and operations retain a central role (Piaget, 1979, pp. 25–27; Piaget et al., 1990/1992, pp. 189–191). Through transformations, individuals construct invariants (i.e., structural relations between entities) that are not inherent in the morphisms they have previously applied to a situation. This is because morphisms are conceptual mappings of *states* constituted by structural relations. By contrast, transformations are operations that *change* states, and in the process the structural relations constituting those states (Barrouillet & Poirier, 1997). Transformations, therefore, modify the morphisms initially utilized to that of another in accordance with the goals of the individual, and in the process create novel morphisms (Piaget et al., 1990/1992, p. 189).

For example, a number of sticks of different lengths, arranged in order of increasing length, can be conceptually mapped as a linear list. However, by definition, the position of any element in a list is immaterial to the relative position of any other element in the list. In this example, though, the position of each stick is related to the sticks that precede or succeed it, as they are arranged in order of increasing length. The transformation (operation) of transitivity, therefore, can modify the initial morphism of a list into that of an ordered series. Consequently, the new morphism of serial order *enforms* the sticks, making their increasing length explicit, information that a linear list cannot capture.

Piaget also considered how the relations between transformations (operations) and morphisms changed with development (Piaget, 1977, p. 351; 1979, pp. 25–27). The correspondences constructed early in development were seen as laying the foundation for the later development of operations (Piaget, 1979, p. 20). These early correspondences may be reciprocal in nature (if A = B, then B = A). However, as there are no negating or inverse correspondences, such correspondences are not reversible. Through the evaluation of empirically observable correspondences between objects (or states of objects) children come to construct an understanding of the operations that are implied by, or that produce, such correspondences. Specifically, independent of the content to which an operation is applied, the form (i.e., class) of the content can be linked together by way of morphisms (functions of comparison). Later with development, correspondences between operations themselves (e.g., the reversible operations of addition and subtraction) arise as a direct consequence of the creation of systematically organized operational structures. At this point, such correspondences are logically necessary and deductively follow from the organization of such operational structures (Piaget, 1979, pp. 25–27). This recognition of a relation between correspondences and operations allowed Piaget to more adequately describe the transition from preoperational to concrete operational thought.

Children's use of morphisms and transformations passes through three levels of development: (a) intramorphic, (b) intermorphic, and (c) transmorphic (Piaget et al., 1990/1992, pp. xx–xxi). We use these levels to describe cognitive development during the second preoperational period and the concrete–operational period. But first we briefly summarize the major characteristics of thought at the first preoperational period, which Piaget (1947/1976, pp. 123–129) also referred to as symbolic and preconceptual thought.

SYMBOLIC AND PRECONCEPTUAL THOUGHT

The onset of the preoperational period is demarcated by the emergence of the semiotic function, which consists of differentiated signifier–signified systems and which, in turn, are a prerequisite for symbolic representation (see Chapter 9, this volume). The semiotic function underlies children's abilities to engage in a number of different activities, such as deferred imitation (i.e., imitation in the absence of the model), pretend play, drawing, psychological functions based on mental images (e.g., recall memory), and language. These activities are practiced and refined during the level of preconceptual thought (approximately 2–4 years of age) (Piaget, 1945/1962, pp. 221–244).

The semiotic function advances cognition in a number of respects. Owing to the semiotic function, cognition (a) transcends the immediate here and now, (b) becomes capable of simultaneously representing two or more states in the world, (c) becomes concerned with truth (and no longer just with practical success), and (d) becomes subject to the influence of social factors in a qualitatively new way (Piaget, 1937/1954, pp. 361–364; 1945/1962, pp. 238–240; 1947/1976, pp. 120–122).

At the same time, preoperational thought is characterized by profound cognitive limitations. These limitations are partly due to the fact that the development of the semiotic function requires that the practical concepts of object, space, causality, and time that had been constructed and only practically understood at the sensorimotor stage be reconstructed on a new symbolic–representational plane. Piaget (1947/1976, p. 148) termed this process of reconstructing concepts at a qualitatively different plane "vertical décalage" (translation: vertical time lag).

To briefly mention one cognitive limitation: Although preconceptual thought is no longer tied to particular objects or events (the here and now), it fails to distinguish between individual members of a concept and the generality of a concept. For example, when Piaget's daughter Jacqueline was 31 months old, she cried, upon seeing a slug, "There it is!" When she saw another slug a few yards further she said, "There's the slug again" (Piaget, 1945/1962, Obs. 107). Concepts thus remain midway between the generality of the concept and the individuality of elements composing it. On the one hand, there is no concept of a general class; on the other hand, particular objects have less individuality and easily lose their identity.[4] Because of this, Piaget termed these concepts preconcepts or prototypes; "the slug" is a prototype representative of all slugs (Piaget, 1945/1962, p. 228).

INTRAMORPHIC

The first morphic level to develop is the intramorphic level, lasting from about 4 to 7 years of age; this level corresponds to what Piaget (1947/1976, p. 129) had previously referred to as the intuitive substage of the level of preoperational thought. The intramorphic level begins when children construct unidirectional cognitive functions (Piaget, Grize,

Szeminska, & Bang, 1968/1977). For example, in the standard Piagetian conservation of substance task (Inhelder, Sinclair, & Bovet, 1974,
pp. 281–284; Piaget, 1975/1985, pp. 94–96; Piaget & Inhelder, 1941/
1974), children are shown a clay ball. The ball is then rolled into a cylinder, thereby *elongating* its length and *thinning* its diameter. Children
are then asked whether the amount of clay (substance) has changed or
remained the same. In the context of this task, *elongating* and *thinning*
consist of two complementary and logically interdependent functions.
As the amount of substance (volume) of clay involved remains constant (invariant) across changes in its form, the effects of *elongating* and
thinning are quantitatively related to one another by a constant mathematical relation: volume $= \pi(\text{diameter}/2)^2 \times \text{length}$. Nevertheless, at the
intramorphic level, the cognitive functions of *elongating* and *thinning*
remain relative to the child's subjective point of view. Thus, if children focus on the act of *elongating* the clay cylinder, they are unaware
that it has simultaneously undergone an act of *thinning*. Consequently,
they will report that the amount of clay has changed (Piaget, 1975/1985,
p. 94).

Owing to their unidirectional understanding of cognitive functions,
children remain unaware of any possible coordination between two, logically interdependent, cognitive functions, as both functions are unable
to occur in cognition simultaneously. Cognition at this level is said to
be centered on only one aspect of any given physical/mental action or
logical system (part and whole relations) under consideration (Piaget,
1947/1976, pp. 130–131, 133; 1970/1976, p. 133; Piaget & Garcia, 1991,
p. 131). As interdependent cognitive functions remain separate in awareness, children cannot begin the process of establishing cognitive structures to logically ground and integrate the cognitive functions involved
(Chapman, 1988, p. 148; Piaget & Garcia, 1991, p. 131). Such reasoning
lacks "reversibility"; that is, children are unaware that logically interdependent functions balance each other *necessarily* and *simultaneously*
(Piaget et al., 1990/1992, pp. xxi, 28).

For example, *elongating* a clay cylinder is *logically* balanced by a
proportional *thinning* of the cylinder's diameter. Lacking such an operational structure, children must rely upon functions that are simple
and instantiated in empirically observable manipulations (Piaget et al.,
1990/1992, pp. xxi, 28). Thus, the only systematic coordination of cognitive functions that children are capable of is "empirical return" (Piaget,
1975/1985, p. 95; Piaget et al., 1990/1992, p. 91). Empirical return
means that children can only reverse (balance) cognitive functions along
their physical paths of manipulation through their *successive* application (Piaget et al., 1990/1992, p. 91). For example, *elongating* a clay

cylinder by three units is balanced, in succession, by *compressing* the same cylinder by three units, thereby returning it to its original shape.

There are a number of reasons why intramorphic reasoning lacks reversibility. First, final states are often all that remain after an empirical manipulation, as initial states are often destroyed in the process. For example, if water is boiled to vapor, it is empirically difficult to return the vapor back into water, although logically the quantity of water has remained the same. In such a case, children are unable to infer from the empirical comparison of initial and final states the logically reversible relation existing between the water and the vapor. Second, children *enform* final states in accordance with their goals. In contrast, initial states are usually imposed from sources outside of children's control. Through the construction of final states, children simultaneously produce an epistemic state. This has the effect of cognitively casting the final state as a "frame of reference." Consequently, reciprocal effects, often the opposite of goal-directed functions, will be excluded from the "frame" and from awareness. That is, children are unable to separate their goals from the activities by which they attempt to attain those goals (Piaget, 1979, p. 22). Third, goal-directed actions are affirmative in that they are observable and actively performed by children, whereas the reciprocal effects of those actions are negative (opposite) in nature in that they are consequential and typically unobservable (Piaget, 1974/1980, pp. 163–164; 1975/1985, pp. 13–15). Children, therefore, understand the affirmative aspects of actions before the negative aspects, the understanding of which children must construct through a process of reflective thought.

Piaget believed that the transition from empirical return to reversibility occurred through a process of cognitive decentration. Rather than understanding cognitive functions in absolute terms, with themselves as the reference point for those functions (egocentric thought), children come to understand cognitive functions as relative to multiple reference points or perspectives (Piaget, 1947/1976, pp. 138–139, 142–143). Thus, if children observe the *elongating* of a clay cylinder, when viewed from a different cognitive perspective that same cylinder will also be thinning at its diameter. Decentration is a consequence of the process of equilibration and involves, among others, the interplay of being confronted with contradictions (e.g., other perspectives, obstacles to goals), the becoming aware of one's own actions, and reflecting abstraction on the coordinations underlying these actions (Piaget, 1975/1985, pp. 36–64; see Chapters 6, 7, and 17, this volume). Through such coordination of viewpoints children's thinking no longer remains bound to the "subjective reciprocity" of a unidirectional viewpoint (i.e., the successive application of cognitive functions from a particular point of view). Instead, children come to coordinate all the viewpoints possible for any given cognitive function into a system of "objective reciprocities" (i.e., not tied to one point of view) (Piaget, 1947/1976, p. 142; Piaget & Inhelder, 1948/1963, pp. 244–245). As a result of this coordination, logically interdependent cognitive functions, such as *elongating* and *thinning*, come to be organized into a single operational system, and the reciprocal coordination of two operations results in reversibility.

INTERMORPHIC

The second morphic level to develop is the intermorphic level and corresponds to what Piaget had previously referred to as the beginning phases of concrete operational thought or "articulated intuitions" (Piaget, 1947/1976, pp. 139–141). For the first time, the systematic coordination of simple cognitive functions becomes possible (Barrouillet & Poirier, 1997). However, those systematic coordinations, being built from the empirically context-specific cognitive functions of the intramorphic level, remain local in their scope of application. In the conservation of substance task, for example, although *elongating* and *thinning* may be coordinated as a *displacement operation*, this operation is still "bound" to the act of displacing a ball of clay. That is, *displacement* has not yet come to be generalized as an abstract, context-free, operation. This dependency on the manipulation of real, empirically verifiable, concrete objects for the ability to use cognitive operations is the defining characteristic of the concrete operational stage of development (Chapman, 1988; Parsons, 1958). Such cognitive operations, although giving structure to children's real-time actions, are dependent on the performance of those actions for their use (Piaget, 1947/1976, p. 146). Consequently, in the absence of objects to physically manipulate, children are incapable of such cognitive operations. For this reason, Piaget did not view the intermorphic level as qualitatively different from the intramorphic level (Barrouillet & Poirier, 1997; Piaget et al., 1990/1992, p. 52). Rather, the intermorphic level involves the successive application of two, interdependent, empirically bound, cognitive functions that were previously only applied successively in isolation from one another at the intramorphic level (Piaget, 1947/1976, p. 138).

Owing to the successive coordination of cognitive functions, a nascent form of reversibility does become possible during the intermorphic level. This early form of reversibility, though lacking logical necessity, does go beyond the successive reversal of cognitive functions along their paths of manipulation (Piaget, 1947/1976, p. 140). Children come to understand, for example, that *elongating* a clay cylinder also produces a *thinning* of its diameter. Therefore, to balance the effects produced by such an act of displacement (rolling the clay cylinder) children must compare both the initial and final states that, respectively, preceded and succeeded the action (Barrouillet & Poirier, 1997). For example, children may compare the initial state of the clay cylinder with its final state after it has been rolled. By noticing that the cylinder is both (a) *thinner* than it was at the start and (b) *longer* than it was at the start, children come to recognize a qualitative relation (empirical correlation) between the functions of *elongating* and *thinning*, as both result from the single operation of displacement (rolling) (Piaget, 1975/1985, p. 95). However, as intermorphic reasoning involves understanding the relation between these two functions in a qualitative and not quantitative sense (e.g., volume $= \pi[\text{diameter}/2]^2 \times \text{length}$), the interdependence between cognitive functions is understood as an empirical fact or certainty rather than as a logical necessity (Cormier & Dagenais, 1983; Miller, 1986). For this reason, children using such reasoning continue to answer the conservation of substance task by stating that the amount of clay has changed, although they preface their answer by indicating that the clay ball will be both "long and thin" (Piaget, 1975/1985, p. 95).

This failure to understand the logical necessity of reversibility is a direct result of children's need to compare initial and final states. Morphisms, as cognitive functions that allow for the conceptual mappings of states, cannot attain logical necessity as they are still empirically bound to the objects they *enform* (Barrouillet & Poirier, 1997; Piaget et al., 1990/1992, p. 28). Therefore, the structural relations between the objects that they map are not yet invariant to those objects' empirical, context-specific, presentation. Consequently, although children compare initial and final states (morphisms) and note the empirical correspondences between them, they have yet to construct invariant relations that change or transform the initial state into the final state (Piaget, 1977, p. 351; Piaget et al., 1990/1992, pp. 190–191). That is, static states (i.e., initial and final) and the actions (i.e., transformations) that modify those states are not yet cognized by children as forming a single, integrated system (Piaget et al., 1990/1992, pp. 190–191).

For example, in a simple transfer of object task (Piaget 1974/1980, pp. 159–164) children are presented with two equal rows of objects. The experimenter's row is then covered and children are asked to transfer n objects from their row to the experimenter's row. Children are then asked how many more objects are in the experimenter's row than in their row. The correct answer is $2n$ (see Piaget et al., 1990/1992, pp. 59–76, for a task using the reciprocal relation, $n/2$). Children with an intermediate understanding of the task approach the problem as if each row represents an independent state and determine the answer by working out the differences between the rows. They compare the initial state of each row with its corresponding final state to determine that each row has changed in number. Finally, as both rows have changed state, they compare the two rows to determine the answer. However, such an empirical strategy (Cormier & Dagenais, 1983) of comparing rows proves ineffective when the rows become too large in number. In contrast, children who use a logical strategy (Cormier & Dagenais, 1983) understand that the answer, $2n$, is invariant across all possible row lengths, owing to the structural relation of a one-to-one correspondence holding between counterposing objects among the two rows. To move an object (n) from one row necessarily entails that a corresponding object (n) in the other row become unmatched (cf. Piaget, 1977, pp. 355–356). Children using this logical strategy understand that the two rows are not independent states but rather together comprise an integrated system that remains balanced at all points in time (cf. Piaget, 1979, pp. 22–23). For this reason, such children no longer need to compare initial and final states but instead focus solely on the transformation performed ($2n$); hence, the length of the rows is inconsequential to their ability to derive the correct answer.

Intermorphic operations, still being "bounded" to context, are not capable of being integrated with each other into a closed transformational system (Piaget, 1941; Piaget et al., 1990/1992, pp. xx, 28). Such an understanding would allow children to decontextualize the operation from the empirical setting and physical manipulations upon which it is dependent for its instantiation. With decontextualization, the operation comes to be grounded in its own logical necessity. Thereafter, the operation is understood to hold invariantly, independent of its empirical instantiation. This new understanding permits children to integrate such operations into a transformational system (Piaget et al., 1990/1992, pp. 28–29). Freed from their empirical context, these operations can now be brought to bear upon novel situations.[5] Such a process changes the *enformations* initially created; that is, children become capable of constructing novel morphisms.

TRANSMORPHIC

The third morphic level to develop is the transmorphic level, starting between 7 and 8 years of age, and it corresponds to what Piaget had previously referred to as the later phases of concrete operational thought (Piaget, 1947/1976, pp. 139–141; 1970/1972, pp. 42–46). Unlike the intermorphic level, where the coordination of functions was the result of trial-and-error observation, transmorphic operations are linked to an understanding of logical necessity (see Chapter 3, this volume). Through reversibility, children come to understand that, by deductive necessity, two interdependent cognitive functions must be systematically related to each other (Piaget, 1947/1976, pp. 36, 141; Piaget et al., 1990/1992, pp. 28–29, 40, 53). Thus, unlike the intermorphic level, children no longer need to compare initial and final states to determine the consequences of an action. Instead, children understand from the start that changes found between initial and final states result from operational transformations (Piaget et al., 1990/1992, p. 53). Children, therefore, shift from an exclusive focus on states (morphisms) toward a focus on the transformations occurring between states (Barrouillet & Poirier, 1997).

Operations of the transmorphic level permit for the first time transformational "freedom" (Piaget et al., 1990/1992, p. 28). That is, independent of the specific empirical context, though not the empirical domain in which they come to be manifest, operations are now relative to any arbitrarily selected application point and logically determined termination point (Piaget et al., 1990/1992, pp. xx, 28). For example, with the conservation of substance task, children understand that even before the clay cylinder is rolled out, for any arbitrarily decided upon length the cylinder's diameter will already be determined out of logical necessity. For this reason, children report that the amount of clay (substance) has remained the same.

However, although transmorphic operations are independent of the local empirical context in which they come to be manifest, such operations are not yet independent of the empirical domain (e.g., substance, liquid, weight, volume) to which they pertain. Transmorphic operations, therefore, are still concrete operations in the sense that they remain bound to a given empirical domain. This discrepancy between understanding logical necessity in one empirical domain yet not in another is referred to as horizontal décalage (Piaget, 1947/1976, p. 147). The reason for such décalages in understanding between domains stems from the potential afforded by each empirical domain for children to experience empirical return. Empirical domains differ from one another in terms of the types of actions children can perform and the ease with which they can observe the empirical consequences of those actions. The greater the difficulty children have in observing the negative (consequential) outcomes of their actions, the greater the difficulty they have in understanding empirical return and thus beginning a process of decentration. For this reason, children must construct cognitive operations in each empirical domain independently (Piaget, 1947/1976, pp. 146–147; see Chapman, 1988), even though such operations will be formally analogous in structure (e.g., conservation). In the next sections, we will illustrate the cognitive advances during childhood in the areas of conservation, transitivity, classification, and number, as these areas have received considerable attention in the child development literature.

CONSERVATION

Conservation, the operational understanding that a whole exists as a *"quantitative* invariant" (Piaget, 1968, p. 18) and therefore remains intact despite the quantitative rearrangement of its parts (Piaget, 1977, p. 355; Piaget & Inhelder, 1941/1974), is considered one of the defining competencies of concrete operational thought. Specifically,

> [P]recisely because they are quantitative, notions of conservation always deal with invariants which are based on the composition of certain transformations, so that we can say that where there is no transformation we cannot speak of conservation. (Piaget, 1968, p. 18)

Throughout the previous discussion we have used the conservation of substance task to illustrate Piaget's morphic account of cognitive development. Two operations are at work in the task: *elongating* and *thinning*. An understanding of conservation entails that children are able to understand the necessary relation existing between these operations and therefore quantitatively coordinate these operations and the transformations they effect upon the clay. This quantitative coordination of operations allows children to understand the whole as a quantitative invariant: "([longer] × thinner = the same amount)" (Piaget, 1968, p. 18). Thus, they say the amount of clay has remained the same. Young children, however, typically focus on only one of the dimensions involved when attempting to solve conservation tasks. Thus, if children focus on the length of the clay cylinder, they will say the amount of clay (substance) has increased.

Piaget (1975/1985, pp. 96–98; 1977, pp. 355–357) proposed that an understanding of conservation can be explained in terms of the coordination of commutability and vicariant relations. Vicariant relations refer to the fact that the same whole (e.g., class, quantity) can be divided in different ways into subclasses and their complements, and that these divisions leave the whole invariant ($A_1 + A_1' = B$, $A_2 + A_2' = B$, etc.). Commutability is the principle that a change resulting in an addition at a terminal point must also be accompanied by, or correspond with, a

removal from an originating point (Piaget, 1979, p. 21). In the conservation of substance task, for example, an understanding of commutability
would mean that children recognize that "what the object loses in one
dimension (diameter) is made up for in another (length)" (Piaget, 1977,
p. 356).

The coordination of commutability and vicariant relations entails the
following. Suppose a whole (B) is composed of two parts, such that $(A_1 + A_1') = B$. It may help to imagine the parentheses ( ) denoting the outside
boundary of a ball of clay. Now imagine that A_1 is moved from the left
side of the ball to the other side, such that $(A_1' + A_1) = B$. Given the previous example of vicariant relations, this scenario is no different from
the arrangement $(A_1' + A_2) = B$. Commutability involves a morphism
(comparison) of identity (Piaget, 1977, p. 355) between A_1 and A_2, such
that children understand them to be the same piece of clay $(A_1 \equiv A_2)$.
Thus, a displacement of the parts has not resulted in a net change in
the quantity of substance (B) involved. However, such a relation of commutability would also hold for A_1' and its corollary, A_2'. This means
that more than one specific instance of a commutable relation exists
in any conservation scenario (e.g., given $A + B + C + D = W$, any part
can be moved to any number of possible locations). There exists, therefore, morphisms (i.e., vicariant relations) between these commutable
relations. Together, the commutable relations that are coordinated with
each other by way of vicariant relations can be considered a category
in the formal mathematical sense of the term: "a collection of objects
with all their possible morphisms" (Piaget, 1979, p. 18). Piaget (1977,
pp. 352, 356) considered this category equivalent to his previous for-
malization of the grouping classification. With regard to conservation,
the coordination of commutability and vicariant relations allows children to conserve the whole despite displacement (commutability) and
rearrangement (vicariant relations) of its parts.

TRANSITIVITY

Transitivity is the mathematical understanding that if in a series, $A < B$
and $B < C$, then it necessarily follows that $A < C$. Children's understanding of transitivity is manifested most readily in their ability to solve seriation tasks. In these tasks children are required to order items in terms
of a binary criterion, such as longer, larger, heavier, etc. For example,
in the standard seriation task (Piaget, 1941/1952, pp. 123–135), children
are presented with a collection of sticks of differing lengths and asked
to arrange them, side by side, from shortest to longest. The differences
between the lengths of the sticks, however, are almost imperceptible,

thereby requiring children to compare sticks two at a time to determine which is longer (Inhelder & Piaget, 1959/1969; Piaget, 1941/1952). Children using intramorphic reasoning, typically 4 to 5 years of age, are only able to produce uncoordinated pairings of sticks (Piaget, 1947/1976, p. 134). Later, children create correct series through trial and error. Finally, with the use of transmorphic/concrete operations, children are able to construct correct series on their first trial. Such children may begin, for example, by finding the shortest stick in the collection, and then the next shortest, and so forth (Piaget, 1947/1976, p. 134); that is, their actions are guided by a principled approach (Leiser & Gillieron, 1990). It is at this point that children also come to understand the logical necessity of transitivity.

From the perspective of Piaget's morphic theory of development, children's failure to understand transitivity results from any exclusive focus on initial and final states. Mathematically, there are two initial states, $A < B$ and $B < C$. These two states, however, cannot be compared to determine the relation, $A < C$, nor the transformations that bring it about, as B is a joint member of each state; to focus on one state ($A < B$) dissolves the other state ($B < C$). Only at the transmorphic level do children construct the invariant relation of transitivity by which the relations between the sticks become integrated into a closed transformational system. Consequently, children focus directly on the operations involved in transitivity rather than the states produced by those operations.

CLASSIFICATION

Classification involves grouping items based upon a common property into sets or collections. Classes are defined in terms of two important features, their intension and their extension (Inhelder & Piaget, 1959/1969, pp. 7–8). The intension of a class is the set of properties that is common to the members of the class and that differentiates them from other classes. The extension of a class is the set of members or individuals comprising that class and the hierarchical relation between classes (i.e., class inclusion: the subordinate class of apples is included in the superordinate class of fruit).[6] Extension is thus a relation between part and whole. For Piaget, then, the development of classification skills involves the coordination of extension (i.e., part–whole relation) with the intension (i.e., similarity and difference of properties).

A criterion for the coordination of intension and extension is the understanding of class inclusion. A typical class inclusion task asks children to compare the number of objects in the including or superordinate class with the number of objects in the most numerous of its subclasses (Inhelder & Piaget, 1959/1969, pp. 100–118). For example, given 12 daisies and 4 roses, children are asked, "Are there more daisies or more flowers?" A correct answer requires that children conserve the including class (B) while making the quantitative comparison between it and the included class (A).

Piaget (1977, pp. 352–353) accounted for children's failure to conserve classes as a result of an inability to coordinate the morphisms of surjection, bijection, and injection holding between subclasses and superordinate classes. For example, children may be presented with pictures of 12 daisies (A) and 4 roses (A'). Together, both subclasses constitute a superordinate class consisting of 16 flowers (A + A' = B). Each daisy can be thought of as possessing two properties: a – an intensional property that defines it as a daisy, and b – an intensional property that defines it as a flower. The relation between the class of daisies (A) and the class of flowers (B) is one of surjection: one-to-many correspondence. That is, the single class of daisies (A) does not exhaust the many number of other classes that together form the superordinate class of flowers (B). This surjective relation, it should be noted, refers specifically to the daises as a class, and not any individual daisy.

With respect to the individual 12 daisies (A) and the superordinate class of flowers (B) there is a relation of injection: a one-to-one correspondence between all elements of one set and a portion of another larger set. That is, each daisy of set (A) corresponds to itself as a member of the flower class (B). However, the flower class (B) is not exhausted by these correspondences as the four roses remain in the superordinate class of flowers (B).

Piaget viewed this injection relation as important in accounting for children's failure at class inclusion. When children fail class inclusion, they compare, for example, the daisies (A) with the roses (A'), thinking that such a comparison has separated the daisies (A) from the flowers (B). Thus, children unintentionally construe the relation between the roses (A') and the flowers (B) to be one of bijection: one-to-one correspondence that is exhaustive of all elements in two equal sets. That is, they treat roses (A') as if they exhaust the class of flowers (B). Children, therefore, fail to realize that there exists a reciprocal relation to the injective relation between the individual daisies (A) and the class of flowers (B). Piaget (1977, p. 352) called this reciprocal relation "subjection": the surjection of the individual members of the flower class (B) into the class of daisies (A) to the extent that those members possess the property a that defines the intension of the daisy class (A). This surjective relation allows children to maintain the unity of the flower class, as children do not need to construct the subclass of daisies (A) by negating the superordinate class of flowers (B); that is, (A = B − A′). Rather, the intensional property, b, that defines a daisy as a flower maintains its membership (injection) in the flower class, whereas the intensional property, a, allows for its subjection into the class of daisies. Without an understanding of this relation, children cannot quantify the flowers (B) and compare them to the number of daisies (A). However, once children can coordinate the injective and subjective relations (morphisms) that construct the classes in question, they can conserve the superordinate class.

Piaget's (1977) morphic account of class inclusion can be seen as an extension of his grouping account of class operations (Davidson, 1988). Specifically, the grouping account was based upon the notion of constructing subclasses through negation under the including class (Inhelder & Piaget, 1959/1969; Piaget, 1941/1952, 1975/1985, p. 103) by the application of an inverse class operation: A = B − A′ and A′ = B − A (Piaget, 1977/2001; Smith, 1982). In contrast, Piaget's (1977, p. 352) morphic account of class inclusion makes no reference to construction under negation but rather focuses solely on the coordination of morphisms that map intensional properties. An advantage of Piaget's morphic account is that the superordinate class is theoretically approached as being positively defined by its own intensional property rather than only being defined by its extension. The morphic account, therefore, helps address the issues of how children first come to construct, through addition, the superordinate class. Specifically, the intensional property of the superordinate class allows children to select the subclasses to include in the superordinate class. This intensional property, and its coordination with the intensional property of the subclasses, is fully taken into account by Piaget's morphic model when providing an account of children's failure at class inclusion. Thus, by describing the grouping structures and class operations in terms of morphisms, the difficulties children have in class inclusion (specifically the surjective relation) can be more readily formalized and studied.

Class inclusion, therefore, illustrates many aspects of Piaget's morphic theory of development. Classes can be conceptualized as representing static states constituted by the morphisms of surjection, injection, and subjection. The coordination of those morphisms gives rise to the class operators of the grouping structures, specifically addition (e.g., A + A′ = B) and subtraction (e.g., B − A′ = A), that transform those states (classes). Unless children have attained a transmorphic level of understanding with respect to class inclusion, they are unable to compare

subclasses and superordinate classes. The reason for this is that understanding the relation between subclasses and superordinate classes can
only be achieved operationally. The strategy of comparing static states
results in failure – focusing on a subclass (part) dissolves the superordinate class (whole) of which it is a part (Barrouillet & Poirier, 1997;
Piaget, 1947/1976, p. 133).

NUMBER

Piaget recognized that although preschoolers may use number words,
they may not understand the cardinal and ordinal properties of numbers. For Piaget, an operational understanding of number begins with
the ability to conserve number (Piaget & Inhelder, 1966/1969, p. 104):
the understanding that the concept of number is independent of the
perceptual configuration of the objects that are counted. Prior to the
development of conservation of number, however, there are only figural collections with their numerosity tied to the physical space they
displace.

In the standard task that assesses the conservation of numerical quantities (Inhelder et al., 1974, pp. 275–277; Piaget, 1941/1952, pp. 65–95),
the experimenter takes six blue buttons and lines them up in a row. The
experimenter then presents the child with red buttons and instructs the
child to select the same number of red ones. At the first level of development, children younger than 4 years of age typically select as many
buttons as necessary to match the spatial length of the experimenter's
row. That is, they judge the number of buttons according to the space
they occupy. At the next level, children construct a one-to-one correspondence between the rows. However, these children fail to conserve
number when the experimenter changes the length of one row, for example, by increasing the spacing between the buttons without adding any
extra buttons. Again, these children understand number in terms of a
figural collection dependent on space. Finally, at the last level, children
conserve number even when the perceptual configuration of the rows is
not the same (Piaget, 1941/1952, pp. 82–85).

The development of an operational concept of number is based on
the synthesis of class operations and seriations (Beth & Piaget, 1966,
pp. 259–272; see Mays, 1987; Smith, 2002a). Class operations account
for the cardinal aspect of number. Seriation accounts for the ordinal
aspect of number. A synthesis of class operation and seriation is required
because (a) class operations by themselves abstract from differences and
treat the elements contained in the class as equivalent, and (b) seriation

by itself focuses on differences and would be unable to determine the relation between one position and its successor:

> Number, then, results primarily from an ignoring of differential quali-
> ties which renders every individual element equivalent to every other
> element: one orange is equivalent to one tree is equivalent to one person
> as far as number is concerned. Once this is established, sets are classi-
> fiable according to inclusion (<): $1 < (1 + 1) < (1 + 1 + 1)$, etc. But
> they are seriable (→), and the only way to tell them apart and not to count
> the same one twice in these inclusions is to serialize them in space or
> in time: one and then another one and then another one; $1 \rightarrow 1 \rightarrow 1$,
> etc. Number thus appears as a synthesis of seriation and inclusion:
> $\{[(1) \rightarrow 1] \rightarrow 1\} \rightarrow$ etc. (Piaget & Inhelder, 1966/1969, p. 105)[7]

CRITICISM OF PIAGET'S THEORY

Piaget's theory of childhood cognitive development received considerable attention in the 1960s and 1970s. This attention was focused on the
age at which children succeed at various concrete–operational tasks. For
the last 20 years, however, the influence of Piagetian theory has been
waning. Piaget is dismissed as a historical figure and his theory regarded
as having been shown to be incorrect and of little value for contemporary developmental research. Specifically, three common criticisms are
the following: (a) Piaget's theory underestimates the age at which children pass different concrete operational tasks; (b) Piaget's notion of stage
implies that children perform consistently across tasks; however, as this
is not the case, Piaget's theory must be wrong; and (c) Piaget described
young children's thinking only in negative terms (for further response to
criticism see Chapter 1, this volume). Not all theorists, however, share
this negative evaluation. Instead, it has been argued that this negative
assessment results from a misinterpretation of Piaget's theory (e.g., see
Chapman, 1988; Desrochers, 2008; Lourenço, & Machado, 1996; Smith,
1992, 2002b). We will briefly describe and respond to these three common criticisms of Piaget's theory.

A common criticism of Piaget's theory of childhood cognitive development is that he underestimated young children's reasoning abilities
because extraneous performance factors in his tasks obscure children's
true competencies. Simplifying the tasks by removing such performance
factors should, therefore, provide a better assessment of children's abilities. Following this logic, a number of researchers set out to simplify
standard Piagetian tasks (e.g., Gelman & Baillargeon, 1983).

For example, Gelman (1972) simplified the conservation of number
task by reducing the number of objects in each row from five to two or

three and found that even 4- to 5-year-olds passed the task. However, it has been argued that simplified tasks, rather than assessing the same competence as standard tasks, but without extraneous performance factors, actually assess completely different competencies (Chapman, 1988; Lourenço & Machado, 1996). In the case of small numbers, what appeared to be conservation of number could be based on perceptual processes ("subitizing" or counting at a glance) rather than on numerical operations (see Desrochers, 2008; von Glasersfeld, 1982). Researchers who adopt such simplified tasks fail to account for the developmental processes that give rise to the competencies assessed by standard tasks, as no relations are drawn between such competencies and children's earlier task-related performances. In contrast, Piaget's morphism model describes the gradual construction of operations from earlier correspondences (comparisons) that are based upon children's interaction with the environment (e.g., experiencing empirical return). Thus, Piaget's morphism model represents an advance over his previous grouping model, as it views the correspondences developed in early childhood as "necessary for the discovery of transformations" (Piaget, 1979, p. 26). Contrary to his critics then, Piaget's morphism model provides a positive account of children's earlier abilities in that it captures subtle differences between different levels of development that are overlooked by the simplified task paradigm.

Another criticism leveled against Piaget's theory is based on a specific and frequent interpretation of Piaget's concepts of stage and structure. According to this interpretation, stages are conceived of as global structures that determine children's thinking, that is, a "hypothetical construct that is related to an observable performance as an antecedent to consequent" (Chapman, 1987, p. 289). Therefore, once children have developed, for example, the structure of concrete operational reasoning they should be able to solve all concrete operational tasks (for sources of this interpretation, see Chapman, 1988; Lourenço & Machado, 1996). However, the abundant evidence of horizontal décalage (inconsistency in reasoning across differing empirical domains) clearly does not fit this prediction. A classic example of asynchrony in development is that children develop conservation first for quantity, then weight, and then volume (Piaget & Inhelder, 1941/1974). From this interpretation of Piaget's concepts of stage and structure, horizontal décalage has been viewed as a significant empirical difficulty for Piaget's theory, one even thought to cast into doubt the structuralist framework of his theory (Siegel & Brainerd, 1978). However, Piaget never assumed that stages are characterized by homogeneity or developmental synchrony (Chapman, 1988). Furthermore, as previously discussed, from Piaget's core insight that thought originates in action it follows that forms of thinking should, at first, be domain specific. According to Piaget, structures develop through the interiorization of actions that are reversible and that later then become coordinated. Such actions will necessarily be content and context specific.

The final criticism that we discuss is the claim that Piaget characterized preschoolers thinking only negatively; that is, in terms of illogical thought and the absence of conservation concepts (Donaldson, 1978; Gelman, 1978; Siegal, 1991). However, Piaget evaluated each level of development positively in terms of its preceding level and negatively in terms of its succeeding level (Lourenço & Machado, 1996). Piaget viewed development as a continuous process in which no particular point in the process can be taken as an absolute starting point (Lourenço & Machado, 1996). Negative and positive assessments of a particular point in development, therefore, are only relative to the particular reference point one selects to conceptualize the developmental process. Consequently, negative and positive assessments of children's thinking are not statements of absolute value but statements of relative value reflecting variations in the accuracy, complexity, and adaptability of thought. For this reason, in his later work on morphisms and functions (as well as in his work on possibility and necessity) Piaget described the preoperational period in positive terms (e.g., unidirectional functions). However, with few exceptions (e.g., Chapman & Lindenberger, 1988; Davidson, 1987, 1988; Kamii, Myiakawa, & Kato, 2007) this later work has received virtually no attention. The claim, therefore, that Piaget only described children's thinking negatively is based to some extent on an incomplete reading of Piaget's work.

CONCLUSION

We have reviewed Piaget's theory and aspects of his vast empirical research program on cognitive development in childhood and responded to common criticisms of Piaget's research in this field. We believe that it is premature to view Piaget's work on cognitive development in childhood as being of just historical interest. Anybody who takes seriously two central features of cognition, its fecundity and logical rigor, cannot bypass Piaget because alternative models of cognition fail to account for these features (Chapman, 1987). In this respect, Piaget's attempt to explain these features in terms of operational groupings and morphisms is still the only game in town.

We indicated that Piaget's later work on morphisms provides an elegant way to describe the different forms of thought and transitions between them in a more fine-grained manner. At the same time, Piaget's theory remains incomplete. The systematic place of morphisms and their relation to operations was not completely worked out by Piaget. Similarly, the relation between further aspects of his later work (Piaget, 1981/1987, 1983/1987; Piaget & Garcia, 1987/1991) and operations is somewhat unclear (see Chapter 7, this volume). There are, therefore, lacunae in Piaget's work that anybody interested in a full account of human rationality is invited to address.[8]

NOTES

1. In his later work, Piaget also drew on modal logic (Piaget, 1981/1987, 1983/1987) and intensional logic (Piaget & Garcia, 1987/1991) to model cognitive development. Arguably, the algebraic and morphic models were developed in more detail. Unfortunately, Piaget never explained the extent to which these different models are consistent with each other and potentially relate to different aspects of the equilibration process.

2. In Piaget's writings, one can find different ways of dividing the developmental process into stages (e.g., Piaget, 1947/1976, 1968/1971, 1970/1972; Piaget & Inhelder, 1966/1969; see also Chapter 17, this volume). In this text, we follow Piaget's (e.g., 1947/1976, pp. 87–155, 1970/1972, pp. 19–51) more fine-grained distinctions.

3. Piaget was very clear that the mathematical descriptions are models applied by the psychologist and he warned against confusing the psychologist's formal mathematical descriptions of the organization of children's thought with the mental content of children's thought (Piaget & Inhelder, 1963/1969, p. 146).

4. Identity is a one-way function (see Piaget, 1968).

5. The transition from the intermorphic to transmorphic level results from the continuing process of equilibration responsible for the transition from the intramorphic to intermorphic level (Piaget, 1975/1985, pp. 36–64; see Chapters 6 and 7, this volume). The same factors (experiencing contradictions, awareness of one's own activities, and reflecting abstraction) involved in decentration continue to play a role in this transition.

6. To study the development of classification, Inhelder and Piaget (1959/1969, pp. 17–46) presented children with a number of objects that differed, for example, in terms of shape (triangles, squares, circles) and color (red, blue, green) and asked children to collect together the objects that were alike. On the basis of the way children grouped the objects, Inhelder and Piaget distinguished between different levels in the graphic and nongraphic levels in the development of classification. Children at these levels cannot construct a stable classification that is independent of space; rather, the perceptual features of the spatial layout determine the extension of a collection. This failure was manifest in the failure to understand class inclusion.

7. In a similar vein, measurement results from a synthesis of seriation and class operations, but the synthesis is applied to spatial relations (see Piaget, Inhelder, & Szeminska, 1948/1960).
8. The preparation of this chapter was supported in part by grants from SSHRC of Canada to all three authors, and from the Human Early Learning Network of Canada to Ulrich Müller and Jeremy Carpendale.

REFERENCES

Barrouillet, P., & Poirier, L. (1997). Comparing and transforming: An application of Piaget's morphisms theory to the development of class inclusion and arithmetic problem solving. *Human Development, 40,* 216–234.

Beth, E. W., & Piaget, J. (1966). *Mathematical epistemology and psychology.* Dordrecht: Reidel.

Chapman, M. (1987). Piaget, attentional capacity, and the functional implications of formal structure. In H. W. Reese (Ed.), *Advances in child development and behavior* (Vol. 20, pp. 229–334). Orlando, FL: Academic Press.

Chapman, M. (1988). *Constructive evolution: Origins and development of Piaget's thought.* Cambridge: Cambridge University Press.

Chapman, M., & Lindenberger, U. (1988). Functions, operations, and decalage in the development of transitivity. *Developmental Psychology, 24,* 542–551.

Cormier, P., & Dagenais, Y. (1983). Class-inclusion developmental levels and logical necessity. *International Journal of Behavioral Development, 6,* 1–14.

Davidson, P. M. (1987). Early function concepts: Their development and relation to certain mathematical and logical abilities. *Child Development, 58,* 1542–1555.

Davidson, P. M. (1988). Piaget's category-theoretic interpretation of cognitive development: A neglected contribution. *Human Development, 31,* 225–241.

Desrochers, S. (2008). From Piaget to specific Genevan developmental models. *Child Development Perspectives, 2,* 7–12.

Donaldson, M. (1978). *Children's minds.* London: Fontana.

Eilenberg, S., & MacLane, S. (1945). General theory of natural equivalences. *Transactions of the American Mathematical Society, 58,* 231–294.

Gelman, R. (1972). Logical capacity of very young children: Number invariance rules. *Child Development, 43,* 75–90.

Gelman, R. (1978). Cognitive development. *Annual Review of Psychology, 29,* 297–332.

Gelman, R., & Baillargeon, R. (1983). A review of some Piagetian concepts. In P. H. Mussen (Series Ed.) & J. H. Flavell & E. M. Markham (Vol. Eds.), *Handbook of child psychology* (Vol. 3, pp. 167–230). New York: Wiley.

Inhelder, B., & Piaget, J. (1958). *The growth of logical thinking: From childhood to adolescence.* New York: Basic Books. (Original work published in 1955)

Inhelder, B., & Piaget, J. (1969). *The early growth of logic in the child.* New York: Norton. (Original work published in 1959)

Inhelder, B., Sinclair, H., & Bovet, M. (1974). *Learning and the development of cognition.* London: Routledge & Kegan Paul.

Kamii, C., Myiakawa, Y., & Kato, T. (2007). Trying to make a lever work at ages 1 to 4: The development of 'functions' (logico-mathematical thinking). *Early Education and Development, 18*, 145–161.

Leiser, D., & Gillieron, C. (1990). *Cognitive science and genetic epistemology – a case study of understanding*. New York: Plenum.

Lourenço, O., & Machado, A. (1996). In defense of Piaget's theory: A reply to 10 common criticisms. *Psychological Review, 103*, 143–164.

MacLane, S. (1971). *Categories for the working mathematician*. New York: Springer-Verlag.

Mays, W. (1987). Piaget on logic and number: The philosophical background. In J. Russell (Ed.), *Philosophical perspectives on developmental psychology* (pp. 220–239). Oxford: Blackwell.

Miller, S. A. (1986). Certainty and necessity in the understanding of Piagetian concepts. *Developmental Psychology, 22*, 3–18.

Parsons, A. (1958). Translators' introduction: A guide for psychologists. In B. Inhelder & J. Piaget (Eds.), *The growth of logical thinking: From childhood to adolescence* (pp. vii–xx). New York: Basic Books.

Piaget, J. (1921). Essai sur quelques aspects du développement de la notion de partie chez l'enfant. *Journal de Psychologie, 18*, 449–480.

Piaget, J. (1941). Le mécanisme du développement mental et les lois du groupement des opérations. *Archives de Psychologie, 28*, 215–285.

Piaget, J. (1942). *Classes, relations et nombres*. Paris: Vrin.

Piaget, J. (1952). *The origins of intelligence in children*. New York: International Universities Press. (Original work published in 1936)

Piaget, J. (1952). *The child's conception of number*. London: Routledge & Kegan Paul. (Abridged translation of Piaget, J., & Szeminska, A. [1941]. *Le genèse du nombre chez l'enfant*. Neuchâtel: Delachaux et Niestlè.)

Piaget, J. (1954). *The construction of reality in the child*. New York: Basic Books. (Original work published in 1937)

Piaget, J. (1956). Les stades du developpement intellectual de l'enfant et de l'adolescent. In P. Osterrieth, J. Piaget, R. Saussure, J. Tanner, H. Wallon, R. Zazzo, B. Inhelder, & A. Rey (Eds.), *Le problème des stades en psychologie de l'enfant* (pp. 33–42). Paris: Presses Universitaires de France.

Piaget, J. (1962). *Play, dreams and imitation in childhood*. New York: W.W. Norton & Co. (Original work published in 1945)

Piaget, J. (1968). *On the development of memory and identity*. Barre, MA: Clark University Press.

Piaget, J. (1970). Piaget's theory. In P. H. Mussen (Ed.), *Carmichael's manual of child psychology, Vol. 1* (3rd ed., pp. 703–710). New York: Wiley.

Piaget, J. (1971). *Structuralism*. London: Routledge & Kegan Paul. (Original work published in 1968)

Piaget, J. (1972). *Judgment and reasoning in the child*. London: Routledge & Kegan Paul. (Original work published in 1924)

Piaget, J. (1972). *Psychology and epistemology: Towards a theory of knowledge*. Middlesex: Penguin Books. (Original work published in 1970)

Piaget, J. (1976). *The psychology of intelligence*. Totowa, NJ: Littlefield, Adams & Co. (Original work published in 1947)

Piaget, J. (1976). The affective and the cognitive unconscious. In B. Inhelder & H. H. Chipman (Eds.), *Piaget and his school* (pp. 63–71). New York: Springer. (Original work published in 1970)

Piaget, J. (1977). Some recent research and its link with a new theory of groupings and conservations based on commutability. *Annals of the New York Academy of Sciences, 291*(1), 350–358.

Piaget, J. (1979). Correspondences and transformations. In F. B. Murray & M. C. Almy (Eds.), *The impact of Piagetian theory* (pp. 17–27). Baltimore, MD: University Park Press.

Piaget, J. (1980). *Experiments in contradiction*. Chicago: University of Chicago Press. (Original work published in 1974)

Piaget, J. (1985). *The equilibration of cognitive structures*. Chicago: University of Chicago Press. (Original work published in 1975)

Piaget, J. (1987). *Possibility and necessity, Vol. 1: The role of possibility in cognitive development*. Minneapolis: University of Minnesota Press. (Original work published in 1981)

Piaget, J. (1987). *Possibility and necessity, Vol. 2: The role of necessity in cognitive development*. Minneapolis: University of Minnesota Press. (Original work published in 1983)

Piaget, J. (2001). *Studies in reflecting abstraction*. Hove, U.K.: Psychology Press. (Original work published in 1977)

Piaget, J., & Garcia, R. (1991). *Toward a logic of meanings*. Hillsdale, NJ: Erlbaum. (Original work published in 1987)

Piaget, J., Grize, J.-B., Szeminska, A., & Bang, V. (1977). *Epistemology and psychology of functions*. Dordrecht: Reidel. (Original work published in 1968)

Piaget, J., Henriques, G., & Ascher, E. (1992). *Morphisms and categories: Comparing and transforming*. Hillsdale, NJ: Erlbaum. (Original work published in 1990)

Piaget, J., & Inhelder, B. (1963). *The child's conception of space*. London: Routledge & Kegan Paul. (Original work published in 1948)

Piaget, J., & Inhelder, B. (1969). Intellectual operations and their development. In P. Fraisse & J. Piaget (Eds.), *Experimental psychology: Its scope and method* (pp. 144–205). New York: Basic Books. (Original work published in 1963)

Piaget, J., & Inhelder, B. (1969). *The psychology of the child*. New York: Basic Books. (Original work published in 1966)

Piaget, J., & Inhelder, B. (1974). *The child's construction of quantities*. London: Routledge & Kegan Paul. (Original work published in 1941)

Piaget, J., Inhelder, B., & Szeminska, A. (1960). *The child's conception of geometry*. New York: Harper Torchbooks. (Original work published in 1948)

Siegal, M. (1991). *Knowing children: Experiments in conversation and cognition*. Hillsdale, NJ: Erlbaum.

Siegel, L., & Brainerd, C. (1978). Preface. In L. Siegel & C. Brainerd (Eds.), *Alternatives to Piaget* (pp. xi–xiv). New York: Academic Press.

Smith, L. (1982). Class inclusion and conclusions about Piaget's theory. *British Journal of Psychology, 73*, 267–276.

Smith, L. (1991). Age, ability, and intellectual development in Piagetian theory. In M. Chandler & M. Chapman (Eds.), *Criteria for competence* (pp. 69–91). Hillsdale, NJ: Erlbaum.

Smith, L. (1992). Judgements and justifications: Criteria for the attribution of children's knowledge in Piagetian research. *British Journal of Developmental Psychology, 10,* 1–23.

Smith, L. (2002a). *Reasoning by mathematical induction in children's arithmetic.* Oxford: Elsevier Pergamon Press.

Smith, L. (2002b). Piaget's model. In U. Goswami (Ed.), *Blackwell handbook of childhood cognitive development* (pp. 515–537). Oxford: Blackwell.

von Glasersfeld, E. (1982). Subitizing – the role of figural patterns in the development of numerical concepts. *Archives de Psychologie, 50,* 191–218.

11 Adolescence

The adolescent stage in Piaget's theory of cognitive development begins – typically about the age of 11 or 12 years – with the emergence of what he called "formal reasoning" or "formal operations." Such reasoning may continue to develop over the course of adolescence and early adulthood, and some individuals may even construct more advanced forms of cognition, but the transition from childhood to adolescence marks the last major qualitative transformation highlighted in Piagetian theory and research. Thus, Piaget's theory differs, on the one hand, from neonativist and other theories that see development as fundamentally a phenomenon of early childhood, and on the other hand from life-span theories that see development as continuing inexorably through adulthood. Piaget's theory leaves open the possibility of more advanced development, but he did not describe a stage beyond formal operations.

By "formal reasoning," Piaget meant hypothetico–deductive reasoning. Even young children make inferences, and by age 7 or 8 their inferences conform to strict rules of deductive logic, but such inferences always begin, Piaget maintained, with what the child believes or accepts. Beginning about age 11 or 12, thinkers explore what can be deduced from propositions deemed hypothetical or even false. This is hypothetico–deductive, or formal, reasoning. Piaget's conception of the emergence of formal reasoning at the transition to adolescence can already be seen in his early work from the 1920s.

Piaget's conceptualization of formal reasoning developed from the 1920s to the 1950s into his theory of formal operations, with subsequent refinements in later work. The major presentation of this theory was, and remains, *The Growth of Logical Thinking From Childhood to Adolescence* (Inhelder & Piaget, 1955/1958), which is the primary basis for the present chapter. First, however, we consider the early treatment of hypothetico–deductive reasoning, not just for historical reasons but because this conception of formal reasoning became and remained central to Piaget's conceptualization of formal operations.

HYPOTHETICO–DEDUCTIVE REASONING

In a chapter entitled "Formal Thought and Relational Judgments" in his early book *Judgment and Reasoning in the Child*, Piaget (1924/1972) presented a study in which "some 40 schoolboys of Geneva between the ages of 9 and 11–12" (p. 63) were presented with the "five absurd phrases" (p. 62) from the Binet-Simon test (an early IQ test). One such phrase, for example, was "I have three brothers: Paul, Ernest, and myself" (p. 63). The others, all somewhat longer, involved matters such as whether a dead cyclist might not recover. In addition to the standard interview intended to induce a scorable answer, reported Piaget,

> we make the child repeat the absurd phrase by heart. The phrase is generally deformed by the child in a significant manner. We then read him the exact text so as to eliminate all factors due to inattention or forgetfulness. Finally, we ask the child to arrange the sentence himself in such a way that "there should no longer be anything silly in it." (pp. 63–64)

Piaget also recommended taking "illustrations from the child's own life" (p. 64). In contrast to the protocol for an IQ test, he was not concerned with standardization but rather with understanding the child's responses. The theoretical challenge was to explain why some problems were solved at earlier ages than others and, more generally, how children's reasoning changed with increasing age.

Examining children's reasoning across problems and ages, Piaget concluded that the age range 11–12 marked the emergence of what he called "formal" reasoning. By reasoning formally he meant "admitting a datum as such and deducing what follows from it" (p. 66). Children of 7 or 8, he argued, already "distinguish hypothesis from reality" (p. 67) and engage in "correct deductive reasoning" (p. 67). "But all reasoning at this stage is still limited by one essential qualification: deduction bears only upon the beliefs which the child has adopted himself, in other words, it deals only with his personal conception of reality" (p. 67).

Until age 11 or 12, that is, "it is almost impossible to make a child assume a suggested hypothesis unless one forces him to believe it and thus changes it into an affirmation" (p. 68). "Formal deduction," then,

> consists in drawing conclusions, not from a fact given in immediate observation, nor from a judgment which one holds to be true without any qualifications (and thus incorporates into reality such as one conceives

it), but in a judgment which one simply assumes, i.e., which one admits without believing it, just to see what it will lead to. This is the form of deduction which we have placed round about the age of 11–12 as opposed to the simpler forms of inference which appear first. (p. 69)

Thus, formal reasoning is "hypothetico–deductive" (p. 69) in the sense that it is deduction from propositions deemed hypothetical rather than those simply accepted. "To be formal," Piaget explained, "deduction must detach itself from reality and take up its stand upon the plane of the purely possible, which is by definition the domain of hypothesis" (p. 71).

THE GROWTH OF LOGICAL THINKING

Three decades after *Judgment and Reasoning,* Piaget and his longtime collaborator Bärbel Inhelder published *The Growth of Logical Thinking From Childhood to Adolescence* (*GLT*; Inhelder & Piaget, 1955/1958). Although Piaget had addressed adolescent cognition elsewhere (e.g., Piaget, 1947/1960, 1953; Piaget & Inhelder, 1951/1976) and continued to revise his theory (e.g., Piaget, 1977/2001, 1981/1987, 1983/1987, 2004/2006; Piaget & Garcia, 1987/1991), *GLT* was and remains the major work on what Piaget now called "formal operations."

Central to *GLT* was a series of 15 ingenious empirical studies designed and conducted by Inhelder and her collaborators. A total of over 1,500 participants (p. 311), ranging in age from 5 through 16 years, were interviewed individually as they explored and theorized about the physical world. In one of Inhelder's studies, for example, they tried to determine how the flexibility of a rod varies as a function of its composition, length, thickness, and cross-sectional form, as well as the weight they placed at its tip. In a similar study, participants examined the oscillation of a pendulum as a function of the length of the string, the weight of the attached object, the height of the dropping point, and the force of the push, if any, with which they started each experiment. Other participants explored the motion of objects varying in size on an inclined plane varying in height, attempted to balance a balance scale, examined the angles of incidence and reflection in a kind of billiards, organized data sets to estimate correlations, predicted whether objects would float or sink, tried to determine what combination of chemicals would turn yellow, or confronted other such scientific challenges.

In each study, each participant's actions, explanations, and justifications, taken as a whole, were classified as preoperational, concrete operational, or formal operational on the basis of theoretical criteria associated with these three stages of development. As expected, preoperational cognition was typical of children under age 7, concrete operational cognition was typical of children beginning about age 7, and formal operational cognition was rarely seen before age 11 but typified adolescence. The distinction between preoperational and concrete operational cognition is discussed in many of Piaget's works, and the logical underpinnings of concrete operations were examined most directly in a later volume by Inhelder and Piaget (1959/1964; see also Chapter 10, this volume). The focus of *GLT* was on the distinction between concrete and formal operations, and thus between the logic of the child and that of the adolescent.

GLT followed *Judgment and Reasoning* in its view of hypothetico-deductive reasoning as central to formal operations:

> [F]ormal thinking is essentially hypothetico-deductive. By this we mean that the deduction no longer refers directly to perceived realities but to hypothetical statements – i.e., it refers to propositions which are formulations of hypotheses or which postulate facts or events independently of whether or not they actually occur. Thus, the deductive process consists of linking up these assumptions and drawing out the necessary consequences. (1955/1958, p. 251)

GLT went beyond the brief treatment in *Judgment and Reasoning*, however, not only in the richness of its empirical base but in at least four aspects of its theorizing. First, it highlighted a profound reversal in the relation of reality to possibility in formal cognition. Second, it identified formal reasoning as second-order (and thus formal) operations, thus providing a structural theory of the distinction between concrete and formal cognition. Third, it identified specific *schemes* (forms of reasoning) associated with formal operations. Finally, and somewhat uncharacteristically, the new volume went beyond the realm of cognition to discuss at some length the implications of formal operations for adolescent personality, social relations, and societal roles.

REALITY AS A SUBSET OF POSSIBILITIES

Already in *Judgment and Reasoning* Piaget associated hypothetico-deductive reasoning with the construction of "a purely possible world which shall be the province of logical deduction" (1924/1972, p. 71). *GLT* elaborated on that theme:

> [I]n formal thought there is a reversal of the direction of thinking between *reality* and *possibility* in the subjects' method of approach. *Possibility* no longer appears merely as an extension of an empirical situation or of

actions actually performed. Instead, it is *reality* that is now secondary to *possibility*. Henceforth, they conceive of the given facts as that sector of a set of possible transformations that has actually come about. (1955/1958, p. 251, italics in original)

Hypothetico-deductive reasoning, in other words, enables the rigorous and systematic elaboration of logical possibilities, which in turn enables one to reconsider reality within a larger hypothetical context. The formal thinker's concern with possibility is not a turn away from reality but a reconceptualization of what it means to understand and explain it. Thus, the construction of formal operations is not just the construction of a new mode of reasoning but, more radically, of a new way of understanding the world. Realms of possibility range from possible experimental outcomes to possible religions, ideologies, and social arrangements. Realities of all sorts are potentially open to critique and reconsideration on the basis of alternative possibilities.

As we will see, this new mode of understanding renders adolescents profoundly different from children and much more like adults. Before we consider the larger implications of this for adolescent life and development, however, we turn to Piaget's structural analysis of formal operations as second-order operations and his description of specific formal operational schemes.

SECOND-ORDER OPERATIONS

Classes and relations are central to logic. Piaget's account of the early development of logical thinking, in very brief form, goes like this: Even infants group and order objects in increasingly logical ways. With the emergence of representational intelligence in the second year of life, children classify and seriate mentally. With the achievement of operational intelligence, typically about age 7, children's actions of classification and seriation become *operations*, meaning they are *reversible* mental actions. They are reversible because they compose equilibrated structures. These structures enable an appreciation of logical necessities as distinct from empirical regularities. For example, children now understand that a subclass (such as all cats) cannot contain more members than a class (such as all animals) that includes it, so there is no need to count. Similarly, seriation operations enable the concrete operational child to infer and understand that if A is longer than B and B is longer than C, then A (no need even to look) must be longer than C. Reversible mental actions of classification and seriation are thus concrete operations (Inhelder & Piaget, 1959/1964).

Formal operations, Piaget proposed, are operations on operations, or second-order operations. Consider, for example, the proportion 10 is to 5 as 4 is to 2. To fully understand the logic of this proportion requires that one see it as a relation between two relations – that is, a second-order relation. The two first-order relations are the relation of 10 to 5 and the relation of 4 to 2. In each case, the first number is twice the second. Thus, the two relations are equal to each other. This equality is a second-order relation – a relation between two relations. Verbal analogies, similarly, have the logical form of a relation (of equality) between two relations. In "hand is to fingers as foot is to toes" the first four words express one relation, the last four words express another relation, and the "as" relates the two relations.

There are also classes of classes. Imagine, for example, a bookshelf. Books on the shelf could be hardcover or paperback. They could be fiction or nonfiction. Multiplying these two classification schemes generates four possible classes of books: hardcover fiction, hardcover nonfiction, paperback fiction, and paperback nonfiction. But how many classes of bookshelves are possible? One possibility is an empty shelf. Four more possibilities are the four ways a shelf could have a single class of books (it could have just hardcover fiction, just hardcover nonfiction, just paperback fiction, or just paperback nonfiction). There are six ways a shelf could have just two classes of books (hardcover fiction and hardcover nonfiction, hardcover fiction and paperback fiction, and so on). There are four ways a shelf could have precisely three classes of books (prove this yourself). And finally there is the possibility of a shelf with all four classes of books, for a total of 16 classes of bookshelves, each of which contains a unique combination of the four classes of books taken zero, one, two, three, or four at a time.

Recall now that the four classes of books were originally derived from two dichotomous variables: cover (hard or paper) and content (fiction or nonfiction). Abstracting from this example, we can see that in any system in which there are two dichotomous variables there will be four possible combinations of the two variables and 16 possible combinations of these four combinations (taken zero, one, two, three, or four at a time). At an abstract level, Piaget referred to the system of 16 possible combinations of the four combinations formed by two dichotomous variables as the "complete combinatorial system" and deemed it central to formal operations.

In particular, Piaget showed that each of the 16 combinations corresponds to a particular logical relation between two variables. Suppose the owner of a particular bookshelf only buys books if they are hardcover or fiction (or both). You might infer that his bookshelf may include hardcover fiction, hardcover nonfiction, and paperback fiction but not paperback nonfiction. Logically, this relation is the inclusive disjunction, which classifies the first three classes into a single class of classes and distinguishes paperback nonfiction, the sole disconfirming case. In analyzing responses to the various tasks designed by Inhelder, Piaget found that formal thinkers could be distinguished from concrete thinkers in that the former examined logical possibilities in a systematic manner consistent with the complete combinatorial system. We see here how the realm of possibility for the formal thinker is not just an imaginative extension of reality, as it is for children, but rather provides a systematic logical framework for investigating empirical phenomena. To see an actual relation between two variables in the context of the system of all possible such relations is to understand reality in a new and deeper way. Thus, Piaget's structural model helps us see how the formal operational conception of reality as a subset of possibilities is not a retreat to fantasy but, quite the contrary, a rigorous basis for experimentation and inference.

At an even deeper level of abstraction, Piaget proposed that the complete combinatorial system, and more generally all formal operational structures, can be understood in terms of two fundamental logico-mathematical structures: the "lattice" and the "group." This is the most technical aspect of his theory in that it refers to work that, in the mid-20th century, was at the cutting edge of logic and mathematics. For present purposes, suffice it to say that these structures were of interest to Piaget in that they represent forms of equilibrium more general and powerful than is possible with the more limited structures he associated with concrete operations (Chapman, 1988a; for later approaches to logic and rationality, see Piaget, 1977/2001, 2004/2006, 1981/1987, 1983/1987; Piaget & Garcia, 1987/1991).

FORMAL SCHEMES

Related to his concern with logical structure, but at a somewhat less technical level, Piaget also identified eight "formal structured operational schemata" (pp. 307–329). He defined these as "the concepts which the subject potentially can organize from the beginning of the formal level when faced with certain kinds of data, but which are not manifest outside these conditions" (p. 308). Developmentally, he maintained, such concepts are "less discovered in objects than deduced or abstracted with the subject's own operational structures serving as the starting point" (p. 309). Theoretically, they could be related to lattice or group structures. Most of these schemata are intuitively meaningful, however, and obviously related to important forms of reasoning. Regardless of their relation to theoretical structures, the formal schemata provide an interesting picture of what adolescents, but not children, can understand and do.

One of the most important formal schemes is referred to by Piaget as "the combinatorial operations" (p. 310). No one but a theorist of logic would explicitly work out the 16 possible classes of classes associated with the complete combinatorial system. Nevertheless, formal operations does entail the ability to elaborate combinations and permutations systematically and comprehensively. In the task of combining chemicals to produce a yellow color, formal thinkers systematically worked through all possible combinations so they were assured of getting the yellow color, whereas preformal children tried various combinations, sometimes including the right one, but had no comprehensive system. Similarly, a preformal child could put four letters into several orders to create several four-letter license plates, but a formal thinker could come up with a system to generate all possible license plates and determine exactly how many possibilities there are. The combinatorial operations are of particular importance in providing mathematical rigor to formal conceptions of reality as a subset of possibilities.

Another formal scheme is proportions. Recognition of proportional relations was seen in adolescents, but not children under age 11, on a number of Inhelder's tasks. This is consistent with the Piagetian analysis of proportion as a second-order relation (noted earlier in connection with second-order operations).

Formal conceptions of probability also constitute a scheme, one studied more directly in an earlier work devoted entirely to the development of conceptions of chance (Piaget & Inhelder, 1951/1976). To understand probability formally, one must conceive a realm of possibility that is not just an extension of reality. Combinatorial operations enable the rigorous elaboration of all possibilities and thus the quantitative determination of precise probabilities.

A fourth formal scheme is correlation, which can be seen as a combination of probability and proportion and can also be related to the complete combinatorial system described previously. Imagine we examine 20 books on a shelf and find 2 are hardcover fiction, 8 hardcover nonfiction, 8 paperback fiction, and 2 paperback nonfiction. Are cover and content correlated? We could note that 8 of the 10 hardcover books are nonfiction whereas 8 of the 10 paperbacks are fiction. Thus, hardcover status is associated with nonfiction content and paperback status with fiction. To assess the correlation quantitatively, we classify the four classes of books into those consistent with the correlation (hardcover nonfiction and paperback fiction) and those not. We see that the number of books consistent with this correlation is 16 and the number inconsistent with it is 4. Thus, there is indeed a correlation between cover and content. Integrating conceptions of probability and proportion with the logic of the complete combinatorial system, adolescents show an understanding of correlation not seen in children.

Formal reasoning also includes the isolation of variables (though this is not listed among the eight formal schemes). If we want to know whether the form of a rod's cross-section makes a difference in its flexibility, we can compare a rod with a round cross-section to one with a square cross-section. But the comparison will be unhelpful if the two rods also differ in length, thickness, or composition, or if we assess flexibility with a heavy weight in one case and a light weight in the other. To determine the effect of cross-section, we must hold all other variables constant. Similarly, on the pendulum task one must isolate a variable to determine its effect on the rate of oscillation. More generally, the isolation of variables is central to scientific reasoning.

ADOLESCENT THINKING

The final chapter of *GLT*, entitled "Adolescent Thinking," addressed the relation of formal operations to adolescent thinking and, beyond that, to adolescent personality and social development. Unlike the earlier presentations of the research, which were written by Inhelder, or the earlier presentations of theory, written by Piaget, the concluding chapter is a "joint production" (p. xxiv). Without questioning the centrality of logical structures to advanced cognition, Inhelder and Piaget remind us (and perhaps themselves) that "there is more to thinking than logic" (p. 335) and more to life than thinking.

Central to the present analysis of formal thinking is that it entails "powers of reflection" (p. 340). That is, formal thinking is "thinking about thought" (p. 341). The formal thinker has "second-order thoughts which deal critically with his own thinking" (p. 340). Reflective analysis of one's own thinking makes if possible to construct explicit "theories" and ideological "systems" (p. 339). The adolescent, moreover, "commits himself to possibilities" (p. 339). Adolescents still live in the real world, of course, but they commit to ideals in a way children cannot.

At the same time, "the adolescent . . . begins to consider himself as the equal of adults and to judge them, with complete reciprocity, on the same plane as himself" (p. 339). Adolescents "participate in the ideas, ideals, and ideologies of a wider group" with the aim of taking their "place in the adult social framework" (p. 341). This involves the elaboration of a life plan, which may include plans for changing the framework itself. "A life plan is also an affirmation of autonomy, and the moral autonomy finally achieved by the adolescent who judges himself the equal of adults is another essential affective feature of the young personality preparing himself to plunge into life" (p. 350).

All of this involves "living responses, always so full of emotion, which the adolescent uses to build his ideals in adapting to society" (p. 342). In many cases, there may be messianic goals of reforming the world. As Piaget always insisted, "Logic is not isolated from life; it is no more than the expression of operational coordinations essential to action" (p. 342).

CURRENT STATUS OF FORMAL OPERATIONS

The core claim of Piaget's theory of formal operations is that there are cognitive competencies often seen in adolescents (and adults) but rarely seen in children below the age of about 11 years (though the precise age is not biologically set and may be a function of educational and social factors). This claim appears to be well supported for concepts and forms of reasoning directly associated with formal operations, including hypothetico–deductive reasoning, explicit conceptions about the validity of inferences, and reflective hypothesis testing. Adolescents and adults also differ from children with regard to related forms and levels of reasoning, understanding, and self-regulation such as dialectical thinking, knowledge about the general nature and justifiability of knowledge, principled forms of moral reasoning, and reflective self-conceptions (for reviews, see Kuhn & Franklin, 2006; Moshman, 1998, 2005, in press).

Inhelder and Piaget (1955/1958) also suggested that formal operations are consolidated by age 14 or 15 years, though Piaget (1972) later softened this claim, acknowledging the role of culture in development and the role of expertise in performance. Piaget's theory is best seen as an account of optimal competence, not a description of typical behavior. Research with adults makes it clear that the use of formal reasoning remains inconsistent, at best, and that we all rely on automatic processes and simple heuristics in much of our thinking (Evans, 2002). Piaget may have been right about the new forms of reasoning that begin to develop about age 11, but it appears that, regardless of age, these new competencies do not consistently generate logical performance. Thus, adolescents are indeed more competent than children, but typical adolescent (and adult) behavior falls far short of what *GLT* seemed to suggest.

Even if Piaget's competence theory overestimates logical performance, however, his critics may be guilty of underestimating logical competence. Many such critics, for example, have emphasized research on the notoriously difficult "selection task," which requires participants to test the truth of a conditional statement (Evans, 2002). The failure of most adolescents and adults to solve this task has been seen by many as a failure to achieve formal operational reasoning. Others have argued, however, that the original abstract version of the selection task, involving an arbitrary relation between meaningless letters and numbers, may not be well suited to assess formal operational competence (Müller, 1999). Performance on versions of the selection task involving meaningful conditional relations shows developmental trends consistent with Piaget's theory (Overton, 1990). With adequate opportunity for discussion and reflection, moreover, college students show formal reasoning even on the original version of the task (Moshman & Geil, 1998).

The most technical aspects of Piaget's theory of formal operations – the complete combinatorial system and the lattice and group structures – have always been subject to reconsideration and revision. Recognizing the limitations of propositional logic, Piaget explored other normative models, especially entailment logic (Piaget, 2004/2006; Piaget & Garcia, 1987/1991). Piaget's conceptualization of formal operations continued to develop right through his final projects and publications; his logical formalizations are best regarded as works in progress.

ADOLESCENCE AFTER PIAGET

Piaget's theory of formal operations was highly influential in the 1960s and 1970s, generating a great deal of research and theoretical controversy (for a sympathetic early review, see Neimark, 1975; for a more critical early review, see Keating, 1980; for subsequent analyses, see Bond, 2001; Byrnes, 1988; Gray, 1990; Kuhn, 2008; Leiser, 1982; Müller, 1999; Ricco, 1993; Smith, 1987). With regard to current research and theory, his ideas and influence are everywhere, sometimes explicitly acknowledged, sometimes implicit in theoretical assumptions. Few current developmentalists, however, would endorse his conception of adolescent cognition in its totality. Even to the extent that Piaget's accounts of concrete and formal operations explain the development of logic, there is more to thinking than logic, as Piaget himself acknowledged, and thus more to cognitive development than the development of logic. Piaget's view was that "the structural transformation [from concrete to formal operations] is like a center from which radiate the various more visible modifications of thinking which take place in adolescence" (p. 335). A more common view today might be that logic is an important domain but not the core of all cognition. Adolescents may indeed develop something like what Piaget called formal operations, but even if this is a new stage in the development of logic, it is not so clearly a general stage of cognitive development.

Within the realm of education, *GLT* had a powerful impact on both research and practice. It apparently changed the life, or at least the career, of at least one physics professor, who turned to research in physics education and developed a cross-disciplinary college program based on the theory of formal operations (Fuller, 2008). Today, the theory of formal operations remains a staple in introductory texts in education and psychology but generally receives brief treatment as the final stage of development in Piaget's historic theory, leaving readers with little more than a vague sense that Piaget thought adolescents reason more abstractly than children.

Research on adolescent development has expanded dramatically since the publication of *GLT*, initially inspired by the theory of formal operations and then, especially since the 1980s, increasingly moving in a variety of new directions. In general, the major post-Piaget trends are consistent with Piaget's own view that there is more to thinking than logic but take this much further than he did.

Perhaps the most important trend of the past several decades in the study of advanced cognitive development has been the recognition that much of later cognitive development consists of the development of what we now call *metacognition*, including the awareness, understanding, and control of inference that we normally associate with thinking (Kuhn & Franklin, 2006; Moshman, 1990, 1998, 2005, in press). *GLT* did not use the term *metacognition* but was clear that what indicates formal thinking is not the competence to make deductive inferences (which is present years earlier) but the ability to control those inferences in a realm of possibility (hypothetico–deductive reasoning). The references in the final chapter to "powers of reflection" (p. 340) and "thinking about thought" (p. 341) further indicate a metacognitive conceptualization of adolescent cognition (Kuhn, 2008).

There is no indication, however, of how this metacognitive conceptualization can be squared with the structural conceptualization that dominates the book. Thinking about thinking is second-order thinking, but it is not clear how this relates to the logic of second-order operations. Campbell and Bickhard (1986) provided a neo-Piagetian theory that downplays Piaget's structuralism and highlights instead his constructivist conception of development as a process of reflective abstraction in which each stage constitutes an explicit reconceptualization of knowledge implicit in the previous stage. Applying this metacognitive conception of development to the domain of logic, Moshman (1990) proposed sequential stages of metalogical understanding that correspond roughly to Piagetian stages. Development, in this view, is a matter of becoming increasingly aware of the logic implicit in our inferences.

Another important trend in theoretical understanding of cognition and development has been the increasing recognition that even as children, adolescents, and adults make progress toward explicit knowledge and deliberate, self-controlled inferences, people of all ages continue to rely heavily on immediate intuitions and automatic cognitive processes. Dual-processing theories (e.g., Klaczynski, 2004) suggest that, even to the extent that we make progress toward increasingly explicit knowledge about logic and deliberate control of inference (both central to Piaget's theory), such competencies supplement – rather than replace – our earlier, more automatic, and more intuitive modes of functioning. Even to the extent that there is cognitive progress, moreover, it is not clear that it fits the Piagetian pattern of a single sequence of stages. Without abandoning Piaget's rational constructivist vision of developmental progress, some developmentalists have suggested that evidence of cognitive diversity is best addressed within a pluralist (rather than a universalist) version of rational constructivism that recognizes progress, and thus development, without insisting on a single highest stage (Chapman, 1988b; Moshman, 1998, 2005).

Current work on the development of various types of thinking and levels of understanding thus supports the Piagetian view that adolescents have advanced qualitatively beyond the level of children, though such research goes far beyond the logical scope of Piaget's analysis. There is also substantial evidence that principled forms of morality and self-achieved forms of identity, which can be argued to require something like formal operations as a cognitive prerequisite, are not seen before adolescence. Here too current work transcends, but is arguably consistent with, Piaget's conception of a structural transition between childhood and adolescence (Moshman, 2005). Piaget's theory of formal operations has not been the last word on adolescent cognition, but it remains a vital part of the ongoing conversation.

REFERENCES

Bond, T. (2001). Building a theory of formal operational thinking: Inhelder's psychology meets Piaget's epistemology. In A. Tryphon & J. Vonèche (Eds.), *Working with Piaget: Essays in honour of Bärbel Inhelder* (pp. 65–84). Hove, UK: Psychology Press.

Byrnes, J. P. (1988). Formal operations: A systematic reformulation. *Developmental Review, 8*, 1–22.

Chapman, M. (1988a). *Constructive evolution: Origins and development of Piaget's thought.* Cambridge: Cambridge University Press.

Chapman, M. (1988b). Contextuality and directionality of cognitive development. *Human Development, 31*, 92–106.

Evans, J. St. B. T. (2002). Logic and human reasoning: An assessment of the deduction paradigm. *Psychological Bulletin, 128*, 978–996.

Fuller, R. G. (2008). Can one book really transform your career? *Journal of Applied Developmental Psychology, 29*, 412–414.

Gray, W. M. (1990). Formal operational thought. In W. F. Overton (Ed.), *Reasoning, necessity, and logic: Developmental perspectives* (pp. 227–253). Hillsdale, NJ: Erlbaum.

Inhelder, B., & Piaget, J. (1958). *The growth of logical thinking from childhood to adolescence.* New York: Basic Books. (Original work published in 1955)

Inhelder, B., & Piaget, J. (1964). *The early growth of logic in the child: Classification and seriation.* London: Routledge. (Original work published in 1959)

Keating, D. P. (1980). Thinking processes in adolescence. In J. Adelson (Ed.), *Handbook of adolescent psychology* (pp. 211–246). New York: Wiley.

Klaczynski, P. A. (2004). A dual-process model of adolescent development: Implications for decision making, reasoning, and identity. In R. V. Kail (Ed.), *Advances in child development and behavior, Vol. 32* (pp. 73–123). Amsterdam: Elsevier.

Kuhn, D. (2008). Formal operations from a twenty-first century perspective. *Human Development, 51*, 48–55.

Kuhn, D., & Franklin, S. (2006). The second decade: What develops (and how)? In D. Kuhn & R. Siegler (Eds.), *Handbook of child psychology, Vol. 2: Cognition, perception, and language* (6th ed., pp. 953–993) (W. Damon & R. Lerner, Series Eds.). Hoboken, NJ: Wiley.

Leiser, D. (1982). Piaget's logical formalism for formal operations: An interpretation in context. *Developmental Review, 2*, 87–99.

Moshman, D. (1990). The development of metalogical understanding. In W. F. Overton (Ed.), *Reasoning, necessity, and logic: Developmental perspectives* (pp. 205–225). Hillsdale, NJ: Erlbaum.

Moshman, D. (1998). Cognitive development beyond childhood. In W. Damon (Series Ed.) & D. Kuhn & R. Siegler (Vol. Eds.), *Handbook of child psychology: Vol. 2. Cognition, perception, and language* (5th ed., pp. 947–978). New York: Wiley.

Moshman, D. (2005). *Adolescent psychological development: Rationality, morality, and identity* (2nd ed.). Mahwah, NJ: Erlbaum.

Moshman, D. (in press). The development of rationality. In H. Siegel (Ed.), *Oxford handbook of philosophy of education.* Oxford: Oxford University Press.

Moshman, D., & Geil, M. (1998). Collaborative reasoning: Evidence for collective rationality. *Thinking & Reasoning, 4*, 231–248.

Müller, U. (1999). Structure and content of formal operational thought: An interpretation in context. *Archives de Psychologie, 67*, 21–35.

Neimark, E. D. (1975). Intellectual development during adolescence. In F. D. Horowitz (Ed.), *Review of child development research, Vol. 4* (pp. 541–594). Chicago: University of Chicago Press.

Overton, W. F. (1990). Competence and procedures: Constraints on the development of logical reasoning. In W. F. Overton (Ed.), *Reasoning, necessity, and logic: Developmental perspectives* (pp. 1–32). Hillsdale, NJ: Erlbaum.

Piaget, J. (1953). *Logic and psychology*. Manchester: Manchester University Press.

Piaget, J. (1960). *Psychology of intelligence*. Totowa, NJ: Littlefield, Adams. (Original work published in 1947)

Piaget, J. (1972). *Judgment and reasoning in the child*. London: Routledge & Kegan Paul. (Original work published in 1924)

Piaget, J. (1972). Intellectual evolution from adolescence to adulthood. *Human Development, 15*, 1–12.

Piaget, J. (1987). *Possibility and necessity, Vol. 1*. Minneapolis: University of Minnesota Press. (Original work published in 1981)

Piaget, J. (1987). *Possibility and necessity, Vol. 2*. Minneapolis: University of Minnesota Press. (Original work published in 1983)

Piaget, J. (2001). *Studies in reflecting abstraction*. Hove: Psychology Press. (Original work published in 1977)

Piaget, J. (2006). Reason. *New Ideas in Psychology, 24*, 1–29. (Original work published in 2004)

Piaget, J., & Garcia, R. (1991). *Toward a logic of meanings*. Hillsdale, NJ: Erlbaum. (Original work published in 1987)

Piaget, J., & Inhelder, B. (1976). *The origin of the idea of chance in children*. New York: Norton. (Original work published in 1951)

Ricco, R. B. (1993). Revising the logic of operations as a relevance logic: From hypothesis testing to explanation. *Human Development, 36*, 125–146.

Smith, L. (1987). A constructivist interpretation of formal operations. *Human Development, 30*, 341–354.

12 Piaget's Theory of Moral Development

How children come to construct and respect moral norms was the central problem Piaget addressed in his major work on moral development, *The Moral Judgment of the Child* (1932/1965),[1] with additional essays published in the *Sociological Studies* (1977/1995). One formulation of this is the problem of "understanding how human societies have come to constitute and recognize law, that is, to construct rules that the social group considers valid and obligatory" (Piaget, 1977/1995, p. 159; see Chapter 3, this volume). The fact that this problem still tends to be neglected gives Piaget's work continuing relevance. Piaget dealt with issues in 1932 that are present in current debates, and he offers an approach that is still missing in psychology. Although it is assumed that Kohlberg built on and extended Piaget's initial work, in fact Kohlberg rejected critical aspects of Piaget's approach, which resulted in problems not present in Piaget's own approach. I introduce Piaget's approach to moral development in the context of his general epistemological approach and discuss the development of children's understanding and use of rules in the context of different social relationships and other aspects of children's practical moral activity such as their understanding of lying and justice. Finally, I consider the implications of Piaget's views for current approaches to moral development.

INDIVIDUALISM, COLLECTIVISM, AND RELATIONISM

Piaget's approach to moral judgment is consistent with his approach to the development of thought in general. He rejected Durkheim's view of society as shaping the behavior of individuals – that all morality is "imposed by the group upon the individual and by the adult upon the child" (Piaget, 1932/1965, p. 341). A current version of the collectivist or socialization view that morality is imposed on children by the previous generation is the "narrative" approach to morality (e.g., Day & Tappan, 1996). The child is assumed to passively adopt and follow local social norms, and thus morality is equated with conformity. Such accounts are problematic because they do not explain how moral norms initially develop. This position also entails relativism because morality is reduced to conforming to current local beliefs with no way to evaluate the moral beliefs of different collectives. Piaget noted that "the danger of the sociological explanation – and Durkheim was the first to notice it – is that it may compromise morality by identifying it with reasons of state, with accepted opinions, or with collective conservatism; in a word, with everything that the greatest reformers have attacked in the name of conscience" (Piaget, 1932/1965, p. 344). The majority is not always right, and moral leaders may defy the moral and legal standards of their countries in following a moral principle.

Piaget also criticized individualistic approaches according to which morality is an aspect of human nature arising from the individual. These approaches, often emphasizing biological aspects, are still present in current debates. This is epitomized by a convergence between theorists arguing that moral intuitions, rather than reasoning (Haidt, 2001), are primary in morality, and others attempting to localize the brain regions associated with these evolved gut reactions (e.g., Greene & Haidt, 2002). The primary role for reasoning is reduced to justifying one's gut emotional reactions and persuading others. This approach does not define morality in Piaget and Kohlberg's sense and thus tends to overlook the problems Piaget was concerned with regarding how children develop progressively more adequate forms of understanding aspects of morality such as truth-telling and justice.

The current debate, as set up by de Waal (2006), is between "veneer theorists" who think of morality as a thin layer imposed by cultures on top of an underlying selfish nature, and others arguing that morality is biologically based. de Waal provides evidence that nonhuman primates are not purely selfish by nature. But de Waal's argument that morality has biological roots still leaves two possibilities that differ in how biology is conceptualized and the role given to social interaction in the development of morality. First, there is the individualistic position that emphasizes evolved moral intuitions or gut feelings. Accounting for normativity, however, becomes an issue for neuroscience in attempting to bridge the gap between causal processes in neurons and the space of human reasons (Changeux & Ricoeur, 2000) – from what is the case to what ought to be the case (e.g., MacIntyre, 1998). Researchers taking a neuroscience approach tend to reduce norms to causal neurological processes (Greene, 2003; Greene & Cohen, 2004), thus overlooking Piaget's main problem of the development of normativity (Smith, 2006; Carpendale, Sokol, & Müller, in press).

Biological reductionism is only one way of viewing humans as part of the natural order. Piaget (1970/1972) argued that biological factors alone are insufficient to account for the development of knowledge and that equilibration and the coordination of action are also necessary (see Chapter 6, this volume). An alternative way of rooting morality in the natural world is to consider the role of forms of social interaction in the development of normativity (Cash, 2009; MacArthur, 2004). Thus, a second possibility is that evolved adaptations such as emotional reactions make possible the forms of human social interaction in which morality can develop. This is consistent with Piaget's position that "it cannot be denied that the idea of equality or of distributive justice possesses individual or biological roots which are necessary but not sufficient conditions for its development," and that the idea of justice and "equalitarianism can never be regarded as a sort of instinct or spontaneous product of the individual mind" (Piaget, 1932/1965, p. 318). For Piaget, "the primary condition of the moral life – the need for reciprocal affection" (p. 176) is the foundation that makes the relationships possible in which morality develops. True equality and justice is the "product of a life lived in common," and it "must be born of the actions and reactions of individuals upon each other" (p. 318).

Although Piaget recognized that biology must have a part in the story, biological adaptations make possible the forms of social interaction in which morality can develop. Thus, for Piaget morality cannot be found either in the collective or in the individual, but rather it develops within relations between people. The idea of justice cannot be completely explained by biology nor is it imposed on the child by the collective, but rather it naturally emerges within interpersonal relations. It is the logic of those relations: "Logic is the morality of thought just as morality is the logic of action" (Piaget, 1932/1965, p. 398). Morality is the logic of action in the sense that it follows from coordinating conflicting perspectives. Piaget's third solution in place of individualism or collectivism is that "the aspiration toward justice characteristic of all human societies is the expression, not of factors prior to social evolution (a 'human nature' innate in the individual) but of laws of equilibrium immanent in society" (Piaget, 1977/1995, p. 161). "This third, equilibration-based solution amounts to saying that two or three individuals who have lived their entire lives on a desert island would necessarily come up with the idea of justice, without implying that they had it in them to start with" (Piaget, 1977/1995, p. 161). The ideas of truth-telling and justice do not

pre-exist either in the collective or in the individual, but rather these norms emerge within relations. It is not that justice is predetermined but rather that the potential for its emergence exists.

The potential for certain forms of morality to develop only exists, however, within certain forms of relationships. Piaget argued that once we recognize that social life influences development, it is not enough to simply talk about social interaction in general; we need to specify particular forms of social interaction. Piaget described a continuum of relationships from constraint to cooperation. Relationships of cooperation, based on mutual respect, are best suited for reaching mutual understanding because people feel obliged to explain and justify their position as well as to listen to and understand the positions taken by others. A sense of justice and fairness is based on persons being equally valued. This is an emergent property of the child's cooperative relations with others based on mutual respect. The potential for cooperation is embedded in the preconditions for interaction. There is a natural tendency to move from constraining relations toward more cooperative relations because constraint is unstable and cooperation is the ideal equilibrium toward which relationships tend. The extent to which this is realized depends on how equilibrated the interaction is. Clearly there is a great deal of injustice in the world, and all relationships certainly are not based on cooperation, but cooperation seems "to be the limiting term, the ideal equilibrium to which all relations of constraint tend" (Piaget, 1932/1965, p. 90). This results from "a permanent tendency toward more equality, more reciprocity, more justice, because all of these are forms of a more complete or advanced stage of equilibrium." This is "a necessary state of equilibrium toward which social relations tend, and not from a structure prior to every society" (Piaget, 1977/1995, p. 161). In other words, "the earliest social relations contain the germs of cooperation" (Piaget, 1932/1965, p. 86), the potential to develop into a cooperative relationship. Cooperation does not provide a set of moral rules; instead it provides a method or process for reaching moral decisions, for resolving moral conflicts.

FOLLOWING RULES AND FORMING RULES

Piaget argued that games can contain a complex system of rules that is passed on and regulates behavior just as moral norms do. The rules of games are one type of norm (see von Wright, 1963) and thus are relevant for studying the development of children's construction and application of norms in general. In the context of games, children create or recreate and apply their own rules, which are passed on from one generation to the next and are "preserved solely by the respect that is felt for them by individuals" (Piaget, 1932/1965, p. 14). Although it might appear that rules of games are merely conventional and thus not moral, the process of deciding upon rules that concern how to interact with others is a normative process, and studying children's games is a window onto the development of such forms of thinking. Piaget (1932/1965) began his book, *The Moral Judgment of the Child*, with a study of how children play games and apply rules (marbles with boys and hopscotch with girls). He was interested in the relations between children's practice of using rules and their understanding of the nature of rules (see Chapter 13, this volume). This methodology allowed Piaget to investigate the two Kantian aspects regarding children's developing ability to act in accordance with norms as well as to create and justify norms they consider valid (Forst, 2005).

Although Piaget referred to stages in forms of children's thinking, he is clear that it "is convenient for the purpose of exposition to divide the children up in age-classes or stages, but the facts present themselves as a continuum which cannot be cut up into sections" (p. 27). Piaget also emphasized that average ages were just for the groups of children studied and could vary depending on social experience. In Piaget's study of children's practice involving rules, 3-year-old children are unaware of rules; their play and motor regularities are purely individual and the rules are not collective and obligatory. The second stage, from 3 to 6 years of age on average, involves the imitation of older children but also the idiosyncratic application of rules; children play "in an individualistic manner with material that is social" (p. 37). This stage is *egocentric* in the sense that children play on their own even if they are side by side – they may think that they can both win. *Cooperation* begins in the third stage, from about 7 to 12 years of age. Children's play is now coordinated with rules, and winning has a social definition, that is, doing better than others while observing common rules. The game has now become social, but the rules are still vague and children play a simplified game. The fourth stage involves the *codification* or mastery of rules.

Children's consciousness of rules was assessed with questions such as: "Can rules be changed? Have rules always been the same as they are today? How did rules begin" (p. 54)? Can you make up a new rule? Would it be real? "Would it be alright to play like that with your pals" (p. 25)? To begin with, young children engage in their own action and have no sense of obligatory rules. The second stage begins when children start to imitate others and want to play in conformity with rules received from the outside. In this stage rules are considered sacred and untouchable – they cannot be changed. Of course, Piaget (pp. 74–75) realized that children did not reflect on rules until he questioned them. But he argued that the children's "answers were dictated by the feelings which the game had aroused in them in varying intensity" (p. 75), and these answers reflect the feeling children have of the adult origin and unchanging nature of rules, indicating that these children think that the rules of the game cannot be changed. The paradoxical point is that these children who insist that rules cannot be changed are the very same children who in actual practice did not follow the rules consistently.

In the third stage, beginning at about the age of 9 to 10, children understand rules as originating in mutual consent as the outcome of a free decision. Children agree to a change in the rules if everyone agrees; rules should be respected if they are based on mutual consent, but not otherwise. At this point autonomy replaces the heteronomy of the previous stage: "The rule of a game appears to the child no longer as an external law, sacred in so far as it has been laid down by adults; but as the outcome of a free decision and worthy of respect in the measure that it has enlisted mutual consent" (p. 65).

This evidence led Piaget (1932/1965, p. 76) to ask, "How is it that democratic practice is so developed in the games of marbles played by boys of 11 to 13, whereas it is still so unfamiliar to the adult in many spheres of life?" Piaget's answer is that boys stopped playing marbles at about 14 to 15 years; therefore, the 12- to 13-year-old boys had no seniors imposing rules upon them. The resulting cooperation among equals allowed the boys to understand others' perspectives and thus to construct an understanding of rules. In cooperative relationships based on equality, mutual respect, and reciprocity, equals value the views of others and individuals must be aware of others' points of view. This contrasts with relationships of constraint that involve unilateral respect and differences of power, status, authority, or prestige, in which beliefs and rules are imposed on others who have less power or status. "The great difference between constraint and cooperation or between unilateral respect and mutual respect, is that the first imposes beliefs or rules that are ready made and to be accepted *en bloc*, while the second only suggests a method – a method of verification and reciprocal control in the intellectual field, of justification and discussion in the domain of morals" (p. 97). The rules that are formed in cooperative relationships and are thus dependent on mutual consent are *constituted* rules. Piaget contrasted these rules with *constitutive* rules or principles that are the procedures that define the cooperative social relations in which constituted rules can be formed (p. 98).

No relationship, however, is pure constraint or cooperation; any actual relationship is some mixture: "Constraint is never unadulterated, nor, therefore, is respect ever purely unilateral" (p. 90). Relationships of constraint, according to Piaget, are unstable, and there is a tendency for them to become more cooperative: "Cooperation, indeed, seems rather to be the limiting term, the ideal equilibrium to which all relations of constraint tend" (p. 90). "Mutual respect is, in a sense, the state of equilibrium toward which unilateral respect is tending when differences between child and adult, younger and older are becoming effaced" (p. 96). Note that what is important here is not just children's age but rather the structure of the relationships that the children experience. Thus, it follows that in relationships of constraint even adults may have difficulty understanding others' perspectives, resulting in "sociocentrism" (Piaget, 1977/1995, p. 137).

MORAL REALISM AND SUBJECTIVE RESPONSIBILITY

In contrast to studying the rules for games, where Piaget could observe children's practice as well as their consciousness of the rules, in studying aspects of morality such as stealing and lying he could only study children's consciousness of or judgments about moral issues. Piaget employed a method of telling pairs of stories to 6- to 12-year-old children. A well-known example involving intention and clumsiness is the story of a boy named John who accidentally breaks 15 cups when he is called for dinner, compared to a story about Henry who breaks only 1 cup, but it happens when he is stealing jam.

Children were asked if the pairs of story characters were equally guilty, or if one of the two was naughtier, and if so, why. Piaget recorded two main types of answers that expressed *moral realism* and *subjective responsibility*. Moral realism is characterized by children judging actions by the objective consequences and not by the intentions underlying the actions; that is, morality is thought of as real or objective rather than depending on the actor's intentions. For example, from the perspective of moral realism a child who breaks 15 cups by accident is judged to be naughtier than the child who breaks 1 cup while trying to steal forbidden jam because the material damage is greater with 15 broken cups compared to 1. In contrast, from the perspective of subjective responsibility, intentions must be considered in evaluating actions, so the child who breaks 1 cup while stealing is naughtier than the child who broke 15 cups while trying to help. Piaget found that although there were no clear stages and children may answer differently depending on the particular story, younger children tended to focus on the material damage and ignore the story character's motives, whereas this was reversed with the older children. "These two attitudes may co-exist at the same age and even in the same child, but broadly speaking, they do not synchronize. Objective responsibility diminishes on the average as the child grows older, and subjective responsibility gains correlatively in importance" (p. 133).

Ironically, it has been assumed that Piaget thought children under the age of 9 did not understand intentions (for a review and critique of this view, see Dean & Youniss, 1991), even though the children retold the stories to make sure that they were well understood and Piaget stated that the children gave these answers "in spite of the fact that they have perfectly well understood the story and consequently the intentions of its characters" (p. 127). Further, when the children talked about similar events occurring in their own lives, they clearly understood the intentions involved. "These answers show what fine shades even some of the youngest children we questioned could distinguish and how well able they were to take intentions into account" (pp. 130–131). Piaget argued that children's evaluations in terms of moral realism were not due to difficulty in understanding intentions but rather were the result of their experience with adult constraint because "generally speaking adults deal very harshly with clumsiness" (p. 131). Again, understanding the child's moral activity is brought back to the relationships children experience with their parents. Within relationships of constraint it is difficult for children to understand the reasons for rules.

TRUTH-TELLING AND RELATIONSHIPS

The development of a norm for truth-telling was investigated by asking children to compare pairs of stories about different lies. For example, Piaget found that young children thought a lie that a child had seen a dog as big as a cow was worse than a lie that a child had received a good mark at school because the mother might believe the second lie but not the first. This suggests that children's understanding of lying as bad was because they get punished for saying certain things, but they did not understand why. Interestingly, the older children used the same reasons to argue for the opposite position – the lie about the dog as big as a cow is now thought to be less naughty because the mother would not believe it. The older children thought that "a lie is bad precisely in so far as it achieves its aim and succeeds in deceiving the other person" (p. 171). Therefore, the lie about the good marks in school is more serious because the mother might believe it. Piaget (pp. 155–156) found that there were no clear stages; children used a mixture of forms of reasoning depending on the story, but objective responsibility gradually lost importance in the older children.

Piaget (1932/1965, pp. 165–166) suggested that, "The child is almost led to tell lies – or what seem to us as lies from our point of view – by the very structure of his spontaneous thought." Young children have a natural tendency to imagine the world in the way they want it to be, and thus the "child, owing to his unconscious egocentrism, tends spontaneously to alter the truth in accordance with his desires" (p. 163). This is accepted by adults in play, but children are surprised when something they say is called a lie by an adult and punished. "Moral realism and objective responsibility are the inevitable outcome of so paradoxical a situation" (p. 166). The adult's command is external and does not resonate with the child's understanding. "The rule that one must not lie, imposed by adult authority, will therefore seem all the more sacred in his eyes and will demand all the more 'objective' an interpretation just because it does not in fact correspond with any felt inner need on his part" (p. 163). Because the child fails to understand the spirit of the command, this only leaves the letter of the law to be obeyed.

Piaget (p. 165) argued that it is through contact with others that "truth will begin to acquire value in the child's eyes and will consequently become a moral demand that can be made upon him." Children must feel "a real desire to exchange thoughts with others in order to discover all that a lie can involve" (pp. 166–167). This kind of interchange of thoughts occurs within cooperative interaction but not in relationships of constraint where the inequality is too great.

> For the need to speak the truth and even to seek it for oneself is only conceivable in so far as the individual thinks and acts as one of a society, and not just any society (for it is the constraining relations between superior and inferior that often drive the latter to prevarication) but of a society founded on reciprocity and mutual respect, and therefore on cooperation. (p. 164)

COOPERATION, CONSCIOUS REALIZATION, AND DEVELOPING THE IDEA OF JUSTICE

Piaget described three general forms or phases of thought in the development of children's conception of justice. To begin with, the idea of justice is subordinated to adult authority – the idea of just or unjust is not differentiated from duty and obedience; whatever adults say must be just. Rules must be stuck to – the letter of the law must be followed because the spirit of the rule cannot be understood. Then there is a period of progressive equalitarianism. Finally, this endorsement of equality is tempered by considerations of equity; that is, the complexity of the situation is taken into account.

In contrast to the common view that morality is passed on to children from parents and that peers can be a bad influence, Piaget argued that the idea of justice cannot be imposed by adult authority and instead must develop within cooperative social interaction:

> The sense of justice, though naturally capable of being reinforced by the precepts and the practical example of the adult, is largely independent of these influences, and requires nothing more for its development than the mutual respect and solidarity which holds among children themselves. It is often at the expense of the adult and not because of him that the notions of just and unjust find their way into the youthful mind. (Piaget, 1932/1965, p. 198)

This is the case even if adult authority acts in conformity with justice because the child will tend to identify justice with rules. A child's understanding of justice cannot develop simply by being imposed by adult authority because in relationships of constraint the child cannot fully understand the other perspectives involved, and thus the child will understand justice in terms of rules rather than as a process – this is the letter of the law rather than the spirit.

> In contrast to a given rule, . . . such as the rule of not telling lies, the rule of justice is a sort of immanent condition of social relationships or a law governing their equilibrium. And as the solidarity between children grows we shall find this notion of justice gradually emerging in almost complete autonomy. (Piaget, 1932/1965, p. 198)

But it is within particular forms of interaction that such an understanding can develop. If

> we wish to distinguish between opinion and reason, between the observance of custom and that of moral norms, we must at the same time make a vigorous distinction between a social process such as constraint, which simply consecrates the existing order of things, and a social process such as cooperation, which essentially imposes a method and thus allows for the emancipation of what ought to be from what is. (Piaget, 1932/1965, p. 349)

It may be "that mutual respect is never to be found pure and unadulterated, but is only an ideal form of equilibrium towards which unilateral respect is guided as the inequalities of age and of social authority tend to disappear" (p. 385). Coordinating conflicting perspectives is possible with cooperative interaction and develops first, for Piaget, within the child's practical moral activity. It later becomes an aspect of verbal activity through the process of *conscious realization*, which is needed "to transfer what is already acquired on the plane of action onto the plane of thought" (Piaget, 1977/1995, p. 22). This is not simply copying from one level to another. It does not just repeat practical action; there are "distortions inherent in the very mechanism of reflection" (p. 184). Thus, "conscious realization is a reconstruction and consequently a new and original construction superimposed upon the constructions already formed by action" (p. 177). According to Piaget (p. 85), it is arbitrary "to cut mental reality up into stages" because children's conscious understanding of rules develops through a gradual process of "conscious realization," and this results in a time lag between their earlier practical moral activity and later verbal or reflective moral understanding. This means that the

> appearance of a new type of rule on the practical plane does not necessarily mean that this rule will come into the subject's consciousness, for each mental operation has to be relearnt on the different planes of action and of thought.... We cannot therefore speak of global or inclusive stages characterized as such by autonomy or heteronomy, but only of phases of heteronomy or autonomy which define a process that is repeated for each new set of rules or for each new plane of thought or reflection. (pp. 85–86)

IMPLICATIONS OF PIAGET'S WORK FOR CURRENT DEBATES ON MORAL DEVELOPMENT

It is commonly assumed that Kohlberg (e.g., 1969) built on and extended Piaget's theory. In fact, however, Kohlberg based his theory of moral judgment on the standard interpretation or "received view" of Piaget's work on cognitive development, and therefore he rejected important aspects of Piaget's views on moral development. This view of stages, which arguably was not Piaget's own position (Chapters 1 and 10, this volume; Chapman, 1988), results in the prediction of consistency in moral reasoning across situations. The evidence of variability in moral reasoning does not support this prediction (Krebs, Denton, Vermeulen, Carpendale, & Bush, 1991). This aspect of Kohlberg's theory clashes with his view of moral reasoning as ideal perspective taking – a position that is closer to Piaget (Carpendale, 2000).

Although Kohlberg was certainly inspired by Piaget, he took the opposite approach to the relations between judgment and action (Wright, 1982; Youniss & Damon, 1992). Kohlberg studied the development of progressively more complex forms of moral reasoning, but his separation of reasoning and action results in the problem of how to put them back together. For Kohlberg this is by "figuring out" the right thing to do and then doing it; that is, "He who knows the good chooses the good" (Kohlberg, 1981, p. 189). The relation is inverted for Piaget – action precedes verbal reflection. Piaget was interested in children's practical moral activity – "the morality of the queue rather than of the pulpit" (Tesson & Youniss, 1995, p. 106) – and he thought that children gradually become consciously aware of the moral activity that they have worked out in actual social relations (Wright, 1982, 1983; Youniss & Damon, 1992). Piaget's concern with children's practical moral life involves relating to persons in situations. This contrasts with Kohlberg's interest in theoretical morality, involving relating to persons as ideas and not persons. There may be times when this is called for, but understanding persons as ideas must originate in actually relating to people (Wright, 1982).

Research on Piaget's views on moral development has been generally supportive (Lapsley, 1996; Lickona, 1976), although there have also been some mixed results reported, partly because some of the hypotheses tested might not be positions actually endorsed by Piaget. For example, two common criticisms of Piaget are that he underestimated the age at which children developed various competences and that he predicts consistency in moral judgment (Lickona, 1976). In fact, Piaget did not make claims about ages. In a significant footnote, Piaget (1932/1965, p. 46n) stated that most of his research involved "children from the poorer parts of Geneva. In different surroundings the age averages would certainly have been different." Lickona (1976) also reviews research on the issue of stages or consistency of moral judgment, in spite of Piaget's repeated statements about the lack of clear-cut stages. This may be the result of a more general view of Piaget's theory as predicting consistency in reasoning (but see Chapman, 1988, and Chapters 1 and 10, this volume).

Current research on moral development from the perspective of social domain theory (e.g., Nucci, 2004; Smetana, 2006; Turiel, 2006) has built on Piaget's constructivist approach to moral development and his insight that children develop social knowledge within particular forms of interaction (Turiel, 1997). The domain approach in emphasizing children's multifaceted lives and development through experience of different forms of social interaction seems to fit well with Piaget's action-based view of development (Sokol & Chandler, 2004).

Social domain theorists critique the idea attributed to Piaget that children develop from a general position of heteronomy, where norms are accepted from adults as ready made, to autonomous reasoning (e.g., Turiel, 1997, 2006; Turiel & Smetana, 1998). Turiel (e.g., 1997) argues that young children do not just accept the adult perspective and that young children can already distinguish moral situations from situations involving social conventions. Clearly Piaget's insights and early empirical work should be critiqued as well as elaborated on; however, several points should be considered here. First, Piaget emphasized that children's thinking on these topics should not be thought of as forming general stages. Instead, the two types of answers (heteronomous and autonomous) "coexist at the same age" (p. 133), and children's thinking varied with the particular story presented, although there was a shift with age in the proportion of children's thinking from heteronomous to autonomous (see Chapman, 1988, and Chapters 1 and 10, this volume, on the point that Piaget did not take a global view of stages). A second and related consideration is that for Piaget, with his emphasis on development within relationships, children may use heteronomous reasoning and objective responsibility not because they cannot understand and consider the intentions underlying an act but because in their experience adults do not consider intentions. Piaget's sample of Swiss children in the 1920s and 1930s likely experienced authoritarian parenting, thus differing from more recent research. Thus, it is not always that young children cannot reason autonomously; it is that they do not tend to do so in relationships of constraint. Some of Piaget's child participants did reason autonomously when talking about their own experience, and he also reported children being critical of adults (e.g., p. 281). In fact, some research from the social domain perspective showing that participants' (ages 11 to 23) views about the morality of punishment depend on the information they are given about parenting seems consistent with Piaget's findings (Wainryb, 1991, 1993).

However, children still have to develop the ability to reason autonomously. Here the domain approach fits with Piaget's view that such development occurs in the context of particular forms of interaction. According to the social domain approach, early in development children already distinguish the moral, the social conventional, and the personal domains, which are organized systems of social knowledge that arise "from children's experience of different types of regularities in the social environment" (Smetana, 2006, p. 120). For example, "Parents or teachers tend to use explanations pertaining to needs, rights, and consequences for acts entailing harm to others, whereas they use explanations pertaining to rules and social order for violations of social conventions" (Turiel, 1997, p. 93). From this it seems to follow that children's ability to first distinguish the domains and then develop within them would be influenced by the nature of their social experience and perhaps in particular their interaction with their parents. It seems possible that if authoritarian parents did not use "explanations pertaining to needs, rights and consequences for acts entailing harm to others" their children might be delayed relative to others in making this distinction. As mentioned, it seems likely that parenting styles have changed considerably since Piaget's research in Switzerland in the 1920s, and this should be considered in evaluating his empirical research.

CONCLUSIONS

Chapman (1992) suggested that the significance of a theory should be judged in terms of the importance of the problems it deals with. In these terms Piaget's work on moral development remains significant in that current approaches to moral development tend to overlook the problems he addressed regarding how children form or reconstruct as well as how they follow the moral norms they consider valid. What remains to be done in following up on Piaget's work is to apply and further develop Piaget's insights regarding the social process through which children develop moral norms through coordinating action with others. This is still overlooked in research today. Although the potential for such interaction must be rooted in biological adaptations that facilitate human forms of interaction, the normativity that emerges within social interaction cannot be reduced to such adaptations. For Piaget, reflective morality develops through conscious realization (*prise de conscience*) of the practical morality that develops within the child's activity with others. Conscious realization involves the gradual translation of the rules of organization of the functioning of the child's practical morality into reflective activity. This is a reconstruction on a reflective level of the functional relations among people, or the logic of interaction (see also Chapter 7, this volume). Thus, there is a lag between children's earlier practical moral activity and their ability to reflect verbally on their functional relations with others. This occurs within cooperative interaction: "Criticism is born of discussion and discussion is only possible among equals; cooperation alone will therefore accomplish what intellectual constraint failed to bring about" (Piaget, 1932/1965, p. 402). This "means that social life is necessary if the individual is to become conscious of the functioning of his own mind and thus to transform into norms properly so called the simple functional equilibria immanent to all mental and even all vital activity" (p. 400). Cooperation leads to "a conscious realization of the logic of relations" (p. 403). The ideas of justice and truth-telling emerge from cooperative relations; they are the constitutive rules, the procedures that structure these relationships.[2]

NOTES

1. The pagination of the English and U.S. translations differs.
2. The preparation of this chapter was supported in part by a grant from the Social Science and Humanities Research Council of Canada. I thank Dennis Krebs and Bryan Sokol for helpful comments on earlier drafts of this chapter.

REFERENCES

Carpendale, J. I. M. (2000). Kohlberg and Piaget on stages and moral reasoning. *Developmental Review, 20,* 181–205.

Carpendale, J. I. M., Sokol, B., & Müller, U. (in press). Is a neuroscience of morality possible? In P. Zelazo, M. Chandler, & E. Crone (Eds.), *Developmental social cognitive neuroscience.* New York: Psychology Press.

Cash, M. (2009). Normativity is the mother of intention: Wittgenstein, normative practices and neurological representations. *New Ideas in Psychology, 27,* 133–147.

Changeux, J.-P., & Ricoeur, P. (2000). *What makes us think?* Princeton, NJ: Princeton University Press.

Chapman, M. (1988). *Constructive evolution: Origins and development of Piaget's thought.* New York: Cambridge University Press.

Chapman, M. (1992). Equilibration and the dialectics of organization. In H. Beilin & P. Pufall (Eds.), *Piaget's theory: Prospects and possibilities* (pp. 39–59). Hillsdale, NJ: Erlbaum.

Day, J. M., & Tappan, M. B. (1996). The narrative approach to moral development: From the epistemic subject to dialogical selves. *Human Development, 39,* 67–82.

Dean, A. L., & Youniss, J. (1991). The transformation of Piagetian theory by American psychology: The early competence issue. In M. Chandler & M. Chapman (Eds.), *Criteria for competence: Controversies in the conceptualization and assessment of children's abilities* (pp. 93–109). Hillsdale, NJ: Erlbaum.

de Waal, F. (2006). *Primates and philosophers: How morality evolved.* Princeton, NJ: Princeton University Press.

Forst, R. (2005). Moral autonomy and the autonomy of morality: Toward a theory of normativity after Kant. *Graduate Faculty Philosophy Journal, 26,* 65–88.

Greene, J. (2003). From neural 'is' to moral 'ought': What are the moral implications of neuroscientific moral psychology? *Nature Reviews: Neuroscience, 4,* 847–850.

Greene, J., & Cohen, J. (2004). For the law, neuroscience changes nothing and everything. *Philosophical Transactions of the Royal Society, 359,* 1775–1785.

Greene, J., & Haidt, J. (2002). How (and where) does moral judgment work? *Trends in Cognitive Science, 16,* 517–523.

Haidt, J. (2001). The emotional dog and its rational tail: A social intuitionist approach to moral judgment. *Psychological Review, 108,* 814–834.

Kohlberg, L. (1969). Stage and sequence: The cognitive-developmental approach to socialization. In D. A. Goslin (Ed.), *Handbook of socialization theory and research* (pp. 347–480). Chicago: Rand McNally & Company.

Kohlberg, L. (1981). From is to ought: How to commit the naturalistic fallacy and get away with it in the study of moral development. In L. Kohlberg, *Essays in moral development: The philosophy of moral development* (pp. 101–189). San Francisco: Harper & Row.

Krebs, D., Denton, K., Vermeulen, S., Carpendale, J., & Bush, J. (1991). The structural flexibility of moral judgment. *Journal of Personality and Social Psychology, 61,* 1012–1023.

Lapsley, D. K. (1996). *Moral psychology*. Boulder, CO: Westview Press.

Lickona, T. (1976). Research on Piaget's theory of moral development. In T. Lickona (Ed.), *Moral development and behavior: Theory, research, and social issues* (pp. 219–240). New York: Holt, Rinehart and Winston.

MacArthur, D. (2004). Naturalizing the human or humanizing nature: Science, nature, and the supernatural. *Erkenntnis, 61*, 29–51.

MacIntyre, A. (1998). *A short history of ethics*. 2nd ed. London: Routledge.

Nucci, L. (2004). Social interaction and the construction of moral and social knowledge. In J. I. M. Carpendale & U. Müller (Eds.), *Social interaction and the development of knowledge* (pp. 195–213). Mahwah, NJ: Erlbaum.

Piaget, J. (1965). *The moral judgment of the child*. New York: The Free Press. (Original work published 1932)

Piaget, J. (1972). *Psychology and epistemology: Towards a theory of knowledge*. New York: The Viking Press. (Original work published 1970)

Piaget, J. (1995). *Sociological studies*. London: Routledge. (Original work published 1977)

Smetana, J. (2006). Social-cognitive domain theory: Consistencies and variations in children's moral and social judgments. In M. Killen & J. Smetana (Eds.), *Handbook of moral development* (pp. 119–153). Mahwah, NJ: Erlbaum.

Smith, L. (2006). Norms in human development: Introduction. In L. Smith & J. Vonèche (Eds.), *Norms in human development* (pp. 1–31). Cambridge: Cambridge University Press.

Sokol, B. W., & Chandler, M. J. (2004). A bridge too far: On the relations between moral and secular reasoning. In J. I. M. Carpendale & U. Müller (Eds.), *Social interaction and the development of knowledge* (pp. 155–174). Mahwah, NJ: Erlbaum.

Tesson, G., & Youniss, J. (1995). Micro-sociology and psychological development: A sociological interpretation of Piaget's theory. In N. Mandell (Ed.), *Sociological studies of children* (Vol. 7, pp. 101–126). Greenwich, CT: JAI Press.

Turiel, E. (1997). Beyond particular and universal ways: Contexts for morality. In H. D. Saltzstein (Ed.), *Culture as a context for moral development: New perspectives on the particular and the universal* (pp. 87–105). San Francisco: Jossey-Bass.

Turiel, E. (2006). Thought, emotions, and social interactional processes in moral development. In M. Killen & J. Smetana (Eds.), *Handbook of moral development* (pp. 7–35). Mahwah, NJ: Erlbaum.

Turiel, E., & Smetana, J. G. (1998). Limiting the limits on domains: A commentary on Fowler and heteronomy. *Merrill-Palmer Quarterly, 44*, 293–312.

von Wright, G. H. (1963). *Norm and action*. London: Routledge & Kegan Paul.

Wainryb, C. (1991). Understanding differences in moral judgments: The role of informational assumptions. *Child Development, 62*, 840–851.

Wainryb, C. (1993). The application of moral judgments to other cultures: Relativism and universality. *Child Development, 64*, 924–933.

Wright, D. (1982). Piaget's theory of moral development. In S. Modgil & C. Modgil (Eds.), *Jean Piaget: Consensus and controversy* (pp. 207–217). London: Holt, Rinehart and Winston.

Wright, D. (1983). "The moral judgment of the child" revisited. In H. Weinreich-Haste & D. Locke (Eds.), *Morality in the making* (pp. 141–155). New York: Wiley.

Youniss, J., & Damon, W. (1992). Social construction in Piaget's theory. In H. Beilin & P. B. Pufall (Eds.), *Piaget's theory: Prospects and possibilities* (pp. 267–286). Hillsdale, NJ: Erlbaum.

13 Piaget's Enduring Contribution to a Science of Consciousness

This chapter provides an analysis of Piaget's views about consciousness and whether they deserve more sustained attention than they get in recent writings about consciousness, of which the *Blackwell Companion to Consciousness* (2007) and the *Cambridge Handbook of Consciousness* (2007) provide good examples.[1] I will argue that they do: Although nothing said in either handbook is false – indeed, Zelazo, Gao, and Todd (2007) give a good overview of some key aspects of Piaget's thoughts about consciousness – all of these accounts are seriously impoverished versions of a much richer narrative.

In general, for many scholars writing today, what is problematic about consciousness is its "phenomenal quality" or the fact that "there is something it is like" to be conscious (Nagel, 1974). Piaget does not address this issue head-on but rather through addressing the more important problem of how subjects develop a meaningful understanding of themselves and the world. Thus, his theory addresses two fundamental epistemological concerns central to any theory of the qualities of conscious experience: (1) the subject–object relationship implicated in any type of knowing, and (2) the physical–mental relationship within the knowing subject (but not its specific mechanism). Piaget adopts a unique form of "internal interactionism" that develops over the life span to address the first issue, and a sophisticated form of parallelism that draws on cybernetics and structuralism to address the second. Ultimately, Piaget aimed for an integrative monism that coordinates information from neuroscience, cognitive science, and logic while providing compelling reasons why such a monism will always have a built-in dualism between biological mechanical causality and psychological implication.

PIAGET'S FRAMING OF A SCIENCE OF CONSCIOUSNESS

When a local interviewer asked Piaget (1971), "What, in your opinion, is the object of psychology?" Piaget answered, "Conduct. [la conduite]." But he immediately added,

> By conduct, we mean the entirety [ensemble] of behaviour; that is, actions as well as the consciousness subjects have of them. But consciousness for psychology is always understood as inserted into the context of behaviour, because consciousness can be very lacunary [lacunaire] and distorting [déformante]. We become conscious of the results of reasoning but not at all of its mechanism. This escapes the subject's own analysis. (p. 60)[2] Piaget continued:
>
> The object of psychology is conduct in the full sense of the term. Psychologists seek mechanisms. We are very far from the psychology of philosophers who analyze lived experience [le vécu], inner experience – something that we don't, however, ignore, because such knowledge poses [scientific] problems. (p. 60)

What this interview and many similar writings show is that consciousness was never unscientific for Piaget, as it was for many behaviorists. In fact, throughout his career, Piaget sought to address the problem of consciousness as part of a comprehensive psychology typical for French psychologists of the generation before him.

What Did Piaget Mean by a Scientific Study of Consciousness?

There are many ways to understand the term "consciousness,"[3] and so it is important to know what Piaget means and how he proposed to study consciousness scientifically. Piaget's most detailed early account of the role of consciousness in his psychology is presented in a 1953 conference on "problems of consciousness" (published in 1954). However, this paper works out a position already elaborated a few years before in volume 3 of his *Introduction to Genetic Epistemology* (1950c) and elaborates views already found in his early novel *Recherche* (1918). According to Piaget (1954, p. 136), there are two ways the nature and function of consciousness are typically analyzed scientifically: (1) study its earliest or most elementary forms, or (2) study conditions under which we can observe consciousness disappearing or reappearing. (This is the approach still adopted in most contemporary scientific studies of consciousness.)

Piaget, however, offered a third approach: studying developmental changes in states of consciousness. He hypothesized that the appearance of new states of consciousness can be scientifically documented through their effect on changes in language or judgment and believed this developmental approach would also shed light on the relations between physiological mechanisms and conscious states. Piaget (1954, pp. 137–138) organized his discussion of the development of consciousness around one archetypal example: the emergence of "consciousness of logical necessity" that appears around age 7 in the forms of necessary and generalized conservation (e.g., of length, quantity, matter, weight). In fact,

> [Consciousness][4] of logical necessity can, it seems, best be explained as follows: this kind of consciousness is the manifestation of certain operational structures that do not seem to exist before the seven- or eight-year old level. They evolve... together with the progressive reversibility of thought. Operations never develop separately but always in coordinated systems (e.g., of addition, subtraction, identity, etc.)... and obey certain definite laws of composition (if $B = A + A_1$, then $B - A_1 = A$, etc.) "[consciousness] of necessity" follows. (1954, p. 139)

This position remains essentially unchanged from the 1950s until the end of Piaget's life, although he increasingly refines it (Smith, 1999a, 1999b; Chapter 3, this volume). Twenty years later, in his major work on the development of consciousness, *La Prise de Conscience* (1974a/ 1976) – the primary source for Zelazo and colleagues (2007) – Piaget writes that becoming conscious "requires reconstructions, and cannot be reduced simply to a process of illumination:... the process of becoming conscious of an action scheme transforms it into a concept; thus becoming conscious consists essentially in conceptualization" (p. 261, my translation). Indeed, it is this ability to explicitly conceptualize logical necessity and how that ability emerged from embodied action in the world that was a guiding idea behind much of Piaget's research program. Oddly, it is a problem that has not received much attention in the contemporary science of consciousness, which focuses on how experience can be embodied and conceptualized in what Piaget would have considered very concrete ways.

For Piaget, then, understanding consciousness involves understanding both how the individual subject acquires necessary knowledge of abstract and physical objects and how the cognitive and physical systems involved in generating such knowledge relate to each other. Let us begin by exploring how Piaget explains subject–object relations through a unique form of interactionism.

TRANSFORMING THE SUBJECT–OBJECT RELATIONSHIP: PIAGET'S INTERNAL INTERACTIONISM

Becoming conscious, for Piaget, presupposes at least an implicit distinction between the conscious subject (the knower) and the object of consciousness (the known). Considering a subject's knowledge usually evokes a traditional dichotomy that either privileges the subject's activities (idealism) or the object (realism) or some sort of interaction between the two (Piaget, 1950a, 1970a, 1970b). Piaget sets out to avoid these standard positions by proposing a "fourth solution" that is an innovative synthesis of idealism and realism: *internal interactionism*.[5] Let me illustrate his ideas through two examples:

Example 1: Knowing mathematical objects. Piaget's (1950a) fourth solution to the relationship between reality and mathematical knowledge (which is essentially operatory) involves "attributing mathematical relationships neither to the subject alone (apriorism), nor to the object alone (empiricism), nor to an actual interaction between the subject and an object external to him, but to an interaction between the two that resides inside the subject himself" (p. 338). Piaget illustrates the difference between these positions with a thought experiment: "Imagine that objects, and thus physical reality, were different: would mathematics and logic remain identical to our own" (p. 338)? For *apriorism*, the answer would be "yes" (being abstracted from laws inherent to the mind); but it would be "no" for traditional empiricism and external interactionism, because physical experience would be the unique or partial source of mathematical thought. The answer would also be "no" for Piaget's internal interactionism, but for a very different reason:

> ... It is not physical experience, thus the external action of the object on the subject that would impose this modification, since logic and mathematics issue from the coordination of the subject's actions and not from specific actions that connect him/her to objects. Now, since the physical world would be other than it is, these coordinations themselves would be modified for a much deeper reason ...: because, in a different world, mental and physiological structuresof the subject in general would be different, and life itself would have issued from a physico-chemical structure distinct from our own. It is thus from the interior, and to the extent that the subject draws his functioning of reality from his biological and physio-chemical roots, and [339] not when engaging in external activities, that the subject is in interaction with the object as far as the general coordination of his acts are concerned, and that is why these coordinations always agree with reality, from which they proceed at their source.... (1950a, pp. 338–339)

In other words, a radically different kind of knowing subject living in a different world would necessarily construct different kinds of mathematical knowledge because its very constitution, and thus its potential to act both physically and abstractly, would by definition be different.

Example 2: Knowing physical objects. Piaget (1950b: especially c. 4 and 8; see also 1970) also brings internal interactionism to the problem of knowing the physical world. The difference between such knowledge and mathematical knowledge is that, when applied to physical actions like pushing or weighing, knowledge necessarily remains tributary to the success and efficacy of the subject's action. That is, externally produced results always implicate physical resistance by objects and effort by subjects that do not arise when coordinating logical or mathematical actions such as arranging a series, classifying, or counting objects. Still, within Piaget's antiempiricist epistemology, the subject never simply records "objects" existing in the "external world" but must structure and reconstruct them through his actions; becoming conscious – conceptualization – is thus tied to the practical actions and ultimately to optimizing adaptation to the environment. Although this internal interaction between subject and object is entirely a lived and embodied experience, it is an understanding that ultimately transcends that experience.

Thus, internal interactionism aims to reconcile the subjective aspects of becoming conscious of both mathematical and physical objects with the realist notion of a physical world that exists interdependently with us. Piaget's internal interactionism is intimately bound up with his ideas about how consciousness develops and remains unrivaled in the contemporary science of consciousness. It repudiates Searle's (1998, 2004) simple realism by suggesting that our developing experience of the world determines our understanding of external reality. In this, it is much closer to the enactive approach introduced by Varela, Thompson, and Rosch (1991; see also Colombetti & Thompson, 2008; Thompson, 2007), as we will see in the next section. But unlike contemporary scientific efforts to explain conscious experience, Piaget is sensitive of the need to incorporate both neurobiology and logical implications (normativity) into his account. Conscious experience hovers between biology and logic for Piaget, which is why he is so adamant that one must explain the development of consciousness of logical and mathematical necessity as something quite distinct from physical causality.

THE DEVELOPMENT OF CONSCIOUSNESS

Some may argue that Piaget did not directly address "the hard problem" of consciousness – that is, the subjective nature of conscious experience (Chalmers, 1996, 2007; McGinn, 1991, 1999) – but focused instead on conscious realization (*la prise de conscience*) (l974a, 1974b) as a "continuously active dynamic system" (1974a/1976, p. 261, my translation).

But, in fact, the subjective nature of experience was not a "hard problem" for Piaget, who is closer to William James, Bergson, or Merleau-Ponty in this regard. For all of these thinkers, experience emerges necessarily from our lived and embodied engagement with the world (Müller & Newman, 2008; Vonèche, 2008). The main problem for Piaget was thus to describe the transition from inarticulate practical knowledge of how to successfully accomplish some task (i.e., know-how) to articulate conceptual knowledge, ultimately logical or mathematical knowledge (i.e., abstract meanings).

For example, although children may be able to successfully hit a target with a slingshot (practical knowledge), they still need to construct an articulate and coherent understanding of exactly how and why their action is successful, as shown empirically by their faulty initial understanding of the reasons for their success (Piaget, 1974a/1976). In *Réussir et Comprendre* (Success and Understanding) (1974b/1978), the companion volume to *La Prise de Conscience* (Conscious Realization) (1974a/1976), Piaget explores the transition from practical success to conceptual understanding in more complex tasks in which understanding is constructed gradually. In both books, Piaget sets out to examine how and why conscious realization occurs. Piaget claims that *how* it occurs is through successive equilibrations of cognitive structures via a process of reflecting abstraction. This is best captured by the inner experience of logical necessity that allows an ever more comprehensive and coherent experience of reality. *Why* it occurs is due to what Piaget calls the periphery-to-center law. This law states that, based on the results of individuals' conduct given the objectives pursued, they necessarily proceed from the periphery (or surface) of experience to a more central understanding both of the internal mechanism of actions – the subject pole or consciousness (*la prise de conscience*) – and of the internal structure or essential features of objects – the object pole, or objective knowledge of reality (*la prise de connaissance*; see Figure 13.1). Only by acting on objects does one gain an increasingly sophisticated and abstract understanding of one's own subjective capacity for knowing. To repeat, this is why, for Piaget, psychology is situated between biology and logic in his circle of the sciences (Piaget, 1950c).

Affective and Perceptual Consciousness

Reading only Piaget's (1974a/1976, 1974b) books on *prise de conscience* leaves the impression that Piaget considered cognitive knowledge the essence of conscious experience and that conceptualization results from purely individual activity – an impression endorsed by both Chafe (2007)

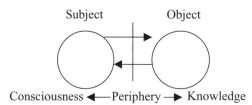

Figure 13.1. The law of consciousness (adapted from Piaget, 1974/1976, p. 335).

and Zelazo and colleagues (2007). However, in Piaget's (1950c, 1954) early detailed account of consciousness, he was careful to consider both affective and perceptual aspects of consciousness and how they relate to cognitive conceptualization, including that of more elementary pre-operative structures. In these writings, Piaget makes clear that we also become increasingly conscious of affective and perceptual meanings. "In affectivity, consciousness constitutes a system of values. Interest is per-haps the most primitive affective mechanism in the child" (Piaget, 1954, p. 144). As with cognition, affective meaning is established by implica-tion. Early on, systems of value may be fleeting and unstable but, later, under social pressure that includes moral rules, they can become coher-ent and permanent.

> [*Consciousness*] *of obligation* is in the area of affectivity what [*conscious-ness*] of necessity is in the cognitive field. . . . While causal mechanisms, physiologic or social, can explain the unconscious determinants of emo-tional life, consciousness of values is obviously a reality in the field of affective behavior. It deals with implication of value rather than of knowledge, but is otherwise as irreducible, specific, and original as cog-nitive implication. Therefore affective and cognitive consciousness are parallel rather than opposed to each other. These two aspects of con-sciousness can, of course, never be separated even though they are dis-tinct. (1954, p. 144, italics in original)

It is in these terms that Piaget understands Freud's discussion of the affective unconscious (see Piaget, 1954/1981). The same is true at a more basic level for perceptual experience because, even here, for Piaget, "consciousness always represents a system of meanings" (p. 144) so that meanings are never isolated: One fact always implies others. The difference is that for higher cognitive processes meanings are represented by (analogous) symbols or (arbitrary) signs experienced as distinct from what is signified, whereas in perception they are not.

Whereas cognitive, affective, and perceptual aspects of consciousness are conceptually distinct, Piaget (1954) acknowledges that they are never isolated in experience. To understand how this is so, we can return to

Piaget's (1928, 1930) early writings on religious experience as immanent divinity:

> [I]t is not in searching for them, as such, that we achieve rational norms. It is working scientifically that we discover them and feel them impose themselves upon us. It is the same with the divine. It is not in seeking it for itself that we lay hold of it, because that only leads to a way to reassure ourselves – just an idol fabricated for our own use. It is in acting in a way that, psychologically and sociologically, conscience/consciousness [conscience] flourishes. Wherever there exists free intellectual inquiry, absolute sincerity, forgetting individual affirmation toward the profit of truth, that one participates in the normative activity of thought.... The spinoziste identification of love and reason must be really lived. Then conscience/consciousness has the *sui generis* experience of agreeing with Thought that is the supreme mystical experience. From hesitations of inquiry and conduct there thus follows, step-by-step, those moments of illumination during which a plenitude of inner equilibrium gives a certainty of participating in the Real. Going forward and regression towards the source then seem to conscience/consciousness as one and the same. (Piaget, 1928, pp. 39–40; note since the French word *conscience* can mean both conscience and consciousness, both are integrated in this passage – MF)

Whether or not one endorses even the immanent reality of the divine, one can agree with the importance of gaining a depth of experience that unites activity, affect, cognition, and reflection. Rather than a purely rational basis to morality, one can endorse Spinoza's marriage of love and reason (Damasio, 2003; Sokol & Hammond, this volume). So although Piaget did not emphasize it in his later writings, his theory already embraced recent efforts to integrate cognition and emotion (Damasio, 2003; Fischer & Bidell, 2006; Johnson, 2007; Lewis, 2005; Piaget, 1928; Thompson, 2007; Tucker, 2007). But in the 1920s, the young Piaget had not considered how to integrate neurobiology into his account of the most profound of human experiences – something he did address in his later writings.

CONSCIOUSNESS AND NEURAL ACTIVITY: PIAGET AND PROPERTY DUALISM

Descartes's Dilemma

Any complete analysis of the origin and development of consciousness that wishes to integrate biology immediately encounters the problem of relating the structure and processes of the brain's functioning to those of the mind; that is, of explaining how the brain allows both conscious and unconscious mental activity. Much of our current difficulty with this issue stems from how Descartes (1641/1996) (following Pythagoras, Plato, and Augustine) framed the modern debate with his substance dualism (a view that provoked many of today's objections as soon as it appeared, most famously in Hobbes's third and Gassendi's fifth set of objections to Descartes' *Meditations*, 1641/1996).

Cartesian dualism continues to exert a large influence on psychology, not only in medicine, psychiatry, and clinical psychology, but in even the experimental study of consciousness (Dennett, 1991, 2005; Müller & Newman, 2008; Thompson, 2007). Recent efforts to naturalize phenomenology – that is to explain how phenomenology is embodied (De Preester, 2006; Johnson, 2007; Roy, Petitot, Pachoud, & Varela, 1999; Thompson, 2007) – provide a clear and compelling alternative to the Cartesian mind–body problem, recasting it as what Thompson (2007) (following Varela) calls the "body–body" problem (i.e., why certain neurobiological bodily processes generate or support phenomenal consciousness, whereas others do not).

Although writing before these efforts to integrate phenomenology into neuroscience (and although quite critical of phenomenology in its original form), Piaget's approach seems very much allied to recent efforts to naturalize phenomenology (Müller & Newman, 2008; Vonèche, 2008). But unlike most contemporary authors, the epistemological problem of explaining how logical necessity emerges through enaction was one of Piaget's central concerns.

Contra Johnson (2007, 2008), Piaget warns us to be alert to uncritically importing metaphors such as "psychological force" or "psychic energy" that apply to physical causality into discussions of psychology. For Piaget (1970a), "sciences more advanced than our own [i.e., than psychology]" (p. 161) have long understood that for intractable problems or crises, the solution often requires a retroactive look at scientific concepts and their scope, engaging in "an internal epistemological critique that is independent of philosophy" (p. 161). Piaget sets out to perform just such a critique of the "mind–body problem" by introducing the notion of structural isomorphism as a synthesis between traditional dual-aspect theory and any strict parallelism between brain activity and experience.

For Piaget (1970a), "Isomorphism (in the sense of a correspondence of structures abstracted of their contents) can be sought between two series of complementary events – described in essentially different languages – avoiding the disagreeable feeling of two analogous series, of which one is useless and a mere duplication or mirror of the other" (p. 161). Piaget does grant a dualism between reality and our idea of it, and that

that dualism extends "to those regions where the neurological functioning that accompanies consciousness differs from those functioning
without consciousness" (p. 161); however, "and this remains essential,
there can be isomorphism despite this dualism, and one that becomes
more and more elaborate starting from initial global forms right up
to higher rationality and aesthetics" (pp. 161–162). As Vonèche (2008)
points out, this presents a paradox in Piaget's view on consciousness
that is hard to understand: How can we have both dualism and continuity between mind and body? Still, Piaget tries mightily to sustain this
position.

In the third volume of his *Introduction to Genetic Epistemology*
(1950c), Piaget opts for a qualified parallelism "between consciousness and its organic concomitants" (1950c, p. 161), and more generally
between biology and logic – the two disciplines between which psychology oscillates – each of which requires its own explanatory system.
The brain and central nervous system (i.e., the *physiological aspect* of
experience) are in the domain of *physical causality*. The relationship
between physical process A (e.g., a tactile stimulus) and physiological
process B (e.g., a pattern of neural firing) obeys a material (i.e., physical,
chemical, or electrical) determinism by which event A *produces* event B.
Much of the contemporary science of consciousness seems concerned
with generating precisely this sort of explanation for some biological
concomitant to conscious experience.

But for Piaget, the *psychological aspect of experience (consciousness)*
involves *logical implication*. In an implicative connection, the relation
between the state or phenomenon of consciousness A (i.e., recognizing
an object) and that of conscious phenomenon B (i.e., desiring that object)
follows a (psycho)logical determinism according to which A *entails* or
implies B by necessity, constraint, or consequence – an intentional,
subjective connection that exists within the conscious experience of
the subject that makes an object or event *mean* something to someone.

"Hypothetically," writes Piaget in 1954, "we assume that all development of operational structures can be causally explained by neurology.
Also, that the structures of conscious thought are always isomorphous
with those of the nervous system" (p. 142). However, if consciousness
is neither a substance nor an energy (two misleading physical metaphors often used in characterizing it), what then is it? For Piaget, consciousness "has very specific and original qualities that become evident
through psychologic analysis of operatory structures [which] cannot easily be explained by materialistic relationships: consciousness is at the
source of connections that depend on systems of meanings" (p. 142). We
see this clearly in explaining mathematics:

> Maybe all mathematical operations could be explained causally in terms of neurological structures, which we believe to be true. Such causal determination would still not explain the deductive necessity in operations such as $2 + 2 = 4$. ... There is causality only when implicitly seen from the physiological point of view. [In the case of visual perception of a visual scene] it sets in motion, and therefore is the cause, of the cortical processes that ends in the judgment that there is nonconservation of quantity. But from the point of view of consciousness statements that concern the perception are not the cause of the judgment, but rather its reason ... we therefore find a relation by implication to be the basic relationship between two states of consciousness, whereas physiological connections are characterized by causal relationships. (1954, pp. 142–143)

Piaget goes on to say that in the early stages of development these relations of implication add little to the causal relationship that corresponds to them physiologically. But at later developmental stages, especially formal operations, "we have seen them lead to deductive necessity, logical or mathematical ... sciences whose fundamentals remain unexplained by physical or physiologic considerations" (p. 143).

Although Piaget's (1970a) main emphasis was on isomorphism between cognitive and neurobiological structures, he did grant that in certain narrow and psychologically basic instances, like EEG studies of attention, there may be a very close concordance – so close as to consider them essentially two aspects of the same process. More generally, Piaget believed that some relations between neurobiology and conscious experience are close enough to hope for an eventual dissolution of the observed parallelism in favor of the sort of integrative monism proposed by the contemporary enactive approach to the science of consciousness. But how would this work exactly? In a very subtle move, Piaget (1949, 1954) proposes that mental actions and operations use the same biological machinery as overt sensorimotor actions but, because they involve structuring thought, they need not be associated with any overt behavior. And this is what allows the eventual possibility of an integration of neurobiological and psychological explanations, a point that is difficult to reconcile with his claim that both kinds of explanation are essentially different (Vonèche, 2008). Clearly, though, for Piaget (as for Johnson, 2007) symbolic and other forms of abstract knowledge begin in embodied action used to imagine creative possibilities by analogy to bodily action (e.g., opening one's mouth as analogous to opening a box of matches) (see Vonèche, 2008, for a detailed presentation of this progression from action to symbolic thought). Piaget (1950c, p. 160) perhaps makes his point clear when he suggests that "between its initial and final states, the construction of the mind [esprit] involves a progressive differentiation of physical causality and mental implication" that genetic epistemology of conscious experience must explain.

Piaget's Imagined Future Integration of Consciousness and Neuroscience

Piaget's isomorphism. Thus, despite their ultimate fundamental differences, Piaget stresses that psychological and neurobiological modes of explanation are more or less isomorphic to each other, because implicative connections share the same structural and functional elements as biological causes of experience (i.e., assimilation, accommodation, anticipation, retroaction, equilibration) and develop out of it in stages (Piaget, 1949, 1950c, 1967/1971, l970a). For Piaget (1970a), equilibration provides an example in which isomorphism was almost complete; that is, it shows "the parallelism that clearly imposes itself between the causal and sequential process of equilibration" (p. 167). However, there is still this difference: The causal sequential process of neurobiological equilibration consists in a string of physiological rhythms, regulations, or self-regulations, whereas the implicative process of cognitive equilibration is a system of compensations between real or virtual activity, one that allows actual or possible reversible operations of transformation (Piaget, 1970a). How does one go from biological rhythm or regulation to cognitive operations that establish norms? Vonèche (2008) suggests that Piaget believed in a rule-seeking capacity of the human mind, and that every biological (and by extension cognitive) system tends to optimize its equilibration, which is by definition immanent to it. But why? Piaget does not say. Such activity is perhaps what Taylor (1989) would call a hypergood that cannot itself be questioned.

Envisioned integration/transformation of psychology and neuroscience. Piaget (1950c) suggests that neuroscience and psychology may eventually reciprocally assimilate each other to constitute a common science, just as biochemistry and molecular biology have. To the extent that the same methods of scientific research could be used to explore questions that span now neighboring disciplines of psychology and physiology (cf. his circle of the sciences), each of these sciences would become not only more exact but simultaneously more theoretical and formalized.

> A complete physiology of perception and intelligence would be, in effect, a sort of physics that is simultaneously deductive and experimental: its deductive aspect becoming no doubt partially fused with the implicative

schemes constructed by psychology. . . . Only then, by the way, would we discover the true relations between the body and the mind: the entire question would be, in effect, to know whether the [psychological operations embodying] logic and mathematics occurring in this exact physiology would finally explain experimental data from physiology or if the inverse would be the case; for our part, we believe that *the assimilation would be reciprocal and that this reciprocal assimilation would even lead to our simultaneously understanding the relations between mind [esprit] and body as well as between subject and object!* (Piaget, 1950c, p. 148: our italics)

Piaget's study of biological systems, his continuing interest in the work of Prigogine, and his collaboration with Garcia all suggest that late in his career Piaget believed that developmental sciences would eventually converge around principles of self-organization in dynamic systems that offer a common language and conceptual framework for studying physical and psychological development (Chapman, 1991; Piaget, 1977/2001; Piaget & Garcia, 1987/1991) – an idea still very much alive today (Johnson, 2007; Lewis, 2000, 2005; Thompson, 2007). Indeed, some studies in cognitive neuroscience – for example, studies of mathematical learning like those conducted and described by Dehaene (2007), Olivier and Houdé (2003), Houdé and Tzourio-Mazoyer (2003), and Ansari, Price, and Holloway (in press) – seem to approach, at least in their conception, the sort of integration that Piaget was hoping for.

A CRITICAL EVALUATION OF PIAGET'S VIEWS ON CONSCIOUSNESS

I agree with McGinn (1991) that any naturalistic account of consciousness must explain both how the physical body generates conscious experience (subjectivity) and how a physical organism can have intentionality (mental representation). What many find most characteristic about consciousness and most problematic about any attempt to account for conscious experience is its "phenomenal quality" or the fact that "there is something it is like" to be conscious (Nagel, 1974).

Tye (2007) provides a useful but by no means exhaustive list of such problems – some dating back to the dawn of modern science or before: (1) the ownership (and privacy) of experiences; (2) perspectival subjectivity (i.e., that we need to have had an experience to really understand it); (3) how we experience the unity of, for example, shape and color that are conceptually distinct and generated by different neural mechanisms (i.e., the "binding problem"); (4) the underlying mechanisms by which the brain operates to produce conscious states; (5) what to make of "divided consciousness" in split-brain patients; (6) the transparency of experience to subjects (i.e., we see "things," not "visual experiences of things"); (7) whether anyone could tell if they experience a color spectrum inverted relative to anybody else; and (8) whether duplicates (i.e., zombies) without phenomenal consciousness are possible.

How does Piaget's theory address these problems? Let's consider them one by one.

The ownership (and privacy) of experiences is not a problem for Piaget. Although actions are public and can be used to infer things about the structure of experience – critical for a science of consciousness – experiences themselves are the product of internal interaction between subject and object, and so they are necessarily private. Nor is *perspectival subjectivity* problematic for Piaget. Again, internal interactionism means that we can no more share others' experiences than we can digest their food (although in digesting our own food, we can have some insight into what it might be like for other people, and even other organisms, to do so). Likewise, our *experience of the unity of conceptually distinct aspects of experience generated by different neural mechanisms* (i.e., the "binding problem") is an illusory problem for Piaget. At least, it is perfectly consistent with this theory that our understandings of all aspects of an object are unified by the meaning implications that emerge from our interactions with them. Our increasingly conscious mental schemes are constructed based on our own actions and are constructed by engaging the world and objects as a whole. So, as for Searle (2004), there is no "color" or "line" perception in the abstract, but only as part of a conscious field from which these are abstracted. That different meanings or aspects of the field arise in different parts of the brain is no more a problem than the fact that it takes the coordinated action of two hands to tie our shoes.

True, Piaget did not make a special study of the underlying mechanisms by which the brain operates to produce conscious states, but he did claim that the same machinery is involved in physical actions on the world.[6] This is an empirical claim to be tested, but we do find, for example, that visual perception and mental imagery appear to use the same biological machinery, although this claim is still debated (Ganis, Thompson, & Kosslyn, 2004; Kosslyn et al., 1999). Thus, it is no surprise that when links between parts of that machinery that formerly worked together are severed, the same biological mechanisms can continue to operate semi-independently, producing the *"divided consciousness"* of split-brain patients whose corpus callosum has been severed for medical reasons (Gazzaniga, 2005; Sperry, 1984).

For Piaget, the problem of *the transparency of experience to subjects* is misconceived, or at least needs to be reconceived developmentally. According to internal interactionism and the periphery to center law, our very notions of "things" and "visual experiences" are constructed out of our reflecting abstractions about actions on our environment. Because we are oriented toward acting on that environment, we begin by experiencing the "surface" – the goals and objects of our actions – as things, perhaps at birth (Johnson, 2007). But as subjects develop, they begin to understand the "visual experiences of things" in ways that acknowledge visual illusions (e.g., the visual experience that two lines are of different lengths in the Müller–Lyer illusion, when one knows they are in fact equal).

Indeed, only two of Tye's problems remain problems for Piaget, as they do for all functional theories of conscious experience. The first is *whether anyone could tell if they experience a color spectrum inverted relative to anybody else*. For a functional theory, it does not matter whether someone who is red-green colorblind sees raspberries as red, green, or some other color. It only matters that they can conceptually distinguish them (assimilate them) to an understanding of fruit or distinguish them as different from blackberries. But surely, one might say, there really is a qualitative and experienced difference between black, red, and green that is more than their functional utility in telling things apart. According to Piaget, the personal qualitative experience of color is beyond the reach of science: We must remain in the realm of what Dennett (1991, 2005) calls "heterophenomenology" inferred through differences in conduct under experimental testing.

This problem leads into Tye's final problem: *whether duplicates (i.e., zombies) without phenomenal consciousness are possible*. There seems to be no way in principle that Piaget's theory can distinguish between people who are awake and conscious and those who are sleepwalking through life without conscious experiences. Piaget might take the premise of this problem to be absurd, because what is to be explained is how people have the conscious experiences they do in fact have (an issue that was at the heart of Piaget's concern with conscious experience from his earliest efforts to draw on Bergson and modern biology to help explain conscious experience) (Piaget, 1918). But there seems to be no way in principle to distinguish a purely mechanical and unconscious use of mental schemes (as one might imagine a computer program might develop, especially if developed through its actions on the environment, like those being tested by Rodney Brooks and his colleagues at MIT) from the subjective experience of "what it is like" to see color – even if it remains impossible to determine how veridical or unchanging those qualitative experiences might be (cf. Dennett, 1991, 2005).

Finally, beyond these classic problems, let me close by considering a few ways Piaget's theory might be extended. As Taylor (1985) points out in his generally sympathetic critique of Piaget's genetic psychology, any genetic or developmental psychology "operates with two major ranges of basic theoretical notions, whose development touch on the nature of maturity – the *terminus ad quem* of development [its model of maturity] – and those which define innate structures – the *terminius ad quo*" (p. 163). Within this scheme development can be understood in two very different ways: one way strives for greater objectification through intellectual decentering and reversibility (as does Piaget); the other is incapable of such objective disinvolvement because "the significance of what we are trying to put in perspective is a shared significance" (Taylor, p. 160). This second sort of genetic development instead strives to gain a truer perspective on any particular predicament – something characteristic of narrative or psychoanalysis (Oatley, 2007; Taylor, 1985). In either case, we cannot divorce genetic psychology from values about what we think living a full human life entails.

Taylor's genetic psychology seems in line with Foucault's (2004) claim that self-knowledge can be used to "care for the self" (one's own self and that of others) – a characteristic of personal wisdom – at least in theories like those of Staudinger, Dörner, and Mickler (2005), Ardelt (2003, 2005), or Pascual-Leone (1990, 2000). Although he does not say so, Piaget might hold that such narrative self-understanding itself has a structure, as shown in neo-Piagetian studies of adolescents' developing understanding of narrative (McKeough & Griffiths, in press). Clearly, such narratives can be increasingly conceptualized and made conscious – through therapy, personal insight, or mindfulness meditation, for example – all of which are ways to attend to one's personal stream of consciousness and make it more explicit, personally meaningful, and coherent. In this way, one might extend Piaget's theory to account for these more narrative aspects of conscious experience.

Despite its limitations (shared by many other accounts of the biological basis of consciousness), Piaget's theory has one strength other contemporary scientific theories of consciousness seem to lack: He was alert to the fact that that conscious experience must be explained in ways that incorporate both biology and logic, without conflating the two. True, it is not clear that Piaget's theory manages to fully bridge the gap between biological causality and the conscious experience of implication; in particular, it is not clear why abstracted and internalized (conceptualized) action is experienced as qualitatively different from sensorimotor meaning. But Piaget does explain how experience might progressively be abstracted from overt actions by the experiencing organism, given that our conscious experiences do exist and do develop to incorporate increasingly coherent understandings of logical necessity. Thus, Piaget's theory of consciousness remains among the most interesting around today and certainly deserves more attention than it has received by people working in this field.[7]

NOTES

1. In the 774-page *Blackwell Companion to Consciousness* (2007), the name Jean Piaget appears twice in two different chapters: neither mention about his views on consciousness. Piaget fares a little better in the 981-page *Cambridge Handbook of Consciousness* (2007). Piaget is again mentioned in only two chapters, but at least both discuss his understanding of consciousness. The first is a single dismissive mention concerning Piaget's views on the relations between language and consciousness (Chafe, 2007, p. 355); the second, by Zelazo, Gao, and Todd (2007), is more sustained. Piaget is classed among the influential early accounts of the development of consciousness; however, they misleadingly claim that "for 'early theorists' like Piaget... consciousness was *the* problem to be addressed by the new science of psychology" (p. 407). Piaget is mentioned twice more in the article, once in reference to modifying sensorimotor schemes (p. 414), and once regarding Piaget's claim that symbolic thought emerges only in the second year (p. 421), highlighting the fact that consciousness was actually not the main issue for Piaget, but rather something to be explained within a comprehensive account of how norms and logical necessity can emerge from contingent embodied action. Zelazo and colleagues' discussion of Piaget's ideas closes with a cryptic quotation from the last paragraph of the 1976 translation of *La Prise de Conscience* – published (under the rather awkward title of "The Grasp of Consciousness") – that, unfortunately, is translated in a way that makes it difficult, if not impossible, to understand.

2. Translations from work unavailable in English, or when the existing English translation was considered misleading, are mine.

3. See Guzeldere, 1997, Searle, 2004, Velmans and Schneider (2007), and Zelazo, Moscovitch, and Thompson (2007) for a tour of the field.

4. The translator of Piaget's 1954 text notes that she translates the French *conscience* by both awareness and consciousness according to context. This is needlessly confusing, so all references to awareness have been replaced by the word consciousness, placed in brackets to denote the change.

5. For a concise summary of many contemporary positions on this problem consult Popper (1994), Searle (2004), or Smith (1999a, 1999b).

6. However, recent research has refined Piaget's basic insights, seeming to suggest that the brain is not a universal information-processing device

proposed by early cybernetic models of mind like Piaget's, but rather a collection of specialized processors that work together as a dynamic system. Tucker (2007) proposes at least three ways the brain is not a homogenous structure: (1) front-to-back differences, (2) right-to-left hemispheric differences, and (3) primitive core to enveloping shell differences. Hence more complexly structured brain activity, to the extent it is isomorphic to experience, must involve the coordination of subabilities and skills in ways that are yet to be fully worked out but might resemble the sorts of coordinated brain activity advocated by Varela, Thompson, or Ansari. Furthermore, Piaget does not emphasize the fact that seeing, imagining, remembering an object or a scene are mentally very different activities that require their own isomorphism, because they imply different basic meanings to the living body (Thompson, 2007).

7. This text develops part of an unpublished book manuscript on the history of the scientific understanding of consciousness by the late Adrien Pinard, and a previous paper, Ferrari, Pinard, and Runions (2001). This work was supported in part by a grant from the Social Sciences and Humanities Council of Canada.

REFERENCES

Ansari, D., Price, G., & Holloway, I. (in press). Typical and atypical development of basic magnitude representations: Perspectives from behavioral and neuroimaging studies. In M. Ferrari & L. Vuletic (Eds.), *The developmental interplay of mind, brain and education: Essays in honor of Robbie Case.* Amsterdam: Springer.

Ardelt, M. (2003). Empirical assessment of a three-dimensional Wisdom Scale. *Research on Aging, 25,* 275–324.

Ardelt, M. (2005). How wise people cope with crises and obstacles in life. *Revision: A Journal of Consciousness and Transformation, 28,* 7–19.

Chafe, W. (2007). Language and consciousness. In P. D. Zelazo, M. Moscovitch, & E. Thompson (Eds.), *The Cambridge handbook of consciousness* (pp. 355–373). New York: Cambridge University Press

Chalmers, D. J. (1996). *The conscious mind: In search of a fundamental theory.* New York: Oxford University Press.

Chalmers, D. (2007). The hard problem of consciousness. In M. Velmans & S. Schneider (Eds.), *The Blackwell companion to consciousness* (pp. 225–235). Oxford: Blackwell.

Chapman, M. (1991). Self-organization as developmental process: Beyond the organismic and mechanistic models? In P. Van Geert & L. P. Mos (Eds.), *Annals of theoretical psychology,* Vol. 7 (pp. 335–348). New York & London: Plenum Press.

Colombetti, G., & Thompson, E. (2008). The feeling body: Toward an enactive approach to emotion. In W. F. Overton, U. Müller, & J. L. Newman (Eds.), *Developmental perspectives on embodiment and consciousness* (pp. 45–68). Mahwah, NJ: Erlbaum.

Damasio, A. (2003). *Looking for Spinoza: Joy, sorrow, and the human brain.* Orlando, FL: Harcourt Brace.

Dehaene, S. (2007). A few steps toward a science of mental life. *Mind, Brain, and Education, 1*, 28–47.

Dennett, D. C. (1991). *Consciousness explained.* Cambridge, MA: Bradford/MIT Press.

Dennett, D. C. (2005). *Sweet dreams: Philosophical obstacles to a science of consciousness.* Cambridge, MA: MIT Press.

De Preester, H. (2006). Naturalism and transcendentalism in the naturalization of phenomenology. *New Ideas in Psychology, 24*, 41–62.

Descartes, R. (1996). *Œuvres de Descartes* (Édition de Charles Adam et Paul Tannery). Paris: Librairie Philosophique J. Vrin. (Original work published in 1641)

Ferrari, M., Pinard, A., & Runions, K. (2001). Piaget's framework for a scientific study of consciousness. *Human Development, 44*, 195–213.

Fischer, K. W., & Bidell, T. R. (2006). Dynamic development of action, thought, and emotion. In R. M. Lerner (Ed.), *Handbook of child psychology, Vol. 1. Theoretical models of human development* (6th ed., pp. 313–399). New York: Wiley.

Foucault, M. (2004). *The hermeneutics of the subject: Lectures at the Collège de France,* 1981–82. New York: Palgrave Macmillan.

Ganis, G., Thompson, W. L., and Kosslyn, S. M. (2004). Brain areas underlying visual mental imagery and visual perception: an fMRI study. *Cognitive Brain Research, 20*, 226–241.

Gassendi, P. (1996). *Fifth set of objections to Descartes' Meditations. Volume VII in Œuvres de Descartes* (Édition de Charles Adam & Paul Tannery). Paris: Librairie Philosophique J. Vrin. (Original work published in 1641)

Gazzaniga, M. S. (2005). Forty-five years of split-brain research and still going strong. *Nature Reviews Neuroscience, 6*, 653–659.

Guzeldere, G. (1997). The many faces of consciousness: A field guide. In N. Block, O. Flanagan, & G. Guzeldere (Eds.), *The nature of consciousness: Philosophical debates* (pp. 1–67). Cambridge, MA: Bradford/MIT Press.

Johnson, M. (2007). *The meaning of the body: Aesthetics of human understanding.* Chicago: University of Chicago Press.

Johnson, M. (2008). The meaning of the body. In W. F. Overton, U. Müller, & J. L. Newman (Eds.), *Developmental perspectives on embodiment and consciousness* (pp. 19–43). Mahwah, NJ: Erlbaum.

Kosslyn, S. M., Pascual-Leone, A., Felician, O., Camposano, S., Keenan, J. P., Thompson, W. L., et al. (1999). The role of area 17 in visual imagery: Convergent evidence from PET and rTMS. *Science, 284*, 167–170.

Lewis, M. D. (2000). The promise of dynamic systems approaches for an integrated account of human development. *Child Development, 71*, 36–43.

Lewis, M. D. (2005). Bridging emotion theory and neurobiology through dynamic systems modeling (target article). *Behavioral and Brain Sciences, 28*, 169–245.

McGinn, C. (1991). *The problem of consciousness: Essays toward a resolution.* Oxford; Cambridge, MA: Blackwell.

McGinn, C. (1999, June). Can we ever understand consciousness? *New York Review of Books,* p. 44.

McKeough, A., & Griffiths, S. (in press). Adolescent narrative thought: Developmental and neurological evidence in support of a central social structure.

In M. Ferrari & L. Vuletic (Eds.), *The developmental interplay of mind, brain and education: Essays in honor of Robbie Case*. Amsterdam: Springer.

Müller, U., & Newman, J. L. (2008). The body in action: Perspectives on embodiment and development. In W. F. Overton, U. Müller, & J. L. Newman (Eds.), *Developmental perspectives on embodiment and consciousness* (pp. 313–342). Mahwah, NJ: Erlbaum.

Nagel, T. (1974). What is it like to be a bat? *Philosophical Review, 83*, 435–450.

Oatley, K. (2007). Narrative modes of consciousness and selfhood. In P. D. Zelazo, M. Moscovitch, & E. Thompson (Eds.), *The Cambridge handbook of consciousness* (pp. 375–402). New York: Cambridge University Press.

Pascual-Leone, J. (1990). An essay on wisdom: Toward organismic processes that make it possible. In R. J. Sternberg (Ed.), *Wisdom: Its nature, origins, and development* (pp. 244–278). New York: Cambridge University Press.

Pascual-Leone, J. (2000). Mental attention, consciousness, and the progressive emergence of wisdom. *Journal of Adult Development, 7*, 241–254.

Piaget, J. (1918). *Recherche*. Lausanne: La Concorde.

Piaget, J. (1928). L'Immanence. In J. Piaget & J. De la Harpe (Eds.), *Deux types d'attitudes religieuses: Immanence et Transcendance* (pp. 7–40). Editions de l'association Chretienne d'Etudiants de Suisse Romande. Dépôt central: Labor à Genève.

Piaget, J. (1930). *Immanentisme et foi religieuse*. Genève: Librarie H. Robert.

Piaget, J. (1949). Le problème neurologique de l'intériorisation des actions en opérations reversibles. *Archives de Psychologie, 32*, 241–258.

Piaget, J. (1950a). *Introduction à l'épistémologie génétique: Tome 1. La pensée mathématique*. Paris: Presses Universitaires de France.

Piaget, J. (1950b). *Introduction à l'épistémologie génétique: Tome 2. La pensée physique*. Paris: Presses Universitaires de France.

Piaget, J. (1950c). *Introduction à l'épistémologie génétique: Tome 3. La pensée biologique, la pensée psychologique et la pensée sociologique*. Paris: Presses Universitaires de France.

Piaget, J. (1954). The problem of consciousness in child psychology: Developmental changes in awareness. In H. A. Abramson (Ed.), *Problems of consciousness* (pp. 136–177). New York: Josiah Macy Jr. Foundation.

Piaget, J. (1970a). Les explications psychologiques et le problème du parallélisme psychophysiologique. In J. Piaget, P. Fraisse, & M. Reuchlin (Eds.), *Traité de psychologie experimentale. Vol. 1. Histoire et méthode* (pp. 131–170, 3rd ed.). Paris: Presses Universitaires de France. (First edition published in 1963)

Piaget, J. (1970b). *Epistémologie des sciences de l'homme*. Paris: Gallimard.

Piaget, J. (1971). *Biology and knowledge*. Edinburgh: Edinburgh University Press. (Original work published in 1967)

Piaget, J. (1971). A quelle image de l'homme conduit la psychologie?: Le professeur Piaget répond. *Etudes et Carrières: Revue d'information Professionnele Universitaire, 6–7*, 60–61.

Piaget, J. (1974a). *La prise de conscience*. Paris: Presses Universitaires de France. Translated as: Piaget, J. (1976). *The grasp of consciousness*. Cambridge, MA: Harvard University Press.

Piaget, J. (1974b). *Réussir et comprendre*. Paris: Presses Universitaires de France. Translated as: Piaget, J. (1978). *Success and understanding*. Cambridge, MA: Harvard University Press.

Piaget, J. (1981). *Intelligence and affectivity*. Palo Alto, CA: Annual Reviews, Inc. (Original work published in 1954)

Piaget, J. (2001). *Studies in reflecting abstraction*. Hove: Psychology Press. (Original work published in 1977)

Piaget, J. & Garcia, R. (1991). *Toward a logic of meaning*. Hillsdale, NJ: Erlbaum. (Original work published in 1987)

Popper, K. R. (1994). *Knowledge and the body-mind problem: In defence of interaction*. New York: Routledge.

Roy, J.-M., Petitot, J., Pachoud, B., & Varela, F. (1999). Beyond the gap: An introduction to naturalizing phenomenology. In J. Petitot, F. J. Varela, B. Pachoud, & J.-M. Roy (Eds.), *Naturalizing phenomenology: Issues in contemporary phenomenology and cognitive science* (pp. 1–80). Stanford, CA: Stanford University Press.

Searle, J. R. (1998). *Mind, language and society: Philosophy in the real world*. New York: Basic Books.

Searle, J. R. (2004). *Mind: A brief introduction*. New York: Oxford University Press.

Smith, L. (1999a). Epistemological principles for developmental psychology in Frege and Piaget. *New Ideas in Psychology, 17*, 83–117.

Smith, L. (1999b). Eight good questions for developmental epistemology and psychology. *New Ideas in Psychology, 17*, 137–147.

Sperry, R. (1984). Consciousness, personal identity and the divided brain. *Neuropsychologia, 22*, 661–673.

Staudinger, U. M., Dörner, J., & Mickler, C. (2005). Wisdom and personality. In R. J. Sternberg & J. Jordan (Eds.), *A handbook of wisdom: Psychological perspectives* (pp. 191–219). New York: Cambridge University Press.

Taylor, C. (1985). What is involved in a genetic psychology? In C. Taylor (Ed.), *Human agency and language* (pp. 139–163). New York: Cambridge University Press.

Taylor, C. (1989). *Sources of the self: The making of modern identity*. New Haven, CT: Yale University Press.

Thompson, E. (2007). *Mind in life: Biology, phenomenology, and the sciences of the mind*. Cambridge, MA: Belknap Press/Harvard University Press.

Tucker, D. M. (2007). *Mind from body: Experience from neural structure*. New York: Oxford University Press.

Tye, M. (2007). Philosophical problems of consciousness. In M. Velmans & S. Schneider (Eds.), *The Blackwell companion to consciousness* (pp. 23–35). Oxford: Blackwell.

Varela, F. J., Thompson, E., & Rosch, E. (1991). *The embodied mind: Cognitive science and human experience*. Cambridge, MA: MIT Press.

Velmans, M., & Schneider, S. (Eds.). (2007). *The Blackwell companion to consciousness*. Oxford: Blackwell.

Vonèche, J. (2008). Action as the solution to the mind-body problem in Piaget's theory. In W. F. Overton, U. Müller, & J. L. Newman (Eds.), *Developmental perspectives on embodiment and consciousness* (pp. 69–98). Mahwah, NJ: Erlbaum.

Zelazo, P. D., Gao, H. H., & Todd, R. (2007). The development of consciousness. In P. D. Zelazo, M. Moscovitch, & E. Thompson (Eds.), *The Cambridge handbook of consciousness* (pp. 405–432). New York: Cambridge University Press.

Zelazo, P. D., Moscovitch, M., & Thompson, E. (Eds.). (2007). *The Cambridge handbook of consciousness*. New York: Cambridge University Press.

14 Piaget and Affectivity

Despite various attempts to adjust the current "received view" of Piaget's theory (e.g., Bearison & Zimiles, 1986; Carpendale & Lewis, 2004; Chapman, 1988; Gouin-Décarie, 1965; Lapsley, 1996; Xypas, 2001), the general impression that Piaget really had nothing substantive to contribute regarding the development of children's affective lives pervades much of contemporary psychology. Piaget, at least as most of us know him, is the "cold cognitivist," whose affinities with Kant's rationalism led him to eschew all things affective or emotional. Much like Piaget's contributions to sociology (Carpendale & Lewis, 2004; Piaget, 1965/1995), his work on affectivity and emotions is largely forgotten, despite his various attempts to note the significance of individuals' affective lives in several of his major publications.[1]

Dispelling this impression, or at least naïve versions of it, will be a central aim of this chapter. In doing so, we plan to revisit Piaget's lectures at the Sorbonne (1953–1954), published in the journal *Bulletin de Psychologie* (Piaget, 1954) and later translated as *Intelligence and Affectivity* (Piaget, 1954/1981), as well as his lectures at the Menninger Clinic in the United States (Piaget, 1962a, 1962b). Although it is certainly true that Piaget's epistemological interests overshadowed much of his work on affectivity (Brown, 1996; Chapman, 1988, pp. 377–379), he nevertheless offers a variety of developmental insights regarding the relationship between intelligence and affectivity that bear repeating and remembering. How well these insights are remembered here will depend on our success at negotiating two hurdles that have, in the past, stood in the way of understanding Piaget's broader theoretical framework and where affectivity falls within it.

HURDLE ONE: RECOVERING THE PIAGET THAT TIME
FORGOT (OR NEVER UNDERSTOOD IN THE FIRST PLACE)

The first of these hurdles concerns a general tendency among psychologists to view historical contributions to the field through presentist lenses (Danziger, 1997). That is, Piaget's theory is commonly viewed through contemporary conceptual lenses that distort the way that he, and many others contributing to the field at the beginning of the 20th century, approached psychological phenomena. Present-day developmental and educational psychologists, for instance, drive a wedge between cognitive and affective matters, such as IQ and EQ, or emotional intelligence (Goleman, 1995), in a way that would have appeared unusual to Piaget and his contemporaries. Although the separation of affect and intelligence has a time-honored philosophical pedigree (Cowan, 1978, p. 50), this divide is now often taken as proven fact, and rarely, if ever, critically examined (Brown & Kozak, 1998), particularly with the kind of rigor seen in much of Piaget's analysis.

Piaget, as history reports, was greatly influenced by Binet's studies of intelligence (Sternberg, 1990) and, as a result, did not approach intelligence as we often do now as a distinct "faculty" or as "an isolated and sharply differentiated class of cognitive processes" (Piaget, 1947/1950, p. 6). Rather Piaget assumed a much more general approach to intelligence, treating it as a broad ability to be adaptive and flexible in one's behavior. As he remarked, "intelligence . . . is essentially a system of living and action operations. It is the most highly developed form of mental adaptation . . . " (p. 7). The action–orientation embedded in this view is as radical now as it was then and is the likely source for various misguided charges of "rampant intellectualism" in Piaget's theory, both past and present.[2]

Like John Dewey's pragmatist philosophy, which also emerged during Piaget's lifetime, affect and intelligence were understood as inextricably linked in the "unity of activity" (Dewey, 1896, p. 360). Where affect is typically portrayed as the diametric opposite of intelligence, Piaget's approach, much like Dewey's, avoided a dualistic separation of the two (Cowan, 1981). For this reason, Piaget claimed that just as it is "impossible to find behavior arising from affectivity alone," so too it is "impossible to find behavior composed only of cognitive elements" (Piaget, 1954/1981, p. 2). That is, Piaget saw cognitive and affective aspects of intelligence in a way unlike many others, as complementary features of individuals' adaptive activities. Again, as he suggested:

> What common sense calls "feelings" and "intelligence," regarding them
> as two opposed "faculties," are simply behaviour relating to persons

and behaviour affecting ideas or things; but in each of these forms of behaviour, the same affective and cognitive aspects of action emerge, aspects which are in fact always associated and in no way represent independent faculties. (Piaget, 1947/1950, p. 6)

In addition to holding a broad view of intelligence, Piaget, we should remember, worked within a philosophical tradition of system building (Vidal, 1998) – sometimes framed as the "sociogenetic perspective" (Valsiner & van der Veer, 2000) – that generally approached the mental activities of cognition, affection, and conation (or will) as functioning within a broad network of relations. The multiple levels of analysis within such system building not only frequently blurred the boundaries between various psychological functions but also between individual and social phenomena. In fact, Piaget's lectures from the Sorbonne, *Intelligence and Affectivity* (1954/1981), can be read as a kind of position statement regarding his particular developmental stance toward cognition, affection, and conation – that is, the classic "trilogy of mind" (Hilgard, 1980) – and how each mental function fit within a broader system of social norms and values. From these lectures, it is clear that Piaget understood affectivity as the basis for developing an ordered set of personal values. Such values, he claimed, when compared to the structures of cognitive growth, formed a "veritable logic of feelings" (Piaget, 1954/1981, p. 13) that also came to share the same "conservations and invariants" (p. 60) that were seen to arise in children's cognitive development.

Moreover, within the system building tradition of his time, Piaget's work also remained closely tied to that of James Mark Baldwin (see Cahan, 1984; Cairns, 1992; Müller & Runions, 2003), who, in addition to promoting a similar constructivist account of knowledge as Piaget, also saw important connections between cognition and affectivity. Baldwin went so far as to relate psychological matters of affectivity with transcendental notions of spirit, or *pancalism*, and the divine (Baldwin, 1906–1915/1974). Piaget's own interests in the divine are particularly evident in his early works (e.g., Piaget, 1918; Piaget, 1923; see also discussion in Brown & Weiss, 1987; Chapman, 1988; Vidal, 1998), as well as in such claims as "the identification of God with life was an idea that moved me to almost ecstasy because it allowed me, from that moment onward, to see in biology the explanation of all things, even of the spirit . . . " (Piaget, 1976; cited in Brown & Weiss, 1987, p. 59). Not only does such spiritualism run counter to current materialist and reductionist trends in psychology, but also very few contemporary approaches to psychological phenomena take seriously the systems orientation that prevailed during Piaget's times. Although Piaget was a transitional figure during this time, his work reflects the merging of various scholarly interests – psychology, biology, philosophy, theology, sociology, and history, to name only a few – that today are commonly treated as distinct disciplines in their own right. Altogether this is only the first hurdle standing in the way of a proper understanding of Piaget's account of affectivity.

HURDLE TWO: MAKING SENSE OF PIAGET'S AMBIVALENCE

Even with the interpretive generosity that such historical reorienting might afford, the tougher, and perhaps more interesting, hurdle to negotiate in coming to understand Piaget's views on affectivity is his own ambivalence toward the topic. Piaget was apparently "both passionate and ambivalent about values throughout his career" (Brown, 1996, p. 137), as well as "conflicted" (Dupont, 1994, p. xix) in developing his ideas of how they related more broadly to matters of affectivity. The evident conflict was already in full swing by the time he delivered his Sorbonne and Menninger lectures. Indeed, Piaget seemed to have delivered the Sorbonne lectures under coercion from his students (Brown, 1996).

Counter, then, to his more radical conceptions of the action-based unity between affectivity and intelligence, Piaget has at times both dismissed and venerated affectivity. For instance, in one of his lectures at the Menninger Clinic, Piaget describes an "uncontestable role" (1962a, p. 129) for affectivity in persons' intellectual growth, going so far to suggest that "without affect there would be no interest, no need, no motivation; and consequently . . . there would be no intelligence" (1962a, p. 129). Yet, at other times, he seems to dismiss affectivity. For example, although remarking on its lack of inherent structure, Piaget suggests that affectivity has "no interest [to him] as a scientific inquiry because it isn't a problem of knowledge . . . " (Bringuier, 1980, p. 49). Moreover, he concedes that others have already successfully developed lines of inquiry into individuals' affective lives, commenting that because "Freud focused on emotions," he instead "chose intelligence" (Gouin-Décarie, 1978, p. 183).

The nuances of Piaget's account fall somewhere in between the extremes of radical unity and disinterested neglect. Piaget tries, with mixed success, to strike a balance in his Sorbonne lectures (1954/1981), his best-developed contribution to understanding the topic of affectivity. There, he simultaneously acknowledges that "affective structures are isomorphic with intellectual structures" (p. 9) while also cautioning that "the comparison between affective states and acts of intelligence cannot be pushed too far" (p. 15).

Piaget's caution here, and related ambivalence to the topic of affectivity, has contributed to various speculations surrounding his own emotional development (Brown & Weiss, 1987). Some have even suggested that Piaget's personal disappointments with psychotherapy led him to reject the then-dominant psychoanalytic view of emotions (Dupont, 1994).[3] The merits of this line of scholarship, however, are unclear, particularly given some of Piaget's more favorable remarks about psychotherapy (e.g., Piaget, 1920). What is less open to speculation – and the line pursued here – is where Piaget's interests in structuralism, or formalism, eventually led him (for better or worse) to view affectivity as standing outside his interests in epistemology. With this structural orientation as a backdrop, the reasons for Piaget's ambivalent posturing toward the study of affectivity appear to be at least threefold. The first, and most central, of these requires that we understand Piaget as a "competence theorist" (Overton, 1991).

According to Overton (1991), "[C]ompetence refers to an idealization of the organization, pattern, design, form, or structure of the event or system being explained" (p. 19). In Piaget's case, the competence in question is simply knowledge, and its various idealized forms, that eventually culminates in "thinking that is coherent, noncontradictory, and precise (i.e., logical reasoning)" (Overton, 1991, p. 27). Having circumscribed his primary theoretical interests in this way, Piaget's approach to affectivity is unavoidably constrained. Such constraints are clearly in operation with the way that he delineates the two possible approaches of relating affect and intelligence at the structural level. The first is that "affectivity speeds up or slows down intellectual functioning without modifying the structures of intelligence as such" (Piaget, 1954/1981, p. 1). The second is that "affectivity changes intellectual structures and is, therefore, the source of new knowledge or new cognitive operations" (Piaget, 1954/1981, p. 1). Given Piaget's manner of defining the formal features of knowledge, particularly logical–mathematical knowledge, he very predictably chooses to defend the first approach, adding that affect is at best "a necessary condition in the constitution of intelligence but ... not a sufficient one" (Piaget, 1962a, p. 129).

Had the formal or structural features of affectivity been more readily identifiable by Piaget his demurral of affection and emotion may have been otherwise. This raises the second potential reason for his ambivalence. Although Piaget makes several suggestive claims about the structuring of affectivity into an organized system of values (Piaget, 1954/1981, p. 59), a fuller rendering of these ideas appears to get derailed by his complacency with the psychoanalytic tradition of his time. On the psychoanalytic view, at least as Piaget seems to have understood it, mental life functions as a kind of hydraulic system by which affectivity provides the energetics and intelligence the rational channels providing direction. Occasionally such energetics are seen to bubble over and disrupt the rational structures of the typical functioning individual, suggesting that affectivity, at least within a psychoanalytic framework, serves as a destabilizing force. That is, affectivity and emotions are associated with disorder, not order. As such, Piaget feared that an affect-centered approach to knowledge – that is, one that allowed affectivity to change intellectual structures – could quickly lead to an unconstrained form of subjectivism.[4] Piaget notes, for example, that some have gone as far as to say that "the estimation of distance . . . is due to the *desire* to reach distant objects, and not to the [actual] distance of the objects" (Piaget, 1962a, p. 129, italics added). To avoid such solipsistic claims, Piaget argued that at least "in structure formation . . . cognition, is autonomous" (Piaget, 1962a, p. 129). Affectivity, in turn, was left to serve a motivating function that "like gasoline . . . activates the motor of an automobile but does not modify its structure" (Piaget, 1962a, p. 5). The upshot of such claims, even if not consistently held by Piaget, is that his account of affectivity never gets entirely off the ground. As Brown and Weiss (1987) remark, it is as if Piaget and his collaborators "stand at the threshold of a cognitive–affective synthesis, but lacking an explicit model of how structures and procedures articulate, they cannot cross it" (p. 68; see also Nucci, 2001, pp. 107–110, for further discussion).

The third and final reason for Piaget's ambivalence toward affectivity revolves around a more general tension in his theory of moving between, and ultimately attempting to unify, epistemological and psychological questions (see Chapter 3, this volume). Returning to Overton's (1991) claims about competence, this tension is sometimes framed as the need to relate competence and procedures, or as he describes:

> Competence . . . necessarily leads to procedures, because procedural explanation offers explanation for how competence may be accessed, implemented, and expressed. . . . Procedural explanation is offered to explain the manifest or real-time activities that access and implement competence. (p. 28)

·Although Piaget was well versed in this kind of levels analysis, coming to terms with the vagaries of individual psychological growth was not a key priority within his system of thought. Moreover, his strengths as a theorist resided primarily at the level of competence explanations (Chapman, 1988) where stability and order were more clearly

TABLE 14.1. *The Six Parallel Stages of Intelligence and Affectivity*

A. *Sensorimotor intelligence*	B. *Intraindividual feelings*
1. Hereditary organization	1. Hereditary organizations
2. First acquired schemes	2. First acquired feelings
3. Sensorimotor intelligence	3. Affect regulating intentional behavior
B. *Verbal intelligence*	B. *Interpersonal feelings*
4. Preoperational representations	4. Intuitive affects
5. Concrete operations	5. Normative affects
6. Formal operations	6. Idealistic feelings

(adapted from Piaget, 1954/1981, p. 14).

articulated. As a consequence, matters of affectivity, which naturally seemed to fit better at the real-time procedural level of psychological functioning, became increasingly tangential in his program of work (Brown & Weiss, 1987).

BEYOND THE HURDLES: PIAGET'S POSITIVE CONTRIBUTION TO AFFECTIVE DEVELOPMENT

Given these various conceptual hurdles, it is perhaps all the more remarkable that Piaget stands to make a positive contribution to understanding the development of children's affective lives. He does this by presenting a series of stages of affective growth that closely parallels his more commonly known account of cognitive development (see also Wadsworth, 1996; Xypas, 2001, for further discussion).

Piaget sees affective development "correspond exactly to the stages of the development of [cognitive] structures" (Piaget, 1962a, p. 130). However, this is somewhat misleading, as it suggests that "affect" might develop in isolation, when Piaget "specifically den[ied] that affectivity can create new structures" (Piaget, 1954/1981, p. 15). It is perhaps better to say that what are traditionally thought of as intellectual structures, such as the conception of space and the permanence of objects, develops alongside what are traditionally thought of as affective structures, such as morality and personality.

Piaget notes six parallel stages of affective and intellectual development (see Table 14.1).[5] The first three are forms of sensorimotor intelligence and *intra*individual feelings. The latter three are related to verbal intelligence and *inter*personal feelings. Just as in standard intellectual development, the developmental pattern of affect is one of progressive *decentrations*. The first forms of affectivity are centered on the infant; then, at the level of reflection and awareness, extend to objects; then goals; and then to other people, morality, and society.[6]

The first stage, hereditary organization, shows little differentiation between what is typically called affect and intelligence. Indeed the term *drive*, as a form of interest, and *instinct*, as a form of organization, are often used synonymously (Piaget, 1954/1981, p. 17). Piaget's important point is that whatever there is initially – and he is skeptical that most of it is truly unlearned – is transformed through development (Piaget, 1954/1981, p. 20). In contrast to Freudian psychoanalytic theory, where primordial affect wells up into each situation, Piaget argues that feelings are "constructed and reconstructed on each occasion" (Piaget, 1954/1981, p. 51).

The second stage sees the infant develop feelings, such as pleasures and pains, linked to circular reactions (Piaget, 1954/1981, p. 21). With the behaviorists, Piaget recognizes that pleasures and pains play a role in learning in that the child's activities will differentiate based on pleasure and pain. If pulling a cord on a crib mobile is pleasurable, an infant will do so more often. However, Piaget stresses that these pleasures and pains are themselves constructed. If the role of intelligence in the construction of feelings is ignored, then "the belief that affectivity is the source of knowledge is a small step [away]" (Piaget, 1954/1981, p. 2).

The third stage, which includes sensorimotor stages IV–VI, sees the emergence of what Piaget defines as "the beginning of intelligent acts" (Piaget, 1954/1981, p. 26), and affectivity becomes similarly complex. Here is where the child begins to develop a hierarchy of values. To discuss how this occurs, it is important to distinguish synchronic (in the moment) and diachronic (over time) affectivity, even though Piaget admits these two forms of evaluation are "difficult to discern at first" (Piaget, 1954/1981, p. 32).

A concrete example is a child reaching for a toy on a blanket. The child pulls on the blanket to bring the toy closer. The child values, and wants, the blanket, but only insofar as the blanket brings the toy; in other words, the toy is valued over the blanket. The first form of valuation is when the child evaluates the success of his or her actions in the moment with feelings of success, failure, etc. This is a form of regulation, dictating when to stop activity through feelings of success or failure. The second form of valuation occurs as these momentary evaluations are organized into a hierarchy of values proper, "bit by bit into a system that is broader, more stable, and distinct from the system of energetic regulations" (Piaget, 1954/1981, p. 32). This larger value system "determines the energies employed in action" (Piaget, 1954/1981, p. 42).

The synchronous and diachronic modes of affect, regulation, and valuation "find their juncture in the mechanism of interest" (Piaget,

1954/1981, p. 32). Interest is both synchronous in that a particular activity is chosen in a particular situation and diachronic in that a person develops and engages in his or her interests over time. Piaget (1954/1981, p. 5) notes that his thoughts on interest closely resemble those of Dewey (e.g., Dewey, 1896).

The fourth stage sees the development of interpersonal feelings and the beginning of normative feelings. The child is at first filled with spontaneous thoughts and fantastical ideas; he or she has spontaneous likes and dislikes. The child, with language, can re-create feelings experienced. Feeling, like thinking, becomes *normative* (though spontaneous feelings, as ideas, persist) as action schemes are conserved (Piaget, 1954/1981, p. 50). Piaget makes a point of noting that "it is not feeling that is conserved but a certain scheme of interaction with other people" (Piaget, 1954/1981, p. 50). At first these feelings are only seminormative. They suggest what "is necessary and just what . . . is desirable or preferable" (Piaget, 1954/1981, p. 55). However, this manifests initially as a feeling of *obligation*, corresponding to heteronomous moral reasoning (see Chapter 12, this volume).

The fifth stage sees these feelings become autonomous. With such autonomy, feelings of *respect* and *justice*, which can be applied to all social partners, emerge and displace more heteronomic feelings of obligation linked to authority figures (Vidal, 1998, p. 591). The transition to "a system of relatively fixed values to which [individuals] feel obligated to adhere" (Piaget, 1954/1981, p. 65) is different than prior feelings of obligation. That is, autonomous moral feelings are akin to logical–mathematical operations such as "$2 + 2 = 4$": No external authority provokes the answer to this equation; it is true by necessity. Following such reasoning, Piaget remarks that "[m]orality is . . . a logic of action in the same way that logic is a morality of thought" (Piaget, 1954/1981, p. 13).

A concrete example of how this system of values functions is provided in Piaget's discussion of the *will* (see esp. Piaget, 1962b). The will is classically defined as that which resolves a conflict between a predominant response and a weaker one by elevating, and selecting, the weaker of the two; Piaget cites William James's example of an urge to go for a pleasant walk and a competing need to keep working (Piaget, 1962b, p. 140). In Piaget's terminology, the "act of will corresponds . . . to the conservation of values; it consists of subordinating a given situation to a permanent scale of values" (Piaget, 1954/1981, p. 65). Willing is accomplished through "an act of decentration" (Piaget, 1962b, p. 142). Piaget illustrates the will at work by way of his famous task of conservation of number, where two rows of coins are laid out at equal distances, and then one of the rows is spread out wider. Just like decentration with objects, we can be fooled (or weak-willed) and choose the predominant response, that there are "more" in the wider row. Of course, the coin example is easy for an adult to solve. But moral dilemmas that plague children (homework or play) might (or might not) be similarly simple for adults to manage.

The sixth stage sees the development of personality. Personality is marked by "idealistic feelings" (Piaget, 1954/1981, p. 70), in that adolescents can project their ideas of how things *should be* onto the workings of the world. Interestingly, and contrary to normal use, Piaget links personality to the "subordination of the self to the collective ideal" (Piaget, 1954/1981, p. 71). He refers to his discussion of the adolescent's idea of homeland, eventually published in *Sociological Studies* (Piaget, 1965/1995). Through the process of decentration, adolescents are able to look beyond aspects of their life that are "accidental," such as being born in a particular country, to more formalistic and potentially universalizable features, such as the desire to learn about the world.

FUTURE HURDLES: WHAT LIES AHEAD?

Even if underdeveloped, many aspects of Piaget's affective theory are absolutely essential to his broader system of thought. This is perhaps most true for his account of morality, which is based on mutual respect (see Chapter 12, this volume), as well as his approach to education (see Chapter 15, this volume). Still, another important extension of Piaget's work lies with developing his third stage of affective development, where he discusses the synchronic and diachronic aspects of valuation. Here, Piaget hints at the role of the value system in selecting activities, a process that has been related to current theorizing about "emotional expectancies" (e.g., Krettenauer, Malti, & Sokol, 2008). On these lines, Brown (1994) argues that "the purpose of affectivity is to select perceptions, ideas, and actions.... psychological selection depends... on evaluative criteria.... [that] appear to consciousness in the form of feelings" (p. 173). In many ways, conceiving of feelings as evaluative judgments resembles current functionalist approaches to emotion in both psychology (e.g., Barrett, 1995) and philosophy (e.g., Nussbaum, 2001; Solomon, 2003). From a functionalist perspective, "emotions are much more than feelings. They are adaptive patterns of behavior arising from a person's appraised relation to ongoing events" (Mascolo & Fischer, 1995, p. 65). The brunt of this view is that emotions are ordered, controllable, and, insofar as they involve accurate cognitive appraisals, rational. Had such an account been available to Piaget when he was developing his own ideas about affectivity, his ambivalence toward affect and emotion may have never surfaced.

Such speculation notwithstanding, in order to extend the promise of Piaget's insights on affective development, it will be critical to move beyond the more limiting structuralist assumptions that he sometimes makes. To do this, some Piagetian scholars have suggested a wholesale reinterpretation of Piaget as the "main action theorist in development[al] psychology" (Boesch, 1984, p. 173; Brown, 1994, 1996; Sokol & Chandler, 2004; Youniss, 1981, 1987) rather than treating him as an exemplar of the "structural–developmental" movement (Chapman, 1988, p. 379). *Action theory* posits a transactional framework (Meacham, 1977) for exploring the inherently relational activities of individuals and their surroundings in any situation.

In this vein, affectivity would play a role in the selection of activity, the consciousness of activity, and the evaluation of successful or failed activity. Having such selection and evaluation functions in place is essential to developing a psychological interpretation of Piaget's "epistemic subject" (e.g., Bickhard, 1980; Ciompi, 1997, p. 162); indeed, Piaget came close to this interpretation in his later writings, such as in the *Grasp of Consciousness* (Brown, 1996, p. 152; Piaget, 1974/1976).

The amount of work that remains might suggest a temptation to dismiss Piaget's theory of affect as an "excursion from the main axis of [Piaget's] work" (Flavell, 1963, p. 81). Two key details, however, speak against this view. First, other Piagetian "excursions" into morality, philosophy, and sociology are justly regarded as serious and noteworthy efforts. Affect could be a similarly important voyage. The second reason follows Chapman's groundbreaking representation of Piaget's work as a lifelong project to "reconcile science and value" (Chapman, 1988, p. vii). Indeed, Piaget's early work was marked by interest in values, immanence, and even democracy (Vidal, 1998). In marked contrast to Piaget's "retrospective view . . . values, and therefore feelings, were the primary focus in [Piaget's] early days" (Brown & Weiss, 1987, p. 59). Although thinkers are certainly allowed to evolve and discard ideas and theories, clinging to Piaget's work on affect, we would argue along with Boesch (1984), carries the promise of "a magnificent view of the total unity of psychological development" (p. 174).

NOTES

1. *The moral judgment of the child* (Piaget, 1932/1965), for example, bases morality on reciprocal affection (Chapter 12, this volume; Vidal, 1998), and various passages in *Play, dreams, and imitation in childhood* (Piaget,

1945/1962), *The origins of intelligence in children* (Piaget, 1936/1952), *The psychology of intelligence* (1947/1950), and *Six psychological studies* (Piaget, 1964/1967) foreshadow the importance of affectivity.

2. Such a criticism is seen in philosopher Merleau-Ponty's (2001 [1949–1952], p. 275) critique of Piaget's epistemic subject as "disembodied" or "quasi-divine." During Piaget's tenure at the Sorbonne, in which he was Merleau-Ponty's sucessor, Piaget was made "well aware" (Piaget, 1965/1971, p. 143) of these accusations (see also Xypas, 2001, pp. 13–26). As an early commentator pointed out, the philosopher's criticism was, strictly speaking, false, though there were other reasons to charge Piaget with intellectualism (Amado, 1969, p. 78). We touch on some of these reasons later in the chapter.

3. As Dupont (1994) remarks, Piaget "never managed to free himself from the notion that to study feelings and emotions was tantamount to doing psychoanalysis" (p. xix).

4. Piaget harbored a similar view regarding phenomenology, which, he imagined, also came dangerously close to radical subjectivism (Piaget, 1971). By having intellect do the structuring, Piaget felt knowledge was more securely tied to reality.

5. The sensorimotor stages Piaget describes in *Intelligence and Affectivity* collapse his earlier formulations of the sensorimotor stages (e.g., Piaget & Inhelder, 1966/1969) into stages 2 (II, III) and 3 (IV, V, VI); for the fluidity of stages, see Smith (2002, pp. 517–519).

6. Piaget's contemporaries assailed him for taking the position that the infant was "centred" (i.e., asocial) rather than fundamentally social. At issue seems to be a misunderstanding of Piaget's divide between action schemes and reflective knowledge. Piaget would acknowledge that children have emotional relations with others from birth (action scheme); however, he would postpone reflective knowledge of people *as people* until a later age (e.g., Piaget, 1954/1981, pp. 19, 26).

REFERENCES

Amado, G. (1969). *L'affectivité de l'enfant*. Paris: PUF.

Baldwin, J. M. (1906–1915). *Thought and things: A study in the development and meaning of thought, or genetic logic* (4 vols.). New York: Putnam. (Reprinted by Arno Press, New York, 1974)

Barrett, K. C. (1995). A functionalist approach to shame and guilt. In J. P. Tangney & K. W. Fischer (Eds.), *Self-conscious emotions: The psychology of shame, guilt, embarrassment, and pride* (pp. 25–63). New York: Guilford.

Bearison, D. J., & Zimiles, H. (Eds.). (1986). *Thought and emotion: Developmental perspectives*. Hillsdale, NJ: Erlbaum.

Bickhard, M. H. (1980). *Cognition, convention, and communication*. New York: Praeger.

Boesch, E. E. (1984). The development of affective schemata. *Human Development, 27*, 173–183.

Bringuier, J. (1980). *Conversations with Jean Piaget*. Chicago: University of Chicago Press. (Original work published in 1977)

Brown, T. A. (1994). Affective dimensions of meaning. In W. F. Overton & D. S. Palermo (Eds.), *The nature and ontogenesis of meaning* (pp. 167–190). Hillsdale, NJ: Erlbaum.

Brown, T. A. (1996). Values, knowledge, and Piaget. In E. S. Reed, E. Turiel, & T. Brown (Eds.), *Values and knowledge* (pp. 137–170). Mahwah, NJ: Erlbaum.

Brown, T. A., & Kozak, A. (1998). Emotion and the possibility of psychologists entering into heaven. In M. F. Mascolo & S. Griffin (Eds.), *What develops in emotional development?* (pp. 135–155). New York: Plenum Press.

Brown, T. A., & Weiss, L. (1987). Structures, procedures, heuristics, and affectivity. *Archives de Psychologie, 55,* 59–94.

Cahan, E. D. (1984). The genetic psychologies of James Mark Baldwin and Jean Piaget. *Developmental Psychology, 20,* 128–135.

Cairns, R. B. (1992). The making of a developmental science: The contributions and intellectual heritage of James Mark Baldwin. *Developmental Psychology, 28,* 17–24.

Carpendale, J. I. M., & Lewis, C. (2004). Constructing an understanding of mind. *Behavioral and Brain Sciences, 27,* 79–151.

Chapman, M. (1988). *Constructive evolution.* New York: Cambridge University Press.

Ciompi, L. (1997). The concept of affect logic. *Psychiatry, 60,* 158–170.

Cowan, P. A. (1978). *Piaget with feeling.* New York: Holt, Rinehart & Winston.

Cowan, P. A. (1981). Preface. In J. Piaget (Ed.), *Intelligence and affectivity* (pp. ix–xiv). Palo Alto, CA: Annual Reviews.

Danziger, K. (1997). *Naming the mind: How psychology found its language.* London: Sage.

Dewey, J. (1896). The reflex arc concept in psychology. *Psychological Review, 3,* 357–370.

Dupont, H. (1994). *Emotional development, theory and applications.* Westport, CT: Praeger.

Flavell, J. H. (1963). *The developmental psychology of Jean Piaget.* New York: D. Van Nostrand.

Goleman, D. (1995). *Emotional intelligence.* New York: Bantam Books.

Gouin-Décarie, T. (1965). *Intelligence and affectivity in early childhood.* New York: International Universities Press.

Gouin-Décarie, T. (1978). Affect development and cognition in a Piagetian context. In M. Lewis & L. A. Rosenblum (Eds.), *The development of affect* (pp. 183–204). New York: Plenum Press.

Hilgard, E. R. (1980). The trilogy of mind: Cognition, affection, and conation. *Journal of the History of the Behavioral Sciences, 16,* 107–117.

Krettenauer, T., Malti, T., & Sokol, B. W. (2008). The development of moral emotion expectancies and the happy victimizer phenomenon: A critical review of theory and application. *European Journal of Developmental Science, 2,* 221–235.

Lapsley, D. K. (1996). *Moral psychology.* Boulder, CO: Westview Press.

Mascolo, M., & Fischer, K. W. (1995). Developmental transformations of appraisals in pride, shame, and guilt. In J. P. Tangney & K. W. Fischer (Eds.), *Self-conscious emotions: The psychology of shame, guilt, embarrassment, and pride* (pp. 64–113). New York: Guilford.

Meacham, J. (1977). A transactional model of remembering. In N. Datan & H. W. Reese (Eds.), *Life-span developmental psychology: Dialectical perspectives on experimental research* (pp. 261–284). New York: Academic.

Merleau-Ponty, M. (2001). *Psychologie et pédagogie de l'enfant: Cours de Sorbonne 1949–1952* [Psychology and pedagogy of the child: Sorbonne courses 1949–1952]. Paris: Verdier.

Müller, U., & Runions, K. (2003). The origins of understanding self and other: James Mark Baldwin's theory. *Developmental Review, 23*, 29–54.

Nucci, L. P. (2001). *Education in the moral domain*. Cambridge: Cambridge University Press.

Nussbaum, M. C. (2001). *Upheavals of thought: The intelligence of emotions*. Cambridge: Cambridge University Press.

Overton, W. F. (1991). Competence, procedures, and hardware: Conceptual and empirical considerations. In M. Chandler & M. Chapman (Eds.), *Criteria for competence: Controversies in the conceptualization and assessment of children's abilities* (pp. 19–42). Hillsdale, NJ: Erlbaum.

Piaget, J. (1918). *Recherche*. Lausanne: La Concorde.

Piaget, J. (1920). La psychanalyse dans ses rapports avec la psychologie de l'enfant [Psychoanalysis and its links with child psychology]. *Bulletin Mensuel de la Société Alfred Binet, 1–3*, 18–34, 41–58.

Piaget, J. (1923). La psychologie et les valeurs religieuses [Psychology and religious values]. In Association Chrétienne d'Etudiants de la Suisse Romande (Ed.), *Saint Croix 1922* (pp. 38–82). Lausanne: Imprimerie de la Concorde.

Piaget, J. (1950). *The psychology of intelligence*. London: Routledge & Kegan Paul. (Original work published in 1947)

Piaget, J. (1952). *The origins of intelligence in children*. New York: International Universities Press. (Original work published in 1936)

Piaget, J. (1954). Les relations entre l'intelligence et l'affectivité dans le développement de l'enfant [The relations between intelligence and affectivity in the development of the child]. *Bulletin de Psychologie* [Psychological Bulletin], *7*, 143–150, 346–361, 522–535, 699–701.

Piaget, J. (1962). *Play, dreams, and imitation in childhood*. New York: Norton Library. (Original work published in 1945)

Piaget, J. (1962a). The relation of affectivity to intelligence in the mental development of the child. *Bulletin of the Menninger Clinic, 26*, 129–137.

Piaget, J. (1962b). Will and action. *Bulletin of the Menninger Clinic, 26*, 138–145.

Piaget, J. (1965). *The moral judgment of the child*. New York: The Free Press. (Original work published in 1932)

Piaget, J. (1967). *Six psychological studies*. New York: Random House. (Original work published in 1964)

Piaget, J. (1971). *Insights and illusions of philosophy*. New York: World Publishing Company. (Original work published in 1965)

Piaget, J. (1976). Autobiographie. *Revue Européene des Sciences Sociales et Cahiers Vilfredo Pareto, 36/39*, 1–43.

Piaget, J. (1976). *The grasp of consciousness*. Cambridge, MA: Harvard University press. (Original work published in 1974)

Piaget, J. (1981). *Intelligence and affectivity*. Palo Alto, CA: Annual Reviews. (Original work published in 1954)

Piaget, J. (1995). *Sociological studies*. New York: Routledge. (Original work published in 1965)

Piaget, J., & Inhelder, B. (1969). *The psychology of the child*. New York: Basic Books. (Original work published in 1966)

Smith, L. (2002). Piaget's model. In U. Goswami (Ed.), *Blackwell handbook of childhood cognitive development* (pp. 515–537). Malden, MA: Blackwell.

Sokol, B. W., & Chandler, M. J. (2004). A bridge too far: On the relations between moral and secular reasoning. In J. I. M. Carpendale & U. Müller (Eds.), *Social interaction and the development of knowledge* (pp. 155–174). Mahwah, NJ: Erlbaum.

Solomon, R. (2003). *Not passion's slave: Emotion and choice*. Oxford: Oxford University Press.

Sternberg, R. J. (1990). *Metaphors of mind: Conceptions of the nature of intelligence*. Cambridge: Cambridge University Press.

Valsiner, J., & van der Veer, R. (2000). *The social mind: Construction of the idea*. Cambridge: Cambridge University Press.

Vidal, F. (1998). Immanence, affectivité et démocratie dans *Le jugement moral chez l'enfant* [Immanence, affectivity and democracy in *The moral judgment of the child*]. *Bulletin de Psychologie, 51,* 585–597.

Wadsworth, B. J. (1996). *Piaget's theory of cognitive and affective development* (5th ed.). White Plains, NY: Longman Publishers.

Xypas, C. (2001). *Les stades du développement affectif selon Piaget* [The stages of affective development according to Piaget]. Paris: L'Harmattan.

Youniss, J. (1981). A revised interpretation of Piaget (1932). In I. E. Sigel, D. M. Brodzinsky, & R. M. Golinkoff (Eds.), *New directions in Piagetian theory and practice* (pp. 191–201). Hillsdale, NJ: Erlbaum.

Youniss, J. (1987). Social construction and moral development: Update and expansion of an idea. In W. M. Kurtines & J. L. Gewirtz (Eds.), *Moral development through social interaction* (pp. 131–148). New York: Wiley.

15 Piaget's Pedagogy

> Education, for most people, means trying to lead the child to resemble
> the typical adult of his society (whereas) for me, education means making
> creators, even if there aren't many of them, even if one's creations are
> limited by comparison with those others. (Piaget, 1977/1980, p. 132)[1]

INTRODUCTION

Education is a complex business and one of its parts is pedagogy, that
is, the process of education in which knowledge or skills are imparted
through teaching. My chapter on Piaget's pedagogy (PP) runs directly
into a problem.[2] Piaget's work is commonly interpreted as a pedagogy-
free zone with teaching adding next to nothing to children's development. In this chapter, I want to do three things. First, I revisit the educational critique of Piaget's work to show that this critique is flawed –
good evidence shows that PP works well in practice. Then I provide PP's
re-analysis to show that its main principles are theoretically alive and
well. Finally, the last section contains a review of my argument with
pointers to future directions.

PIAGET'S PEDAGOGY IN PRACTICE

Piaget's work has attracted attention with regard to its educational
potential and promise. The predominant view, however, has been that
it failed to deliver; that is, the outcome of the educational critique has
commonly been negative. In this section, I review this negative critique
and then state a counter-argument to show that it is flawed.

A preliminary clarification first. Psychology is an empirical science
with multiple divisions.[3] Education is an interdisciplinary study that
includes all the human sciences. Thus, psychology and education are

324

different, and there are several ways in which they could be related (Smith, 2005):

(a) Independence: psychology and education pass each other by like ships in the dark.

(b) Relevance: psychological ideas with a global import for education, whether in the minds of individuals or as a *zeitgeist* in the culture.

(c) Implication: psychological theories with testable consequences that could impact on education.

(d) Application: implications actually tested in education and shown to work in practice.

(e) Interdependence: two-way implications between psychological and educational theories, successfully tested in practice.

Taking Piaget's work, a case can be made for each of these. Many commentaries adopt (a) – indeed, Piaget (1932/1932, pp. 413–414) was acutely aware that educational conclusions could not be "read off" from his psychology. Under (b), educational relevance has been noted for PP's distinctive commitment to child-centered education (Donaldson, 1992). Relevance amounts to a sign of promise, but promises still have to be made good. Piaget disavowed some uses of his work, notably the reforms leading to "modern mathematics taught by archaic methods" (Piaget, 1966/1998, p. 235; Piaget, 1977/1980, p. 128). Under (e) is Piaget's (1951/1998) professional work as director of the International Bureau of Education. However, Piaget (1932/1932, p. 414; 1951/1998, p. 269) repeatedly observed that too little empirical investigation using controlled methods had been carried out in educational science. So I plan to steer clear of these three alternatives. Instead my focus is on (c) and (d).

The educational critique has been predominantly negative on both fronts. Under (c), PP's implications are regarded as problematic, and under (d), its application not to work at all.[4] Straddling both is the "American question" (Bruner, 1986), so called because Piaget's presentations in the United States usually led to the question "Can one accelerate the stages indefinitely?"

Piaget's (1971, p. 7) answer was "Yes." As he put this elsewhere: "Some pedagogical interventions can, of course, accelerate and complete spontaneous development" (Piaget, 1970/1983, p. 111). But he also added qualifications. One was about whether there is any advantage because a principal issue in education is not "how fast" but "how far" (Piaget, 1971, p. 7). Another was that successful interventions "cannot change the order of the constructions" (Piaget, 1970/1983, p. 111). A third was that "each time one prematurely teaches a child something he could have discovered for himself, that child is kept from inventing it and consequently understanding it completely" (Piaget, 1970/1983, p. 113).[5] Piaget's answer was combined with a thought-experiment about a boy who in counting pebbles had

> lined them up in a row, counted them from left to right, and got ten. Then, just for fun, he counted them from right to left [and] was astonished that he got ten again. (Piaget, 1970, pp. 16–17; cf. 1970/1983, p. 119)

Piaget's point was that the boy had come to realize the mathematical rule for commutativity.[6] Since rules are norms and norms are complex, his point was that grasping a norm is a complex business – more on this in the following section.

In the educational critique, PP's answer was interpreted to be "No" on the grounds that the thought-experiment serves as a false model with its implication that all learning is self-discovery in which teachers are unnecessary. Thus, Hughes (1986, p. 17) interpreted PP as the view that "to a large extent mathematical concepts cannot be taught" and that "mathematics is not essentially difficult for it is something children will for the most part do" – for themselves and without a teacher in sight. Clearly, a ridiculous position! But is it true of PP?

Others seem to think so. The "American question" amounts to a bridge from psychology to education. On one side is Piaget's stage theory, dependent on two essential parts about developmental sequences and mechanisms. In this critique, both were challenged in that Piagetian sequences marked by stages are problematic, with each stage having a corresponding structure "difficult to define, to explicate, and to operationalize" (Case, 1985, p. 415); and the main Piagetian mechanism was interpreted to be similarly problematic – "globally defined and explicated [and so] quite difficult to operationalize" (p. 416). The evidence attested the presence of décalages with low inter-task correlations alleged to be incompatible with stage-like progressions (Case, 1992, 1999).[7] On the other side is Piaget's position on teaching/learning. This was interpreted to be "child-centered" (Donaldson, 1992) in that "children are encouraged to explore as wide a variety of situations as possible on their own, and to reflect on the results of their own activity" (Case, 1985, p. 408), and so "a theory of teaching is almost lacking" (Ginsburg, 1981) because learning is "independent and spontaneous" (Hughes, 1986, p. 17) – that is, it is the child's own "discovery learning." Bryant (1984) regarded this as anomalous: Teachers are "doomed to be peripheral at best and ineffective at worst." Brainerd (2003, p. 283) summarized the evidence from training studies, concluding that four types of "passive" procedures promote good learning, whereas discovery methods were not found to be superior to them. In this critique, "the mystique of discovery learning [is based on] the weakest part of the theory [i.e., equilibration]" (Sullivan, 1967, p. 34).

This educational critique with its negative conclusion is open to the challenge that there is good evidence to show that PP works well in practice. This evidence is part of the ongoing research-program over three decades due to Michael Shayer and Philip Adey. My review is in four parts, covering evidence about successful assessments and interventions.

Diagnostic Assessment

Using a national sample ($n = 10,000$) in 1975, Shayer and Adey (1981) assessed youngsters using Piagetian tasks and Piagetian stage interpretations (concrete and formal operations). The findings were that, by 16 years, about 30% of the youngsters were thinking at the level of formal operations. Crucially, the pass rate in public examinations in Science was about 30%. These findings imply that Piagetian stages and achievement in national examinations are related.

Criterion-Referenced Assessment

Assessment is norm-referenced in psychometrics where scores are interpreted in terms of standardized performances of other individuals. This is a descriptive – not value-laden – interpretation of norms (see point 4 in the next section). Assessment is criterion-referenced when scores are interpreted in terms of some external criterion. Using the previous findings as the 1975 baseline, criterion-referenced Piagetian tasks have been used to document anti-Flynn effects, that is, declining performance in successive cohorts.[8] The findings from a national sample ($n = 10,023$) in 2003 revealed (Shayer, Ginsburg, & Coe, 2007; Wylam & Shayer, 1980):

- the disappearance of the original boy–girl differential of 0.5 SD;
- a decrease in boys' performance by 1.04 SD;
- an increase in girls' performance by 0.55 SD.

This is an educationally significant finding, once again based on Piagetian stage theory.

Formative Assessment

Teaching can make a contribution to better learning through formative assessment; that is, the assessment design is itself educative in promoting learning (Black & Wiliam, 1998; Shepard, 2000; Torrance & Pryor,

1998). In *Thinking Science*, Adey, Shayer, and Yates (1989) adapted Piagetian tasks for collaborative work in the classroom combined with individual reflection. Under the negative critique, that was a futile exercise. By contrast, *Thinking Science* attests PP's classroom utility.

Interventions

As well, *Thinking Science* was put to work. The aim of the first intervention study was to increase beyond 30% the number of youngsters gaining a good Pass in national examinations (Adey & Shayer, 1994). In a quasi-experimental design controlled for school effects, the classroom tasks were used 1 hour biweekly over 2 school years (11–13 years). Delivery was subject-specific in Science. The main outcome measure was in national examinations taken at 15–16 years. The improvement was tested in three core subjects – Science, Mathematics, English – where circa 54% of the youngsters in the experimental classes gained "good" Passes, that is, well in excess of the 30% Pass rate in the control classes. Thus, this intervention was significant, durable, and transferable. Crucially, too, it was replicable, leading to a similar level of improvement in a second intervention (Shayer & Adey, 2002). Further, this research-program is generalizable both to children aged 5–7 years (Adey, 2007; Shayer, 2008) and to comparable designs internationally (Hautamäki, 2007). In short, this evidence shows that PP works well in practice.

In conclusion, this section has presented a review of PP's negative critique in education. It was followed by a counterargument showing that educational assessments and interventions based on PP do work in practice. Using the five positions at the outset of the second section, this means that PP fits (d) – quite an achievement because most psychological theories remain somewhere between (a) and (c). The key issue, then, is no longer whether PP works – it does – but rather why it does so. This is taken up in the next section.

PIAGET'S PEDAGOGY: THEORY AND RE-ANALYSIS

The conclusion in the last section was that PP does work in practice. This section provides a re-analysis of PP with specific reference to its main constructs in the clarification of PP's explanatory scope.

The motivation for this re-analysis was a challenge comprising ten questions about PP (Smith, 2004). Due to space limitations, only the first and last – questions 1 and 10 – are re-stated here to bring out two things.

Question 1: Is Piaget's Work on Education Well Understood?

Educationalists with interests in PP included Isaacs (1930, pp. 78–79), who criticized PP for its over-estimation of social factors in education, and Vygotsky (1994a, pp. 351–352; 1994b, pp. 365–366) for its under-estimation. These criticisms are contraries, so they cannot both be right. Actually, Piaget (1931 and 1962/2000, respectively) challenged both, pointing out that a *tertium quid*, or third factor, operating interdependently with society and heredity too, was equilibration; and this had been ignored. Do not rush to judgment!

Question 10: For Piaget, Equilibration Is the Central Construct and a Road to Nowhere?

Commentators see major problems in its use at all (Bryant, 2001; Case, 1999; Ginsburg, 1981; Sullivan, 1967). Yet equilibration is Piaget's central construct, and it is intelligible (Chapters 3 and 6, this volume). Any judgment about PP is inconclusive without a fuller analysis of this central construct. PP's negative critique is inconclusive because its analysis is, at best, incomplete and, at worst, absent altogether.

This pair of questions is the reminder that PP is subtle and complex – subtle because PP has long been open to incompatible interpretations, complex because its main construct is equilibration, a notion that defies straightforward interpretation. Thus, something more has to be said about PP with a view to clarifying both.

The re-analysis is intended as a contribution to PP's clarification through four principles: (1) education as a value-laden exchange relation, (2) intelligence and affectivity, (3) instructional strategies, and (4) knowing through right reasons. This quartet is no doubt incomplete. But it serves to identify essential principles that may serve in the de-mystification of Piaget's central construct, equilibration.

(1) Education Is an Exchange Relation Between a Learner and the Educator's Values

In PP, education is defined as a relationship between the growing individual and the social, intellectual, and moral values into which the educator is charged with initiating that individual (Piaget, 1935/1971, p. 137).

Notice four things here. One: it depicts education as a two-termed relationship – a learner as a developing person (child, adult) and an educator (parent, peer, tutor). It is the educator's values that frame their relationship. Two: the definition refers to human growth, that is, development. But this is ambiguous for the reason given by Dewey (1966, p. 49): "Education is development (though) everything depends on *how* development is conceived." For Piaget, the key issue is what use the learner makes of the values invoked by the teacher. Under this definition, education is a relation in which values are exchanged. Three: central to the exchange are the values that the educator plans to impart. What is valued can be anything at all, doubtless reflecting the diversity of human values. Using Piaget's (1965/1995, p. 25) examples, this could be, for example, initiation into the Hitler Youth or an introduction to school mathematics. If the values are intellectual, it is for the educator to identify important knowledge – a value-laden choice.[9] Four: an educator is specifically required in that "each individual is led to think and re-think the system of collective notions" (Piaget, 1950/1995, p. 76). This is an important admission about the indispensability of teaching.

Collective notions are notions publicly available in the culture. "Thinking" them is an essential first step for anyone, and it is specifically stated that each individual is "led" to do so; that is, the educator is required to provide assistance to the learner. As well, "re-thinking" is also required, and Piaget's point is that this is an individual matter – it is for me to make my mind up, whether rightly or wrongly, even when you are assisting me. This is Piaget's (1962/2000, pp. 251–252) individualism, and it is in the best tradition of "education for intellectual freedom" (1945/1998, p. 162).

So this principle comprises two explicit denials. One is the denial of human development in terms of the "solitary knower." The other is the denial of learning and knowing without teaching. At a stroke, this shows that Piagetian constructivism includes an essentially social element (*pace* Vygotsky, 1994b, p. 352; cf. Piaget, 1962/2000).

(2) Knowing Is Always Mediated by Affectivity Intrinsic to It

From (1), education is value-laden in virtue of the educator's values. But the educator is a person, and so is the learner who, by implication, has values too. Thus, an open question is the interaction between the learner's and educator's values. In turn, this means that although knowing is a cognitive matter, it always has an affective counterpart. In Piaget's work, living organisms adapt to their environment, where an intrinsic aspect of adaptation is organization, that is, to adapt to the world is to organize the world. In turn, organization includes both affectivity and intelligence.

TABLE 15.1. *Adaptation and Organization*

Biological Functions		Intellectual Functions	Categories		
Organization		Regulative	Totality	×	Reciprocity
			Ideal (goal)	×	Value (means)
Adaptation	Assimilation	Implicative	Quality	×	Class
			Quantitative relationship	×	Number
	Accommodation	Explicative	Object	×	Space
			Causality	×	Time

Source: Adapted from Piaget (1953, p. 9).

This principle was austerely formulated in Piaget's (1936/1953) first infancy book (Table 15.1). The table seems obscure and irrelevant to human intelligence. Yet it pinpoints the inter-dependence of "cold cognition" and "hot motivation" in Piaget's account.[10] Its later elaboration is instructive (Piaget, 1954/1981). Affectivity includes feelings, motivation, values, and the self. Organisms have likings and interests and their opposites, and these become organized through the choices made in terms of what is good or bad from my perspective as opposed to yours (Piaget, 1954/1981, pp. 31–34). Values proliferate to form value systems. These systems may be loose or exact, implicit in what an agent does or in intellectual acts, but either way without any requirement for the agent to be conscious of them (see Chapter 14, this volume). Crucially, "valued objects or people provide the agent with new goals" (Piaget, 1954/1981, p. 43*), and they do so in becoming more specific and more stable. Unlike the logic of intelligence, these systems never become fully coherent, Piaget (1954/1981, p. 60) claimed. This is because the use of a value system can – and does – lead to contrary outcomes, to value conservation, or to paralogisms (Piaget, 1954/1981, p. 60).[11] For Piaget, the function of affectivity is internal regulation by ordering preferences both as energetics or as the economy of an agent's activities, and as finality in ordering mean/ends relationships (Piaget, 1954/1981, p. 42). In general, "affectivity can cause accelerations and retardations" (Piaget, 1954/1981, p. 73). Even so, affectivity "can neither engender nor modify structures" (Piaget, 1954/1981, p. 73) – that is, cognitive structures.

In short, educational relationships always involve a learner's and educator's value systems. A value can be causally imposed and compliance may follow, but its internalization and autonomous acceptance is another matter. "My tutor requires me to do this – but I won't" is not a contradiction. This does not mean that learners "should do anything they want; (rather it means that) they should want to do what they do (in that) they should act, not that they should be acted upon" (Piaget, 1935/1971, p. 152).[12] The contribution by affectivity is necessary in PP, but it is not sufficient without something else pointing in the right direction. Two such pointers follow as (3) and (4).

(3) Knowing Is a Spontaneous Activity That Benefits from Pedagogical Assistance

An extrinsic pointer is due to educators' strategies. Kant argued that the mind has both receptive capacities and spontaneous capabilities, both operative in human knowledge. For Kant (1787/1933, B74, B93), knowledge has its origin in sensory capacities to receive representations and in intellectual capabilities for knowing objects through them. Thus, intellectual capabilities were interpreted to be inherently spontaneous with regard to which concepts are used in assigning meaning to which representations. Piaget had a comparable view that is pedagogically important. "Memory, passive obedience, imitation of the adult, and the receptive factors in general are all as natural to the child as spontaneous activity" (Piaget, 1935/1971, p. 139). Play in a child is a specific example of spontaneity (1954/1981, p. 19) or, more generally, any human action freely performed. The point is that although learners will spontaneously do some things, such activities are not thereby conducive to intellectual development, for example, if factual memorization or conformity to peers are valued as ends in themselves. Learners may be disinclined to accept control; they may be willing to rely on receptivity rather than engagement. That is why instructional assistance is required. Further, it is made available in PP through three instructional strategies.

Formative assessment. Formative assessment was identified in the previous section as the educator's design of assessment tasks with a view to making learning possible, easier, or better. For Piaget (1945/1998, p. 163) "children have to be taught to think.... To think is to search for oneself, that is, to criticize freely, and to demonstrate autonomously." Anarchy and autonomy are not the same thing, and teaching has a contribution to make in exchanging the former, which is spontaneous, for the latter, which is a human development. Secondly, "a teacher creates a learning context which evokes a spontaneous elaboration of the part of the learner" (Piaget, 1962/2000, p. 252). The difference between "creating learning" and "creating a context for learning" is an important difference, invoked by Piaget and comparable to Vygotsky's position (1994b, p. 366). Once again, for Piaget, pedagogical input is required for the growth of autonomy. Third, this means that the teacher is less "a person who gives 'lessons' and is rather someone who organizes situations that will give rise to curiosity and solution-seeking in the child, and who will support such behavior by means of appropriate arrangements" (Piaget, 1973, p. 85). This is because "the role of *the teacher becomes central* as the animator of discussions *in consequence of having been the instigator*, within each child, of the taking of possession of that remarkable power of intellectual construction which is manifest in all genuine activity" (Piaget, 1949/1998, p. 191; my emphasis). One qualification is that Piaget's own work did not provide relevant evidence. True, but his pedagogy is another matter. Others have used Genevan tasks in exactly this way, including *Thinking Science* (Adey, Shayer, & Yates, 1989–; see the previous section). Further, novel tasks have been used for formative assessment purposes.[13]

Group learning. PP officially and repeatedly included recommendations for collaborative learning; that is, the educator has to – note this obligation – ensure that no learner works solely as a solitary knower. "The active school necessarily presupposes collaboration in work" (Piaget, 1930/1998, pp. 45–46). This is because, for Piaget, there are three benefits: "group work is in principle more 'active' than purely individual work" (1935/1971, p. 158); "the group develops the intellectual independence of its members" (p. 159); and "weak and lazy pupils, far from being abandoned to their lot, are stimulated and obligated by the group" (1945/1998, p. 166). This recommendation is not ad hoc because it follows from the principles that "human knowledge is essentially collective, and social life constitutes an essential factor in the creation and growth of knowledge, both pre-scientific and scientific" (1950/1995, p. 30). Related to this is the thought-experiment devised by Piaget (1932/1932, pp. 348–49) and re-stated like this. "Imagine a society in which almost all individuals were contemporaries, having experienced little of the family and school constraints which affected preceding generations and exercising hardly any on the next generation" (1950/1995, p. 57) – what would human development be like? Piaget's analysis was threefold (Smith, 2002b). One: the "essential instrument of transmission" would be absent, a profound loss to the learner of the knowledge and values of previous generations. Two: this loss would not preclude development because the children would have social interactions with their contemporaries – thus, they would be able to learn collaboratively with their peers. Three: though causally abnormal, this society would be normatively typical. The children – both individually and collectively – would have their own normative capabilities whose use is required for any development, that is, right use – this is taken up in (4).[14]

Self-government. Again, this recommendation was repeatedly made in PP. "The method of self-government consists in attributing to pupils a share in the responsibility for scholarly discipline" (Piaget, 1945/1998, p. 167).[15] Self-government is polymorphic in assuming different forms (1934/1998, p. 122), including

- national and international collaborations (1951/1995, p. 262) in as much as "nothing teaches the humanity of judgment and true modesty so much as daily contact with equals exercising free speech and possessing a spirit of comradeship" (1934/1998, p. 136);
- institutional control such as "the simple organization of work in common by the pupils themselves, responsibility for collective discipline, extra-mural organisations (scholarly societies, clubs, etc)" (1951/1998, p. 273);
- personal development as the "rediscovery by oneself" (1930/1998, p. 46) as well as being "a process of social education aiming, like all of the others, to teach individuals how to escape from their egocentrism so as *to* collaborate between themselves and to submit to shared rules" (1934/1998, p. 128);
- self-discipline as the foundation of personal development: "It is therefore not wasting a child's time to let him acquire by himself the habit of work and of inner discipline" (1932/1932, p. 369).

Notice that self-government is inclusive in covering both social relationships (I will work with every other person in the class – or will I work only with my best friend?) and self-discipline (I will read all the essential texts on this course – or will I rely on Wikipedia?). Notice too that its basis is normative. National governments issue laws where laws are norms in regulation for the public good. Self-government is similarly normative regulation. "Helen – you will lead the *Hamlet* seminar." In that case, there are things that Helen has to do – her actions are intentional, and so norm-directed (Eckensberger, 2006) – for her to act appropriately on her tutor's commands that are themselves norms (Smith, 2006a).

In short, this principle contributes to "fleshing out" respects in which knowing is a spontaneous activity that requires the three forms of instructional assistance.

(4) Knowing Is Successful Only If It Is Due to the Right Reasons

An intrinsic pointer is the formation of reasons as an essential aspect of the inferential process that Piaget (2004/2006, note 1) regarded equilibration to be. Reasons amount to "what subjects regard as proof or 'reason' for what they regard as a truth [that is] the 'why' therefore the 'reason' for something's being so" (Piaget 2004/2006, p. 7). This dense remark is now unpacked in four steps (for a complementary, see Chapter 3, this volume).

From values to norms. Piaget (1932/1932, p. 354) acknowledged the difference between *le bien et le devoir*, between goodness and duty. They differ in that affectivity – feelings, values – marks out what is good, whereas norms are imperatives concerning duties. Piaget generalized this to all acts of knowing – anything can be valued as good, just as anything can become an imperative. This does not mean that the valorization is the right one, nor that the imperative is good – human constructions are fallible.[16] Following von Wright (1963, p. 176), "norms are intrinsically value-directed" in that an operative norm is assigned a value in that person's value-system *hic et nunc*, in these particular circumstances.

Varieties of norms. In psychology, norms are used in norm-referencing as the normal or average performance in the demarcation of what people think or do, typically as opposed to atypically. But this cannot be a complete interpretation of normativity. In his American Psychological Association (APA) address, Martin Luther King commended psychologists for their focus on maladjustment – a descriptive, causal focus – and then made this normative commitment: "I am sure that we all *recognize* that there are some things in our society [to] which we must always be maladjusted, if we are to be people of good will" (King, 1968). This commitment is normative, not causal. As well, there are non-moral norms. Most 21st-century U.S. adults believe that biological life is due to intelligent design, not to evolution (Harris, 2004). These adults have normal beliefs – more than half the adult population holds them. But are their beliefs thereby the right beliefs to hold? An adequate answer to this question invokes a norm because norms lay down what is right/wrong. In this norm-laden sense, there are many varieties of norms whose six main types are rules, commands, directives, customs, moral principles, and ideals (Smith, 2006a). The "has to" of normativity has an intrinsically binding force on action or thought, thereby differentiating normativity from causality.

In PP, norms available biologically or socio-culturally can always be constructed and reconstructed – that is what underlies the previous claim about "being led to think and re-think." Thereby do norms have their origin in human actions and are constituted in their serial use through time. This is a fallible process with examples included in Chapter 3 (this volume).

Norms are manifest in reasons. Norms occur in frameworks with their network of relations to other norms. For Piaget, human development is the construction of richer and better action frameworks. The norms in a framework may be operative without being consciously accessed by their user; they can also become consciously realized and so become manifest in action or thought [see Chapter 13, this volume]. The specific character of a framework is revealed in two ways – the agent's several actions in any context and the reasons for them.

Here is an example. In a study of children's reasoning by mathematical induction, two containers had equal contents to which the children made serial and equal additions. The children were then asked to add "any number at all, any number you like as long as it is the same number." A boy gave a knowing smile, saying:

> You're putting in any number you like and it's actually the same number, because you're adding your favourite number into one and your favourite number into the other. (Smith, 2002a, p. 92)

His response was correct, but his reason was idiosyncratic, marred by the conflation – no doubt primed by the investigator's question – in which "any number at all" became "favourite number." Compare this with

> because you said any number to that and the same to that, so it is going to be the same, isn't it? (p. 92)

There is an elegance and clarity of thought in this sound reasoning of a 7-year-old girl.

Good reasons are necessities. Necessitating reasons are the royal road to true knowledge, and they comprise three types: pre-conditions, implied consequences, and over-arching linkages (Piaget, 2004/2006, pp. 8–9). There is a proviso that even a good reason may turn out to be replaceable by a better reason; that is, it is recast in the sequel, whether by the same person or by someone else. The ability to formulate reasons is not the whole of education, of course. It is, however, a prerequisite of "re-thinking" the collective notions that any learner has been led to "think" in the first place.

The characterization of a framework is a normative matter. The identification of which framework is in-use is an empirical matter about normative facts (Smith, 2006b, 2009). Complementary to this is the empirical identification of pseudo-rational norms, masquerading as the real thing. For Piaget (1975/1985, p. 38*), there are "all the intermediaries between this subjective evidence and logical necessity," that is, between subjective affectivity and norms of necessity.

In sum, this principle has two consequences. One is for Piaget's epistemology: A "critical method" (Smith, 2002a, chapter 5) should be used in psychological studies to ascertain how children understand the questions that have to be addressed for good understanding. The other consequence is that if good understanding is an educational goal, then it can only be attained through improvements in the learner's reasons (Smith, 2002a, chapter 8).

CONCLUSION: FUTURE DIRECTIONS

I have argued for two conclusions about PP. One: its negative critique in education is itself flawed. That critique has ignored PP's applications that have repeatedly been shown to work well in practice. Two: my re-analysis includes four principles that are distinctive in being essential to equilibration, Piaget's central construct. Further, their implications are testable. The third conclusion follows on as to ways ahead.

Take Epistemology Seriously

Piaget's epistemology has been noticed in educational commentary but not strenuously elaborated in view of a pre-occupation with its psychology. One way to label the difference is to contrast the psychological focus on the causality of teaching/learning with an epistemological focus on the normativity of knowing. There is ample research on the former (Moshman, 2008), hardly any on the latter (Smith, 2002a, chapter 8).

Take Values Seriously in the Empirical Study of Knowing

Values are central, both learners' and educators' values. The point is not merely that values are investigable as an independent aspect of personal education or moral development (Nucci, 2005). Rather, all intellectual and instructional interactions require this. Piaget's work provides dual guides, including empirical (1951/1995) and formal (1941/1995) studies.

Take Norms, and So Right Reasons, Seriously Too

Normative commitment can be made without reasons. Yet reasons are always implied and serve to identify exactly what any commitment amounts to. In instructional contexts, educators standardly operate in imperative mode in their directions about what is to be done and by making judgments based on norm-laden criteria. Asking learners to display their reasons is standard practice (Ginsburg, 1997; Mercer, 2008). Diagnostic and formative assessment directed on learners' necessitating reasons in instructional contexts is a rarity. Yet principles in psychological studies are there for educational adaptation (Smith, 2006b; see also Chapters 8, 10, 11, and 12, this volume).

Take Pedagogical Interventions Seriously

This implication complements the previous trio. PP's pedagogical principles are typically long-standing (Parrat-Dayan & Tryphon, 1998). They have been appropriated and shown to work (Adey, 2007; Shayer, 2008). This provides a good grounding to take things further.

Finally, two general conclusions are worth noticing. One is about Piaget's constructivism. Its central tenet is the strict denial that human knowledge amounts to ready-made representations (Bickhard, 2006). Instead, all – note this "all" – human understanding amounts to a continual construction and re-construction of knowledge. That is why education is creative – see Piaget's (1977/1980, p. 132) arresting quotation at the outset of this chapter. Piaget's pedagogy is sensitive to key aspects of this creative process. The other is about scientific theories and their dual functions, namely for understanding the world and for use in the world. Usually, these functions are interpreted as linear and uni-directional – understanding precedes use (Hilgard, 1970). Using Pasteur's work as a paradigm, Stokes (1997) has argued that some scientific theories make novel advances jointly in understanding and in use. Apparently, Piaget's work fits this paradigm.

NOTES

1. Piaget's papers published in English books are identified through the date of their original (usually French) publication, where * indicates my emended translation.
2. Pedagogy has had rare mentions in educational research in England (Simon, 1980/1999) unlike teaching and knowledge in curriculum theory (Stenhouse, 1975).
3. The American Psychological Association (APA, 2008) currently lists 56 divisions.
4. Predominantly, not universally (DeVries, 1987; Duckworth, 1996).
5. See his book title (Piaget, 1948/1976).
6. In arithmetical addition, sum is independent of order. Currently, our knowledge of children's development of commutativity is "fragmentary"

(Cowan, 2003). Because commutativity is a normative principle, Piaget's point was about how norms are in fact acquired and legitimated, notably in mathematics (Smith, 2009).

7. Chapman (1988) had already argued that this interpretation conflates formal and functional aspects of Piaget's account.

8. Flynn effects are the linear rise in norm-referenced IQ scores during the 20th century, thereby requiring these tests to be serially recalibrated (Neisser, 1998).

9. Is "intelligent design" to be included in the school biology curriculum or not?

10. For commentary, see Brown (1996; Brown & Weiss, 1987).

11. I want a high mark on my course and I also want a good social life. Tonight – do I work or play?

12. This leads directly to matching problems as to (a) intended and actual commitments, and (b) task demands and knower's capabilities (Bennett, 1984).

13. Duckworth (1996, chapter 10) asked a sample of teachers what "east" means to probe their grasp of the incompatibilities arising from "east is along the latitude to where the sun rises" and "east lies 90 degrees from north in the direction of rising sun."

14. Vygotsky (1994a, p. 351) re-visited Piaget's thought-experiment but drew the contrary conclusion that number-development would be non-existent. Arguably, Vygotsky missed the main point about the normativity of human development (Smith, 2002b, 2006b).

15. Piaget's French text used the English term "self-government."

16. See pseudo-obligated conjunctions (Piaget, 2004/2006, note 12).

REFERENCES

Adey, P. (2007). The CASE for a general factor in intelligence. In M. J. Roberts (Ed.), *Integrating the mind: Domain general versus domain specific processes in higher cognition* (pp. 369–386). Hove: Psychology Press.

Adey, P., & Shayer, M. (1994). *Really raising standards*. London: Routledge.

Adey, P., Shayer, M., & Yates, C. (1989). *Thinking science*. London: Macmillan.

American Psychological Association (APA). (2008). http://www.apa.org/about/division.html.

Bennett, N. (1984). *The quality of pupil learning experiences*. London: Erlbaum Associates Ltd.

Bickhard, M. H. (2006). Developmental normativity and normative development. In L. Smith & J. Vonèche (Eds.), *Norms in human development* (pp. 57–76). Cambridge: Cambridge University Press.

Black, P., & Wiliam, D. (1998). Assessment and classroom learning. *Assessment in Education, 5*, 7–74.

Brainerd, C. (2003). Jean Piaget, learning research and American education. In B. Zimmerman & D. Schunk (Eds.), *Educational psychology: A century of contributions* (pp. 251–286). Mahwah, NJ: Erlbaum.

Brown, T. (1996). Values, knowledge, and Piaget. In E. Reed, E. Turiel, & T. Brown (Eds.), *Values and knowledge* (pp. 137–170). Mahwah, NJ: Erlbaum.

Brown, T., & Weiss, L. (1987). Structures, procedures, heuristics and affectivity. *Archives de Psychologie, 55*, 59–94.

Bruner, J. (1986). *Actual minds, possible worlds.* Cambridge, MA: Harvard University Press.

Bryant, P. (1984). Piaget, teachers and psychologists. *Oxford Review of Education, 10*, 251–259.

Bryant, P. (2001). Learning in Geneva: The contribution of Bärbel Inhelder and her colleagues. In A. Tryphon & J. Vonèche (Eds.), *Working with Piaget: Essays in honour of Bärbel Inhelder* (pp. 129–140). Hove: Psychology Press.

Case, R. (1985). *Intellectual development: Birth to adulthood.* London: Academic Press.

Case, R. (1992). *The mind's staircase.* Hillsdale, NJ: Erlbaum.

Case, R. (1999). Conceptual development in the child and in the field: A personal view of the Piagetian legacy. In E. Scholnick, K. Nelson, S. Gelman, & P. Miller (Eds.), *Conceptual development: Piaget's legacy* (pp. 23–52). Mahwah, NJ: Erlbaum.

Chapman, M. (1988). *Constructive evolution.* Cambridge: Cambridge University Press.

Cowan, R. (2003). Does it all add up? In A. Broody & A. Bowker (Eds.), *The development of arithmetic concepts and skills* (pp. 35–74). Mahwah, NJ: Erlbaum.

DeVries, R. (1987). *Programs of early education.* London: Longman.

Dewey, J. (1966). *Democracy and education.* New York: The Free Press.

Donaldson, M. (1992). *Human minds.* London: Allen Lane Press.

Eckensberger, L. H. (2006). Contextualizing moral judgment: Challenges of interrelating the normative (ought judgments) and the descriptive (knowledge of facts), the cognitive and the affective. In L. Smith & J. Vonèche (Eds.), *Norms in human development* (pp. 141–168). Cambridge: Cambridge University Press.

Ginsburg, H. (1981). Piaget and education. In I. Sigel, D. Brodzinsky, & R. Golinkoff (Eds.), *New directions in Piagetian theory and practice* (pp. 315–330). Hillsdale, NJ: Erlbaum.

Ginsburg, H. (1997). *Entering the child's mind.* Cambridge: Cambridge University Press.

Harris, S. (2004). *The end of faith: Religion, terror, and the future of reason.* London: Free Press.

Hautamäki, J. (2007). *Same reason, different outcomes: Epidemiological considerations of epistemological (formal operational) reasoning in Finnish schools.* Paper presented at the Annual Meeting, Jean Piaget Society, Amsterdam.

Hilgard, E. (1970). A perspective on the relationship between learning theory and educational practices. In E. Stones (Ed.), *Readings in educational psychology* (pp. 54–78). London: Methuen.

Hughes, M. (1986). *Children and number.* Oxford: Blackwell.

Isaacs, S. (1930). *Intellectual growth in young children.* London: George Routledge & Sons Ltd.

Kant, I. (1933). *Critique of pure reason* (2nd ed.). London: Macmillan. (Original work published in 1787)

King, M. L. (1968). The role of the behavioural scientist in the Civil Rights movement. *American Psychologist, 23*, 180–186.

Mercer, N. (2008). Talk and the development of reasoning and understanding. *Human Development, 51,* 90–100.

Moshman, D. (2008). Epistemic development and the perils of Pluto. In M. F. Shaughnessy, M. Veenman, & C. Kleyn-Kennedy (Eds.), *Meta-Cognition: A recent review of research, theory and perspectives* (pp. 161–174). New York: Nova Science.

Neisser, U. (1998). *The rising curve: Long-term gains in IQ and related measures.* Washington, DC: American Psychological Association.

Nucci, L. (2005). *Conflict, contradiction, and contrarian elements in moral development and education.* Mahwah, NJ: Erlbaum.

Parrat-Dayan, S., & Tryphon, A. (1998). Introduction. In J. Piaget, *De la pédagogie* (pp. 7–24). Paris: Odile Jacob.

Piaget, J. (1931). Le développement intellectuel chez les jeunes enfants: Étude critique. *Mind, 40,* 137–160.

Piaget, J. (1932). *The moral judgment of the child.* London: Routledge & Kegan Paul. (Original work published in 1932)

Piaget, J. (1953). *The origins of intelligence in the child.* London: Routledge & Kegan Paul. (Original work published in 1936)

Piaget, J. (1970). *Genetic epistemology.* New York: Columbia University Press.

Piaget, J. (1971). The new methods: Their psychological foundations. In J. Piaget, *Science of education and the psychology of the child* (pp. 135–180). London: Longman. (Original work published in 1935)

Piaget, J. (1971). The theory of stages in cognitive development. In D. Green, M. Ford, & G. Flamer (Eds.), *Measurement and Piaget* (pp. 1–11). New York: McGraw-Hill.

Piaget, J. (1973). Comments on mathematical education. In A. Howson (Ed.), *Developments in mathematical education* (pp. 79–87). Cambridge: Cambridge University Press.

Piaget, J. (1976). *To understand is to invent: The future of education.* London: Penguin. (Original work published in 1948)

Piaget, J. (1980). Concerning creativity: Three methods. In J.-C. Bringuier (Ed.), *Conversations with Jean Piaget* (pp. 126–132). Chicago: University of Chicago Press. (Original work published in 1977)

Piaget, J. (1981). *Intelligence and affectivity.* Palo Alto, CA: Annual Review Monographs. (Original work published in 1954)

Piaget, J. (1983). Piaget's theory. In P. Mussen (Ed.), *Handbook of child psychology, Vol. 1* (4th ed., pp. 103–128). New York: Wiley. (Original work published in 1970)

Piaget, J. (1985). *The equilibration of cognitive structures.* Chicago: University of Chicago Press. (Original work published in 1975)

Piaget, J. (1995). Essay on the theory of qualitative value in static sociology. In J. Piaget, *Sociological studies* (pp. 97–133). London: Routledge. Original work published in 1941)

Piaget, J. (1995). Explanations in sociology. In J. Piaget, *Sociological studies* (pp. 30–96). London: Routledge. (Original work published in 1950)

Piaget, J. (1995). The development in the child of the idea of homeland and of foreign relationships. In J. Piaget, *Sociological studies* (pp. 248–275). London: Routledge. (Original work published in 1951)

Piaget, J. (1995). Preface. In J. Piaget, *Sociological studies* (pp. 23–29). London: Routledge. (Original work published in 1965)

Piaget, J. (1998). Les procédés de l'éducation morale. In J. Piaget, *De la pédagogie* (pp. 25–62). Paris: Odile Jacob. (Original work published in 1930)

Piaget, J. (1998). Remarques psychologiques sur le *self-government*. In J. Piaget, *De la pédagogie* (pp. 121–138). Paris: Odile Jacob. (Original work published in 1934)

Piaget, J. (1998). L'éducation de la liberté. In J. Piaget, *De la pédagogie* (pp. 161–168). Paris: Odile Jacob. (Original work published in 1945)

Piaget, J. (1998). Remarques psychologiques sur l'enseignement élémentaire des science naturelles. In J. Piaget, *De la pédagogie* (pp. 177–192). Paris: Odile Jacob. (Original work published in 1949)

Piaget, J. (1998). Plan d'action de l'Unesco. In J. Piaget, *De la pédagogie* (pp. 259–279). Paris: Odile Jacob. (Original work published in 1951)

Piaget, J. (1998). L'éducation artistique et la psychologie de l'enfant. In J. Piaget, *De la pédagogie* (pp. 199–202). Paris: Odile Jacob. (Original work published in 1954)

Piaget, J. (1998). L'initiation aux mathématiques, les mathématiques modernes et la psychologie de l'enfant. In J. Piaget, *De la pédagogie* (pp. 231–236). Paris: Odile Jacob. (Original work published in 1966)

Piaget, J. (2000). Commentary on Vygotsky. *New Ideas in Psychology, 18*, 241–259. (Original work published in 1962)

Piaget, J. (2006). Reason. *New Ideas in Psychology, 24*, 1–29. (Original work published in 2004)

Shayer, M. (2008). Intelligence for education: As described by Piaget and measured by psychometrics. *British Journal of Educational Psychology, 78*, 1–29.

Shayer, M., & Adey, P. (1981). *Towards a science of science teaching*. London: Heinemann.

Shayer, M., and Adey, P. (2002). *Learning intelligence*. Buckingham, UK: Open University Press.

Shayer, M., Ginsburg, D., Coe, R. (2007). Thirty years on – a large anti-Flynn effect? The Piagetian test Volume & Heaviness norms 1975–2003. *British Journal of Educational Psychology, 77*, 25–41.

Shepard, L. (2000). The role of assessment in a learning culture. *Educational Researcher, 29*, 4–14.

Simon, B. (1999). Why no pedagogy in England? In J. Leach & B. Moon (Eds.), *Learners and pedagogy* (pp. 15–39). London: Paul Chapman. (Original work published in 1980)

Smith, L. (2002a). *Reasoning by mathematical induction in children's arithmetic*. Oxford: Elsevier Pergamon Press.

Smith, L. (2002b). Piaget's model. In U. Goswami (Ed.), *Blackwell handbook of childhood cognitive development* (pp. 515–537). Oxford: Blackwell.

Smith, L. (2004). Developmental and Education. In J. Carpendale & U. Müller (Eds.), *Social interaction and the development of knowledge* (pp. 175–194). Mahwah, NJ: Erlbaum.

Smith, L. (2005). Education. In B. Hopkins (Ed.), *The Cambridge encyclopedia of child development* (pp. 487–490). Cambridge: Cambridge University Press.

Smith, L. (2006a). Norms in human development: Introduction. In L. Smith & J. Vonèche (Eds.), *Norms in human development* (pp. 1–31). Cambridge: Cambridge University Press.

Smith, L. (2006b). Norms and normative facts in human development. In L. Smith & J. Vonèche (Eds.), *Norms in human development* (pp. 103–137). Cambridge: Cambridge University Press.

Smith, L. (2009). Wittgenstein's rule-following paradox: How to resolve it with lessons for psychology. *New Ideas in Psychology, 27,* 228–242.

Stenhouse, L. (1975). *An introduction to curriculum research and development.* London: Heinemann.

Stokes, D. (1997). *Pasteur's quadrant.* Washington, DC: Brookings Institution.

Sullivan, E. (1967). *Piaget and the school curriculum.* Toronto, Ontario, Canada: Ontario Institute for Studies in Education.

Torrance, H., & Pryor, J. (1998). *Investigating formative assessment.* Milton Keynes, UK: Open University Press.

von Wright, G. H. (1963). *The varieties of goodness.* London: Routledge & Kegan Paul.

Vygotsky, L. (1994a). The problem of the environment. In R. van der Veer & J. Valsiner (Eds.), *The Vygotsky reader* (pp. 338–354). Oxford: Blackwell.

Vygotsky, L. (1994b). The development of academic concepts in school aged children. In R. van der Veer & J. Valsiner (Eds.), *The Vygotsky reader* (pp. 355–370). Oxford: Blackwell.

Wylam, H., & Shayer, M. (1980). *CSMS science reasoning tasks.* Windsor, UK: NFER Publishing.

16 Piaget in the United States, 1925–1971

In the 20th century, U.S. psychologists' reception of Jean Piaget's work interwove with many social and intellectual events that brought Piaget to prominence in social sciences. This chapter examines this reception chronologically from his first introduction in 1925 to the era of "Piaget rediscovered," ending in 1971 when he became a paramount figure in developmental psychology and education. I will divide this historical review into three periods: the early 1920s to 1939, 1940 to 1955, and 1956 to 1971. Following Flavell (1963, p. 1), the phrase, "Piaget's work" stands for Piaget, his collaborators and assistants as a whole. Additionally, because the translations of Piaget's early books in psychology were first made available in England, and British psychologists' evaluation of Piaget's work exerted an influence on U.S. psychologists, some early British psychologists' views will be included. Although the discourse about Piaget's work has been an international phenomenon that transcended ideological barriers and cultural boundaries, the focus of this chapter is on the connection between Piaget's work and social and intellectual events in the United States. This focus leads us to consider the theory of social institution design in developmental psychology (White, 2003a) that will be discussed in the conclusion.

1925–1939

This first period saw the U.S. economy going up and down with unprecedented significance. Laura Spelman Rockefeller Memorial funneled large funds into the child study movement, education, and industrial research. But these deliberately promoted social movements dwindled or halted following the Great Depression. Similarly, translations and reviews of Piaget's work, which had increased in the 1920s, made a fast downturn after 1930. During this period Piaget's first two books on children's language and thinking attracted the most attention. However, unknown to most psychologists was a bold application of his work that occurred in industrial research, resulting in his first honorary degree at Harvard University. Meanwhile, a number of psychologists with a steely empiricist bent found Piaget's work not being par for what they believed was objective science, and their critical evaluation of his work set a tone that could be heard even decades later.

Early Introductions

Piaget received his first U.S. review in *Psychological Bulletin* (Diserens, 1921) in the year when he began working at the Jean-Jacques Rousseau Institute. Four earlier mentions of Piaget's work appeared in *Psychological Bulletin* (Fernberger, 1922a, 1922b) and *American Journal of Psychology*. In the latter, E. G. Boring (1923, 1924), a leading experimental psychologist and historian, made two brief mentions of Piaget's journal articles. Similarly, Bird T. Baldwin (1923, 1924) made a quick mention of Piaget's work in a review of the fields of educational psychology and mental development.

A vivid introductory description of Piaget's work came from Édouard Claparède, the founder of the Rousseau Institute. On G. Stanley Hall's invitation, Claparède (1925a) introduced the Rousseau Institute to the U.S. audience, explaining that Piaget supervised students in observing children in public schools of Geneva "with the method known as that of 'clinical examination'" (p. 94). Citing Piaget's work, he stated, "[Piaget] has supplied us with a totally new conception of the child's mind" (p. 101), offering explanations of a mass of previously unexplained facts. In the same year, Claparède (1925b) wrote to Laura Spelman Rockefeller Memorial (LSRM), asking for financial support, especially to help Piaget continue his innovative research at the institute. Viewing the Rousseau Institute as a flagship of child study movements in Europe, the memorial provided its initial 3-year funding to the institute (Hsueh, 2002b, 2004), a philanthropic act that foreshadowed future events involving Piaget's legacy in the United States. Pierre Bovet, director of the Rousseau Institute, who had already in 1926 talked to U.S. educators and intellectuals about the institute during his study tour supported by LSRM, also wrote to an English-speaking audience about Piaget's work (Bovet, 1928).

Piaget's early five books on children's thinking were first published in French between 1923 and 1932. Kegan Paul Trench Trubner in London brought these five books (Piaget, 1923/1926, 1924/1927, 1926/1929, 1927/1930, 1932) to the attention of English-speaking educators, philosophers, child advocates, and psychologists. But most readers at that time, including Soviet psychologists like Luria and Vygotsky, read mostly the first two (van der Veer & Valsiner, 1991; Vygotsky, 1934/1986). From the published reviews, replications, and critiques of Piaget's work in this period, one can observe this limited exposure in the United States (Hsueh, 2002a, 2004). Rarely did a reviewer or commentator up to 1935 examine the five books as a whole.

The Famous Book

A survey I conducted of 18 psychology journals and monographs, 2 British psychology journals, and 1 journal of the Society for Research in Child Development (SRCD), available in the United States between 1921 and 1941, showed 68 articles that referred to Piaget's work in form of meticulous review, mention in passing, and validations with varied methods. But these 68 pieces were from only 12 of the 21 psychological journals and monographs. The rest did not yield any articles mentioning Piaget's work (e.g., *Journal of Psychology, Journal of General Psychology*, and *Journal of Experimental Psychology*).

Although 37 reviews and remarks from these 12 journals covered Piaget's five early books in descriptive and evaluative terms, most empirical studies and validations inspired by Piaget tended to pay attention only to *The Language and Thought of the Child* (Piaget, 1923/1926). Salient are SRCD's publications in the 1930s: Twelve articles in *Child Development* along with three monographs explicitly referred to Piaget's work. But 11 of these publications devoted their attention mostly or only to *The Language and Thought of the Child*. In fact, *The Language and Thought of the Child* (Piaget, 1923/1926) was widely reviewed shortly after its translation into English (e.g., Baldwin, 1930; Fernberger, 1927; Isaacs, 1929a; McCarthy, 1930; Mitchell, 1927; Thouless, 1927; White, 1927). Later, regardless of the fact that Piaget's five early books were all available in English by 1932, these empirical studies seemed to favor the first two books (Piaget, 1923/1926, 1924/1927) on language issues – a fact that led Piaget (1952) later to regret his early books had focused so heavily on language. This trend in the SRCD publications had a social and intellectual context.

In 1933, the birth of SRCD, formerly known as the Committee on Child Development (CCD) founded in 1924, was an important event at the end of the so-called decade of the child (Smuts, 1986), a child study movement that was greatly facilitated by LSRM and the Social Science Research Council (Cahan, 1991; Cameron & Hagen, 2005; Cross, 1994; Senn, 1975; Siegel & White, 1982). CCD was created in part to join the force of progressive education to raise "the whole child" and in part to provide sound scientific evidence to advance and correct educational practice. In other words, basic research and applied research in child development were two parallel goals that were often conflicting (Cahan, 1991). LSRM played a critical role in establishing child study centers in U.S. universities devoted to both kinds of research to "achieve concrete improvement in the conditions of life and to contribute realistically to the public welfare," and in all the endeavors "scientific research occupied an important place" (LSRM, 1933, p. 10).

In this context, there were numerous empirical studies in *Child Development* on Piaget's notions of egocentrism and verbal forms in relation to children's questions, criticisms, and vocabulary acquisition, not only because of the primacy effect of Piaget's first child psychology book, but also because of the social call for understanding children's language skills and vocabulary growth. U.S. soldiers' poor verbal ability as evidenced by intelligence testing suggested that low intelligence among young recruits in World War I was widespread. CCD's concern with this alarming finding (Cameron & Hagen, 2005) can be seen in the publications during the first decade of *Child Development*, referring mainly to Piaget's (1923/1926) *The Language and Thought of the Child*. In the second half of the 20th century, Piaget was often remembered as the author who made his fame with this book.

Critical Evaluations

Critical evaluations during this period fell approximately into four areas: academic psychology, child psychology, education, and psychoanalysis. U.S. academic psychologists paid attention to Piaget's work much earlier than others did. But their reviews tended to matter-of-factly mention Piaget's work without commentary. As noted earlier, *American Journal of Psychology* and *Psychological Bulletin*, two long-standing APA journals, yielded 18 reviews altogether and kept pace with Piaget's steady research output. Of these 18 reviews (Baldwin, 1923, 1924, 1930 Boring, 1923, 1924; Chrisof, 1938; Diserens, 1921; Fernberger, 1922a, 1922b, 1924, 1927; Gould, 1928; Henmon, 1929, 1930; Murray, 1931; Peterson, 1929, 1932, 1935), 14 were based on Piaget's original French texts! One up-to-date review of child psychology between 1923 and 1928 that B. T. Baldwin (1930) posthumously published comprises three books and three articles of Piaget. Probably nothing is more indicative of the acceptance of Piaget's work in child psychology than the inclusion of his chapter (Piaget, 1931, 1933) on children's philosophies in the first two editions of *A Handbook of Child Psychology*.

With the increasing publications of Piaget's work, the reviews became evaluative and critical. Academic psychologists and some child psychologists, especially those who published in *Child Development*, commended Piaget's innovative approach to studying children's language and his massive observation-based methods. However, they were critical and skeptical of Piaget's method and findings; some staunchly remarked on his notions and findings as nonscientific because Piaget did not measure children's intelligence in the first place (Peterson, 1932, 1935). In his review of Piaget's (1927) *La Causalité Physique Chez L'enfant*, Joseph Peterson (1929) of Peabody College tactfully offered what he saw as a scientific view by emphasizing the importance of "accuracy of the control of experiments and in objectively established results. Accurate researches into the thinking processes of children of different ages and of adults of various degrees of training would constitute valuable contributions to psychology and to the progress of science in general" (p. 482). Obviously, Peterson did not believe that Piaget's work showed this objectivity or accuracy.

Skeptical of Piaget's notion of egocentrism, Victoria Hazlitt (1927, 1932) of University of London cited Cyril Burt as saying there is "no evidence of any specific process of thought that could not be performed by a child of seven," and she went on to criticize Piaget's view of the developmental socialization of children's thought, arguing, "The truth seems to be that the child's egocentrism is largely due to his lack of experience" (1927, p. 360). This view on the primacy of experience was similar to that of Susan Isaacs (1930/1966), a prominent British educationalist and child psychoanalyst who wrote a series of reviews of Piaget's work (Isaacs, 1929a, 1929b, 1931, 1934) and in 1927 welcomed his visit to her Cambridge Malting House School, an experimental nursery school. About Piaget's notion of children's concepts of natural phenomena, Isaacs questioned: "But how *can* the child know the true relation of the movements of the sun and the earth and his own body until he has been taught them" (Isaacs, 1930/1966, p. 93)? Both Hazlitt and Isaacs held the empiricist view that children's knowledge of the world was shaped at a young age by adults. Unmistakenly, empiricist criticisms, not without a behaviorist tone, could be heard from both U.S. and British psychologists who found Piaget's work interesting at best and lacking scientifically objective method at worst, not to speak of the difficulty his writings presented to the reader. In the later part of the 20th century when Piaget was "rediscovered," arguments about objective science and empiricist principles persisted in various forms.

Applications in Changing Society

The year of 1936 was full of exciting events in Geneva. The Rousseau Institute and the International Bureau of Education, both of which Piaget directed, moved into Palais Wilson by Lake Geneva, a converted hotel building named after U.S. President Woodrow Wilson. This move provided much-needed space for Piaget's persistent and ambitious efforts to promote international understanding of public education (Hsueh, 2005b). He was a high-profile participant in the New Education movement in Europe (Abbiss, 1998; Brehony, 2004) and attended the inauguration of the International Montessori Association in Denmark in 1929 (AMI, 1999). Meanwhile, the first of his three infancy books, *The Origins of Intelligence in Children*, was published; he and Bärbel Inhelder advanced the notion of conservation in children's thinking that he presented at the Tercentenary of Harvard University as a keynote speaker, replacing Ivan Pavlov, a Nobel laureate. On that occasion, he also received his first honorary degree. This was his second visit to the United States after having attended the ninth International Congress of Psychology at Yale University in 1929.

The reason why Harvard University looked at Piaget as a leading scientist of the world can be traced to 1927 when a group of Harvard researchers from industrial research, biochemistry, sociology, and anthropology began to read Piaget's work. These researchers called themselves "the human relations group" and wrestled with problems of industrial management and workers' morale. Elton Mayo and Lawrence J. Henderson, two leaders of this group, were funded by LSRM, which also supported the Rousseau Institute in Geneva. They found Piaget's theory and method most suitable to attacking industrial problems. Mayo and his colleagues helped the Hawthorne plant of the Western Electric Company outside Chicago interview 20,000 workers, using Piaget's method. In this interview program, the interviewer investigated workers' thoughts and feelings about the workplace by following the accounts of their work life. Copious notes were taken for analysis to improve management and productivity. This program became a landmark in U.S. organizational psychology with an international significance (Gillespie, 1991; Hsueh, 2001, 2002b; Trahair, 1984).

Harvard gave Piaget his first honorary degree, *not* in psychology but in literature to acknowledge his contributions to social scientists' understanding of social learning in the changing society (Hsueh, 2004). The Harvard Psychology Department never considered nominating Piaget. His name and Lewis Terman's were put forth to the Executive Committee of Tercentennial Celebration only after the word came that Ivan Pavlov, the Nobel laureate, could no longer travel. After a month-long deliberation, the committee concluded, "To restore the balance in the Symposium on 'Factors Determining Human Behavior' occasioned by the very probable absence of Pavlov, the Committee nominated Professor Jean Piaget" (Executive Committee, 1935).

Piaget's first honorary degree at Harvard epitomized the intellectual ideals that LSRM, Henderson, Mayo and their colleagues advocated. Mayo, who was behind the success at the Hawthorne interview program (Hsueh, 2002b; Trahair, 1984), saw the practical value of Piaget's work not only in raising worker morale but also in raising socially responsible children, parental education, guidance for delinquency, and a range of social topics embedded in the progressive movements at the time (Mayo, 1927, 1928, 1930, 1931, 1934a, 1934b, 1936). Consistently positive reviews (Mitchell, 1927; Reed, 1930; Robinson, 1929; Smith, 1933) during this period appeared in *Progressive Education*, the mouth piece of the Progressive Education Association. All these reviews explicitly took Piaget's work beyond a matter-of-fact description to offer some implications for education. One reviewer (Schoen, 1933) marveled at the message *The Moral Judgment of the Child* might bring to people's life: "The book should be pondered long and seriously by our moral guardians, whether parents, teachers or ministers" (p. 157).

As many progressive educators began to favor Freudian ideas that were gaining ground in the United States of the 1930s (Cremin, 1961), many in psychoanalytical circles found Piaget inspiring. William White (1927, 1929a, 1929b, 1931, 1933, 1941), editor of *Psychoanalytical Review*, who reviewed four of Piaget's five books, plus his speech at Harvard Tercentennial Celebration, stated, "[Piaget's] book, in the reviewer's opinion, is of the highest significance not only for those who are interested in the child but for psychiatrists, psychoanalysts and psychopathologists generally" (White, 1929b, p. 411). In a study about reasoning and communications in schizophrenics, Cameron (1938) closely followed Piaget to note, "It has been abundantly shown that the development of adult logical form is the product of necessity and develops with the increase in the child's socialization" (p. 11). In abnormal psychology, Stone (1929, 1930) went so far as to say, "Piaget's writings are not merely splendid examples of ingenuity and cautiousness of method; they are vital revelations of the nature of the child mind" (Stone, 1930, p. 94). In short, in psychoanalysis and related fields, people found Piaget an enlightening addition to psychoanalytic practice in the 1920s and 1930s, although by the 1940s the Freudians who were at the forefront of helping professions started to ignore Piaget's work.

Studies in the Late 1930s

Starting from 1935, reviews of Piaget's work in U.S. psychological journals began to dwindle. Only one rather negative review (Crisof, 1938) stood out, giving *The Origins of Intelligence in Children* some fleeting attention by suggesting it was not good enough to be "a sound descriptive psychology" (p. 201). In the meantime, a few Piaget-inspired attempts at replication via quantitative approaches cast profound doubt on Piaget's findings. The most provocative study was Deutsche's (1937) *The Development of Children's Concept of Causal Relations*, demonstrating that only 4 out of Piaget's 17 types of causal thinking "are found in large enough frequency to warrant further analysis" (p. 97). Other more sympathetic researchers were interested in taking Piaget's work further in their own areas. Wayne Dennis's (1938) historical review claimed that studies of child animism had disappeared for 20 years until Piaget's scientific work brought it back to life. Lane and Kinder (1939) examined relativism, as in "your brother relative to your brother's brother" (see Piaget, 1924/1927) among "subnormal people's" thinking using Piaget's notion and method. One important publication in *Journal of Genetic Psychology* was by Piaget's student, Edith Meyer (1937), who like Inhelder was involved in initial research in Geneva on children's notions of spatial relationships in 1934. However, despite this early introduction to a new line of Geneva research, the U.S. audience entirely failed to recognize its importance until 20-some years later after the translation of Piaget and Inhelder's (1948/1956) book on this topic.

Interestingly, during this period, a few U.S. students completed their studies at the Rousseau Institute and returned to the United States to become faculty members, such as Harold Anderson (Rabin, 1991), Eugene Lerner (1937, also see 1941), and Daniel Prescott (1930). They all carried on the spirit of the Geneva research, but their efforts in this respect were not especially noted in the literature. Even though Edith Meyer (1940) published another experimental study of preschoolers' conception of spatial relations, her later work shifted to child psychiatry as she moved from Yale University to Boston Children's Hospital. However, regardless of the declining reception, James Mark Baldwin (1934) confidently predicted that one of the most promising future psychologies was "the child study movement centered in the J. J. Rousseau Institute and in the work of the group led by Piaget" (p. 28).

During this first period in U.S. psychology, there is a trajectory from brief mentions of Piaget's work to critical reviews and then to validations of Piaget's work. U.S. psychologists focused on his work about children's language, assessing his method and findings with interest and disapproval. These reactions reflected a lively empiricist tradition firmly established in the U.S. research culture in response to societal needs. The large-scale application of Piaget's work to industrial research at Hawthorne was ignored by academic psychologists, but philanthropists and other social scientists, including psychoanalytically inclined people, valued his work for its societal and practical implications. Behind the scene, LSRM played a vital role in promoting Piaget's work via its support to the Rousseau Institute, education, and industrial research. These features would reappear in varied forms over the next three decades.

1940–1955

Interest in Piaget's work came to a halt during World War II. But a few years after the war, translations and reviews of his steady publications began to resume. In the early 1950s, as Piaget emerged as an internationally known psychologist and scientist, philanthropies like Rockefeller Foundation and Ford Foundation found in his work the future leadership for social sciences. Piaget and his colleagues' increased presence on the U.S. scene, along with more translation of his psychological studies, helped revive the U.S. child psychology.

The Paucity of Translations and Reviews

World War II threw the world into chaos. Many U.S. psychologists put their research on hold to participate in the war effort. European psychologists experienced more devastating interruptions, but Piaget was an exception (Piaget, 1952; Terman, 1953). During the war, Piaget himself was willing to "put science aside temporarily to fight against dictatorship" (Rijsman, 2007, p. 119), but his research productivity remained at a steady pace (see Bond & Tryphon, 2007, p. 8). However, the translation of his work for English readers completely stopped. In 1951, Edith Meyer, a well-placed observer of both European and U.S. psychology, wrote a review of the English translation of Piaget's (1947/1950) *Psychology of Intelligence*, a book based on his six lectures at the College of France. She stated that this translation was "the first of Piaget's books to appear in English since 1932" (Meyer, 1951, p. 606). For nearly 20 years, this paucity of translation starkly contrasted the early steadfast efforts to recognize and criticize Piaget.

Nevertheless, there were a few exceptions. Among them were R. W. Russell and Wayne Dennis, whose persistent interest in animism produced most of the publications with reference to Piaget in this period (e.g., Dennis, 1942, 1943, 1947, 1953; Dennis & Mallinger, 1949; Dennis & Russell, 1940; Russell, 1940a, 1940b; Russell & Dennis, 1939, 1941; Russell, Dennis, & Ash, 1940). Their psychoanthropological studies (Dennis, 1943; Dennis & Russell, 1940) to explore animism among Zuni children became well known for, among other things, providing the anthropological verification of Piaget's work that Margaret Mead had attempted in 1927. Dennis (1951a, 1951b) often included Piaget as an important historical and contemporary influence. But as the saying goes, "one waving hand does not make a clap." This rather lone effort did not arouse much lively interest among other researchers, except sporadic studies, including one on human play (Britt & Janus, 1941) and a study on egocentricity and abstraction (Prothro, 1943). As the war raged on, Piaget was dropped from the discourse that had critically assessed his work.

In the United States, the war was not the only reason why the translations and reviews of Piaget's work stopped for two decades. Several events eclipsed the efforts to engage Piaget's ongoing research. In the field of psychology, Hilgard (1987) believed that the revised edition of *Behaviorism* (Watson, 1930) was "reaching the widest public" (p. 90) in the 1930s. Although the impetus of Watsonian behaviorism was set back with his downfall from academia, his behaviorism ushered in a variety of neobehaviorisms represented by Edwin Guthrie, Clark Hull, B. F. Skinner, Edward Tolman (Hothersall, 2004), and learning theory (Miller & Dollard, 1941). With such a zeitgeist, it is not surprising that Piaget's method, observations, and interpretations were often found incompatible with "objective" science. In the meantime, Freudian theories began permeating education (Cremin, 1961). Child therapy and child psychiatry emerged before and after the war (Landreth, 2002; Shaefer & Kaduson, 2007; Smith, 1983), holding the attention of many child psychologists. Even behaviorist leaders like Guthrie, Hull, and Skinner showed keen interest in psychoanalysis, hypnosis, and clinical psychology (Hothersall, 2004).

Disinterest in Piaget since 1932 among U.S. psychologists derived also from some evaluations of his work, one of which was that he had no theory. A doctoral student at Harvard in 1938, apparently unaware of the honorary degree Piaget received 2 years earlier, Jerome Bruner (1983) recalled, "It never occurred to any of us graduate students at Harvard that [Piaget] had any bearing on anything aside from the phenomena to which he addressed himself" (p. 134); "I found him fascinating, but not as a *theorist*" (p. 133). This memory resonates with Chisof's (1938) review of *The Origins of Intelligence in Children*: "[Piaget's] carefully elaborated account does not differ substantially from those of earlier writers who concerned themselves with teleological speculations on the development of intellectual life" (p. 201). These critiques added to the earlier voices faulting Piaget's method as not rigorous or numerical, irreplicable, and ironically, too speculative. Piaget's (1931, 1933) chapter "Children's Philosophies" in *A Handbook of Child Psychology* was dropped in the third edition probably for this reason, because as the editor of this volume remarked, "The speculative period in child psychology is definitely past" (Carmichael, 1946, p. v).

For two decades, the paucity of translations and reviews of Piaget's groundbreaking research can thus be attributed to a variety of factors, but chief among them is the booming of various forms of behaviorisms, which manifested an enthusiasm for scientific psychology to treat human mental activities as part of the objectified world. Behaviorist theories and experiments bore clear stripes of the empiricism seen in both British and U.S. psychologists' critiques of Piaget's theory, method, and interpretation during the previous period. Few understood where Piaget came from and what his research program was about. Even fewer came to his defense as Meyer (1951) did when she commented on U.S. psychologists' evaluation of Piaget's work to date: "Attempts to duplicate these [Piaget's] findings with simplified methods and a quantitative approach are doomed to failure, as would be similar endeavors on material obtained with other interview methods" (p. 608). Although new forms of behaviorism thrived in many fields of psychology, the once-vigorous field of child psychology took a plunge in the late 1940s.

The Plight of Child Psychology

The bleak reaction to Piaget's work may also be attributable to the plight in which child psychology found itself. In the late 1940s, child psychology showed little sign of vitality. In the inaugural volume of *Annual Review of Psychology*, Jones and Bailey (1950) deplored the situation in the field as "growth, development, and decline" (p. 1). In the next volume, Roger Barker (1951) observed that "Child psychology... lacks vigor. By every index available – number of publications, number of papers presented at scientific meetings, membership in scientific societies, and establishments of research institutes – child psychology shows little life" (p. 1). Promising research was concentrated in the few child study centers, led by physicians, clinical psychologists, and psychoanalysts. Harry Beilin, a well-known experimental child psychologist at the Graduate Center of City University of New York, recalled his time at the Institute of Child Welfare of the University of Minnesota as follows: "Between 1953 and 1956, I was among the minority on the [child psychology] faculty who were experimentally inclined" (personal communication, June 12, 1998). The desolation in U.S. child psychology and the lagging effort in experimental approach set a backdrop for Bärbel Inhelder's U.S. study tour.

Mounting Presence in the United States

Sponsored by the Rockefeller Foundation, Inhelder, Piaget's closest collaborator, took a study tour in the United States, which was initiated in 1947 and implemented in 1954. The foundation officers had closely followed the activities in Geneva since the 1920s and provided generous funding. Inhelder's tour took place amid a series of events that were important to Piaget's rise in the United States, to name a few: Piaget's grant application in 1952 for creating a center for interdisciplinary research, his first U.S. honorary degree in *psychology* at the University of Chicago soon after his participation in the Fourth Macy Conference on the problems of consciousness in 1953, his 3-month visit at the Institute for Advanced Study in Princeton in 1954 after being elected president of the 3-year-old International Union of Scientific Psychology (Langfeld, 1954), and eventually the founding of the International Center for Genetic Epistemology in 1955 with the support from the Rockefeller Foundation and the Ford Foundation. These foundations' roles in promoting Piaget's theory and basic research cannot be overestimated for the later booming reception of his work. Together, these events remarkably increased Piaget and his colleagues' presence in the United States and amplified their international influence. In psychological journals, reviews of his newer research also stepped up.

After the English translation of *Psychology of Intelligence, The Child's Conception of Number* (Piaget, 1941/1952) became available in English and attracted much attention (e.g., Churchill, 1958; Dodwell, 1957, 1960; Estes, 1956; Millichamp, 1954; Hunt, 1954). Meanwhile, Piaget's three infancy books were translated (Piaget, 1936/1952, 1937/1954, 1945/1951) with reviews quickly in tow (e.g., Magaret, 1952; Garner, 1953, 1955; Anderson, 1955). Interestingly, the last of these three books, *Play, Dreams and Imitation in Childhood*, was first translated in association with the New Education Fellowship in Europe. This association is significant in view of the reception of Piaget discussed previously (Abbiss, 1998; AMI, 1999; Brehony, 2004; Hsueh, 1997a, 1997b; Lauwerys, 1945). The book received multiple reviews (Magaret, 1952; Sigel, 1953; Spoerl, 1955) and the recognition of his theory became explicit. An associate editor of *The Journal of Consulting Psychology* said of the book, "In dealing with behavior which is often subtle and elusive, Piaget is, as usual, the careful observer, meticulous recorder, and imaginative theorizer" (Magaret, 1952, p. 414). Another reviewer stated, "[T]hose who take the time to gain a thorough mastery of this little book will be richly rewarded by gaining new insight into a theory which took Piaget a lifetime to formulate" (Holtzman, 1951, p. 537).

Awareness of Piaget's recent work began entering the consciousness of U.S. psychology.

To summarize, from 1940 to 1955, the thriving empiricist spirit of neobehaviorisms, the popularity of psychoanalysis, and the impact of World War II contributed to the near absence of Piaget in the U.S. psychological discourse. Many psychologists who read Piaget failed to recognize his contributions as a theorist. The significant decline of child psychology in the late 1940s was a result of the converging effect of these intellectual and social movements. However, the Rockefeller Foundation and other philanthropic institutions continued to promote, through their scholar networks, the intellectual value that Piaget's work represented in psychology and education, although his genetic epistemology was less discussed. The increasing presence of Piaget and Inhelder now in the United States paved the way for the major events in the next period.

1956–1971

The onset of the cognitive revolution in 1956 paralleled the reintroduction of Piaget's work to the U.S. psychological community. Inhelder proclaimed in 1957 to U.S. psychologists that a developmental psychology that integrated general and experimental psychology was on the horizon. Psychologists, educators, and policymakers realized that Piaget's work was worth mining to meet societal needs and bring child psychology out of its plight. Around 1960, Piaget was still an unfamiliar name to the U.S. public, but two key events brought him to the forefront of national discourse in psychology and education, and thus to the public's attention. This reception culminated in the first symposium of the Jean Piaget Society in Philadelphia in 1971.

The Rise of Developmental Psychology

In the early 1950s, Piaget probably found himself in a rather awkward position in the United States, where he was mostly celebrated for his early "famous five books" published a quarter of a century ago, although he had already gone beyond his early writings. "The younger generation [of psychologists] in this country has learned to consider him a venerable, though outmoded, name rather than a living force in psychology" (Meyer, 1951, p. 606). Even one decade later, Flavell (1962) noted, "It is a fair guess that the average psychologist today is still likely to respond 'animism' to the stimulus word 'Piaget'" (p. 14). From the mid-1950s onward, however, a host of U.S. social, political, and intellectual needs brought Piaget's recent work across the Atlantic. The intellectual arena was particularly lively against the backdrop of the postwar international politics. Roger Brown (1970) recalled, "Then computer simulation, psycholinguistics, [post-Sputnik] curriculum reform, and mathematical models altered our notions of the scientific enterprise in such a way as to cause us to see Piaget as a very modern psychologist... the great psychologist of cognitive development" (p. x). The cognitive revolution began to pick up momentum in 1956 (Baars, 1986; Gardner, 1985). In this context rose Piaget, now, as a psychologist, a theorist, and a scientist who was thought to possess urgently needed insights into science education, which was a critical lever for the United States in international politics.

In the eighth volume of *Annual Review of Psychology*, Inhelder (1957) announced that the new field of developmental psychology, rejuvenated by the Genevan theory and experimental approach, would "bring child psychology out of its current isolation in order to reintegrate it into general psychology." Sheldon White (1992) observed that child psychology re-emerged with new vitality in 1959 by the name of developmental psychology. Further, he pointed out that the Civil Rights movement and the Head Start program prepared a social cradle that rocked Piaget's influence into fast growth (personal communication, May 2, 2000). By certain accounts, the 1960 interdisciplinary conference that William Kessen (1962) organized in Dedham, Massachusetts, reintroduced Piaget to American psychology (Mandler, 2000). Inhelder once again made a keynote presentation there. Two years later, she spent a semester at Harvard University and interacted with, among others, science curriculum leaders of the Elementary Science Studies Project, a group of MIT scientists, engineers, and curriculum workers who knew nothing about Piaget (Duckworth, 1996; ESS, 1970). The ramifications of developmental psychology being integrated with mainstream psychology, as Inhelder foresaw, quickly went beyond the psychological field.

"The Most Illuminating Light"

In the 1950s, more and more researchers, enthusiastic or skeptical, took seriously Piaget's theory, method, and interpretations. The growth of research publications was led by a steady stream of translations of Piaget's psychological writings in both the United States and England. Nathan Isaacs (1960/1972), husband of the late Susan Isaacs, explained to preschool teachers about Piaget, "The sequence of books translated between 1927 and 1932, though very stimulating, seemed open to a good many doubts. However, the volumes published in English during the last decade, and others still untranslated, have shown beyond question how much Professor Piaget can help us to understand children's intellectual growth" (p. 15). Isaacs suggested that Piaget's work cast "the most illuminating light" (p. 65) on children's number concept formation and on their mental development as a whole. At the same time, similar effort in the United States to popularize Piaget's work began.

The Woods Hole Conference in 1959 on science education and curriculum brought Inhelder into a discussion and debate with U.S. scientists, researchers, scholars, and curriculum workers about the nature of learning and teaching (Bruner, 1960). Hunt's (1961) textbook gave college students a well-organized introduction to Piaget's research enterprise and theory of intelligence from 1923 to 1957, based on 50 books and articles by Piaget and his colleagues. Piaget's work was hailed as being complementary to the already popular psychoanalysis (Cobliner, 1963). Such excitement about Piaget's work anticipated two noteworthy events: the publication of Flavell's book in 1963 and the publication of conference proceedings entitled *Piaget Rediscovered*. These two events are widely recognized as instrumental to uplifting Piaget to a paramount figure in developmental psychology and education.

Two Major Events

The first major event was the publication of Flavell's (1963) book *The Developmental Psychology of Jean Piaget*. It presented the first comprehensive introduction of Piaget's theory and experiments and dramatically brought U.S. psychologists and educators up to date. It also provided a set of thoughtful critiques of Piaget's theory, method, and interpretations. "The book is a first-class discussion of the work of Piaget" (Peel, 1963, p. 107). It summarized most of the major studies done after 1950 to validate Piaget's experiments and provided comments on earlier criticisms of Piaget's vague writing, replication difficulties, and overinterpretations of data (Flavell, 1963; also see Smith, 1992, 1996, for more critical assessments from this period onward). Based on this comprehensive introduction, Flavell offered new ideas for future research in developmental psychology.

The second major event started with the visit of Piaget as a consultant on science curriculum, in part at the invitation of the U.S. Office of Education in 1964. This event is also known as the Cornell-Berkeley conference on curriculum where Piaget gave two lectures. Recognizing the changing nature of his audience, Piaget (1964) concluded his first presentation at this conference with a constructivist remark: "[My theory] is indeed a stimulus–response theory, if you will, but first you add operations and then you add equilibration" (p. 19). The conference resulted in a book entitled, *Piaget Rediscovered* (Ripple & Rockcastle, 1964). The phrase "Piaget rediscovered" caught on immediately. Interestingly, this phrase was coined first by Eleanor Duckworth, a student of Piaget in the late 1950s. Beginning in 1962, Duckworth joined the aforementioned project of Elementary Science Studies. As a Geneva-trained psychologist, she initially felt at a loss in trying to apply Piaget's work to developing science curriculum. Only after a long period of struggles in the curriculum field did she rediscover the important connections between Piaget's theory and elementary science education (Duckworth, 1964, 1996). And yet, this idiosyncratic phrase quickly became a historical expression rather than a personal reflection. Later, the mention of Flavell's book would probably evoke the phrase, "Piaget rediscovered" in the minds of U.S. psychologists.

The Jean Piaget Society

By the end of the 1960s, an American Psychological Association (APA) survey that asked U.S. psychology department chairpersons to rank the ten *all-time* most influential psychologists did not find Piaget on the list. Rather, as Brown (1970) pointed out, the survey did find Piaget among the top ten most influential *contemporary* psychologists (Sebkriiagen & Moore, 1969; also see Wright, 1970). In 1969, the APA gave an award for distinguished scientific contribution to Piaget, the first European to receive this award (APA, 1970). But a more enduring honor came at the initiative of a group of Philadelphia educators: establishing a Jean Piaget Society in 1970. Piaget and Inhelder came to the society's first-annual symposium held in McGonigle Hall of Temple University on Wednesday, May 26, 1971 (Annesley, 1971; Macomber, 1971). They addressed "some 3000 teachers, students and sundry educational workers and thinkers" (Temple University, 1971, p. 19). Today, nearly 40 years later, the Jean Piaget Society (www.piaget.org) remains a unique international forum for people from diverse knowledge fields to meet and discuss their intellectual pursuits in honor of Jean Piaget.

In short, from the mid-1950s to 1971, Piaget rose steadily in the United States from a psychologist with five "old," "outmoded" books to a contemporary theorist and scientist in developmental psychology and education. His work was seen to have great relevance to many intellectual, social, and political efforts in the United States. Inhelder's proclamation about the advent of developmental psychology as an integrated discipline earmarked a new era of Piaget's influence. In a sense, Flavell's introduction crowned Piaget in developmental psychology, but so much as a psychologist that Piaget (1963) characterized the book as being "too exclusively psychological and insufficiently epistemological" (p. viii). Nevertheless, as Piaget's renown grew, philanthropists, social institutions, educators, and grass roots enthusiasts looked to his work for potential solutions to intellectual, social and political problems of the era.

CONCLUSION

In recent decades, there has been growing scholarly interest in the societal, historical, and intellectual contexts in which Piaget lived (e.g., Bond & Tryphon, 2007; Chapman, 1988; Ducret, 1984; Hsueh, 1997a, 1998, 2002a, 2004, 2005a; Perret-Clermont & Barrelet, 2007; Parrat-Dayan, 1993a, 1993b; Vidal, 1987, 1989, 1994). Some believe that Piaget's research career and international fame were critically linked to the societal, economic, and educational changes in the United States. This chapter has examined the historical context in which Piaget rose to prominence in developmental psychology and beyond.

The changing reception of Piaget's work from 1925–1971 reflected the impact of social, intellectual, and political change in U.S. society. Throughout, philanthropists played a critical role in facilitating the introduction, application, and advance of Piaget's work. But three intellectual receptions remained stable amidst the change over time: (1) the positive recognition of his work in education and psychoanalysis, (2) repeated critiques of Piaget merely as a psychologist of cognitive development rather than as a epistemologist, and (3) the explicit and persistent criticism, grounded in psychology, that Piaget's work was not consistent with an empiricist epistemology.

As this chapter describes, from the early introduction of Piaget's work to the culmination of his influence in the United States, the reception has been a series of coordinated social acts in response to the societal needs. This perspective is consistent with the institutional design theory (Cahan & White, 1992; White, 2002, 2003a, 2003b; White & Phillips, 2000) that explains the history of developmental psychology through its social, economic, and political context. It demonstrates that the child study movements in the 1920s and 1960s that welcomed Piaget were human social initiatives. This institutional design theory postulates that what underlies developmental psychology is an array of conscious and deliberate human thoughts that create a pattern of human activity to serve human purposes with rules of human design. From the early introductions of Piaget in the 1920s to the creation of the Jean Piaget Society in 1970, event after event was preceded and ensued by a series of purposeful activities to design social and scientific institutions inside and outside universities to facilitate human social development as an integral part of a changing society.

The 45-year history suggests that the U.S. reception of Piaget's work over time reflected diverse viewpoints that altered and filtered our understanding of the contributions of a major scientist in the 20th century. Psychologists' attempts to examine the work of Piaget as a psychologist with an inventive bent, not as an epistemologist invested in psychology as a means, have not infrequently failed to confront the interdisciplinary nature of his work and to understand his view on science and humanity as a whole to be studied through an empirical constructive epistemology. It is likely that the increasing call for interdisciplinary research programs in the 21st century may urge developmental scientists to cast an eye back on Piaget for inspiration in the future.

REFERENCES

Abbiss, J. (1998). The "New Education Fellowship" in New Zealand: Its activity and influence in the 1930s and 1940s. *New Zealand Journal of Educational Studies, 33*(1), 81–93.

American Psychological Association (APA) (1970). Distinguished scientific contribution awards (1969). *American Psychologist, 25*, 65–79.

AMI (1999). 70 years of AMI. *Communications* (official journal of Montessori Association International), *4*, 46–47.

Anderson, J. E. (1955). [Review of the book *The construction of reality in the child*]. *Psychological Bulletin, 52*(6), 526–528.

Annesley, F. R. (1971, May). *Letter to Philadelphia teachers*. Jean Piaget Society. Harvard University, Cambridge, MA.

Baars, B. (1986). *The cognitive revolution in psychology*. New York: Guilford.

Baldwin, B. T. (1923). General review: Mental development of children. *The Psychological Bulletin, 20*, 665–683.

Baldwin, B. T. (1924). Educational psychology. *The Psychological Bulletin, 21*, 203–224.

Baldwin, B. T. (1930). Child psychology: A review of the literature, January 1, 1923 to March 31, 1928. *The Psychological Bulletin, 25*, 629–697.

Barker, R. G. (1951). Child psychology. *Annual Review of Psychology, 2*, 1–22.

Bond, T. G., & Tryphon, A. (2007). Piaget's legacy as reflected in the *Handbook of Child Psychology* (1998 ed.). Online manuscript of Jean Piaget Society. Retrieved May 1, 2008, from http://www.piaget.org/news/docs/Bond-Tryphon-2007.pdf.

Boring, E. G. (1923). J. Piaget. "Une forme verbale de la comparaison chez l'enfant: un cas de transition entre le jugement predicatif et le jugement de relation." *Archives de Psychologie. American Journal of Psychology, 34*, 141.

Boring, E. G. (1924). J. Piaget et P. Rossello. Note sur les types de description d'images chez l'enfant. *Archives de Psychologie* (Tomes xviii, No. 3 and No. 4, pp. 209–210). *American Journal of Psychology, 35*, 299.

Bovet, P. (1928). Jean-Jacques Rousseau Institute and its work. In P. Bovet, *The child's religion: A study of the development of the religious sentiment* (pp. 191–200). New York: E. P. Dutton. (Original work published in 1923)

Brehony, K. (2004). A new education for a new era: The contributions of the conferences of the New Education Fellowship to the disciplinary field of education, 1921–1938. *Paedagogica Historica: International Journal of the History of Education, 40*(5–6), 733–755.

Britt, S. H., & Janus, S. Q. (1941). Toward a social psychology of human play. *The Journal of Social Psychology, 13,* 351–384.

Brown, R. (1970). Introduction. In Society for Research in Child Development: *Cognitive development in children: Five monographs of the Society for Research in Child Development* (pp. viii–xii). Chicago: University of Chicago Press.

Bruner, J. (1960). *The process of education.* Cambridge, MA: Harvard University Press.

Bruner, J. (1983). *In search of mind: Essays in autobiography.* New York: Harper & Row.

Cahan, E. D. (1991). Science, practice, and gender roles in early American child psychology. In F. S. Kessel & M. H. Bornstein (Eds.), *Contemporary constructions of the child: Essays in honor of William Kessen* (pp. 225–249). Mahwah, NJ: Erlbaum.

Cahan, E. D., & White, S. H. (1992). Proposals for a second psychology. *American Psychologist, 47,* 224–235.

Cameron, N. (1938). Reasoning, regression and communication in schizophrenics. *Psychological Monographs, 50,* 1–34.

Cameron, C. E., & Hagen, J. W. (2005). Women in child development: Themes from the SRCD Oral History Project. *History of Psychology, 8,* 289–316.

Carmichael, L. (1946). *A manual of child psychology.* Worcester, MA: Clark University Press.

Chapman, M. (1988). *Constructive evolution.* Cambridge: Cambridge University Press.

Chrisof, C. (1938). [Review of the book *La naissance de l'intellignece chez l'enfant*]. *American Journal of Psychology, 51,* 200–201.

Churchill, E. M. (1958). The number concepts of the young child. *Researches and Studies, University of Leeds Institute of Education, 17,* 34–49.

Claparède, E. (1925a). The psychology of the child at Geneva and the J. J. Rousseau Institute. *Pedagogical Seminary, 32,* 92–104.

Claparède, E. (1925b). *Letter to Ruml.* Folder 340, Box 32, Series III, Laura Spelman Rockefeller Memorial Collection. Rockefeller Archive Center. Tarrytown, NY.

Cobliner, W. G. (1963). The Geneva school of genetic psychology and psychoanalysis: Parallels and counterparts. In R. A. Spitz (Ed.), *The first year of life: A psychoanalytic study of normal and deviant development of object relations* (pp. 301–356). New York: International Universities Press.

Cremin, L. A. (1961). *The transformation of the school: Progressivism in American Education 1876–1957.* New York: Knopf.

Cross, S. J. (1994). *Designs for living: Lawrence K. Frank and the progressive legacy in American social science.* Ann Arbor, MI: UMI Dissertation Services.

Dennis, W. (1938). Historical notes on child animism. *The Psychological Review, 45,* 257–266.

Dennis, W. (1942). Piaget's questions applied to a child of known environment. *Journal of Genetic Psychology, 60,* 307–320.

Dennis, W. (1943). Animism and related tendencies in Hopi children. *The Journal of Abnormal and Social Psychology, 38*(1), 21–36.

Dennis, W. (1947). Animistic thinking in the feebleminded. *Mental Health Bulletin, 25,* 16.

Dennis, W. (1951a). Developmental theories. In W. Dennis, R. Leeper, H. F. Harlow, J. J. Gibson, D. Krech, D. M. Rioch, W. S. McCulloch, & H. Feigle (Eds.), *Current trends in psychological theory* (pp. 1–20). Pittsburgh: University of Pittsburgh Press.

Dennis, W. (Ed.). (1951b). *Readings in child psychology.* New York: Prentice-Hall.

Dennis, W. (1953). Animistic thinking among college and university students. *Scientific Monthly, 76,* 247–249.

Dennis, W., & Mallinger, B. (1949). Animism and related tendencies in senescence. *Journal of Gerontology, 4,* 218–221.

Dennis, W., & Russell, R. W. (1940). Piaget's questions applied to Zuni children. *Child Development, 11,* 181–187.

Deutsche, J. M. (1937). *The development of children's concept of causal relations.* Minneapolis: University of Minnesota Press.

Diserens, C. M. (1921). Mental development in man: Piaget, J., *Essai sur quelques aspects du developpment de la notion de partie chez l'enfant. Journal de Psychologie, 18,* 449–480. *The Psychological Bulletin, 18,* 562–563.

Dodwell, P. C. (1957). The evolution of number concepts in the child. *Mathematics Teaching, 5,* 5–11.

Dodwell, P. C. (1960). Children's understanding of number and related concepts. *Canadian Journal of Psychology/Revue Canadienne de Psychologie, 4,* 191–205.

Duckworth, E. (1964). Piaget rediscovered. In R. E. Ripple & V. N. Rockcastle (Eds.), *Piaget rediscovered* (pp. 1–5). Ithaca, NY: Cornell University.

Duckworth, E. (1996). *The having of wonderful ideas* (2nd ed.). New York: Teachers College Press.

Ducret, J. (1984). *Jean Piaget: Savant et philosophe.* Geneva, Switzerland: Droz.

Elementary Science Study (ESS) (1970). *Elementary Science Study: A history.* Watertown, MA: Education Services Incorporated.

Estes, B. W. (1956). Some mathematical and logical concepts in children. *Journal of Genetic Psychology, 88,* 219–222.

Executive Committee (1935, November 26). *Meeting minute.* In Folder: Executive Committee: Business, Box 26, UAV 827.114. Cambridge, MA: Harvard University Archives.

Fernberger, S. W. (1922a). Mental development in man: Piaget, J., *Essai sur la Multiplication Logique et les Debuts de la Pensée Formelle chez l'Enfant.*

Journal de Psychologie, 19, 222–261. *The Psychological Bulletin, 20,* 159–160.

Fernberger, S. W. (1922b). Mental development in man: Piaget, J., and Rossellò, P., *Note sur les Types de Description d'Images chez l'Enfant. Journal de Psychologie, 18,* 208–234. *The Psychological Bulletin, 20,* 268–269.

Fernberger, S. W. (1924). Mental development in man: Piaget, J., *La pensée symbolique et le pensée de l'enfant. Journal de Psychologie, 19,* 222–261. *The Psychological Bulletin, 21,* 139.

Fernberger, S. W. (1927). Special reviews: Jean Piaget, *The Language and Thought of the Child. Psychological Bulletin, 24,* 506.

Flavell, J. (1962). Historical and bibliographical note. In W. Kessen & C. Kuhlmann (Eds.), *Society for research in child development monograph, 27*(2). *Thought in the young child: Report of a conference on intellective development with particular to the work of Jean Piaget (1962),* pp. 8–15.

Flavell, J. (1963). *The developmental psychology of Jean Piaget.* Princeton, NJ: Van Nostrand.

Gardner, H. (1985). *The mind's new science: A history of the cognitive revolution.* New York: Basic Books.

Garner, A. M. (1953). [Review of the book *The origins of intelligence in children*]. *Journal of Consulting Psychology, 17,* 467.

Garner, A. M. (1955). [Review of the book *The construction of reality in the child*]. *Journal of Consulting Psychology, 19,* 77.

Gillespie, R. (1991). *Manufacturing knowledge: A history of Hawthorne experiments.* New York: Cambridge University Press.

Gould, M. C. (1928). Book review: *La representation du monde chez l'enfant. American Journal of Psychology, 40,* 658–659.

Hazlitt, V. (1927). Children's thinking. *British Journal of Psychology, 20,* 354–361.

Hazlitt, V. (1932). [Review of the book *The child's conception of physical causality*]. *Pedagogical Seminary and the Journal of Genetic Psychology, 40,* 243–249.

Henmon, V. A. (1929). Educational psychology. *The Psychological Bulletin, 26,* 445–456.

Henmon, V. A. (1930). Educational psychology. *The Psychological Bulletin, 27,* 417–430.

Hilgard, E. R. (1987). *Psychology in America: A historical survey.* San Diego, CA: Harcourt Brace Jovanovich.

Holtzman, W. H. (1951). [Review of the book *The psychology of intelligence*]. *Psychological Bulletin, 48,* 535–537.

Hunt, J. M. (1961). *Intelligence and experience.* New York: Ronald Press.

Hsueh, Y. (1997a). *Jean Piaget, spontaneous development and constructivist teaching.* Unpublished doctoral dissertation, Harvard University, Cambridge, MA.

Hsueh, Y. (1997b, June). *Jean Piaget and the Jean Jacques Rousseau Institute.* Presentation at the Annual Meeting of Jean Piaget Society, Santa Monica, CA.

Hsueh, Y. (1998). Some notes on Bärbel Inhelder's 1954 study tour in the US. *Archives de Psychology, 66,* 239–254.

Hsueh, Y. (2001). Basing much of the reasoning upon the work of Jean Piaget: 1927–1936. *Archives de Psychologie, 69*, 39–62.

Hsueh, Y. (2002a). The usefulness of misunderstanding. *The Constructivist, 14*(1), 12–18.

Hsueh, Y. (2002b). The Hawthorne experiments and the introduction of Jean Piaget in American industrial psychology, 1929–1932. *History of Psychology, 5*, 163–189.

Hsueh, Y. (2004). "He sees the development of children's concepts upon a background of sociology" – Jean Piaget's honorary degree at Harvard University in 1936. *History of Psychology, 7*, 45–64.

Hsueh, Y. (2005a). The lost and found experience: Piaget rediscovered. *The Constructivist, 16*(1), ISSN 1091–4072. Retrieved April 1, 2009, from http://www.odu.edu/educ/act/journal/vol16no1/hsueh.pdf

Hsueh, Y. (2005b, June). *Jean Piaget: An unclaimed and forgotten educator.* Presentation at Annual Meeting of Jean Piaget Society, Vancouver, Canada.

Hunt, W. A. (1954). [Review of the book *The child's conception of number*]. *Journal of Consulting Psychology, 18*, 76.

Inhelder, B. (1957). Developmental psychology. *Annual Review of Psychology, 8*, 139–162.

Isaacs, N. (1972). *A brief introduction to Piaget.* New York: Agathon Press. (Original work published in 1960)

Isaacs, S. (1929a). [Review of the books *The language and thought of the child, Judgment and reasoning in the child, The child's conception of the world*]. *Pedagogical Seminary and the Journal of Genetic Psychology, 37*, 597–607.

Isaacs, S. (1929b). [Review of the book *The child's conception of the world*]. *Mind: A Quarterly Review of Psychology and Philosophy, 38*, 506–513.

Isaacs, S. (1931). [Review of the book *The child's conception of causality*]. *Mind: A Quarterly Review of Psychology and Philosophy, 40*, 89–93.

Isaacs, S. (1934). [Review of the book *The moral judgment of the child*]. *Mind: A Quarterly Review of Psychology and Philosophy, 43*, 85–99.

Isaacs, S. (1966). *Intellectual growth in young children.* New York: Schocken. (Original published in 1930)

Jones, H., & Bayley, N. (1950). Child psychology. *Annual Review of Psychology, 1*, 1–8.

Kessen, W. (1962). "Stage" and "structure" in the study of children. Thought in the young child: Report of a conference on intellective development with particular attention to the work of Jean Piaget. *Monographs of the Society for Research in Child Development, 27*(2), 65–86.

Landreth, G. L. (2002). *Play therapy: The art of relationship.* New York: Psychology Press.

Lane, E. B., & Kinder, E. (1939). Relativism in the thinking of subnormal subjects as measured by certain of Piaget's tests. *Pedagogical Seminary and the Journal of Genetic Psychology, 54*, 107–118.

Langfeld, H. S. (1954). International union of scientific psychology. *American Psychologist, 19*, 765.

Lauwerys, J. A. (1945). *Letter to Piaget.* September 18, 1945. A1.79.973. Box 35, BIE Library, Office of International Education, UNESCO.

Lerner, E. (1937). New techniques for tracing cultural factors in children's personality organization. *Journal of Educational Sociology, 10*(8), 479–486.

Lerner, E. (1941). Edouard Claparède: 1873–1940. *The American Journal of Psychology, 54*(2), 296–299.

LSRM (1933). *The Laura Spelman Rockefeller Memorial: Final report.* New York: Rockefeller Foundation.

Macomber, L. (1971, June 22). *Letter to director of the physical plant of Temple University.* Jean Piaget Society Archives, Harvard University, Cambridge, MA.

Magaret, A. (1952). [Review of the book *Play, dreams and imitation in childhood*]. *Journal of Consulting Psychology, 16*, 413–414.

Mandler, G. (2000). Obituary: William Kessen (1925–1999). *American Psychologist, 55*, 758–759.

Mayo, E. (1927). *The dynamics of family relations.* Carton 5, Folder 28, G54, Elton Mayo Papers, 1909–1960, Harvard Business School Archives.

Mayo, E. (1928). Notes on *Maladjustment of the industrial worker 1928/1929.* Carton 5, Folder 33, G54, Elton Mayo Papers, 1909–1960, Harvard Business School Archives.

Mayo, E. (1930). The work of Jean Piaget. *Ohio State University Bulletin, 35*(3), 140–146.

Mayo, E. (1934a). *To Seabury, F., November 25, 1934.* Carton 5, Folder 130, G54, Elton Mayo Papers, 1909–1960, Harvard Business School Archives.

Mayo, E. (1934b). *Training the child for responsibility to his world.* Carton 5, Folder 130, G54, Elton Mayo Papers, 1909–1960, Harvard Business School Archives.

Mayo, E. (1936). *The effect of social change upon the developing child.* Lecture notes at Woods School of Langhorne, April 1936. Carton 5, Folder 33, G54, Elton Mayo Papers, 1909–1960, Harvard Business School Archives.

McCarthy, D. A. (1930). *The language development of the preschool child.* Minneapolis: University of Minnesota Press.

Meyer, E. (1937). The child's conception of spatial relationships. *Progressive Education, 14*, 199–207.

Meyer, E. (1940). Comprehension of spatial relations in preschool children. *Pedagogical Seminary and the Journal of Genetic Psychology, 57*, 119–151.

Meyer, E. (1951). [Review of the book *Psychology of intelligence*]. *The Journal of Abnormal and Social Psychology, 46*(4), 606–608.

Miller, N. E., & Dollard, J. (1941). *Social learning and imitation.* New Haven, CT: Yale University Press.

Millichamp, D. A. (1954). [Review of the book *The child's conception of number*]. *Canadian Journal of Psychology/Revue Canadienne de Psychologie, 8*, 42–43.

Mitchell, L. S. (1927). [Review of the book *Language and thought of the child*]. *Progressive Education, 4*, 136–139.

Murray, E. (1931). [Review of the book *The child's conception of the world*]. *American Journal of Psychology, 43*, 154–156.

Parrat-Dayan, S. (1993a). La réception de l'œuvre de Piaget dans le milieu pédagogique des années 1920–1930. [The reception of Piaget's work in the psychological context between 1920 and 1930]. *Revue Française de Pédagogie, 104*, 73–83.

Parrat-Dayan, S. (1993b). Le texte et ses voix: Piaget lu par ses pairs dans le milieu psychologique des années 1920–1930. [The text and tone: Interpretations of Piaget's work in the psychological context between 1920 and 1930]. *Archives de Psychologie, 61,* 127–152.

Peel, E. A. (1963). The developmental psychology of Jean Piaget by John H. Flavell. *British Journal of Educational Studies, 12,* 107.

Perret-Clermont, A. N., & Barrelet, J. (Eds.) (2007). *Jean Piaget and Neuchâtel: The learner and the scholar.* New York: Psychology Press.

Peterson, J. (1929). [Review of the book *La causalité physicque chez l'enfant*]. *American Journal of Psychology, 41,* 481–483.

Peterson, J. (1932). [Review of the book *The child's conception of physical causality*]. *American Journal of Psychology, 44,* 612.

Peterson, J. (1935). [Review of the book *Moral judgment of the child*]. *American Journal of Psychology, 47,* 523–525.

Piaget, J. (1926). *The language and thought of the child.* London: Kegan Paul Trench Trubner. (Original work published in 1923)

Piaget, J. (1927). *Judgment and reasoning in the child.* London: Kegan Paul Trench Trubner. (Original work published in 1924)

Piaget, J. (1929). *The child's conception of the world.* London: Kegan Paul Trench Trubner. (Original work published in 1926)

Piaget, J. (1930). *The child's conception of physical causality.* Translated by Marjorie Gabain. Totowa; London: Kegan Paul Trench Trubner. (Original work published in 1927)

Piaget, J. (1931). Children's philosophies. In C. Murchinson (Ed.), *A handbook of child psychology* (pp. 377–391). Worcester, MA: Clark University Press.

Piaget, J. (1932). *The moral judgment of the child.* London: Kegan Paul Trench Trubner.

Piaget, J. (1933). Children's philosophies. In C. Murchinson (Ed.), *A handbook of child psychology: 2nd ed.* (Revised) (pp. 534–547). Worcester, MA: Clark University Press.

Piaget, J. (1950). *Psychology of intelligence.* London: Routledge and Kegan Paul. (Original work published in 1947)

Piaget, J. (1951). *Play, dreams and imitation in childhood.* New York: W.W. Norton. (Original work published in 1945)

Piaget, J. (1952). Jean Piaget. In E. G. Boring, H. Werner, H. S. Langfeld, & R. M. Yerkes (Eds.), *A history of psychology in autobiography, 4.* Worcester, MA: Clark University Press.

Piaget, J. (1952). *The child's conception of number.* London: Routledge and Kegan Paul. (Original work published with A. Szeminska in 1941)

Piaget, J. (1952). *The origins of intelligence in children.* New York: W.W. Norton. (Original work published in 1936)

Piaget, J. (1954). *The construction of reality in the child.* New York: Basic Books. (Original work published in 1937)

Piaget, J. (1963). Foreword. In J. Flavell, *The developmental psychology of Jean Piaget* (pp. vii–ix). Princeton, NJ: Van Nostrand.

Piaget, J. (1964). Development and learning. In R. E. Ripple & V. N. Rockcastle (Eds.), *Piaget rediscovered* (pp. 7–19). Ithaca, NY: Cornell University.

Piaget, J., & Inhelder, B. (1956). *The child's conception of space*. London: Rout-ledge and Kegan Paul. (Original work published in 1948)

Prescott, D. A. (1930). *Education and international relations: A study of the social forces that determine the influence of education. Harvard Studies in Education, 14*. Cambridge, MA: Harvard University Press.

Prothro, E. T. (1943). Egocentricity and abstraction in children and in adult aments. *The American Journal of Psychology, 56*, 66–77.

Rabin, A. I. (1991). Harold Homer Anderson (1897–1990). *American Psychologist, 46*, 982.

Reed, F. (1930). [Review of the book *The child's conception of physical causality*]. *Progressive Education, 7*, 424–426.

Rijsman, J. (2007). An intellectual and technological panorama of Piaget's world. In A. N. Perret-Clermont & J. Barrelet (Eds.), *Jean Piaget and Neuchâtel: The learner and the scholar* (pp. 119–136). New York: Psychology Press.

Ripple, R. E., & Rockcastle, V. N. (Eds.). *Piaget rediscovered*. Ithaca, NY: Cornell University.

Robinson, V. P. (1929). [Review of the book *Judgment and reasoning in the child* and *The child's conception of the world*]. *Progressive Education, 6*, 374–376.

Russell, R. W. (1940a). Studies in animism: II. The development of animism. *Journal of Genetic Psychology, 56*, 353–366.

Russell, R. W. (1940b). Studies in animism: IV. An investigation of concepts allied to animism. *Journal of Genetic Psychology, 57*, 83–91.

Russell, R. W., & Dennis, W. (1939). Studies in animism: I. A standardized pro-cedure for the investigation of animism. *Journal of Genetic Psychology, 55*, 389–400.

Russell, R. W., & Dennis, W. (1941). Note concerning the procedure employed in investigating child animism. *Journal of Genetic Psychology, 58*, 423–424.

Russell, R. W., Dennis, W., & Ash, F. E. (1940). Studies in animism. III. Animism in feebleminded subjects. *Journal of Genetic Psychology, 57*, 57–63.

Schoen, M. (1933). [Review of the book *The moral judgment of the child*]. *The Journal of Educational Psychology, 24*, 157–158.

Sebkriiagen, L. W., & Moore, M. H. (1969). A note on ranking the important psychologists. *Proceedings of the 77th Annual Convention of the American Psychological Association, 4*(Pt. 2), 849–850.

Senn, M. J. E. (1975). Insights on the child development movement in the United States. *Monographs of the Society for Research in Child Development, 40*(3–4), 1–107.

Shaefer, C. E., & Kaduson, H. (2007). *Contemporary play therapy: Theory, research and practice*. New York: Guilford.

Siegel, A. W., & White, S. H. (1982). The child study movement: Early growth and development of the symbolized child. *Advances in Child Behavior and Development, 17*, 233–285.

Sigel, I. (1953). [Review of the book *Play, dreams and imitation in childhood*]. *Psychological Bulletin, 50*, 226–227.

Smith, C. A. (1983). *The children's hospital of Boston: Built better than they knew*. Boston: Little, Brown.

Smith, L. (1992). *Jean Piaget: Critical assessments* (4 Vols.). London: Routledge.

Smith, L. (1996). *Critical readings on Piaget*. London: Routledge.

Smith, R. B. (1933). [Review of the book *The moral judgment of the child*]. *Progressive Education, 10*, 237–238.

Smuts, A. B. (1986). The National Research Council Committee on Child Development and the founding of the Society for Research in Child Development, 1925–1933. *Monographs of the Society for Research in Child Development, 50*(4), 108–125.

Spoerl, D. T. (1955). [Review of the book *Play, dreams and imitation in childhood*]. *The Journal of Abnormal and Social Psychology, 50*, 151–153.

Stone, C. L. (1929). [Review of the book *Judgment and reasoning in the child*]. *Journal of Abnormal Psychology and Social Psychology, 24*, 239–240.

Stone, C. L. (1930). [Review of the book *The child's conception of the world*]. *Journal of Abnormal Psychology and Social Psychology, 25*, 93–94.

Temple University (1971, Summer). *Temple University alumni review*. Philadelphia: Temple University.

Terman, L. M. (1953). [Review of the book *A history of psychology in autobiography, 4*]. *Psychological Bulletin, 50*(6), 477–481.

Thouless, R. H. (1927). [Review of the book *The language and thought of the child*]. *British Journal of Psychology, 17*, 258–259.

Trahair, R. (1984). *The humanist temper: The life and work of Elton Mayo*. New Brunswick, NJ: Transaction Books.

van der Veer, R., & Valsiner, J. (1991). *Understanding Vygotsky: A quest for synthesis*. Oxford: Blackwell.

Vidal, F. (1987). Jean Piaget and psychoanalysis: A historical and biographical note (up to the 1930s). In S. Bem & H. Rappard (Eds.), *Studies in the history of psychology and the social sciences, 4* (pp. 315–329). Leiden: Psychologisch Instituut van de Rijksuniversiteit Leiden.

Vidal, F. (1989). *Jean Piaget and the liberal Protestant tradition. Psychology in Twentieth-Century Thought and Society*. Cambridge: Cambridge University Press.

Vidal, F. (1994). *Piaget before Piaget*. Cambridge, MA: Harvard University Press.

Vygotsky, L. S. (1986). *Thought and language*. Cambridge, MA: MIT Press. (Original work published in 1934)

Watson, J. B. (1930). *Behaviorism* (rev. ed.). New York: W. W. Norton.

White, S. H. (1992). The rise of developmental psychology. *Contemporary Psychology, 36*, 469–473.

White, S. H. (2002). Notes towards a philosophy of science for developmental psychology. In W. Hartup & R. Weinberg (Eds.), *Child psychology in retrospect and prospect: 32nd Minnesota Symposium on Child Psychology* (pp. 207–226). Mahwah, NJ: Erlbaum.

White, S. H. (2003a). Developmental psychology in a world of designed institutions. In W. Koops & M. Zuckerman (Eds.), *Beyond the century of the child* (pp. 204–224). Philadelphia: University of Pennsylvania Press.

White, S. H. (2003b). The contemporary reconstruction of developmental psychology. In T. C. Dalton & R. B. Evans (Eds.), *The life cycle of psychological ideas: Understanding prominence and the dynamics of intellectual change* (pp. 281–297). New York: Kluwer.

White, S. H., & Phillips, D. A. (2000). Designing Head Start: Roles played by developmental psychologists. In D. L. Featherman & M. Vinovskies (Eds.), *Social science and policy making* (pp. 83–118). Ann Arbor: University of Michigan Press.

White, S. H., & Pillemer, D. B. (Eds.). (2005). *Developmental psychology and social change*. New York: Cambridge University Press.

White, W. A. (1927). [Review of the book *The language and thought of the child*]. *Psychoanalytic Review, 14*, 359–360.

White, W. A. (1929a). [Review of the book *The language and thought of the child, judgment and reasoning of the child*]. *Psychoanalytic Review, 16*, 312–321.

White, W. A. (1929b). [Review of the book *The child's conception of the world*]. *Psychoanalytic Review, 16*, 411–421.

White, W. A. (1931). [Review of the book *The child's conception of physical causality*]. *Psychoanalytic Review, 18*, 85–89.

White, W. A. (1933). [Review of the book *The moral judgment of the child*]. *Psychoanalytic Review, 20*, 215–220.

White, W. A. (1941). [Review of the book *Factors determining human behavior*]. Cambridge, MA: Harvard University Press.

Wright, G. D. (1970). A further note on ranking the important psychologists. *American Psychologist, 25*, 650–651.

17   The Mind's Staircase Revised

This chapter focuses on two related questions, both of which were central to Piaget's thinking. The first question concerns the extent to which there are nontrivial regularities in cognitive development and what these regularities consist in. The second question pertains to the development of necessary knowledge. I briefly show that in addressing these questions Piaget picks up a thread that can be traced back to the philosophers Hegel and Kant, respectively. Both questions are intricately intertwined with one of the most important but also most heavily criticized aspects of Piaget's work – his stage theory. Stages are important not just for the classification of abilities and problem-solving strategies: Stage theory is an instrument that clarifies the development of different aspects of human intelligence itself – logical thinking, imagination, symbolic functioning, bodily movements, etc. It is impossible to make reference to Piaget's stage theory without discussing the manifold criticisms leveled against it. These criticisms led many psychologists to abandon Piaget's theory and work with modular theories. Yet, as will be shown, modular theories fail to explain regularities in cognitive development as well as the genesis of necessary knowledge. The most important objections against Piagetian stage theory are evaluated before the main features of his theory are reconstructed and the concepts of level, substage, and level transition explained. It will turn out that Piaget's stage theory must be modified in some minor but important details. These alterations cast new light on developmental regularities and the genesis of necessary knowledge.

THE HEGELIAN VIEW

In many of his writings, Piaget claimed that in cognitive development some of the main processes occur repeatedly (e.g., Inhelder & Piaget, 1955/1958, pp. 342–343; Piaget, 1947/1976, p. 122). The German philosopher Habermas (1976, pp. 12, 74, 82, 164, 232) suspected that Piaget defended nothing less than a *developmental logic*, and Habermas pointed out several analogies between Piaget's genetic epistemology and Hegel's theory of conceptual development (Habermas, 1983/1990, p. 8).

Indeed, Piaget and Hegel made similar claims concerning cognitive development and its regularities. Both distinguished different developmental levels and described their succession in a similar way, explaining the origin of the cognitive content in level $n + 1$ by a process of reflection on the cognitive form(s) from level n (e.g., Hegel, 1816/1951, p. 481; Piaget, 1961/1966, pp. 246–247, 1970/1972, pp. 63–64, 1975/1985, p. 51, 1977/2001, pp. 305–306). Therefore, both described intellectual development as a process, which, at the same time, is proactive (i.e., leading to progress) and retroactive (i.e., driven by reflection on the structures previously constructed). Moreover, both metaphorically described the transition from one level to the next as a reversal of the direction of consciousness or perspectives (e.g., Hegel, 1807/1977, p. 55; Piaget, 1936/1952, p. 155, 1950b, p. 78, 1967, p. 1257, 1975/1985, p. 72; see Kesselring, 1981, pp. 69–73, 164). Finally, both referred to cognitive development as a cyclical process: Piaget (e.g., 1954/1973, p. 172, 1968/1971, p. 34, 1977/2001, p. 306) used the image of a *spiral* to illustrate this process; Hegel used the image of a *circle of circles* (1816/1951, p. 484). There are also some profound differences between both authors: According to Hegel, intellectual development passes through a serious contradiction at the end of each level, whereas Piaget speaks only of disequilibria, which he attributes to the initial phases of a level and not to the final ones. Nonetheless, these analogies are far from being trivial and they merit an explication, especially in light of Piaget's following comment: "I think . . . there is a clear parallel between Hegelian dialectic and psychogenesis and this is a pure convergence without influence because, unfortunately, I have not yet read Hegel" (J. Piaget, personal communication, December 13, 1976, translated by editors). In this article I reconstruct, without further reference to Hegelian dialectics (see Kesselring, 1981, 1984), Piaget's developmental theory in such a way that these regularities, or at least some of them, become intelligible.

THE KANTIAN VIEW

In his *Critique of Pure Reason*, Kant tried to answer the question of how geometry and sciences based on mathematics and natural sciences, mainly physics, are possible (Kant 1787/1933, B X). Kant held that both the necessity of mathematical knowledge and the necessity of natural sciences are not analytical but rather *synthetic* and *a priori* (i.e., not given by experience). Instead, he argued that human knowledge is based on necessarily true judgments. Kant did not explain the origin of these judgments but assumed that they were attained by abstraction from the activity of the soul, which structures, according to eternal laws, its experiences (Kant, 1770/1968, § 8, § 15, corollary).

Two hundred years later, Piaget reformulated this question from a more psychological perspective. It is no coincidence that he referred to Kant as "the father of us all" (Piaget, 1965/1971, p. 220). Several researchers (e.g., Lourenço & Machado, 1996; Smith, 1993) consider the question about the origin of necessary truth one of the central issues of Piagetian epistemology. Indeed, Piaget's investigations into object permanence, conservation of quantities, and operational knowledge – concepts that form the bedrock of mathematics and natural sciences – are directly related to the Kantian question. Piaget dedicated a great deal of his scientific effort to the analysis of the emergence of operational thinking and necessary knowledge. Is their genesis itself necessary (Smith, 1993, p. 183)? How far is their genesis independent of empirical facts "of factors in nature and nurture" (Smith, 1993, p. 174)? Is it possible that a contingent genesis can lead to necessary knowledge?

This essay will not try to resolve these complex problems, but the question about the regularities in cognitive development is intertwined with them. How far do these regularities go, and how can they be explained? There is evidence that the search for developmental regularities was one of the main reasons Piaget elaborated a stage theory (e.g., Piaget, 1970/1972, p. 102). Given that this theory was the target of serious objections, these need to be reviewed first.

MAIN OBJECTIONS TO PIAGET'S STAGE CONCEPT

> "One tries to construct stages, because this is an *indispensable instrument* for the analysis of processes." (Piaget, 1956/1977, p. 817)

Genetic psychology resembles a landscape with a rich diversity of reliefs, and genetic epistemology is the map of this landscape. If this map is exact, it allows us to recapitulate all possible routes a child can travel in cognitive development, those which are recommended by educators and those which are not. Like on a map a contour indicates a height, in genetic epistemology a level or stage indicates a type of structural complexity related to a cognitive ability. Evidently, a stage concept is not a bidimensional but a multidimensional map, and one of its dimensions is time. Piaget distinguished several epistemic levels or stages (I use these terms interchangeably), the sequence of which is irreversible. The activity specific to each stage does not emerge before the organization of the preceding stage has reached a certain equilibrium. Writing, for example, presupposes oral language use, the acquisition of which, in turn, presupposes the child's ability to recognize both objects (significations) and sounds (signs). Piaget used to subdivide each level into several substages, the sequence of which he held to be irreversible, too. Morover, he described cognitive development in terms of structures. Every scheme, every operation has its structural aspects. The developmental timing depends on how intensely the child is stimulated by his social environment (Piaget, 1962/1973). The specific age at which he reaches a certain level therefore differs according to the social conditions.

There are at least nine different objections to Piaget's stage theory. I briefly mention them here and discuss them in more detail in a later section.

(1)   The stage theory is "too monolithic [and] universal" (Case, 1992a, p. 10): Its claims are too far-reaching and too general. It does not explain domain-specific development and it does not consider individual differences in and cultural influences on cognitive development (Case, 1992a, pp. 10, 17; 1992b, p. 166).

(2)   Lack of intertask correlations: Between different tasks that assess abilities that are characteristic of the same stage, like conservation, classification, and seriation, significant correlations have not been found (Pinard & Laurendeau, 1969). Furthermore, different children master these tasks in a different order, and it was shown that special training could have "an impact on one class of task without affecting any other task that was supposed to be 'structurally related'" (Case, 1992b, p. 165).

(3)   Horizontal and vertical *décalages*: In many cases, when a synchronic acquisition of apparently structurally similar abilities, like understanding conservation of number, mass, weight, and volume, would be expected, asynchrony was found (Lourenço & Machado, 1996, p. 151). Piaget (1956/1977, p. 816) referred to this phenomenon as *horizontal* décalage and distinguished it from *vertical* décalage, which refers to the reconstruction of a structure at different developmental levels. Asynchrony in tasks based on a similar logical structure has puzzled many developmental psychologists (e.g., Case, 1985, p. 27; Case, 1992a, p. 38). Both types of observation – those mentioned in (2) and in (3) – undermine the idea of a logical structure that sustains different types of cognitive abilities.

(4) Lack of discontinuity: The term *stage* suggests that stage transitions are discontinuous (Habermas, 1976, p. 67), as the sequence *caterpillar – cocoon – butterfly* illustrates. Therefore, a stage sequence can only be verified if the cognitive abilities between individuals belonging to the same stage are more similar to each other than those of individuals belonging to different stages (Brainerd, 1978; Goswami, 2001, p. 267).

(5) Age dependency: Piaget often used age as an indicator of stage. Cognitive development is age-related, but this does not imply that a specific ability appears "at a specific point of time" (Smith 1993, p. 39; see also Smith, 1991).

(6) To what extent are cognitive structures real? As a biologist, Piaget (1941, p. 46) assumed that cognitive structures are real. Piaget seemed to have attributed these structures to the child's or adolescent's mind. It has been argued, however (Vonèche & Vidal, 1985, p. 125), that when we try to understand how children and adolescents think, we may draw on ways of formalizing these structures that are different from those chosen by Piaget (1949/1972). Indeed, in his later work, Piaget (Piaget & Garcia, 1987/1991; Piaget, Henriques, & Ascher, 1992) himself used different ways of formalizing these structures.

(7) Structural causality: Piaget admitted that structures have the power to exert a causal influence (Inhelder & Piaget 1955/1958, pp. 263–264). This expression is problematic for three reasons. First, there is no way to see how a concrete operational system – for example, the logic of sets or classes – can "move" and "transform" itself, by its own "causality," to a formal operational system – for example, a logic of propositions. Second, it contradicts Piaget's basic assumption that the ultimate source of cognitive development is the subject's *activity* and nothing else. Third, operational thinking is basic for human reasoning, but a reason is not a cause.

(8) Paradox: It is not clear how cognitive structures can at the same time be stable and rigid, and therefore, like operational systems, make possible some type of necessary knowledge (Smith, 1993, p. 146) and nevertheless continue developing. This is the old question of how *genesis* (which involves time) and cognitive *validity* or even *necessity* (which are timeless) can be reconciled (Lask, 1911).

(9) The stage theory is incoherent: Piaget described levels and stages (and their relations) in many different ways (Smith, 2002; Vuyk, 1981, p. 191).

The overall impression is that these objections to Piaget's stage theory are devastating.

THE MODULAR THEORY AND ITS SHORTCOMINGS

Since the 1980s, partly in response to the problems encountered by Piaget's stage theory, the view has become popular, if not dominant, that "cognitive development is domain-specific or even modular" (Goswami, 2001, p. 265). This view is based on a series of assumptions (Case, 1992a, p. 45):

(1) Cognitive development is no longer forced into a straitjacket. In different domains knowledge develops differently. Modular learning processes are regarded as being age independent.

(2) Specific competences develop in different modules, and there are no particular relations between them (Fodor, 1992; Goswami, 2001, p. 265).

(3) Many modular theories are based on sophisticated stimulus-response schematisms, information processing, and biologically determined programs.

(4) There is no difference between learning and development. Development *is* cumulative learning (Case, 1992a, p. 8).

However, the modular paradigm runs into problems, too (Case, 1992a, p. 9). Most of them are directly opposite to those encountered by Piaget's theory. Modular theories rule out the possibility of intertask correlations and the occurrence of vertical décalages, although both *do* occur in cognitive development. Furthermore, the assumption that children are able to learn anything at any time is false. The findings from training studies are inconclusive at best (Field, 1987), and children younger than the age of 5 fail at conservation tasks even after extensive training (Halford, 1989). Modular theories do not explain these facts.

From an epistemological perspective, a person is a uniform being who interprets the different parts of her conscious knowledge in a coherent fashion (or at least tries to do this). How do modular theories explain this search for coherence? And how do they explain necessary knowledge, which hardly can be domain-specific (Smith, 1993, p. 5)?

Apparently, the modular paradigm has its shortcomings, too, and these do not seem to be any less detrimental than the alleged drawbacks of Piagetian theory. What is to be concluded from this state of affairs? Case (1992a, p. 48) suggested that there is a "dialectical progression" and that neo-Piagetian theories represent a synthesis of universal and atomistic theories of development (see Chapter 18, this volume). However, in this instance the use of the genuine Piagetian device of reconciling two opposing theories by a *tertium quid* does not work because Case did not consider that atomism excludes a universal view, which, in turn, excludes atomism. What we need is a paradigm, which, on the one hand, is strong enough to tackle necessary knowledge, and which, on the other hand, is mobile and flexible enough to accommodate domain-specific knowledge. Such a theory can hardly be atomistic. What we need is an *organic* theory – a theory that considers the human mind as a uniform but differentiated and flexible organ. Organs are supple and capable of adapting to different situations and domains. Finally, they are open to development, and this is precisely what "stable systems" (Case, 1992a, p. 5) are not. But organs are much more complex than such systems, and it is much more difficult to understand them.

CAN PIAGET'S STAGE THEORY BE REPAIRED?

If it turned out that Piaget's stage theory has to be abandoned, then what else would remain of his theory if not just ruins – and, of course, Piaget's early biological work about mollusks in Swiss lakes (see, e.g., Piaget, 1914, 1929)?

Therefore, in the following I address the different criticisms that have been raised with respect to Piaget's stage theory. I first deal with the criticisms that are based on simple misunderstandings (1) to (5). Then I comment on the different versions of Piaget's stage theory (9). Finally, I tackle the more serious objections (6) to (8) and suggest revisions of Piaget's theory that address these objections.

Misunderstandings of Piaget's Stage Theory

Many readers of Piaget seem to associate stages with stairs (Kärn, 1978), floors, and buildings. Case gives one of his books (1992a) the metaphorical title *The Mind's Staircase*. This title can be read in three different ways: (a) There is a staircase in the mind; (b) The mind lives in a staircase; (c) The mind is the creator (or architect) of the staircase, but the staircase neither exists in the mind nor does the mind live in a staircase. If understood in one of the first two ways, the expression sounds ironic. The staircase metaphor loses its ironic meaning, however, when we read it in the third way. Objections (1) to (4) make sense only if we attribute either meaning (a) or (b) to the expression. Somebody who has developed up to stage n may be seen as dwelling in the nth floor, and his further development as being an act of building up new floors. But this

interpretation runs the risk of bringing about serious misunderstandings. Buildings are stable and rigid, and they do not move from one
place to another. The higher up their occupants live, the more panoramic
their view; but, of course, nobody's view transcends his or her horizon.
Whoever wants to expand his view has to leave the building and move
to a new region. Yet, once that has been done, he may prefer to construct another building at the new location instead of returning to the
old one.

Speaking nonmetaphorically: If we succeed in showing that Piaget's
theory is supple and organic instead of being a compound of "stable systems" (Case, 1992a, p. 5), then the objection that domain-specific development is neglected can be refuted. Other misunderstandings related to
the building metaphor can be eliminated as well: the idea that moving
from one stage to the next is a sudden, discontinuous process, or the
assumption that all children climb from one floor to the next at the
same age – as if they moved simultaneously from one class to the next.
Even if we concede that climbing up stages is controlled by biological
processes, it does not follow that stages have strict age limits. To say
that it is not possible to teach a child anything at any age does not mean
that development follows an exact timetable. In other words: Age "is
at best an indicator, not a criterion, of development stage" (Lourenço &
Machado, 1996, p. 147; see Smith, 1993, p. 110).

The décalage objection (3) concerns a more specific aspect of Piaget's
theory. The fact that some structurally similar abilities are acquired at
different time points can have different reasons: Either the empirical
setting of the tasks includes different degrees of difficulty (Bringuier,
1977/1980, p. 59) or the tasks are only apparently but not in fact structurally similar. Or they are structurally similar but related to different
cognitive planes (vertical décalage). Piaget discovered many cases of vertical décalage, and this may have been one of his major motivations for
searching for stage criteria.

There is no doubt that Piaget's insistence in claiming that developmental processes run through stage sequences made his doctrine appear
dogmatic. Moreover, some of Piaget's own explanations are misleading, if not enigmatic. In this sense, the criticisms (6) to (8) have to be
taken seriously. Completely untenable is the idea that structures exert
some form of causal influence (7). The question about the "real" location of cognitive structures (6) and how systems that permit necessary
knowledge can evolve (8) become crucial with respect to Piaget's treatises on formalizing operational structures (1949, 1972). I return to these
questions later. But first I consider the objection that Piaget's theory is
inconsistent in terms of the number of stages (9).

Which of Piaget's Stage Theories Is Most Promising?

Rita Vuyk (1981, p. 191) stated that, "[I]t is rather confusing that Piaget's system of numbering levels or stages of achievements differs from one book to the next." There are mainly two types of inconsistencies that must be cleared up.

(1) "In many recent books level I corresponds to failure, level II to relative success and level III to complete success" (Vuyk, 1981, p. 191). This is, for instance, the case in Piaget's research on the development of physical conservation concepts (Piaget & Inhelder, 1941/1974). In other works, the concept of level refers to different kinds of cognitive activities that arise successively (sensorimotor intelligence, symbolic function and representation, operational thinking). As a result of the inconsistent uses of the level concept, Piagetian levels have often been understood as bound to a value hierarchy. Higher levels indicate correct thinking, whereas lower levels indicate cognitive deficiencies. However, used in the second way (i.e., reference to successively emerging abilities), the level concept is not related to total failure or total success.

(2) Even when restricted to the second sense, Piaget's level concept is not used consistently. "In some publications Piaget distinguishes three stages, in others five, but generally there are four with substages" (Vuyk, 1981, p. 192).

Let me address these inconsistencies in turn. As to the first inconsistency, it is true that a type n of cognitive activity (e.g., operational thinking), which emerges later than another type $n-1$ of cognitive activity (e.g., symbolic function), presupposes the elaboration of the latter – at least until a specific equilibrium is reached. Therefore, type n appears later than type $n-1$, but this has no value implication, because with each level transition the cognitive style and the corresponding world view of the subject also change. Piaget often referred to this as "genetic relativity" (1936/1952, p. 380, 1950a, p. 51): Our world view and value system(s) are always internal. Consequently there is no stage-external view and no absolutely valid value system (Piaget, 1967, p. 1269). Therefore, it would be erroneous to associate Piaget's stage theory with a value hierarchy, even though Piaget was not always coherent with respect to this point and, as a scientist, used to share a highly optimistic view concerning scientific progress (Piaget, 1950c, pp. 312–313; see also Wetzel, 1984).

The second inconsistency is less puzzling than the first, but nevertheless it merits some comments. The decision between a three- or four-level theory (the five-level version does not play a major role in Piaget's theory, but there is a six-stage version[1] in Piaget 1954/1981) has consequences for how we handle the difference between horizontal and vertical décalages. Furthermore, the understanding of the very nature of concrete operations depends on how we decide this question.

In the years between 1923 and 1929, Piaget represented cognitive development as a process with three major stages (1923/1955, 1924/1976). The first stage he called a period of autism (Piaget, 1928/1995, pp. 199–200) – a notion he adopted from Freud (e.g., Piaget, 1924/1976, p. 158). This stage was supposed to last until the end of the third year of life (1924/1976, p. 246, 1927/1960, p. 302). In this period, the child's thinking is adualistic and nondirected. The second period he called egocentric (the child is not able to distinguish clearly between his perspective and that of another person), and this period was supposed to last from 3 years until 7 years (Piaget, 1927/1960, p. 303). Finally, the third period is characterized by deductive reasoning and social reciprocity (Piaget 1924/1976, pp. 251–253, 1928/1995, pp. 207–208). This first version of a three-stage sequence is vulnerable to the criticism that it is committed to a notion of progress in an evaluative sense. Piaget, however, had abandoned this stage theory, at the latest, by 1936 (see Kesselring, 1981, p. 164).

From 1936 on, Piaget advocated a different stage concept. Due to the meticulous observation of his own children's development during the first 2 years of their life, he substituted the idea of an autistic period with that of a period of sensorimotor development (which lasted until about $1\frac{1}{2}$ years; see Chapter 9, this volume). Furthermore, he observed some similarities between the order in which some early cognitive abilities develop during the first 18 months and that in which some "higher-level" capacities develop in later periods (Piaget, 1937/1954, pp. 364–380, 1945/1962, pp. 237–273, 1947/1976, pp. 122–123). Whereas before 1930 he described cognitive development altogether as a *decentration* process, he distinguished from 1936 on decentration processes in sensorimotor from those in preoperational intelligence. In the 1950s, Piaget identified a decentration process also at the level of formal operations (Inhelder & Piaget, 1955/1958, pp. 343–346).

But this latter type of stage theory exists in two versions. In some books and articles Piaget distinguished three main levels (Inhelder & Piaget, 1955/1958, pp. 342–343, 1970, 1975/1985). Smith (1993, p. 40) adheres to this version. In other publications, Piaget (e.g., 1970/1972) distinguished four stages. Many interpreters prefer this latter taxonomy (e.g., Case, 1985; Goswami, 2001; Kesselring, 1999; Vuyk, 1981). In still other works (e.g., Piaget & Inhelder, 1966/1969, pp. 93–96), Piaget presents a mixture of both versions.

Aside from the mere number of levels, the two versions differ in terms of the emphasis Piaget placed on decentration processes. In the three-level version, Inhelder and Piaget interpreted preoperational and concrete operational thinking as two parts of one decentration process (1955/1958, p. 343). By contrast, in the four-level version, concrete operations mark a level by themselves, which suggests that the preoperational decentration process has terminated (Goswami, 2001). In the following, I further analyze implications of the three- and four-level versions.

TOWARD AN ORGANIC INTERPRETATION OF PIAGETIAN
STAGE THEORY: A NEW PROPOSAL

In this section, I show that Piaget's stage theory can be considered in a different way, if one succeeds in responding to the objections (6) to (8) and transforms the stage doctrine into a supple theory about a flexibly functioning human mind. Building on my writings (Kesselring, 1981, 1984, 1990, 1993, 1999), I propose what I term an organic interpretation of Piaget's theory. If we do not attribute to levels whole structural systems, but rather "construction schemes," then the reasons for most of the objections vanish. As I show, what develops across levels and stages are not structures or structural systems built up by a child or adolescent, but blueprints (patterns, schemes) according to which structures are constructed. In what follows, I elaborate this thesis. The elaboration amounts to a reformulation of some parts of Piaget's theory, and I illustrate these modifications in terms of reflecting abstraction and equilibration, grasp of consciousness, and decentration. Recasting Piaget's theory in this manner should make intelligible why cognitive structures may work differently in different domains, but nevertheless belong to the same level, instead of representing different nonrelated modular entities.

The Suspended Spiral Line

Cognitive development was repeatedly illustrated by Piaget with a spiral line or pyramid (1970/1972, p. 67), which is suspended at its top and grows downward. The top is just a point, but downward the spiral line broadens – like a snail's shell. This metaphor can be interpreted as follows: Though the spiral line or pyramid increases in height – growth is *proactive* or *constructive* (Piaget, 1962/2000, p. 244, 1967,

p. 1263, 1967/1971, pp. 320/321, 1980, pp. 10, 216), the process that produces height is oriented backward – *retroactive* or *reflexive* (1950a, p. 76, 1950c, pp. 314, 319, 1974/1980, p. 90). This description (which, by the way, corresponds exactly to how Hegel describes intellectual development, see Hegel, 1816/1951, pp. 477–481) suggests that the process underlying cognitive development is reflective. To this double process Piaget attributes the necessary construction, which at the same time is "always open for new improvements" (1967, p. 1249, my translation).

Reflecting abstraction. It makes sense to consider reflecting abstraction, and not equilibration, as being the driving force of development – again, in analogy to Hegel (Kesselring, 1981). Equilibration only explains how given structures are balanced and become coherent but not how structures themselves are built up. The problems that arise if we take equilibration as the structure building process have been analyzed but not solved by Smith (1993, p. 146).

Blueprint. The suspended spiral or pyramid has the character neither of a staircase nor of a building but of a slowly growing *pattern* or *blueprint*. This pattern can be regarded as an instrument for making knowledge possible – in the same sense in which Kant held that the empirical sciences depend on some mental abilities – *intuition* and *categories* – the functioning of which is *a priori* (Kant, 1787/1933, B XVI). There are other metaphors suitable for describing the nature and "rationale" of the spiral: that of a *stamp*, which is impressed on the objects of knowledge; of *glasses* through which we perceive more clearly what our environment looks like. But, more exactly, a *blueprint* is a *program* for creating or building up something – comparable to the program followed by bees when they build honeycombs. Yet this blueprint is neither static nor immobile but open for development. Piaget (1967/1971, pp. 201–213) came closest to this view in his discussion of regulations that control the functioning of organic processes and evolve into sensorimotor behavior patterns. He did not himself use the term *blueprint*; instead, he used the term *scheme*, but a scheme is a pattern, regulating a behavior or action, not a construction plan.

A pattern or blueprint is autoregulated and regulates cognitive construction processes.[2] A blueprint does not assimilate or accommodate to anything. Neither does it make sense to say, for instance, that a given logical or mathematical operation assimilates objects or accommodates itself to them. Assimilation occurs when the subject learns to do something, such as, to take an example from mathematics, to extract a root. This learning implies the building up of a specific structural framework and the training of the operations related to it. To an operational

ability corresponds what for sensorimotor intelligence is a scheme; but
an operational ability is far more complex. It includes several functions:
a construction program for a structural framework, operational know-
how related to this framework, and the ability to differentiate between
situations and recognize what operation is adequate in a given situation.
These functions do not necessarily arise simultaneously.

The blueprint is not itself a structured object, in the same way in
which the bee's blueprint for building honeycombs is not itself a honey-
comb. In other words, the blueprint does not have the structural properties of its products. A beehive is formed when bees produce honeycombs – one after the other. All honeycombs are formed by the same
blueprint. The same thing occurs when a structural framework is built
up. But whereas beehives are always built according to the same pattern,
human knowledge is produced according to evolving patterns. This has
two theoretically important implications.

(1) Human beings are able to build up cognitive structures of a grad-
     ually growing complexity; in other words, the type of construc-
     tion itself changes over time. As the infant has many different
     schemes at her disposal, the adolescent has many different con-
     struction plans at his disposal. It makes sense to assume that
     there are even blueprints for constructing blueprints (of a lower
     type, which, in turn, are programs for building up more elemen-
     tary schemes).
(2) What develops is the blueprint and not the structures, the con-
     struction of which it regulates. This is, for a variety of reasons,
     an important point. *First*, it would be odd to say that one oper-
     ational system (e.g., the logic of classes) develops further and
     becomes another operational system (e.g., propositional logic).
     Second, the development of the blueprint up to a certain point
     does not imply the complete construction of a structural system
     and, thus, the subject's ability to perform all operations related
     to that system. That is why becoming able to deal with proposi-
     tional logic does not necessarily mean becoming able to apply *all*
     operations related to propositional logic. Some aspects of proposi-
     tional logic are similar to those of class logic and therefore may be
     learned earlier than others with which the subject is not famil-
     iar (Lourenço & Machado, 1996, p. 157). *Third*, the blueprint
     itself has no hierarchical structure, even if it is a program for
     building up hierarchical structures (e.g., the concrete operational
     ability of class inclusion).[3] There is a simple reason for that:

Structures built up according to the blueprint are due to activities (of a certain type), and it is the *iteration* of these activities that creates hierarchical structures. Platonism becomes compatible with constructivism as soon as we distinguish systematically between blueprint and structural systems. The dilemma described by Campbell and Bickhard (1986, pp. 4, 52) and Smith (1993, p. 148) that a system which permits necessary knowledge is rigid and therefore cannot evolve, and a system which changes cannot permit necessary knowledge, disappears. *Fourth*, the question of whether the logical and algebraic structures Piaget tried to formalize really exist in the child's or adolescent's mind no longer arises. What we attribute to the child's mind are some blueprints (i.e., construction programs); the structural systems, however, are creations of the cognitive activity of human beings and belong to what Popper called the world 3 (i.e., they do not belong to either the material or the subjective world; Popper, 1979). The truism that validity of a cognitive system cannot be explained by its genesis, and its genesis cannot be explained on the basis of its validity (Lask, 1911), should no longer bother genetic epistemology. *Fifth*, the blueprint naturally is not a cognitive operation either. Logical and mathematical operations (e.g., $7 + 7 = 14$) are bound to cognitive systems (e.g., a system of groupings or groups), but these systems do not "exist" as pre-established framework in a person's mind. *Sixth*, it becomes evident, too, why equilibration cannot be the driving force behind the construction of the system. Equilibration is neither a power of construction nor an architect who surveys a construction. Equilibration is just the process by which a structural system gets adjusted and regulated. The system itself is constructed by reflecting abstraction.

There is evidence that Piaget himself did not carefully distinguish between the plane of blueprints and that of structures built up according to a blueprint (Piaget, 1983/1987, pp. 141–142, is a rare exception). Sometimes, Piaget (1949/1972) used the concept of structure(s) not only when he described and analyzed cognitive abilities (e.g., children's and adolescents' problem-solving behavior) but also when he defined levels and stages. But structures are built up by an activity regulated by a blueprint, whereas levels are subsequent phases in the development of the blueprint. Furthermore, structures are not strictly bound to developmental periods or levels, because an earlier structure (e.g., sensorimotor intelligence) does not lose its significance in later developmental periods.[4]

Same Blueprint, Different Types of Structures

The cognitive abilities of human beings ultimately form a unity. This unity covers different patterns, which regulate different cognitive functions. But it does not make sense to assume that there is an indefinite number of blueprints coexisting in an atomistic manner without relation among each other. To explain how necessary knowledge can be built up, it is more convenient to think of a rather small number of blueprints, which, moreover, are related to each other.

A blueprint specific to a particular level permits the generation of structural patterns of more than just one type, which may be applied to different tasks specific to this level. If we interpret the cognitive mechanisms in this way, then we understand more easily why it often happens that a child is able to pass one task but not a structurally similar task. It becomes also clear why structures built up in a specific domain may become productive later on in a different domain. Structural patterns constitute the basis for particular tasks. Though structural patterns, which issue from the same blueprint, are in some way similar, there is no reason to assume that a child activates them all at the same time. The order in which apparently similar tasks are solved may differ from child to child. Let me provide two examples that illustrate the similarities and differences between structural patterns relying on the same blueprint.

Sensorimotor invariance. Object permanence is a scheme Piaget used for describing the concept of invariance the infant acquires at the transition from sensorimotor to preoperational intelligence (see Chapter 9, this volume). I suggest that there is not just one invariance scheme but a whole family of schemes linked by a sort of family resemblance.

(1) Object permanence in the strict sense implies that the infant knows that different sensory images correspond to a material object and that an object exists independently of whether it is actually represented by some sensory image.

(2) Permanence relates to persons, too ("people also become objectified and spatialized," Piaget, 1954/1981, p. 40). Mirror self-recognition (e.g., Bertenthal & Fischer, 1981; Brooks-Gunn & Lewis, 1984; Hoffman, 2000, pp. 69, 71) seems to be a consequence of the acquisition of the permanence concept of persons.

The permanence scheme has its importance also in language acquisition because a child has to understand intuitively that a word and its meaning stay the same in different situations.

Concrete operational thinking. Piaget took reversibility and compensation as two of the main criteria for concrete operational thinking, and he demonstrated the importance of these criteria for tasks that required the conservation of quantities. Again, there is a whole family of examples for reversibility and compensation. Do they represent the same scheme or different ones? The following examples show that to distinguish operational reversibility and compensation from the type of invariance found in sensorimotor and early preoperational intelligence, an additional criterion may be useful: the amenability to iteration. Iteration permits the discovery of regularities and thus is an essential aspect of operational necessity.

(1)   Classification is an operational activity by which a child coordinates two relations – a vertical (subsumption) and a horizontal one (relation between subsumed elements); a relation itself is constructed by an operation, and this constructive process can be reiterated: Flippy is a dog; a dog is a mammal; a mammal is a vertebrate, etc.

(2)   Semantic relations are analogous to those of classification, but their order is inverted: The term *dog* implies the term *mammal*, which, in turn, implies the term *vertebrate*, etc. With each step, information decreases and class extension increases. Again, the constructive process can be iterated.

(3)   One-to-one correspondence involves the coordination of two relations: seriation (one after the other) and correspondence. The operation by which order is established is amenable to iteration.

(4)   For the understanding of natural numbers, it is important to consider class inclusion between subsequent numbers. This aspect is more important than mere coordination between seriation and one-to-one correspondence (Smith, 1993, p. 153). Class inclusion is itself coordinated with seriation, and both permit iteration *ad libitum*. Again, the amenability to iteration is a crucial criterion for concrete operational thinking.

How Is Development Explained?

The fact that a blueprint develops has the effect that the set of blueprints in which development manifests itself changes over time: New patterns develop and older ones are deactivated. Therefore, there is no discontinuity, even when there is a transition from one level to the next. In this section, I elaborate on some of the processes that play a central role in the development of a blueprint.

Grasp of consciousness. Piaget (1974/1976, see Chapter 13, this volume) described becoming aware as a process that starts at the periphery of the action and progresses in the direction of its regulatory center. As long as the subject is not conscious of himself, he is not able to clearly differentiate between himself and his surroundings (between the I and the external world). Piaget (1962/2000) called this cognitive attitude *egocentrism*. It often marks the attitude at the beginning of a developmental level. As long as the subject is not fully conscious of himself and of his perspective, he is blind to the difference between what is subjective and what is objective. Another consequence of this adualism is what Piaget calls *realism* (1926/1960, p. 126) or *phenomenism* (i.e., the reduction of one's own perspective and cognitive activity to the effects of external phenomena; 1950b, p. 78). The process of overcoming this adualism and, later on, of coordinating different perspectives, is called *decentration*.

When adualism is overcome, the subject becomes conscious of distinctions and – bound to them – relations. These relations first remain uncoordinated and later on become coordinated with each other. This process of differentiation and coordination underlies the development of a blueprint and shapes the structures, which are built up accordingly (thus influencing the subject's worldview). To be able to understand the specific level of development of the blueprint, we have to make sure on which cognitive plane the differentiation and coordination processes occur. This plane is essential for the determination of a level.

Reflecting abstraction. The driving force of development is reflecting abstraction. Reflecting abstraction is not the same process as the grasp of consciousness, but there are some similarities: Reflecting abstraction also starts at the periphery of an action and advances toward its regulatory center. However, the results of reflecting abstraction are different from those of the grasp of consciousness. Reflecting abstraction mainly focuses on certain *aspects* of cognitive activity and *relations* between different (aspects of) cognitive activities. Reflecting abstraction does not lead to a clear consciousness – neither of the object nor of the subject – but to a further elaboration of the regulatory pattern underlying the cognitive action, thus promoting its further development. On the other hand, reflecting abstraction does not lead to decentration because decentration is caused by an increasing dawn of consciousness.

Construction of levels and level transitions. The four cognitive stages Piaget referred to are those of (I) sensorimotor intelligence, (II) preoperational thinking, (III) concrete operations, and (IV) formal operations. In many of his works Piaget subdivided each level into two substages and a transition phase (except on the sensorimotor level where he assumed six substages). It makes sense to adopt this division and distinguish on each level two substages and a transition phase (Kesselring, 1993).

Form and content. Piaget provided a detailed description of how different types of cognitive activity are built up from level to level. In this context, he used to apply the concepts *form* and *content* and argued that they are related such that the forms belonging to level n become the content of level $n + 1$. To quote Piaget:

> The sensorimotor structures are forms in relation to the simple movements they coordinate, but content in relation to the interiorized and conceptualized actions of the subsequent level; "concrete" operations are forms in relation to these latter actions, but content with respect to the already formal operations...; and these again are only content in relation to the operations applying to them at later levels. (1970/1972, pp. 67–68)

This statement is decisive for understanding how Piaget conceptualized the succession of levels. There are no essential cognitive structures, which were extracted by empirical abstraction from the world outside. In other words, the subject's construction program (i.e., blueprint) integrates exclusively schemes or patterns of his own cognitive activities from the preceding level. In other words, behavioral patterns or construction programs, which developed at earlier levels, are integrated into the patterns of subsequent levels. But, once again, this does not mean that the structures of class inclusion (level III) are integrated into propositional logic (which Piaget attributed to level IV), because the notions of form and content refer to the formation of a blueprint. When the forms of level n become the content of level $n + 1$, they are transformed, thus losing their status as forms.

Level Transitions

As criteria for level transitions one may think first about (a) *logical reversibility* and *compensation* for operational intelligence (Piaget, 1957, 1975/1985, pp. 94–108) and *empirical reversibility* for sensorimotor intelligence (Piaget, 1937/1954, pp. 79–86) and (b) schemes or concepts of *invariance* and *conservation* (permanent object, mass invariance, proportionality, etc.; Piaget & Inhelder 1941/1974). But there are some further criteria that in the Piagetian literature have often been neglected: (c) When he described development as a decentration process, Piaget frequently characterized the level transition as a *conversion* or a reversal of consciousness – in strict analogy to Hegel, who in his dialectics described level transitions in exactly the same way (Kesselring,

1981). Often Piaget refers to this reversal as the *Copernican Revolution* (1962/2000, p. 243, 1962/1973, p. 16, p. 13, 1970/1972, p. 21, Piaget & Inhelder, 1966/1969, p. 13): The subject looks back at his own (prior) cognitive standpoint and considers herself an object of reflection, like in the Copernican theory Earth became an object of astronomical reflection. In Piaget's words, the subject must "become just one element in the universe he constructs" (Piaget & Inhelder, 1941/1974, p. 62).[5] This self-reflection indicates that a new, higher plane of reflection – which always marks a new cognitive plane – has been reached; and this is a fourth criterion (d) of level transitions. The introduction of a new cognitive level thus leads to the construction of new types of entities and, with this, to a deep change in the subject's worldview.[6] In this respect, a level transition resembles a paradigm change in the sense of Thomas Kuhn (1970). Piaget used to mention criterion (d) in the context of explaining transitions from level I to level II and from level III to level IV, but he did not invoke it when he explained the transition from level II to level III (this, by the way, may have been one of the reasons why he was uncertain as to whether concrete operational thinking marks a level on its own).

Transition I–II. At the transition from level I to level II, it is the plane of representation or imagination that makes symbolic function, language acquisition, and preoperational thinking possible. At level I, the infant has acquired the scheme of a sensory image: The infant remains attentive to a sensory image only as long as she remains in direct sensorial contact with it; when she loses contact, she behaves as if the image had no permanent substrate. At level II, the infant has the scheme of the permanent object at her disposal. To permanent objects she refers in a completely different way than to sensory images. An object is identical with itself, notwithstanding whether it is present or absent or whether it is seen from its front or back side.

Transition III–IV. Piaget (Inhelder & Piaget, 1955/1958, pp. 251–255) describes a couple of cognitive novelties that emerge in the transition from level III to level IV (see Chapter 11, this volume). Thinking becomes hypothetical and deductive. This means that reality receives the status of just one among many possible worlds. The adolescent begins to reflect upon his own position in society, his future life, etc. These cognitive novelties are due to the emergence of a new cognitive plane: The adolescent acquires the ability to reflect on his operational thinking and thus starts to exercise *second-order operations* (operations on operations). With this he starts constructing new types of cognitive objects, such as combinatorial logic, probabilities, logical necessity, proportionality, function (in the mathematical sense), and transfinite numbers.

(a)   ● ● ● ● ●   ○   ○
(b)   ● ● ● ● ●

Figure 17.1. Class inclusion: Comparison of superordinate class (a) with larger subclass (b).

It is evident that this cognitive change, too, transforms the subject's ontology.

The Transition II–III

But what happens at the transition from level II to level III? I discuss this question more extensively because Piaget's own analysis seems to me incomplete. Let me provide some examples.

Class inclusion involves the understanding that a subclass is included in its superordinate class. Class inclusion is assessed by showing a preschool child, for example, seven wooden marbles, five of which are black and two of which are white. When the preschooler is asked whether there are more wooden marbles or more black ones, he commonly answers "more black ones" (Piaget, 1941/1952, pp. 161–184). This may at first glance be surprising because this task seems simple. However, children fail in comparing the whole class with the bigger of its two mutually exclusive subclasses. Even if they repeat the question correctly, most of them are not able to give the correct answer. What kind of difficulty do they encounter? If the five black marbles are separated from the whole, then only two white ones remain. Therefore, the child only compares the two subclasses and does not consider the whole. Piaget attributed this behavior to a lack of reversibility: The child cannot anticipate the recomposition of the whole.

But this cannot be the whole story. In order to solve the class inclusion problem, the child must (a) put all the marbles, black and white ones, into one and the same (superordinate) class, and (b) consider the subclass of the five black marbles independently, as if they constituted a smaller class by themselves. It is impossible to physically execute these two operations simultaneously because, as shown in Figure 17.1, the subclass of black marbles is either put together with the subclass of white marbles or kept separate from it.

Following this analysis, the difficulty of class inclusion does not consist in representing the larger subclass aside from the whole class (preoperational children are even able to represent a set of absent objects) but rather in comparing two different classes – the subclass of black marbles and the superordinate class of all marbles. This is difficult because only one of these classes is materially present, whereas the other one must be imagined as being present. To solve the class inclusion problem, a *second-order representational act* is required.

A set or class is something immaterial that we can only imagine: A set is "each collection C of some distinct objects given in our *representation or thinking*" (Cantor, 1895/1932, p. 282; translation and emphasis added by the author). The idea of iteration, which is essential for the concept of natural number, is bound to the concept of class inclusion – an operational process that depends on the ability to execute second-order representational acts. Piaget (1940/1967, p. 63) himself does mention second-order representation, but only in the context of formal operational thinking.

Inversion of left and right, when a person turns 180 degrees. Here two relations (that between left and right and that between too opposite positions) need to be coordinated (Piaget, 1924/1976, pp. 98–101). Iteration is possible, and with the second rotation the original position is re-established. A 4- to 5-year-old who is sitting in front of another person may be perfectly able to imagine what it is like to sit at that person's place, but she is not yet able to coordinate left and right in a system of spatial relations involving two persons, one sitting opposite to the other. To overcome this difficulty, she has to imagine the whole situation from an external perspective. Again, the coordination requires a second-order representational act.

The conservation of quantity or mass. In analyzing the conservation of mass, Piaget & Inhelder, 1941/1974) emphasized children's use of reversibility, compensation, and identity arguments: The ball–sausage transformation can be reversed, the sausage is thinner, but also longer, and during the transformation process nothing has been taken away from nor added to the mass of clay. But these arguments are insufficient for proving the conservation of mass. When a ball of clay is transformed into a sausage, the sum of length and (medium) thickness does not remain constant. Why, then, is the child convinced that mass is conserved? Rather than simply comparing length and thickness of the ball and the sausage, he has to imagine several phases of the transformation (its iteration) and compare the length and thickness differences at these different phases. Here again, a second-order representational act is required. Of course, the child does not have the concept of a mathematical function at his disposal, but the conservation of mass is its concrete operational precursor.

The discussion of these examples may suffice for demonstrating that a second-order representational act is necessary for the realization of concrete operations. The new level of representation permits the child to compare not only things with things and then relations with relations (as preoperational children do), but also differences between (e.g., quantitative) relations with differences between other relations. But the concrete operational child can display this new ability only if his imagination is supported by concrete material or by drawings. That is why Piaget called these operations *concrete*. In using these operations, children construct concepts that represent new types of entities – sets, classes, numbers (*natural* numbers), quantitative differences. These entities are all constructed in the imagination. The newly acquired operations can be iterated, and with their help children become, for the first time, able to construct hierarchical operational systems.

The transition from level II to level III is, once again, accompanied by a pervasive change in the child's ontology. He discovers new properties such as the property of something being logical or illogical, explicable or inexplicable. And from now on the world is seen as endowed with the property of being calculable – open to mathematical (and logical) treatment. Thus, preoperational and concrete operational intelligence apparently belong to different levels. The three-stage view defended by Smith (1993, p. 40) turns out to be untenable.

There is no reason to believe that a child who has reached a new level in one cognitive domain must have reached it in other domains, too. That a blueprint enables a child to build up a special kind of structural pattern does not imply that all possible structures of the same pattern must arise simultaneously. In other words, the theory does not make any claims pertaining to when, where, and how the child uses this kind of structural pattern in other cognitive domains.

Is the Child Conscious of a Level Transition?

Though level transitions are processes of a special type, they do not occur in a discontinuous way, as some of Piaget's critics have claimed (see previous discussion). To use an analogy, level transitions are similar to the crossing of a timberline. Normally, different climate zones that an alpinist passes through when climbing a high mountain are not separated by a clear-cut borderline. Nonetheless, the concept of climate zones makes sense. To assume that the transition from one level to the next is marked by a quick and discontinuous step or even a quantum leap (e.g., Brainerd, 1978, p. 210) is as strange as holding that when crossing the timberline, an alpinist behaves in a special manner, such as jumping over it, hurrying up, or suffering a crisis.

The notion of level transition does not create any obligation to impute to the child a consciousness of this transition (most passengers in an airplane crossing the equator do not pay any attention to this fact). The child can only become conscious that his way of thinking has changed when he remembers clearly how he used to think before. This consciousness, however, does not accompany every change in the way of thinking, and not every such change is related to a level transition.

A final issue concerns the overcoming of egocentrism and the emergence of self-consciousness. Piaget described the transition from level I to level II, as well as the transition from level III to level IV, as periods in which a decentration process ends at one level and gives way, at the next level, to a new and more complex form of egocentrism (e.g., Inhelder & Piaget, 1955/1958, pp. 343–344). In both of these transitions, there is a significant enrichment of self-consciousness: The infant (transition from level I to level II) who recognizes herself in the mirror has attained a new understanding of her own embodiment (Piaget, 1937/1954, p. 208, 1954/1981, p. 40; see Chapter 9, this volume). An adolescent (transition from level III to level IV), after passing a substage of strong egocentrism, starts reflecting upon his own position in society and on how he is perceived by his peers (Inhelder & Piaget, 1955/1958, pp. 346–347).

But what happens at the transition from level II to level III? Piaget apparently did not observe any behavior indicative of an initial egocentrism at the beginning of the concrete operational level. It seems that the opposite occurs: The child's thinking becomes logical and social (Piaget, 1923/1955, 1924/1976), and the child who plays a game involving rules learns to pay attention to the rules because he is now able to put himself at another person's position (Piaget, 1932/1965, pp. 84–100). For the same reason, he acquires the attitude of mutual respect and understands the *Golden Rule*: Don't do to others what you don't want the others to do to you (Piaget, 1932/1965, pp. 395–406). Thus, it seems that there is no clear centration or egocentrism at the beginning of level III.

But if we look closer and move beyond Piaget's writings, we easily discover a special type of centration typical for level III: In the cognitive domain prevails a centration on *given things* ("natural" numbers, instead of negative and/or rational numbers; *real* states of affair instead of *possible* ones). And in the social and ethical domain the child's thinking remains centered on the small group of persons he lives with. Initially, this group is represented by his family and, later on, by a group of friends or peers with whom the child likes to play, cooperate, and exchange ideas (Lickona, 1983, chapter 9). During this period he understands a moral norm as a rule that is based on the mutual expectations of the members of such a group.

This mental attitude, however, shows an extreme form of centration in the social domain. We easily may imagine a mafia group the members of which respect each other and cooperate successfully but commit crimes against people who do not belong to the group. Such behavior usually counts as being amoral. In Kohlberg's theory (1981, 1984), the difference between a group morality and a morality related to society as a whole is manifest in his distinction between levels III and IV. Reflection on human rights takes place only on the postconventional level (i.e., after level IV). For establishing criteria of a moral norm applicable to the larger society, it is worthwhile to refer to *human rights*.

CONCLUSION

To address Hegel's question, I have argued that a revised version of Piaget's stage theory captures developmental regularities and recurrent processes.[7] These regularities occur, among others, due to the construction of different cognitive planes. This construction leads regularly to a cognitive reversal (i.e., Copernican Revolution) that produces a through-going and lasting transformation of children's way of thinking and world view.

With respect to Kant's question about the origin of necessary knowledge, this chapter leads to two conclusions. First, the necessity of knowledge is bound to operational systems. In this chapter, I proposed to interpret these systems not as stage-related cognitive structures, but rather as the result of a construction process guided by a blueprint, which itself evolves and regulates the creation of different and domain-specific structural systems (representation, symbol function, logical and mathematical operations). Properties such as reversibility, compensation, and criteria of identity belong to such systems. The subject becomes aware of them through reflecting abstraction. All operational systems are, on the one hand, constructed, but, on the other hand, belong to world 3 (Popper, 1979).

Second, the necessary character of these systems itself is neither constructed nor merely subjective. The construction plan (blueprint) develops according to lawlike regularities that result from the subject's reflecting abstraction on his action and coordinatory schemes. In this respect – but only in this respect – the direction of cognitive development appears to be necessary.[8]

NOTES

1. This six-stage version is compatible with the four-stage version, but the three substages in the first stage or level count as if they were each their own stage.

2. Piaget (1983/1987, p. 142) compared the organizational principles of an organism to those of cognition: The organs built up in an organism correspond to the structures built up in the cognitive subject.

3. Piaget unfortunately confused these points (see, e.g., 1967, p. 1249).

4. If Piaget had described levels and stages only in relation to blueprints (schemes), then he would have saved his theory from much confusion.

5. In the preface of his *Critique of Pure Reason*, Kant (1787/1933, B XVI) refers in the same way to the Copernican Revolution. He points out that for explaining the possibility of scientific knowledge about (physical) objects we have to reflect on central cognitive functions (*intuition and categories*). According to Piaget, however, the reversal of the attentional focus of the mind does not happen just once but several times – namely at every level transition.

6. The reconstruction of Piaget's stage theory by Case (1992) is, in several respects, similar to what is proposed in this chapter. However, because Case does not consider criteria (c) and (d), he arrives at completely different results.

7. Further examples to illustrate the developmental regularities can be found in Kesselring (1981, 1984, 1990, 1993, 1999).

8. Many thanks to Ulrich Müller for helpful suggestions and comments on earlier versions of this chapter.

REFERENCES

Bertenthal, B. I., & Fischer, K. W. (1981). Development of self-recognition in the infant. *Developmental Psychology, 14*, 44–50.

Brainerd, C. J. (1978). The stage question in cognitive developmental theory. *Behavioral and Brain Sciences, 2*, 173–182.

Bringuier, J.-C. (1980). *Conversations with Jean Piaget*. Chicago: University of Chicago Press. (Original work published in 1977)

Brooks-Gunn, J., & Lewis, M. (1984). The development of early visual self-recognition. *Developmental Review, 4*, 215–239.

Cantor, Georg (1932). *Gesammelte Abhandlungen mathematischen und philosophischen Inhalts*. Berlin: Springer. (Original work published in 1895)

Case, R. (1985). *Intellectual development: Birth to adulthood*. New York: Academic Press.

Case, R. (1992a). *The mind's staircase: Exploring the conceptual underpinnings of children's thought and knowledge*. Mahwah, NJ: Erlbaum.

Case, R. (1992b). Neo-Piagetian theories of child development. In R. J. Sternberg & C. Berg (Eds.), *Intellectual development* (pp. 161–196). New York: Cambridge University Press.

Field, D. (1987). A review of preschool conservation training: An analysis of analyses. *Developmental Review, 7*, 210–251.

Fodor, J. A. (1992). A theory of the child's theory of mind. *Cognition, 44*, 283–296.

Goswami, U. (2001). No stages please – we're British. *British Journal of Psychology, 92*, 257–277.

Habermas, J. (1976). *Zur Rekonstruktion des Historischen Materialismus.* Frankfurt: Suhrkamp.

Habermas, J. (1990). *Moral consciousness and communicative action.* Cambridge, MA: MIT Press. (Original work published in 1983)

Halford, G. S. (1989). Reflections on 25 years of Piagetian cognitive development psychology, 1963–1988. *Human Development, 32,* 325–337.

Hegel, G. W. F. (1951). *Science of logic.* New York: Macmillan. (Original work published in 1816)

Hegel, G. W. F. (1977). *Phenomenology of spirit.* Oxford: Oxford University Press. (Original work published in 1807)

Hoffman, M. I. (2000). *Empathy and moral development: Implications of caring and justice.* Cambridge, MA: Cambridge University Press.

Inhelder, B., & Piaget, J. (1958). *The growth of logical thinking from childhood to adolescence.* New York: Norton. (Original work published in 1955)

Kant, I. (1933). *Critique of pure reason* (2nd ed.). London: Macmillan. (Original work published in 1787)

Kant, I. (1968). On the form and principles of the sensible and intelligible world. In I. Kant (Ed.), *Selected precritical writings and correspondence with Beck* (pp. 45–92). New York: Barnes & Noble. (Original work published in 1770)

Kärn, M. (1978). Vorsicht Stufe! Ein Kommentar zur Stufentheorie der moralischen Entwicklung. In G. Portele (Ed.), *Sozialisation und Moral. Neue Ansätze zur moralischen Entwicklung und Erziehung* (pp. 81–100). Weinheim: Beltz.

Kesselring, T. (1981). *Entwicklung und Widerspruch.* Frankfurt: Suhrkamp.

Kesselring, T. (1984). *Die Produktivität der Antinomie.* Frankfurt: Suhrkamp.

Kesselring, T. (1990). Os quatro níveis de conhecimento em Jean Piaget. *Educação e Realidade, 15,* 3–21.

Kesselring, T. (1993). Egocentrism and equilibration. In D. Maurice & J. Montangero (Eds.), *Equilibrium and equilibration* (pp. 63–78). Geneva: Fondation Archives Jean Piaget.

Kesselring, T. (1999). *Jean Piaget* (2nd ed.). München: Beck.

Kohlberg, L. (1981). *The philosophy of moral development: Moral stages and the idea of justice.* San Francisco: Harper & Row.

Kohlberg, L. (1984). *The psychology of moral development: The nature and validity of moral stages.* San Francisco: Harper & Row.

Kuhn, T. S. (1970). *The structure of scientific revolutions* (2nd ed.). Chicago: University of Chicago Press.

Lask, E. (1911). *Die Logik der Philosophie und die Kategorienlehre.* Tübingen: Mohr.

Lickona, T. (1983). *Raising good children.* New York: Bantam.

Lourenço, O., & Machado, A. (1996). In defense of Piaget's theory: A reply to 10 common criticisms. *Psychological Review, 103,* 143–164.

Piaget, J. (1914). L'espèce mendelienne a-t-elle une valeur absolue? *Zoologischer Anzeiger, 44,* 328–331.

Piaget, J. (1929). L'adaptation de la limnaea stagnalis aux milieux lacustres de la Suisse romande. *Revue Suisse de Zoologie, 36,* 263–531.

Piaget, J. (1941). Esprit et réalité. *Jahrbuch der Schweizerischen Gesellschaft, 1,* 40–47.

Piaget, J. (1950a). *Introduction à l'épistémologie génétique, Vol. 1: La pensée mathématique*. Paris: Presses Universitaires de France.

Piaget, J. (1950b). *Introduction à l'épistémologie génétique, Vol. 2: La pensée physique*. Paris: Presses Universitaires de France.

Piaget, J. (1950c). *Introduction à l'épistémologie génétique, Vol. 3: La pensée biologique, la pensée psychologique et la pensée sociologique*. Paris: Presses Universitaires de France.

Piaget, J. (1952). *The origins of intelligence in children*. New York: International Universities Press. (Original work published in 1936)

Piaget, J. (1952). *The child's conception of number*. London: Routledge and Kegan Paul. (Original work published with A. Szeminska in 1941)

Piaget, J. (1954). *The construction of reality in the child*. New York: Basic Books. (Original work published in 1937)

Piaget, J. (1955). *The language and thought of the child*. New York: Meridian. (Original work published in 1923)

Piaget, J. (1957). Logique et équilibre dans les comportements du sujet. In L. Apostel, B. Mandelbrot, & J. Piaget (Eds.), *Études d'épistémologie génétique II: Logique et équilibre* (pp. 27–117). Paris: Presses Universitaires de France.

Piaget, J. (1960). *The child's conception of the world*. Totowa, NJ: Littlefield, Adams & Co. (Original work published in 1926)

Piaget, J. (1960). *The child's conception of causality*. Totowa, NJ: Littlefield, Adams & Co. (Original work published in 1927).

Piaget, J. (1962). *Play, dreams and imitation in childhood*. New York: W.W. Norton & Co. (Original work published in 1945)

Piaget, J. (1965). *The moral judgment of the child*. New York: The Free Press. (Original work published in 1932)

Piaget, J. (1966). *Part II*. In E. Beth & J. Piaget (Eds.), *Mathematical epistemology and psychology* (pp. 131–304). Dordrecht: Reidel. (Original work published in 1961)

Piaget, J. (1967). The mental development of the child. In J. Piaget (Ed.), *Six psychological studies* (pp. 3–73). New York: Random House. (Original work published in 1940)

Piaget, J. (1967). *Logique et connaissance scientifiques*. Paris: Encyclopédie de la Pléjade.

Piaget, J. (1970). Piaget's theory. In P. H. Mussen (Ed.), *Carmichael's manual of child psychology, Vol. 1* (3rd ed., pp. 703–730). New York: Wiley.

Piaget, J. (1971). *Insights and illusions of philosophy*. New York: World Publishing Company. (Original work published in 1965)

Piaget, J. (1971). *Biology and knowledge*. Chicago: University of Chicago Press. (Original work published in 1967)

Piaget, J. (1971). *Structuralism*. London: Routledge & Kegan Paul. (Original work published in 1968)

Piaget, J. (1972). *Essai de logique opératoire*. Paris: Dunod. (2nd ed., Traité de logique, 1949)

Piaget, J. (1972). *The principles of genetic epistemology*. New York: Basic Books. (Original work published in 1970)

Piaget, J. (1973). Life and thought. In J. Piaget, *The child and reality* (pp. 163–172). New York: Grossman Publishers. (Original work published in 1954)

Piaget, J. (1973). Time and the intellectual development of the child. In J. Piaget, *The child and reality* (pp. 1–30). New York: Grossman Publishers. (Original work published in 1962)

Piaget, J. (1976). *Judgment and reasoning in the child.* Totowa, NJ: Littlefield, Adams. (Original work published in 1924)

Piaget, J. (1976). *The psychology of intelligence.* Totowa, NJ: Littlefield, Adams, & Co. (Original work published in 1947)

Piaget, J. (1976). *The grasp of consciousness.* Cambridge, MA: Harvard University Press. (Original work published in 1974)

Piaget, J. (1977). The stages of intellectual development in childhood and adolescence. In H. E. Gruber & J. J. Vonèche (Eds.), *The essential Piaget* (pp. 814–819). New York: Basic Books. (Original work published in 1956)

Piaget, J. (1980). *Adaptation and intelligence: Organic selection and phenocopy.* Chicago: University of Chicago Press. (Original work published in 1974)

Piaget, J. (1980). *Les formes élémentaires de la dialectique.* Paris: Gallimard.

Piaget, J. (1981). *Intelligence and affectivity.* Palo Alto, CA: Annual Reviews. (Original work published in 1954).

Piaget, J. (1985). *The equilibration of cognitive structures.* Chicago: University of Chicago Press. (Original work published in 1975)

Piaget, J. (1987). *Possibility and necessity: The role of necessity in cognitive development.* Minneapolis: University of Minnesota Press. (Original work published in 1983)

Piaget, J. (1995). Genetic logic and sociology. In J. Piaget, *Sociological studies* (pp. 184–214). London: Routledge. (Original work published in 1928)

Piaget, J. (2000). Commentary on Vygotsky. *New Ideas in Psychology, 18,* 241–259. (Original work published in 1962)

Piaget, J. (2001). *Studies in reflecting abstraction.* Hove: Taylor & Francis. (Original work published in 1977)

Piaget, J., & Garcia, R. (1991). *Toward a logic of meanings.* Hillsdale, NJ: Erlbaum. (Original work published in 1987)

Piaget, J., Henriques, G., & Ascher, E. (1992). *Morphisms and categories: Comparing and transforming.* Hillsdale, NJ: Erlbaum.

Piaget, J., & Inhelder, B. (1969). *The psychology of the child.* New York: Basic Books. (Original work published in 1966)

Piaget, J., & Inhelder, B. (1974). *The child's construction of quantities.* London: Routledge & Kegan Paul. (Original work published in 1941)

Pinard, A., & Laurendeau, M. (1969). 'Stage' in Piaget's cognitive-developmental theory: Exegesis of a concept. In D. Elkind & J. H. Flavell (Eds.), *Studies in cognitive development* (pp. 121–170). New York: Oxford University Press.

Popper, K. (1979). *Objective knowledge* (2nd ed.). Oxford: Oxford University Press.

Smith, L. (1991). Age, ability, and intellectual development in Piagetian theory. In M. Chandler & M. Chapman (Eds.), *Criteria for competence* (pp. 69–91). Hillsdale, NJ: Erlbaum.

Smith, L. (1993). *Necessary knowledge: Piagetian perspectives on constructivism*. Hillsdale, NJ: Erlbaum.

Smith, L. (2002). Piaget's model. In U. Goswami (Ed.), *Blackwell handbook of childhood cognitive development* (pp. 515–537). Oxford: Blackwell.

Vonèche, J., & Vidal, F. (1985). Jean Piaget and the child psychologist in Jean Piaget. *Synthese, 65*, 121–138.

Vuyk, R. (1981). *Overview and critique of Piaget's genetic epistemology 1965–1980, Vol.* 1. London: Academic Press.

Wetzel, F. G. (1984). Elemente des Rationalismus in der Erkenntnistheorie Jean Piagets. In G. Steiner (Ed.), *Kindlers Psychologie des 20.Jahrhunderts, Vol.* 1 (pp. 41–63). Zurich: Kindler.

18 Dynamic Development

A Neo-Piagetian Approach

The questions Piaget raised, and his concepts and observations for addressing them, have shaped virtually all research and theory in cognitive development over the last 50 years. Even those who rejected Piaget's conclusions shaped their work in terms of his questions. Some approaches built upon his work directly whereas others sought to oppose it. The focus of this chapter is primarily on the former – research and theory that has built directly on Piaget to address new, revised, and expanded questions.

The primary question raised in neo-Piagetian work is variability: the dynamic ways that people's actions differ and change. At all ages and in all cultures, people's actions vary dramatically across contexts, tasks, and emotional states. For example, in class Christina, a fifth-grade student, can read and explain a paragraph about how the eye works, but she cannot give the same explanation at home on her own. Seth, a high school freshman, can solve a math problem about the cost of schoolbooks when he does it with his mother's support, but in class the next day he is unable to solve the same problem. On the other hand, for a similar problem about the cost of new jeans, he solves it easily across all situations. This sort of variation can be frustrating, but it is normal, and it happens every day with everyone. Modern neo-Piagetian research and theory embrace this variability, using it to create better explanations of the complexity and diversity of human knowledge and action.

In this chapter we argue that the modern neo-Piagetian framework provides a solution to the long-standing problem of variability by analyzing the dynamics of the organization of action and thought. Classical explanations of development and learning often analyze action and thought in terms of static forms instead of dynamically varying structures. They explain Christina's descriptions of how the eye works in terms of her logical understanding of the mechanisms of the eye, but they do not explain how that understanding seems to disappear outside

400

of class. They explain Seth's variable math skill in calculating the costs of books and jeans in terms of his knowledge of equations with algebraic variables, but they do not explain how that skill differs across objects and contexts.

By directly analyzing such variability in people's knowledge and action, the modern neo-Piagetian approach explains the stability and variability of what people know. With a focus on the dynamics of variation and stability, neo-Piagetian research and theory have built eloquent explanations for the richness of development and learning and have helped reconcile long-standing tensions in the field related to stages, developmental range, and variation in age of acquisition. Neo-Piagetians have constructed a powerful set of concepts, methods, and tools to ground research and theory in developmental science for years to come. One recent but important tool of neo-Piagetian dynamic structuralism is mathematical modeling, which has opened a new window on the study of developmental phenomena.

NEO-PIAGETIAN THEORY: DYNAMIC PSYCHOLOGICAL STRUCTURE

The broad goal of the neo-Piagetian perspective is to explain universals in development and epistemology that Piaget so elegantly described and to account for the pervasive variability that underpins all development and learning. The focus of this chapter is the fundamental neo-Piagetian postulate of psychological structure as *dynamic organization*. First we explicate this argument and contrast it with the assumption of static form embedded in traditional theories of growth and change. In developmental and cognitive science, static views of structure have been the rule, not the exception – a static property of the mind existing separately from the behavior it organizes (Chomsky, 1957, 1965; Fodor, 1983). In subsequent sections we show how a dynamic perspective is essential for explaining variability.

If the search for universal structures has taught us anything, it is this: Structures (knowledge, action, emotion) are both organized and variable, continually changing systematically as a function of multiple characteristics of person and context. Action in sports illustrates this principle nicely. Even the relatively simple act of throwing a ball, for example, is not a fixed action that happens identically every time. Context matters! At a baseball game the pitcher throws differently depending on a range of factors working together: temperature, crowd noise, fatigue, having a runner on base, and lighting (to name but a few factors). Understanding the pitcher's performance, including its natural variability, depends on analyzing how such factors function in the immediate context, which includes the person throwing the ball, of course. This kind of dynamic process characterizes all actions and knowledge (Rose & Fischer, in press).

In classic structural explanations, structure has been confounded with form. Piaget (1968/1970) clearly stated that *structure* refers to the system of relations by which complex entities such as psychological activities and biological organisms are organized. In the human body, for example, the nervous system, skeletal system, and cardiovascular system all work together through constant interconnecting activity by which each system adapts dynamically to the other systems and to the functioning of the body as a whole. In the structure of a body set patterns can be detected, such as the way the nervous system creates changes in the cardiovascular system when a person experiences stress.

Piaget recognized the dynamic nature of psychological structure and believed that activity is the foundation of learning and development, but the core metaphor for stage theory (universal logic defining the developmental trajectories of each person) is profoundly static. Because stage theory equates structure (the dynamic organization of mental activity) with static form (formal logic), it does not provide a full characterization of the complex mechanisms that underpin variability and change in psychological development (Fischer & Bidell, 2006). If Piaget had an opportunity to craft his approach to cognition and development in the 21st century, we suspect he would have emphasized the dynamics of knowledge and growth.

The problem of classic concepts of structure is that they treat structure as form – an abstraction existing in its own right – instead of as dynamic organization that emerges from the components organizing themselves together. Consider an orange – a piece of fruit that has its own structure of cells and tissue that self-organizes into a spherical shape. The orange has a *dynamic* structure, starting with a developmental history of growth from a tree, maintaining equilibrium as a stable piece of fruit, and decaying (if it is not eaten or put to other use). In contrast to the orange itself, the concept of sphere is an abstract form that describes one characteristic of the dynamic structure – its shape – which applies across many situations. The Greek philosopher Plato (1941) suggested that these abstract, idealized forms actually exist in an arena beyond the physical world. The uniformity of the formal sphere concept makes it useful for characterizing many objects, such as balls, peaches, marbles, and planets.

Classic concepts of structure use an abstract description to characterize reality as if it were static like the concept of sphere. This form fallacy is not limited to science: People commonly use categories in this idealized way, expecting objects, events, and people to fit such abstract concepts instead of showing the natural dynamic variation central to all living things. In social interactions, for example, people may expect others to fit the stereotype of a category, such as a wife, a scientist, an outgoing person, or a member of an ethnic minority (Greenwald et al., 2002; Rosch & Lloyd, 1978). In the same way, scientists who focus exclusively on the form of the sphere will be surprised at the differences between baseballs, basketballs, oranges, and peaches. The spherical shape of the orange specifies an abstract property that applies across different objects, not an ideal form that specifies the nature of the objects. Likewise, researchers who emphasize the role of innate forms in knowledge of number will focus on the capacity of infants to discriminate arrays with one, two, or three dots (Dehaene, 1997; Spelke, 2005) and thus will be surprised to discover that a 3-year-old does not understand the nature of numbers one, two, and three as ordered sets. The child must construct the number line to understand how numbers work in mathematics. The fallacy of form applies broadly to human behavior, from stereotypes to the nativist explanation of number.

The neo-Piagetian movement was created by scholars working to preserve many of Piaget's core epistemological assumptions (i.e., constructive knowledge, hierarchical development, structural relations between levels of knowledge) while moving beyond Piaget's most problematic concept – the assertion of universal structures of formal logic. These scholars replaced the logic model of the mind with a more dynamic, domain-specific, task-dependent, culturally embedded view of psychological structure. During the 1980s, several scholars put forward accounts of development that laid a conceptual foundation for modern neo-Piagetian research (e.g., Biggs & Collis, 1982; Case, 1985; Fischer, 1980; Halford, 1982; Pascual-Leone, 1987; Shayer, Demetriou, & Pervez, 1988). Over the past 25 years, the neo-Piagetian framework has expanded into all areas of developmental science. It is testament to its ubiquitous influence that we cannot possibly do justice to all that is neo-Piagetian theory and research in a single chapter. Instead of chronicling the evolution of neo-Piagetian ideas or cataloging theoretical differences, we focus on the key issues of variability and stability.

To explain variability and stability together, the neo-Piagetian approach replaces traditional static views of structure with dynamic ones. Psychological structures do not exist outside of activity – like the concept of a sphere – but instead they arise from action systems embedded in what people do on a daily basis. Through the dynamic analysis of psychological structure, neo-Piagetian scholars have been able to identify and explain specific patterns of developmental variability and have reconciled long-standing issues in the field related to stage and synchrony, developmental range, and variation in age of acquisition of knowledge.

STAGE AND SYNCHRONY: GETTING BEYOND THE CRISIS OF VARIABILITY

Piaget (1970/1983) postulated a series of stages of cognitive development, which he characterized as specific logical structures that shaped the mind, including concrete operations in childhood and formal operations in adolescence. One powerful criticism of his stage theory has been the overwhelming evidence of asynchrony in children's development (Fischer, 1980). Piaget predicted that as a new logic emerged in the mind, it would catalyze the whole mind into a new kind of intelligence. However, research has consistently found unevenness instead of monolithic transformation, even with logically equivalent tasks. For example, the conservation of number with items like stones or dolls is usually acquired around age 5 or 6; however, conservation of amount of liquid such as water or orange juice is not acquired until age 7 or 8 (Piaget & Inhelder, 1968/1973). Skills for different kinds of conservation develop along separate pathways. This unevenness is difficult to reconcile with universal stages: If the mind is governed by underlying logical structures, why would they manifest themselves at one age in some contexts but not until later ages in others?

Piaget acknowledged this variability (Piaget, 1972) – which he called "décalage" – and distinguished two specific forms: He called variability in age of a given logical form "horizontal décalage," and he called parallels across stages (logically distinct forms that share important characteristics) "vertical décalage" (Piaget, 1941). However, although these categories of décalage may be a starting point for the study of variation, they are *not* in and of themselves an explanation. Defining forms of variability is not the same as explaining them. Explanation requires specifying the processes by which logical stage structures interact with environmental influences, or "resistances," to make one kind of task develop later than another. Equally important, the explanations need to deal with the pervasive differences across individuals in developmental pathways, timing, and skill related to tasks, context, social support, and experience. In short, although stage theory offers important insight into the general shape of cognitive development, it does not explain the many kinds of variation (Fischer & Bidell, 2006).

The limitations of Piaget's assumptions about the uniform logic behind stages were forcefully exposed when, in the 1960s and 1970s, a large body of research began to accumulate, revealing remarkable variability in every aspect of cognitive development studied. As replication studies continued to proliferate into the 1980s and researchers continued to introduce new changes to Piaget's tasks and procedures, departures from stability predicted by stage theory proved to be the norm, not the exception. Although the evidence did not undermine the constructivism in Piaget's theory, it rendered untenable the postulate that universal forms of mental logic created stages of development. As evidence for variability became overwhelming and the failure of universal structure obvious, the field of developmental science was thrust into an explanatory crisis, which we call the Crisis of Variability (Fischer & Bidell, 2006).

One result of extensive research showing unevenness was an abandonment of the concept of stage, with many scientists and educators asserting that there were no stages but only learning sequences within limited domains, such as a sequence for the domain of conservation of number and a separate sequence for conservation of liquid. However, starting with dynamic explanations of variability and grounded in a view of structure as organization, neo-Piagetian researchers have been able to illuminate the long-standing stage debate. Arguments used to be overly simple: "Children develop in clear stages, as described by Piaget," countered by "No, they don't. Development is uneven, and there are no stages." But these arguments centered on the assumption of static forms of structure. When variation is systematically embedded into assessments and analyzed directly, both general characteristics of developmental processes and the stage-like nature of change are revealed as two sides of the same coin. In other words, the neo-Piagetian approach shifts the dialogue to determining the *circumstances* under which development shows stage-like properties and under which it shows continuous change.

An important characteristic of dynamic systems is that they commonly show abrupt changes, which have been variously called "reorganizations," "emergent properties," or "catastrophes" (Abraham & Shaw, 1992; van der Maas & Molenaar, 1992). Human action and knowledge grow out of dynamic systems, and dynamic models of brain functioning, cognitive development, and learning all show times of rapid, discontinuous change (Fischer & Rose, 1996; van der Maas, Verschure, & Molenaar, 1990). In other words, neo-Piagetian analysis of dynamic growth and variation demonstrates that development and learning regularly show stage-like jumps and reorganizations of action and thought. Importantly, these discontinuities appear most commonly when people perform at their highest level of skill, their *optimal level*. That is, for optimal level people perform the most complex skill they are capable of

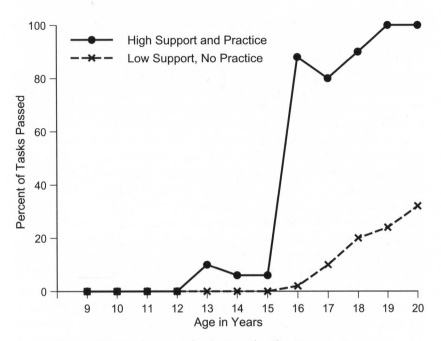

Figure 18.1. Development of mappings of arithmetic operations.

for a specific task, and methods called "high support" have been devised to assess optimal level performance.

An example of a rapid, dramatic jump in performance comes from a study of the development of understanding arithmetic operations (addition, subtraction, multiplication, and division) in 9- to 20-year-olds (Fischer & Kenny, 1986). Students did arithmetic tasks under two conditions – low support, in which they simply performed the tasks, and high support, in which key ideas needed for the tasks were primed to create optimal-level performance. The problems required explaining arithmetic operations and the relationships between them. In the low-support condition, the researcher asked the student to explain the operations and their relationships. In the high-support condition, the researcher offered prototypical answers to each problem. To offer adequate practice time and ensure optimal-level performance, the conditions were repeated 2 weeks later. For tasks shown in Figure 18.1, correct performance required that students give a truly abstract response about arithmetic relationships that went beyond a concrete answer. Instead of "addition and subtraction are related because 4 + 6 = 10 and 10 − 4 = 6," they had to explain the relationship in general terms and apply it to a concrete problem: "Addition and subtraction are related because in addition you put numbers together, while in subtraction you take numbers apart – they are opposite operations."

In this study, analysis of high- and low-support conditions led to a profound realization about the shapes of growth and change. Under the low-support condition (functional level) performance improved gradually and did not reach very high levels overall (see Figure 18.1), whereas the high-support condition (optimal level) produced a consistent and dramatic spurt at the age of 16. Under the high-support condition no student showed understanding of more than one abstract relationship at age 15, but all students understood a majority of the relationships at age 16. This did not happen under low support, where all students showed poor understanding.

Similar powerful spurts have been demonstrated in multiple domains and age ranges in several cultures, including reflective judgment (Kitchener, Lynch, Fischer, & Wood, 1993), moral reasoning (Dawson, 2000), self-understanding (Fischer & Kennedy, 1997), and vocabulary (Ruhland & van Geert, 1998). Across familiar tasks, optimal-level performance spurts to higher levels at specific points in the construction of knowledge. Importantly, the modal ages of these spurts typically correspond to those Piaget posited for his four main stages (as well as additional ones), but the ages can vary across individuals, cultures, and domains. What remains constant is the place in the learning sequence where the spurts occur.

These discontinuities form a common scale for development that seems to be universal, once the dynamic variability in performance is taken into account. Table 18.1 shows this scale as a sequence of ten levels, for all of which there is extensive research evidence. A complete description of these discontinuities is presented elsewhere (Fischer & Bidell, 2006). Note that analysis of variability in growth curves has led to reframing the stage question and resolving the stage debate. Piaget's analysis of stages turns out to have been partly correct, but how it is correct becomes evident only within a dynamic neo-Piagetian framework.

SOCIAL SUPPORT AND DEVELOPMENTAL RANGE

The analysis of variability goes far beyond identifying when stage-like changes occur and when they do not. It forms the foundation for analyzing processes of learning and development in general. Research has made clear that people never function at a single developmental level but instead vary the levels of their actions across a broad range depending on context, bodily state, goals, and other factors. Humans adapt their skill level to the needs of the situation instead of being stuck at one level.

TABLE 18.1. *Developmental Scale of Levels of Skills*

Tiers	Levels	Age of Emergence of Optimal Level
	Ab4. Principles	23–25 years
Abstractions	Ab3. Systems	18–20 years
	Ab2. Mappings	14–16 years
	Rp4/Ab1. Single Abstractions	10–12 years
Representations	Rp3. Systems	6–7 years
	Rp2. Mappings	3½–4½ years
	Sm4/Rp1. Single Representations	2 years
Actions	Sm3. Systems	11–13 months
	Sm2. Mappings	7–8 months
	Sm1. Single Actions	3–4 months

This range of variation is sometimes called the "developmental range" (Fischer & Bidell, 2006) and sometimes the "zone of proximal development," a phrase from Lev Vygotsky (1978). This variation is often driven by support from other people, such as parents, teachers, and siblings, as well as by cultural tools, such as books and computers. People learn ways of acting and thinking from their culture, and support from other people and cultural tools help them become expert members of their culture.

Two main kinds of variation in the developmental range illuminate how learning, development, and enculturation occur. First, people (especially children) often perform activities with others who are more expert, thereby participating in the activity at a level of complexity they are unable to sustain on their own (Rogoff, 2003). A 3-year-old child builds a pyramid from a puzzle of interlocking blocks with his mother facilitating the process. Without his mother's aid, he would fail miserably in his effort to build the pyramid. But with his mother unobtrusively giving him hints and supports (often subtle), he spends 40 minutes working with the blocks and succeeds in building the whole pyramid (Wood & Middleton, 1975). Similarly, a 14-year-old needs to write a 500-word essay on global warming, and her father discusses with her what her argument could be, what examples she could use, and how she can begin her argument. He supports her writing of the essay, although she actually writes almost all of it herself. Through these kinds of support, more knowledgeable people engage closely with learners to help guide them to build skill and knowledge (Fischer & Rose, 2001).

The second kind of variation in the developmental range focuses on novel tasks or situations. When people encounter something novel that they do not understand, the most fruitful strategy for coping with it seems to be to drop down to a lower skill level – acting like a child – and explore the new situation to understand its components. For example, in one study graduate students encountered Lego robots before these gadgets had been marketed, when they had just been invented at the Media Laboratory at MIT (Fischer & Granott, 1995; Granott, Fischer, & Parziale, 2002). With these novel, mobile objects, the students explored them through sensorimotor actions – acting in many ways like a small child, gradually building knowledge about how the robots worked. Similarly, when learning a new language, people seem to learn more effectively if they play with the sounds and grammar and thus learn the most basic elements, which is similar to the ways that babies and toddlers babble and play with speech sounds and words.

DOMAINS, SEQUENCES, AND CONSTRUCTION OF KNOWLEDGE

Beginning in the 1970s many researchers seeking to address the Crisis of Variability abandoned stage explanations altogether and opted for a framework that emphasized the domain-specific nature of knowledge. They turned atomistic, crafting a modular approach to the mind, which postulated that behavior could be divided into core domains that were themselves built on general psychological structures (Fodor, 1983; Gardner, 1983). This domain assumption has been influential in developmental science and helped move the field beyond conceptions of monolithic universal stages. However, many domain models remain grounded in a static conception of structure, seeking a logical structure for each domain – for example, treating spatial reasoning and musical thinking as encapsulated each to itself and fundamentally separate from the other. Skills do not work that way. Action and knowledge are based on acting in the world, where there are not sharp demarcations between domains of action unless cultures create them. Babies do all sorts of actions to, say, a rattle. They grasp it, chew it, look at it, shake it, listen to it, smell it, bang it, throw it, and they try to connect the results of all those activities. Cultures, on the other hand, often establish strong demarcations between socially defined fields or disciplines, such as architecture, music performance, and history (Gardner, 1999).

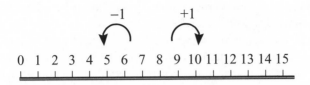

The metaphor of a number line forms the foundation for the central conceptual structure for number. In this simple version, adding 1 moves the number higher and to the right, and subtracting 1 moves it lower and to the left.

Figure 18.2. Number line, foundation for a central conceptual structure.

The extensive research on domains has shown that many possible domains do not actually exist as distinct cognitive entities. They do not group together as closely related skills. For example, educators often nominate critical thinking as an important domain, and surely critical thinking skills play an important role in education. But describing a kind of skill does not make it an actual domain. For critical thinking, the skills do not cohere as a domain (Willingham, 2007). Thinking critically about international politics, for example, does not seem to involve the same skills as thinking critically about the physics of energy.

Neo-Piagetian research, however, has begun to uncover how knowledge is built in some domains that do cohere, including development of mathematics and literacy. We will focus on the development of arithmetic in the early years, where researchers and educators have discovered learning sequences for the construction of mathematical knowledge and have shown how educators can systematically facilitate learning based on movement through those sequences.

Case, Griffin, and their colleagues identified what they characterize as a *central conceptual structure* for number in early childhood, which shows powerful generalization across tasks (Case et al., 1996; Griffin & Case, 1997). Infants demonstrate two kinds of simple numerical knowledge, one for enumeration (one or two or three) and another for relative magnitude (proportionate comparison of sets of objects, like many vs. few buttons). These elementary number systems form a foundation for understanding arithmetic, but they are not sufficient by themselves. Children need specific experience about numbers to build the complex knowledge foundation for understanding numbers and arithmetic.

The central conceptual structure that they have to build is an elementary number line (Figure 18.2), with numbers varying along the line, increasing one unit at a time in one direction (two to three, or six to seven) and decreasing in the other direction. The number line represents a fundamental change (beyond the two infant systems) in the structure that children have available for addressing quantitative problems, and children have to build it with numerical experience over many months. When they succeed in building the skill for the number line, that knowledge facilitates reasoning across a wide range of tasks that differ greatly except for their focus on number, such as doing arithmetic problems in school and telling time with a clock.

Many children grow up in an environment that supports learning the number line, such as their family or preschool, and they gradually construct the number line between 2 to 4 years of age. In one study researchers used simple tasks to assess children's understanding of number, asking them to choose a particular number of objects, for example, "three dinosaurs" or "one dinosaur" (Le Corre, Van de Walle, Brannon, & Carey, 2006). The children built the number line one digit at a time. First, they understood *one* as a number (one and only one dinosaur) but treated other numbers as meaning "many" dinosaurs. A few months later, they added *two* as a number, with three and four meaning "many." After a few more months they added *three* as a number, and then still later *four*, until finally at age 3.5 to 4 years they understood that one, two, three, and four all go together to form a number line, and the number of objects can be determined by counting. This is the beginning of the number-line framework that becomes the foundation of arithmetic and mathematics.

Case, Griffin, and their colleagues devised a curriculum for teaching the number line to young children, focusing on playing games that included the number line. Such games have been popular with children for centuries, such as Chutes and Ladders (called Snakes and Ladders in its classic form). In these games children move objects along a number line, forward and backward, and this activity is a key part of learning the number line quickly and efficiently. Notably, as little as 10 weeks of training produced substantial improvement in number tasks that were taught – as well as in number tasks outside the curriculum (such as counting presents at a birthday party and understanding musical scales). In contrast, training did not improve performance on non-numerical tasks such as social narratives. The power of the number-line construct is evident in both the size of the effects (explaining nearly 50 percent of the variance in performance over time – a huge effect, much larger than for most curricula) and in the fact the curriculum has been successful with children from disadvantaged communities and in multiple countries (Case et al., 1996).

So why did Case and Griffin succeed in the search for structure where others had failed? First, their concept of structure extends beyond static notions of abstract form and beyond logic: Children deal with objects in activities organized in a framework of concepts, such as the number line. In games they play with semantic relationships between those concepts, all linked with their everyday activities. Second, Case and Griffin made use of what children actually do when counting and dealing with number and made tasks that were grounded in what the children already knew about number. Finally, an important advantage may be that the number line is built into everyday language as a basic metaphor for number, which means that children already possess key elements of the concept that they have learned implicitly through their language.

LOOKING BACKWARD: AGE VARIATION AND THE PRECOCIOUS INFANT

An important criticism leveled against Piaget's theory was that it underestimated the competence of infants and young children (Carey & Gelman, 1991; Spelke, Breinlinger, Macomber, & Jacobson, 1992). In response to this criticism, the neo-nativist movement emerged as a theoretical alternative to Piagetian stage theory and surged forth in the 1970s to characterize many previously unknown abilities in early development within domains such as language, number, space, and object concept. Researchers who adopted this view of development have worked tirelessly to show that Piagetian tasks can mask the real abilities of children (e.g., Halford, 1989). For neo-nativists the goal is to find "essential" knowledge: to strip away the factors that limit performance as much as possible to get at the underlying competence. Over the past several decades, researchers have simplified the questions, instructions, scoring criteria, and procedural details in assessment tasks, and in the process have developed new versions of Piaget's tasks.

Take, for example, the idea of object permanence, the notion that objects continue to exist beyond what a child can perceive. Piaget used successful retrieval of a hidden object as a measure of object permanence and found it emerged in infants around 8 months (Piaget, 1937/1954). In contrast, others have used the reaction of surprise as the criterion (rather than the active search for hidden objects) and have concluded infants have this competence as early as 3 to 4 months (Spelke et al., 1992). Some researchers have used this body of evidence to argue against Piaget's major claims about knowledge development (Baillargeon, 1987).

Obviously, such discrepancies raise the question: How do we explain the origin of this early knowledge? Nativists argue that the knowledge is innate, demonstrating inborn, genetically determined competence modules. Sensorimotor limitations, they say, prevent infants from demonstrating what they know in most experimental paradigms. This *argument from precocity* has been used to claim innate determination for a wide range of concepts beyond object permanence, including space, number, language, and theory of mind (Carey & Spelke, 1994; Saxe, Carey, & Kanwisher, 2004; Spelke et al., 1992).

This position fails because its argument is based on structure as *form*: The first glimmer of infant behavior related to a domain such as object permanence is taken to show a general competence – knowledge of the permanence of objects. Yet infants fail almost every single aspect of knowledge of object permanence. The first glimmer is only a small beginning.

The neo-Piagetian dynamic perspective puts forth a powerful, comprehensive explanation: Knowledge varies across tasks based on their complexity, familiarity, and other factors, and within a domain children develop skills in a learning sequence, an ordering of tasks along a developmental pathway. Nativist research has selectively focused on downward variation in age of onset for concepts like object permanence and has ignored the complementary and widely observed upward variation in age for other tasks and conditions (Pinard, 1981). For a theory of development to be useful, it cannot simply opt out of explaining change – explanation is required! Neo-Piagetian learning sequences describe how object permanence involves many skills arrayed along strands in a developmental web, which starts with the abilities of young infants that neo-nativists have uncovered and moves toward complex, diverse knowledge and action in the same domain. As shown in Figure 18.3, development begins with the basic knowledge of objects, space, and number, and gradually over time children build more complex knowledge along multiple strands for each domain. With number, for example, they construct the number line as their development proceeds, especially when they receive experience and instruction to facilitate their understanding.

Fortunately, research often helps resolve theoretical debates like those between nativism and Piaget: The learning sequence for understanding number described previously came from bringing together nativist and neo-Piagetian research. The nativist approach predicted that understanding the number line would spontaneously develop in young children such as 2-year-olds. However, when nativist researchers tested how young children understand numbers, their findings instead coincided with Case and Griffin's neo-Piagetian research: Children build the number line gradually one digit at a time during the preschool years (Le Corre et al., 2006). The learning sequence for number knowledge begins with infants' capacities for simple enumeration and relative magnitude,

Domains

Number   Space   Objects

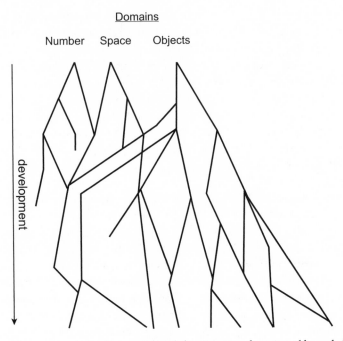

development

Figure 18.3. A developmental Web for Piagetian domains of knowledge.

but it takes several years to develop, moving through construction of the number line toward complex understanding of mathematics.

LOOKING FORWARD: MODELING DEVELOPMENT

The concepts of neo-Piagetian dynamic structuralism have influenced research and theory in development. However, concepts are not enough. To get beyond endless (and typically unproductive) arguments about vague metaphors, like whether stages exist, theoretical concepts must be grounded in explicit models capable of capturing the dynamics of growth and change. Happily such tools are now available owing to remarkable advances in dynamic systems theory and modeling in the last 50 years (Abraham & Shaw, 1992). These mathematical tools provide powerful methods to pin down processes of development and learning, allowing for a new kind of empirical theoretical psychology (van Geert, 1996), where any rigorously defined theory can be put in mathematical terms and analyzed to see what kinds of growth and other patterns it actually produces. The ability of researchers to directly experiment with theories in models moves the field toward greater sophistication and precision. In this section we offer a glimpse of the dynamic models being used

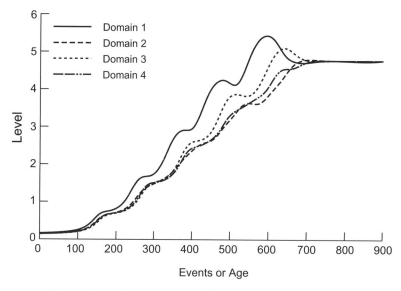

Figure 18.4a. Attractor pattern of hierarchical growth model.

in current developmental research (Fischer & Bidell, 2006; Thelen & Smith, 2006; van Geert, 2000) and discuss ways that models can help advance the field of developmental science in the future.

At this early point in research with models, it is already clear that developmental processes demonstrate considerable variability as well as predictable points of stability. For example, in hierarchical growth a more complex structure (or skill) emerges from the coordination and differentiation of simpler structures, which is a common theme in most Piagetian and neo-Piagetian models. Figure 18.4a shows a model for four different strands (domains), each growing as a series of five hierarchically organized skills, where later skills are built on earlier ones within each strand (Fischer & Bidell, 2006). Every skill is represented by a growth function (based on the universal growth equation, which is logistic). In each domain, skills are linked hierarchically such that later skills cannot begin until earlier skills reach a specific level (just as standing is a fundamental prerequisite for walking). Across each domain, skills are connected in different ways (such as supportive vs. competitive) and at different levels of strength (from no connection to weakly connected to moderately connected). All connections can influence the shape of a particular growth function, as can the initial value and growth rate of each component. As a result, development in the model, as in real life, often shows complex patterns.

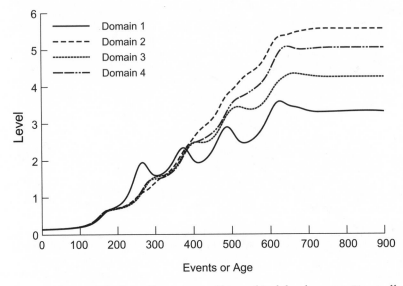

Figure 18.4b. Spreading pattern of hierarchical development: Piaget effect.

Each strand in Figure 18.4a shows clear stage-like characteristics including movement toward a common value, which is called an "attractor pattern" in dynamics. The dynamics of growth create this attractor pattern, which produces stage-like change in several domains (strands), as is evident in the graph. Interestingly, small changes to one value in the model can dramatically alter growth patterns – for example, giving rise to the spread-out trajectories in the graph in Figure 18.4b. This growth pattern is called "the Piaget effect" because it illustrates Piaget's argument against unnatural efforts to speed up early development, such as training children to perform complex tasks in the way that circus trainers teach bears to ride bicycles (e.g., Piaget, 1936/1952, 1975/1985). Such perturbations in normal development can produce the unintended consequence of disturbing natural patterns of development. This model illustrates how dynamic modeling can reconcile what appear to be disparate aspects of growth (different trajectories for similar types of abilities) while also revealing unexpected outcomes (the Piaget effect) that stimulate empirical research. In short, the model shows how widely different patterns can emerge from the exact same underlying model of growth!

Importantly, the hierarchical growth model only characterizes one of several families of developmental shapes. Other models relevant to development include predator–prey models that specify the dynamic relationship between components that show support and competition but no hierarchical integration (Thatcher, 1998). For example, cats and mice show a stable predator–prey relationship: The number of mice available at any one time will, in part, determine the number of cats that survive. If there are many mice, more cats will survive in a given season. However, too many cats in turn lead to fewer mice the following season, which in turn constrains the number of cats that survive in the next season. Research has found that similar predator–prey relationships exist for cognitive and neurological processes, such as the development of connections between cortical regions (Fischer & Rose, 1996).

Developmental processes are highly nonlinear, heterogeneous, and dependent on a wide range of factors. For this reason, dynamic models are well suited for the study of cognitive development, bringing together many interacting factors to specify patterns of development and learning rigorously and precisely. In short, dynamic modeling offers tools to better understand development and learning in their full complexity, integrating influences involving person, context, and culture.

CONCLUSION: STABILITY GROWS FROM THE DYNAMICS OF VARIATION

From grand theories of stable monolithic development to atomistic theories that focus on domain-specific change, neo-Piagetian work on development has created a balanced model in the form of dynamic structuralism. It is crystal clear that stability and variability are complementary hallmarks of development, not separate issues. Capturing the richness and complexity of development requires models capable of analyzing both of these simultaneously. Dynamic structuralism shifts the understanding of structure beyond static form toward dynamic organization, which depends not on prespecified innate representations but instead on continual real-time interactions between person, context, and culture. When development is viewed through the lens of dynamic structuralism, many classic controversies – such as whether stages exist – are revealed as artifacts of misconceptions. The organization of behavior clearly develops systematically, as Piaget described, and it also varies from moment to moment. These facts are only contrary for overly simple concepts of stage and variation.

We human beings construct knowledge through our own unique bodies and distinct sociocultural relationships, thus producing highly variable patterns of behavior. If this variability is ignored or marginalized, it serves only as noise to disguise the nature of developmental processes, and it will often mislead researchers and educators. However, if the full range of methods, tools, and concepts are used to study the dynamic and complex properties of behavior, then patterns of variability can be revealed and illuminate the nature and development of knowledge and action.

REFERENCES

Abraham, R. H., & Shaw, C. D. (1992). *Dynamics: The geometry of behavior* (2nd ed.). New York: Addison-Wesley.

Baillargeon, R. (1987). Object permanence in 31/2- and 41/2-month-old infants. *Developmental Psychology, 23,* 655–664.

Biggs, J., & Collis, K. (1982). *Evaluating the quality of learning: The SOLO taxonomy (structure of the observed learning outcome).* New York: Academic Press.

Carey, S., & Gelman, R. (Eds.). (1991). *The epigenesis of mind: Essays on biology and knowledge.* Hillsdale, NJ: Erlbaum.

Carey, S., & Spelke, E. (1994). Domain-specific knowledge and conceptual change. In L. A. Hirschfeld & S. A. Gelman (Eds.), *Mapping the mind: Domain specificity in cognition and culture* (pp. 169–200). Cambridge, UK: Cambridge University Press.

Case, R. (1985). *Intellectual development: Birth to adulthood.* New York: Academic Press.

Case, R., Okamoto, Y., Griffin, S., McKeough, A., Bleiker, C., Henderson, B., et al. (1996). The role of central conceptual structures in the development of children's thought. *Monographs of the Society for Research in Child Development, 61*(5–6, Serial No. 246).

Chomsky, N. (1957). *Syntactic structures.* The Hague: Mouton.

Chomsky, N. (1965). *Aspects of the theory of syntax.* Cambridge, MA: MIT Press.

Dawson, T. L. (2000). Moral reasoning and evaluation reasoning about the good life. *Journal of Applied Measurement, 1,* 372–397.

Dehaene, S. (1997). *The number sense: How the mind creates mathematics.* New York: Oxford.

Fischer, K. W. (1980). A theory of cognitive development: The control and construction of hierarchies of skills. *Psychological Review, 87,* 477–531.

Fischer, K. W., & Bidell, T. R. (2006). Dynamic development of action and thought. In W. Damon & R. M. Lerner (Eds.), *Theoretical models of human development. Handbook of child psychology* (6th ed., Vol. 1, pp. 313–399). New York: Wiley.

Fischer, K. W., & Granott, N. (1995). Beyond one-dimensional change: Parallel, concurrent, socially distributed processes in learning and development. *Human Development, 38,* 302–314.

Fischer, K. W., & Kennedy, B. (1997). Tools for analyzing the many shapes of development: The case of self-in-relationships in Korea. In E. Amsel & K. A. Renninger (Eds.), *Change and development: Issues of theory, method, and application* (pp. 117–152). Mahwah, NJ: Erlbaum.

Fischer, K. W., & Kenny, S. L. (1986). The environmental conditions for discontinuities in the development of abstractions. In R. Mines & K. Kitchener (Eds.), *Adult cognitive development: Methods and models* (pp. 57–75). New York: Praeger.

Fischer, K. W., & Rose, L. T. (2001). Webs of skill: How students learn. *Educational Leadership, 59*, 6–12.

Fischer, K. W., & Rose, S. P. (1996). Dynamic growth cycles of brain and cognitive development. In R. Thatcher, G. R. Lyon, J. Rumsey, & N. Krasnegor (Eds.), *Developmental neuroimaging: Mapping the development of brain and behavior* (pp. 263–279). New York: Academic Press.

Fodor, J. (1983). *The modularity of mind: An essay on faculty psychology*. Cambridge, MA: MIT Press.

Gardner, H. (1983). *Frames of mind: The theory of multiple intelligences*. New York: Basic Books.

Gardner, H. (1999). *The disciplined mind*. New York: Simon & Schuster.

Granott, N., Fischer, K. W., & Parziale, J. (2002). Bridging to the unknown: A transition mechanism in learning and problem-solving. In N. Granott & J. Parziale (Eds.), *Microdevelopment: Transition processes in development and learning* (pp. 131–156). Cambridge, UK: Cambridge University Press.

Greenwald, A. G., Banaji, M. R., Rudman, L., Farnham, S., Nosek, B. A., & Mellott, D. (2002). A unified theory of implicit attitudes, stereotypes, self-esteem, and self-concept. *Psychological Review, 109*, 3–25.

Griffin, S., & Case, R. (1997). Rethinking the primary school math curriculum. *Issues in Education: Contributions from Educational Psychology, 3*, 1–49.

Halford, G. S. (1982). *The development of thought*. Hillsdale, NJ: Erlbaum.

Halford, G. S. (1989). Reflections on 25 years of Piagetian cognitive developmental psychology, 1963–1988. *Human Development, 32*, 325–357.

Kitchener, K. S., Lynch, C. L., Fischer, K. W., & Wood, P. K. (1993). Developmental range of reflective judgment: The effect of contextual support and practice on developmental stage. *Developmental Psychology, 29*, 893–906.

Le Corre, M., Van de Walle, G., Brannon, E. M., & Carey, S. (2006). Re-visiting the competence/performance debate in the acquisition of counting as a representation of the positive integers. *Cognitive Psychology, 52*, 130–169.

Pascual-Leone, J. (1987). Organismic processes for neo-Piagetian theories: A dialectical causal account of cognitive development. *International Journal of Psychology, 22*, 531–570.

Piaget, J. (1941). Le mécanisme du développement mental et les lois du groupement des opérations. *Archives de Psychologie, 28*, 215–285.

Piaget, J. (1952). *The origins of intelligence in children*. New York: International Universities Press. (Original work published in 1936)

Piaget, J. (1954). *The construction of reality in the child*. New York: Basic Books. (Original work published in 1937)

Piaget, J. (1970). *Structuralism*. New York: Basic Books. (Original work published in 1968)

Piaget, J. (1972). Intellectual evolution from adolescence to adulthood. *Human Development, 15*, 1–12.

Piaget, J. (1983). Piaget's theory. In W. Kessen (Ed.), *History, theory, and methods* (Vol. 1, pp. 103–126). New York: Wiley. (Original work published in 1970)

Piaget, J. (1985). *The equilibration of cognitive structures: The central problem of cognitive development.* Chicago: University of Chicago Press. (Original work published in 1975)

Piaget, J., & Inhelder, B. (1973). *Memory and intelligence.* New York: Basic Books. (Original work published in 1968)

Pinard, A. (1981). *The concept of conservation.* Chicago: University of Chicago Press.

Plato. (1941). *The republic.* London: Oxford University Press.

Rogoff, B. (2003). *The cultural nature of human development.* Oxford: Oxford University Press.

Rosch, E., & Lloyd, B. (1978). *Cognition and categorization.* Hillsdale, NJ: Erlbaum.

Rose, L. T., & Fischer, K. W. (in press). Dynamic systems theory. In R. Shweder, T. Bidell, A. Dailey, S. Dixon, P. J. Miller, & J. Modell (Eds.), *Chicago companion to the child.* Chicago: University of Chicago Press.

Ruhland, R., & van Geert, P. (1998). Jumping into syntax: Transitions in the development of closed class words. *British Journal of Developmental Psychology, 16,* 65–95.

Saxe, R., Carey, S., & Kanwisher, N. (2004). Understanding other minds: Linking developmental psychology and functional neuroimaging. *Annual Review of Psychology, 55,* 87–124.

Shayer, M., Demetriou, A., & Pervez, M. (1988). The structure and scaling of concrete operational thought: Three studies in four countries. *Genetic, Social, and General Psychology Monographs, 114,* 308–375.

Spelke, E. S. (2005). Big answers from little people. *Scientific American, 16*(3), 38–43.

Spelke, E. S., Breinlinger, K., Macomber, J., & Jacobson, K. (1992). Origins of knowledge. *Psychological Review, 99,* 605–632.

Thatcher, R. W. (1998). A predator-prey model of human cerebral development. In K. Newell & P. Molenaar (Eds.), *Applications of nonlinear dynamics to developmental process modeling* (pp. 87–128). Mahwah, NJ: Erlbaum.

Thelen, E., & Smith, L. B. (2006). Dynamic systems theories. In W. Damon & R. M. Lerner (Eds.), *Theoretical models of human development. Handbook of child psychology* (Vol. 1, 6th ed., pp. 258–312). New York: Wiley.

van der Maas, H., & Molenaar, P. (1992). A catastrophe-theoretical approach to cognitive development. *Psychological Review, 99,* 395–417.

van der Maas, H., Verschure, P. F. M. J., & Molenaar, P. C. M. (1990). A note on chaotic behavior in simple neural networks. *Neural Networks, 3,* 119–122.

van Geert, P. (1996). The dynamics of Father Brown: Essay review of book *A dynamic systems approach to the development of action and thought* by E. Thelen and B. Smith. *Human Development, 39,* 57–66.

van Geert, P. (2000). The dynamics of general developmental mechanisms: From Piaget and Vygotsky to dynamic systems models. *Current Directions in Psychological Science, 9,* 64–68.

Vygotsky, L. (1978). *Mind in society: The development of higher psychological processes*. Cambridge, MA: Harvard University Press.

Willingham, D. T. (2007). Critical thinking: Why is it so hard to teach? *American Educator, 31*, 8–19.

Wood, D., & Middleton, D. (1975). A study of assisted problem-solving. *British Journal of Psychology, 66*, 181–191.

INDEX